THE LETTERS OF J.R.R. TOLKIEN

D1429781

February 4th. 1938.

Dear Mr Furth,

I enclose copy of Chapter I 'A Long-expected Party' of possible sequel to The Hobbit.

I received safely 4 additional copies of The Hobbit.

I received a letter from a young reader in Boston (Lincs) enclosing a list of _errata_. I then put on my youngest son, lying in bed with a bad heart, to find any more at twopence a time. He did. I enclose the results — which added to those already submitted should (I hope) make an exhaustive list. I also hope they may one day be required.

Yours sincerely
JRR Tolkien.

THE LETTERS
OF J.R.R. TOLKIEN

A SELECTION EDITED BY

Humphrey Carpenter

WITH THE ASSISTANCE OF

Christopher Tolkien

HOUGHTON MIFFLIN COMPANY
BOSTON · NEW YORK

First Houghton Mifflin paperback edition 2000.

This edition first published in Great Britain in 1995.
First published in Great Britain by George Allen & Unwin in 1981.
Copyright © 1981 by George Allen & Unwin (Publishers) Ltd.

ALL RIGHTS RESERVED

Library of Congress Cataloging-in-Publication data is available.

ISBN 0-618-05699-8

For information about permission to reproduce selections from
this book, write to Permissions, Houghton Mifflin Company,
215 Park Avenue South, New York, New York 10003.

Visit our Web site: www.hmco.com/trade.

 ® is a registered trademark of the
J.R.R. Tolkien Estate Limited

Printed in the United States of America

QUM 10 9 8 7 6 5 4 3 2 1

Contents

Introduction

Towards the end of his life, J. R. R. Tolkien was deprived for a few weeks of the use of his right arm. He told his publisher: 'I found not being able to use a pen or pencil as defeating as the loss of her beak would be to a hen.'

An immense amount of Tolkien's time was taken up with the written word: not just his academic work and the stories of 'Middle-earth', but also letters. Many of these had to be written in the way of business, but in any case letter-writing was on most occasions a favourite activity with him. The consequence is that an immense number of letters by Tolkien survive; and when, with the help of Christopher Tolkien, I began work on this selection, it became obvious that an enormous quantity of material would have to be omitted, and that only passages of particular interest could be included. Naturally, priority has been given to those letters where Tolkien discusses his own books; but the selection has also been made with an eye to demonstrating the huge range of Tolkien's mind and interests, and his idiosyncratic but always clear view of the world.

Among the omissions is the very large body of letters he wrote between 1913 and 1918 to Edith Bratt, who was his fiancée and then his wife; these are highly personal in character, and from them I have chosen only a few passages which refer to writings in which Tolkien was engaged at the time. Between 1918 and 1937 few letters survive, and such as have been preserved record (unfortunately) nothing about Tolkien's work on *The Silmarillion* and *The Hobbit*, which he was writing at this time. But from 1937 onwards there is an unbroken series of letters to the end of his life, giving, often in great detail, an account of the writing of *The Lord of the Rings*, and of later work on *The Silmarillion*, and often including lengthy discussions of the meaning of his writings.

Within the letters chosen for publication, all passages omitted have been indicated by a row of *four* dots, thus: . . . . In cases where *three* dots appear, this is the usage employed by Tolkien himself in the letter. In almost all cases, omissions have been made simply for reasons of space, and only very rarely has it been necessary to leave a passage out of a letter for reasons of discretion.

Tolkien's original text has been left unaltered except in the case of the address and date, which have been given according to the same system throughout the book. and in the matter of titles of Tolkien's books. He

1

himself employed a number of different systems for giving titles: for instance, *the Hobbit*, the 'Hobbit', *The Hobbit*, *'the Hobbit'*, *'The Hobbit'*; so also with *The Lord of the Rings*. In general, editorial practice has been to regularise these titles according to the usual system, though the original form has been left where it is of interest.

Some letters are printed from carbon copies kept by Tolkien; he only began to make carbons of his letters towards the end of his life, and this explains why there is no trace of earlier letters unless the originals themselves can be discovered. Other letters in the book are printed from a draft or drafts which differ from the text that he actually sent (if he sent one at all), and in certain instances a continuous text has been assembled from several fragments of drafts: in cases where this has been done, the letter is headed 'Drafts'. The frequency of such drafts among his correspondence, and the great length of many of them, was partly explained by Tolkien in a letter to his son Michael:

Words beget words, and thoughts skid off into side-track. . . . . The 'laconic' is by me only occasionally achieved as an 'art form' by the cutting out of ¾ or more of what I have written and so is, of course, in fact more time-taking and laborious than 'free length'.

Where only a portion of a letter has been printed, the address and opening salutation have been omitted, together with the ending and signature; in such cases the letter is headed 'From a letter to ——.' All footnotes to letters are Tolkien's own.

Where I have thought it necessary, letters are preceded by a headnote giving the context of the correspondence. All other notes will be found at the back of the book; the existence of such a note is indicated by a superior numeral in the text. Notes are numbered consecutively throughout each letter, and are identified letter by letter (rather than page by page) at the back of the book. The notes have been compiled according to the principle of providing such information as is necessary for comprehension, but the aim has been brevity, too, and it is assumed that the reader will have a fairly thorough knowledge of *The Hobbit* and *The Lord of the Rings*. Bearing in mind the large number of editions of the latter book, with their different paginations, Tolkien's page-references to it in his letters are explained in the notes, with a citation of the passage to which he is referring.

In the editorial notes, four books are cited by brief titles: *Pictures, Unfinished Tales, Biography, Inklings.* These are, in full: *Pictures by J. R. R. Tolkien*, with foreword and notes by Christopher Tolkien (1979); J. R. R. Tolkien, *Unfinished Tales*, edited by Christopher Tolkien (1980); Humphrey Carpenter, *J. R. R. Tolkien, a biography*

(1977); and Humphrey Carpenter, *The Inklings* (1978). All four books are published in Britain by George Allen & Unwin Ltd., and in America by the Houghton Mifflin Company.

The division of labour between myself and Christopher Tolkien has been as follows. I myself collected and transcribed all the letters, and the initial selection was mine; he commented on the selection and transcription, and made various suggestions for changes, which we discussed further, and adopted with various emendations. We then found it necessary to reduce the text quite severely, for considerations of space; again, I proposed the initial cuts, he made comments on my suggestions, and we agreed on a final procedure. With the notes, too, I wrote the original text, and he again commented on what I had done and supplied certain additional pieces of information. The book as published therefore reflects my own taste and judgement rather more than his, but it is also the product of our joint work; and I am very grateful to him for sparing many hours, and for guiding and encouraging me.

Finally I am, of course, very grateful too to those many people who lent letters. Most of these are acknowledged in the book, in that their names appear as the recipients of the letters; in those few cases where letters were lent but have not been included, I must both thank those concerned and apologise to them for the fact that their letter or letters were omitted for reasons of space. I must also thank the various organisations and individuals who helped me: members of the Tolkien Society of Great Britain, the American Tolkien Society, and the Mythopoeic Society, who publicised our wish to trace letters, and in some cases put us in touch with owners of letters; the BBC Written Archives, the Bodleian Library, the Oxford University Press and its Dictionary Department, the Humanities Research Center of the University of Texas at Austin, and the Wade Collection at Wheaton College, Illinois, all of whom made letters available to us; the various executors (especially the Rev. Walter Hooper) and other people who helped us trace letters to persons now deceased; and finally Douglas Anderson, who helped greatly and generously in a number of ways with the preparation of the book. He and Charles Noad kindly read proofs for us.

Despite the length of this volume, and the great number of letters we have collected, there can be no doubt that much of Tolkien's correspondence still remains untraced. Any reader knowing of further letters which might deserve publication is encouraged to contact the publishers of this book, in the hope that it may be possible to add them to a second edition.

Humphrey Carpenter

3

LETTERS

1 To Edith Bratt

[Tolkien became engaged to Edith Bratt, whom he had met during his adolescence in Birmingham, in January 1913, when he was twenty-one. The following letter was written during his final year as an undergraduate at Oxford, when he was studying English Language & Literature, and at the same time was drilling in the University Officers' Training Corps as a preparation for joining the army.]

[Not dated; October 1914]   Exeter College, Oxford

My Edith darling:

Yes I was rather surprised by your card of Sat. morning and rather sorry because I knew my letter would have to wander after you. You do write splendid letters to me, little one; I am such a pig to you though. It seems age[s] since I wrote. I have had a busy (and very wet!) week end.

Friday was completely uneventful and Sat too though we had a drill all afternoon and got soaked several times and our rifles got all filthy and took ages to clean afterwards.

I spent most of the rest of those days indoors reading: I had an essay, as I told you, but I didn't get it finished as Shakespeare came up and then (Lieutenant) Thompson[1] (very healthy and well in his new uniform) and prevented me doing work on the Sabbath, as I had proposed to do. . . . . I went to St Aloysius for High Mass – and I rather enjoyed it – it is such ages since I heard one for Fr. F.[2] wouldn't let me go when I was at the Oratory last week.

I *had* to pay a duty call to the Rector[3] in the afternoon which was very boring. His wife really is appalling! I got away as soon as possible and fled back in the rain to my books. Then I went and saw Mr Sisam[4] and told him I could not finish my essay till Wed: and stayed and talked with him for some time, then I went and had an interesting talk with that quaint man Earp[5] I have told you of and introduced him (to his great delight) to the 'Kālevalā' the Finnish ballads.

Amongst other work I am trying to turn one of the stories – which is really a very great story and most tragic – into a short story somewhat on the lines of Morris' romances with chunks of poetry in between. . . . .[6]

I have got to go to the college library now and get filthy amongst dusty books – and then hang about and see the Bursar. . . . .

R.[7]

2 From a letter to Edith Bratt   27 November 1914

I did about 4 hrs. [work] 9.20–1 or so in the morning: drilled all afternoon went to a lecture 5–6 and after dinner (with a man called Earp) had to go to a meeting of the Essay Club – an informal kind of last gasp [?]. There was a bad paper but an interesting discussion. It was also composition meeting and I read 'Earendel' which was well criticised.[1]

3 From a letter to Edith Bratt   26 November 1915

[After graduating at Oxford with a First Class in English, Tolkien was commissioned in the Lancashire Fusiliers. This letter was written from Rugeley Camp in Staffordshire, where he was training. Meanwhile he was working on a poem, 'Kortirion among the Trees', suggested by Warwick, where Edith Bratt was living. The poem describes a 'fading town upon a little hill', where 'linger yet the Lonely Companies . . . . The holy fairies and immortal elves.' For 'the T.C.B.S.' see no. 5.]

The usual kind of morning standing about and freezing and then trotting to get warmer so as to freeze again. We ended up by an hour's bomb-throwing with dummies. Lunch and a freezing afternoon. All the hot days of summer we doubled about at full speed and perspiration, and now we stand in icy groups in the open being talked at! Tea and another scramble – I fought for a place at the stove and made a piece of toast on the end of a knife: what days! I have written out a pencil copy of 'Kortirion'. I hope you won't mind my sending it to the T.C.B.S. I want to send them something: I owe them all long letters. I will start on a careful ink copy for little you now and send it tomorrow night, as I don't think I shall get more than one copy typed (it is so long). No on second thoughts I am sending you the pencil copy (which is very neat) and shall keep the T.C.B.S. waiting till I can make another.

4 From a letter to Edith Bratt   2 March 1916

This miserable drizzling afternoon I have been reading up old military lecture-notes again:— and getting bored with them after an hour and a half. I have done some touches to my nonsense fairy language – to its improvement.[1]

I often long to work at it and don't let myself 'cause though I love it so it does seem such a mad hobby!

5 To G. B. Smith

[While they were at King Edward's School, Birmingham, in 1911, Tolkien and three friends, Rob Gilson, Geoffrey Smith and Christopher Wiseman, formed themselves into an unofficial and semi-secret society which they called 'the T.C.B.S.', initials standing for 'Tea Club and Barrovian Society', an allusion to their fondness for having tea in the school library, illicitly, and in Barrow's Stores near the school. Since leaving King Edward's, the T.C.B.S. had kept in close touch with each other, and in December 1914 had held a 'Council' at Wiseman's London home, following which Tolkien had begun to devote much energy to writing poetry – the result, he believed, of the shared ideals and mutual encouragement of the T.C.B.S. Wiseman was now serving in the Navy, Gilson and Smith were sent out to the Somme, and Tolkien arrived on that battlefield, as Battalion Signalling Officer to the 11th Lancashire Fusiliers, just as the Allied offensive of 1 July was beginning. On that day, Rob Gilson was killed in action, but news of his death did not reach the other members of the T.C.B.S. for some weeks. Geoffrey Smith sent Tolkien a note about it, and later passed him a letter from Christopher Wiseman.]

12 August 1916   11th Lancashire Fusiliers, B.E.F., France
My dear old Geoffrey,

Thank you indeed for Christopher's letter. I have thought much of things since – most of them incommunicable thoughts until God brings us together again if it be only for a space.

I don't agree with Chris – although of course he does not say much. I agree most heartily of course with the part you underlined – but strangely enough not in the least now with the part I marked and commented. I went out into the wood – we are out in camp again from our second bout of trenches still in the same old area as when I saw you – last night and also the night before and sat and thought.

I cannot get away from the conclusion that it is wrong to confound the greatness which Rob has won with the greatness which he himself doubted. He himself will know that I am only being perfectly sincere and I am in no way unfaithful to my love for him – which I only realise now, more and more daily, that he has gone from the four – when I say that I now believe that if the greatness which we three certainly meant (and meant as more than holiness or nobility alone) is really the lot of the TCBS, then the death of any of its members is but a bitter winnowing of those who were not meant to be great – at least directly. God grant that this does not sound arrogant – I feel humbler enough in truth and immeasurably weaker and poorer now. The greatness I meant was that of a great instrument in God's hands – a mover, a doer, even an achiever of great things, a beginner at the very least of large things.

The greatness which Rob has found is in no way smaller – for the greatness I meant and tremblingly hoped for as ours is valueless unless steeped with the same holiness of courage suffering and sacrifice – but is of a different kind. His greatness is in other words now a personal matter with us – of a kind to make us keep July 1st as a special day for all the years God may grant to any of us – but only touches the TCBS on that precise side which perhaps – it is possible – was the only one that

9

Rob really felt – 'Friendship to the Nth power'. What I meant, and thought Chris meant, and am almost sure you meant, was that the TCBS had been granted some spark of fire – certainly as a body if not singly – that was destined to kindle a new light, or, what is the same thing, rekindle an old light in the world; that the TCBS was destined to testify for God and Truth in a more direct way even than by laying down its several lives in this war (which is for all the evil of our own side with large view good against evil).

So far my chief impression is that something has gone crack. I feel just the same to both of you – nearer if anything and very much in need of you – I am hungry and lonely of course – but I don't feel a member of a little complete body now. I honestly feel that the TCBS has ended – but I am not at all sure that it is not an unreliable feeling that will vanish – like magic perhaps when we come together again. Still I feel a mere individual at present – with intense feelings more than ideas but very powerless.

Of course the TCBS may have been all we dreamt – and its work in the end be done by three or two or one survivor and the part of the others be trusted by God to that of the inspiration which we do know we all got and get from one another. To this I now pin my hopes, and pray God that the people chosen to carry on the TCBS may be no fewer than we three. . . . .

I do however dread and grieve about it – apart from my own personal longings – because I cannot abandon yet the hope and ambitions (inchoate and cloudy I know) that first became conscious at the Council of London. That Council was as you know followed in my own case with my finding a voice for all kinds of pent up things and a tremendous opening up of everything for me:— I have always laid that to the credit of the inspiration that even a few hours with the four always brought to all of us.

There you are – I have sat solemnly down and tried to tell you drily just what I think. I have made it sound very cold and distant – and if it is incoherent that is due to its being written at different sittings amongst the noise of a very boring Company mess.

Send it on to Chris if you think it worth while. I do not know what is to be our move next or what is in store. Rumour is as busy as the universal weariness of all this war allows it to be. I wish I could know where you are. I make a guess of course.

I could write a huge letter but I have lots of jobs on. The Bde. Sig. Offr. is after me for a confabulation, and I have two rows to have with the QM and a detestable 6.30 parade – 6.30 pm of a sunny Sabbath.

Write to me when you get the ghost of a chance.

Yours
John Ronald.

6 To Mrs E. M. Wright

[In 1920 Tolkien was appointed Reader in English Language at Leeds University, a post that was later converted into a Professorship; see no. 46 for an account of the interview leading to his appointment. Tolkien was now married to Edith Bratt; by 1923 he had two children, John and Michael. In 1922 he published a glossary to a Middle English Reader edited by his former tutor, Kenneth Sisam. He also began work with E. V. Gordon on an edition of *Sir Gawain and the Green Knight*. The following letter, acknowledging receipt of an article about that poem, is addressed to the wife of Joseph Wright, editor of the *English Dialect Dictionary* ('E.D.D.'). Tolkien had studied philology with Wright at Oxford.]

13 February 1923   The University, Leeds

Dear Mrs Wright,

I am very grateful to you for the offprint – and also for your kind remarks about the glossary. I certainly lavished an amount of time on it which is terrible to recall, and long delayed the Reader bringing curses on my head; but it was instructive.

I need hardly say that I am quite convinced by your article and am delighted to feel confident that another rough patch in 'Sir G.' is now smoothed out finally by you.

We have just passed through a somewhat disastrous Christmas, as the children chose that time to sicken for measles – by the beginning of January I was the only one in the house left up, the patients including the wife & nursemaid. The vacation work lay in ruins; but they (not the work) are all better now and not much the worse. I escaped. I hope you are well, and that Professor Wright is well – I have not heard any news of him lately, which I have interpreted favourably.

Middle English is an exciting field – almost uncharted I begin to think, because as soon as one turns detailed personal attention on to any little corner of it the received notions and ideas seem to crumple up and fall to pieces – as far as language goes at any rate. E.D.D. is certainly indispensable, or 'unentbehrlich' as really comes more natural to the philological mind, and I encourage people to browze in it.

My wife wishes to be remembered to you both and joins her greetings to mine.

Yours sincerely

J. R. R. Tolkien.

Philology is making headway here. The proportion of 'language' students is very high, and there is no trace of the press-gang! JRRT.

11

7 To the Electors of the Rawlinson and Bosworth Professorship of Anglo-Saxon, University of Oxford

[In the summer of 1925 the Professorship of Anglo-Saxon at Oxford was advertised, following the resignation of W. A. Craigie. Tolkien decided to apply, though he was only thirty-three. This is his formal letter of application, dated 27 June 1925.]

Gentlemen,

I desire to offer myself as a candidate for the Rawlinson and Bosworth Professorship of Anglo-Saxon.

A Chair which affords such opportunity of expressing and communicating an instructed enthusiasm for Anglo-Saxon studies and for the study of the other Old Germanic languages is naturally attractive to me, nor could I desire anything better than to be reassociated in this way with the Oxford English School. I was a member of that School both as undergraduate and as tutor, and during my five years' absence in Leeds am happy to have remained in touch with it, more especially, in the last two years, as an Examiner in the Final Schools.

I entered Exeter College as Stapledon Exhibitioner in 1911. After taking Classical Moderations in 1913 (in which I specialized in Greek philology), I graduated with first class honours in English in 1915, my special subject being Old Icelandic. Until the end of 1918 I held a commission in the Lancashire Fusiliers, and at that date entered the service of the Oxford English Dictionary. I was one of Dr. Bradley's[1] assistants until the spring of 1920, when my own work and the increasing labours of a tutor made it impossible to continue.

In October 1920 I went to Leeds as Reader in English Language, with a free commission to develop the linguistic side of a large and growing School of English Studies, in which no regular provision had as yet been made for the linguistic specialist. I began with five hesitant pioneers out of a School (exclusive of the first year) of about sixty members. The proportion to-day is 43 literary to 20 linguistic students. The linguists are in no way isolated or cut off from the general life and work of the department, and share in many of the literary courses and activities of the School; but since 1922 their purely linguistic work has been conducted in special classes, and examined in distinct papers of special standard and attitude. The instruction offered has been gradually extended, and now covers a large part of the field of English and Germanic philology. Courses are given on Old English heroic verse, the history of English*, various Old English and Middle English texts*, Old and Middle English philology*, introductory Germanic philology*, Gothic, Old Icelandic (a second-year* and third-year course), and Medieval Welsh*. All these courses I have from time to

12

time given myself; those that I have given personally in the past year are marked *. During this last session a course of voluntary reading of texts not specially considered in the current syllabus has attracted more than fifteen students, not all of them from the linguistic side of the department.

Philology, indeed, appears to have lost for these students its connotations of terror if not of mystery. An active discussion-class has been conducted, on lines more familiar in schools of literature than of language, which has borne fruit in friendly rivalry and open debate with the corresponding literary assembly. A Viking Club has even been formed, by past and present students of Old Icelandic, which promises to carry on the same kind of activity independently of the staff. Old Icelandic has been a point of special development, and usually reaches a higher standard than the other special subjects, being studied for two years and in much the same detail as Anglo-Saxon. . . . .

The large amount of teaching and direction which my post has hitherto involved, supplemented by a share in the general administration of a growing department, and latterly by the duties of a member of Senate at a time of special difficulty in University policy, has seriously interfered with my projects for publishable work; but I append a note of what I have found time to do. If elected to the Rawlinson and Bosworth Chair I should endeavour to make productive use of the opportunities which it offers for research; to advance, to the best of my ability, the growing neighbourliness of linguistic and literary studies, which can never be enemies except by misunderstanding or without loss to both; and to continue in a wider and more fertile field the encouragement of philological enthusiasm among the young.

I remain,

Gentlemen,

Your obedient servant,

J. R. R. Tolkien.

8   From a letter to the Vice Chancellor of Leeds University
22 July 1925

My election to the Rawlinson & Bosworth professorship at Oxford has just been announced to me, & I have accepted – it takes effect from next October 1st – only with feelings of great regret at this sudden severance, in spite of this unexpected turn of fortune for myself.

Only the sudden resignation of my predecessor has thrust this upon me so soon – I dimly coveted it as a thing perhaps for the more distant years, but now after this University's kindness, and the great happiness of my brief period of work here, I feel ungrateful in asking to be released from my appointment so soon. I hope for your forgiveness.

9   To Susan Dagnall, George Allen & Unwin Ltd.

[Tolkien wrote the greater part of *The Hobbit* during his first seven years as Professor of Anglo-Saxon at Oxford. A text was in existence by the winter of 1932, when it was read by C. S. Lewis, though at this stage the typescript apparently lacked the final chapters, and broke off shortly before the death of the dragon Smaug. This typescript was eventually seen by Susan Dagnall, an Oxford graduate working for the London publishing house of Allen & Unwin, and she encouraged Tolkien to complete the story and offer it for publication. See nos. 163, 257, and 294 for Tolkien's account of her involvement with the book, though two of these later letters are in error in suggesting that Susan Dagnall was still an Oxford student when she read the manuscript. See further *Biography* p. 180. It was on 3 October 1936 that Tolkien sent the completed typescript to Allen & Unwin. Stanley Unwin, founder and chairman of the firm, replied on 5 October that they would give their 'immediate and careful consideration' to the book. No further correspondence survives until the following letter. By the time that Tolkien wrote it, the book had been accepted for publication, and he was already preparing maps and illustrations.]

4 January 1937   20 Northmoor Road, Oxford
Dear Miss Dagnall,
                            Maps &c. for '*The Hobbit*'.
   I am sorry for the long delay. I was unwell for some time, and then faced by a family laid low one by one by influenza, brought back from school for the entire ruin of Christmas. I succumbed myself on New Year's Eve. It has been difficult to do anything, and what I have done is I fear poor enough. I have redrawn two items: the chart, which has to be tipped in (in Chapter I), and the general map. I can only hope – as I have small skill, and no experience of preparing such things for reproduction – that they may possibly serve. The other maps I have decided are not wanted.

   I have redrawn (as far as I am capable) one or two of the amateur illustrations of the 'home manuscript', conceiving that they might serve as endpapers, frontispiece or what not. I think on the whole such things, if they were better, might be an improvement. But it may be impossible at this stage, and in any case they are not very good and may be technically unsuitable. It would be kind if you would return the rejected.

                                            Yours sincerely
                                            J. R. R. Tolkien.

10 To C. A. Furth, Allen & Unwin

[Some time between 1932 and 1937, Tolkien wrote and illustrated a short book for children entitled *Mr Bliss*. For a description of it, see *Biography* p. 163. It was shown to Allen & Unwin at the same time that *The Hobbit* was submitted. The publishers said they would be happy to accept it, providing Tolkien could reduce the number of colours in the drawings.]

17 January 1937   20 Northmoor Road, Oxford

Dear Sir,

'Mr Bliss' returned safely. I can only say that I was surprised to receive your kind letter the following morning. I did not imagine that he was worth so much trouble. The pictures seem to me mostly only to prove that the author cannot draw. But if your firm really think that he is worth publishing, I will try and make the illustrations more easy to reproduce. Certainly it would be a great help, if you would be so kind as to call, as you suggest, and give me some advice. I am at present endeavouring to earn a grant for 'research',[1] in addition to my ordinary duties, but I may find some odd moments in the near future, especially as I am freed from the burden of examining for two years.

I am also grateful and pleasantly surprised that the drawings for 'the Hobbit' can be used. I leave it in your hands as to the best way of reproducing and using them. Actually the *chart* – the map with runes – was intended to be tipped in (folded) in Chapter I, opposite the first mention of it: 'a piece of parchment rather like a map', towards the end of the chapter. The *other map* in the 'home MS.' came at the end, and the long narrow drawing of *Mirkwood*[2] was at the beginning. The *Elvenking's Gate* came at the end of Ch. VIII, *Lake Town* in Ch. X, *The Front Gate* in Ch. XI after the description of the adventurers' first sight of it: 'they could see the dark cavernous opening in a great cliff-wall'. In considering the matter closer I see that this concentrates all the maps and pictures, in place or reference, towards the end. This is due to no plan, but occurs simply because I failed to reduce the other illustrations to even passable shape. I was also advised that those with a geographical or landscape content were the most suitable – even apart from my inability to draw anything else.

I now enclose 6 more.[3] They all are obviously defective, and quite apart from this may, each or some, present difficulties of reproduction. Also you may be quite unwilling to consider thus belatedly any more complications, and a change of plan. So that I shall be neither pained nor surprised if you return them, all or any. . . . .

I am yrs. truly,

J. R. R. Tolkien.

11 From a letter to Allen & Unwin 5 February 1937

[Concerning the reproduction of illustrations in *The Hobbit*.]

I approve the rough prints. Reduction has improved all except 'the Trolls'. On this there are one or two defects, probably simply due to the impression. I have marked them: the thin white outline of one of the background trees is slightly broken; some of the tiny dots outlining a flame have failed to come out; the dot after 'Trolls.' also.

In the 'Hall at Bag-End' I misguidedly put in a wash shadow reaching right up to the side beam. This has of course come out black (with disappearance of the key) though not right up to the beam. But the print is I think as good as the original allows. Please note – these are not serious criticisms! I am still surprised that these indifferent pictures have been accepted at all, and that you have taken so much trouble with them – especially against economics (a factor I had not forgotten, and the reason for my originally forswearing illustrations).

12 To Allen & Unwin

[In mid-March, Tolkien returned the proofs of *The Hobbit* to Allen & Unwin, having marked them with a very large number of alterations to the original text. He was told that as a result he might have to pay part of the cost of correction, though the publishers noted that he had devised revisions which would occupy exactly the same space as the original text. With the following letter, he submitted a drawing for the dust-jacket, which included a runic inscription.]

13 April 1937   20 Northmoor Road, Oxford
Dear Sirs,

I return under separate cover the corrected *Revises* of *the Hobbit*, complete. . . . . I note what you so kindly say about the cost of corrections. I must pay what is just, if required; though I shall naturally be grateful for clemency. Thank you for your trouble & consideration. . . . .

You will find with the revised proofs a *draft of the jacket*, for your criticism. I discovered (as I anticipated) that it was rather beyond my craft and experience. But perhaps the general design would do?

I foresee the main objections.

There are too many colours: blue, green, red, black. (The 2 reds are an accident; the 2 greens inessential.) This could be met, with possible improvement, by substituting *white* for *red*; and omitting the sun, or drawing a line round it. The presence of the sun and moon in the sky together refers to the magic attaching to the door.

It is too complicated, and needs simplifying: e.g. by reducing the mountains to a single colour, and simplification of the jagged 'fir-trees'. . . . .

In redrawing the whole thing could be reduced – if you think the runes are attractive. Though magical in appearance they merely run: *The Hobbit or There and Back Again, being the record of a year's journey made by Bilbo Baggins; compiled from his memoirs by J. R. R. Tolkien and published by George Allen & Unwin.* . . . .

Yrs truly

J. R. R. Tolkien.

13   To C. A. Furth, Allen & Unwin

[On 11 May, Allen & Unwin told Tolkien that they had interested 'one of the outstanding firms of American publishers' in *The Hobbit*, and said that this firm 'would like a number of further illustrations in colour and suggested employing good American artists'. Allen & Unwin, however, thought 'it would be better if all the illustrations were from your hand'.]

13 May 1937   20 Northmoor Road, Oxford
Dear Mr Furth,

Thank you for the information concerning prospective American publication. Could you tell me the name of the firm, and what are likely to be the financial arrangements?

As for the illustrations: I am divided between knowledge of my own inability and fear of what American artists (doubtless of admirable skill) might produce. In any case I agree that all the illustrations ought to be by the same hand: four professional pictures would make my own amateurish productions look rather silly. I have some 'pictures' in my drawer, but though they represent scenes from the mythology on the outskirts of which the Hobbit had his adventures, they do not really illustrate his story. The only possible one is the original coloured version of *Mirkwood*[1] (re-drawn in black and white for 'the Hobbit'). I should have to try and draw some five or six others for the purpose. I will attempt this, as far as time allows in the middle of term, if you think it advisable. But I could not promise anything for some time. Perhaps the matter does not allow of much delay? It might be advisable, rather than lose the American interest, to let the Americans do what seems good to them – as long as it was possible (I should like to add) to veto anything from or influenced by the Disney studios (for all whose works I have a heartfelt loathing). I have seen American illustrations that suggest that excellent things might be produced – only too excellent for their companions. But perhaps you could tell me how long there is

17

before I must produce samples that might hope to satisfy Transatlantic juvenile taste (or its expert connoisseurs)? . . . .

Yours sincerely

J. R. R. Tolkien

14 To Allen & Unwin

[The publishers had suggested to Tolkien that *The Hobbit* should be published in October 1937, just after the beginning of the Michaelmas Term at Oxford. They also told him that they had forwarded his letter about illustrations (no. 13) to the Houghton Mifflin Company of Boston, Massachusetts, who were to publish the book in America.]

28 May 1937   20 Northmoor Road, Oxford

Dear Sirs,

. . . . *Date of publication*. This is, of course, your business, and entails many considerations outside my knowledge. In any case the final decision is now, I suppose, made; and America has also to be considered. But as far as G.B. is concerned, I cannot help thinking that you are possibly mistaken in taking Oxford University and its terms into account; and alternatively, if you do, in considering early October better than June. Most of O.U. will take no interest in such a story; that part of it that will is already clamouring, and indeed beginning to add The Hobbit to my long list of never-never procrastinations. As far as 'local interest' is concerned it is probably at its peak (not that at its best it will amount to much reckoned in direct sales, I imagine). In any case late June between the last preparations for exams and the battle with scripts (affecting only a minority of seniors) is a quiescent interlude, when lighter reading is sought, for immediate use and for the vacation. October with the inrush of a new academic year is most distracted.

Mr Lewis of Magdalen,[1] who reviews for the Times Literary Supplement, tells me that he has already written urging a review and claiming the book as a specialist in fairy-stories; and he is now disgruntled because he will get 'juveniles' that he does not want, while the Hobbit will not reach him until the vacation is over, and will have to wait till December to be read & written up properly. Also if the book had been available before the university disintegrates I could have got my friend the editor of the O.U. Magazine,[2] who has been giving it a good dose of my dragon-lore recently, to allocate it and get a review at the beginning of the autumn term. However, I say these things too late I expect. In any case I do not suppose it makes in the long run a great deal of difference. I have only one personal motive in regretting this delay: and that is that I was anxious that it should appear as soon as possible, because I am under research-contract since last October, and not supposed to be indulging

18

in exams or in 'frivolities'. The further we advance into my contract time, the more difficulty I shall have (and I have already had some) in pretending that the work belongs wholly to the period before October 1936. I shall now find it very hard to make people believe that this is not the major fruits of 'research' 1936–7!

Houghton Mifflin Co. I was perturbed to learn that my letter had been sent across the water. It was not intended for American consumption unedited: I should have expressed myself rather differently. I now feel even greater hesitation in posing further as an illustrator. . . . . However, I enclose three coloured 'pictures'.[3] I cannot do much better, and if their standard is too low, the H.M.Co can say so at once and without offence, as long as they send them back. These are casual and careless pastime products, illustrating other stories. Having publication in view I could possibly improve the standard a little, make drawings rather bolder in colour & less messy and fussy in detail (and also larger). The Mirkwood picture is much the same as the plate in *the Hobbit*, but illustrates a different adventure. I think if the H.M.Co wish me to proceed I should leave that black and grey plate and do four other scenes. I will try my hand at them as soon as possible, which is not likely to be before their verdict arrives, if cabled . . .

Yours truly,
J. R. R. Tolkien.

15 To Allen & Unwin

[Enclosed with this letter was a coloured version of the drawing 'The Hill: Hobbiton-across-the-Water'. Tolkien had already sent four new coloured drawings: 'Rivendell', 'Bilbo woke with the early sun in his eyes', 'Bilbo comes to the Huts of the Raft-elves', and 'Conversation with Smaug'. All of these except the 'Huts of the Raft-elves' were used in the first American edition, and all except 'Bilbo woke with the early sun in his eyes' were added to the second British impression.]

31 August 1937   20 Northmoor Road, Oxford
Dear Mr Furth,

I send herewith the coloured version of the frontispiece. If you think it good enough, you may send it on to the Houghton Mifflin Co. Could you at the same time make it finally clear to them (it does not seem easy): that the first *three* drawings were *not* illustrations to 'the Hobbit', but only samples: they cannot be used for that book, and may now be returned. Also that the ensuing *five* drawings (*four* and now *one*) were specially made for the H.M.Co, and for 'the Hobbit'. They are, of course, at liberty to reject or use all or any of these *five*. But I would point out that they are specially selected so as to distribute illustration

19

fairly evenly throughout the book (especially when taken in conjunction with the black-and-white drawings).

I suppose no question of remuneration arises? I have no consciousness of merit (though the labour was considerable), and I imagine that the 'gratis' quality of my efforts compensates for other defects. But I gathered that the H.M.Co's original terms simply covered 'The Hobbit', as you produced it, and that they then proposed to top up with coloured pictures, as a selling attraction of their own, employing good American artists. They would have had to pay these independently. At the moment I am in such difficulties (largely owing to medical expenses) that even a very small fee would be a blessing. Would it be possible to suggest (*when* they have decided if they want any of these things) that a small financial consideration would be gracious?

Perhaps you will advise me, or tell me where I get off? I need hardly say that such an idea only occurs to me with regard to the Americans – who have given a lot of unnecessary trouble. Even if I did not know that your production costs have been excessive (and that I have been hard on proofs), you are most welcome at any time to anything you think I can do, in the way of drawing or redrawing, that is fit to use on The Hobbit.

I hope Mr Baggins will eventually come to my rescue – in a moderate way (I do not expect pots of troll-gold). I am beginning to have hopes that the publishers (*vide* jacket) may be justified.[1] I have had two testimonials recently, which promise moderately well. For one thing Professor Gordon[2] has actually read the book (supposed to be a rare event); and assures me that he will recommend it generally and to the Book Society. I may warn you that his promises are usually generous – but his judgement, at any rate, is pretty good. Professor Chambers[3] writes very enthusiastically, but he is an old and kindhearted friend. The most valuable is the document I enclose, in case it may interest you: a letter from R. Meiggs (at present editing the Oxford Magazine). He has no reason for sparing my feelings, and is usually a plain speaker. Of course, he has no connexions with reviewing coteries, and is virtually a mere member of the avuncular public.

Yours sincerely

J. R. R. Tolkien.

P.S. I enclose also a commentary on the jacket-flap words for your perusal at leisure – if you can read it.

[When *The Hobbit* was published on 21 September 1937, Allen & Unwin printed the following remarks on the jacket-flap: 'J. R. R. Tolkien. . . . has four children and *The Hobbit* . . . . was read aloud to them in nursery days. . . . . The manuscript . . . . was lent to friends in Oxford and read to their children. . . . . The birth of *The Hobbit* recalls very strongly that of *Alice in Wonderland*. Here again a professor of an abstruse subject is at play.' Tolkien now sent the following commentary on these remarks.]

By the way. I meant some time ago to comment on the additional matter that appears on the jacket. I don't suppose it is a very important item in launching *The Hobbit* (while that book is only one minor incident in your concerns); so I hope you will take the ensuing essay in good part, and allow me the pleasure of explaining things (the professor will out), even if it does not appear useful.

I am in your hands, if you think that is the right note. Strict truth is, I suppose, not necessary (or even desirable). But I have a certain anxiety lest the H.M.Co seize upon the words and exaggerate the inaccuracy to falsehood. And reviewers are apt to lean on hints. At least I am when performing that function.

Nursery: I have never had one, and the study has always been the place for such amusements. In any case is the age-implication right? I should have said 'the nursery' ended about 8 when children go forth to school. That is too young. My eldest boy was thirteen when he heard the serial. It did not appeal to the younger ones who had to grow up to it successively.

Lent: we must pass that (though strictly it was forced on the friends by me). The MS. certainly wandered about, but it was not, as far as I know, ever read *to* children, and only read *by* one child (a girl of 12–13), before Mr Unwin tried it out.

Abstruse: I do not profess an 'abstruse' subject – not qua 'Anglo-Saxon'. Some folk may think so, but I do not like encouraging them. Old English and Icelandic literature are no more remote from human concerns, or difficult to acquire cheaply, than commercial Spanish (say). I have tried both. In any case – except for the runes (Anglo-Saxon) and the dwarf-names (Icelandic), neither used with antiquarian accuracy, and both regretfully substituted to avoid abstruseness for the genuine alphabets and names of the mythology into which Mr Baggins intrudes – I am afraid my professional knowledge is not directly used. The magic and mythology and assumed 'history' and most of the names (e.g. the epic of the Fall of Gondolin) are, alas!, drawn from unpublished inventions, known only to my family, Miss Griffiths[1] and Mr Lewis. I believe they give the narrative an air of 'reality' and have a northern atmosphere. But I wonder whether one should lead the unsuspecting to imagine it all comes out of the 'old books', or tempt the knowing to point out that it does not?

'Philology' – my real professional bag of tricks – may be abstruse, and perhaps more comparable to Dodgson's maths. So the real parallel (if

21

one exists: I feel very much that it breaks down if examined)* lies in the fact that both these technical subjects in any overt form are absent. The only philological remark (I think) in *The Hobbit* is on p. 221 (lines 6–7 from end):[2] an odd mythological way of referring to linguistic philosophy, and a point that will (happily) be missed by any who have not read Barfield[3] (few have), and probably by those who have. I am afraid this stuff of mine is really more comparable to Dodgson's amateur photography, and his song of Hiawatha's failure than to *Alice*.

Professor: a professor at play rather suggests an elephant in its bath – as Sir Walter Raleigh[4] said of Professor Jo Wright in a sportive mood at a *viva*.[5] Strictly (I believe) Dodgson was not a 'professor', but a college lecturer – though he was kind to my kind in making the 'professor' the best character (unless you prefer the mad gardener) in *Sylvie & Bruno*. Why not 'student'? The word has the added advantage that Dodgson's official status was Student of Christ Church. If you think it good, and fair (the compliment to *The Hobbit* is rather high) to maintain the comparison – *Looking-glass* ought to be mentioned. It is much closer in every way. . . . .

J. R. R. Tolkien.

16 To Michael Tolkien

[Tolkien's second son Michael, now aged sixteen, was a pupil at the Oratory School in Berkshire, together with his younger brother Christopher. He was hoping to get into the school rugby football team.]

3 October 1937   20 Northmoor Road, Oxford
Dearest Mick,

It was nice to have a letter from you. I hope all is going well. I thought the new flats[1] looked as if they would be presentable when furnished. It is good of you to keep a kindly eye on Chris, as far as you can. I expect he will make a mess of things to begin with, but he ought soon to find his bearings and be no more trouble to you or himself.

I am sorry and surprised you are not (yet) in the team. But many a man ends up in it and even with colours, who is rejected at first. It was so with me – and for same reason: too light. But one day I decided to make up for weight by (legitimate) ferocity, and I ended up a house-captain at end of that season, & got my colours the next. But I got rather damaged – among things having my tongue nearly cut out – and as I am on the whole rather luckier than you, I should really be quite happy if you remain uninjured though not in the team! But God bless you & keep

---

*Is the presence of 'conundrums' in *Alice* a parallel to echoes of Northern myth in *The Hobbit*?

you anyway. There is no very special news. Mummy seems to have taken to car-riding. We have been two since you left, and I have now got to take her, P. and J.B.[2] out this afternoon instead of writing. So this must be all for the moment. With v. much love indeed.

Your own
Father

17   To Stanley Unwin, Chairman of Allen & Unwin

[Unwin had sent Tolkien a letter from the author Richard Hughes, who had been given a copy of *The Hobbit* by Allen & Unwin. Hughes wrote to Unwin: 'I agree with you that it is one of the best stories for children I have come across for a very long time. . . . . The only snag I can see is that many parents . . . . may be afraid that certain parts of it would be too terrifying for bedside reading.' Unwin also mentioned that his own eleven-year-old son Rayner, who had written the report on the manuscript of *The Hobbit* which had led to its publication (see *Biography* pp. 180–81), had been re-reading the book now that it was in print. Unwin concluded by warning Tolkien that 'a large public' would be 'clamouring next year to hear more from you about Hobbits!']

15 October 1937   20 Northmoor Road, Oxford
Dear Mr Unwin,

Thank you very much for your kind letter of October 11th, and now for the copy of Richard Hughes' letter. I was particularly interested in this, since we are quite unknown to one another. The reviews in The Times and its Literary Supplement were good – that is (unduly) flattering; though I guess, from internal evidence, that they were both written by the same man,[1] and one whose approval was assured: we started with common tastes and reading, and have been closely associated for years. Still that in no way detracts from their public effect. Also I must respect his opinion, as I believed him to be the best living critic until he turned his attention to me, and no degree of friendship would make him say what he does not mean: he is the most uncompromisingly honest man I have met! . . . .

No reviewer (that I have seen), although all have carefully used the correct *dwarfs* themselves, has commented on the fact (which I only became conscious of through reviews) that I use throughout the 'incorrect' plural *dwarves*. I am afraid it is just a piece of private bad grammar, rather shocking in a philologist; but I shall have to go on with it. Perhaps my *dwarf* – since he and the *Gnome*[2] are only translations into approximate equivalents of creatures with different names and rather different functions in their own world – may be allowed a peculiar plural. The real 'historical' plural of *dwarf* (like *teeth* of *tooth*) is

23

dwarrows, anyway: rather a nice word, but a bit too archaic. Still I rather wish I had used the word *dwarrow*.

My heart warms to your son. To read the faint and close typescript was noble: to read the whole thing again so soon was a magnificent compliment.

I have received one postcard, alluding I suppose to the Times' review: containing just the words:

sic hobbitur ad astra.[3]

All the same I am a little perturbed. I cannot think of anything more to say about *hobbits*. Mr Baggins seems to have exhibited so fully both the Took and the Baggins side of their nature. But I have only too much to say, and much already written, about the world into which the hobbit intruded. You can, of course, see any of it, and say what you like about it, if and when you wish. I should rather like an opinion, other than that of Mr C. S. Lewis and my children, whether it has any value in itself, or as a marketable commodity, apart from hobbits. But if it is true that *The Hobbit* has come to stay and more will be wanted, I will start the process of thought, and try to get some idea of a theme drawn from this material for treatment in a similar style and for a similar audience – possibly including actual hobbits. My daughter would like something on the Took family. One reader wants fuller details about Gandalf and the Necromancer. But that is too dark – much too much for Richard Hughes' snag. I am afraid that snag appears in everything; though actually the presence (even if only on the borders) of the terrible is, I believe, what gives this imagined world its verisimilitude. A safe fairy-land is untrue to all worlds. At the moment I am suffering like Mr Baggins from a touch of 'staggerment', and I hope I am not taking myself too seriously. But I must confess that your letter has aroused in me a faint hope. I mean, I begin to wonder whether duty and desire may not (perhaps) in future go more closely together. I have spent nearly all the vacation-times of seventeen years examining, and doing things of that sort, driven by immediate financial necessity (mainly medical and educational). Writing stories in prose or verse has been stolen, often guiltily, from time already mortgaged, and has been broken and ineffective. I may perhaps now do what I much desire to do, and not fail of financial duty. Perhaps!*

I think 'Oxford' interest is mildly aroused. I am constantly asked how my hobbit is. The attitude is (as I foresaw) not unmixed with surprise and a little pity. My own college is I think good for about six copies, if only in order to find material for teasing me. Appearance in The Times

---

*Not that 'examining' is very profitable. Quite small sales would surpass it. £100 requires nearly as much labour as a full-sized novel.

convinced one or two of my more sedate colleagues that they could admit knowledge of my 'fantasy' (i.e. indiscretion) without loss of academic dignity. The professor of Byzantine Greek[4] bought a copy, 'because first editions of "Alice" are now very valuable'. I did hear that the Regius Professor of Modern History was recently seen reading 'The Hobbit'. It is displayed by Parkers[5] but not elsewhere (I think).

I am probably coming to town, to hear Professor Joseph Vendryes at the Academy on Wednesday Oct. 27th. I wonder would that be a suitable day for the luncheon you kindly asked me to last summer? And in any case, I could bring *Mr Bliss* to the office so as to get the definite advice on what is needed to make it reproducible promised by Mr Furth?

Yours sincerely

J. R. R. Tolkien.

PS. I acknowledge safe receipt of the specimen 'pictures' sent to America.

18 From a letter to Stanley Unwin   23 October 1937

[On 19 October, Unwin wrote to Tolkien: 'I think there is cause for your faint hope. . . . . It is seldom that a children's writer gets firmly established with one book, but that you will do so very rapidly I have not the slightest doubt. . . . . You are one of those rare people with genius, and, unlike some publishers, it is a word I have not used half a dozen times in thirty years of publishing.']

Thank you in return for your encouraging letter. I will start something soon, & submit it to your boy at the earliest opportunity.

19 To Stanley Unwin

[Tolkien lunched with Unwin in London on 15 November, and told him about a number of his writings which already existed in manuscript: the series of *Father Christmas Letters*, which he had addressed to his children each Christmas since 1920; various short tales and poems; and *The Silmarillion*. Following this meeting, he handed to Allen & Unwin the 'Quenta Silmarillion', a prose formulation of the latter book, together with the long unfinished poem 'The Gest of Beren and Lúthien'. These were shown to one of the firm's outside readers, Edward Crankshaw, who reported unfavourably on the poem, but praised the prose narrative for its 'brevity and dignity', though he said he disliked its 'eye-splitting Celtic names'. His report continued: 'It has something of that mad, bright-eyed beauty that perplexes all Anglo-Saxons in face of Celtic art.' These comments were passed on to Tolkien.]

16 December 1937   20 Northmoor Road, Oxford
Dear Mr Unwin,

I have been ill and am still rather tottery, and have had others of the common human troubles, so that time has slipped out of my hands: I have accomplished next to nothing of any kind since I saw you. Father Christmas' 1937 letter is unwritten yet. . . . .

My chief joy comes from learning that the Silmarillion is not rejected with scorn. I have suffered a sense of fear and bereavement, quite ridiculous, since I let this private and beloved nonsense out; and I think if it had seemed to you to be nonsense I should have felt really crushed. I do not mind about the verse-form, which in spite of certain virtuous passages has grave defects, for it is only for me the rough material. But I shall certainly now hope one day to be able, or to be able to afford, to publish the Silmarillion! Your reader's comment affords me delight. I am sorry the names split his eyes – personally I believe (and here believe I am a good judge) they are good, and a large part of the effect. They are coherent and consistent and made upon two related linguistic formulae, so that they achieve a reality not fully achieved to my feeling by other name-inventors (say Swift or Dunsany!). Needless to say they are not Celtic! Neither are the tales. I do know Celtic things (many in their original languages Irish and Welsh), and feel for them a certain distaste: largely for their fundamental unreason. They have bright colour, but are like a broken stained glass window reassembled without design. They are in fact 'mad' as your reader says – but I don't believe I am. Still I am very grateful for his words, and particularly encouraged that the style is good for the purpose and even gets over the nomenclature.

I did not think any of the stuff I dropped on you filled the bill. But I did want to know whether any of the stuff had any exterior non-personal value. I think it is plain that quite apart from it, a sequel or successor to The Hobbit is called for. I promise to give this thought and attention. But I am sure you will sympathize when I say that the construction of elaborate and consistent mythology (and two languages) rather occupies the mind, and the Silmarils are in my heart. So that goodness knows what will happen. Mr Baggins began as a comic tale among conventional and inconsistent Grimm's fairy-tale dwarves, and got drawn into the edge of it – so that even Sauron the terrible peeped over the edge. And what more can hobbits do? They can be comic, but their comedy is suburban unless it is set against things more elemental. But the real fun about orcs and dragons (to my mind) was before their time. Perhaps a new (if similar) line? Do you think Tom Bombadil, the spirit of the (vanishing) Oxford and Berkshire countryside, could be made into the hero of a story? Or is he, as I suspect, fully enshrined in the enclosed verses?[1] Still I could enlarge the portrait.

Which are the four coloured illustrations you are using?[2] Have the five originals yet returned? Is there a spare one available of the dragon on his hoard? I have to give a lecture on *dragons*, (at the Natural History Museum!!!) and they want a picture to make a slide of.[3]

Could I have four more copies of *the Hobbit* at author's rates, to use as Christmas presents?

May I wish you bon voyage – and a safe return.[4] I am supposed to be broadcasting from BBC on Jan 14th, but that will I suppose be after your return.[5] I shall look forward to seeing you again.

Yours sincerely

J. R. R. Tolkien

P.S. I have received several queries, on behalf of children and adults, concerning the *runes* and whether they are real and can be read. Some children have tried to puzzle them out. Would it be a good thing to provide a runic alphabet? I have had to write one out for several people. Please excuse scrawling and rambling nature of this letter. I feel only half-alive. JRRT.

I have received safely by a later post the *Geste* (in verse) and the *Silmarillion* and related fragments.

20 To C. A. Furth, Allen & Unwin

[On 17 December, Furth wrote to Tolkien: 'The demand for *The Hobbit* became so acute with the beginning of the Christmas orders that we had to rush the reprint though. . . . . At the last minute the crisis was so acute that we fetched part of the reprint from our printers at Woking in a private car.']

19 December 1937   20 Northmoor Road, Oxford
Dear Mr Furth,

Thank you for the account of recent events with regard to 'the Hobbit'. It sounds quite exciting.

I have received *four* copies of the new impression charged to me, as ordered in my letter to Mr Unwin. I think the coloured pictures have come out well . . . I am sorry that the Eagle picture (to face p. 118) is not included – merely because I should have liked to see it reproduced. I marvel that four can have been included without raising the price. Perhaps the Americans will use it? Odd folk . . .

I have written the first chapter of a new story about Hobbits – 'A long expected party'.[1] A merry Christmas.

Yrs sincerely

J. R. R. Tolkien.

27

[P.S.] . . . . Mr Arthur Ransome[2] objects to *man* on p. 27 (line 7 from end). Read *fellow* as in earlier recension? He also objects to *more men* on p. 294 l. 11. Read *more of us*? *Men* with a capital is, I think, used in text when 'human kind' are specifically intended; and *man*, *men* with a minuscule are occasionally and loosely used as 'adult male' and 'people'. But perhaps, although this can be mythologically defended (and is according to Anglo-Saxon usage!), it may be as well to avoid raising mythological issues outside the story. Mr Ransome also seems not to like Gandalf's use of *boys* on p. 112 (lines 11, 13). But, though I agree that his insult was rather silly and not quite up to form, I do not think anything can be done about it now. Unless *oaves* would do? JRRT.

21 From a letter to Allen & Unwin   1 February 1938

Would you ask Mr Unwin whether his son, a very reliable critic, would care to read the first chapter of the sequel to *The Hobbit*? I have typed it. I have no confidence in it, but if he thought it a promising beginning, could add to it the tale that is brewing.

22 To C. A. Furth, Allen & Unwin

4 February 1938   20 Northmoor Road, Oxford
Dear Mr Furth,
   I enclose copy of Chapter I 'A Long-expected Party' of possible sequel to *The Hobbit*. . . . .
   I received a letter from a young reader in Boston (Lincs) enclosing a list of *errata* [in *The Hobbit*]. I then put my youngest son, lying in bed with a bad heart,[1] to find any more at twopence a time. He did. I enclose the results – which added to those already submitted should (I hope) make an exhaustive list. I also hope they may one day be required.
                                Yours sincerely,
                                J. R. R. Tolkien.

23 To C. A. Furth, Allen & Unwin

[The publishers had again been considering the possibility of publishing *Mr Bliss*, for which see the introductory note to no. 10.]

17 February 1938   20 Northmoor Road, Oxford
Dear Mr Furth,
   'Mr Bliss' returned safely. I am sorry you have had so much trouble with him. I wish you could find someone to redraw the pictures

properly. I don't believe I am capable of it. I have at any rate no time now – it is easier to write a story at odd moments than draw (though neither are easy). . . . .

They say it is the first step that costs the effort. I do not find it so. I am sure I could write unlimited 'first chapters'. I have indeed written many. The Hobbit sequel is still where it was, and I have only the vaguest notions of how to proceed. Not ever intending any sequel, I fear I squandered all my favourite 'motifs' and characters on the original 'Hobbit'.

I will write and get your advice on 'Mr Bliss' before I do anything. It will hardly be before the Long Vacation, or the end of my 'research fellowship'.[1]

Yours sincerely

J. R. R. Tolkien.

24 To Stanley Unwin

[On 11 February, Unwin reported that his son Rayner was 'delighted with the first chapter' of the new story.]

18 February 1938   20 Northmoor Road, Oxford

Dear Mr Unwin,

I am most grateful to your son Rayner; and am encouraged. At the same time I find it only too easy to write opening chapters – and for the moment the story is not unfolding. I have unfortunately very little time, made shorter by a rather disastrous Christmas vacation. I squandered so much on the original 'Hobbit' (which was not meant to have a sequel) that it is difficult to find anything new in that world.

Mr C. S. Lewis tells me that you have allowed him to submit to you 'Out of the Silent Planet'. I read it, of course; and I have since heard it pass a rather different test: that of being read aloud to our local club (which goes in for reading things short and long aloud). It proved an exciting serial, and was highly approved. But of course we are all rather like-minded.

It is only by an odd accident that the hero is a philologist (one point in which he resembles me) and has your name.[1] The latter detail could I am sure be altered: I do not believe it has any special significance.

We originally meant each to write an excursionary 'Thriller': a Space-journey and a Time-journey (mine) each discovering Myth.[2] But the Space-journey has been finished, and the Time-journey remains owing to my slowness and uncertainty only a fragment, as you know.[3]

Yours sincerely

J. R. R. Tolkien.

25 To the editor of the 'Observer'

[On 16 January 1938, the *Observer* published a letter, signed 'Habit', asking whether hobbits might have been suggested to Tolkien by Julian Huxley's account of 'the "little furry men" seen in Africa by natives and . . . . at least one scientist'. The letter-writer also mentioned that a friend had 'said she remembered an old fairy tale called "The Hobbit" in a collection read about 1904', in which the creature of that name 'was definitely frightening'. The writer asked if Tolkien would 'tell us some more about the name and inception of the intriguing hero of his book. . . . . It would save so many research students so very much trouble in the generations to come. And, by the way, is the hobbit's stealing of the dragon's cup based on the cup-stealing episode in *Beowulf*? I hope so, since one of the book's charms appears to be its Spenserian harmonising of the brilliant threads of so many branches of epic, mythology, and Victorian fairy literature.' Tolkien's reply, though it was not intended for publication (see the conclusion of no. 26), was printed in the *Observer* on 20 February 1938.]

Sir, – I need no persuasion: I am as susceptible as a dragon to flattery, and would gladly show off my diamond waistcoat, and even discuss its sources, since the Habit (more inquisitive than the Hobbit) has not only professed to admire it, but has also asked where I got it from. But would not that be rather unfair to the research students? To save them trouble is to rob them of any excuse for existing.

However, with regard to the Habit's principal question there is no danger: I do not remember anything about the name and inception of the hero. I could guess, of course, but the guesses would have no more authority than those of future researchers, and I leave the game to them.

I was born in Africa, and have read several books on African exploration. I have, since about 1896, read even more books of fairy-tales of the genuine kind. Both the facts produced by the Habit would appear, therefore, to be significant.

But are they? I have no waking recollection of furry pigmies (in book or moonlight); nor of any Hobbit bogey in print by 1904. I suspect that the two hobbits are accidental homophones, and am content* that they are not (it would seem) synonyms. And I protest that my hobbit did not live in Africa, and was not furry, except about the feet. Nor indeed was he like a rabbit. He was a prosperous, well-fed young bachelor of independent means. Calling him a 'nassty little rabbit' was a piece of vulgar trollery, just as 'descendant of rats' was a piece of dwarfish malice – deliberate insults to his size and feet, which he deeply resented. His feet, if conveniently clad and shod by nature, were as elegant as his long, clever fingers.

*Not quite. I should like, if possible, to learn more about the fairy-tale collection, c. 1904.

As for the rest of the tale it is, as the Habit suggests, derived from (previously digested) epic, mythology, and fairy-story – not, however, Victorian in authorship, as a rule to which George Macdonald is the chief exception. *Beowulf* is among my most valued sources; though it was not consciously present to the mind in the process of writing, in which the episode of the theft arose naturally (and almost inevitably) from the circumstances. It is difficult to think of any other way of conducting the story at that point. I fancy the author of *Beowulf* would say much the same.

My tale is not consciously based on any other book – save one, and that is unpublished: the 'Silmarillion', a history of the Elves, to which frequent allusion is made. I had not thought of the future researchers; and as there is only one manuscript there seems at the moment small chance of this reference proving useful.

But these questions are mere preliminaries. Now that I have been made to see Mr. Baggins's adventures as the subject of future enquiry I realise that a lot of work will be needed. There is the question of nomenclature. The dwarf-names, and the wizard's, are from the Elder Edda. The hobbit-names from Obvious Sources proper to their kind. The full list of their wealthier families is: Baggins, Boffin, Bolger, Bracegirdle, Brandybuck, Burrowes, Chubb, Grubb, Hornblower, Proudfoot, Sackville, and Took. The dragon bears as name – a pseudonym – the past tense of the primitive Germanic verb *Smugan*, to squeeze through a hole: a low philological jest. The rest of the names are of the Ancient and Elvish World, and have not been modernised.

And why *dwarves*? Grammar prescribes *dwarfs*; philology suggests that *dwarrows* would be the historical form. The real answer is that I knew no better. But *dwarves* goes well with *elves*; and, in any case, *elf, gnome, goblin, dwarf* are only approximate translations of the Old Elvish names for beings of not quite the same kinds and functions.

These dwarves are not quite the dwarfs of better known lore. They have been given Scandinavian names, it is true; but that is an editorial concession. Too many names in the tongues proper to the period might have been alarming. Dwarvish was both complicated and cacophonous. Even early elvish philologists avoided it, and the dwarves were obliged to use other languages, except for entirely private conversations. The language of hobbits was remarkably like English, as one would expect: they only lived on the borders of The Wild, and were mostly unaware of it. Their family names remain for the most part as well known and justly respected in this island as they were in Hobbiton and Bywater.

There is the matter of the Runes. Those used by Thorin and Co., for special purposes, were comprised in an alphabet of thirty-two letters (full list on application), similar to, but not identical, with the runes of

Anglo-Saxon inscriptions. There is doubtless an historical connection between the two. The Feanorian alphabet, generally used at that time, was of Elvish origin. It appears in the curse inscribed on the pot of gold in the picture of Smaug's lair, but had otherwise been transcribed (a facsimile of the original letter left on the mantelpiece can be supplied).

*

And what about the Riddles? There is work to be done here on the sources and analogues. I should not be at all surprised to learn that both the hobbit and Gollum will find their claim to have invented any of them disallowed.

Finally, I present the future researcher with a little problem. The tale halted in the telling for about a year at two separate points: where are they? But probably that would have been discovered anyway. And suddenly I remember that the hobbit thought 'Old fool', when the dragon succumbed to blandishment. I fear that the Habit's comment (and yours) will already be the same. But you must admit that the temptation was strong. – Yours, etc.,

J. R. R. Tolkien.

26 To Stanley Unwin

[On 2 March, Unwin sent Tolkien an extract from a reader's report on C. S. Lewis's *Out of the Silent Planet*. The reader commented: 'Mr Lewis is quite likely, I dare say, to write a worth while novel one day. This one isn't good enough – quite.' The reader judged the creatures of the planet Malacandra to be 'bunk'. Unwin asked Tolkien for his opinion of the book.]

4 March 1938   20 Northmoor Road, Oxford
Dear Mr Unwin,

I wrote you the enclosed letter[1] some time ago; but I hesitated to send it, knowing that you would wish to send Mr Lewis' work to your reader, and not wishing to interfere beyond getting you to consider it. Lewis is a great friend of mine, and we are in close sympathy (witness his two reviews of my Hobbit): this may make for understanding, but it may also cast an unduly rosy light. Since you ask for my opinion, here it is.

I read the story in the original MS. and was so enthralled that I could do nothing else until I had finished it. My first criticism was simply that it was too short. I still think that criticism holds, for both practical and artistic reasons. Other criticisms, concerning narrative style (Lewis is always apt to have rather creaking stiff-jointed passages), inconsistent details in the plot, and philology, have since been corrected to my satisfaction. The author holds to items of linguistic invention that do not appeal to me (Malacandra, Maleldil – eldila, in any case, I suspect to be due to the influence of the *Eldar* in the Silmarillion – and Pfifltriggi); but this is a matter of taste. After all your reader found my invented names, made with cherished care, eye-splitting. But the linguistic inventions and the philology on the whole are more than good enough. All the part about language and poetry – the glimpses of its Malacandrian nature and form – is very well done, and extremely interesting, far superior to what one usually gets from travellers in untravelled regions. The language difficulty is usually slid over or fudged. Here it not only has verisimilitude, but also underlying thought.

I was disturbed by your reader's report. I am afraid that at the first blush I feel inclined to retort that anyone capable of using the word 'bunk' will inevitably find matter of this sort – bunk. But one must be reasonable. I realize of course that to be even moderately marketable such a story must pass muster on its surface value, as a *vera historia* of a journey to a strange land. I am extremely fond of the genre, even having read *Land under England*[2] with some pleasure (though it was a weak example, and distasteful to me in many points). I thought *Out of the Silent Planet* did pass this test very successfully. The openings and the actual mode of transportation in time or space are always the weakest points of such tales. They are well enough worked here, but there should be more narrative given to adventure on Malacandra to balance and justify them. The theme of three distinct rational species (*hnau*) requires more attention to the third species, *Pfifltriggi*. Also the central episode of the visit to Eldilorn is reached too soon, artistically. Also would not the book be in fact practically rather short for a narrative of this type?

But I should have said that the story had for the more intelligent reader a great number of philosophical and mythical implications that enormously enhanced without detracting from the surface 'adventure'. I found the blend of *vera historia* with *mythos* irresistible. There are of course certain satirical elements, inevitable in any such traveller's tale, and also a spice of satire on other superficially similar works of 'scientific' fiction – such as the reference to the notion that higher intelligence will inevitably be combined with ruthlessness. The underlying myth is of course that of the Fall of the Angels (and the fall of man on this our silent planet); and the central point is the sculpture of the planets revealing the erasure of the sign of the Angel of this world. I cannot understand how any one can say this sticks in his gullet, unless (a) he thinks this particular myth 'bunk', that is not worth adult attention (even on a mythical plane); or (b) the use of it unjustified or perhaps unsuccessful.

The latter is perhaps arguable – though I dissent – but at any rate the critique should have pointed out the existence of the myth. Oyarsa is not of course a 'nice kind scientific God',[3] but something so profoundly different that the difference seems to have been unnoticed, namely an Angel. Yet even as a nice kind scientific God I think he compares favourably with the governing potentates of other stories of this kind. His name is not invented, but is from Bernardus Silvestris, as I think is explained at the end of the book (not that I think that this learned detail matters, but it is as legitimate as pseudo-scientific learning). In conclusion I might say that in designating the *Pfifltriggi* as the 'workers' your reader also misses the point, and is misled by current notions that are not applicable. But I have probably said more than enough. I at any rate should have bought this story at almost any price if I had found it in print, and loudly recommended it as a 'thriller' by (however and surprisingly) an intelligent man. But I know only too sadly from efforts to find anything to read even with an 'on demand' subscription at a library that my taste is not normal. I read 'Voyage to Arcturus'[4] with avidity – the most comparable work, though it is both more powerful and more mythical (and less rational, and also less of a story – no one could read it merely as a thriller and without interest in philosophy religion and morals). I wonder what your reader thinks of it? All the same I shall be comforted on my own behalf, if the second reader supports my taste a bit more!

*

The sequel to *The Hobbit* has now progressed as far as the end of the third chapter. But stories tend to get out of hand, and this has taken an unpremeditated turn. Mr Lewis and my youngest boy are reading it in bits as a serial. I hesitate to bother your son, though I should value his criticisms. At any rate if he would like to read it in serial form he can. My Christopher and Mr Lewis approve it enough to say that they think it is better than the *Hobbit*; but Rayner need not agree!

I have received a copy of the American edition. Not so bad. I am glad they have included the eagle picture, but I cannot imagine why they have spoilt the Rivendell picture, by slicing the top and cutting out the ornament at the bottom. All the numerous textual errors are of course included. I hope it will some day be possible to get rid of them.

I don't know whether you saw the long and ridiculous letter in *The Observer* of Feb. 20, and thought I had suddenly gone cracked. I think the editor was unfair. There was a letter signed Habit in the paper in January (asking if the hobbit was influenced by Julian Huxley's lectures on furry African pygmies, and other questions). I sent this jesting reply with a stamped envelope for transmission to Habit; and also a short and fairly sane reply for publication. Nothing happened for a month, and then I woke up to find my ill-considered joke occupying nearly a column.

With best wishes. Yours sincerely,
J. R. R. Tolkien.

27 To the Houghton Mifflin Company

[An extract from a letter apparently addressed to Tolkien's American publishers, and probably written in March or April 1938. Houghton Mifflin seem to have asked him to supply drawings of hobbits for use in some future edition of *The Hobbit*.]

I am afraid, if you will need drawings of hobbits in various attitudes, I must leave it in the hands of someone who can draw. My own pictures are an unsafe guide – e.g. the picture of Mr. Baggins in Chapter VI and XII. The very ill-drawn one in Chapter XIX is a better guide than these in general impressions.

I picture a fairly human figure, not a kind of 'fairy' rabbit as some of my British reviewers seem to fancy: fattish in the stomach, shortish in the leg. A round, jovial face; ears only slightly pointed and 'elvish'; hair short and curling (brown). The feet from the ankles down, covered with brown hairy fur. Clothing: green velvet breeches; red or yellow waistcoat; brown or green jacket; gold (or brass) buttons; a dark green hood and cloak (belonging to a dwarf).

Actual size – only important if other objects are in picture – say about three feet or three feet six inches. The hobbit in the picture of the gold-hoard, Chapter XII, is of course (apart from being fat in the wrong places) enormously too large. But (as my children, at any rate, understand) he is really in a separate picture or 'plane' – being invisible to the dragon.

There is in the text no mention of his acquiring of boots. There should be! It has dropped out somehow or other in the various revisions – the bootings occurred at Rivendell; and he was again bootless after leaving Rivendell on the way home. But since leathery soles, and well-brushed furry feet are a feature of essential hobbitness, he ought really to appear unbooted, except in special illustrations of episodes.

[On 1 June, Unwin told Tolkien that Houghton Mifflin had now sold approximately three thousand copies of the American edition of *The Hobbit*. In April, the book had been awarded a $250 prize by the *New York Herald Tribune* for the best juvenile story of the season. Meanwhile Rayner Unwin had criticised the second and third chapters of the new story for having too much 'hobbit talk'.]

4 June 1938   20 Northmoor Road, Oxford

Dear Mr Unwin,

Thank you for your comforting news. It is indeed comforting, for in spite of unexpected strokes of luck, such as the American prize, I am in considerable difficulties; and things will not be improved in September, when I vacate my research fellowship. That will mean, of course, that the pressure on my writing time will be less, except that as far as I can see I shall have to return to the examination treadmill[1] to keep the boat afloat.

Your previous letters of April 29 and May 3 have I fear long lain unanswered. I meant long ago to have thanked Rayner for bothering to read the tentative chapters, and for his excellent criticism. It agrees strikingly with Mr Lewis', which is therefore confirmed. I must plainly bow to my two chief (and most well-disposed) critics. The trouble is that 'hobbit talk' amuses me privately (and to a certain degree also my boy Christopher) more than adventures; but I must curb this severely. Although longing to do so, I have not had a chance to touch any story-writing since the Christmas vacation. With three works in Middle English and Old English going to or through the press, and another in Old Norse in a series of which I am an editor under my hand on behalf of the author who is abroad,[2] and students coming in July from Belgium and Canada to work under my direction, I cannot see any loophole left for months! . . . .

Yours sincerely

J. R. R. Tolkien.

P.S. My answer was delayed, because your letter arrived in the midst of our little local strife. You may not have noticed that on June 2 the Rev. Adam Fox[3] was elected Professor of Poetry, defeating a Knight and a noble Lord. He was nominated by Lewis and myself, and miraculously elected: our first public victory over established privilege. For Fox is a member of our literary club of *practising poets* – before whom the *Hobbit*, and other works (such as *the Silent Planet*) have been read. We are slowly getting even into print. One of Fox's works is *Old King Coel*, a rhymed tale in four books (Oxford).

[Allen & Unwin had negotiated the publication of a German translation of *The Hobbit* with Rütten & Loening of Potsdam. This firm wrote to Tolkien asking if he was of 'arisch' (aryan) origin.]

I must say the enclosed letter from Rütten and Loening is a bit stiff. Do I suffer this impertinence because of the possession of a German name, or do their lunatic laws require a certificate of 'arisch' origin from all persons of all countries?

Personally I should be inclined to refuse to give any *Bestätigung*[1] (although it happens that I can), and let a German translation go hang. In any case I should object strongly to any such declaration appearing in print. I do not regard the (probable) absence of all Jewish blood as necessarily honourable; and I have many Jewish friends, and should regret giving any colour to the notion that I subscribed to the wholly pernicious and unscientific race-doctrine.

You are primarily concerned, and I cannot jeopardize the chance of a German publication without your approval. So I submit two drafts of possible answers.

30   **To Rütten & Loening Verlag**

[One of the 'two drafts' mentioned by Tolkien in the previous letter. This is the only one preserved in the Allen & Unwin files, and it seems therefore very probable that the English publishers sent the other one to Germany. It is clear that in that letter Tolkien refused to make any declaration of 'arisch' origin.]

25 July 1938   20 Northmoor Road, Oxford

Dear Sirs,

Thank you for your letter. . . . . I regret that I am not clear as to what you intend by *arisch*. I am not of *Aryan* extraction: that is Indo-iranian; as far as I am aware none of my ancestors spoke Hindustani, Persian, Gypsy, or any related dialects. But if I am to understand that you are enquiring whether I am of *Jewish* origin, I can only reply that I regret that I appear to have *no* ancestors of that gifted people. My great-great-grandfather came to England in the eighteenth century from Germany: the main part of my descent is therefore purely English, and I am an English subject – which should be sufficient. I have been accustomed, nonetheless, to regard my German name with pride, and continued to do so throughout the period of the late regrettable war, in which I served in the English army. I cannot, however, forbear to comment that if impertinent and irrelevant inquiries of this sort are to become the rule in matters of literature, then the time is not far distant when a German name will no longer be a source of pride.

Your enquiry is doubtless made in order to comply with the laws of your own country, but that this should be held to apply to the subjects of another state would be improper, even if it had (as it has not) any bearing whatsoever on the merits of my work or its suitability for publication, of which you appear to have satisfied yourselves without reference to my *Abstammung*.[1]

I trust you will find this reply satisfactory, and

remain yours faithfully

J. R. R. Tolkien.

31 To C. A. Furth, Allen & Unwin

[Among the stories that Tolkien showed to his publishers during 1937, as a possible successor to *The Hobbit*, was a short version of *Farmer Giles of Ham*. Allen & Unwin liked it, but felt that it would need the companionship of other stories to make it into a book of sufficient length. They also, of course, encouraged Tolkien to write the sequel to *The Hobbit*.]

24 July 1938   20 Northmoor Road, Oxford

Dear Mr Furth,

The Hobbit ought to have come out this year not last. Next year I should have probably had time and mood for a follower. But pressure of work as a 'research fellow', which has to be wound up if possible by September, has taken all my time, and also dried up invention. The sequel to *the Hobbit* has remained where it stopped. It has lost my favour, and I have no idea what to do with it. For one thing the original Hobbit was never intended to have a sequel – Bilbo 'remained very happy to the end of his days and those were extraordinarily long': a sentence I find an almost insuperable obstacle to a satisfactory link. For another nearly all the 'motives' that I can use were packed into the original book, so that a sequel will appear either 'thinner' or merely repetitional. For a third: I am personally immensely amused by hobbits as such, and can contemplate them eating and making their rather fatuous jokes indefinitely; but I find that is not the case with even my most devoted 'fans' (such as Mr Lewis, and ? Rayner Unwin). Mr Lewis says hobbits are only amusing when in unhobbitlike situations. For a last: my mind on the 'story' side is really preoccupied with the 'pure' fairy stories or mythologies of the *Silmarillion*, into which even Mr Baggins got dragged against my original will, and I do not think I shall be able to move much outside it – unless it is finished (and perhaps published) – which has a releasing effect. The only line I have, quite outside that, is 'Farmer Giles' and the Little Kingdom (with its capital at Thame). I rewrote that to about 50% longer, last January, and read it to the Lovelace Society[1] in lieu of a paper 'on' fairy stories. I was very much surprised at the result. It took nearly twice as long as a proper 'paper' to read aloud; and the audience was apparently not bored – indeed they were generally convulsed with mirth. But I am afraid that means it has taken on a rather more adult and satiric flavour. Anyway I have not written the necessary two or three other stories of the Kingdom to go with it!

It looks like *Mr Bliss*. If you think that is worthy of publication. I can bring it back to you, if you wish. I do not think that I personally can do anything to improve it.

I am really very sorry: for my own sake as well as yours I would like to produce something. But September seems quite out of the question this year. I hope inspiration and the mood will return. It is not for lack of wooing that it holds aloof. But my wooing of late has been perforce intermittent. The Muses do not like such half-heartedness.

Yours sincerely
J. R. R. Tolkien.

32   To John Masefield

[Masefield, then Poet Laureate, together with Nevill Coghill organised an entertainment in Oxford during the summers of 1938 and 1939, entitled *Summer Diversions*. In 1938 he invited Tolkien to impersonate Chaucer and recite from memory the *Nun's Priest's Tale*. He wrote to Tolkien enclosing some lines of verse with which he proposed to introduce him.]

27 July 1938   20 Northmoor Road, Oxford
Dear Mr Masefield,

I have no prelude of my own to fire off, and no objection as a performer to being preceded by the lines you send. In any case you are Master of the Diversions, and I am under your good authority.

Privately, as one student of Chaucer to another, I might perhaps say that these lines seem to me to allude to the erroneous imagination that Chaucer was the first English poet, and that before and except for him all was dumb and barbaric. That is of course not true, and is perhaps, even as a way of emphasizing the fact that he possessed a peculiar genius, which would at any period have produced work having a novel flavour, rather misleading. I do not personally connect the North with either night or darkness, especially not in England, in whose long 1200 years of literary tradition Chaucer stands rather in the middle than the beginning. I also do not feel him springlike but autumnal (even if of the early autumn) and not kinglike but middle-class. However, as I say, these are professional matters, about which the present occasion is hardly one to join battle.

I am not at all happy about the effect of Chaucer in general, or the Nonnes Prestes Tale in particular, in a supposed 14th. C. pronunciation. I will do my best, but I hope it will be sufficiently intelligible for some of the sense to get over. Personally I rather think that a modified modern pronunciation (restoring rhymes but otherwise avoiding archaism) is the best – such as I once heard you use on the Monk's Tale a good many years ago.

Yours sincerely
J. R. R. Tolkien.

33 To C. A. Furth, Allen & Unwin

31 August 1938   20 Northmoor Road, Oxford
Dear Mr Furth,

I am not so much pressed, as oppressed (or depressed). Further troubles which I need not detail have occurred, and I collapsed (or bent) under them. I have been unwell, since I saw you – in fact I reached the edge of a breakdown, and was ordered by the doctor to stop short. I have done nothing for a week or two – being in fact quite unable. But I am beginning to feel a good deal better. I am now (tomorrow) going away for a fortnight's holiday; which I had not planned and cannot afford, though it seems required by my own health and my youngest son's. . . . .

I did not entirely forget 'Farmer Giles': I had it typed. I submit it now, for your consideration in its rather altered scope and tone. A good many folk have found it very diverting (I think that is the right word): but that is as may be! I see that it is *not* long enough to stand alone probably – at least not as a commercial proposition (if indeed it cd. ever be such a thing). It probably requires more of its kind. I have planned out a sequel[1] (though it does not need one), and have an unfinished pseudo-Celtic fairy-story of a mildly satirical order, which is also amusing as far as it has gone, called the *King of the Green Dozen*.[2] These I might finish off if *Giles* seems to you worthy of print and companionship.

In the last two or three days, after the benefit of idleness and open air, and the sanctioned neglect of duty, I have begun again on the sequel to the 'Hobbit' – The Lord of the Ring. It is now flowing along, and getting quite out of hand. It has reached about Chapter VII and progresses towards quite unforeseen goals. I must say I think it is a good deal better in places and some ways than the predecessor; but that does not say that I think it either more suitable or more adapted for its audience. For one thing it is, like my own children (who have the immediate serial rights), rather 'older'. I can only say that Mr Lewis (my stout backer of the Times and T.L.S.) professes himself more than pleased. If the weather is wet in the next fortnight we may have got still further on. But it is no bed-time story. . . . .

Yours sincerely,
J. R. R. Tolkien.

34 To Stanley Unwin

13 October 1938   20 Northmoor Road, Oxford

Dear Mr Unwin,

 . . . . I have worked very hard for a month (in the time which my doctors said must be devoted to some distraction!) on a sequel to *The Hobbit*. It has reached Chapter XI (though in rather an illegible state); I am now thoroughly engrossed in it, and have the threads all in hand – and I have to put it completely aside, till I do not know when. Even the Christmas vacation will be darkened by New Zealand scripts, as my friend Gordon[1] died in the middle of their Honours Exams, and I had to finish setting the papers. But I still live in hopes that I may be able to submit it early next year.

   When I spoke, in an earlier letter to Mr Furth, of this sequel getting 'out of hand', I did not mean it to be complimentary to the process. I really meant it was running its course, and forgetting 'children', and was becoming more terrifying than the Hobbit. It may prove quite unsuitable. It is more 'adult' – but my own children who criticize it as it appears are now older. However, you will be the judge of that, I hope, some day! The darkness of the present days has had some effect on it. Though it is not an 'allegory'. (I have already had one letter from America asking for an authoritative exposition of the allegory of The Hobbit).

Yours sincerely
J. R. R. Tolkien.

35 To C. A. Furth, Allen & Unwin

2 February 1939   20 Northmoor Road, Oxford

Dear Mr Furth,

   By the end of last term the new story – *The Lord of the Rings* – had reached Chapter 12 (and had been re-written several times), running to over 300 MS. pages of the size of this paper and written generally as closely. It will require 200 at least to finish the story that has developed. Could you give me any idea of the *latest* date by which the completed MSS. ought to reach you? I have worked under difficulties of all kinds, including ill-health. Since the beginning of December I have not been able to touch it. Among many other labours and troubles that the sudden death of my friend Professor Eric Gordon bequeathed to me, I had to clear up the New Zealand examinations, which occupied nearly all last vacation. I then caught influenza, from which I have just recovered. But I have other heavy tasks ahead. I am at the 'peak' of my educational financial stress, with a second son clamouring for a university and the youngest wanting to go to school (after a year under heart-specialists), and I am obliged to do exams and lectures and what not. Perhaps you ought to be thinking about *Mr Bliss*. And what about *Farmer Giles*? You had the MSS. of the enlarged form in September or October.

I think *The Lord of the Rings* is in itself a good deal better than *The Hobbit*, but it may not prove a very fit sequel. It is more grown up – but the audience for which *The Hobbit* was written has done that also. The readers young and old who clamoured for 'more about the Necromancer' are to blame, for the N. is not child's play.* My eldest son is enthusiastic, but it would be a relief to me to know that my publishers were satisfied. If the part so far written satisfied you, there need be no fear of the whole. I wonder whether it would not be a wise thing to get what I have done typed and let you see it? I shall certainly finish it eventually whatever you think of it; but if it did not seem to be what you want to follow *The Hobbit* there would be no desperate pressure. The writing of *The Lord of the Rings* is laborious, because I have been doing it as well as I know how, and considering every word. The story, too, has (I fondly imagine) some significance. In spare time it would be easier and quicker to write up the plots already composed of the more lighthearted stories of the Little Kingdom to go with *Farmer Giles*. But I would rather finish the long tale, and not let it go cold.

Let me know what you think. I may get part of the Easter Vac. free. Not all – I shall have some papers to set; and some work in preparation for a possible 'National Emergency' (which will take a week out).[1] I have to go to Scotland either in March or April. It is conceivable I could finish by June. And the MSS. would be final (no knocking page-proofs about). But I should have no time or energy for illustration. I never

---

*Still there are more hobbits, far more of them and about them, in the new story. Gollum reappears, and Gandalf is to the fore: 'dwarves' come in; and though there is no dragon (so far) there is going to be a Giant; and the new and (very alarming) Ringwraiths are a feature. There ought to be things that people who liked the old mixture will find to have a similar taste.

could draw, and the half-baked intimations of it seem wholly to have left me. A map (very necessary) would be all I could do.

Yours sincerely
J. R. R. Tolkien.

36 To C. A. Furth, Allen & Unwin

[On 8 February, Furth sent a royalty cheque for *The Hobbit,* and told Tolkien that the middle of June was the latest date by which Allen & Unwin must have the new story if they were going to publish it by Christmas.]

10 February 1939   20 Northmoor Road, Oxford

Dear Mr Furth,

Thank you very much for your letter – and the enclosed cheque: which was rather a welcome tonic. The influenza has not damaged me much, though it caught me in a state of exam-exhaustion; but my throat seems to be getting worse, and I don't feel very bright. . . . .

I will get my stuff typed and let you have it; and (if it meets with approval, and does not demand extensive rewriting) I think I shall make a special effort, at the expense of other duties, to finish it off before June 15th. . . . .

Did *Farmer Giles* in the enlarged form meet with any sort of approval? (I received the typescript safely.) Is it worth anything? Are two more stories, or any more stories of the Little Kingdom, worth contemplating? For instance the completion in the same form of the adventures of Prince George (the farmer's son) and the fat boy Suovetaurilius (vulgarly Suet), and the Battle of Otmoor. I just wonder whether this local family game played in the country just round us is more than silly.

Yours sincerely
J. R. R. Tolkien.

37 To Stanley Unwin

[Allen & Unwin were publishing a revision by C. L. Wrenn of Clark Hall's translation of *Beowulf.* Tolkien had agreed to write a foreword, and during the second half of 1939 he received several enquiries from the publishers about the progress of this. He left these enquiries unanswered until December, when Stanley Unwin himself wrote to find out what was happening.]

19 December 1939   20 Northmoor Road, Oxford

Dear Mr Unwin,

I was greatly comforted to receive your kind note this morning, even though it heaped hot coals of fire on my head. In spite of my troubles I have not really a sufficient excuse for not at least writing or responding to notes and enquiries. My accident just before the outbreak of war[1] left me very unwell for a long while, and that combined with the anxieties and troubles that all share, and with the lack of any holiday, and with the virtual headship of a department in this bewildered university have made me unpardonably neglectful. I hardly knew how to cope with the further blow of my wife's illness, threatening to come to a climax all through the summer and autumn.

The worst seems over now. I have her back, an invalid but apparently mending at last, and the fear of cancer which was at first entertained apparently dismissed. I am uncommandeered still myself, and shall now probably remain so, as there is (as yet) far too much to do here, and I have lost both my chief assistant and his understudy.

I will try and collect my weary wits and pen a sufficient foreword to the 'Beowulf' translation, *at once*. . . . .

May I turn now to *The Hobbit* and kindred affairs. I have never quite ceased work on the sequel. It has reached Chapter XVI. I fear it is growing too large. I am not at all sure that it will please quite the same audience (except in so far as that has grown up too). Will there be any chance of publication, if I can get it done before the Spring? If you would like to try it on anyone as a serial I am willing to send in chapters. But I have only one fair copy. I have had to go back and revise early chapters as the plot and plan took firmer shape and so nothing has yet been sufficiently definitive to type.

I suppose the German edition of *The Hobbit* will probably never appear now? It was a great disappointment to my son and myself. We had a bet between us on the version of the opening sentence. My son is now in Italy,[2] whither he has carried *The Hobbit*, and occasionally sends enquiries for more of the sequel, which he knew and approved as far as it went. But there is no time, or very little even when one steals from other more dutiful claims.

I wish you would publish poor 'Farmer Giles' in the interim. He is at least finished, though very slender in bulk. But he amuses the same people, although Mr Furth seemed to think he has no obvious public. He has mouldered in a drawer since he amused H. S. Bennett's[3] children when I was in Cambridge last March. Admittedly they are bright children. . . . .

Yours sincerely,
J. R. R. Tolkien.

38 To Stanley Unwin

[Tolkien had still not delivered the foreword to the Clark Hall *Beowulf* translation by 27 March, when Allen & Unwin wrote a desperate letter asking what had happened to it, and telling him that 'a word or two' would be enough. The text sent by Tolkien with the following letter was, despite its length, used in full when the book was published.]

30 March 1940   20 Northmoor Road, Oxford

Dear Mr Unwin,

Apologies would be vain in the face of my vexatious and uncivil behaviour. So I felt long ago – that the only possible reply to your repeated enquiry of March 5 was copy. I have got into worse trouble than I need – in spite of the many disasters that have befallen me* – since I have foolishly wasted much labour and time under a misapprehension, which a more careful consideration of the pagination of the page-proofs might have dispelled.

I knew that a 'word or two' would suffice (though I could not feel that any words under my name would have any particular value unless they said something worth saying – which takes space). But I believed that more was hoped for. I cannot lay my hand on the relative letter, and in any case I now realise that an earlier stage, before page-proof, was envisaged. I can only regret that I did not get something done at an earlier stage. For a fairly considerable 'preface' is really required. The so-called 'Introduction' does not exist, being merely an argument:[2] there is no reference whatever to either a translator's or a critic's problems. I advised originally against any attempt to bring the apparatus of the old book up to date – it can be got by students elsewhere. But I did not expect a reduction to 10 lines, while the 'argument' (the least useful part) was re-written at length.

That being so I laboured long and hard to compress (and yet enliven) such remarks on *translation* as might both be useful to students and of interest to those using the book without reference to the original text. But the result ran to 17 of my MSS. pages (of some 300 words each) – not counting the metrical appendix,[3] the most original part, which is as long again!

I was in this stage early in March, and trying to make up my mind what to jettison, when your letter of March 27th reached me (yesterday). All very foolish. For the pagination indicates clearly my share as a very small one.

---

*It may mitigate your just wrath, if I say that since I wrote in December my wife's health became much worse. I spent most of last term in an attic in a hotel, with my house derelict and damaged.[1] I have been ill myself, and hardly able to cope with university work, which for me has trebled.

All I can do now is to send in what I have done. You might care to consider it (submitting it to Wrenn) for inclusion later, e.g. if a further edition is required. (Retouched it might make a suitable booklet for students. The metrical account, being on a novel plan, and considering the relations of style and metre, might be attractive, as students are usually rather at sea on this subject.)

To meet the immediate emergency – I suggest (with grief, reluctance, and penitence) that the passages marked in *red* (? 1400 words), or those in *blue* (750–800?) might serve. If not too long.

Yours sincerely
J. R. R. Tolkien.

39   From a letter to Michael Tolkien   29 September 1940

[In the late summer of 1940, two women evacuees were billeted for a short time on the Tolkien household.]

Our evacuees went off again this morning, back home to Ashford (they were railway folk), after scenes of comedy and pathos. I have never come across more simple, helpless, gentle and unhappy souls (mother and daughter-in-law). They had been away from their husbands for the first time in their married lives, and found they would prefer to be blown to bits.

40   From a letter to Michael Tolkien   6 October 1940

[In September 1939 Tolkien's second son, then aged nearly nineteen, volunteered for army service, but was instructed to spend one year at university and then enlist. He entered Trinity College, Oxford, and left it again the following summer to train as an anti-aircraft gunner.]

I am very sorry indeed, dear boy, that your Varsity career has been cut in two. It would have been better, if you had been the elder and could have finished before the army took you. But I still hope you will be able to come back again. And certainly you will learn a lot, first! Though in times of peace we get, perhaps (and naturally and for the purpose rightly), too engrossed in thinking of everything as a preparation or training or a making one fit – for what? At any minute it is what we are and are doing, not what we plan to be and do that counts. But I cannot pretend that I myself found that idea much comfort against the waste of time and militarism of the army. It isn't the tough stuff one minds so much. I was pitched into it all, just when I was full of stuff to write, and of things to learn; and never picked it all up again.

41 From a letter to Michael Tolkien   2 January 1941

I have been clearing up arrears of correspondence, and have at last got as far as getting out my story again; but as soon as I get really started, term will be casting its shadow ahead, and I shall have to think of lectures and committees.

42 To Michael Tolkien

[After taking part with his gun-battery in the defence of aerodromes during the Battle of Britain, Michael was injured in an accident with an army vehicle during night training, and was sent to hospital in Worcester. This is one of several letters his father sent to him there.]

12 January 1941   20 Northmoor Road, Oxford
My dearest Mick,

It seems a long time since I wrote: and it has been a rather dreary and busy time, with a foul east wind blowing steadily, day after day, and the weather varying from bone-piercing cold to grey damp chill. . . . . I have had one amusement lately: Dr Havard[1] took me and the Lewis brothers[2] out to a pub at Appleton on a snowy skiddy night last Tuesday. J.B. had given me a little pot of snuff as a birthday present. So I brought it out of my pocket and read out the ancient label: 'AS SUPPLIED to THEIR MAJESTIES the KINGS of HANOVER & BELGIUM etc. the DUKE of CUMBERLAND and the DUCHESS of KENT'. 'Will any one have any?' I said. Many horny hands of yokels were thrust out. And several caplifting explosions followed! You had better not tell J.B. what I did with (a small portion) of the precious Fribourg and Treyer stuff. Major Lewis – unaware that Blackwell[3] lives at Appleton and that the locals were all ears – gave an amusing account of visiting Blackwell's shop with Hugo Dyson.[4] When he came to the point at which the assistant returned to Hugo and said: *Sorry, sir, we have no second-hand copy, but we have a new copy* (and H. replied *Well, rub it on the floor and make it second-hand: it's all the same to me*), there was loud applause. Apart from this brief interlude, life has been rather dull, and much too full of committees and legislative business, which has kept me up late several nights. . . . .

Air Raid warnings are frequent here, but (so far) remain just Warnings . . . I fancy things will 'blow up' earlier this year than last – weather permitting – and that we shall have a pretty hectic time in every corner of this island! It is also plain that our dear old friends the U.S.S.R. are up to some mischief.[5] It is a pretty close race with time. . . . . I don't suppose mere 'citizens' really have any knowledge of what is going on. But plain reasoning seems to show that Hitler must attack this country direct and v. heavily soon, and before the summer.

Meanwhile the 'Daily Worker'[6] is cried in the streets unmolested. We shall have some lively times after the War even if we win it as far as Germany is concerned.

God bless you, my dear son. I pray for you constantly. Remember me. Do you want anything specially? Very much love from your
Father.

43 From a letter to Michael Tolkien 6–8 March 1941

[On the subject of marriage and relations between the sexes.]

A man's dealings with women can be purely physical (they cannot really, of course: but I mean he can refuse to take other things into account, to the great damage of his soul (and body) and theirs); or 'friendly'; or he can be a 'lover' (engaging and blending all his affections and powers of mind and body in a complex emotion powerfully coloured and energized by 'sex'). This is a fallen world. The dislocation of sex-instinct is one of the chief symptoms of the Fall. The world has been 'going to the bad' all down the ages. The various social forms shift, and each new mode has its special dangers: but the 'hard spirit of con-cupiscence' has walked down every street, and sat leering in every house, since Adam fell. We will leave aside the 'immoral' results. These you desire not to be dragged into. To renunciation you have no call. 'Friendship' then? In this fallen world the 'friendship' that should be possible between all human beings, is virtually impossible between man and woman. The devil is endlessly ingenious, and sex is his favourite subject. He is as good every bit at catching you through generous romantic or tender motives, as through baser or more animal ones. This 'friendship' has often been tried: one side or the other nearly always fails. Later in life when sex cools down, it may be possible. It may happen between saints. To ordinary folk it can only rarely occur: two minds that have really a primarily mental and spiritual affinity may by accident reside in a male and a female body, and yet may desire and achieve a 'friendship' quite independent of sex. But no one can count on it. The other partner will let him (or her) down, almost certainly, by 'falling in love'. But a young man does not really (as a rule) want 'friendship', even if he says he does. There are plenty of young men (as a rule). He wants *love*: innocent, and yet irresponsible perhaps. *Allas! Allas! that ever love was sinne!* as Chaucer says. Then if he is a Christian and is aware that there is such a thing as sin, he wants to know what to do about it.

There is in our Western culture the romantic chivalric tradition still strong, though as a product of Christendom (yet by no means the same as Christian ethics) the times are inimical to it. It idealizes 'love' – and as far as it goes can be very good, since it takes in far more than physical pleasure, and enjoins if not purity, at least fidelity, and so self-denial, 'service', courtesy, honour, and courage. Its weakness is, of course, that it began as an artificial courtly game, a way of enjoying love for its own sake without reference to (and indeed contrary to) matrimony. Its centre was not God, but imaginary Deities, Love and the Lady. It still tends to make the Lady a kind of guiding star or divinity – of the old-fashioned 'his divinity' = the woman he loves – the object or reason of noble conduct. This is, of course, false and at best make-believe. The woman is another fallen human-being with a soul in peril. But combined and harmonized with religion (as long ago it was, producing much of that beautiful devotion to Our Lady that has been God's way of refining so much our gross manly natures and emotions, and also of warming and colouring our hard, bitter, religion) it can be very noble. Then it produces what I suppose is still felt, among those who retain even vestigiary Christianity, to be the highest ideal of love between man and woman. Yet I still think it has dangers. It is not wholly true, and it is not perfectly 'theocentric'. It takes, or at any rate has in the past taken, the young man's eye off women as they are, as companions in shipwreck not guiding stars. (One result is for observation of the actual to make the young man turn cynical.) To forget *their* desires, needs and temptations. It inculcates exaggerated notions of 'true love', as a fire from without, a permanent exaltation, unrelated to age, childbearing, and plain life, and unrelated to will and purpose. (One result of that is to make young folk look for a 'love' that will keep them always nice and warm in a cold world, without any effort of theirs; and the incurably romantic go on looking even in the squalor of the divorce courts).

Women really have not much part in all this, though they may use the language of romantic love, since it is so entwined in all our idioms. The sexual impulse makes women (naturally when unspoiled more unselfish) very sympathetic and understanding, or specially desirous of being so (or seeming so), and very ready to enter into all the interests, as far as they can, from ties to religion, of the young man they are attracted to. No intent necessarily to deceive: sheer instinct: the servient, helpmeet instinct, generously warmed by desire and young blood. Under this impulse they can in fact often achieve very remarkable insight and understanding, even of things otherwise outside their natural range: for it is their gift to be receptive, stimulated, fertilized (in many other matters than the physical) by the male. Every teacher knows that. How quickly an intelligent woman can be taught, grasp his ideas, see his point – and how (with rare exceptions) they can go no further, when they leave his hand, or when they cease to take a *personal* interest in *him*. But this is their natural avenue to love. Before the young woman knows

49

where she is (and while the romantic young man, when he exists, is still sighing) she may actually 'fall in love'. Which for her, an unspoiled natural young woman, means that she wants to become the mother of the young man's children, even if that desire is by no means clear to her or explicit. And then things are going to happen: and they may be very painful and harmful, if things go wrong. Particularly if the young man only wanted a temporary guiding star and divinity (until he hitches his waggon to a brighter one), and was merely enjoying the flattery of sympathy nicely seasoned with a titillation of sex – all *quite* innocent, of course, and worlds away from 'seduction'.

You may meet in life (as in literature*) women who are flighty, or even plain wanton – I don't refer to mere flirtatiousness, the sparring practice for the real combat, but to women who are too silly to take even love seriously, or are actually so depraved as to enjoy 'conquests', or even enjoy the giving of pain – but these are abnormalities, even though false teaching, bad upbringing, and corrupt fashions may encourage them. Much though modern conditions have changed feminine circumstances, and the detail of what is considered propriety, they have not changed natural instinct. A man has a life-work, a career, (and male friends), all of which could (and do where he has any guts) survive the shipwreck of 'love'. A young woman, even one 'economically independent', as they say now (it usually really means economic subservience to male commercial employers instead of to a father or a family), begins to think of the 'bottom drawer' and dream of a home, almost at once. If she really falls in love, the shipwreck may really end on the rocks. Anyway women are in general much less romantic and more practical. Don't be misled by the fact that they are more 'sentimental' in words – freer with 'darling', and all that. They do not want a guiding star. They may idealize a plain young man into a hero; but they don't really need any such glamour either to fall in love or to remain in it. If they have any delusion it is that they can 'reform' men. They will take a rotter open-eyed, and even when the delusion of reforming him fails, go on loving him. They are, of course, much more realistic about the sexual relation. Unless perverted by bad contemporary fashions they do not as a rule talk 'bawdy'; not because they are purer than men (they are not) but because they don't find it funny. I have known those who pretended

---

*Literature has been (until the modern novel) mainly a masculine business, and in it there is a great deal about the 'fair and false'. That is on the whole a slander. Women are humans and therefore capable of perfidy. But within the human family, as contrasted with men they are not generally or naturally the more perfidious. Very much the reverse. Except only that women are apt to break down if asked to 'wait' for a man, too long, and while youth (so precious and necessary to a would-be mother) is swiftly passing. They should, in fact, not be asked to wait.

to, but it is a pretence. It may be intriguing, interesting, absorbing (even a great deal too absorbing) to them: but it is just plumb natural, a serious, obvious interest; where is the joke?

They have, of course, still to be more careful in sexual relations, for all the contraceptives. Mistakes are damaging physically and socially (and matrimonially). But they are instinctively, when uncorrupt, mono-gamous. *Men are not.* . . . . No good pretending. Men just ain't, not by their animal nature. Monogamy (although it has long been fundamental to our inherited *ideas*) is for us men a piece of 'revealed' ethic, according to faith and not to the flesh. Each of us could healthily beget, in our 30 odd years of full manhood, a few hundred children, and enjoy the process. Brigham Young (I believe) was a healthy and happy man. It is a fallen world, and there is no consonance between our bodies, minds, and souls.

However, the essence of a *fallen* world is that the *best* cannot be attained by free enjoyment, or by what is called 'self-realization' (usually a nice name for self-indulgence, wholly inimical to the realization of other selves); but by denial, by suffering. Faithfulness in Christian marriage entails that: great mortification. For a Christian man there is *no escape*. Marriage may help to sanctify & direct to its proper object his sexual desires; its grace may help him in the struggle; but the struggle remains. It will not satisfy him – as hunger may be kept off by regular meals. It will offer as many difficulties to the purity proper to that state, as it provides easements. No man, however truly he loved his betrothed and bride as a young man, has lived faithful to her as a wife in mind and body without deliberate conscious exercise of the *will*, without self-denial. Too few are told that – even those brought up 'in the Church'. Those outside seem seldom to have heard it. When the glamour wears off, or merely works a bit thin, they think they have made a mistake, and that the real soul-mate is still to find. The real soul-mate too often proves to be the next sexually attractive person that comes along. Someone whom they might indeed very profitably have married, if only —. Hence divorce, to provide the 'if only'. And of course they are as a rule quite right: they did make a mistake. Only a *very* wise man at the *end* of his life could make a sound judgement concerning whom, amongst the total possible chances, he ought most profitably to have married! Nearly all marriages, even happy ones, are mistakes: in the sense that almost certainly (in a more perfect world, or even with a little more care in this very imperfect one) both partners might have found more suitable mates. But the 'real soul-mate' is the one you are actually married to. You really do very little choosing: life and circumstance do most of it (though if there is a God these must be His instruments, or His appearances). It is notorious that in fact happy marriages are more

51

common where the 'choosing' by the young persons is even more limited, by parental or family authority, as long as there is a social ethic of plain unromantic responsibility and conjugal fidelity. But even in countries where the romantic tradition has so far affected social arrangements as to make people believe that the choosing of a mate is solely the concern of the young, only the rarest good fortune brings together the man and woman who are really as it were 'destined' for one another, and capable of a very great and splendid love. The idea still dazzles us, catches us by the throat: poems and stories in multitudes have been written on the theme, more, probably, than the total of such loves in real life (yet the greatest of these tales do not tell of the happy marriage of such great lovers, but of their tragic separation; as if even in this sphere the truly great and splendid in this fallen world is more nearly achieved by 'failure' and suffering). In such great inevitable love, often love at first sight, we catch a vision, I suppose, of marriage as it should have been in an unfallen world. In this fallen world we have as our only guides, prudence, wisdom (rare in youth, too late in age), a clean heart, and fidelity of *will*. . . . .

My own history is so exceptional, so wrong and imprudent in nearly every point that it makes it difficult to counsel prudence. Yet hard cases make bad law; and exceptional cases are not always good guides for others. For what it is worth here is some autobiography – mainly on this occasion directed towards the points of *age*, and *finance*.

I fell in love with your mother at the approximate age of 18. Quite genuinely, as has been shown – though of course defects of character and temperament have caused me often to fall below the ideal with which I started. Your mother was older than I, and not a Catholic. Altogether unfortunate, as viewed by a guardian.[1] And it *was* in a sense very unfortunate; and in a way very bad for me. These things are absorbing and nervously exhausting. I was a clever boy in the throes of work for (a very necessary) Oxford scholarship. The combined tensions nearly produced a bad breakdown. I muffed my exams and though (as years afterwards my H[ead] M[aster] told me) I ought to have got a good scholarship, I only landed by the skin of my teeth an exhibition of £60 at Exeter: just enough with a school leaving schol[arship] of the same amount to come up on (assisted by my dear old guardian). Of course there was a credit side, not so easily seen by the guardian. I was clever, but not industrious or single-minded; a large part of my failure was due simply to not working (at least not at classics) not because I was in love, but because I was studying something else: Gothic and what not.[2] Having the romantic upbringing I made a boy-and-girl affair serious, and made it the source of effort. Naturally rather a physical coward, I passed from a despised rabbit on a house second-team to school colours in two seasons. All that sort of thing. However, trouble arose: and I had to choose between disobeying and grieving (or deceiving) a guardian who had been a father to me, more than most real fathers, but without any obligation, and 'dropping' the love-affair until I was 21. I don't regret my decision, though it was very hard on my lover. But that was not my fault. She was perfectly free and under no vow to me, and I should have had no just complaint (except according to the unreal romantic code) if she had got married to someone else. For very nearly *three* years I did not see or write to my lover. It was extremely hard, painful and bitter, especially at first. The effects were not wholly good: I fell back into folly and slackness and misspent a good deal of my first year at College. But I don't think anything else would have justified marriage on the basis of a boy's affair; and probably nothing else would have hardened the will enough to give such an affair (however genuine a case of true love) permanence. On the night of my 21st birthday I wrote again to your mother – Jan. 3, 1913. On Jan. 8th I went back to her, and became engaged, and informed an astonished family. I picked up my socks and did a spot of work (too late to save Hon. Mods.[3] from disaster) – and then war broke out the next year, while I still had a year to go at college. In those days chaps joined up, or were scorned publicly. It was a nasty cleft to be in, especially for a young man with too much imagination and little physical courage. No degree: no money: fiancée. I endured the obloquy, and hints becoming outspoken from relatives, stayed up, and produced a First in Finals in 1915. Bolted into the army: July 1915. I found the situation intolerable and married on March 22, 1916. May found me crossing the Channel (I still have the verse I wrote on the occasion!)[4] for the carnage of the Somme.

Think of your mother! Yet I do not now for a moment feel that she was doing more than she should have been asked to do – not that that detracts from the credit of it. I was a young fellow, with a moderate degree, and apt to write verse, a few dwindling pounds p. a. (£20 – 40),[5] and no prospects, a Second Lieut. on 7/6 a day in the infantry where the chances of survival were against you heavily (as a subaltern). She married me in 1916 and John was born in 1917 (conceived and carried during the starvation-year of 1917 and the great U-Boat campaign) round about the battle of Cambrai, when the end of the war seemed as far-off as it does now. I sold out, and spent to pay the nursing-home, the last of my few South African shares, 'my patrimony'.

Out of the darkness of my life, so much frustrated, I put before you the one great thing to love on earth: the Blessed Sacrament. . . . . There you will find romance, glory, honour, fidelity, and the true way of all your loves upon earth, and more than that: Death: by the divine paradox, that which ends life, and demands the surrender of all, and yet by the taste (or foretaste) of which alone can what you seek in your earthly relationships (love, faithfulness, joy) be maintained, or take on that complexion of reality, of eternal endurance, which every man's heart desires.

44 From a letter to Michael Tolkien 18 March 1941

[Tolkien's maternal ancestors, the Suffields, came from the West Midlands, and were particularly associated with Worcestershire.]

Though a Tolkien by name, I am a Suffield by tastes, talents, and upbringing, and any corner of that county [Worcestershire] (however fair or squalid) is in an indefinable way 'home' to me, as no other part of the world is. Your grandmother, to whom you owe so much – for she was a gifted lady of great beauty and wit, greatly stricken by God with grief and suffering, who died in youth (at 34) of a disease hastened by persecution of her faith[1] – died in the postman's cottage at Rednal,[2] and is buried at Bromsgrove.

45 To Michael Tolkien

[Michael was now an Officer Cadet at the Royal Military College, Sandhurst.]

9 June 1941   20 Northmoor Road, Oxford
My dearest Michael,

I was so glad to hear from you. I would have written earlier to-day, only Mummy carried your letter off to Birmingham, before I had time to do more than glance at it. I am afraid that I show up badly as a letter writer: but really I get sick of the pen. Lectures ended on Thursday, and I hoped to get a little while (a) to rest, and (b) to put some order into the garden before 'Schools'[1] begin on Thursday (Corpus Christi). But the everlasting rain has prevented my outdoor work, and lots of extra business prevented any rest. I sympathize with Govt. officials! I have spent most of my time of late drafting rules and regulations,[2] only to find all kinds of loopholes as soon as they are in print, and only to be cursed and criticized by those who have not done the work, and won't try to understand the aims and objects! . . . .

One War is enough for any man. I hope you will be spared a second. Either the bitterness of youth or that of middle-age is enough for a life-time: both is too much. I suffered once what you are going through, if rather differently: because I was very inefficient and unmilitary (and we are alike only in sharing a deep sympathy and feeling for the 'tommy', especially the plain soldier from the agricultural counties). I did not then believe that the 'old folk' suffered much. Now I know. I tell you I feel like a lame canary in a cage. To carry on the old pre-war job – it is just poison. If only I could do something active! But there it is: I am 'permanently reserved', and as such I have my hands too full even to be a Home Guard. And I cannot even get out o'nights to have a crack with a crony.

Still you are my flesh and blood, and carry on the name. It is something to be the father of a good young soldier. Can't you see why I care so much about you, and why all that you do concerns me so closely? Still, let us both take heart of hope and faith. The link between father and son is not only of the perishable flesh: it must have something of *aeternitas* about it. There is a place called 'heaven' where the good here unfinished is completed; and where the stories unwritten, and the hopes unfulfilled, are continued. We may laugh together yet . . .

Did you see Maxwell (the 'tobacco-controller's')[3] account of what the wholesale dealers were doing! They ought to be in quod. . . . . . Commercialism is a swine at heart. But I suppose the major English vice is *sloth*. And it is to sloth, as much or as more than to natural virtue, that we owe our escape from the overt violences of other countries. In the fierce modern world, indeed, sloth does begin almost to look like a virtue. But it is rather terrifying to see so much of it about, when we are grappling with the Furor Teutonicus.

People in this land seem not even yet to realize that in the Germans we have enemies whose virtues (and they are virtues) of obedience and patriotism are greater than ours in the mass. Whose brave men are just about as brave as ours. Whose industry is about 10 times greater. And who are – under the curse of God – now led by a man inspired by a mad, whirlwind, devil: a typhoon, a passion: that makes the poor old Kaiser look like an old woman knitting.

I have spent most of my life, since I was your age, studying Germanic matters (in the general sense that includes England and Scandinavia). There is a great deal more force (and truth) than ignorant people imagine in the 'Germanic' ideal. I was much attracted by it as an undergraduate (when Hitler was, I suppose, dabbling in paint, and had not heard of it), in reaction against the 'Classics'. You have to understand the good in things, to detect the real evil. But no one ever calls on me to 'broadcast', or do a postscript! Yet I suppose I know better than most what is the truth about this 'Nordic' nonsense. Anyway, I have in this War a burning private grudge – which would probably make me a better soldier at 49 than I was at 22: against that ruddy little ignoramus Adolf Hitler (for the odd thing about demonic inspiration and impetus is that it in no way enhances the purely intellectual stature: it chiefly affects the mere will). Ruining, perverting, misapplying, and making for ever accursed, that noble northern spirit, a supreme contribution to Europe, which I have ever loved, and tried to present in its true light. Nowhere, incidentally, was it nobler than in England, nor more early sanctified and Christianized. . . . .

Pray for me. I need it, sorely. I love you.

Your own Father.

46 From a draft to R. W. Chapman 26 November 1941

[George S. Gordon, who died early in 1942, was Tolkien's head of department at Leeds University in the early 1920s, before becoming Professor of English Literature at Oxford and then President of Magdalen College. This draft appears to have been written in reply to a request from Chapman, the Secretary to the Delegates of the Oxford University Press, for reminiscences of Gordon, perhaps to be incorporated into an obituary; Gordon was already known to be terminally ill at the time the letter was written.]

I do not remember dates. Perhaps you know these? I put down some impressions, from which your skill may select a few notes or phrases that may seem appropriate. I associate Leeds with Gordon, although as a matter of fact of my six years there (1920–1925 and one year as a pluralist)[1] the larger part was spent in the company of Abercrombie.[2]

I remember that (before the last war) Gordon's departure from Oxford[3] was viewed with some consternation among the under-graduates of the English School in Oxford; but as a stiff-necked young philologist I did not myself regard the event as important. I first met Gordon at the interview in Leeds (June 1920) for the 'Readership' in English Language: established after the death by drowning of Moorman.[4] I suppose the title (novel in Leeds), and the high salary (as such things go)[5] were both due to Gordon and his farsighted policy. I was, I believe, only a substitute for Sisam[6] (not the least of whose kindnesses was his pointing out the chance to me). But Gordon's kindness and encouragement began at our first meeting. He rescued me from the barren waiting-room, and took me to his house. I remember we spoke of Raleigh[7] on the tram. As (still) a stiff-necked young philologist, I did not in fact think much of Raleigh – he was not, of course, a good lecturer; but some kind spirit prompted me to say that he was 'Olympian'. It went well; though I only really meant that he reposed gracefully on a lofty pinnacle above my criticism.

I was extraordinarily fortunate. And if I speak so of myself, instead of directly and impersonally of Gordon, it is because my prime feeling and first thoughts of him are always of personal gratitude, of a friend rather than of an academic figure. It is not often in 'universities' that a

Professor bothers with the domestic difficulties of a new junior in his twenties; but G. did. He found me rooms himself, and let me share his private room at the University. I do not think that my experience was peculiar. *He was the very master of men.* Anyone who worked under him could see (or at least suspect) that he neglected some sides of his own work: finding, especially, the sort of half-baked 'research', and dreary thesis-writing by the serious minded but semi-educated hunters of the M.A., of which there was far too much, an exceeding weariness, from which he sometimes took refuge in flight. Yet he created not a miserable little 'department', but a team. A team fired not only with a departmental esprit de corps, determined to put 'English' at the head of the Arts departments, but inspired also with a missionary zeal. . . . .

A personal contribution of his was his doctrine of lightheartedness: dangerous, perhaps, in Oxford, necessary in Yorkshire. No Yorkshire-man, or woman, was ever in danger of regarding his class in finals as a matter of indifference (even if it did not have a lifelong effect on his salary as a school teacher): the poet might 'sit in the third and laugh', but the Yorkshire student would not. But he could be, and was, encouraged to play a little, to look outside the 'syllabus', to regard his studies as something larger and more amusing than a subject for an examination. This note Gordon struck and insisted on, and even expressed in print in the little brochure which he had made for the use of his students. There was very little false solemnity, except rarely and that among the students.

As for my side: the foundations were already securely laid for me, and the lines of development marked out. But, subject always to his unobtrusive control, I had a 'free hand'. Every encouragement was given to development on the mediæval and linguistic side; and a friendly rivalry grew up between two, nearly equal, divisions. Each had its own 'seminars'; and there were sometimes combined meetings. Quite the happiest and most balanced 'School' I have seen. I think it might be called a 'School'. Gordon found 'English' in Leeds a departmental subject (I rather fancy you could not get a degree in it alone) and left it a school of studies (in bud). When he arrived he shared a box of glazed bricks, mainly furnished with hot water pipes, with the Professor of French, as their private room. Mere assistants possibly had a hat-peg somewhere. When he left we had 'English House', where every member had a separate room (not to mention a bathroom!) and a common room for students: and with this centre the growing body of students became a cohesive unit, and derived some of the benefits (or distant reflections of them) that we associate with a university rather than a municipal college. It would not have been difficult to build on this foundation. But I fancy that, after he left, the thing just 'ran on', and did not fall into hands of the same quality. In any case numbers fell and finances changed. And

Vice-Chancellors. Sir Michael Sadler I imagine was a helpful superior; and he left about the same time.

47 To Stanley Unwin

[Unwin wrote on 4 December to say that Foyle's bookshop in London were to issue *The Hobbit* under the imprint of their Children's Book Club, and that this had enabled Allen & Unwin to reprint the book. This was all the more desirable as the previous stock of copies had been burnt during an air-raid on London.]

7 December 1942   20 Northmoor Road, Oxford

Dear Mr Unwin,

Thank you for your note, containing two items of hope. I have for some time intended to write and enquire whether in the present situation it was of any use, other than private and family amusement, to endeavour to complete the sequel to *The Hobbit*. I have worked on it at intervals since 1938, all such intervals in fact as trebled official work, quadrupled domestic work, and 'Civil Defence'[1] have left. It is now approaching completion. I hope to get a little free time this vacation, and might hope to finish it off early next year. My heart rather misgives me, all the same. I ought to warn you that it is very long, in places more alarming than 'The Hobbit', and in fact not really a 'juvenile' at all. It has reached Chapter XXXI[2] and will require at least six more to finish (these are already sketched); and the chapters are as a rule longer than the chapters of *The Hobbit*. Is such an 'epic' possible to consider in the present circumstances? Would you like to wait, until it is really finished; or would you care to see a considerable portion of it now? It is in type-script (of various amateur hands) up to about Ch. xxiii. I don't think you will be disappointed with the quality of it. It has had the approval of the original Hobbit audience (my sons and Mr C. S. Lewis), who have read or heard it many times. But it is a question of paper, bulk, and market! It would require two maps.

The burning of *The Hobbit* was a blow. I am to blame in not writing (as I intended) and expressing to you my sympathy with the grievous damage you must have sustained, of which I shared only a very small part. Is any 'compensation' eventually recoverable? . . . .

Would you also consider a volume, containing three or four shorter 'Fairy' stories and some verses? 'Farmer Giles', which I once submitted to you, has pleased a large number of children and grown-ups. If too short, I could add to it one or two similar tales, and include some verse on similar topics, including 'Tom Bombadil' . . . .

Yours sincerely,

J. R. R. Tolkien.

48 To C. S. Lewis

[Lewis kept very few letters, and only two that Tolkien actually sent to him have survived. (For the second, see no. 113.) 'The U.Q.' is an abbreviation for 'Useless Quack', the nickname given by his fellow Inklings to R. E. Havard, Tolkien and Lewis's doctor. 'Ridley' was M. R. Ridley of Balliol College, who, with Tolkien and Lewis, was involved in teaching forces cadets at the university, on the wartime 'short courses'. Lewis was, meanwhile, also travelling around England giving talks on the Christian religion to RAF stations.]

20 April 1943   [20 Northmoor Road, Oxford]
My dear Jack,

V: sorry to hear you are laid low – and with no U.Q. to suggest that it may be your last illness! You must be v: disconsolate. I begin to think that for us to meet on Wednesdays is a duty: there seem to be so many obstacles and fiendish devices to prevent it.

I hope to have a good report of you soon. But do not trouble yourself. Ridley was so astounded at the ignorance of all 22 cadets, revealed in his first class, that he has leaped at the chance of another hour, esp. since otherwise there was no 'Use of E[nglish]' class next week at all. You can (if you wish) shove in 'Arthur'[1] on some other date, when you are recovered fully. The tutorials do not matter.

I fear you are attempting too much. For even if you have merely got 'flu', you are prob. tiring yourself into an easy victim. As a mere 'director', I shall hope v. much to persuade you to ease off in travel (if poss.), and put some weight into this cadet stuff. I am a bit alarmed by it. My lone machine-gun since it started seems to me to have missed the target, and it needs at least one more gun – to depend on – other than the valuable Ridley.

I lunched at the Air Squadron to-day & got a brief whiff of an atmosphere now all too familiar to you, I expect.

Yours affectionately
T[2]

PS. Ridley's first question in the test-paper was a group of words to define – apposite, reverend, venal, choric, secular and a few others. *Not one* cadet got *any* of the words right.

49 To C. S. Lewis (draft)

[A comment on Lewis's suggestion, in *Christian Behaviour* (1943), that 'there ought to be two distinct kinds of marriage': Christian marriage, which is binding and lifelong, and marriage-contracts solemnised only by the State, which make no such demands. The draft, apparently written in 1943, was found tucked into Tolkien's copy of Lewis's booklet.]

My dear L.,

I have been reading your booklet 'Christian Behaviour'.[1] I have never felt happy about your view of Christian 'policy' with regard to *divorce*. I could not before say why – because on the surface your policy seems to be reasonable; and it is at any rate the system under which Roman Catholics already live. For the moment I will not argue whether your policy is in fact right (for today), even an inevitable situation. But I should like to point out that your opinion is in your booklet based on an argument that shows a confusion of thought discoverable from that booklet itself.

p. 34. 'I'd be very angry if the Mohammedans tried to prevent the rest of us from drinking wine.' Justly so. Let us consider this point alone, at first. Why? Well, if we try to ascend straightaway to a rational plane, and leave behind mere anger with anyone who interferes with our habits (good or bad), the answer is: because the Mohammedans would be guilty of injustice. They would be injuring us by depriving us of our share in a *universal human right*, the temperate use of wine, against our will. You made that quite clear in your remarks about *Temperance*, p. 13.

But look now at pp. 26, 30, 31. There you will observe that you are really committed (with the Christian Church as a whole) to the view that *Christian marriage* – monogamous, permanent,[2] rigidly 'faithful' – is in fact the truth about sexual behaviour for *all humanity*: this is the only road of total health[3] (including[4] sex in its proper place) for all[5] men and women. That it is dissonant with men's present sex-psychology does not disprove this, as you see: 'I think it is the instinct that has gone wrong,' you say. Indeed if this were not so, it would be an intolerable injustice to impose permanent[6] monogamy even on Christians. If Christian marriage were in the last analysis 'unnatural' (of the same type as say the prohibition of flesh-meat in certain monastic rules) it could only be imposed on a special 'chastity-order' of the Church, not on the universal Church. No item of compulsory Christian morals is valid only for Christians. (See II Social Morality at the beginning.)[7] Do I not then say truly that your bringing in of Mohammedans on p. 34 is a most stinking red-herring? I do not think you can possibly support your 'policy', by this argument, for by it you are giving away the very foundation of Christian marriage. The foundation is that this is the correct way of 'running the human machine'. Your argument reduces it merely to a way of (perhaps?) getting an extra mileage out of a few selected machines.*

The horror of the Christians with whom you disagree (the great

*Christian marriage is not a prohibition of sexual intercourse, but the correct way of sexual temperance – in fact probably the best way of getting the most satisfying *sexual pleasure*, as alcoholic temperance is the best way of enjoying beer and wine.

majority of all practising Christians) at legal divorce is in the ultimate analysis precisely that: horror at seeing good machines ruined by misuse. I could hope that, if you ever get a chance of alterations, you would make the point clear. Toleration of divorce – if a Christian does tolerate it – is toleration of a human abuse, which it requires special local and temporary circumstances to justify (as does the toleration of usury) – if indeed either divorce or genuine usury should be tolerated at all, as a matter merely of expedient policy.

Under your limitations of space you have not, of course, had opportunity to elaborate[8] your 'policy' – toleration of abuse. But I must suppose you have considered it, as a practical policy in the present world. You do not speak of your two-marriage system as a merely expedient policy, but as if it was somehow related to the Christian virtue of charity. Still I think you can only defend it as an expedient; as a surgeon who, knowing that an operation is necessary for a patient's health, does not operate because he can't (the patient and the patient's foolish advisers won't allow him); or does not even advocate the operation, because the Anti-Surgical League is so powerful and vocal that he is afraid of being beaten up. A Christian of your view is, as we have seen, committed to the belief that all people who practise 'divorce' – certainly divorce as it is now legalized – are misusing the human machine (whatever philosophical defence they may put up), as certainly as men who get drunk (doubtless with a philosophic defence also). They are injuring themselves, other people, and society, by their behaviour. And wrong behaviour (if it is really wrong on universal principles) is progressive, always: it never stops at being 'not very good', 'second best' – it either reforms, or goes on to third-rate, bad, abominable. In no department is that truer than in sex – as you yourself vividly exhibit, in the comparison between a dish of bacon and strip-tease.[9] You show too that you yourself suspect that the break-down of sex-reticence in our time has not made matters better but worse. Anyone in any case can see that the enormous extension and facilitation of 'divorce' in our days, since those of (say) Trollopean society, has done great social harm. It is a slippery slope – leading quickly to Reno,[10] and beyond: in fact already to a promiscuity barely restrained by legalities: for a pair can now divorce one another, have an interlude with new partners, and then 're-marry'. A situation is being, has been, produced in which ordinary unphilosophical and irreligious folk are not only *not* restrained by law from inconstancy, but are actually by law and social custom encouraged to inconstancy. I need hardly add that a situation is thus being produced in which it is intolerably hard to bring up Christian youth in Christian sexual morals (which are ex hypothesi correct morals for all, and which will be lost but which depend upon Christian youth for their maintenance).

61

On what grounds then do you part company with those Christians who resist, step by step, attempts to extend and make divorce easier? (On one point only would I agree. I do *not* view extension of the provisions of the law to all classes (irrespective of rank and money) as an extension of divorce – it is rather justice: if you can have real justice in evil. I think in so desperate a battle (about so fundamental and vital a matter) that resistance even of 'cheapening' of divorce may be defended – why not save the poor by their poverty?; but I admit that as an expedient policy it may be given an ugly twist by the enemy.)

I should like to know on what grounds you base your 'two-marriage' system! From the biological-sociological point of view I gather (from Huxley and others) that monogamy is probably highly beneficial to a community. On that plane, permanence and rigid fidelity would not appear at first sight to be essential. All that the 'social director' requires would seem to be a high degree of sexual continence. But has this ever been, and can it ever be in fact achieved without 'sanctions' or religio-legal ordinance that invests the marriage contract with 'awe'? It does not look like it. The battle may be a losing one, but I cannot help suspecting that those who fight against the *divorce* in this case of law and religion are in the right. Sentire cum ecclesia:[11] how often one finds that this is a true guide. I say this all the more cheerfully, because on this point I myself *dissented* in feeling (not expressly because I am under saving obedience). But I was then still under the delusion that Christian marriage was just a bit of special behaviour of my 'sect or order'.

The last Christian marriage I attended was held under your system: the bridal pair were 'married' twice. They married one another before the Church's witness (a priest), using one set of formulas, and making a vow of lifelong fidelity (and the woman of obedience); they then married again before the State's witness (a registrar, and in this case – adding in my view to the impropriety – a woman) using another set of formulas and making no vow of fidelity or obedience. I felt it was an abominable proceeding – and also ridiculous, since the first set of formulas and vows included the latter as the lesser. In fact it was only not ridiculous on the assumption that the State was in fact saying by implication: I do not recognize the existence of your church; you may have taken certain vows in your meeting-place but they are just foolishness, private taboos, a burden you take on yourself: a limited and impermanent contract is all that is really necessary for citizens. In other words this 'sharp division' is a piece of propaganda, a counter-homily delivered to young Christians fresh from the solemn words of the Christian minister.

[The draft ends here.]

50 From a letter to Christopher Tolkien 25 October 1943

The poplars are now leafless except for one top spray; but it is still a green and leafy October-end down here. At no time do birches look so beautiful: their skin snow-white in the pale yellow sun, and their remaining leaves shining fallow-gold. I have to sleep at Area H.Q.[1] on Friday. Tomorrow night I am going to hobnob, chez Lewis, with – Joad of Joad Hall!

51 From a letter to Christopher Tolkien 27 October 1943

[C. E. M. Joad, well known from his broadcasts on the BBC *Brains Trust*, had just published *The Recovery of Belief*, an indication that he had returned from agnosticism to Christianity. He had been invited to dine with C. S. Lewis at Magdalen College.]

At 9 I went to Magdalen and saw the Joad. He is (except in face) not only very like a toad, but is in character v. like Mr Toad of Toad Hall, & I now perceive that the author of the jest was more subtle than I knew. Still he is intelligent, kindly, and we agreed on many fundamental points. He has the advantage of having been in Russia – and loathing it. He says the 'new towns' do not rise above Willesden level, and the country does not rise at all. He said if you got into a train and looked out of the window, and then read a book for a few hours, and looked out again – there would be nothing outside to see to show that the train had moved at all!

52 From a letter to Christopher Tolkien 29 November 1943

[In the summer of 1943, Christopher, then aged eighteen, was called up into the Royal Air Force. When this letter was written, he was at a training camp in Manchester.]

My political opinions lean more and more to Anarchy (philosophically understood, meaning abolition of control not whiskered men with bombs) – or to 'unconstitutional' Monarchy. I would arrest anybody who uses the word State (in any sense other than the inanimate realm of England and its inhabitants, a thing that has neither power, rights nor mind); and after a chance of recantation, execute them if they remained obstinate! If we could get back to personal names, it would do a lot of good. Government is an abstract noun meaning the art and process of governing and it should be an offence to write it with a capital G or so as to refer to people. If people were in the habit of referring to 'King George's council, Winston and his gang', it would go a long way to clearing thought, and reducing the frightful landslide into Theyocracy.

Anyway the proper study of Man is anything but Man; and the most improper job of any man, even saints (who at any rate were at least unwilling to take it on), is bossing other men. Not one in a million is fit for it, and least of all those who seek the opportunity. And at least it is done only to a small group of men who know *who* their master is. The mediævals were only too right in taking *nolo episcopari*[1] as the best reason a man could give to others for making him a bishop. Give me a king whose chief interest in life is stamps, railways, or race-horses; and who has the power to sack his Vizier (or whatever you care to call him) if he does not like the cut of his trousers. And so on down the line. But, of course, the fatal weakness of all that – after all only the fatal weakness of all good natural things in a bad corrupt unnatural world – is that it works and has worked only when all the world is messing along in the same good old inefficient human way. The quarrelsome, conceited Greeks managed to pull it off against Xerxes; but the abominable chemists and engineers have put such a power into Xerxes' hands, and all ant-communities, that decent folk don't seem to have a chance. We are all trying to do the Alexander-touch – and, as history teaches, that orientalized Alexander and all his generals. The poor boob fancied (or liked people to fancy) he was the son of Dionysus, and died of drink. The Greece that was worth saving from Persia perished anyway; and became a kind of Vichy-Hellas, or Fighting-Hellas (which did not fight), talking about Hellenic honour and culture and thriving on the sale of the early equivalent of dirty postcards. But the special horror of the present world is that the whole damned thing is in one bag. There is nowhere to fly to. Even the unlucky little Samoyedes, I suspect, have tinned food and the village loudspeaker telling Stalin's bed-time stories about Democracy and the wicked Fascists who eat babies and steal sledge-dogs. There is only one bright spot and that is the growing habit of disgruntled men of dynamiting factories and power-stations; I hope that, encouraged now as 'patriotism', may remain a habit! But it won't do any good, if it is not universal.

Well, cheers and all that to you dearest son. We were born in a dark age out of due time (for us). But there is this comfort: otherwise we should not *know*, or so much love, what we do love. I imagine the fish out of water is the only fish to have an inkling of water. Also we have still small swords to use. 'I will not bow before the Iron Crown, nor cast my own small golden sceptre down.'[2] Have at the Orcs, with winged words, hildenæddran (war-adders), biting darts – but make sure of the mark, before shooting.

9 December 1943   20 Northmoor Road, Oxford
My dearest,
   I believe it is a week or more since I wrote to you? I can't really remember, as life has been such a rush. . . . . I haven't seen C.S.L. for weeks or Williams.[1] . . . . The daily round(s) and the common task + + which furnish so much more than one actually asks. No great fun, no amusements; no bright new idea; not even a thin small joke. Nothing to read – and even the papers with nothing but Teheran Ballyhoo.[2] Though I must admit that I smiled a kind of sickly smile and 'nearly curled up on the floor, and the subsequent proceedings interested me no more', when I heard of that bloodthirsty old murderer Josef Stalin inviting all nations to join a happy family of folks devoted to the abolition of tyranny & intolerance! But I must also admit that in the photograph our little cherub W. S. C.[3] actually *looked* the biggest ruffian present. Humph, well! I wonder (if we survive this war) if there will be any niche, even of sufferance, left for reactionary back numbers like me (and you). The bigger things get the smaller and duller or flatter the globe gets. It is getting to be all one blasted little provincial suburb. When they have introduced American sanitation, morale-pep, feminism, and mass production throughout the Near East, Middle East, Far East, U.S.S.R., the Pampas, el Gran Chaco, the Danubian Basin, Equatorial Africa, Hither Further and Inner Mumbo-land, Gondhwanaland, Lhasa, and the villages of darkest Berkshire, how happy we shall be. At any rate it ought to cut down travel. There will be nowhere to go. So people will (I opine) go all the faster. Col. Knox[4] says 1/8 of the world's population speaks 'English', and that is the biggest language group. If true, damn shame – say I. May the curse of Babel strike all their tongues till they can only say 'baa baa'. It would mean much the same. I think I shall have to refuse to speak anything but Old Mercian.
   But seriously: I do find this Americo-cosmopolitanism very terrifying. Quâ mind and spirit, and neglecting the piddling fears of timid flesh which does not want to be shot or chopped by brutal and licentious soldiery (German or other), I am not really sure that its victory is going to be so much the better for the world as a whole and in the long run than the victory of ——.[5] I don't suppose letters *in* are censored. But if they are, or not, I need to you hardly add that them's the sentiments of a good many folk – and no indication of lack of patriotism. For I love England (not Great Britain and certainly not the British Commonwealth (grr!)), and if I was of military age, I should, I fancy, be grousing away in a fighting service, and willing to go on to the bitter end – always hoping that things may turn out better for England than they look like doing.

Somehow I cannot really imagine the fantastic luck (or blessing, one would call it, if one could dimly see why we should be blessed – implying God) that has attended England is running out yet. Chi vincerà? said the Italians (before they got involved poor devils), and answered Stalin. Not altogether right perhaps. Our Cherub above referred to can play a wily hand – one guesses, one hopes, one does not know. . . . .

Your own father.

54 From a letter to Christopher Tolkien 8 January 1944

Remember your guardian angel. Not a plump lady with swan-wings! But – at least this is my notion and feeling – : as souls with free-will we are, as it were, so placed as to face (or to be able to face) God. But God is (so to speak) also behind us, supporting, nourishing us (as being creatures). The bright point of power where that life-line, that spiritual umbilical cord touches: there is our Angel, facing two ways to God behind us in the direction we cannot see, and to us. But of course do not grow weary of facing God, in your free right and strength (both provided 'from behind' as I say). If you cannot achieve inward peace, and it is given to few to do so (least of all to me) in tribulation, do not forget that the aspiration for it is not a vanity, but a concrete act. I am sorry to talk like this, and so haltingly. But I can do no more for you dearest. . . . .

If you don't do so already, make a habit of the 'praises'. I use them much (in Latin): the Gloria Patri, the Gloria in Excelsis, the Laudate Dominum; the Laudate Pueri Dominum (of which I am specially fond), one of the Sunday psalms; and the Magnificat; also the Litany of Loretto (with the prayer Sub tuum præsidium). If you have these by heart you never need for words of joy. It is also a good and admirable thing to know by heart the Canon of the Mass, for you can say this in your heart if ever hard circumstance keeps you from hearing Mass. So endeth Fæder lár his suna.[1] With very much love.

> Longað þonne þy læs þe him con léoþa worn,
> oþþe mid hondum con hearpan grétan;
> hafaþ him his glíwes giefe, þe him God sealde.

From the Exeter Book. Less doth yearning trouble him who knoweth many songs, or with his hands can touch the harp: his possession is his gift of 'glee' (= music and/or verse) which God gave him.

How these old words smite one out of the dark antiquity! 'Longað'! All down the ages men (of our kind, most awarely) have felt it: not necessarily caused by sorrow, or the hard world, but sharpened by it.

[Christopher had now left for South Africa, where he was to train as a pilot. This is the first of a long series of letters to him, which were numbered, for reasons which Tolkien gives here.]

18 January 1944   20 Northmoor Road, Oxford
Fæder his þriddan suna (1)[1]
My dearest,

I am afraid it is a very long time (or it seems so: actually it is about 8 days) since I wrote; but I did not quite know what to do, until we got your letter yesterday. . . . . I am glad my last long letter caught you before you went! We don't know yet, of course, just when that was, or whither. . . . .

I gave 2 lectures yesterday, and then conferred with Gabriel Turville-Petre[2] about Cardiff. . . . . I managed just to catch the last post with my Cardiff report. Then I had to go and sleep (???) at C. HeadQ.[3] I did not – not much. I was in the small C33 room: very cold and damp. But an incident occurred which moved me and made the occasion memorable. My companion in misfortune was Cecil Roth (the learned Jew historian).[4] I found him charming, full of gentleness (in every sense); and we sat up till after 12 talking. He lent me his watch as there were no going clocks in the place: – and nonetheless himself came and called me at 10 to 7: so that I could go to Communion! It seemed like a fleeting glimpse of an unfallen world. Actually I was awake, and just (as one does) discovering a number of reasons (other than tiredness and having no chance to shave or even wash), such as the desirability of getting home in good time to open up and un-black and all that, why I should not go. But the incursion of this gentle Jew, and his sombre glance at my rosary by my bed, settled it. I was down at St Aloysius at 7.15 just in time to go to Confession before Mass; and I came home just before the end of Mass. . . . . I lectured at 11 a.m. (after collecting fish);[5] and managed to have a colloguing with the brothers Lewis and C. Williams (at the White Horse).[6] And that is about all the top off the news as far as I am concerned! Except that the *fouls*[7] do not lay, but I have still to clean out their den. . . . .

I start to-day *numbering* each letter, and *each page*, so that if any go awry you will know – and the bare news of importance can be made up. This is (No. 1) of Pater ad Filium Natu (sed haud alioquin) minimum:[8] Fæder suna his ágnum, þám gingstan nalles unléofestan.[9] (I suppose a professor of Old English may be permitted to use that language to a former pupil?: query for ref. to censor, if any). I can't write Russian and find Polish rather sticky yet. I expect poor old Poptawski[10] will be wondering how I am getting on, soon. It will be a long time before I can be of any assistance to him in devising a new technical vocabulary!!! The vocab. will just happen along anyway (if there are any Poles and Poland left) . . . .

56   From a letter to Christopher Tolkien   1 March 1944 (FS 6)

[For 'The Useless Quack', see the introductory note to no. 48.]

As I have hardly seen anybody in the last few weeks there is no quip, jest, or other item of merriment to record. The Useless Quack has returned to Oxford! Almost the only wire I have ever pulled that has rung a bell. But there he is, uniform, red-beard, slow smile and all, still in Navy, but living at home and working on his research Board (Malaria). He seems pleased, and so do the Board. All done at the Mitre – where I picked up an urgent enquiry as to his whereabouts, as being the one man wanted. He was on the other side of the globe just then. Lewis is as energetic and jolly as ever, but getting too much publicity for his or any of our tastes. 'Peterborough', usually fairly reasonable, did him the doubtful honour of a peculiarly misrepresentative and asinine paragraph in the Daily Telegraph of Tuesday last. It began 'Ascetic Mr Lewis' ——!!! I ask you! He put away three pints in a very short session we had this morning, and said he was 'going short for Lent'. I suppose all the stuff you see in print is about as accurate about Tom, Dick, or Harry. It is a pity newspapers can't leave *people* alone, and don't make some effort to understand what they *say* (if it is worth it): at any rate they might have some standards that would prevent them saying things about people which are quite untrue, even if not actually (as often) painful, angering, or indeed injurious. . . . .

Still very cold. Snow last night. But there is no mistaking the growing power of a March sun. Clumps of yellow crocus are out, and the white-mauve ones beginning; green buds are appearing. I wonder what you think of the season-reverse south of the Line? More or less the equivalent of early September with you, I suppose. My earliest recollection of Christmas is of a blazing hot day.[1]

57   From an airgraph to Christopher Tolkien   30 March 1944 (FS 12)

I saw the two Lewis bros. yesterday, & lunched with C.S.L.: quite an outing for me. The indefatigable man read me part of a new story! But he is putting the screw on me to finish mine. I needed some pressure, & shall probably respond; but the 'vac.' is already half over & the exam. wood only just cleared.

[A description of a visit to Birmingham, where Tolkien was attending a lunch given by the new headmaster of his school, King Edward's, which since his schooldays had moved to new buildings in another part of the city.]

3 April 1944 (FS 13)   20 Northmoor Road, Oxford

My dearest,

I wrote you an airgraph[1] on Thursday last at night; but unfortunately it was not sent off on Friday, and on Saturday I went off early and in a rush to Brum. So it has only gone today. Nothing more has come from you since yours of 13 March (arrived 28). I can't remember much about Friday, except that the morning was wrecked by shopping and queueing: result one slab of pork-pie; and that I had a dreadfully bad and lugubriously dull dinner in college, and was glad to get home before 9 p.m. But I have begun to nibble at Hobbit again. I have started to do some (painful) work on the chapter which picks up the adventures of Frodo and Sam again; and to get myself attuned have been copying and polishing the last written chapter (Orthanc-Stone). Saturday was a memorable day. Grey, damp and unpleasing. But I got off about 9 a.m. Cycled to Pembroke and deposited bike and lamps. Caught the 9.30, which (just, I suppose, because I had time to spare) left Oxford on time (!!!), for the first time in human memory, and reached Brum only a few minutes late. I found myself in a carriage occupied by an R.A.F. officer (this war's wings, who had been to South Africa though he looked a bit elderly), and a very nice young American Officer, New-Englander. I stood the hot-air they let off as long as I could; but when I heard the Yank burbling about 'Feudalism' and its results on English class-distinctions and social behaviour, I opened a broadside. The poor boob had not, of course, the very faintest notions about 'Feudalism', or history at all – being a chemical engineer. But you can't knock 'Feudalism' out of an American's head, any more than the 'Oxford Accent'. He was impressed I think when I said that an Englishman's relations with porters, butlers, and tradesmen had as much connexion with 'Feudalism' as skyscrapers had with Red Indian wigwams, or taking off one's hat to a lady has with the modern methods of collecting Income Tax; but I am certain he was not convinced. I did however get a dim notion into his head that the 'Oxford Accent' (by which he politely told me he meant mine) was not 'forced' and 'put on', but a natural one learned in the nursery – and was moreover not feudal or aristocratic but a very middle-class bourgeois invention. After I told him that his 'accent' sounded to me like English after being wiped over with a dirty sponge, and generally suggested (falsely) to an English observer that, together with American slouch, it indicated a slovenly and ill-disciplined people – well, we got quite friendly. We had some bad coffee in the refreshment room at Snow Hill, and parted.

I then strolled about my 'home town' for a bit. Except for one patch of ghastly wreckage (opp. my old school's site) it does not look much damaged: not by the enemy. The chief damage has been the growth of great flat featureless modern buildings. The worst of all is the ghastly multiple-store erection on the old site. I couldn't stand much of that or the ghosts that rose from the pavements; so I caught a tram from the same old corner at which I used to catch it to go out to the playing fields. Down the shabby (much bomb-pocked) Bristol Road to Edgbaston Park Road at 12.15 (half an hour too soon). I won't weary you with impressions of the ghastly utterly third-rate new school buildings. But if you can imagine a building better than most Oxford colleges being replaced by what looks like a girls' council school, you've got it and my feelings. And apparently the new Head Master's. In a speech after lunch he hinted (or more than that) that they were pretty foul, and the school would never recover from the blow if something was not done about it. There were about 120 Old Boys (out of 220 asked): many of my vintage. I saw faces I had not seen since I was your age – and to many I could give only *initials*, not names. All Old Edwardians remember initials. To my complete surprise I found that I was remembered chiefly for rugger-prowess (!!) and my taste in coloured socks. . . . .

59 From an airgraph to Christopher Tolkien 5 April 1944 (FS 14)

I have seriously embarked on an effort to finish my book, & have been sitting up rather late: a lot of re-reading and research required. And it is a painful sticky business getting into swing again. I have gone back to Sam and Frodo, and am trying to work out their adventures. A few pages for a lot of sweat: but at the moment they are just meeting Gollum on a precipice. What a lot of work you put into the typing, and the chapters written out so beautifully! I wish I still had my amanuensis and critic near at hand.

60 To Christopher Tolkien (airgraph)

[Christopher had now arrived in South Africa, and was at a camp in the Transvaal.]

13 April 1944 (FS 15)   20 Northmoor Road, Oxford
Dearest: your Airletter of 25 March (?), postmd. 28th, arrived this morning: very welcome. By now you should be getting news from me:

have been writing about twice a week. I don't comment on your letter, though I am v. sorry. Know how you feel! Especially about cancelled leave. Your letter was 'deur Sensor oopgemak'[1] by the way. You do not seem to have done anything very useful since September! I miss you hourly also, and am lonely without you. I have friends, of course, but can seldom see them. Things a bit easier for me now, though. Helped in the admission of cadets today (as big a bunch as ever), but as far as I can see they will not concern me further this term – joy! I did see C.S.L. & Charles Williams yesterday for almost 2 hours (cut short by having to meet M. & P.[2] for lunch at 12.20, which proved unobtainable so that we had to return home). I read my recent chapter: it received approbation. I have begun another. Shall have spare copies typed, if possible, & sent out to you. Don't think there's more news at moment. . . . . Am actually going out tonight to Magdalen: C.S.L., Warnie[3] (writing a book: it's catching), C.W., David Cecil,[4] and prob. the Useless Quack (still bearded and uniformed): quite an event for me. . . . . Now I will return to Frodo & Gollum for a brief spell. More tomorrow, when this shall go off. . . . . Saturday 15th. I'm afraid this didn't get off. I had a very pleasant time on Thurs. All turned up except Cecil, & we stayed until after midnight. The best entertainment proved to be the chapter of Major Lewis' projected book – on a subject that does not interest me: the court of Louis XIV; but it was most wittily written (as well as learned). I did not think so well of the concluding chapter of C.S.L.'s new moral allegory or 'vision', based on the mediæval fancy of the Refrigerium, by which the lost souls have an occasional holiday in Paradise. Yesterday morning I managed to get an hour or two writing, & have brought Frodo nearly to the gates of Mordor. Afternoon lawn-mowing. Mrs. C.[5] arrived safely from Carmarthen on Thurs. bringing gifts comestible. . . . . I had a pretty wearing time on 'exercise' up till 10 p.m. & then supped with the family, & then went to 'sleep' at area H.Q. That I did not manage: I had hardly a wink. Post is right on main road: very noisy all night. . . . . M. & I are going to have tea with the Nichol Smiths[6] today, & I am supping with Elaine,[7] and others at a small don-party. Quite a week for me. But term begins next week, & proofs of Wales papers[8] have come. Still I am going to continue 'Ring' in every salvable moment. . . . .

61 From a letter to Christopher Tolkien   18 April 1944 (FS 17)

It has been a great event to-day, all your crowd of letters arriving, and much delaying the eating of breakfast. . . . . Your accounts, which were uncensored, distressed but did not surprise me. How it reminds me of

71

my own experience! Only in one way was I better off: wireless was not invented. I daresay it had some potential for good, but it has in fact in the main become a weapon for the fool, the savage, and the villain to afflict the minority with, and to destroy thought. Listening in has killed listening. I can only hope you won't have any more Altmarks![1] I was always against your choice of service (on the ground it seems a war behind); but at least it should not later land you often in to the animal horror of the life of active service on the earth – such as trenchlife as I knew it. Even HP[2] were a Paradise to that and the Altmark not (prob.) much worse. At least at present you are getting an occasional chance to read. I am glad. God bless you. Ðys dógor þu geþyld hafa wéana gehwylces, swá ic þé wéne to.[3] If the censor (and you) will permit me to quote an ancient *English* poet – and I can't help thinking it comes better from father to son, than from young Béowulf, about your age, to old greybeard Hrothgar! Úre æghwylc sceal ende gebidan worolde lífes: wyrce se þe móte dómes ǽr déaþe.[4] Cold stern counsel; and much depends on 'he who may', and on what you consider to be *dóm*.

I am surprised that, tasting and disliking the very opposite, you should also dislike the 'manners' of life 150 years ago (nearly) as depicted by Jane [Austen]. Little is left of it all, save a few remnants of table-manners (among a decreasing minority). But actually they made life a lot easier, smoother, and less frictional and dubious; and cloaked or indeed held in check (as table-manners do) the everlasting cat, wolf, and dog that lurk at no great depth under our social skin. . . . .

I hope to see C.S.L. and Charles W. tomorrow morning and read my next chapter – on the passage of the Dead Marshes and the approach to the Gates of Mordor, which I have now practically finished. Wasted some time on Sunday answering a letter from the Eighth Army (!). I get a good many of the kind, but this one was rather amusingly written. The 'Regius Professor of English' was asked to adjudicate on a dispute which was rending the Mess of a certain Light A.A. Regt R.A. into a faction-war: how to pronounce the name of the poet *Cowper*. Big Money hangs on the issue. The letter was from the adjutant (who appeared to have read the poet, even *The Task*, 'in his wayward youth'). I can't help thinking that the Army shows spots of more wit and intelligence – you may one day strike some in your service (mais je le doute). Deeming it below the dignity of a 'Regius Prof⸢.' to adjudicate on Big Money, I sent as Delphic an oracular reply as I could, giving the adjt. a good deal more facts, I expect, than he wanted. Not of course that there is any doubt that the poet called himself *Cooper* (of which his name is merely the older spelling): *oup*, *owp* spells *oop* in English: there are no *aups* (in Latin value): so *stoup*, *group*, *soup* and formerly also *droup*, *stoup* (verb), *troup*, *coup(er)*, *whouping*-cough, *loup*, etc. (not to mention *roum, toumb*). Yesterday I had a visit from F. Pakenham,[5] getting up a combined Christian Council of all denominations, for this city, as now in 50 others. I joined, but refused the proffered secretaryship (you bet!). Term has almost begun: I tutored Miss Salu[6] for an hour. The afternoon was squandered on plumbing (stopping overflow) and cleaning out fowls – less grudgingly, as they are laying generously (9 again yesterday). A lovely morning dawned on us this morn. A mist like early Sept. with a pearl-button sun (8 a.m. being really 6 a.m.) that soon changed into serene blue, with the silver light of spring on flower and leaf. Leaves are out: the white-grey of the quince, the grey-green of young apple, the full green of hawthorn, the tassels of flower even on the sluggard poplars. The narcissuses are a marvellous show, but the grass grows so quick that I feel like a barber faced with a never-ending queue (& not a chinaman's either, to be trimmed with one snip).

I cannot tell you how I miss you, dear man. I would not mind it, if you were happier or more usefully employed. How stupid everything is!, and war multiplies the stupidity by 3 and its power by itself: so one's precious days are ruled by $(3x)^2$ when x=normal human crassitude (and that's bad enough). However, I hope that in after days the experience of men and things, if painful, will prove useful. It did to me. As for what you say or hint of 'local' conditions: I knew of them. I don't think they have much changed (even for the worse). I used to hear them discussed by my mother; and have ever since taken a special interest in that part of the world. The treatment of colour nearly always horrifies anyone going out from Britain, & not only in South Africa. Unfort. not many retain that generous sentiment for long. I don't say anything about home conditions. You will (I suppose) hear on radio as much as I could say. We are all well at the moment. We are waiting. I wonder for how long now. Not long I think. I see from paper that Air Crew training in Canada is being cut: fewer A.C. generally are now to be trained. I thought I guessed from your letter that you do not now expect to come to G.B. to finish. I hope that is not so. But who knows? We are in God's hands. Our lot has fallen on evil days: but that cannot be by *mere* ill chance. Take care of yourself in all due ways (aequam serva mentem, comprime linguam[7]) . . . .

62 From an airgraph to Christopher Tolkien   23 April 1944 (FS 18)

I read my second chapter, Passage of the Dead Marshes, to Lewis and Williams on Wed. morning. It was approved. I have now nearly done a third: Gates of the Land of Shadow. But this story takes me in charge, and I have already taken three chapters over what was meant to be one!

And I have neglected too many things to do it. I am just enmeshed in it now, and have to wrench my mind away to tackle exam-paper proofs, and lectures (beginning on Tuesday).

63 To Christopher Tolkien

24 April 1944 (FS 19)   20 Northmoor Road, Oxford

My dearest Chris,

Your airletter . . . . arrived at breakfast this morn. I had the uncommon luxury of lying a-bed with toast and home-made marmalade (a good many oranges *and* lemons lately) and your letter. St George's day passed uneventfully; I sat up 'on duty' till 1.30 this morn. and then decided to retire: it is so warm one can sleep with open windows and hear alerts. I was drawing my curtains when I noted a v. white light S.W., and I was just putting foot in much desired sheets when Ulysses' Peril[1] let off her wail. Did not in fact get to bed till past 3.30, or sleep till 4, or wake till 8.45, or get up till 9.45. . . . . I spent what was left of this morning in town doing odd jobs, among them that of getting my head-harvest reaped: a big crop: still fertile soil evidently. Mitre[2] was locked! Have not tasted beer since Thursday last when our barrel ran dry, & has not yet been replaced. I have to lecture tomorrow, so now I must stop for the moment. . . . .

Wed. 26 April. . . . . Yesterday felt effects of Sunday night. Went off early to town and did some executor's business for Mrs Wright,[3] gave a poor lecture, saw the Lewises and C.W. (White Horse) for ½ hour; mowed three lawns, and wrote letter to John, and struggled with recalcitrant passage in 'The Ring'. At this point I require to know how much later the moon gets up each night when nearing full, and how to stew a rabbit! No Lewis this morning, as he has been appointed Clarke Lecturer in Cambridge, and leaves early to lecture there at 5 p.m. on Wednesdays. . . . .

3.45 Wed. A record college meeting (12½ mins.)! Arrived back to find Biddy had broken another egg (about the 7th), so, despairing that the 'henwife' would attend to it, I have spent an agreeable time catching her (i.e. the bird), cleaning her, trimming her and disinfecting her – and then disinfecting myself. Grr! The fourth lawn will have to wait. I was pleased that you managed to get some church at the end of Holy Week, though not too pleased with your Even-christians (as they called 'em in O. & M.E.).[4] However that cannot be helped. The only salve is the sudden reflection that one of them is prob. making an adverse judgement on oneself, not unreasonable as founded on one's looks and deportment, but as wide of the mark of the inner self as our own are!

God ána wát.[5] But as for sermons! They are bad, aren't they! Most of them from any point of view. The answer to the mystery is prob. not simple; but part of it is that 'rhetoric' (of which preaching is a dept.) is an art, which requires (a) some native talent and (b) learning and practice. The instrument used is v. much more complex than a piano, yet most performers are in the position of a man who sits down to a piano and expects to move his audience without any knowledge of the notes at all. The art can be learned (granted some modicum of aptitude) and can then be effective, in a way, when wholly unconnected with sincerity, sanctity etc. But preaching is complicated by the fact that we expect in it not only a performance, but truth and sincerity, and also at least no word, tone, or note that suggests the possession of vices (such as hypocrisy, vanity) or defects (such as folly, ignorance) in the preacher.

Good sermons require some art, some virtue, some knowledge. Real sermons require some special grace which does not transcend art but arrives at it by instinct or 'inspiration'; indeed the Holy Spirit seems sometimes to speak through a human mouth providing art, virtue and insight he does not himself possess: but the occasions are rare. In other times I don't think an educated person is required to suppress the critical faculty, but it should be kept in order by a constant endeavour to apply the truth (if any), even in cliché form, to oneself exclusively! A difficult exercise. . . . .

I was much amused by your account of your journey to Jo'burg on Maundy Thursday. . . . . If you fetch up at Bloemfontein I shall wonder if the little old stone bank-house (Bank of South Africa) where I was born is still standing. And I wonder if my Father's grave is there still. I have never done anything about it, but I believe my mother had a stone-cross put up or sent out.[6] (A. R. Tolkien died 1896). If not it will be lost now, prob., unless there are any records. . . . .

64 To Christopher Tolkien

30 April 1944 (FS 20)   20 Northmoor Road, Oxford
My dearest:

I have decided to send you another air letter, not an airgraph, in the hope that I may so cheer you up a little more. . . . . I do miss you so, and I do find all this mighty hard to bear on my own account and on yours. The utter stupid waste of war, not only material but moral and spiritual, is so staggering to those who have to endure it. And always was (despite the poets), and always will be (despite the propagandists) – not of course that it has not is and will be necessary to face it in an evil world. But so short is human memory and so evanescent are its generations that in only about 30 years there will be few or no people with that direct experience which alone goes really to the heart. The burnt hand teaches most about fire.

I sometimes feel appalled at the thought of the sum total of human misery all over the world at the present moment: the millions parted, fretting, wasting in unprofitable days – quite apart from torture, pain, death, bereavement, injustice. If anguish were visible, almost the whole of this benighted planet would be enveloped in a dense dark vapour, shrouded from the amazed vision of the heavens! And the products of it all will be mainly evil – historically considered. But the historical version is, of course, not the only one. All things and deeds have a value in themselves, apart from their 'causes' and 'effects'. No man can estimate what is really happening at the present sub specie aeternitatis. All we do know, and that to a large extent by direct experience, is that evil labours with vast power and perpetual success – in vain: preparing always only the soil for unexpected good to sprout in. So it is in general, and so it is in our own lives. . . . . But there is still some hope that things may be better for us, even on the temporal plane, in the mercy of God. And though we need all our natural human courage and guts (the vast sum of human courage and endurance is stupendous, isn't it?) and all our religious faith to face the evil that may befall us (as it befalls others, if God wills) still we may pray and hope. I do. And you were so special a gift to me, in a time of sorrow and mental suffering, and your love, opening at once almost as soon as you were born, foretold to me, as it were in spoken words, that I am consoled ever by the certainty that there is no end to this. Probable under God that we shall meet again, 'in hale and in unity', before very long, dearest, and certain that we have some special bond to last beyond this life – subject of course always to the mystery of free will, by which either of us could throw away 'salvation'. In which case God would arrange matters differently! . . . .

On Thursday I gave 2 lectures and had some troublesome business in town and was too tired to attend the Lewis séance. I hope to see him tomorrow, and read some more of 'the Ring'. It is growing and sprouting again (I did a whole day at it yesterday to the neglect of many matters) and opening out in unexpected ways. So far in the new chapters Frodo and Sam have traversed Sarn Gebir, climbed down the cliff, encountered and temporarily tamed Gollum. They have with his guidance crossed the Dead Marshes and the slag-heaps of Mordor, lain in hiding outside the main gates and found them impassable, and set out for a more secret entrance near Minas Morghul (formerly M. Ithil). It will turn out to be the deadly Kirith Ungol and Gollum will play false. But at moment they are in Ithilien (which is proving a lovely land); there has been a lot of bother about stewed rabbit; and they have been captured by Gondorians, and witnessed them ambushing a Swerting army (dark men of South) marching to Mordor's aid. A large elephant of prehistoric size, a war-elephant of the Swertings, is loose, and Sam has gratified a life-long wish to see an Oliphaunt, an animal about which there was a hobbit nursery-rhyme (though it was commonly supposed to be mythical). In the chapter next to be done they will get to Kirith Ungol and Frodo will be caught. Here is the rhyme cited by Sam: Grey as a mouse,/Big as a house,/Nose like a snake,/I make the earth quake,/As I tramp through the grass;/Trees crack as I pass./With horns in my mouth/I walk in the South/Flapping big ears./Beyond count of years/I've stumped round and round,/Never lie on the ground,/Not even to die./Oliphaunt am I,/Biggest of All,/huge, old, and tall./If ever you'd met me,/You wouldn't forget me./If you never do,/You won't think I'm true;/But old Oliphaunt am I,/and I never lie. I hope that has something of the 'nursery rhyme' flavour. On the whole Sam is behaving well, and living up to repute. He treats Gollum rather like Ariel to Caliban. . . . .

It is full Maytime by the trees and grass now. But the heavens are full of roar and riot. You cannot even hold a shouting conversation in the garden now, save about 1 a.m. and 7 p.m. – unless the day is too foul to be out. How I wish the 'infernal combustion' engine had never been invented. Or (more difficult still since humanity and engineers in special are both nitwitted and malicious as a rule) that it could have been put to rational uses – if any. . . . .

Now we can only link with this flimsy bit of paper! But may it speed to you and arrive safely. I wish that it might be written in Runes beyond the craft of Celebrimbor of Hollin, shining like silver, filled with the visions and horizons that open in my mind. Though I have without you no one to speak my thought. I first began to write the 'H. of the Gnomes'[1] in army huts, crowded, filled with the noise of gramophones – and there you are in the same prison. May you, too, escape – strengthened. Take care of yourself, in soul and body, in all ways proper and possible, for the love that you have to your own Father.

65   From an airgraph to Christopher Tolkien   4 May 1944 (FS 21)

I saw Lewis (solo) on Monday and read another chapter: am busy now with the next; we shall soon be in the shadows of Mordor at last. I will send you some copies, as soon as I can get them made.

I sent off to you yesterday an airgraph, FS 21 (written Thursday), and there was not room to tell you that that morn. (Friday) your airletter (Z) had arrived; now your airletter (Y) has come, and I have 2 to answer. We don't mind your grousing at all – you have no one else, and I expect it relieves the strain. I used to write in just the same way or worse to poor old Fr. Vincent Reade,[1] I remember. Life in camp seems not to have changed at all, and what makes it so exasperating is the fact that all its worse features are unnecessary, and due to human stupidity which (as 'planners' refuse to see) is always magnified indefinitely by 'organization'. But England in 1917, 1918 was in a poor way, and it is a bit thicker that in a land of relative plenty, you shd. have such conditions. And the taxpayers would like to know where are all the millions going, if the pick of their sons are so treated. However it is, humans being what they are, quite inevitable, and the only cure (short of universal Conversion) is not to have wars – nor planning, nor organization, nor regimentation. Your service is, of course, as anybody with any intelligence and ears and eyes knows, a very bad one, living on the repute of a few gallant men, and you are probably in a particularly bad corner of it. But all Big Things planned in a big way feel like that to the toad under the harrow, though on a general view they do function and do their job. An ultimately evil job. For we are attempting to conquer Sauron with the Ring. And we shall (it seems) succeed. But the penalty is, as you will know, to breed new Saurons, and slowly turn Men and Elves into Orcs. Not that in real life things are as clear cut as in a story, and we started out with a great many Orcs on our side. . . . . Well, there you are: a hobbit amongst the Urukhai. Keep up your hobbitry in heart, and think that all *stories* feel like that when you are *in* them. You are inside a very great story! I think also that you are suffering from suppressed 'writing'. That may be my fault. You have had rather too much of me and my peculiar mode of thought and reaction. And as we are so akin it has proved rather powerful. Possibly inhibited you. I think if you could begin to *write*, and find your own mode, or even (for a start) imitate mine, you would find it a great relief. I sense amongst all your pains (some merely physical) the desire to express your *feeling* about good, evil, fair, foul in some way: to rationalize it, and prevent it just festering. In my case it generated Morgoth and the History of the Gnomes. Lots of the early parts of which (and the languages) – discarded or absorbed – were done in grimy canteens, at lectures in cold fogs, in huts full of blasphemy and smut, or by candle light in bell-tents, even some down in dugouts under shell fire. It did not make for efficiency and present-mindedness, of course, and I was not a good officer. . . . .

Nothing much has happened here since I wrote on Thursday. Weather foul. Cold, windy; roads littered with torn leaves, and broken blossom. It has veered from SW > W > NW > NE. Buchan is at it (as usual).[2] I wrote in the morning, wasted an afternoon in footling Board Meetings, and wrote again. P. and Mummy went to the Playhouse at 6. I had some brief peace; a late supper with them (about 9). A new character has come on the scene (I am sure I did not invent him, I did not even want him, though I like him, but there he came walking into the woods of Ithilien): Faramir, the brother of Boromir – and he is holding up the 'catastrophe' by a lot of stuff about the history of Gondor and Rohan (with some very sound reflections no doubt on martial glory and true glory): but if he goes on much more a lot of him will have to be removed to the appendices – where already some fascinating material on the hobbit Tobacco industry and the Languages of the West have gone. There has been a battle – with a monstrous Oliphaunt (the Mâmuk of Harad) included – and after a short while in a cave behind a waterfall, I think I shall get Sam and Frodo at last into *Kirith Ungol* and the webs of the Spiders. Then the Great Offensive will burst out. And so with the death of Theoden (by a Nazgûl) and the arrival of the hosts of the White Rider before the Gates of Mordor we shall reach the denouement and the swift unravelling. As soon as I can get the new matter written legibly, I will have it typed and sent to you.

67 From an airgraph to Christopher Tolkien   11 May 1944 (FS 23)

I completed my fourth new chapter ('Faramir'), which rec'd fullest approbation from C.S.L. and C.W. on Monday morning. I visited church on your behalf. Lunched with Mummy in town. Saw C.S.L. on Tuesday morning. Dined at Pembroke (Rice-Oxley[1] as guest): boring. McCallum seems to think well of Mick's work.[2] Rest of time filled with lectures, house, garden (very exigent just now: lawns, hedges, marrow-beds, weeding) & what can be spared for 'Ring'. Another chapter proceeding, leading to disaster at Kirith Ungol where Frodo is captured. Story then switches back to Gondor, & runs fairly swiftly (I hope) to denouement. Ithilien (you may remember its situation on the map you made) is revealed as rather a lovely land. I wish I had you here, doing something useful and pleasant, completing the maps and typing.

68 From an airgraph to Christopher Tolkien   12 May 1944 (FS 24)

Spent a morning writing and we are now in sight of Minas Morghul. Gardening in sultry (and properly midday) heat this afternoon. . . . . I have done nothing about getting new copies typed to send to you of fresh chapters, as I am pushing on while there is a chance and cannot wait to make fair copy. . . . . Very much love to you, and all my thoughts and prayers. How much I wish to know! 'When you return to the lands of the living, and we re-tell our tales, sitting by a wall in the sun, laughing at old grief, you shall tell me then' (Faramir to Frodo).

69 To Christopher Tolkien

14 May 1944 (FS 25)   20 Northmoor Road, Oxford

Well my dearest, here goes to begin a proper letter again . . . I did a certain amount of writing yesterday but was hindered by two things: the need to clear up the study (which had got into the chaos that always indicates literary or philological preoccupation) and attend to business; and trouble with the moon. By which I mean that I found my moons in the crucial days between Frodo's flight and the present situation (arrival at Minas Morghul) were doing impossible things, rising in one part of the country and setting simultaneously in another. Rewriting bits of back chapters took all afternoon! . . . . Fr C.[1] gave a pretty stirring little sermon, based on Rogation Days (next Mon – Wed) in which he suggested we were all a lot of untutored robots for not saying Grace; and did not suggest but categorically pronounced Oxford to deserve to be wiped out with fire and blood in the wrath of God for the abominations and wickedness there perpetrated. We all woke up. I am afraid it is all too horribly true. But I wonder if it is *specially* true now? A small knowledge of history depresses one with the sense of the everlasting mass and weight of human iniquity: old, old, dreary, endless repetitive unchanging incurable wickedness. All towns, all villages, all habitations of men – sinks! And at the same time one knows that there is always good: much more hidden, much less clearly discerned, seldom breaking out into recognizable, visible, beauties of word or deed or face – not even when in fact sanctity, far greater than the visible advertised wickedness, is really there. But I fear that in the individual lives of all but a few, the balance is debit – we do so little that is positive good, even if we negatively avoid what is actively evil. It must be terrible to be a priest! . . . .

Monday 4 p.m. . . . . I saw C.S.L. from 10.45 to 12.30 this morning: heard 2 chapters of his 'Who Goes Home?'[2] – a new allegory on Heaven and Hell; and I read my 6th new chapter 'Journey to the Cross Roads' with complete approval. So far it has gone well: but I am now coming to the nub, when the threads must be gathered and the times synchronized and the narrative interwoven; while the whole thing has grown so large in significance that the sketches of concluding chapters (written ages ago) are quite inadequate, being on a more 'juvenile' level. . . . .

I suddenly got an idea for a new story (of about length of Niggle[3]) – in church yesterday, I fear. A man sitting at a high window and seeing not the fortunes of a man or of people, but of one small piece of *land* (about the size of a garden) all down the ages. He just sees it illumined, in borders of mist, and things, animals and men just walk on and off, and the plants and trees grow and die and change. One of the points would be that plants and animals change from one fantastic shape to another but men (in spite of different dress) don't change at all. At intervals all down the ages from Palaeolithic to Today a couple of women (or men) would stroll across scene saying exactly the same thing (e.g. It oughtn't to be allowed. They ought to stop it. Or, I said to her, I'm not one to make a fuss, I said, but . . .) . . . .

Your own dear and loving Father.

70 To Christopher Tolkien

21 May 1944 (FS 26)   20 Northmoor Road, Oxford
My dearest,

I am afraid I have not written for some time. . . . . I have taken advantage of a bitter cold grey week (in which the lawns have not grown in spite of a little rain) to write: but struck a sticky patch. All that I had sketched or written before proved of little use, as times, motives, etc., have all changed. However at last with v. great labour, and some neglect of other duties, I have now written or nearly written all the matter up to the capture of Frodo in the high pass on the very brink of Mordor. Now I must go back to the other folk and try and bring things to the final crash with some speed. Do you think *Shelob* is a good name for a monstrous spider creature? It is of course only 'she+lob' (= spider), but written as one, it seems to be quite noisome. . . . .

Monday 22 May. . . . . It was a wretched cold day yesterday (Sunday). I worked very hard at my chapter – it is most exhausting work; especially as the climax approaches and one has to keep the pitch up: no easy level will do; and there are all sorts of minor problems of plot and mechanism. I wrote and tore up and rewrote most of it a good many times; but I was rewarded this morning, as both C.S.L and C.W. thought it an admirable performance, and the latest chapters the best so far. Gollum continues to develop into a most intriguing character. I was on 'key duty' last night and not supposed to retire, but did so at 3.30 a.m. A bit tired this morning. And I have to be on all night at the HQ Post tonight. . . . .

Your own Father.

25 May 1944 (FS 27)   20 Northmoor Road, Oxford

Dearest Chris, Letters, immensely welcome, have poured in. . . . . I was disposed, at last, to envy you a little; or rather to wish I could be with you 'in the hills'. There is something in nativity, and though I have few pictorial memories, there is always a curious sense of reminiscence about any stories of Africa, which always move me deeply. Strange that you, my dearest, should have gone back there. . . . . There is not much to report of self since Monday. That night I never slept at all (quite literally): partly owing to deafening traffic (on moldan ꝩ on úprodore[1]): and gave up trying at 6 a.m. I was not frightfully bright at lecture on Tuesday, as a result. Chief reason, however, is absorption in Frodo, which now has a great grip and takes a lot out of me: chapter on Shelob and the disaster in Kirith Ungol has been written several times. Whole thing comes out of the wash quite different to any preliminary sketch! Apart from making a hen-coop and chick-run (I succumbed at last: couldn't stand the untidy box and jumbled net which did duty on the lawn) I have given most of my energies to that task. Two lectures this morning; and this evening I am taking 'off', and going to Magdalen, where there's supposed to be a full assembly, including Dyson. . . . . I hope you will have some more leave in genuine Africa, ere too long. Away from the 'lesser servants of Mordor'. Yes, I think the orcs as real a creation as anything in 'realistic' fiction: your vigorous words well describe the tribe; only in real life they are on both sides, of course. For 'romance' has grown out of 'allegory', and its wars are still derived from the 'inner war' of allegory in which good is on one side and various modes of badness on the other. In real (exterior) life men are on both sides: which means a motley alliance of orcs, beasts, demons, plain naturally honest men, and angels. But it does make some difference who are your captains and whether they are orc-like per se! And what it is all about (or thought to be). It is even in this world possible to be (more or less) in the wrong or in the right. I could not stand Gaudy Night.[2] I followed P. Wimsey from his attractive beginnings so far, by which time I conceived a loathing for him (and his creatrix) not surpassed by any other character in literature known to me, unless by his Harriet. The honeymoon one (Busman's H.?) was worse. I was sick. . . . . God bless you. Your own Father. Finished 3.45 p.m.: 25 May 1944.

31 May 1944 (FS 28)   20 Northmoor Road, Oxford
Dearest Chris,

About time I wrote again . . . On Thursday I dined in college, myself and the three old gents (Drake, Ramsden, and the Bursar[1]) who were very affable. The Inklings meeting . . . . was very enjoyable. Hugo[2] was there: rather tired-looking, but reasonably noisy. The chief entertainment was provided by a chapter of Warnie Lewis's book on the times of Louis XIV (very good I thought it); and some excerpts from C.S.L.'s 'Who Goes Home?' – a book on Hell, which I suggested should have been called rather 'Hugo's Home'. I did not get back till after midnight. The rest of my time, barring chores in and out door, has been occupied by the desperate attempt to bring 'The Ring' to a suitable pause, the capture of Frodo by the Orcs in the passes of Mordor, before I am obliged to break off by examining. By sitting up all hours, I managed it: and read the last 2 chapters (*Shelob's Lair* and *The Choices of Master Samwise*) to C.S.L. on Monday morning. He approved with unusual fervour, and was actually affected to tears by the last chapter, so it seems to be keeping up. Sam by the way is an abbreviation not of *Samuel* but of Samwise (the Old E. for Half-wit), as is his father's name the Gaffer (Ham) for O.E. Hamfast or Stayathome. Hobbits of that class have very Saxon names as a rule – and I am not really satisfied with the surname Gamgee and shd. change it to Goodchild if I thought you would let me. I am going to get these 8 new chapters, XXXIII – XL, which you have not read, typed almost at once to send out to you, one at a time at short intervals. . . . . I have done no serious writing since Monday. Until midday today I was sweating at Section Papers:[3] & took my MSS. to the Press at 2 p.m. today – the last possible day. . . . . Yesterday: lecture – puncture, after fetching fish, so I had to foot it to town and back, and as bike-repairs are imposs. with Denis[4] ill and working slow, I had to squander afternoon in a grimy struggle, which ended at last in my getting tire off, mending 1 puncture in inner tube, and gash in outer, and getting thing on again. Io! triumphum.[5] But it's hard work at a bob! . . . .

Sunday: June 3. . . . . One of the reasons for this second gap since Wednesday is that since I finished setting papers, and before scripts came in, I have been trying to get some chapters typed so that they can be duplicated and sent out to you. I have got two done. A labour at first, as I have not typed for so long. There is little further news of me beyond this. . . . . Prisca and Mummy went to see Anna Neagle in *Emma* in the play from Jane Austen, and enjoyed it. I walked home with them, after dining at Pembroke. A poor affair. But it is increasingly heartbreaking as the armies draw near to Rome to hear the crass comments of elderly and stupid old gentlemen. I find the present situation of things more and more distressing. I wonder if you were even able to hear any of the Pope's words. A propos of that, but concerning another occasion: that you may judge of the atmosphere of tact and courtesy in my beautiful college. I took Rice-Oxley to dine on the second Tuesday in term. The election to the Rectorship of Lincoln had just been announced: the college had elected K. Murray the young Scotch Bursar responsible for the Turl atrocity.[6] The obvious (and I think proper) person was V. J. Brooke (St Cath's Censor[7]); but Hanbury[8] was also a candidate. Sitting next to *me*, the Master in a loud voice said: 'Thank heaven they did not elect a Roman Catholic to the Rectorship anyway: disastrous, disastrous for the college.' 'Yes, indeed,' echoed Dr Ramsden, 'disastrous.' My guest looked at me and smiled and whispered 'models of tact and courtesy!' . . . .

Your own dear Father.

73 From a letter to Christopher Tolkien   10 June 1944 (FS 30)

[Written four days after the beginning of the Allied invasion of Normandy.]

I got your airletter at tea-time yesterday. . . . . A great deal is happening at this end of the world. But I won't enlarge on that, as doubtless you get the same news as we do, and as quick; and if one knew anything outside that it would be 'indiscreet' to mention it. As a matter of fact I don't. But thank God it really looks like clearing up a bit this evening. It is calmer, warmer, and there are glimpses of sun and blue sky. I fancy weather is of paramount importance. . . . .

I last wrote on D. Day June 6. On Wed. I made special efforts with typing. Of the rest I can only remember that on Thursday I dined lugubriously in Pembroke, and then went to Magdalen, where the Lewises, C. Williams, and Edison (author of Ouroboros)[1] were assembled. From 9 until after 12.30 the time was occupied by reading. A long chapter from the Captain,[2] largely on the system of government in the ancien régime of France, which he managed to make very amusing (though it was very long) followed by Edison with a new chapter from an uncompleted romance[3] – of undiminished power and felicity of expression; myself; and C.S.L. Enjoyable, but no longer amid exams and wars to be taken so lightly as of old – especially as I had arisen at 5 a.m. (or 7 a.m. BDST) to get to Mass for Corpus Christi. . . . .

This morning . . . . was occupied with exams, the afternoon with a mass-meeting at Rhodes House in favour of a local Christian Council. . . . . There was one man . . . . who got up and said that he approved of a C. Council, because he had been Lord Nelson in his previous life, and had much appreciated being in Oxford during part of the present life; but nobody laughed – although he was one of the amiable kind, who would have liked it. He said so. But apparently he has made this speech so often, that it was taken as a matter of course. Just shows how little one can know of one's own home-town, as I had never seen or heard of him before. . . . .

[11 June] I was very interested in all the descriptions: both of your abode and of the country. Your sharpened memory is I imagine due to 2 things (1) sharpened desire (2) new images which do not correspond to the old, and so do not overlay and blur them. Few inhabitants of a town who have never gone away can recall even the major changes in a street during the past year. My own rather sharp memory is probably due to the dislocation of all my childhood 'pictures' between 3 and 4 by leaving Africa: I was engaged in a constant attention and adjustment. Some of my actual visual memories I now recognize as beautiful blends of African and English details. . . . . As for what to try and write: I don't know. I tried a diary with portraits (some scathing some comic some commendatory) of persons and events seen; but I found it was not my line. So I took to 'escapism': or really transforming experience into another form and symbol with Morgoth and Orcs and the Eldalie (representing beauty and grace of life and artefact) and so on; and it has stood me in good stead in many hard years since and I still draw on the conceptions then hammered out. But, of course, there was no time except on leave or in hospital. . . . .

I certainly live on your letters, although my circumstances are so very much more easy. In my case weariness, sheer boredom of sameness is the enemy. If I were younger, I should wish to exchange with you, merely to change! I hope you can read some of this. Certainly six-penn'orth as far as quantity (not quality I fear) goes. More anon.

74   From a letter to Stanley Unwin   29 June 1944

[Unwin wrote on 22 June, enclosing 'a further substantial cheque' for royalties earned by *The Hobbit*, and telling Tolkien that his son Rayner was now reading English at Oxford as a naval cadet: 'He will be away next week on leave, but after his return I should much like him to meet you some time.']

First about Rayner. I was both delighted and grieved at your news. Delighted because I shall have a chance of seeing him. I hope he will treat me in the most unprofessorial manner, and as soon as he gets back, will just let me know how we can meet: whether I can roll into his rooms, and whether he would care at any time to wander up here to my house and have tea (meagre) in my garden (untidy). Grieved because it is abominable to think that the passage of time and the prolongation of this misery has swept him up. My youngest boy, also Trinity, was carried off last July – in the midst of typing and revising the Hobbit sequel and doing a lovely map – and is now far away and very wretched, in the Orange Free State:[1] the fact that it was my native land does not seem to recommend it to him. I have at the moment another son, a much damaged soldier, at Trinity trying to do some work and recover a shadow of his old health.[2] . . . .

I am afraid I have treated you badly. Fortune has treated me pretty rough since I last wrote – though not rougher than many others, alas! – and I have had barely the energy or the time to get through the menial day. But I should have thanked you for your note about Foyles[3] and for the two copies of the edition. Also I might have let you know what was happening to the sequel to the Hobbit. Not a line on it was possible for a year. One of the results (until I was drowned in an abyss of exams) of release from work for R.N. and R.A.F. was that I managed to bring this (great) work to within sight of conclusion, and am now about to conclude it, disregarding all other calls, as far as is possible.

I hope you still have some mild interest in it, in spite of paper shortage – at any rate as a possible future. It is frightfully difficult and/or expensive getting anything typed in this town, and when my typewriter broke down nobody would repair it. I have still only one copy, and that needs revision as the thing nears its end. But I hope at last soon to be able to submit a chunk to you. A pity Rayner is now involved with other and more serious matters. In any case, I fear, the story has grown too long and unjuvenile.

Thank you very much for the cheque. Even halved it will be very useful. I still labour under debts, mainly due to trying to complete a family's education after war had taken most of one's means: not an uncommon experience.

75 To Christopher Tolkien

7 July 1944 (FS 36)   20 Northmoor Road, Oxford

My Dearest: I thought I would try the experiment of an airletter on my midget type.[1] It is certainly as small, and a lot clearer than I could write. It is only two days since I last wrote, but I have a great desire to talk to you. Not that there is anything but the smallest news to tell. I haven't had a chance to do any more writing yet. This morning I had shopping and cadets; and when on my way back to town for the second time my back tire blew up with a loud explosion, the inner tube having oozed through a gash in the outer cover. Fortunately this was not far from Denis, and I was able to console myself at The Gardeners' Arms, not yet discovered by Stars or Stripes,[2] and where they serve a mixture of College Ale and Bitter. But I had to make a third journey after lunch: and from 5 to 8 was occupied enlarging the house, with bits of old wood and salvaged nails, for the new hen-folk, drat 'em. I have just heard the news and so goes the day. There is a family of bullfinches, which must have nested in or near our garden, and they are very tame, and have been giving us entertainment lately by their antics feeding their young, often just outside the diningroom window. Insects on the trees and sowthistle seeds seem their chief delight. I had no idea they behaved so much like goldfinches. Old fat father, pink waistcoat and all, hangs absolutely upside down on a thistle-spray, tinking all the while. There are also a few wrens about. Otherwise nothing of note, though all birds are vastly increased in numbers, after the mild winters, and in these relatively catless days. The garden is its usual wilderness self, all deep green again, and still with abundant roses. The bright summer day turned to rain again by night and we have had a lot more, though not without breaks. . . . .

[9 July] *A propos* of bullfinches, did you know that they had a connexion with the noble art of brewing ale? I was looking at the Kalevala the other day – one of the books which I don't think you have yet read? Or have you? – and I came across Runo XX, which I used to like: it deals largely with the origin of beer. When the fermentation was first managed, the beer was only in birch tubs and it foamed all over the place, and of course the heroes came and lapped it up, and got mightily drunk. *Drunk was Ahti, drunk was Kauko, drunken was the ruddy rascal, with the ale of Osmo's daughter* – Kirby's translation[3] is funnier than the original. It was the bullfinch who then suggested to Osmo's daughter the notion of putting the stuff in oak casks with hoops of copper and storing it in a cellar. *Thus was ale at first created . . . best of drinks for prudent people; Women soon it brings to laughter, Men it warms into good humour, but it brings the fools to raving.* Sound sentiments. Poor old Finns, and their queer language, they look like being scuppered. I wish I could have visited the Land of Ten Thousand Lakes before this war. Finnish nearly ruined my Hon. Mods,[4] and was the original germ of the Silmarillion. . . . .

I wonder how you are getting on with your flying since you first went solo – the last news we had of this. I especially noted your observations on the skimming martins. That touches to the heart of things, doesn't it? There is the tragedy and despair of all machinery laid bare. Unlike art which is content to create a new secondary world in the mind, it attempts to actualize desire, and so to create power in this World; and that cannot really be done with any real satisfaction. Labour-saving machinery only creates endless and worse labour. And in addition to this fundamental disability of a creature, is added the Fall, which makes our devices not only fail of their desire but turn to new and horrible evil. So we come inevitably from Daedalus and Icarus to the Giant Bomber. It is not an advance in wisdom! This terrible truth, glimpsed long ago by Sam Butler, sticks out so plainly and is so horrifyingly exhibited in our time, with its even worse menace for the future, that it seems almost a world wide mental disease that only a tiny minority perceive it. Even if people have ever heard the legends (which is getting rarer) they have no inkling of their portent. How could a maker of motorbikes name his product Ixion cycles! Ixion, who was bound for ever in hell on a perpetually revolving wheel! Well, I have got over 2 thousand words onto this little flimsy airletter; and I will forgive the Mordor-gadgets some of their sins, if they will bring it quickly to you. . . . .

76 From a letter to Christopher Tolkien   28 July 1944 (FS 39)

As to Sam Gamgee. I quite agree with what you say, and I wouldn't dream of altering his name without your approval; but the object of the alteration was precisely to bring out the comicness, peasantry, and if you will the Englishry of this jewel among the hobbits. Had I thought it out at the beginning, I should have given all the hobbits very English names to match the shire. The Gaffer came first; and Gamgee followed as an echo of old Lamorna jokes.[1] I doubt if it's English. I knew of it only through Gamgee (Tissue) as cottonwool was called being invented by a man of that name last century. However, I daresay all your imagination of the character is now bound up with the name. Plain news is on the airgraph; but the only event worth of talk was the performance of Hamlet[2] which I had been to just before I wrote last. I was full of it then, but the cares of the world have soon wiped away the impression. But it emphasised more strongly than anything I have ever seen the folly of reading Shakespeare (and annotating him in the study), except as a concomitant of seeing his plays acted. It was a very good performance, with a young rather fierce Hamlet; it was played fast without cuts; and came out as a very exciting play. Could one only have seen it without ever having read it or knowing the plot, it would have been terrific. It was well produced except for a bit of bungling over the killing of Polonius. But to my surprise the part that came out as the most moving, almost intolerably so, was the one that in reading I always found a bore: the scene of mad Ophelia singing her snatches.

Neglecting other duties I've put in a good many hours typing and am now nearly at the end of the new stuff in the Ring; so soon I may go on and finish; and I hope shortly to send you another batch. . . . . Binney was here on Sat. to tea, in a v. pleasant mood; it cheered P. up, as she too is v. lonely with only a couple of old grousers, and nothing to do but read. She's just read *Out of the S. Planet* and *Perelandra*; and with good taste preferred the latter. But she finds it hard to realise that Ransom is not meant to be a portrait of me (though as a philologist I may have some part in him, and recognize some of my opinions and ideas Lewisified in him). . . . . The news is good today. Things may begin to move fast now, if not quite so fast as some think. I wonder how long von Papen will manage to keep above ground?[1] But when the burst comes in France, then will be the time to get excited. How long? And what of the red Chrysanthemum in the East? And when it is all over, will ordinary people have any freedom left (or right) or will they have to fight for it, or will they be too tired to resist? The last rather seems the idea of some of the Big Folk. Who have for the most part viewed this war from the vantage point of large motor-cars. Too many are childless.But I suppose the one certain result of it all is a further growth in the great standardised amalgamations with their mass-produced notions and emotions. Music will give place to jiving: which as far as I can make out means holding a 'jam session' round a piano (an instrument properly intended to produce the sounds devised by, say, Chopin) and hitting it so hard that it breaks. This delicately cultured amusement is said to be a 'fever' in the U.S.A. O God! O Montreal! O Minnesota! O Michigan! What kind of mass manias the Soviets can produce remains for peace and prosperity and the removal of war-hypnotism to show. Not quite so dismal as the Western ones, perhaps (I hope). But one doesn't altogether wonder at a few smaller states still wanting to be 'neutral'; they are between the devil and the deep sea all right (and you can stick which D you like on to which side you like). However it's always been going on in different terms, and you and I belong to the ever-defeated never altogether subdued side. I should have hated the Roman Empire in its day (as I do), and remained a patriotic Roman citizen, while preferring a free Gaul and seeing good in Carthaginians. *Delenda est Carthago.*[2] We hear rather a lot of that nowadays. I was actually taught at school that that was a fine saying; and I 'reacted' (as they say, in this case with less than the usual misapplication) at once. There lies still some hope that, at least in our beloved land of England, propaganda defeats itself, and even produces the opposite effect. It is said that it is even so in Russia; and I bet it is so in Germany. . . . .

[1 August] I hear that there is just coming out *First Whispers of the Wind in the Willows*; and the reviews seem favourable. It is published by Kenneth Grahame's widow, but it is not, I gather, notes for the book, but stories (about Toad and Mole etc.) that he wrote in letters to his son. I must get hold of a copy, if poss. I'm afraid I have made a great mistake in making my sequel too long and complicated and too slow in coming out. It is a curse having the epic temperament in an overcrowded age devoted to snappy bits!

78 From a letter to Christopher Tolkien   12 August 1944 (FS 43)

It is longer than I meant to leave since my airgr. of Aug. 8 . . . I read your letters carefully, and of course as is quite right you open your rather troubled heart to us; but do not think that any detail of your exterior life, your friends, acquaintance, or the most minor events, are not worth writing or of interest. I am glad that you are finding it (at times) easier to rub along. I shouldn't worry too much, if the process sometimes seems to be a declension from the highest standards (intellectual and aesthetic, at any rate, not moral). I don't think you are in the least likely permanently to decline upon the worse; and I should say that you need a little thickening of the outer skin, if only as a protection for the more sensitive interior; and if you acquire it, it will be of permanent value in any walk of later life in this tough world (which shows no signs of softening). And of course, as you already discover, one of the discoveries of the process is the realization of the values that often lurk under dreadful appearances. Urukhai is only a figure of speech. There are no genuine Uruks, that is folk made bad by the intention of their maker; and not many who are so corrupted as to be irredeemable (though I fear it must be admitted that there are human creatures that seem irredeemable short of a special miracle, and that there are probably abnormally many of such creatures in Deutschland and Nippon – but certainly these unhappy countries have no monopoly: I have met them, or thought so, in England's green and pleasant land). All you say about the dryness, dustiness, and smell of the satan-licked land reminds me of my mother; she hated it (as a land) and was alarmed to see symptoms of my father growing to like it. It used to be said that no English-born woman could ever get over this dislike or be more than an exile, but that Englishmen (under the freer conditions of peace) could and usually did get to love it (as a land; I am saying nothing of any of its inhabitants). Oddly enough all that you say, even to its detriment, only increases the longing I have always felt to see it again. Much though I love and admire little lanes and hedges and rustling trees and the soft rolling contours of a rich champain, the thing that stirs me most and comes nearest to heart's satisfaction for me is space, and I would be willing to barter barrenness for it; indeed I think I like barrenness itself, whenever I have seen it. My heart still lingers among the high stony wastes among the morains and mountain-wreckage, silent in spite of the sound of thin chill water. Intellectually and aesthetically, of course; man cannot live on stone and sand, but I at any rate cannot live on bread alone; and if there was not bare rock and pathless sand and the unharvested sea, I should grow to hate all green things as a fungoid growth. . . . .

I am absolutely dry of any inspiration for the Ring and am back where I was in the Spring, with all the inertia to overcome again. What a relief it would be to get it done. How I miss you on that count alone! I forgot to make a note of when I sent the MSS. off, but I suppose it must have been about a month ago and you may soon be getting it. I shan't send any more until I know your next address, though the subsequent chapters are better. I shall be very eager to know what you think of them. This book has come to be more and more addressed to you, so that your opinion matters more than any one else's.

79 From a letter to Christopher Tolkien   22 August 1944 (FS 45)

[A reply to Christopher's comments on Kroonstad, where he was stationed, and on Johannesburg.]

Kroonstad is the real product of our culture, as it now lives and is; Jo'burg (in its good spots) is what it would like to be, but only can be in special economic circumstances which are quite unstable and imperma-nent. In England, and there less than in most other European countries, it has up to now been softened and concealed by the relics of a former age (not confined to ruinous buildings). There will be a good many Kroonstads, architecturally, morally, and mentally, in this land in ten to twenty years time, when the Portal Houses, 'temporary', are blistered and bent like rotting tin mushrooms but nothing else is forthcoming. As in the former dark age, the Christian Church alone will carry over any considerable tradition (not unaltered, nor, it may be, undamaged) of a higher mental civilization, that is, if it is not driven down into new catacombs. Gloomy thoughts, about things one cannot really know anything [of]; the future is impenetrable especially to the wise; for what is really important is always hid from contemporaries, and the seeds of what is to be are quietly germinating in the dark in some forgotten corner, while everyone is looking at Stalin or Hitler, or reading illus-trated articles on Beveridge ('The Master of University College At Home') in *Picture Post*. . . . .

This morning I lectured, and found the Bird and Baby[1] closed; but was hailed in a voice that carried across the torrent of vehicles that was once St Giles, and discovered the two Lewises and C. Williams, high and very dry on the other side. Eventually we got 4 pints of passable ale at the King's Arms – at a cost of 5/8. . . . . I hope to see the lads tomorrow; otherwise life is as bright as water in a ditch. . . . .

Here I am at the best end of the day again. The most marvellous sunset I have seen for years: a remote pale green-blue sea just above the horizon, and above it a towering shore of bank upon bank of flaming cherubim of gold and fire, crossed here and there by misty blurs like purple rain. It may portend some celestial merriment in the morn, as the glass is rising.

80   From an airgraph to Christopher Tolkien
3 September 1944 (FS 46)

[On G. K. Chesterton.]

P[riscilla] . . . . has been wading through The Ballad of the White Horse for the last many nights; and my efforts to explain the obscurer parts to her convince me that it is not as good as I thought. The ending is absurd. The brilliant smash and glitter of the words and phrases (when they come off, and are not mere loud colours) cannot disguise the fact that G.K.C. knew nothing whatever about the 'North', heathen or Christian.

81   To Christopher Tolkien

[Christopher had moved to a camp at Standerton in the Transvaal.]

23–25 September 1944 (FS 51)   20 Northmoor Road, Oxford
My dearest,

We have had another airgraph from you this morn, just on the eve of your departure to Standerton. . . . . I am pleased that the Chapters meet with your approval. As soon as I get them back, I'll send the next lot; which I think are better (Of Herbs and Stewed Rabbit; Faramir; The Forbidden Pool; Journey to the Crossroads; The Stairs of Kirith Ungol; Shelob's Lair; and The Choices of Master Samwise). . . . . There is not much more Home news. Lights are steadily increasing in Oxford. More and more windows are being unblacked; and the Banbury Road now has a double row of lamps; while some of the side-roads have ordinary lamps. I actually went out to an 'Inklings' on Thursday night, and rode in almost peacetime light all the way to Magdalen for the first time in 5 years. Both Lewises were there, and C. Williams; and beside some pleasant talk, such as I have not enjoyed for moons, we heard the last chapter of Warnie's book and an article of CSL, and a long specimen of his translation of Vergil.[1] I did not start home till midnight, and walked with C.W. part of the way, when our converse turned on the difficulties of discovering what common factors if any existed in the notions associated with *freedom*, as used at present. I don't believe there are any, for the word has been so abused by propaganda that it has ceased to have any value for reason and become a mere emotional dose for generating heat. At most, it would seem to imply that those who domineer over you should speak (natively) the same language – which in the last resort is all that the confused ideas of race or nation boil down to; or class, for that matter, in England. . . . . The western war-news of course occupies a good deal of our minds, but you know as much about it as we do. Anxious times, in spite of the rather premature shouting. The armoured fellows are right in the thick of it, and (I gather) think there is going to be a good deal more of the thick yet. I cannot understand the line taken by BBC (and papers, and so, I suppose, emanating from M[inistry] O[f] I[nformation]) that the German troops are a motley collection of sutlers and broken men, while yet recording the bitterest defence against the finest and best equipped armies (as indeed they are) that have ever taken the field. The English pride themselves, or used to, on 'sportsmanship' (which included 'giving the devil his due'), not that attendance at a league football match was not enough to dispel the notion that 'sports-manship' was possessed by any very large number of the inhabitants of this island. But it is distressing to see the press grovelling in the gutter as low as Goebbels in his prime, shrieking that any German commander who holds out in a desperate situation (when, too, the military needs of his side clearly benefit) is a drunkard, and a besotted fanatic. I can't see much distinction between our popular tone and the celebrated 'military idiots'. We knew Hitler was a vulgar and ignorant little cad, in addition to any other defects (or the source of them); but there seem to be many v. and i. l. cads who don't speak German, and who given the same chance would show most of the other Hitlerian characteristics. There was a solemn article in the local paper seriously advocating systematic exterminating of the entire German nation as the only proper course after military victory: because, if you please, they are rattlesnakes, and don't know the difference between good and evil! (What of the writer?) The Germans have just as much right to declare the Poles and Jews exterminable vermin, subhuman, as we have to select the Germans: in other words, no right, whatever they have done. Of course there is still a difference here. The article was answered, and the answer printed. The Vulgar and Ignorant Cad is not yet a boss with power; but he is a very great deal nearer to becoming one in this green and pleasant isle than he was. And all of that you know. Still you're not the only one who wants to let off steam or bust, sometimes; and I could make steam, if I opened the throttle, compared with which (as the Queen said to Alice) this would be only a scent-spray. It can't be helped. You can't fight the Enemy with his own Ring without turning into an Enemy; but unfortunately Gandalf's wisdom seems long ago to have passed with him into the True West. . . . .

The NW gale in the 'Straits of Dover' has passed, and we are back in a mild September day with a silver sun gleaming through very high mottled clouds moving still fairly fast from the NW. I must try and get on with the Pearl and stop the eager maw of Basil Blackwell.[2] But I have the autumn wanderlust upon me, and would fain be off with a knapsack on my back and no particular destination, other than a series of quiet inns. One of the too long delayed delights we must promise ourselves, when it pleases God to release us and reunite us, is just such a perambulation, together, preferably in mountainous country, not too far from the sea, where the scars of war, felled woods and bulldozed fields, are not too plain to see. The Inklings have already agreed that their victory celebration, if they are spared to have one, will be to take a whole inn in the country for at least a week, and spend it entirely in beer and talk, without reference to any clock! . . . God be with you and guide you in all your ways. All the love of your own

Father.

82   From an airgraph to Christopher Tolkien
30 September 1944 (FS 52)

We three have just come back through the rainy end of a golden day, from a v. poor production at Playhouse of 'Arms and the Man', which does not wear well. I saw the good lady (in the theatre with C. Williams) who is typing Ring and have hopes of more to send soon. I don't think I should write any more, but for the hope of your seeing it. At moment I'm engaged in revision, as I can't get on without having back stuff fresh in mind. Do you remember chapter 'King of the Golden Hall'? Seems rather good, now it is old enough for a detached view.

83   From a letter to Christopher Tolkien   6 October 1944 (FS 54)

It has been rather an unusually interesting week. You know how, even if you are not hard up, the finding of a forgotten bob in an old pocket gives you a curious feeling of wealth. I am not referring to the fact that I netted about £51 from my vacation labours on Cadets, though that wasn't too bad. But to the fact that I am a *week* up. Term does not begin today but next week! It has given me a wonderful (if fictitious and later to be paid for) sense of leisure. . . . . . On Tuesday at noon I looked in at the Bird and B. with C. Williams. There to my surprise I found Jack and Warnie[1] already ensconced. (For the present the beer shortage is over, and the inns are almost habitable again). The conversation was pretty lively – though I cannot remember any of it now, except C.S.L.'s story of an elderly lady that he knows. (She was a student of English in the past days of Sir Walter Raleigh. At her *viva* she was asked: *What period would you have liked to live in Miss B? In the 15th C.* said she. *Oh come, Miss B., wouldn't you have liked to meet the Lake poets? No, sir, I prefer the society of gentlemen.* Collapse of viva.) – & I noticed a strange tall gaunt man half in khaki half in mufti with a large wide-awake hat, bright eyes and a hooked nose sitting in the corner. The others had their backs to him, but I could see in his eye that he was taking an interest in the conversation quite unlike the ordinary pained astonishment of the British (and American) public at the presence of the Lewises (and myself) in a pub. It was rather like Trotter at the Prancing Pony,[2] in fact v. like. All of a sudden he butted in, in a strange unplaceable accent, taking up some point about Wordsworth. In a few seconds he was revealed as Roy Campbell (of *Flowering Rifle* and *Flaming Terrapin*). Tableau! Especially as C.S.L. had not long ago violently lampooned him in the Oxford Magazine, and his press-cutters miss nothing. There is a good deal of Ulster still left in C.S.L. if hidden from himself. After that things became fast and furious and I was late for lunch. It was (perhaps) gratifying to find that this powerful poet and soldier desired in Oxford chiefly to see Lewis (and myself). We made an appointment for Thursday (that is last) night. If I could remember all that I heard in C.S.L.'s room last night it would fill several airletters. C.S.L. had taken a fair deal of port and was a little belligerent (insisted on reading out his lampoon again while R.C. laughed at him), but we were mostly obliged to listen to the guest. A window on a wild world, yet the man is in himself gentle, modest, and compassionate. Mostly it interested me to learn that this old-looking war-scarred Trotter, limping from recent wounds, is 9 years younger than I am, and we prob. met when he was a lad, as he lived in O[xford] at the time when we lived in Pusey Street (rooming with Walton the composer,[3] and going about with T. W. Earp, the original twerp, and with *Wilfrid Childe*[4] your godfather – whose works he much prizes). What he has done since beggars description. Here is a scion of an Ulster prot. family resident in S. Africa, most of whom fought in both wars, who became a Catholic after sheltering the Carmelite fathers in Barcelona – in vain, they were caught & butchered, and R.C. nearly lost his life. But he got the Carmelite archives from the burning library and took them through the Red country. He speaks Spanish fluently (he has been a professional bull-fighter). As you know he then fought through the war on Franco's side, and among other things was in the van of the company that chased the Reds out of Malaga in such haste that their general (Villalba I believe) could not carry off his loot – and left on his table St. Teresa's hand with all its jewels. He had most interesting things to say about the situation at Gib, since the war (in Spain). But he is a patriotic man, and has fought for the B. Army since. Well, well. Martin D'Arcy[5] vouches for him, and told him to seek us out. But I wish I could remember half his picaresque stories, about poets and musicians etc. from Peter Warlock to Aldous Huxley. The one I most enjoyed was the tale of greasy Epstein (the sculptor) and how he fought him and put him in hospital for a week. However it is not possible to convey an impression of such a rare character, both a soldier and a poet, and a Christian convert. How unlike the Left – the 'corduroy panzers' who fled to America (Auden among them who with his friends got R.C.'s works 'banned' by the Birmingham T. Council!). I hope to see this man again next week. We did not leave Magdalen until midnight, and I walked up to Beaumont Street with him. C.S.L.'s reactions were odd. Nothing is a greater tribute to Red propaganda than the fact that he (who knows they are in all other subjects liars and traducers) believes all that is said against Franco, and nothing that is said for him. Even Churchill's open speech in Parliament left him unshaken. But hatred of our church is after all the real only final foundation of the C of E – so deep laid that it remains even when all the superstructure seems removed (C.S.L. for instance reveres the Blessed Sacrament, and admires nuns!). Yet if a Lutheran is put in jail he is up in arms; but if Catholic priests are slaughtered – he disbelieves it (and I daresay really thinks they asked for it). But R.C. shook him a bit. . . . .

Do 'ramble on'. Letters need not be only about exterior events (though all details are welcome). What you are thinking is just as important: Christmas, bee-noises, and all the rest. And why you should think the encounter with the chemist-botanist . . . . unworthy of record, I can't say. I thought it most interesting. . . . . It is not the *not-man* (e.g. weather) nor *man* (even at a bad level), but the *man-made* that is ultimately daunting and insupportable. If a ragnarök[6] would burn all the slums and gas-works, and shabby garages, and long arc-lit suburbs, it cd. for me burn all the works of art – and I'd go back to trees.

84 From an airgraph to Christopher Tolkien
12 October 1944 (FS 55)

I began trying to write again (I would, on the brink of term!) on Tuesday, but I struck a most awkward error (one or two days) in the synchronization, v. important at this stage, of movements of Frodo and the others, which has cost labour and thought and will require tiresome small alterations in many chapters; but at any rate I have actually begun Book Five (and last: about 10 chapters per 'book'). I have today sent Leaf by Niggle to Dublin Review, as the editor wrote asking for verse or narrative.

85 From an airgraph to Christopher Tolkien
16 October 1944 (FS 56)

I have been struggling with the dislocated chronology of the Ring, which has proved most vexatious, and has not only interfered with other more urgent and duller duties, but has stopped me getting on. I think I have solved it all at last by small map alterations, and by inserting an extra day's Entmoot, and extra days into Trotter's chase and Frodo's journey (a small alteration in the first chapter I have just sent: 2 days from Morannon to Ithilien). But now I have lectures again, and also Pearl.

86 From a letter to Christopher Tolkien 23 October 1944 (FS 57)

I have just been out to look up: the noise is terrific: the biggest for a long time, skywide Armada. I suppose it is allright to say so, as by the time that this reaches you somewhere will have ceased to exist and all the world will have known about it and already forgotten it. . . . .

There seems no time to do anything properly; and I feel tired all the time, or rather bored. I think if a jinn came and gave me a wish – *what would you really like?* – I should reply: *Nothing. Go away!* . . . .

With regard to the blasphemy, one can only recall (when applicable) the words *Father, forgive them, for they know not what they do* – or say. And somehow I fancy that Our Lord actually is more pained by offences we commit against one another than those we commit against himself, esp. his incarnate person. And linguistically there is not a great deal of difference between a *damn you*, said without reflection or even knowledge of the terror and majesty of the One Judge, and the things you mention. Both the sexual and the sacred words have ceased to have any content except the ghost of past emotion. I don't mean that it is not a bad thing, and it is certainly very wearisome, saddening and maddening, but it is at any rate not *blasphemy* in the full sense.

87   To Christopher Tolkien

25 October 1944   20 Northmoor Road, Oxford

Dearest man, Here is a little more of 'the Ring' for your delectation (I hope), and criticism, but not for return. Two more chapters to complete the 'Fourth Book', & then I hope to finish the 'Fifth' and last of the Ring. I have written a long airletter today, & shall write again (of course) before your birthday. I am afraid this little packet won't get to you in time for it.

'Dear Mr Tolkien, I have just finished reading your book The Hobbit for the 11th time and I want to tell you what I think of it. I think it is the most wonderful book I have ever read. It is beyond description . . . Gee Whiz, I'm surprised that it's not more popular . . . If you have written any other books, would you please send me their names?'

John Barrow 12 yrs.
West town School, West town, Pa.'

I thought these extracts from a letter I got yesterday would amuse you. I find these letters which I still occasionally get (apart from the smell of incense which fallen man can never quite fail to savour) make me rather sad. What thousands of grains of good human corn must fall on barren stony ground, if such a very small drop of water should be so intoxicating! But I suppose one should be grateful for the grace and fortune that have allowed me to provide even the drop. God bless you beloved. Do you think 'The Ring' will come off, and reach the thirsty?
Your own Father.

It's nice to find that little American boys do really still say 'Gee Whiz'.

88   From a letter to Christopher Tolkien   28 October 1944 (FS 58)

This empty year is fading into a dull grey mournful darkness: so slow-footed and yet so swift and evanescent. What of the new year and the spring? I wonder.

98

7–8 November 1944 (FS 60)   20 Northmoor Road, Oxford

. . . . Your reference to the care of your guardian angel makes me fear that 'he' is being specially needed. I dare say it is so. . . . . It also reminded me of a sudden vision (or perhaps apperception which at once turned itself into pictorial form in my mind) I had not long ago when spending half an hour in St Gregory's before the Blessed Sacrament when the Quarant' Ore[1] was being held there. I perceived or thought of the Light of God and in it suspended one small mote (or millions of motes to only one of which was my small mind directed), glittering white because of the individual ray from the Light which both held and lit it. (Not that there were individual rays issuing from the Light, but the mere existence of the mote and its position in relation to the Light was in itself a line, and the line was Light). And the ray was the Guardian Angel of the mote: not a thing interposed between God and the creature, but God's very attention itself, personalized. And I do not mean 'personi-fied', by a mere figure of speech according to the tendencies of human language, but a real (finite) person. Thinking of it since – for the whole thing was very immediate, and not recapturable in clumsy language, certainly not the great sense of joy that accompanied it and the realiza-tion that the shining poised mote was myself (or any other human person that I might think of with love) – it has occurred to me that (I speak diffidently and have no idea whether such a notion is legitimate: it is at any rate quite separate from the vision of the Light and the poised mote) this is a finite parallel to the Infinite. As the love of the Father and Son (who are infinite and equal) is a Person, so the love and attention of the Light to the Mote is a person (that is both with us and in Heaven): finite but divine: i.e. angelic. Anyway, dearest, I received comfort, part of which took this curious form, which I have (I fear) failed to convey: except that I have with me now a definite awareness of you poised and shining in the Light – though your face (as all our faces) is turned from it. But we might see the glimmer in the faces (and persons as apprehended in love) of others. . . . .

On Sunday Prisca and I cycled in wind and rain to St Gregory's. P. was battling with a cold and other disability, and it did not do her much immediate good, though she's better now; but we had one of Fr. C's best sermons (and longest). A wonderful commentary on the Gospel of the Sunday (healing of the woman and of Jairus' daughter), made intensely vivid by his comparison of the three evangelists. (P. was espec. amused by his remark that St Luke being a doctor himself did not like the suggestion that the poor woman was all the worse for them, so he toned that bit down). And also by his vivid illustrations from modern miracles. The similar case of a woman similarly afflicted (owing to a vast uterine tumour) who was cured instantly at Lourdes, so that the tumour could not be found, and her belt was twice too large. And the most moving story of the little boy with tubercular peritonitis who was *not* healed, and was taken sadly away in the train by his parents, practically dying with 2 nurses attending him. As the train moved away it passed within sight of the Grotto. The little boy sat up. 'I want to go and talk to the little girl' – in the same train there was a little girl who had been healed. And he got up and walked there and played with the little girl; and then he came back, and he said 'I'm hungry now'. And they gave him cake and two bowls of chocolate and enormous potted meat sand-wiches, and he ate them! (This was in 1927). So Our Lord told them to give the little daughter of Jairus something to eat. So plain and matter of fact: for so miracles are. They are intrusions (as we say, erring) into real or ordinary life, but they do intrude into real life, and so need ordinary meals and other results. (Of course Fr. C could not resist adding: and there was also a Capuchin Friar who was mortally ill, & had eaten nothing for years, and he was cured, and he was so delighted about it that he rushed off and had two dinners, and that night he had not his old pains but an attack of plain ordinary indigestion). But at the story of the little boy (which is a fully attested *fact* of course) with its apparent sad ending and then its sudden unhoped-for happy ending, I was deeply moved and had that peculiar emotion we all have – though not often. It is quite unlike any other sensation. And all of a sudden I realized what it was: the very thing that I have been trying to write about and explain – in that fairy-story essay that I so much wish you had read that I think I shall send it to you. For it I coined the word 'eucatastrophe': the sudden happy turn in a story which pierces you with a joy that brings tears (which I argued it is the highest function of fairy-stories to produce). And I was there led to the view that it produces its peculiar effect because it is a sudden glimpse of Truth, your whole nature chained in material cause and effect, the chain of death, feels a sudden relief as if a major limb out of joint had suddenly snapped back. It perceives – if the story has literary 'truth' on the second plane (for which see the essay) – that this is indeed how things really do work in the Great World for which our nature is made. And I concluded by saying that the Resurrec-tion was the greatest 'eucatastrophe' possible in the greatest Fairy Story – and produces that essential emotion: Christian joy which produces tears because it is qualitatively so like sorrow, because it comes from those places where Joy and Sorrow are at one, reconciled, as selfishness and altruism are lost in Love. Of course I do not mean that the Gospels tell what is *only* a fairy-story; but I do mean very strongly that they do tell a fairy-story: the greatest. Man the story-teller would have to be redeemed in a manner consonant with his nature: by a moving story. *But* since the author if it is the supreme Artist and the Author of Reality, this one was also made to Be, to be true on the Primary Plane. So that in the Primary Miracle (the Resurrection) and the lesser Christian miracles too though less, you have not only that sudden glimpse of the truth behind the apparent Ananke[2] of our world, but a glimpse that is actually a ray of light through the very chinks of the universe about us. I was riding along on a bicycle one day, not so long ago, past the Radcliffe Infirmary, when I had one of those sudden clarities which sometimes come in dreams (even anaesthetic-produced ones). I remember saying aloud with absolute conviction: 'But of course! Of course that's how things really do work'. But I could not reproduce any argument that had led to this, though the sensation was the same as having been convinced by *reason* (if without reasoning). And I have since thought that one of the reasons why one can't recapture the wonderful argument or secret when one wakes up is simply because there was not one: but there was (often maybe) a direct appreciation by the mind (sc. reason) but without the chain of argument we know in our time-serial life. However that's as may be. To descend to lesser things: I knew I had written a story of worth in 'The Hobbit' when reading it (after it was old enough to be detached from me) I had suddenly in a fairly strong measure the 'eucatastrophic' emotion at Bilbo's exclamation: 'The Eagles! The Eagles are coming!' . . . . And in the last chapter of The Ring that I have yet written I hope you'll note, when you receive it (it'll soon be on its way) that Frodo's face goes livid and convinces Sam that he's dead, just when Sam gives up *hope*.

And while we are still, as it were, on the porch of St Gregory's on Sunday 5 Nov. I saw the most touching sight there. Leaning against the wall as we came out of church was an old tramp in rags, something like sandals tied on his feet with string, an old tin can on one wrist, and in his other hand a rough staff. He had a brown beard, and a curiously 'clean' face, with blue eyes, and he was gazing into the distance in some rapt thought not heeding any of the people, cert. not begging. I could not resist the impulse of offering him a small alms, and he took it with grave kindliness, and thanked me courteously, and then went back to his contemplation. Just for once I rather took Fr. C. aback by saying to him that I thought the old man looked a great deal more like St Joseph than the statue in the church – at any rate St Joseph on the way to Egypt. He seems to be (and what a happy thought in these shabby days, where poverty seems only to bring sin and misery) a holy tramp! I could have sworn it anyway, but P. says Betty[3] told her that he had been at the early mass, and had been to communion, and his devotion was plain to see, so plain that many were edified. I do not know just why, but I find that immensely comforting and pleasing. Fr. C says he turns up about once a year.

This is becoming a very peculiar letter! I hope it does not seem all very incomprehensible; for events have directed me to topics that are not really treatable without erasions and re-writings, impossible in air letters! . . . . Let us finish the diary. . . . . On Monday (I think) a hen died – one of the bantam twins; cert. it was buried that day. Also I saw C.S.L. and C.W. from about 10.40 to 12.50, but can recollect little of the feast of reason and flow of soul, partly because we all agree so. It was a bright morning, and the mulberry tree in the grove just outside C.S.L.'s window shone like fallow gold against colbalt blue sky. But the weather worsened again, and in the afternoon I did one of the foulest jobs. I grease-banded all the trees (apple) tying 16 filthy little pantelettes on. It took 2 hours, and nearly as long to get the damned stuff off hands and implements. I neglected it last year, and so lost ½ a glorious crop to 'moth'. It will be like this 'cacocatastrophic' fallen world, if next year there ain't no blossom. Tuesday: lectures and a brief glimpse, at 'The Bird', of the Lewis Bros. and Williams. The Bird is now gloriously empty, with improved beer, and a landlord wreathed in welcoming smiles! He lights a special fire for us! . . . .

A propos of yr. reminder about 'Lord Nelson' – it was in the preliminary meeting to form a United Christian Council – he's always about. I forgot to tell you that at Gielgud's 'Hamlet' he seized on a quiet moment to yell from the Dress Circle 'A very fine performance, and I'm enjoying it very much, but cut out the swear-words!' He did the same at the Playhouse. He was nearly lynched in the New Theatre. But he goes on his odd way. . . . .

Your own Father.

90 To Christopher Tolkien

24 November 1944 (FS 64)   20 Northmoor Road, Oxford

My dearest, there has been a splendid flow of letters from you, since I last wrote. . . . . We were most amused by your account of the Wings ceremony. I wonder how the 'native band' enjoyed being whizzed through the air! I also wondered how you came to have seen and to have remembered the quotation from the Exeter Book Gnomics – which (though I had not thought of it before) does cert. provide a most admirable plea in defence of singing in one's bath. It cheered me a lot to see a bit of Anglo-Saxon, and I hope indeed that you'll soon be able to return and perfect your study of that noble idiom. As the father said to his son: 'Is nu fela folca þætte fyrngewrıtu healdan wille, ac him hyge brosnað.' Which might be a comment on the crowding of universities and the decline of wit. 'There is now a crowd of folks that want to get hold of the old documents, but their wits are decaying!' I have to teach or talk about Old English to such a lot of young persons who simply are not equipped by talent or character to grasp it or profit by it. . . . . Yesterday 2 lectures, re-drafting findings of Committee on Emergency Exams . . . . and then a great event: an evening Inklings. I reached the Mitre at 8 where I was joined by C.W. and the Red Admiral (Havard), resolved to take fuel on board before joining the well-oiled diners in Magdalen (C.S.L. and Owen Barfield). C.S.L. was highly flown, but we were also in good fettle; while O.B. is the only man who can tackle C.S.L. making him define everything and interrupting his most dogmatic pronouncements with subtle *distinguo's*. The result was a most amusing and highly contentious evening, on which (had an outsider eavesdropped) he would have thought it a meeting of fell enemies hurling deadly insults before drawing their guns. Warnie was in excellent majoral form. On one occasion when the audience had flatly refused to hear Jack discourse on and define 'Chance', Jack said: 'Very well, some other time, but if you die tonight you'll be cut off knowing a great deal less about Chance than you might have.' Warnie: 'That only illustrates what I've always said: every cloud has a silver lining.' But there was some quite interesting stuff. A short play on Jason and Medea by Barfield, 2 excellent sonnets sent by a young poet to C.S.L.; and some illuminating discussion of 'ghosts', and of the special nature of Hymns (CSL has been on the Committee revising Ancient and Modern). I did not leave till 12.30, and reached my bed about 1 a.m. this morn. . . . .

Your own father.

91 To Christopher Tolkien

29 November 1944   20 Northmoor Road, Oxford
My dearest,

Here is a small consignment of 'The Ring': the last two chapters that have been written, and the end of the Fourth Book of that great Romance, in which you will see that, as is all too easy, I have got the hero into such a fix that not even an author will be able to extricate him without labour and difficulty. Lewis was moved almost to tears by the last chapter. All the same, I chiefly want to hear what you think, as for a long time now I have written with you most in mind.

I see from my Register that I sent 3 chapters off on October 14th, and another 2 on October 25th. Those must have been: Herbs and Stewed

Rabbit; Faramir; and The Forbidden Pool; and Journey to the Cross-roads; and the Stairs of Kirith Ungol. The first lot should have reached you by now, I hope about your birthday; the second should soon come; and I hope this lot will get to you early in the New Year. I eagerly await your verdict. Very trying having your chief audience Ten Thousand Miles away, on or off The Walloping Window-blind. Even more trying for the audience, doubtless, but authors, qua authors, are a hopelessly egotist tribe. Book Five and Last opens with the ride of Gandalf to Minas Tirith, with which The Palantir, last chapter of Book Three closed. Some of this is written or sketched. Then should follow the raising of the siege of Minas Tirith by the onset of the Riders of Rohan, in which King Theoden falls; the driving back of the enemy, by Gandalf and Aragorn, to the Black Gate; the parley in which Sauron shows various tokens (such as the mithril coat) to prove that he has captured Frodo, but Gandalf refuses to treat (a horrible dilemma, all the same, even for a wizard). Then we shift back to Frodo, and his rescue by Sam. From a high place they see all Sauron's vast reserves loosed through the Black Gate, and then hurry on to Mount Doom through a deserted Mordor. With the destruction of the Ring, the exact manner of which is not certain – all these last bits were written ages ago, but no longer fit in detail, nor in elevation (for the whole thing has become much larger and loftier) – Baraddur crashes, and the forces of Gandalf sweep into Mordor. Frodo and Sam, fighting with the last Nazgul on an island of rock surrounded by the fire of the erupting Mount Doom, are rescued by Gandalf's eagle; and then the clearing up of all loose threads, down even to Bill Ferny's pony, must take place. A lot of this work will be done in a final chapter where Sam is found reading out of an enormous book to his children, and answering all their questions about what happened to everybody (that will link up with his discourse on the nature of stories in the Stairs of Kirith Ungol).[1] But the final scene will be the passage of Bilbo and Elrond and Galadriel through the woods of the Shire on their way to the Grey Havens. Frodo will join them and pass over the Sea (linking with the vision he had of a far green country in the house of Tom Bombadil). So ends the Middle Age and the Dominion of Men begins, and Aragorn far away on the throne of Gondor labours to bring some order and to preserve some memory of old among the welter of men that Sauron has poured into the West. But Elrond has gone, and all the High Elves. What happens to the Ents I don't yet know. It will probably work out very differently from this plan when it really gets written, as the thing seems to write itself once I get going, as if the truth comes out then, only imperfectly glimpsed in the preliminary sketch. . . . .

All the love of your own father.

Your news of yourself does not in some ways add to my equanimity: a dangerous trade, but may God keep you, dear boy; but as you seem to be enjoying part of it more than anything up to now, I take comfort in that. I should feel happier, if your time was better organized, so that you could get reasonable rest: training by straining seems irrational. But I fear an Air Force is a fundamentally irrational thing *per se*. I could wish dearly that you had nothing to do with anything so monstrous. It is in fact a sore trial to me that any son of mine should serve this modern Moloch. But such wishes are vain, and it is, I clearly understand, your duty to do as well in such service as you have the strength and aptitude to do. In any case, it is only a kind of squeamishness, perhaps, like a man who enjoys steak and kidney (or did), but would not be connected with the butchery business. As long as war is fought with such weapons, and one accepts any profits that may accrue (such as preservation of one's skin and even 'victory') it is merely shirking the issue to hold war-aircraft in special horror. I do so all the same. . . . .

This morning . . . . I saw C.S.L. for a while. His fourth (or fifth?) novel is brewing, and seems likely to clash with mine (my dimly projected third). [1] I have been getting a lot of new ideas about Prehistory lately (via Beowulf and other sources of which I may have written) and want to work them into the long shelved time-travel story I began. C.S.L. is planning a story about the descendants of Seth and Cain. We also begin to consider writing a book in collaboration on 'Language' (Nature, Origins, Functions). [2] Would there were time for all these projects!

I am v. glad that you enjoyed the next three ch. of the Ring. The 3rd consignment shd. reach you about Dec. 10 and the last on 14 Jan. I shall be eager for more comments when you have time. Cert. Sam is the most closely drawn character, the successor to Bilbo of the first book, the genuine hobbit. Frodo is not so interesting, because he has to be highminded, and has (as it were) a vocation. The book will prob. end up with Sam. Frodo will naturally become too ennobled and rarefied by the achievement of the great Quest, and will pass West with all the great figures; but S. will settle down to the Shire and gardens and inns. C. Williams who is reading it all says the great thing is that its *centre* is not in strife and war and heroism (though they are understood and depicted) but in freedom, peace, ordinary life and good liking. Yet he agrees that these very things require the existence of a great world outside the Shire

– lest they should grow stale by custom and turn into the humdrum. . . . .

By the way, you wrote *Harebell* and emended it to *Hairbell*. I don't know whether it will interest you, but I looked up the whole matter of this name once – after an argument with a dogmatic scientist. It is plain (a) that the ancient name is *harebell* (an animal name, like so many old flower-names), and (b) that this meant the *hyacinth* not the *campanula*. *Bluebell,* not so old a name, was coined for the campanula, and the 'bluebells' of Scotland are, of course, not the hyacinths but the campanulas. The transference of the name (in England, not in Scotland, nor indeed in uncorrupted country-speech in parts of England) and its fictitious alteration *hairbell* seems to be due to ignorant (of etymology) and meddlesome book-botanists of recent times, of the sort that tried *folk'sglove* for *foxglove*!, by whom we've been led astray. As for the latter, the only part of the name that is doubtful is the *glove*, not the *fox*. *Foxes glófa* occurs in Anglo-Saxon but also in form *-clófa*: in old herbals, where it seems pretty rashly applied to plants with big broad leaves, e.g. *burdock* (called also *foxes clife*, cf. *clifwyrt**=foxglove*). The causes of these ancient associations with animals are little known or understood. Perhaps they sometimes depend on lost beast-fables. It would be tempting to try and make some fables to fit the names.

Are you still inventing names for the nameless flowers you meet? If so, remember that the old names are not always descriptive, but often mysterious! My best inventions (in elvish of the Gnomish dialect) were *elanor* and *nifredil*; though I like A-S *symbelmynë* or *evermind* found on the Great Mound of Rohan. I think I shall have to invent some more for Sam's garden at the end.

94 To Christopher Tolkien

28 December 1944 (FS 71)   20 Northmoor Road, Oxford
My dearest:

You have no need to reproach yourself! We are getting lots of letters from you, and v. quickly. . . . . I am glad the third lot of Ring arrived to date, and that you liked it – although it seems to have added to yr. homesickness. It just shows the difference between life and literature: for anyone who found himself actually on the stairs of Kirith Ungol would wish to exchange it for almost any other place in the world, save Mordor itself. But if lit. teaches us anything at all, it is this: that we have in us an eternal element, free from care and fear, which can survey the things that in 'life' we call evil with serenity (that is not without

---

*Since *clifian*='cleave, stick', it is plain that *foxes clife* and *clifwyrt* originally=burdock. *clófa* is prob. an MS error for *glófa* through mixing the names.

appreciating their quality, but without any disturbance of our spiritual equilibrium). Not in the same way, but in some such way, we shall all doubtless survey our own story when we know it (and a great deal more of the Whole Story). I am afraid the next two chapters won't come for some time (about middle of Jan) which is a pity, as not only are they (I think) v. moving and exciting, but Sam has some interesting comments on the rel. of stories and actual 'adventures'. But I count it a triumph that these two chapters, which I did not think as good as the rest of Book IV, could distract you from the noise of the Air Crew Room! . . . .

The weather has for me been one of the chief events of Christmas. It froze hard with a heavy fog, and so we have had displays of Hoarfrost such as I only remember once in Oxford before (in the other house[1] I think) and only twice before in my life. One of the most lovely events of Northern Nature. We woke (late) on St Stephen's Day to find all our windows opaque, painted over with frost-patterns, and outside a dim silent misty world, all white, but with a light jewelry of rime; every cobweb a little lace net, even the old fowls' tent a diamond-patterned pavilion. I spent the day (after chores, that is from about 11.30, as I got up late) out of doors, well wrapped up in old rags, hewing old brambles and making a fire the smoke of which rose in a still unmoving column straight up into the fog-roof. . . . . The rime was yesterday even thicker and more fantastic. When a gleam of sun (about 11) got through it was breathtakingly beautiful: trees like motionless fountains of white branching spray against a golden light and, high overhead, a pale translucent blue. It did not melt. About 11 p.m. the fog cleared and a high round moon lit the whole scene with a deadly white light: a vision of some other world or time. It was so still that I stood in the garden hatless and uncloaked without a shiver, though there must have been many degrees of frost. . . . .

Mr Eden in the house[2] the other day expressed pain at the occurrences in Greece 'the home of democracy'. Is he ignorant, or insincere? δημοκρατὶα was not in Greek a word of approval but was nearly equivalent to 'mob-rule'; and he neglected to note that Greek Philosophers – and far more is Greece the home of philosophy – did *not* approve of it. And the great Greek states, esp. Athens at the time of its high art and power, were rather Dictatorships, if they were not military monarchies like Sparta! And modern Greece has as little connexion with ancient Hellas as we have with Britain before Julius Agricola. . . . .

Your own Father.

I read till 11.50, browsing through the packed and to me enthralling pages of Stenton's *Anglo-Saxon England*. A period mostly filled with most intriguing Question Marks. I'd give a bit for a time-machine. But of course my mind being what it is (and wholly different from Stenton's) it is the things of racial and linguistic significance that attract me and stick in my memory. Still, I hope one day you'll be able (if you wish) to delve into this intriguing story of the origins of our peculiar people. And indeed of us in particular. For barring the Tolkien (which must long ago have become a pretty thin strand) you are a Mercian or Hwiccian (of Wychwood) on both sides.

96   To Christopher Tolkien

30 January 1945 (FS 78)   20 Northmoor Road, Oxford
My dearest Chris,

   . . . . The minor imp of Slubgob's brood who specially attends to preventing C.S.L. and myself from meeting provided a special attraction in the morning with the leaking of the scullery tap coinciding with the blocking of the sink! It took me until nearly 11 a.m. to get that cleared up. But I got to Magdalen, where after a brief shiver over 2 depressing elm-logs (elm won't burn) we decided to seek warmth and beer at the Mitre: we got both (pubs manage their business better than bursars: upon my word, I don't think the latter gentry would even hold down a Kiwi job in the R.A.F.!). A good many things happened then. My rest was rudely broken by a 'phone call on business from which quite incidentally I learned the startling news that Prof. H. C. Wyld[1] died on Saturday. God rest his soul. But he leaves me a legacy of terrestrial trouble. For one thing I've got to make up mind what to do about the succession. Five years ago I'd have been thinking of how to get the Merton chair myself: my ambition was to get C.S.L. and myself into the 2 Merton Chairs.[2] It would be marvellous to be both in the same college – and for me to be in a real college and shake off the dust of miserable Pembroke. But I think prob. not – even if there was a chance . . . To continue the tale. About supper time the glass fell and the therm. rose, and a great downfall of snow with a wind (W to SW) began. It was piled high against the doors before midnight, but was really thawing underneath, so that although it went on, off and on, all night it was nowhere much over ½ a foot except in knee high drifts. All the same coal, coke, and fowls had vanished, and I had a most laborious morning digging things out before going to lecture. I arrived late (after an appalling acrobatic ride) attired like a 'Skegness' fisherman,[3] and my apology for being late on the platform (Taylorian theatre) as I had been catching sardines, was very well received, better indeed than my subsequent disquisition on Offa of Angel, or on the itinerary of Israel from Egypt to the Red Sea. At the subsequent Bird and B. session (thank heaven, no fish arrived in port!) the UQ (alias Honest Humphrey) arrived tricked out in mountaineering kit. When asked why he was out of uniform he replied: 'I am not in the Swiss Navy. The British Navy does not come out in snow.' Alas, he's being transferred to Liverpool soon. Indescribable mixture of ice and slush. I fell off three times, and was, of course, hustled into the gutter and drenched in fountains of filthy squelch by those amiable people who drive 'private cars'. It took me till nigh 3.30 to finish the clearance of snow and clear drains, and then I settled down to your delightful letters. I hadn't a moment to look at them when they arrived at breakfast time. But they had their effect by merely arriving, as you can see by my skittishness on the platform and from C.S.L.'s remark at the B & B.: 'What's the matter with him this morning, he's quite above himself?' . . . .

As for Eden. I think most Christians, except the v. simple and uneducated or those protected in other ways, have been rather bustled and hustled now for some generations by the self-styled scientists, and they've sort of tucked Genesis into a lumber-room of their mind as not very fashionable furniture, a bit ashamed to have it about the house, don't you know, when the bright clever young people called: I mean, of course, even the *fideles* who did not sell it secondhand or burn it as soon as modern taste began to sneer. In consequence they have indeed (myself as much as any), as you say, forgotten the beauty of the matter even 'as a story'. Lewis recently wrote a most interesting essay (if published I don't know)[4] showing of what great value the 'story-value' was, as mental nourishment – of the whole Chr. story (NT especially). It was a defence of that kind of attitude which we tend to sneer at: the fainthearted that loses faith, but clings at least to the beauty of 'the story' as having some permanent value. His point was that they do still in that way get some nourishment and are not cut off wholly from the sap of life: for the beauty of the story while not necessarily a guarantee of its truth is a concomitant of it, and a *fidelis* is meant to draw nourishment from the beauty as well as the truth. So that the faintheart 'admirer' is really still getting something, which even one of the faithful (stupid, insensitive, shamefaced) may be missing. But partly as a development of my own thought on my lines and work (technical and literary), partly in contact with C.S.L., and in various ways not least the firm guiding hand of Alma Mater Ecclesia, I do not now feel either ashamed or dubious on the Eden 'myth'. It has not, of course, historicity of the same kind as the NT, which are virtually contemporary documents, while Genesis is separated by we do not know how many sad exiled generations from the Fall, but certainly there was an Eden on this very unhappy earth. We all long for it, and we are constantly glimpsing it: our whole nature at its best and least corrupted, its gentlest and most humane, is still soaked with the sense of 'exile'. If you come to think of it, your (very just) horror at the stupid murder of the hawk, and your obstinate memory of this 'home' of yours in an idyllic hour (when often there is an illusion of the stay of time and decay and a sense of gentle peace) – ἐίθε γενοίμην,[5] 'stands the clock at ten to three, and is there honey still for tea' – are derived from Eden. As far as we can go back the nobler part of the human mind is filled with the thoughts of *sibb*, peace and goodwill, and with the thought of its *loss*. We shall never recover it, for that is not the way of repentance, which works spirally and not in a closed circle; we may recover something like it, but on a higher plane. Just as (to compare a small thing) the converted urban gets more out of the country than the mere yokel, but he cannot become a real landsman, he is both more and in a way less (less truly earthy anyway). Of course, I suppose that, subject to the permission of God, the whole human race (as each individual) is free not to rise again but to go to perdition and carry out the Fall to its bitter bottom (as each individual can singulariter[6]). And at certain periods, the present is notably one, that seems not only a likely event but imminent. Still I think there will be a 'millenium', the prophesied thousand-year rule of the Saints, i.e. those who have for all their imperfections never finally bowed heart and will to the world or the evil spirit (in modern but not universal terms: mechanism, 'scientific' materialism, Socialism in either of its factions now at war).

I am so glad you felt that 'the Ring' is keeping up its standard, and (it seems) achieving that difficult thing in a long tale: maintaining a difference of quality and atmosphere in events that might easily become 'samey'. For myself, I was prob. most moved by Sam's disquisition on the seamless web of story, and by the scene when Frodo goes to sleep on his breast, and the tragedy of Gollum who at that moment came within a hair of repentance – but for one rough word from Sam. But the 'moving' quality of that is on a different plane to *Celebrimbor* etc. There are two quit diff. emotions: one that moves me supremely and I find small difficulty in evoking: the heart-racking sense of the vanished past (best expressed by Gandalf's words about the Palantir); and the other the more 'ordinary' emotion, triumph, pathos, tragedy of the characters. That I am learning to do, as I get to know my people, but it is not really so near my heart, and is forced on me by the fundamental literary dilemma. A story must be told or there'll be no story, yet it is the untold stories that are most moving. I think you are moved by *Celebrimbor* because it conveys a sudden sense of endless *untold* stories: mountains seen far away, never to be climbed, distant trees (like Niggle's) never to be approached – or if so only to become 'near trees' (unless in Paradise or N's Parish).

Well my space will soon run out, and also it is 9 p.m., and I have some letters of necessity to write, and 2 lectures tomorrow, so I must be thinking of closing down soon. I read eagerly all details of your life, and the things you see and do – and suffer, Jive and Boogie-Woogie among them. You will have no heart-tug at losing that (for it is essentially vulgar, music corrupted by the mechanism, echoing in dreary un-nourished heads), but you'll remember the other things, even the storms and the dry veld and even the smells of camp, when you return to this other land. I can see clearly now in my mind's eye the old trenches and the squalid houses and the long roads of Artois, and I would visit them again if I could. . . . .

I have just heard the news. . . . . Russians 60 miles from Berlin. It does look as if something decisive might happen soon. The appalling destruc-tion and misery of this war mount hourly: destruction of what should be (indeed is) the common wealth of Europe, and the world, if mankind were not so besotted, wealth the loss of which will affect us all, victors or not. Yet people gloat to hear of the endless lines, 40 miles long, of miserable refugees, women and children pouring West, dying on the way. There seem no bowels of mercy or compassion, no imagination, left in this dark diabolic hour. By which I do not mean that it may not all, in the present situation, mainly (not solely) created by Germany, be necessary and inevitable. But why gloat! We were supposed to have reached a stage of civilization in which it might still be necessary to execute a criminal, but not to gloat, or to hang his wife and child by him while the orc-crowd hooted. The destruction of Germany, be it 100 times merited, is one of the most appalling world-catastrophes. Well, well – you and I can do nothing about it. And that shd. be a measure of the amount of guilt that can justly be assumed to attach to any member of a country who is not a member of its actual Government. Well the first War of the Machines seems to be drawing to its final inconclusive chapter – leaving, alas, everyone the poorer, many bereaved or maimed and millions dead, and only one thing triumphant: the Machines. As the servants of the Machines are becoming a privileged class, the Machines are going to be enormously more powerful. What's their next move?
. . . . All the love of your own father.

I've wasted some precious time this week-end writing a letter to the Catholic Herald. One of their sentimentalist correspondents wrote about the etymology of the name *Coventry*, and seemed to think that unless you said it came from *Convent*, the answer was not 'in keeping with Catholic tradition'. 'I gather the convent of St Osburg was of no consequence,' said he: boob. As *convent* did not enter English till after 1200 A.D. (and meant an 'assembly' at that) and the meaning 'nunnery' is not recorded before 1795, I felt annoyed. So I have asked whether he would like to change the name of Oxford to Doncaster; but he's probably too stupid to see even that mild quip.

98   To Stanley Unwin

[Unwin's elder son David – the children's writer 'David Severn' – had read Tolkien's story 'Leaf by Niggle' in the *Dublin Review*, where it was published in January 1945. He commended it to his father, calling it an 'exquisite piece of work', and suggested that it be published in a volume along with other short stories by Tolkien. Stanley Unwin passed this suggestion to Tolkien.]

[Undated; *circa* 18 March 1945]   20 Northmoor Road, Oxford
Dear Unwin,

I have written several imaginary letters to you, and half an actual one, in the past few months, before I got your note of 24 February. Especially I have meant to enquire after Rayner. I hope you have good news of him. The R.A.F. cadets of his course seem all to have had a wretched time since, but the Navy is rather less irrational and wasteful; so he may have been spared some of the worse squalors and frustrations now inflicted (too often quite unnecessarily) on young men.

Also my third son, Christopher, has been for a long time at Standerton in the Transvaal, and there one of his great friends has been Chris Unwin.[1] .... My boy, I hear today, is 'In Transit' for England, after a year and a quarter away, so I hope Unwin is too. Certainly they were still together on March 3rd. But already one of the group has been killed, in his first flight in a Hurricane, my boy's stable-companion, and the one who came out top of the Course. And there you have one of the explanations of my unproductiveness and (seeming) neglect. My heart is gnawed out with anxiety. And anyway my Christopher was my real primary audience, who has read, vetted, and typed all of the new Hobbit, or The Ring, that has been completed. He was dragged off in the middle of making maps. I have squandered almost the only time I have had to spare for writing in continuing our interrupted conversations by epistle: he occupied the multiple position of audience, critic, son, student in my department, and my tutorial pupil![2] But he has received copies of all the chapters I wrote in a spurt last year. Since when I have been more than ever burdened, or the ratio between duty and weariness has been more unfavourable. . . . .

Since you have seen 'Leaf by Niggle' – I was going to advert to it myself, as part apologia, part confession – I need say no more. Except that that story was the only thing I have ever done which cost me absolutely no pains at all. Usually I compose only with great difficulty and endless rewriting. I woke up one morning (more than 2 years ago) with that odd thing virtually complete in my head. It took only a few hours to get down, and then copy out. I am not aware of ever 'thinking' of the story or composing it in the ordinary sense. All the same I do not feel so detached as not to be cheered, indeed rather bowled over, by your son's comment. The only notice of, or observation on, the 'Leaf' that I have had at all, outside my own circle.

Well! 'Niggle' is so unlike any other short story that I have ever written, or begun, that I wonder if it would consort with them. Two others, of that tone and style, remain mere budding leaves like so many of silly Niggle's.[3] Would it be of any use, if I put together in a bundle what I can find, and let you say whether with re-writing of this, omission of that, or addition of the other, they have any chance of making a volume? There are one or two short verse narratives (some have already appeared in print in the Oxford Magazine) which might pass, tactfully sandwiched in. Were you considering 'Farmer Giles' as a possibility? It is rather a long short. The corrected and properly typed copy is 'out', on its usual travels, at the moment; but I've a tolerable home-made copy which I am sending for 'David Severn's' perusal. (The sequel is plotted but unwritten, and likely to remain so. The heart has gone out of the Little Kingdom, and the woods and plains are aerodromes and bomb-practice targets). But another comic fairy story of a similar genre, 'The King of the Green Dozen', is half-written, and could be finished without much pain, if 'Farmer Giles' is approved.

As for larger work. Of course, my only real desire is to publish 'The Silmarillion':* which your reader, you may possibly remember, allowed to have a certain beauty, but of a 'Celtic' kind irritating to Anglo-Saxons. Still there is the great 'Hobbit' sequel – I use 'great', I fear, only in quantitative sense. It is much too 'great' for the present situation, in that sense. But it cannot be docked or abbreviated. I cannot do better than I have done in this, unless (as is possible enough) I am no judge. But it is not finished. I made an effort last year to finish it and failed. Three

---

*Especially as I find allusions and references to it creeping into Mr Lewis' work, such as his latest novel.[4]

weeks with nothing else to do – and a little rest and sleep first – would probably be sufficient. But I don't see any hope of getting them; and it simply is not the kind of stuff for odd moments. Like Niggle I want a 'public pension', and am equally unlikely to get one! You shall, of course, have it for consideration the moment it is done, if it ever is. I did say, I believe, that I would let you have a part of it, to judge of. But it is so closely knit, and under a process of growth in all its parts, that I find I have to have all the chapters by me – I am always, you see, hoping to get at it. And anyway only one copy (home-typed or written by various filial hands and my own), that is legible by others, exists, and I've feared to let go of it; and I've shirked the expense of professional typing in these hard days, at any rate until the end, and the whole is corrected. But would you now really wish to see some of it? It is divided into Five Parts, of 10–12 chapters each (!). Four are completed, and the last begun. I could send it to you, Part by Part, with all its present imperfections on it – riders, alternatives, variable proper names – until you cry 'halt! This is enough! It must go the way of "The Silmarillion" into the Limbo of the great unpublishables!'

I must stop, or you will be feeling the time and paper could be better spent on writing not talking about it. I have 'special exams' until Easter, and some trouble with the University of Wales. Also all the trouble caused by the death of my colleague, H. C. K. Wyld, to find whose successor will chiefly devolve on me this vacation. I am in trouble with Blackwell who has set up my translation of *Pearl*, and needs corrections and an introduction. I am in trouble with the widow of Professor E. V. Gordon of Manchester, whose posthumous work on *Pearl* I undertook, as a duty to a dead friend and pupil, to put in order; and have failed to do my duty. But I suppose I may get a few weeks in the year to myself. Though I'm also in serious trouble with the Clarendon Press; and with my lost friend Mlle. Simonne d'Ardenne, who has suddenly reappeared, having miraculously survived the German occupation, and the Rundstedt offensive (which rolled over her) waving the MSS. of a large work we began together and promised to the Early English Text Soc.[5] Which has not forgotten it – nor my own book on *The Ancrene Riwle*,[6] which is all typed out. If instead of B.D.S.T.[7] you could invent a scheme for doubling the day (and relieve me of house-boy's duties), I'd drown you in stuff, like Tom, Dick, and Harry. But I do remain very deeply grateful for your kindness and concern.

Yours sincerely,
J. R. R. Tolkien.

99 To 'Michal' Williams, widow of Charles Williams

[Written on the day that Williams died, following an operation.]

15 May 1945   20 Northmoor Road, Oxford

Dear Mrs Williams,

My heart goes out to you in sympathy, and I can say no more. I share a little in your loss, for in the (far too brief) years since I first met him I had grown to admire and love your husband deeply, and I am more grieved than I can express.

Later, if you find that there is anything in which I might be of service to you and your son, please tell me. Fr. Gervase Mathew is saying Mass at Blackfriars on Saturday at 8 a.m., and I shall serve him; but of course I shall have you all in my prayers immediately and continually: for such as they are worth. Forgive this halting note.

Yours very sincerely,
J. R. R. Tolkien.

100 From a letter to Christopher Tolkien   29 May 1945

[After returning from South Africa, Christopher was stationed with the R.A.F. in Shropshire. He was hoping to arrange a transfer to the Fleet Air Arm.]

It would be at least some comfort to me if you escaped from the R.A.F. And I hope, if the transfer goes through, it will mean a real transfer, and a re-commission. It would not be easy for me to express to you the measure of my loathing for the Third Service – which can be nonetheless, and is for me, combined with admiration, gratitude, and above all pity, for the young men caught in it. But it is the aeroplane of war that is the real villain. And nothing can really amend my grief that you, my best beloved, have any connexion with it. My sentiments are more or less those that Frodo would have had if he discovered some Hobbits learning to ride Nazgûl-birds, 'for the liberation of the Shire'. Though in this case, as I know nothing about British or American imperialism in the Far East that does not fill me with regret and disgust, I am afraid I am not even supported by a glimmer of patriotism in this remaining war. I would not subscribe a penny to it, let alone a son, were I a free man. It can only benefit America or Russia: prob. the latter. But at least the Americo-Russian War won't break out for a year yet.

101 From a letter to Christopher Tolkien   3 June 1945

There is a stand-down parade of Civil Defence in the Parks in the afternoon, to which I shall prob. have to drag myself. But I am afraid it all seems rather a mockery to me, for the War is not over (and the one that is, or the part of it, has largely been lost). But it is of course wrong to fall into such a mood, for Wars are always lost, and The War always goes on; and it is no good growing faint!

102 From a letter to Christopher Tolkien 9 August 1945

The news today about 'Atomic bombs' is so horrifying one is stunned. The utter folly of these lunatic physicists to consent to do such work for war-purposes: calmly plotting the destruction of the world! Such explosives in men's hands, while their moral and intellectual status is declining, is about as useful as giving out firearms to all inmates of a gaol and then saying that you hope 'this will ensure peace'. But one good thing may arise out of it, I suppose, if the write-ups are not overheated: Japan ought to cave in. Well we're in God's hands. But He does not look kindly on Babel-builders.

103 From a letter to Christopher Tolkien 11 October 1945

[Following his election to the Merton Professorship of English Language and Literature, Tolkien left Pembroke College and became a Professorial Fellow of Merton College. This letter describes his first impressions of Merton.]

I was duly admitted yesterday at 10 a.m. and then had to endure the most formidable College Meeting I have ever seen – went on till 1.30 p.m. without cessation and then broke up in disorder. The Warden talked almost unceasingly. I lunched in Merton and made a few arrangements, putting my name down at the Estates Bursary on the housing list;[1] and getting a Master Key to all gates and doors. It is incredible belonging to a real college (and a very large and wealthy one). I am looking forward to showing you round. I walked round this afternoon with Dyson[2] who was duly elected yesterday, and is now ensconced in the rooms I hoped for, looking out over the meadows! I am going to the Inklings tonight. We shall think of you.

104 From a letter to Christopher Tolkien 22 October 1945

I dined for the first time at Merton high table on Thursday, and found it very agreeable; though odd. For fuel-economy the common room is not heated, and the dons meet and chat amiably on the dais, until someone thinks there are enough there for grace to be said. After that they sit and dine, and have their port, and coffee, and smoke and evening newspapers all at high table in a manner that if agreeably informal is rather shocking to one trained in the severer ceremonies and strict precedence of mediæval Pembroke. At about 8.45 Dyson and I strolled through 'our grounds' to Magdalen and visited Warnie and Havard – Jack was away. We broke up about 10.30.

105 To Sir Stanley Unwin

[Unwin, who had been knighted, wrote to enquire about the progress of *The Lord of the Rings*.]

21 July 1946   20 Northmoor Road, Oxford

Dear Sir Stanley,

I have treated you very badly. I think you would be disposed to forgive me, if you knew the true tale of my troubles, domestic and academic. But I will spare you that, and attempt to do better.

I have been ill, worry and overwork mainly, but am a good deal recovered; and am at last able to take some steps to see that at least the overwork, so far as it is academic, is alleviated. For the first time in 25 years, except the year I went on crutches (just before The Hobbit came out, I think), I am free of examining, and though I am still battling with a mountain of neglects, out of which I have just dug a good many letters from George Allen and Unwin, and with a lot of bothers in this time of chaos and 'reconstruction', I hope after this week actually to – write. For one thing, I shall not be left all alone to try and run our English School. I have ceased to be the Professor of Anglo-Saxon. I have removed to Merton, as the Merton Professor of English Language and Literature: Professor Wrenn, from King's College, London, is coming in October to take Anglo-Saxon off my shoulders; and we are about to elect another Merton professor (of modern literature). It ought to be C. S. Lewis, or perhaps Lord David Cecil, but one never knows.

But I did not begin this letter primarily to talk about myself. I wanted to say first how sorry I am that I did not, as I intended, write as soon as ever I heard, to congratulate you on your own honour, which gave me very great pleasure. Also I very much want news of Rayner. I hope earnestly that it is good, though one is still hesitant to ask news of sons. But my Christopher, who transferred to the Fleet Air arm, and is still technically in the Navy, has gone back this term to Trinity; and I wondered if there is any chance of Rayner returning soon. I should very much like to see him again. . . . .

I do not know whether David Severn still wants to look at Farmer Giles. In case he does, I am sending it now, after more than a year's delay. If I could have a little leisure, I could add a few things of the same sort, still not finished. But *Niggle* has never bred any thing that consorts with himself at all.

I do not know whether any more information about so literally 'promising' and not performing an author will interest you at all. But I made a very great effort to finish the Hobbit sequel, and chapters went out to Africa and back to my chief critic and collaborator, Christopher, who is doing the maps. But I failed. Troubles and ill health became too thick. I shall now have to study my own work in order to get back to it. But I really do hope to have it done before the autumn term, and at any rate before the end of the year. Though I wonder if you will find any paper, even supposing that the work commends itself.

I have, by the way, published a story in verse[1] in the Welsh Review of Dec. 1945; am about to publish a much expanded version of an essay on Fairy Stories, originally delivered as a lecture at St Andrews, in a memorial volume to the late Charles Williams; and I have in a fortnight of comparative leisure round about last Christmas written three parts of another book,[2] taking up in an entirely different frame and setting what little had any value in the inchoate *Lost Road* (which I had once the impudence to show you: I hope it is forgotten), and other things beside. I hoped to finish this in a rush, but my health gave way after Christmas. Rather silly to mention it, till it is finished. But I am putting *The Lord of the Rings*, the *Hobbit* sequel, before all else, save duties that I cannot wriggle out of.

My very best wishes.
Yours sincerely,
J. R. R. Tolkien.

106   From a letter to Sir Stanley Unwin   30 September 1946

[Allen & Unwin expressed enthusiasm for *Farmer Giles of Ham*, but asked if Tolkien could provide other stories to make up a sufficiently large volume.]

I should, of course, be delighted if you see your way to publish 'Farmer Giles of Ham' . . . With leisure I could give him company, but I am in a tough spot academically, and see no hope of leisure until the various new professors come along. I could not promise to complete anything soon. At least I suppose I could, but it would be difficult – and really the Hobbit sequel is so much better (I think) than these things, that I should wish to give it all spare hours. I picked it up again last week and wrote (a good) chapter, and was then drowned with official business – in which I have waded since your kind letter came 10 days ago.

I have never tried illustrating 'Farmer Giles' and do not know of any one.

107 From a letter to Sir Stanley Unwin 7 December 1946

[On the subject of a German edition of *The Hobbit*.]

I continue to receive letters from poor Horus Engels[1] about a German translation. He does not seem necessarily to propose himself as a translator. He has sent me some illustrations (of the Trolls and Gollum) which despite certain merits, such as one would expect of a German, are I fear too 'Disnified' for my taste: Bilbo with a dribbling nose, and Gandalf as a figure of vulgar fun rather than the Odinic wanderer that I think of. . . . .

I am shortly moving to a small house (3 Manor Road)[2] and so hoping to solve the intolerable domestic problems which thieve so much of the little time that is left over. I still hope shortly to finish my 'magnum opus': the Lord of the Rings: and let you see it, before long, or before January. I am on the last chapters.

108 From a letter to Allen & Unwin 5 July 1947

[Allen & Unwin had decided to publish *Farmer Giles of Ham* as a separate volume.]

I am now sending back (a week late) under separate cover the MS. of *Farmer Giles of Ham*, revised for the press. I have as you will see gone through it carefully, making a good many alterations, for the better (I think and hope) in both style and narrative. . . . .

You will note that, whoever may buy it, this story was *not* written *for* children; though as in the case of other books that will not necessarily prevent them from being amused by it. I think it might be as well to emphasize the fact that this is a tale specially composed for reading aloud: it goes very well so, for those that like this kind of thing at all. It was, in fact, written to order, to be read to the Lovelace Society at Worcester College; and was read to them at a sitting.

For that reason I should like to put an inscription to C. H. Wilkinson[1] on a fly-leaf, since it was Col. Wilkinson of that College who egged me to it, and has since constantly egged me to publication.

109 To Sir Stanley Unwin

[Tolkien lunched with Unwin in London on 9 July, and agreed that Rayner Unwin should see Book I of *The Lord of the Rings* which was in 'fair' typescript. On 28 July, Tolkien was sent Rayner's comments; Rayner wrote: 'The tortuous and contending currents of events in this world within a world almost overpower one . . . . The struggle between darkness and light (sometimes one suspects leaving the story proper to become pure allegory) is macabre and intensified beyond that in "Hobbit" .... Converting the original Ring into this new and powerful instrument takes some explaining away and Gandalf is hard put to it to find reasons for many of the original Hobbit's actions, but the linking of the books is well done on the whole .... Quite honestly I don't know who is expected to read it . . . If grown ups will not feel infra dig to read it many will undoubtedly enjoy themselves .... The proof reader will have to correct a number of omitted changes from "Hamilcar" to "Belisarius".' Despite these criticisms and hesitations, Rayner judged the book to be 'a brilliant and gripping story'. Tolkien wrote the following reply on 31 July, but did not send it until 21 September, for reasons given in the letter of that date.]

31 July 1947   Merton College, Oxford
Dear Unwin,

I will certainly address you so, cum permissu, though it hardly seems a fair exchange for the loss of 'professor', a title one has rather to live down than to insist on.

I was surprised to get the instalment of The Ring back so quickly. It may be a large book, but evidently it will be none too long in the reading for those who have the appetite. And it was very kind of you to send me Rayner's impressions. Any criticism from outside the small circle that has known the thing as it has grown (and becoming familiar with its world have long ceased to be overpowered) would be welcome; but this critic is worth listening to.

I must now wait with patience until he has seen more. I will send another instalment at the end of August. And I have now another urgent reason, in addition to the clamour of the circle, for finishing it off, so that it can be finally judged.

I return Rayner's remarks with thanks to you both. I am sorry he felt overpowered, and I particularly miss any reference to the comedy, with which I imagined the first 'book' was well supplied. It may have misfired. I cannot bear funny books or plays myself, I mean those that set out to be all comic; but it seems to me that in real life, as here, it is precisely against the darkness of the world that comedy arises, and is best when that is not hidden. Evidently I have managed to make the horror really horrible, and that is a great comfort; for every romance that takes things seriously must have a warp of fear and horror, if however remotely or representatively it is to resemble reality, and not be the merest escapism. But I have failed if it does not seem possible that mere mundane hobbits could cope with such things. I think that there is no horror conceivable that such creatures cannot surmount, by grace (here appearing in mythological forms) combined with a refusal of their nature and reason at the last pinch to compromise or submit.

But in spite of this, do not let Rayner suspect 'Allegory'. There is a 'moral', I suppose, in any tale worth telling. But that is not the same thing. Even the struggle between darkness and light (as he calls it, not me) is for me just a particular phase of history, one example of its pattern, perhaps, but not The Pattern; and the actors are individuals – they each, of course, contain universals, or they would not live at all, but they never represent them as such.

Of course, Allegory and Story converge, meeting somewhere in Truth. So that the only perfectly consistent allegory is a real life; and the only fully intelligible story is an allegory. And one finds, even in imperfect human 'literature', that the better and more consistent an allegory is the more easily can it be read 'just as a story'; and the better and more closely woven a story is the more easily can those so minded find allegory in it. But the two start out from opposite ends. You can make the Ring into an allegory of our own time, if you like: an allegory of the inevitable fate that waits for all attempts to defeat evil power by power. But that is only because all power magical or mechanical does always so work. You cannot write a story about an apparently simple magic ring without that bursting in, if you really take the ring seriously, and make things happen that would happen, if such a thing existed.

Rayner has, of course, spotted a weakness (inevitable): the linking. I am glad that he thinks that the linking has on the whole been well done. That is the best that could be hoped. I have done the best I could, since I had to have hobbits (whom I love), and must still have a glimpse of Bilbo for old times' sake. But I don't feel worried by the discovery that the ring was more serious than appeared; that is just the way of all easy ways out. Nor is it Bilbo's actions, I think, that need explanation. The weakness is Gollum, and his action in offering the ring as a present.[1] However, Gollum later becomes a prime character, and I do not rely on Gandalf to make his psychology intelligible. I hope it will come off, and Gandalf finally be revealed as perceptive rather than 'hard put to it'. Still I must bear this in mind, when I revise chapter II for press: I intend, in any case, to shorten it. The proper way to negotiate the difficulty would be slightly to remodel the former story in its chapter V. That is not a practical question; though I certainly hope to leave behind me the whole thing revised and in final form, for the world to throw into the waste-paper basket. All books come there in the end, in this world, anyway.

As for who is to read it? The world seems to be becoming more and more divided into impenetrable factions, Morlocks and Eloi, and others. But those that like this kind of thing at all, like it very much, and cannot get anything like enough of it, or at sufficiently great length to appease hunger. The taste may be (alas!) numerically limited, even if, as I suspect, growing, and chiefly needing supply for further growth. But where it exists the taste is not limited by age or profession (unless one excludes those wholly devoted to machines). The audience that has so far followed The Ring, chapter by chapter, and has re-read it, and clamours for more, contains some odd folk of similar literary tastes: such as C. S. Lewis, the late Charles Williams, and my son Christopher; they are probably a very small and unrequiting minority. But it has included others: a solicitor, a doctor (professionally interested in cancer), an elderly army officer, an elementary school-mistress, an artist, and a farmer.[2] Which is a fairly wide selection, even if one excludes professionally literary folk, whose own interests would seem to be far removed, such as David Cecil.

At any rate the proof-reader, if it ever comes to that, will, I hope, have very little to do. I was bowed under other work and had no time to look over the chapters I sent in. Belisarius must have been scribbled as a suggestion over the name Hamilcar[3] in a few cases. The choice matters little, though the change had a purpose; but at any rate I hope that most detestable slovenliness of not keeping even a minor character's name firm will not disfigure the final form. Also: it is inevitable that the knowledge of the previous book should be presumed; but there is in existence a Foreword, or opening chapter, 'Concerning Hobbits'. That gives the gist of Chapter V 'Riddles in the Dark', and retells the information supplied in the first two pages or so of the other book, besides explaining many points that 'fans' have enquired about: such as tobacco, and references to policemen and the king (p. 43),[4] and the appearance of houses in the picture of Hobbiton. The Hobbit was after all not as simple as it seemed, and was torn rather at random out of a world in which it already existed, and which has not been newly devised just to make a sequel. The only liberty, if such it is, has been to make Bilbo's Ring the One Ring: all rings had the same source, before ever he put his hand on it in the dark. The horrors were already lurking there, as on page 36, and 303;[5] and Elrond saw that they could not be banished by any White Council.

Well, I have talked quite long enough about my own follies. The thing is to finish the thing as devised and then let it be judged. But forgive me! It is written in my life-blood, such as that is, thick or thin; and I can no other. I fear it must stand or fall as it substantially is. It would be idle to pretend that I do not greatly desire publication, since a solitary art is no art; nor that I have not a pleasure in praise, with as little vanity as fallen man can manage (he has not much more share in his writings than in his children of the body, but it is something to have a function); yet the chief thing is to complete one's work, as far as completion has any real sense.

I am deeply grateful for being taken seriously by a busy man who has dealt and deals with many men of greater learning and talent. I wish you and Rayner a good voyage, successful business, and then great days among the Mountains.[6] How I long to see the snows and the great heights again!

Yours sincerely,
J. R. R. Tolkien.

Talking about revising *The Hobbit*. Any alteration of any radical kind is of course impossible, and unnecessary. But there are still quite a number of misprints in it. I have twice, I think, sent in lists of these, and I hope they have been corrected this time. Also there are minor errors, which the researches of fans have revealed, and some closer attention of my own has discovered. I wish there could be a chance of putting them right. I enclose a list again.

110 From a letter to Allen & Unwin   20 September 1947

[Tolkien's American publishers, the Houghton Mifflin Co., applied to Allen & Unwin for permission to use several riddles from *The Hobbit* in an anthology of poetry. Allen & Unwin suggested to Tolkien that 'the riddles were taken from common folk lore and were not invented by you'.]

As for the Riddles: they are 'all my own work' except for 'Thirty White Horses' which is traditional, and 'No-legs'. The remainder, though their style and method is that of old literary (but not 'folk-lore') riddles, have *no models* as far as I am aware, save only the egg-riddle which is a reduction to a couplet (my own) of a longer literary riddle which appears in some 'Nursery Rhyme' books, notably American ones. So I feel that to try and use them without fee would be about as just as walking off with somebody's chair because it was a Chippendale copy, or drinking his wine because it was labelled 'port-type'. I feel also constrained to remark that 'Sun on the Daisies' is not in verse (any more than 'No-legs') being but the etymology of the word 'daisy', expressed in riddle-form.

I wrote to you on the last day of July, but I put the letter aside, as it seemed too much of a pother about my works. . . . .

Hyde (or Jekyll) has had to have his way, and I have been obliged to devote myself mainly to philology, especially as my colleague from Liege,[1] with whom I had been embarking on 'research' before the war, was staying here to help to get our work ready for press.

Now I am about to go off again for a few days on college business. It is my turn to go with the Warden and Bursar to inspect estates in Cambridge and Lincolnshire. So rather than leave your letter of July 28 unanswered any longer, I send along herewith my original and now rather tattered answer. With it I send Rayner's comments; also some notes on The Hobbit; and (for the possible amusement of yourself and Rayner) a specimen of re-writing of Chapter V of that work, which would simplify, though not necessarily improve, my present task.

I have tried unsuccessfully to squeeze in, in the intervals of 'research' and journeys, some revision of Book II of The Lord of the Rings. But, as I should like very much to benefit by Rayner's reading (and yours, if you have any time), I send it along under separate cover, with its many defects of detail. But Rayner may note, if he has time to bother with this packet, that Chapter XIV has been re-written, to match the re-writing of Chapter II 'Ancient History' which he has read. Chapter II is now called 'The Shadow of the Past' and most of its 'historical' material has been cut out, while a little more attention is paid to Gollum. So that if XIV seems repetitive, it is not actually so; practically nothing now in XIV will appear in II.

I send also the preliminary chapter of Foreword to the whole: 'Concerning Hobbits', which acts as a link to the earlier book and at the same time answers questions that have been asked.

112   **To Katherine Farrer**

[A postcard, apparently written on 30 November 1947, using the system of runes employed in *The Hobbit*; a transcription will be found on p. 441. Mrs Farrer, a writer of detective stories, was married to the theologian Austin Farrer, then Chaplain of Trinity College, Oxford. She had apparently asked Tolkien to sign her copy of *The Hobbit*.]

PROFESSOR TOLKIEN
MERTON COLLEGE
OXFORD

3, MANOR ROAD
OXFORD
Telephone: 47106

113 To C. S. Lewis

[The exact circumstances behind this letter are not clear, but it seems that Tolkien and Lewis had been corresponding about criticisms that Tolkien had made of a piece of Lewis's work read aloud to the Inklings. This may have been part of Lewis's *English Literature in the Sixteenth Century*, in the Oxford History of English Literature ('OHEL') series, which is referred to in the letter.]

Septuagesima 1948

My dear Jack,

It was good of you to write in return. But you write largely on 'offence'; though surely I amended 'offended' in my letter to 'pained'? Pained we cannot help being by the painful. I knew well enough that you wd. not allow pain to grow into resentment, not even if (or still less because) that may be a tendency of your nature. Woe to him, though, by

125

whom the temptations come. I regret causing pain, even if and in so far as I had the right; and I am very sorry indeed still for having caused it quite excessively and unnecessarily. My verses and my letter were due to a sudden very acute realization (I shall not quickly forget it) of the pain that may enter into authorship, both in the making and in the 'publication', which is an essential part of the full process. The vividness of the perception was due, of course, to the fact that you, for whom I have deep affection and sympathy, were the victim and I myself the culprit. But I felt myself tingling under the half-patronizing half-mocking lash, with the small things of my heart made the mere excuse for verbal butchery.

I have been possessed on occasions (few, happily) with a sort of *furor scribendi*, in which the pen finds the words rather than head or heart; and this was one of them. But nothing in your speech or manner gave me any reason to suppose that you felt 'offended'. Yet I could see that you *felt* – you would have been hardly human otherwise –, and your letter shows how much. I daresay under grace that will do good rather than harm, but that is between you and God. It is one of the mysteries of pain that it is, for the sufferer, an opportunity for good, a path of ascent however hard. But it remains an 'evil', and it must dismay any conscience to have caused it carelessly, or in excess, let alone wilfully. And even under necessity or privilege, as of a father or master in punishment, or even of a man beating a dog, it is the rod of God only to be wielded with trepidation. There may have been one or two of my comments that were just or valid, but I should have limited myself to them, and expressed them differently. He is a savage physician who coats a not wholly unpalatable pill with a covering of gall!

But as for your feelings about me as a 'critic', whether exercising the function wisely or foolishly. I am *not* a critic. I do not want to be one.* I am capable on occasion (after long pondering) of 'criticism', but I am not naturally a critical man. I have been partly and in a sense unnaturally galvanized into it by the strongly 'critical' tendency of the brotherhood. I am not really 'hyper-critical'. For I am usually only trying to express 'liking' not universally valid criticism. As a rule I am in fact merely lost in a chartless alien sea. I need *food* of particular kinds, not exercise for my analytical wits (which are normally employed in other fields). For I have something that I deeply desire to *make*, and which it is the (largely

---

*I think 'criticism' – however valid or intellectually engaging – tends to get in the way of a writer who has anything personal to say. A tightrope walker may require *practice*, but if he starts a theory of equilibrium he will lose grace (and probably fall off). Indeed (if I dare yet venture on any criticism again) I should say that I think it gets in your way, *as a writer*. You read too much, and too much of that analytically. But then you are also a born critic. I am not. You are also a born reader.

frustrated) bent of my nature to make. Without any vanity or exaggerated notion of the universal importance of this, it remains a fact that other things are *to me* less important. I am sure that most of them are a great deal more important to the world. But that does not help my situation. I think this prevents me from being a critic worth considering, as a rule; and it probably makes me at my *worst* when the other writer's lines come too near (as do yours at times): there is liable to be a short circuit, a flash, an explosion – and even a bad smell, one ingredient of which may be mere jealousy. Still, it would be fairer to say of me not that I tend to be imprisoned in my own taste, so much as to be burdened with my own small but peculiar 'message'. In fact, suffering (for a variety of reasons, not all blameworthy) from 'suppressed composition'. Indeed a savage creature, a soreheaded bear (if I can liken myself to anything so large), a painful friend. But God bless you for your goodness. And instead of confessing as sinful the natural and inevitable feeling of pain and its reactions (I am sure never unresisted, and immediately), do me the great generosity of making me a present of the pains I have caused, so that I may share in the good you have put them to.

I do not know if I make myself clear. But I suppose that it is in our power, as members of Christ, to make such gifts effectively. In the simplest case: if a man has stolen something from me, then before God I declare it a gift. That is, of course, a simple way of making use of a wrong, and getting rid of the sting, but that is not the direct object (or it would not be effective); for it seems to me probable that such a gift has effect on the culprit's situation before God, and in any case in any true desire to 'forgive' the desire that that should be so must be present. It would be wonderful when summoned to judgement, to answer innumerable charges of wrongdoing to one's brethren, to find unexpectedly that many were not going to be preferred at all! And indeed that instead one had a share in the good made of one's evil. And no less wonderful for the giver. An eternal interaction of relief and gratitude. (But the culprit must be sorry. Otherwise I suppose in the terrible realms of doom the coals of fire would burn intolerably).

(What happens when the culprit is genuinely repentant, but the sufferer is deeply resentful and witholds all 'forgiveness'? It is a terrible thought, to deter anyone from running the risk of needlessly causing such an 'evil'. Of course, the power of mercy is only delegated and is always exercised with or without cooperation by Higher Authority. But the joys and healing of cooperation must be lost?)

While I was thinking of all this, I came across a passage dealing with the charming relations between G. M. Hopkins and his 'pen-friend' Canon Dixon. Two men starved of 'recognition'. Poor Dixon whose *History of the Church of England* (and whose poems) received but a casual glance, and Hopkins unappreciated in his own order. H. seems clearly to have seen that 'recognition' with some understanding is in this world an essential part of authorship, and the want of it a suffering to be distinguished from (even when mixed with) mere desire for the pleasures of fame and praise. Dixon was rather bowled over by being appreciated by Hopkins; and much moved by Burne-Jones' words (said to H. who quoted them) that 'one works really for the one man who may rise to understand one'. But H. then demurred, perceiving that Burne-Jones' hope can also in this world be frustrated, as easily as general fame: a painter (like Niggle) may work for what the burning of his picture, or an accident of death to the admirer, may wholly destroy. He summed up: The only just literary critic is Christ, who admires more than does any man the gifts He Himself has bestowed. Then let us 'bekenne either other to Crist'. God keep you.

I write only because I find it easier so to say such things as I really want to say. If they are foolish or seem so, I am not present when they fall flat. (My whispering asides are most often due to sheer pusillanimity, and a fear of being laughed at by the general company.)

This requires no answer. But as for yourself: rest in peace, as far as I am any 'critic' of behaviour. At least you are the fautlest freke[1] that I know. 'Loudness' did you say?[2] Nay! That is largely a self-defensive rumour put about by Hugo. If it has any basis (for him), it is but that noise begets noise. We are safe in your presence and presidency from contention, ill will, detraction, or accusations without evidence. Doubtless, as you say, I have as a member of the brotherhood a right to criticize, an[3] I please. But I shall not lightly forget my vision of the wounds; and I shall be deterred from rash dispraise, for myself. Indeed, I do not really think that for any man valuable 'criticism' is usually to be attained hot on the spot: it is then too mixed with mere reaction. Let us *listen* again more patiently. And let me beg of you to bring out OHEL, with no coyness.

But I warn you, if you bore me, I shall take my revenge. (It is an Inkling's duty to be bored willingly. It is his privilege to be a borer on occasion). I sometimes conceive and write other things than verses or romance! And I may come back at you. Indeed, if our beloved and esteemed physician is to pose us with problems of the earth as a dynamo, I can think of other problems as intricate if more petty to present to his notice – if only for the malicious delight of seeing Hugo (if present), slightly heated with alcohol, giving an imitation of the intelligent boy of the class. But Lord save you all! I don't find myself in any need of practising *forbearance* towards any of you – save on the rarest occasions, when I myself am tired and exhausted: then I find mere *noise* and vulgarity trying. But I am not yet so hoar (nor so refined) that that has

128

become a permanent state. I want noise often enough. I know no more pleasant sound than arriving at the B. and B.[4] and hearing a roar, and knowing that one can plunge in.

Yours

J.R.R.T.

As you see, I have delayed nearly a week in sending this. Re-reading it, I do not think it will do any harm. And in any case, I send it lest you shd. think that my recent absences from the Inklings are in any way connected. I have missed three: one because I was desperately tired, the others for domestic reasons – the last because my daughter (bless her! always mindful of Thursdays) was obliged to go out that evening.

114   From a letter to Hugh Brogan   7 April 1948

[Brogan, then a schoolboy, had written to Tolkien praising *The Hobbit* and asking for more information about the world it described.]

I am glad you enjoyed 'the Hobbit'. I have in fact been engaged for ten years on writing another (longer) work about the same world and period of history, in which at any rate all can be learned about the Necromancer and the mines of Moria. Only the difficulty of writing the last chapters, and the shortage of paper have so far prevented its printing. I hope at least to finish it this year, and will certainly let you have advance information. I wrote long ago (and passed the proofs a year ago) another (short) work on a rather different period: *Farmer Giles of Ham*. I don't know what, beyond paper, is holding it up, but it should appear this autumn or winter. But it will not satisfy any curiosity about the older world. I am afraid you would not find any information about that in ordinary works of reference, since I possess all the documents, and publishers won't publish them. What you really require is *The Silmarillion*, which is virtually a history of the Eldalië (or Elves, by a not very accurate translation) from their rise to the Last Alliance, and the first temporary overthrow of Sauron (the Necromancer): that would bring you nearly down to the period of 'The Hobbit'. Also desirable would be some maps, chronological tables, and some elementary information about the Eldarin (or Elvish) languages. I have got all those things, of course, and they are known in a small circle which includes my sons (all once at the Dragon School).[1] If I can find some time and way of reproducing them, or part of them, say in typescript, and you remain interested in this little-explored region of pre-history, I will let you have some of the documents.

129

[Mrs Farrer had apparently expressed a desire to read *The Silmarillion* and related manuscripts.]

15 June [year not given; possibly 1948]   Merton College, Oxford

Dear Mrs Farrer,

I am sorry that I have been so long in replying and so may have seemed ungrateful, when I was really very touched by your kind letter – and also excited. For though I have (in the cracks of time!) laboured at these things since about 1914, I have never found anyone but C.S.L. and my Christopher who wanted to read them; and no one will publish them. I have spent what time I could spare since you wrote in collecting out of the unfinished mass such things as are more or less finished and readable (I mean legible). You may find the 'compendious history' or *Silmarillion* tolerable – though it is only really half-revised.

The long tales out of which it is drawn (by 'Pengolod')[1] are either incomplete or not up to date.

> The Fall of Gondolin
> The Lay of Beren and Lúthien (verse)
> The Children of Húrin

I am distressed (for myself) to be unable to find the 'Rings of Power', which with the 'Fall of Númenor' is the link between the *Silmarillion* and the Hobbit world. But its essentials are included in Ch. II of *The Lord of the Rings*. That book would, of course, be easier to write, if the *Silmarillion* were published first!

I will bring you round some *unique MSS.* some time to-day.

Thank you for your remembrance in prayer.

Yrs sincerely

Ronald Tolkien.

116 From a letter to Allen & Unwin 5 August 1948

[The artist Milein Cosman had been chosen to illustrate *Farmer Giles of Ham,* and the publishers had asked Tolkien for his opinion of some specimen drawings, which Miss Cosman had only provided after many delays.]

I am not for myself much interested in the fashionableness of these drawings, or in their resemblance to Topolski or Ardizzone. I find their lack of resemblance to their text more marked. This is a definitely located story (one of its virtues if it has any): Oxfordshire and Bucks, with a brief excursion into Wales. The places in it are largely named, or fairly plainly indicated. There is no attempt by the illustrator to represent any of this. The incident of the dog and dragon occurs near Rollright, by the way, and though that is not plainly stated at least it clearly takes place in Oxfordshire.

The giant is passable – though the artist is a poor drawer of trees. The dragon is absurd. Ridiculously coy, and quite incapable of performing any of the tasks laid on him by the author. I cannot help wondering why he should be so fatuously looking over his right shoulder SE when an obvious if sketchy dog is going off NW. In defiance of the fact that the dog happily did not come on the head end first, but turned his own tail as soon as he came on the dragon's. The Farmer, a large blusterer bigger than his fellows, is made to look like little Joad at the end of a third degree by railway officials. He would hardly have used as a cowshed the shambling hut at which the miller and parson are knocking. He was a prosperous yeoman or franklin.

I gather you do not share my sentiments. Well, if you think that illustrations of this sort, wholly out of keeping with the style or manner of the text, will do, or will for reasons of contemporary taste be an advantage, I am so far in your hands. But are you ever going to induce Miss C. to impart such finish as will not exhaust her or make her too unhappy – in fact to finish the job? And when do you expect to get this book out?

117   From a letter to Hugh Brogan   31 October 1948

I managed to go into 'retreat' in the summer, and am happy to announce that I succeeded at last in bringing the 'Lord of the Rings' to a successful conclusion. Also, it has been read and approved by Rayner Unwin, who (the original reader of 'The Hobbit') has had time to grow up while the sequel has been made, and is now here at Trinity. I think there is a chance of it being published though it will be a massive book far too large to make any money for the publisher (let alone the author): it must run to 1200 pages. However length is no obstacle to those who like that kind of thing. If only term had not caught me on the hop again, I should have revised the whole – it is astonishingly difficult to avoid mistakes and changes of name and all kinds of inconsistencies of detail in a long work, as critics forget, who have not tried to make one – and sent it to the typists. I hope to do so soon, and can only say that as soon as I have a spare copy you shall have the loan of one, plus a good deal of explanatory matter, alphabets, history, calendars, and genealogies reserved for the real 'fans'. I hope this may be possible soon, so that you could have it during the Christmas holidays; but I cannot promise. This university business of earning one's living by teaching, delivering philological lectures, and daily attendance at 'boards' and other talk-meetings, interferes sadly with serious work.

[A note of Christmas greetings, not dated but possibly written at Christmas 1948. It is in a form of *Angerthas* or dwarf-runes close to that used in *The Lord of the Rings* but not identical, and in two versions of Fëanorian script, the first using *tehtar* (marks above the consonants) to indicate vowels, the second with vowels represented by full letters. For a transcription, see p. 442].

119 From a letter to Allen & Unwin 28 February 1949

I have not time to type [*Farmer Giles*] again, and I don't think it is really necessary. I am finding the labour of typing a fair copy of the 'Lord of the Rings' v. great, and the alternative of having it professionally typed prohibitive in cost. . . . . I believe that after 25 years service I am shortly going to be granted a term of 'sabbatical' leave, partly on medical grounds. If so, I may really finish a few things.

120 From a letter to Allen & Unwin 16 March 1949

[The services of Milein Cosman had now been dispensed with, and
Pauline Baynes had been contracted to illustrate *Farmer Giles of Ham*.]

Miss Baynes' pictures must have reached Merton on Saturday; but
owing to various things I did not see them till yesterday. I merely write
to say that I am pleased with them beyond even the expectations aroused
by the first examples. They are more than illustrations, they are a
collateral theme. I showed them to my friends whose polite comment
was that they reduced my text to a commentary on the drawings.

121 From a letter to Allen & Unwin 13 July 1949

[On the subject of a sequel to *Farmer Giles of Ham*.]

As for further 'legends of the Little Kingdom': I put a reference to one in
the Foreword, in case they should ever come to anything, or a manuscript of the fragmentary legend should come to light. But Georgius and
Suet remains only a sketch, and it is difficult now to recapture the spirit
of the former days, when we used to beat the bounds of the L.K. in an
ancient car. The 'children' now range from 20 to 32. But when I have at
last got the 'Lord of the Rings', of which I have nearly completed a final
fair copy, the released spring may do something.

122 To Naomi Mitchison

[Mrs Mitchison had written in praise of *Farmer Giles of Ham*, which was
published in the autumn of 1949.]

18 December 1949   3 Manor Road, Oxford
Dear Mrs Mitchison,
    It was extremely kind of you to write to me. . . . . As for 'Farmer
Giles' it was I fear written very light-heartedly, originally of a 'no time'
in which blunderbusses or anything might occur. Its slightly donnish
touching up, as read to the Lovelace Soc., and as published, makes the
Blunderbuss rather glaring – though not really worse than all mediæval
treatments of Arthurian matter. But it was too embedded to be changed,
and some people find the anachronisms amusing. I myself could not
forgo the quotation (so very Murrayesque) from the Oxford Dictionary.
Greek Fire must have been more like a flammenwerfer: as used on their
ships it seems to have been quite deadly. But in the Isle of Britain in
archaeological fact there can have been nothing in the least like a
fire-arm. But neither was there fourteenth century armour.

I find 'dragons' a fascinating product of imagination. But I don't think the Beowulf one is frightfully good. But the whole problem of the intrusion of the 'dragon' into northern imagination and its transformation there is one I do not know enough about. Fáfnir in the late Norse versions of the Sigurd-story is better; and Smaug and his conversation obviously is in debt there.

I know Icelandic pretty well (as I should), and a little Welsh, but in spite of efforts I have always been rather heavily defeated by Old Irish, or indeed its modern descendants. The mix-up was politically and culturally great and complex – but it left very little linguistic trace on Icelandic, save in the borrowing of certain names notably Brian and Nial which became used in Iceland. On Irish the influence was more considerable. But in any case names that were at all similar in sound tended to be equated or confused. . . . .

I hope to give you soon two books, about which at least one criticism will be possible: that they are excessively long! One is a sequel to 'The Hobbit' which I have just finished after 12 years (intermittent) labour. I fear it is 3 times as long, not *for* children (though that does not mean wholly unsuitable), and rather grim in places. I *think* it is very much better (in a different way). The other is pure myth and legend of times already remote in Bilbo's days.

Thank you again for writing. I hope the reply is in places legible. With best wishes.

Yours sincerely,
J. R. R. Tolkien.

123 From a draft to Milton Waldman 5 February 1950

[At about the time that he was finishing *The Lord of the Rings*, Tolkien was introduced to Milton Waldman, an editor with the London publisher Collins. Waldman expressed great interest in the new book, and also in *The Silmarillion*, which Tolkien hoped would be published in conjunction with *The Lord of the Rings*. As Allen & Unwin had not accepted *The Silmarillion* when Tolkien offered it to them in 1937, he now believed that he should try to change his publisher; accordingly he showed Waldman those parts of *The Silmarillion* of which there were fair copies. Waldman said he would like to publish it if Tolkien would finish it. Tolkien then showed him *The Lord of the Rings*. Waldman was again enthusiastic, and offered to publish it providing Tolkien had 'no commitment either moral or legal to Allen & Unwin'. The reply that Tolkien sent cannot be traced, but what follows is part of a draft for it.]

I am sorry that the days have slipped by since I got your note. . . . . As soon as I had dumped the MS. [of *The Lord of the Rings*] on you, I felt bad about it: weighing down your holiday with a labour that only an author's egotism could have inflicted at such a time. And examining my conscience I had to confess that – as one who has worked alone in a corner and only had the criticism of a few like-minded friends – I was moved greatly by the desire to hear from a fresh mind whether my labour had any wider value, or was just a fruitless private hobby.

All the same I don't think that in fact I burdened you under false pretences. . . . . I believe myself to have no *legal* obligation to Allen and Unwin, since the clause in *The Hobbit* contract with regard to offering the next book seems to have been satisfied either (a) by their rejection of *The Silmarillion* or (b) by their eventual acceptance and publication of *Farmer Giles*. I should (as you note) be glad to leave them, as I have found them in various ways unsatisfactory. But I have friendly personal relations with Stanley (whom all the same I do not much like) and with his second son Rayner (whom I do like very much). It has always been supposed that I am writing a sequel to *The Hobbit*. Rayner has read most of *The Lord of the Rings* and likes it – as a small boy he read the MS. of *The Hobbit*. Sir Stanley has long been aware that *The Lord of the Rings* has outgrown its function, and is not pleased since he sees no money in it for anyone (so he said); but he is anxious to see the final result all the same. If this constitutes a moral obligation then I have one: at least to explain the situation. Did I say something of all this in my letter of Dec. 13th? I certainly meant to. However, I certainly shall try to extricate myself, or at least the *Silmarillion* and all its kin, from the dilatory coils of A. and U. if I can – in a friendly fashion if possible.

124   To Sir Stanley Unwin

[Allen & Unwin had passed on a reader's enquiry as to whether Tolkien had written an 'Authentic History of Faery'.]

24 February 1950   Merton College, Oxford

Dear Unwin,

I am, I fear, a most unsatisfactory person. I am at present 'on leave', and away off and on; though the effort to cope with a mass of literary and 'learned' debts, that my leave was supposed to assist, has proved too much for me, especially as I have been troubled with my throat and have felt often far from well.

But at any rate I should long ago have answered your query, handed on from Mr Selby. Though dated Jan. 31st, it was in fact addressed to me on Dec. 31st.

I cannot imagine and have not discovered what Mr Selby was referring to. I have, of course, not written an 'Authentic history of Faery' (and should not in any case have chosen such a title); nor have I caused any prophecy or rumour of any such work to be circulated. I must suppose that Mr Selby associates me with 'Faery', and has attached my name to someone else's work It seems hardly likely that he can have come across some literary chat (of which in any case I am ignorant) in which somebody has referred to my *Silmarillion* (long ago rejected, and shelved). The title is not particularly fitting, and the work has been read in MS. only by about five persons, counting two of my children and your reader.

That, however, brings me to a more important topic (to me at any rate). In one of your more recent letters you expressed a desire still to see the MS. of my proposed work, *The Lord of the Rings*, originally expected to be a sequel to *The Hobbit*. For eighteen months now I have been hoping for the day when I could call it finished. But it was not until after Christmas that this goal was reached at last. It is finished, if still partly unrevised, and is, I suppose, in a condition which a reader could read, if he did not wilt at the sight of it.

As the estimate for typing a fair copy was in the neighbourhood of £100 (which I have not to spare), I was obliged to do nearly all myself. And now I look at it, the magnitude of the disaster is apparent to me. My work has escaped from my control, and I have produced a monster: an immensely long, complex, rather bitter, and very terrifying romance, quite unfit for children (if fit for anybody); and it is not really a sequel to *The Hobbit*, but to *The Silmarillion*. My estimate is that it contains, even without certain necessary adjuncts, about 600,000 words. One typist put it higher. I can see only too clearly how impracticable this is. But I am tired. It is off my chest, and I do not feel that I can do anything more about it, beyond a little revision of inaccuracies. Worse still: I feel that it is tied to the *Silmarillion*.

You may, perhaps, remember about that work, a long legendary of imaginary times in a 'high style', and full of Elves (of a sort). It was rejected on the advice of your reader many years ago. As far as my memory goes he allowed to it a kind of Celtic beauty intolerable to Anglo-Saxons in large doses. He was probably perfectly right and just. And you commented that it was a work to be drawn upon rather than published.

Unfortunately I am not an Anglo-Saxon and though shelved (until a year ago), the *Silmarillion* and all that has refused to be suppressed. It has bubbled up, infiltrated, and probably spoiled everything (that even remotely approached 'Faery') which I have tried to write since. It was kept out of *Farmer Giles* with an effort, but stopped the continuation. Its shadow was deep on the later parts of *The Hobbit*. It has captured *The Lord of the Rings*, so that that has become simply its continuation

136

and completion, requiring the *Silmarillion* to be fully intelligible – without a lot of references and explanations that clutter it in one or two places.

Ridiculous and tiresome as you may think me, I want to publish them both – *The Silmarillion* and *The Lord of the Rings* – in conjunction or in connexion. 'I want to' – it would be wiser to say 'I should like to', since a little packet of, say, a million words, [1] of matter set out in extenso that Anglo-Saxons (or the English-speaking public) can only endure in moderation, is not very likely to see the light, even if paper were available at will.

All the same that is what I should like. Or I will let it all be. I cannot contemplate any drastic re-writing or compression. Of course being a writer I should like to see my words printed; but there they are. For me the chief thing is that I feel that the whole matter is now 'exorcized', and rides me no more. I can turn now to other things, such as perhaps the Little Kingdom of the Wormings, [2] or to quite other matters and stories.

I am sorry that this letter is so long, and so full of myself. I am not really filled with any overweening conceit of my absurd private hobbies. But you have been very patient – expecting during the long years a sequel to *The Hobbit*, to fit a similar audience; though I know that you are aware that I have been going off the rails. I owe you some kind of explanation.

You will let me know what you think. You can have all this mountain of stuff, if you wish. It will take a reader who really reads a long time, I fear; though he may make up his mind with a sample. But I shall not have any just grievance (nor shall I be dreadfully surprised) if you decline so obviously unprofitable a proposition; and ask me to hurry up and submit some more reasonable book as soon as I can.

Yours sincerely

J. R. R. Tolkien.

P.S. Rayner, poor man, has of course read a large part of *The Lord of the Rings*, though not to the bitter end: I only finished the last 'book' quite recently. I hope he is prospering. How is little *Farmer Giles* doing, I wonder?

JRRT.

125 To Sir Stanley Unwin

[Unwin replied on 6 March, asking if the problem of the combined length of the two books might be solved by splitting them into 'three or four to some extent self-contained volumes'. In response to Tolkien's enquiry about *Farmer Giles of Ham,* he reported that, out of the first printing of

10 March 1950   3 Manor Road, Oxford

Dear Unwin,

Thank you for your letter of March 6th. I see in it your good will; but also, I fear, your opinion that this mass of stuff is not really a publisher's affair at all, but requires an endowment. I am not surprised.

With regard to your enquiry about its divisibility. A work of great length can, of course, be divided up artificially into more handy bulks: the sort of process that produced sections of the big Oxford Dictionary labelled 'ONOMASTICAL – OUTING' and 'SIMPLE TO SLEEP'. But the whole Saga of the Three Jewels and the Rings of Power has only one natural division into two parts (each of about 600,000 words): *The Silmarillion* and other legends; and *The Lord of the Rings*. The latter is as indivisible and unified as I could make it.

It is, of course, divided into sections for narrative purposes (six of them), and two or three of these, which are of more or less equal length, could be bound separately, but they are not in any sense self-contained.

I now wonder (I must confess, though as a 'seller' I suppose I should show more confidence) whether many beyond my friends, not all of whom have endured to the end, would read anything so long, even if they liked that kind of thing in moderation. I wonder still more if they would read, not to mention purchase, it serially, and if the pot, as it were, went off the boil. You must know much more about that than I do.

I realise the financial difficulties, and the remote chance of recovering the great cost. I have no money to sink in the bog, and I can hardly expect you to sink it. Please do not think that I shall feel that I have a just grievance if you decline to become involved, without much hesitation. After all the understanding was that you would welcome a sequel to *The Hobbit*, and this work can not be regarded as such in any practical sense, or in the matter of atmosphere, tone, or audience addressed.

I am sorry that I presented such a problem. Wilfully, it may seem, since I knew long ago that I was courting trouble and producing the unprintable and unsaleable, most likely. I have not at the moment anything else completed to submit; but I am quite prepared to make something simpler and shorter soon. I feel, at the end of my leave of absence, a return of energy, and when the present time of trial is over (the process of removing all my teeth began yesterday, and that of removing my household goods begins shortly) I hope to feel still more. I think I shall soon put in hand other things long *in petto*.

All the same it would have been more encouraging if *Farmer Giles* could report better of his luck. Rather a donnish little squib after all? I cannot discover that he has been widely heard of. He does not seem to have been very forcibly brought to notice.

I always thought, that in so far as he has virtue, it would have been improved by other stories of the same kingdom and style; but the domination of the remoter world was so great that I could not make them. It may now prove different.

With best wishes,
Yours sincerely,
J. R. R. Tolkien.

126 To Milton Waldman (draft)

10 March 1950   3 Manor Road, Oxford

Dear Waldman,

Sir Stanley Unwin has at length replied personally. The pertinent paragraph is:

'Your letter has indeed set us a problem! It would not have been easy to solve before the War; it is much more difficult now with costs of production about three times what they were then. In order to see more precisely what is involved would you tell us whether there is any possibility of breaking the million words into, say, three or four to some extent self-contained volumes. You may perhaps remember that when we published Murasaki's great work *The Tale of Genji*, we started by issuing it in six separate volumes, each under a different title, though the first four were, of course, all the Tale of Gengi, and the last two were more about his son.'

I have replied to the effect that I see in his letter his good will, but also perceive his opinion that this mass of stuff is not suitable for ordinary publication and requires endowment. (I had in my letter made a strong point that the *Silmarillion* etc. and *The Lord of the Rings* went together, as one long Saga of the Jewels and the Rings, and that I was resolved to treat them as one thing, however they might formally be issued.) I noted that the mass naturally divides only between *The Silmarillion* and *The Lord* (each about 600,000 words), but that the latter is not divisible except into artificial fragments. I added that I shall not be surprised if he declines to become involved in this monstrous Saga; and that now it is off my chest, I am very willing to turn out something simpler and shorter (and even actually 'juvenile') for him, soon.

There at the moment the matter waits. I profoundly hope that he will let go without demanding the MS. and two months for 'reading'. But I am not sanguine. But time runs short. I shall soon be plunged back into business – I already am involved, as I find things getting very out of hand during my absence; and I shall not be free again for writing until I return from Ireland at the beginning of July.

Unwin tells me that *Farmer Giles* has only sold 2000 copies. I have replied that I have observed no advertisements. . . .

With best wishes.

Yours sincerely

J. R. R. Tolkien.

I move to 99 Holywell,[1] but the date is uncertain, as the house needs a lot of repair. I hope but hardly expect to be settled before St George's Day. Merton will always find me. JRRT.

127 To Sir Stanley Unwin

[On 3 April, just as Tolkien had sent him a note requesting a reply to his letter of 10 March, Unwin wrote to say that he had asked the opinion of his son Rayner, who was now studying in America, at Harvard University. He enclosed Rayner's comments, though they were not really intended for Tolkien's eyes. Rayner Unwin wrote: '*The Lord of the Rings* is a very great book in its own curious way and deserves to be produced somehow. *I* never felt the lack of a *Silmarillion* when reading it. . . . . Surely this is a case for an editor who would incorporate any *really* relevant material from *The Silmarillion* into *The Lord of the Rings*. . . . . If this is not workable I would say publish *The Lord of the Rings* as a prestige book, and after having a second look at it, drop *The Silmarillion*.']

14 April 1950   3 Manor Road, Oxford

Dear Unwin,

It was odd that our letters crossed. I might have waited a day longer; but the matter is for me becoming urgent. Weeks have become precious. I want a decision yes, or no: to the proposal I made, and not to any imagined possibilities.

Your letters[1] were, as always, very kind; though I was puzzled by the first, and its enclosure of an extract from a letter of Rayner's. This was not, as you remarked, intended for me; which made it all the more interesting to me (and I do not refer to the compliment that it contained). The puzzling thing was that it seemed unsuitable for my eye (from your point of view); and I wonder precisely why you sent it to me.

My present conclusion is that you are in general agreement with Rayner, and thought that letting me see his advice was a good way of telling me what is the most I can hope for – since he is about as favourable a critic as I am likely to get. But I should like to be sure.

The kick is plainly in the last sentence of the excerpt (before the remembrance to me): 'If this is not workable, etc.' This is surely to reveal policy a little nakedly. Also it shows a surprising failure to understand the situation, or my letter. But I will say no more until I hear from you. . . . .[2]

Yours sincerely,
J. R. R. Tolkien.

128   From a letter to Allen & Unwin   1 August 1950

[Following Tolkien's ultimatum, Sir Stanley Unwin replied: 'As you demand an *immediate* "yes" or "no" the answer is "no"; but it might well have been yes given adequate time and the sight of the complete typescript.' The matter rested there for the time being. In July, Allen & Unwin sent Tolkien the proofs of a new edition of *The Hobbit*, incorporating minor corrections to the text, and – much to Tolkien's surprise – substituting, for the original, the new version of part of Chapter V, 'Riddles in the Dark', which he had sent them in 1947 merely as 'a specimen of re-writing' (see no. 111), and which he had not necessarily intended for publication.]

The Hobbit: I return the proofs herewith. They did not require much correction, but did need some consideration. The thing took me much by surprise. It is now a long while since I sent in the proposed alteration of Chapter V, and tentatively suggested the slight remodelling of the original *Hobbit*.[1] I was then still engaged in trying to fit on the sequel, which would have been a simpler task with the alteration, besides saving most of a chapter in that over-long work. However, I never heard any more about it at all; and I assumed that alteration of the original book was ruled out. The sequel now depends on the earlier version; and if the revision is really published, there must follow some considerable rewriting of the sequel.

I must say that I could wish that I had had some hint that (in any circumstances) this change might be made, before it burst on me in page-proof. However, I have now made up my mind to accept the change and its consequences. The thing is now old enough for me to take a fairly impartial view, and it seems to me that the revised version is in itself better, in motive and narrative – and certainly would make the sequel (if ever published) much more natural.

I did not mean the suggested revision to be printed off; but it seems to have come out pretty well in the wash.

129 From a letter to Sir Stanley Unwin 10 September 1950

[Allen & Unwin asked Tolkien to supply a 'precise wording' for a note in the new edition of *The Hobbit* which would explain the changes in the new text.]

Well, there it is: the alteration is now made, and cannot, I suppose, be unmade. Such people as I have consulted think that the alteration is in itself an improvement (apart from the question of a sequel). That is something. But when I tried to consider 'a precise wording' for a note on the revision in an English edition, I did not find the matter as simple as I had thought.

I have now on my hands two printed versions of a crucial incident. Either the first must be regarded as washed out, a mere miswriting that ought never to have seen the light; or the story as a whole must take into account the existence of two versions and use it. The former was my original simpleminded intention, though it is a bit awkward (since the Hobbit is fairly widely known in its older form) if the literary pretence of historicity and dependence on record is to be maintained. The second can be done convincingly (I think), but not briefly explained in a note.

In the former case, or in doubt, the only thing to do, I fancy, is just to say nothing. I am in doubt, so I propose at the moment just to say nothing; though I do not like it. There is, in any case, I take it, no question of inserting a note into the American reprint. And you will no doubt warn me in good time when an English one becomes necessary.

In the meanwhile I send you a specimen of the kind of thing that I should want to insert in an altered reprint – if I decide to recognise two versions of the Ring-finding as part of the authentic tradition. This is not intended as copy; but if you would return it, with any comment you like, it would be helpful.

130 From a letter to Sir Stanley Unwin 14 September 1950

[Further consideration led Tolkien to decide that an explanatory note would definitely be needed in the new edition.]

I have decided to accept the existence of both versions of Chapter Five, so far as the sequel goes – though I have no time at the moment to rewrite that at the required points. I enclose, therefore, a copy of the briefest form of the prefatory note: which is intended as copy, if you should think it well to use it in the reprint.[1]

[After Allen & Unwin, under pressure from Tolkien to make up their minds, had reluctantly declined to publish *The Lord of the Rings* together with *The Silmarillion*, Tolkien was confident that Milton Waldman of Collins would shortly issue both books under his firm's imprint. In the spring of 1950, Waldman told Tolkien that he hoped to begin typesetting the following autumn. But there were delays, largely caused by Waldman's frequent absences in Italy and his ill-health. By the latter part of 1951 no definite arrangements for publication had yet been made, and Collins were becoming anxious about the combined length of both books. It was apparently at Waldman's suggestion that Tolkien wrote the following letter – of which the full text is some ten thousand words long – with the intention of demonstrating that *The Lord of the Rings* and *The Silmarillion* were interdependent and indivisible. The letter, which interested Waldman so much that he had a typed copy made (see the end of no. 137), is not dated, but was probably written late in 1951.]

My dear Milton,

You asked for a brief sketch of my stuff that is connected with my imaginary world. It is difficult to say anything without saying too much: the attempt to say a few words opens a floodgate of excitement, the egoist and artist at once desires to say how the stuff has grown, what it is like, and what (he thinks) he means or is trying to represent by it all. I shall inflict some of this on you; but I will append a mere resume of its contents: which is (may be) all that you want or will have use or time for.

In order of time, growth and composition, this stuff began with me – though I do not suppose that that is of much interest to anyone but myself. I mean, I do not remember a time when I was not building it. Many children make up, or begin to make up, imaginary languages. I have been at it since I could write. But I have never stopped, and of course, as a professional philologist (especially interested in linguistic aesthetics), I have changed in taste, improved in theory, and probably in craft. Behind my stories is now a nexus of languages (mostly only structurally sketched). But to those creatures which in English I call misleadingly Elves* are assigned two related languages more nearly completed, whose history is written, and whose forms (representing two different sides of my own linguistic taste) are deduced scientifically from a common origin. Out of these languages are made nearly all the *names* that appear in my legends. This gives a certain character (a cohesion, a consistency of linguistic style, and an illusion of historicity) to the nomenclature, or so I believe, that is markedly lacking in other

---

*Intending the word to be understood in its ancient meanings, which continued as late as Spenser – a murrain on Will Shakespeare and his damned cobwebs.

comparable things. Not all will feel this as important as I do, since I am cursed by acute sensibility in such matters.

But an equally basic passion of mine *ab initio* was for myth (not allegory!) and for fairy-story, and above all for heroic legend on the brink of fairy-tale and history, of which there is far too little in the world (accessible to me) for my appetite. I was an undergraduate before thought and experience revealed to me that these were not divergent interests – opposite poles of science and romance – but integrally related. I am *not* 'learned'* in the matters of myth and fairy-story, however, for in such things (as far as known to me) I have always been seeking material, things of a certain tone and air, and not simple knowledge. Also – and here I hope I shall not sound absurd – I was from early days grieved by the poverty of my own beloved country: it had no stories of its own (bound up with its tongue and soil), not of the quality that I sought, and found (as an ingredient) in legends of other lands. There was Greek, and Celtic, and Romance, Germanic, Scandinavian, and Finnish (which greatly affected me); but nothing English, save impoverished chap-book stuff. Of course there was and is all the Arthurian world, but powerful as it is, it is imperfectly naturalized, associated with the soil of Britain but not with English; and does not replace what I felt to be missing. For one thing its 'faerie' is too lavish, and fantastical, incoherent and repetitive. For another and more important thing: it is involved in, and explicitly contains the Christian religion.

For reasons which I will not elaborate, that seems to me fatal. Myth and fairy-story must, as all art, reflect and contain in solution elements of moral and religious truth (or error), but not explicit, not in the known form of the primary 'real' world. (I am speaking, of course, of our present situation, not of ancient pagan, pre-Christian days. And I will not repeat what I tried to say in my essay, which you read.)

Do not laugh! But once upon a time (my crest has long since fallen) I had a mind to make a body of more or less connected legend, ranging from the large and cosmogonic, to the level of romantic fairy-story – the larger founded on the lesser in contact with the earth, the lesser drawing splendour from the vast backcloths – which I could dedicate simply to: to England; to my country. It should possess the tone and quality that I desired, somewhat cool and clear, be redolent of our 'air' (the clime and soil of the North West, meaning Britain and the hither parts of Europe: not Italy or the Aegean, still less the East), and, while possessing (if I could achieve it) the fair elusive beauty that some call Celtic (though it is rarely found in genuine ancient Celtic things), it should be 'high', purged of the gross, and fit for the more adult mind of a land long now

*Though I have thought *about* them a good deal.

steeped in poetry. I would draw some of the great tales in fullness, and leave many only placed in the scheme, and sketched. The cycles should be linked to a majestic whole, and yet leave scope for other minds and hands, wielding paint and music and drama. Absurd.

Of course, such an overweening purpose did not develop all at once. The mere stories were the thing. They arose in my mind as 'given' things, and as they came, separately, so too the links grew. An absorbing, though continually interrupted labour (especially since, even apart from the necessities of life, the mind would wing to the other pole and spend itself on the linguistics): yet always I had the sense of recording what was already 'there', somewhere: not of 'inventing'.

Of course, I made up and even wrote lots of other things (especially for my children). Some escaped from the grasp of this branching acquisitive theme, being ultimately and radically unrelated: *Leaf by Niggle* and *Farmer Giles*, for instance, the only two that have been printed. *The Hobbit*, which has much more essential life in it, was quite independently conceived: I did not know as I began it that it belonged. But it proved to be the discovery of the completion of the whole, its mode of descent to earth, and merging into 'history'. As the high Legends of the beginning are supposed to look at things through Elvish minds, so the middle tale of the Hobbit takes a virtually human point of view – and the last tale blends them.

I dislike Allegory – the conscious and intentional allegory – yet any attempt to explain the purport of myth or fairytale must use allegorical language. (And, of course, the more 'life' a story has the more readily will it be susceptible of allegorical interpretations: while the better a deliberate allegory is made the more nearly will it be acceptable just as a story.) Anyway all this stuff* is mainly concerned with Fall, Mortality, and the Machine. With Fall inevitably, and that motive occurs in several modes. With Mortality, especially as it affects art and the creative (or as I should say, sub-creative) desire which seems to have no biological function, and to be apart from the satisfactions of plain ordinary biological life, with which, in our world, it is indeed usually at strife. This desire is at once wedded to a passionate love of the real primary world, and hence filled with the sense of mortality, and yet unsatisfied by it. It has various opportunities of 'Fall'. It may become possessive, clinging to the things made as 'its own', the sub-creator wishes to be the Lord and God of his private creation. He will rebel against the laws of the Creator – especially against mortality. Both of these (alone or together) will lead to the desire for Power, for making the will more quickly effective, – and so to the Machine (or Magic). By the last I intend all use

---

*It is, I suppose, fundamentally concerned with the problem of the relation of Art (and Sub-creation) and Primary Reality.

of external plans or devices (apparatus) instead of development of the inherent inner powers or talents – or even the use of these talents with the corrupted motive of dominating: bulldozing the real world, or coercing other wills. The Machine is our more obvious modern form though more closely related to Magic than is usually recognised.

I have not used 'magic' consistently, and indeed the Elven-queen Galadriel is obliged to remonstrate with the Hobbits on their confused use of the word both for the devices and operations of the Enemy, and for those of the Elves. I have not, because there is not a word for the latter (since all human stories have suffered the same confusion). But the Elves are there (in my tales) to demonstrate the difference. Their 'magic' is Art, delivered from many of its human limitations: more effortless, more quick, more complete (product, and vision in unflawed correspondence). And its object is Art not Power, sub-creation not domination and tyrannous re-forming of Creation. The 'Elves' are 'immortal', at least as far as this world goes: and hence are concerned rather with the griefs and burdens of deathlessness in time and change, than with death. The Enemy in successive forms is always 'naturally' concerned with sheer Domination, and so the Lord of magic and machines; but the problem: that this frightful evil can and does arise from an apparently good root, the desire to benefit the world and others* – speedily and according to the benefactor's own plans – is a recurrent motive.

The cycles begin with a cosmogonical myth: the *Music of the Ainur*. God and the Valar (or powers: Englished as gods) are revealed. These latter are as we should say angelic powers, whose function is to exercise delegated authority in their spheres (of rule and government, *not* creation, making or re-making). They are 'divine', that is, were originally 'outside' and existed 'before' the making of the world. Their power and wisdom is derived from their Knowledge of the cosmogonical drama, which they perceived first as a drama (that is as in a fashion we perceive a story composed by some-one else), and later as a 'reality'. On the side of mere narrative device, this is, of course, meant to provide beings of the same order of beauty, power, and majesty as the 'gods' of higher mythology, which can yet be accepted – well, shall we say baldly, by a mind that believes in the Blessed Trinity.

It moves then swiftly to the *History of the Elves*, or the *Silmarillion* proper; to the world as we perceive it, but of course transfigured in a still half-mythical mode: that is it deals with rational incarnate creatures of

*Not in the Beginner of Evil: his was a sub-creative Fall, and hence the Elves (the representatives of sub-creation par excellence) were peculiarly his enemies, and the special object of his desire and hate – and open to his deceits. Their Fall is into possessiveness and (to a less degree) into perversion of their art to power.

more or less comparable stature with our own. The Knowledge of the Creation Drama was incomplete: incomplete in each individual 'god', and incomplete if all the knowledge of the pantheon were pooled. For (partly to redress the evil of the rebel Melkor, partly for the completion of all in an ultimate finesse of detail) the Creator had not revealed all. The making, and nature, of the Children of God, were the two chief secrets. All that the gods knew was that they would come, at appointed times. The Children of God are thus primevally related and akin, and primevally different. Since also they are something wholly 'other' to the gods, in the making of which the gods played no part, they are the object of the special desire and love of the gods. These are the *First-born*, the Elves; and the *Followers* Men. The doom of the Elves is to be immortal, to love the beauty of the world, to bring it to full flower with their gifts of delicacy and perfection, to last while it lasts, never leaving it even when 'slain', but returning – and yet, when the Followers come, to teach them, and make way for them, to 'fade' as the Followers grow and absorb the life from which both proceed. The Doom (or the Gift) of Men is mortality, freedom from the circles of the world. Since the point of view of the whole cycle is the Elvish, mortality is not explained mythically: it is a mystery of God of which no more is known than that 'what God has purposed for Men is hidden': a grief and an envy to the immortal Elves.

As I say, the legendary *Silmarillion* is peculiar, and differs from all similar things that I know in not being anthropocentric. Its centre of view and interest is not Men but 'Elves'. Men came in inevitably: after all the author is a man, and if he has an audience they will be Men and Men must come in to our tales, as such, and not merely transfigured or partially represented as Elves, Dwarfs, Hobbits, etc. But they remain peripheral – late comers, and however growingly important, not principals.

In the cosmogony there is a fall: a fall of Angels we should say. Though quite different in form, of course, to that of Christian myth. These tales are 'new', they are not directly derived from other myths and legends, but they must inevitably contain a large measure of ancient wide-spread motives or elements. After all, I believe that legends and myths are largely made of 'truth', and indeed present aspects of it that can only be received in this mode; and long ago certain truths and modes of this kind were discovered and must always reappear. There cannot be any 'story' without a fall – all stories are ultimately about the fall – at least not for human minds as we know them and have them.

So, proceeding, the Elves have a fall, before their 'history' can become storial. (The first fall of Man, for reasons explained, nowhere appears – Men do not come on the stage until all that is long past, and there is only

147

a rumour that for a while they fell under the domination of the Enemy and that some repented.) The main body of the tale, the *Silmarillion* proper, is about the fall of the most gifted kindred of the Elves, their exile from Valinor (a kind of Paradise, the home of the Gods) in the furthest West, their re-entry into Middle-earth, the land of their birth but long under the rule of the Enemy, and their strife with him, the power of Evil still visibly incarnate. It receives its name because the events are all threaded upon the fate and significance of the *Silmarilli* ('radiance of pure light') or Primeval Jewels. By the making of gems the sub-creative function of the Elves is chiefly symbolized, but the Silmarilli were more than just beautiful things as such. There was Light. There was the Light of Valinor made visible in the Two Trees of Silver and Gold.* These were slain by the Enemy out of malice, and Valinor was darkened, though from them, ere they died utterly, were derived the lights of Sun and Moon. (A marked difference here between these legends and most others is that the Sun is not a divine symbol, but a second-best thing, and the 'light of the Sun' (the world under the sun) become terms for a fallen world, and a dislocated imperfect vision).

But the chief artificer of the Elves (Fëanor) had imprisoned the Light of Valinor in the three supreme jewels, the Silmarilli, before the Trees were sullied or slain. This Light thus lived thereafter only in these gems. The fall of the Elves comes about through the possessive attitude of Fëanor and his seven sons to these gems. They are captured by the Enemy, set in his Iron Crown, and guarded in his impenetrable stronghold. The sons of Fëanor take a terrible and blasphemous oath of enmity and vengeance against all or any, even of the gods, who dares to claim any part or right in the Silmarilli. They pervert the greater part of their kindred, who rebel against the gods, and depart from paradise, and go to make hopeless war upon the Enemy. The first fruit of their fall is war in Paradise, the slaying of Elves by Elves, and this and their evil oath dogs all their later heroism, generating treacheries and undoing all victories. *The Silmarillion* is the history of the War of the Exiled Elves against the Enemy, which all takes place in the North-west of the world (Middle-earth). Several tales of victory and tragedy are caught up in it; but it ends with catastrophe, and the passing of the Ancient World, the world of the long *First Age*. The jewels are recovered (by the final intervention of the gods) only to be lost for ever to the Elves, one in the sea, one in the deeps

---

*As far as all this has symbolical or allegorical significance, Light is such a primeval symbol in the nature of the Universe, that it can hardly be analysed. The Light of Valinor (derived from light before any fall) is the light of art undivorced from reason, that sees hings both scientifically (or philosophically) and imaginatively (or subcreatively) and says that they are good' – as beautiful. The Light of Sun (or Moon) is derived from the Trees only after they were sullied by Evil.

148

of earth, and one as a star of heaven. This legendarium ends with a vision of the end of the world, its breaking and remaking, and the recovery of the Silmarilli and the 'light before the Sun' – after a final battle which owes, I suppose, more to the Norse vision of Ragnarök than to anything else, though it is not much like it.

As the stories become less mythical, and more like stories and romances, Men are interwoven. For the most part these are 'good Men' – families and their chiefs who rejecting the service of Evil, and hearing rumours of the Gods of the West and the High Elves, flee westward and come into contact with the Exiled Elves in the midst of their war. The Men who appear are mainly those of the Three Houses of the Fathers of them, whose chieftains become allies of the Elflords. The contact of Men and Elves already foreshadows the history of the later Ages, and a recurrent theme is the idea that in Men (as they now are) there is a strand of 'blood' and inheritance, derived from the Elves, and that the art and poetry of Men is largely dependent on it, or modified by it.* There are thus two marriages of mortal and elf – both later coalescing in the kindred of Earendil, represented by Elrond the Half-elven who appears in all the stories, even *The Hobbit*. The chief of the stories of the *Silmarillion*, and the one most fully treated is the *Story of Beren and Lúthien the Elfmaiden*.† Here we meet, among other things, the first example of the motive (to become dominant in Hobbits) that the great policies of world history, 'the wheels of the world', are often turned not by the Lords and Governors, even gods, but by the seemingly unknown and weak – owing to the secret life in creation, and the part unknowable to all wisdom but One, that resides in the intrusions of the Children of God into the Drama. It is Beren the outlawed mortal who succeeds (with the help of Lúthien, a mere maiden even if an elf of royalty) where all the armies and warriors have failed: he penetrates the stronghold of the Enemy and wrests one of the Silmarilli from the Iron Crown. Thus he wins the hand of Lúthien and the first marriage of mortal and immortal is achieved.

As such the story is (I think a beautiful and powerful) heroic-fairy-romance, receivable in itself with only a very general vague knowledge of the background. But it is also a fundamental link in the cycle, deprived of its full significance out of its place therein. For the capture of the Silmaril, a supreme victory, leads to disaster. The oath of the sons of Fëanor becomes operative, and lust for the Silmaril brings all the kingdoms of the Elves to ruin.

---

*Of course in reality this only means that my 'elves' are only a representation or an apprehension of a part of human nature, but that is not the legendary mode of talking.

†It exists indeed as a poem of considerable length, of which the prose version in *The Silmarillion* is only a reduced version.[1]

There are other stories almost equally full in treatment, and equally independent and yet linked to the general history. There is the *Children of Húrin*, the tragic tale of Túrin Turambar and his sister Níniel – of which Túrin is the hero: a figure that might be said (by people who like that sort of thing, though it is not very useful) to be derived from elements in Sigurd the Volsung, Oedipus, and the Finnish Kullervo. There is the *Fall of Gondolin*: the chief Elvish stronghold. And the tale, or tales, of *Earendil the Wanderer*.* He is important as the person who brings the Silmarillion to its end, and as providing in his offspring the main links to and persons in the tales of later Ages. His function, as a representative of both Kindreds, Elves and Men, is to find a sea-passage back to the Land of the Gods, and as ambassador persuade them to take thought again for the Exiles, to pity them, and rescue them from the Enemy. His wife Elwing descends from Lúthien and still possesses the Silmaril. But the curse still works, and Earendil's home is destroyed by the sons of Feanor. But this provides the solution: Elwing casting herself into the Sea to save the Jewel comes to Earendil, and with the power of the great Gem they pass at last to Valinor, and accomplish their errand – at the cost of never being allowed to return or dwell again with Elves or Men. The gods then move again, and great power comes out of the West, and the Stronghold of the Enemy is destroyed; and he himself [is] thrust out of the World into the Void, never to reappear there in incarnate form again. The remaining two Silmarils are regained from the Iron Crown – only to be lost. The last two sons of Fëanor, compelled by their oath, steal them, and are destroyed by them, casting themselves into the sea, and the pits of the earth. The ship of Earendil adorned with the last Silmaril is set in heaven as the brightest star. So ends *The Silmarillion* and the tales of the First Age.

The next cycle deals (or would deal) with the Second Age. But it is on Earth a dark age, and not very much of its history is (or need be) told. In the great battles against the First Enemy the lands were broken and ruined, and the West of Middle-earth became desolate. We learn that the Exiled Elves were, if not commanded, at least sternly counselled to return into the West, and there be at peace. They were not to dwell permanently in Valinor again, but in the Lonely Isle of Eressëa within sight of the Blessed Realm. The Men of the Three Houses were rewarded for their valour and faithful alliance, by being allowed to dwell 'western-

---

*His name is in actual origin Anglo-Saxon: *earendel* 'ray of light' applied sometimes to the morning-star, a name of ramified mythological connexions (now largely obscure). But that is a mere 'learned note'. In fact his name is Elvish signifying the Great Mariner or Sea-lover.

most of all mortals', in the great 'Atlantis' isle of *Númenóre*.* The doom or gift of God, of mortality, the gods of course cannot abrogate, but the Númenóreans have a great span of life. They set sail and leave Middle-earth, and establish a great kingdom of mariners just within furthest sight of Eressëa (but not of Valinor). Most of the High Elves depart also back into the West. Not all. Some Men akin to the Númenóreans remain in the land not far from the shores of the Sea. Some of the Exiles will not return, or delay their return (for the way west is ever open to the immortals and in the Grey Havens ships are ever ready to sail away for ever). Also the Orcs (goblins) and other monsters bred by the First Enemy are not wholly destroyed. And there is *Sauron*. In the *Silmarillion* and Tales of the First Age Sauron was a being of Valinor perverted to the service of the Enemy and becoming his chief captain and servant. He repents in fear when the First Enemy is utterly defeated, but in the end does not do as was commanded, return to the judgement of the gods. He lingers in Middle-earth. Very slowly, beginning with fair motives: the reorganising and rehabilitation of the ruin of Middle-earth, 'neglected by the gods', he becomes a reincarnation of Evil, and a thing lusting for Complete Power – and so consumed ever more fiercely with hate (especially of gods and Elves). All through the twilight of the Second Age the Shadow is growing in the East of Middle-earth, spreading its sway more and more over Men – who multiply as the Elves begin to fade. The three main themes are thus The Delaying Elves that lingered in Middle-earth; Sauron's growth to a new Dark Lord, master and god of Men; and Numenor-Atlantis. They are dealt with annalistically, and in two Tales or Accounts, *The Rings of Power* and the *Downfall of Númenor*. Both are the essential background to *The Hobbit* and its sequel.

In the first we see a sort of second fall or at least 'error' of the Elves. There was nothing wrong essentially in their lingering against counsel, still sadly with[3] the mortal lands of their old heroic deeds. But they wanted to have their cake without eating it. They wanted the peace and bliss and perfect memory of 'The West', and yet to remain on the ordinary earth where their prestige as the highest people, above wild Elves, dwarves, and Men, was greater than at the bottom of the hierarchy of Valinor. They thus became obsessed with 'fading', the mode in which the changes of time (the law of the world under the sun) was perceived by them. They became sad, and their art (shall we say) antiquarian, and their efforts all really a kind of embalming – even though they also retained the old motive of their kind, the adornment of earth, and the

---

*A name that Lewis derives from me and cannot be restrained from using, and mis-spelling as Numinor. Númenóre means in 'Elvish' simply Westernesse or Land in the West, and is not related to *numen* numinous, or νούμενον![2]

healing of its hurts. We hear of a lingering kingdom, in the extreme North-west more or less in what was left in the old lands of *The Silmarillion*, under Gilgalad; and of other settlements, such as Imladris (Rivendell) near Elrond; and a great one at Eregion at the Western feet of the Misty Mountains, adjacent to the Mines of Moria, the major realm of the Dwarves in the Second Age. There arose a friendship between the usually hostile folk (of Elves and Dwarves) for the first and only time, and smithcraft reached its highest development. But many of the Elves listened to Sauron. He was still fair in that early time, and his motives and those of the Elves seemed to go partly together: the healing of the desolate lands. Sauron found their weak point in suggesting that, helping one another, they could make Western Middle-earth as beautiful as Valinor. It was really a veiled attack on the gods, an incitement to try and make a separate independent paradise. Gilgalad repulsed all such overtures, as also did Elrond. But at Eregion great work began – and the Elves came their nearest to falling to 'magic' and machinery. With the aid of Sauron's lore they made *Rings of Power* ('power' is an ominous and sinister word in all these tales, except as applied to the gods).

The chief power (of all the rings alike) was the prevention or slowing of *decay* (i.e. 'change' viewed as a regrettable thing), the preservation of what is desired or loved, or its semblance – this is more or less an Elvish motive. But also they enhanced the natural powers of a possessor – thus approaching 'magic', a motive easily corruptible into evil, a lust for domination. And finally they had other powers, more directly derived from Sauron ('the Necromancer': so he is called as he casts a fleeting shadow and presage on the pages of *The Hobbit*): such as rendering invisible the material body, and making things of the invisible world visible.

The Elves of Eregion made Three supremely beautiful and powerful rings, almost solely of their own imagination, and directed to the preservation of beauty: they did not confer invisibility. But secretly in the subterranean Fire, in his own Black Land, Sauron made One Ring, the Ruling Ring that contained the powers of all the others, and controlled them, so that its wearer could see the thoughts of all those that used the lesser rings, could govern all that they did, and in the end could utterly enslave them. He reckoned, however, without the wisdom and subtle perceptions of the Elves. The moment he assumed the One, they were aware of it, and of his secret purpose, and were afraid. They hid the Three Rings, so that not even Sauron ever discovered where they were and they remained unsullied. The others they tried to destroy.

In the resulting war between Sauron and the Elves Middle-earth, especially in the west, was further ruined. Eregion was captured and destroyed, and Sauron seized many Rings of Power. These he gave, for their ultimate corruption and enslavement, to those who would accept them (out of ambition or greed). Hence the 'ancient rhyme' that appears as the leit-motif of *The Lord of the Rings*,

> Three Rings for the Elven-Kings under the sky,
> Seven for the Dwarf-lords in their halls of stone,
> Nine for Mortal Men doomed to die,
> One for the Dark Lord on his dark throne
> In the Land of Mordor where the shadows lie.

Sauron became thus almost supreme in Middle-earth. The Elves held out in secret places (not yet revealed). The last Elf-Kingdom of Gilgalad is maintained precariously on the extreme west-shores, where are the havens of the Ships. Elrond the Half-elven, son of Eârendil, maintains a kind of enchanted sanctuary at *Imladris* (in English *Rivendell*) on the extreme eastern margin of the western lands.* But Sauron dominates all the multiplying hordes of Men that have had no contact with the Elves and so indirectly with the true and unfallen Valar and gods. He rules a growing empire from the great dark tower of Barad-dûr in Mordor, near to the Mountain of Fire, wielding the One Ring.

But to achieve this he had been obliged to let a great part of his own inherent power (a frequent and very significant motive in myth and fairy-story) pass into the One Ring. While he wore it, his power on earth was actually enhanced. But even if he did not wear it, that power existed and was in 'rapport' with himself: he was not 'diminished'. Unless some other seized it and became possessed of it. If that happened, the new possessor could (if sufficiently strong and heroic by nature) challenge Sauron, become master of all that he had learned or done since the making of the One Ring, and so overthrow him and usurp his place. This was the essential weakness he had introduced into his situation in his effort (largely unsuccessful) to enslave the Elves, and in his desire to establish a control over the minds and wills of his servants. There was another weakness: if the One Ring was actually *unmade*, annihilated, then its power would be dissolved, Sauron's own being would be diminished to vanishing point, and he would be reduced to a shadow, a mere memory of malicious will. But that he never contemplated nor feared. The Ring was unbreakable by any smithcraft less than his own. It was indissoluble in any fire, save the undying subterranean fire where

---

*Elrond symbolises throughout the ancient wisdom, and his House represents Lore – the preservation in reverent memory of all tradition concerning the good, wise, and beautiful. It is not a scene of *action* but of *reflection*. Thus it is a place visited on the way to all deeds, or 'adventures'. It may prove to be on the direct road (as in *The Hobbit*); but it may be necessary to go from there in a totally unexpected course. So necessarily in *The Lord of the Rings*, having escaped to Elrond from the imminent pursuit of present evil, the hero departs in a wholly new direction: to go and face it at its source.

it was made – and that was unapproachable, in Mordor. Also so great was the Ring's power of lust, that anyone who used it became mastered by it; it was beyond the strength of any will (even his own) to injure it, cast it away, or neglect it. So he thought. It was in any case on his finger.

Thus, as the Second Age draws on, we have a great Kingdom and evil theocracy (for Sauron is also the god of his slaves) growing up in Middle-earth. In the West – actually the North-West is the only part clearly envisaged in these tales – lie the precarious refuges of the Elves, while Men in those parts remain more or less uncorrupted if ignorant. The better and nobler sort of Men are in fact the kin of those that had departed to Númenor, but remain in a simple 'Homeric' state of patriarchal and tribal life.

Meanwhile *Númenor* has grown in wealth, wisdom, and glory, under its line of great kings of long life, directly descended from Elros, Earendil's son, brother of Elrond. The *Downfall of Númenor*, the Second Fall of Man (or Man rehabilitated but still mortal), brings on the catastrophic end, not only of the Second Age, but of the Old World, the primeval world of legend (envisaged as flat and bounded). After which the Third Age began, a Twilight Age, a Medium Aevum, the first of the broken and changed world; the last of the lingering dominion of visible fully incarnate Elves, and the last also in which Evil assumes a single dominant incarnate shape.

The Downfall is partly the result of an inner weakness in Men – consequent, if you will, upon the first Fall (unrecorded in these tales), repented but not finally healed. Reward on earth is more dangerous for men than punishment! The Fall is achieved by the cunning of Sauron in exploiting this weakness. Its central theme is (inevitably, I think, in a story of Men) a Ban, or Prohibition.

The Númenóreans dwell within far sight of the easternmost 'immortal' land, Eressëa; and as the only men to speak an Elvish tongue (learned in the days of their Alliance) they are in constant communication with their ancient friends and allies, either in the bliss of Eressëa, or in the kingdom of Gilgalad on the shores of Middle-earth. They became thus in appearance, and even in powers of mind, hardly distinguishable from the Elves – but they remained mortal, even though rewarded by a triple, or more than a triple, span of years. Their reward is their undoing – or the means of their temptation. Their long life aids their achievements in art and wisdom, but breeds a possessive attitude to these things, and desire awakes for more *time* for their enjoyment. Foreseeing this in part, the gods laid a Ban on the Númenóreans from the beginning: they must never sail to Eressëa, nor westward out of sight of their own land. In all other directions they could go as they would. They must not set foot on 'immortal' lands, and so become enamoured of an immortality (within the world), which was against their law, the special doom or gift of Ilúvatar (God), and which their nature could not in fact endure.*

There are three phases in their fall from grace. First acquiescence, obedience that is free and willing, though without complete understanding. Then for long they obey unwillingly, murmuring more and more openly. Finally they rebel – and a rift appears between the King's men and rebels, and the small minority of persecuted Faithful.

In the first stage, being men of peace, their courage is devoted to sea-voyages. As descendants of Earendil, they became the supreme mariners, and being barred from the West, they sail to the uttermost north, and south, and east. Mostly they come to the west-shores of Middle-earth, where they aid the Elves and Men against Sauron, and incur his undying hatred. In those days they would come amongst Wild Men as almost divine benefactors, bringing gifts of arts and knowledge, and passing away again – leaving many legends behind of kings and gods out of the sunset.

In the second stage, the days of Pride and Glory and grudging of the Ban, they begin to seek wealth rather than bliss. The desire to escape death produced a cult of the dead, and they lavished wealth and art on tombs and memorials. They now made settlements on the west-shores, but these became rather strongholds and 'factories' of lords seeking wealth, and the Númenóreans became tax-gatherers carrying off over the sea ever more and more goods in their great ships. The Númenóreans began the forging of arms and engines.

This phase ended and the last began with the ascent of the throne by the thirteenth[4] king of the line of Elros, Tar-Calion the Golden, the most powerful and proud of all kings. When he learned that Sauron had taken the title of King of Kings and Lord of the World, he resolved to put down the 'pretender'. He goes in strength and majesty to Middle-earth, and so vast is his armament, and so terrible are the Númenóreans in the day of their glory that Sauron's servants will not face them. Sauron humbles himself, does homage to Tar-Calion, and is carried off to Númenor as hostage and prisoner. But there he swiftly rises by his cunning and knowledge from servant to chief counsellor of the king, and seduces the king and most of the lords and people with his lies. He denies the existence of God, saying that the One is a mere invention of the jealous Valar of the West, the oracle of their own wishes. The chief of the gods is he that dwells in the Void, who will conquer in the end,

---

*The view is taken (as clearly reappears later in the case of the Hobbits that have the Ring for a while) that each 'Kind' has a natural span, integral to its biological and spiritual nature. This cannot really be *increased* qualitatively or quantitatively; so that prolongation in time is like stretching a wire out ever tauter, or 'spreading butter ever thinner' – it becomes an intolerable torment.

and in the void make endless realms for his servants. The Ban is only a lying device of fear to restrain the Kings of Men from seizing everlasting life and rivalling the Valar.

A new religion, and worship of the Dark, with its temple under Sauron arises. The Faithful are persecuted and sacrificed. The Númenóreans carry their evil also to Middle-earth and there become cruel and wicked lords of necromancy, slaying and tormenting men; and the old legends are overlaid with dark tales of horror. This does not happen, however, in the North West; for thither, because of the Elves, only the Faithful who remain Elf-friends will come. The chief haven of the good Númenóreans is near the mouth of the great river Anduin. Thence the still beneficent influence of Númenor spreads up the River and along the coasts as far north as the realm of Gilgalad, as a Common Speech grows up.

But at last Sauron's plot comes to fulfilment. Tar-Calion feels old age and death approaching, and he listens to the last prompting of Sauron, and building the greatest of all armadas, he sets sail into the West, breaking the Ban, and going up with war to wrest from the gods 'everlasting life within the circles of the world'. Faced by this rebellion, of appalling folly and blasphemy, and also real peril (since the Númenóreans directed by Sauron could have wrought ruin in Valinor itself) the Valar lay down their delegated power and appeal to God, and receive the power and permission to deal with the situation; the old world is broken and changed. A chasm is opened in the sea and Tar-Calion and his armada is engulfed. Númenor itself on the edge of the rift topples and vanishes for ever with all its glory in the abyss. Thereafter there is no visible dwelling of the divine or immortal on earth. Valinor (or Paradise) and even Eressëa are removed, remaining only in the memory of the earth. Men may sail now West, if they will, as far as they may, and come no nearer to Valinor or the Blessed Realm, but return only into the east and so back again; for the world is round, and finite, and a circle inescapable – save by death. Only the 'immortals', the lingering Elves, may still if they will, wearying of the circle of the world, take ship and find the 'straight way', and come to the ancient or True West, and be at peace.

So the end of the Second Age draws on in a major catastrophe; but it is not yet quite concluded. From the cataclysm there are survivors: *Elendil* the Fair, chief of the Faithful (his name means *Elf-friend*), and his sons *Isildur* and *Anarion*. Elendil, a Noachian figure, who has held off from the rebellion, and kept ships manned and furnished off the east coast of Númenor, flees before the overwhelming storm of the wrath of the West, and is borne high upon the towering waves that bring ruin to the west of the Middle-earth. He and his folk are cast away as exiles upon the shores. There they establish the Númenórean kingdoms of Arnor in the north close to the realm of Gilgalad, and Gondor about the mouths of Anduin further south. Sauron, being an immortal, hardly escapes the ruin of Númenor and returns to Mordor, where after a while he is strong enough to challenge the exiles of Númenor.

The Second Age ends with the *Last Alliance* (of Elves and Men), and the great siege of Mordor. It ends with the overthrow of Sauron and destruction of the second visible incarnation of evil. But at a cost, and with one disastrous mistake. Gilgalad and Elendil are slain in the act of slaying Sauron. Isildur, Elendil's son, cuts the ring from Sauron's hand, and his power departs, and his spirit flees into the shadows. But the evil begins to work. Isildur claims the Ring as his own, as 'the Weregild of his father', and refuses to cast it into the Fire nearby. He marches away, but is drowned in the Great River, and the Ring is lost, passing out of all knowledge. But it is not unmade, and the Dark Tower built with its aid still stands, empty but not destroyed. So ends the Second Age with the coming of the Númenórean realms and the passing of the last kingship of the High Elves.

The Third Age is concerned mainly with the Ring. The Dark Lord is no longer on his throne, but his monsters are not wholly destroyed, and his dreadful servants, slaves of the Ring, endure as shadows among the shadows. Mordor is empty and the Dark Tower void, and a watch is kept upon the borders of the evil land. The Elves still have hidden refuges: at the Grey Havens of their ships, in the House of Elrond, and elsewhere. In the North is the Kingdom of Arnor ruled by the descendants of Isildur. Southward athwart the Great River Anduin are the cities and forts of the Númenórean realm of Gondor, with kings of the line of Anárion. Away in the (to these tales) uncharted East and South are the countries and realms of wild or evil men, alike only in their hatred of the West, derived from their master Sauron; but Gondor and its power bars the way. The Ring is lost, for ever it is hoped; and the Three Rings of the Elves, wielded by secret guardians, are operative in preserving the memory of the beauty of old, maintaining enchanted enclaves of peace where Time seems to stand still and decay is restrained, a semblance of the bliss of the True West.

But in the north Arnor dwindles, is broken into petty princedoms, and finally vanishes. The remnant of the Númenóreans becomes a hidden wandering Folk, and though their true line of Kings of Isildur's heirs never fails this is known only in the House of Elrond. In the south Gondor rises to a peak of power, almost reflecting Númenor, and then fades slowly to decayed Middle Age, a kind of proud, venerable, but increasingly impotent Byzantium. The watch upon Mordor is relaxed. The pressure of the Easterlings and Southrons increases. The line of

Kings fails, and the last city of Gondor, Minas Tirith ('Tower of Vigilance'), is ruled by hereditary Stewards. The Horsemen of the North, the Rohirrim or Riders of Rohan, taken into perpetual alliance, settle in the now unpeopled green plains that were once the northern part of the realm of Gondor. On the great primeval forest, Greenwood the Great, east of the upper waters of the Great River, a shadow falls, and grows, and it becomes Mirkwood. The Wise discover that it proceeds from a Sorcerer ('The Necromancer' of *The Hobbit*) who has a secret castle in the south of the Great Wood.*

In the middle of this Age the Hobbits appear. Their origin is unknown (even to themselves)† for they escaped the notice of the great, or the civilised peoples with records, and kept none themselves, save vague oral traditions, until they had migrated from the borders of Mirkwood, fleeing from the Shadow, and wandered westward, coming into contact with the last remnants of the Kingdom of Arnor.

Their chief settlement, where all the inhabitants are hobbits, and where an ordered, civilised, if simple and rural life is maintained, is *the Shire*, originally the farmlands and forests of the royal demesne of Arnor, granted as a fief: but the 'King', author of laws, has long vanished save in memory before we hear much of *the Shire*. It is in the year 1341 of the Shire (or 2941 of the Third Age: that is in its last century) that Bilbo – The Hobbit and hero of that tale – starts on his 'adventure'.

In that story, which need not be resumed, hobbitry and the hobbit-situation are not explained, but taken for granted, and what little is told of their history is in the form of casual allusion as to something known. The whole of the 'world-politics', outlined above, is of course there in mind, and also alluded to occasionally as to things elsewhere recorded in full. Elrond is an important character, though his reverence, high powers, and lineage are toned down and not revealed in full. There are allusions to the history of the Elves, and to the fall of Gondolin and so on. The shadows and evil of Mirkwood provide, in diminished 'fairy-story' mode, one of the major parts of the adventure. Only in one point

*It is only in the time between *The Hobbit* and its sequel that it is discovered that the Necromancer is *Sauron Redivivus*, growing swiftly to visible shape and power again. He escapes the vigilance and re-enters Mordor and the Dark Tower.

†The Hobbits are, of course, really meant to be a branch of the specifically *human* race (not Elves or Dwarves) – hence the two kinds can dwell together (as at Bree), and are called just the Big Folk and Little Folk. They are entirely without non-human powers, but are represented as being more in touch with 'nature' (the soil and other living things, plants and animals), and abnormally, for humans, free from ambition or greed of wealth. They are made *small* (little more than half human stature, but dwindling as the years pass) partly to exhibit the pettiness of man, plain unimaginative parochial man – though not with either the smallness or the savageness of Swift, and mostly to show up, in creatures of very small physical power, the amazing and unexpected heroism of ordinary men 'at a pinch'.

do these 'world-politics' act as part of the mechanism of the story. Gandalf the Wizard* is called away on high business, an attempt to deal with the menace of the Necromancer, and so leaves the Hobbit without help or advice in the midst of his 'adventure', forcing him to stand on his own legs, and become in his mode heroic. (Many readers have observed this point and guessed that the Necromancer must figure largely in any sequel or further tales of this time.)

The generally different tone and style of *The Hobbit* is due, in point of genesis, to it being taken by me as a matter from the great cycle susceptible of treatment as a 'fairy-story', for children. Some of the details of tone and treatment are, I now think, even on that basis, mistaken. But I should not wish to change much. For in effect this is a study of simple ordinary man, neither artistic nor noble and heroic (but not without the undeveloped seeds of these things) against a high setting – and in fact (as a critic has perceived) the tone and style change with the Hobbit's development, passing from fairy-tale to the noble and high and relapsing with the return.

The Quest of the Dragon-gold, the main theme of the actual tale of *The Hobbit*, is to the general cycle quite peripheral and incidental – connected with it mainly through Dwarf-history, which is nowhere central to these tales, though often important.† But in the course of the Quest, the Hobbit becomes possessed by seeming 'accident' of a 'magic ring', the chief and only immediately obvious power of which is to make its wearer invisible. Though for this tale an accident, unforeseen and having no place in any plan for the quest, it proves an essential to success. On return the Hobbit, enlarged in vision and wisdom, if unchanged in idiom, retains the ring as a personal secret.

The sequel, *The Lord of the Rings*, much the largest, and I hope also in proportion the best, of the entire cycle, concludes the whole business – an attempt is made to include in it, and wind up, all the elements and motives of what has preceded: elves, dwarves, the Kings of Men, heroic 'Homeric' horsemen, orcs and demons, the terrors of the Ring-servants and Necromancy, and the vast horror of the Dark Throne, even in style

*Nowhere is the place or nature of 'the Wizards' made fully explicit. Their name, as related to Wise, is an Englishing of their Elvish name, and is used throughout as utterly distinct from Sorcerer or Magician. It appears finally that they were as one might say the near equivalent in the mode of these tales of Angels, guardian Angels. Their powers are directed primarily to the encouragement of the enemies of evil, to cause them to use their own wits and valour, to unite and endure. They appear always as old men and sages, and though (sent by the powers of the True West) in the world they suffer themselves, their age and grey hairs increase only slowly. Gandalf whose function is especially to watch human affairs (Men and Hobbits) goes on through all the tales.

†The hostility of (even good) Dwarves and Elves, a motive that often appears, derives from the legends of the First Age; the Mines of Moria, the wars of Dwarves and Orcs (goblins, soldiery of the Dark Lord) refer to the Second Age and early Third.

it is to include the colloquialism and vulgarity of Hobbits, poetry and the highest style of prose. We are to see the overthrow of the last incarnation of Evil, the unmaking of the Ring, the final departure of the Elves, and the return in majesty of the true King, to take over the Dominion of Men, inheriting all that can be transmitted of Elfdom in his high marriage with Arwen daughter of Elrond, as well as the lineal royalty of Númenor. But as the earliest Tales are seen through Elvish eyes, as it were, this last great Tale, coming down from myth and legend to the earth, is seen mainly though the eyes of Hobbits: it thus becomes in fact anthropocentric. But through Hobbits, not Men so-called, because the last Tale is to exemplify most clearly a recurrent theme: the place in 'world politics' of the unforeseen and unforeseeable acts of will, and deeds of virtue of the apparently small, ungreat, forgotten in the places of the Wise and Great (good as well as evil). A moral of the whole (after the primary symbolism of the Ring, as the will to mere power, seeking to make itself objective by physical force and mechanism, and so also inevitably by lies) is the obvious one that without the high and noble the simple and vulgar is utterly mean; and without the simple and ordinary the noble and heroic is meaningless.

It is not possible even at great length to 'pot' *The Lord of the Rings* in a paragraph or two. . . . . It was begun in 1936,[5] and every part has been written many times. Hardly a word in its 600,000 or more has been unconsidered. And the placing, size, style, and contribution to the whole of all the features, incidents, and chapters has been laboriously pondered. I do not say this in recommendation. It is, I feel, only too likely that I am deluded, lost in a web of vain imaginings of not much value to others – in spite of the fact that a few readers have found it good, on the whole.* What I intend to say is this: I cannot substantially alter the thing. I have finished it, it is 'off my mind': the labour has been colossal; and it must stand or fall, practically as it is.

[The letter continues with a summary (without comments) of the story of *The Lord of the Rings*, after which Tolkien writes:]

That is a long and yet bald resumé. Many characters important to the tale are not even mentioned. Even some whole inventions like the remarkable *Ents*, oldest of living rational creatures, *Shepherds of the Trees*, are omitted. Since we now try to deal with 'ordinary life', springing up ever unquenched under the trample of world policies and events, there are love-stories touched in, or love in different modes, wholly absent from *The Hobbit*. But the highest love-story, that of

*But as each has disliked this or that, I should (if I took all the criticisms together and obeyed them) find little left, and am forced to the conclusion that so great a work (in size) cannot be perfect, nor even if perfect, be liked entirely by any *one* reader.

Aragorn and Arwen Elrond's daughter is only alluded to as a known thing. It is told elsewhere in a short tale, *Of Aragorn and Arwen Undómiel*. I think the simple 'rustic' love of Sam and his Rosie (nowhere elaborated) is *absolutely essential* to the study of his (the chief hero's) character, and to the theme of the relation of ordinary life (breathing, eating, working, begetting) and quests, sacrifice, causes, and the 'longing for Elves', and sheer beauty. But I will say no more, nor defend the theme of mistaken love seen in Eowyn and her first love for Aragorn. I do not feel much can now be done to heal the faults of this large and much-embracing tale – or to make it 'publishable', if it is not so now. A slight revision (now accomplished) of a crucial point in *The Hobbit*, clarifying the character of Gollum and his relation to the Ring, will enable me to reduce Book I chapter II 'The Shadow of the Past', simplify it, and quicken it – and also simplify the debatable opening of Book II a little. If *the other material*, 'The Silmarillion' and some other tales or links such as *The Downfall of Númenor* are published or in process of this, then much explanation of background, and especially that found in the *Council of Elrond* (Bk II) could be dispensed with. But altogether it would hardly amount to the excision of a single long chapter (out of about 72).

I wonder if (even if legible) you will ever read this ??

132 From a letter to John Tolkien   10 February 1952

[This letter, to Tolkien's eldest son, who was now a Catholic priest, describes one of the dinners occasionally held by the Inklings.]

We had a 'ham-feast' with C. S. Lewis on Thursday (an American ham from Dr Firor of Johns Hopkins University), and it was like a glimpse of old times: quiet and rational (since Hugo was not asked!). C.S.L. asked Wrenn[1] and it was a great success, since it pleased him, and he was very pleasant: a good step towards weaning him from 'politics' (academic).

133 To Rayner Unwin

[In the spring of 1952, Tolkien lost patience with the delays at Collins over the publication of his books, and told the firm that they must publish *The Lord of the Rings* immediately or he would withdraw the manuscript. Collins, frightened by the length of the book, decided that they must decline it, together with *The Silmarillion*, and they withdrew from the negotiations. In June, Rayner Unwin wrote to Tolkien to enquire about his poem 'Errantry', which had been brought to Allen & Unwin's notice; he also asked about progress with the publication of *The Lord of the Rings* and *The Silmarillion*.]

22 June 1952   99 Holywell, Oxford
My dear Rayner,

How kind of you to write again! I have behaved badly. You wrote to me on 19 November,[1] and that still remains unanswered. Now disaster has overtaken me, but I cannot again postpone a reply – disaster: I am chairman again of the English examiners, and in the midst of a 7-day week, and a 12-hour day, of labour that will last right on to July 31st, when I shall be cast up exhausted on the shoals of August.

As for 'Errantry': it is a most odd coincidence that you should ask about that. For only a few weeks ago I had a letter from a lady unknown to me making a similar enquiry. She said that a friend had recently written out for her from memory some verses that had so taken her fancy that she was determined to discover their origin. He had picked them up from his son-in-law who had learned them in Washington D.C. (!); but nothing was known about their source save a vague idea that they were connected with English universities. Being a determined person she apparently applied to various Vice-Chancellors, and Bowra[2] directed her to my door. I must say that I was interested in becoming 'folk-lore'. Also it was intriguing to get an oral version – which bore out my views on oral tradition (at any rate in early stages): sc. that the 'hard words' are well preserved,[3] and the more common words altered, but the metre is often disturbed.

There was once a literary club of dons and undergraduates (Tangye Lean of Univ. was a leading junior: we often met in his rooms)[4] and 'Errantry' first appeared in its papers and probably began its oral travels from that point. Though I think the line leading to Sir John Burnet-Stuart[5] and his son-in-law probably (on internal evidence) goes back to a printed version which appeared later in *The Oxford Magazine*, November 9th 1933. Probably your correspondent's too. That version might be called the A.V. I sent my enquirer a copy of it, and one of an R.V.,[6] and I gather the making of a 'critical text' kept a house-party amused for a day, while their hostess (Mrs Roberts of Lightwater Manor) was laid low with a broken arm.

She says she cannot 'understand how the verses have remained unpublished' disregarding the O.M., 'so long. I fear your publicity manager must be incompetent.' The answer is, of course, that I am too busy officially to give such things due attention. But also that I have *tried* often to get 'Errantry' and such things published, but unsuccessfully. The O.M. used at one time (especially under Nowell Smith)[7] to accord me space; but no one else. I should, of course, be very pleased to submit a collection to you when I have a moment. But 'Errantry' is the most attractive. It is for one thing in a metre I invented (depending on trisyllabic assonances or near-assonances, which is so difficult that

162

except in this one example I have never been able to use it again – it just blew out in a single impulse).[8]

As for *The Lord of the Rings* and *The Silmarillion*, they are where they were. The one finished (and the end revised), and the other still unfinished (or unrevised), and both gathering dust. I have been both off and on too unwell, and too burdened to do much about them, and too downhearted. Watching paper-shortages and costs mounting against me. But I have rather modified my views. Better something than nothing! Although to me all are one, and the 'L of the Rings' would be better far (and eased) as part of the whole, I would gladly consider the publication of any part of this stuff. Years are becoming precious. And retirement (not far off) will, as far as I can see, bring not leisure but a poverty that will necessitate scraping a living by 'examining' and such like tasks.

When I have a moment to turn round I will collect the *Silmarillion* fragments in process of completion – or rather the original outline which is more or less complete, and you can read it. My difficulty is, of course, that owing to the expense of typing and the lack of time to do my own (I typed nearly all of *The Lord of the Rings*) I have no spare copies to let out. But what about *The Lord of the Rings*? Can anything be done about that, to unlock gates I slammed myself?

I feel very conscience-stricken about you. I know you have married. I knew the date. But though indeed I wished you well, and wished to write, I did not. I never recovered from the confusion of my affairs when I had a terrible bout of fibrositis and neuritis of the arm last October, and cd. not write at all (or bear myself) for a month. I have been chasing lost days ever since. And somehow I always postponed because (I suppose) I wished to deal with my wretched literary affairs as well as your personal ones. It is a great blessing to have importunate and determined friends who will not let one relapse into permanent silence. I am most grateful to you for writing again.

My wife and Priscilla send you our best wishes. Do call again! I'll find time, whatever I am doing.

                    Yrs sincerely
                    J. R. R. Tolkien.

I enclose the only copy I can find of the R.V. of 'Errantry'.

134   From a letter to Rayner Unwin   29 August 1952

[Rayner Unwin replied on 1 July, praising 'Errantry', and asking if Tolkien could send one of his copies of the typescript of *The Lord of the Rings* by registered post. He told Tolkien: 'We do *want* to publish for you

– it's only ways and means that have held us up.' He also asked to see *The Silmarillion*, as well as anything else that Tolkien had written, and suggested that he and Tolkien should meet.]

I am at last turning to my own affairs. The situation is this: I am anxious to publish *The Lord of the Rings* as soon as possible. I believe it to be a great (though not flawless) work. Let other things follow as they may. But as the expense of typing proved prohibitive, I had to do it all myself, and there is only one (more or less) fair copy in existence. I dare not consign that to the post, and in any case I am now going to devote some days to correcting it finally. For this purpose, I am retiring tomorrow from the noise and stench of Holywell to my son's cottage on Chiltern-top while he is away with his children.[1] . . . . I shall return on September 10th. After that I could call with my burden at Museum Street[2] on some date convenient to you . . . . or, if that is not asking too much, you could call on me (as you so kindly suggest might be possible). . . . .

I have recently made some tape-recordings of parts of the Hobbit and The Lord (notably the Gollum-passages and some pieces of 'Elvish') and was much surprised to discover their effectiveness as recitations, and (if I may say so) my own effectiveness as a narrator, I do a very pretty Gollum and Treebeard. Could not the BBC be interested? The tape-reel is in the possession of George Sayer (English Master at Malvern) and I am sure he would forward it for your or anyone else's trial. It was unrehearsed and impromptu and could be improved.[3]

I should love to come to London, if only for the purpose of seeing you and meeting your wife. But I am cutting even the 'seventh International Congress of Linguists' (Sept 1), of which I am an official – time is so miserably short, and I am tired. I have on my plate not only the 'great works', but the overdue professional work I was finishing up at Cambridge (edition of the *Ancrene Wisse*); the W. P. Ker lecture at Glasgow; *Sir Gawain*; and new lectures! But your continued interest cheers me. I have a constant 'fan-mail' from all over the English-speaking world for 'more' – curiously enough often for 'more about the Necromancer', which the Lord certainly fulfils.

135 From a letter to Rayner Unwin   24 October 1952

[Rayner Unwin visited Tolkien at Oxford on 19 September, and the manuscript of *The Lord of the Rings* was given to him by Tolkien shortly afterwards. On 23 October, Rayner Unwin reported that, according to a printer's estimate, the book would have to be priced at £3. 10s. (at least) in order to recover its costs, and that the price would be even higher if it were divided into two volumes. He had now sent the manuscript to another printer, and was waiting to hear if a cheaper estimate could be obtained.]

I regret very much (in some ways) having produced such a monster in such unpropitious days; and I am very grateful to you for the trouble you are taking. But I hope very much that you will be able before very long to say 'yea' or 'nay'. Uncertainty is a great weight on the heart. The thing weighs on my mind, for I can neither dismiss it as a disaster and turn to other matters, nor get on with it and things concerned with it (such as the maps).

£3.10.0 (or more) would certainly be a very big price for any book, even today. Were you to contemplate publishing a monster at such a price, what number would you print? And how many must you sell to indemnify you, at the least? There are, of course, a larger number of people than might be supposed who are avid of such fare; they are usually delighted with length, and sometimes able to pay for it – esteeming one large book better than four small, and not surprised to find it 4 times as expensive as one small book. But I would not like to hazard a guess at their total numbers, or the chance of making contact with them!

I am at last after three weeks incessant labour of the most exacting and dreariest sort, getting into rather calmer water. I have shuffled off the Chairmanship of the Board, and concluded a number of tasks, and now, barring lecturing and teaching, have only to face (before preparation for Schools begins in February) examination of a tiresome thesis (on Fairy Tales!), reading and editing a monograph for a series, producing a contribution to 'Essays and Studies' by December 2nd,[1] completing my edition of *Ancrene Wisse*, and writing the W. P. Ker Lecture for Glasgow.[2] And also (if I can) finding somewhere else to live and moving! This charming house has become uninhabitable – unsleepable-in, unworkable-in, rocked, racked with noise, and drenched with fumes. Such is modern life. Mordor in our midst. And I regret to note that the billowing cloud recently pictured did not mark the fall of Barad-dûr, but was produced by its allies – or at least by persons who have decided to use the Ring for their own (of course most excellent) purposes.[3]

136   To Rayner Unwin

[Allen & Unwin decided to publish *The Lord of the Rings* in three volumes, priced at twenty-one shillings each. Tolkien's contract stipulated that the manuscript of the book should be delivered, ready for the printer, by 25 March 1953. The publishers had also asked him to write a description of the book for publicity purposes, in not more than a hundred words.]

24 March 1953   99 Holywell, Oxford

Dear Rayner,

I have intended for some time to write to you, as the 'contract day', 25 March, steadily drew nearer, and found me still enmeshed in troubles that gathered upon me the moment I had signed. And here I am on the eve.

In brief what has happened to me is above all my wife's increasing ill health, which has involved me in various distresses since November. On a doctor's ultimatum I was obliged to spend most of what time I could spare from duties in finding and negotiating for the purchase of a house on high dry soil and in the quiet. I am in fact now in 'articulo mortis', or it almost feels like that – in fact in the very act of a household-removal. Nothing could be more disastrous. In addition the ill will of Mordor decreed that I myself should lose most of the vital Christmas Vacation being ill. There was no chink in the armour of last term; and I am now still involved as chairman in controlling the setting of all the honours English papers for June, and a week behind at that.

I am afraid I must ask for your lenience in the matter of the date. But I see some hope in your letter, since it appears that the *first 2 books* would suffice to keep the ball rolling. I practically completed a detailed revision of these before disasters overtook me; and I can let you have them by the end of this month.

Would it be useful if I sent now at once the *first book* (the longest of all), which is quite ready, and is matched by a spare corrected copy? If you care to wire or phone me, I could despatch Book I tomorrow.

I am v. sorry to be a nuisance; but you may guess how painful it is to me that what should be a labour of delight should have been transformed into a nightmare, by the gathering upon 1953 of so many duties and troubles.

Between 23 April and June 17 I hope to have enough leisure to put the bulk of the later books (which need little revision) into order, so as not to hold things up once started. But I go into a tunnel of examinations from 17 June to 27 July which will give me 12 hours work a day. After that I shall lift my battered head, I hope. I am resigning from Exams anyway; but I could not get out of it this year.

If you could give me any hints as to what your publicity department requires, it would help my battered wits. How can I describe the book clearly and emphasize its special interest in a hundred words? Perhaps I could get someone else who has read it, like C.S.L., to help? . . . .

Yours ever

J. R. R. Tolkien.

166

P.S. I have given some thought to the matter of sub-titles for the volumes, which you thought were desirable. But I do not find it easy, as the 'books', though they must be grouped in pairs, are not really paired; and the middle pair (III/IV) are not really related.

Would it not do if the 'book-titles' were used: e.g. *The Lord of the Rings*: Vol. I *The Ring Sets out* and *The Ring Goes South*; Vol. II *The Treason of Isengard*, and *The Ring goes East*; Vol. III *The War of the Ring*, and *The End of the Third Age*?[1]

If not, I can at the moment think of nothing better than: I *The Shadow Grows* II *The Ring in the Shadow* III *The War of the Ring* or *The Return of the King*. JRRT.

137 To Rayner Unwin

11 April 1953   76 Sandfield Road, Headington, Oxford

Dear Rayner,

I am extremely sorry that it is already eleven days after the end of the month (March)! But I have had a very bad time indeed, far worse even than I feared. In spite of every care the move proved disastrously dislocating, and instead of two days I have spent ten in endless labour; and I still cannot lay my hands on many papers and notes that I need. In addition things have gone wrong with the examination business which is under my unhappy charge; and I leave on Tuesday morning for Glasgow to deliver a W. P. Ker Lecture which is still only half prepared.

I have at last completed the revision for press – I hope to the last comma – of Part I: *The Return of the Shadow*: of *The Lord of the Rings*, Books I and II. I have unfortunately missed the posts today; but I will send the MSS off in two packets on Monday.

I am sending in the original Foreword, which of course need not be printed yet, since I cannot find my note of the additions or alterations which you thought would be required in view of the publication of the work in three volumes. Also, the matter of 'appendices' at the end of volume III, after the final and rather short sixth 'book', has not been decided. It is no good promising things that are not going actually to appear; but I very much hope that precisely what is here promised, in however reduced a form, will in fact prove possible.[1]

I am not at this time returning, re-drawn, the design required in Book II Ch. iv,[2] since I have not had a chance to re-draw it. But I will attend to that as soon as it is needed.*

*That is, I will draw it as much better as my little skill allows, in black. But it should of course properly appear in white line on a black background, since it represents a silver line in the darkness. How does that appeal to the Production Department?

As for the 'facsimiles' of the burned and torn pages of the Runic Book, originally planned to appear at the beginning of Book II Ch. v,[3] I am retaining them for the present. I think their disappearance is regrettable; but in spite of what you have said, I think line-blocks are for this purpose impracticable. A page each is required, or the things will be too illegible to be interesting (or too unveracious to be worth inclusion). I earnestly hope it may be found possible to include them in the 'appendix'.

I shall not make such heavy weather with the remainder of the work. The first two books were written first a very long time ago, have been often altered, and needed a close consideration of the whole to bring them into line. As a result the later parts are nearly done; and two more books can follow as soon as you want them (that is, Vol. II). Can you give me any idea when anything will be likely to need my attention, such as proofs or what not? After such long delays I, of course desire nothing more than to press on, once publication has begun. But I am horribly trammelled this year. I shall have a little elbow-room until about the 20th of June; after that no time at all for anything but exam-scripts until about August 1. I shall then be tired, but my time will be free (more or less) during August and September.

Maps are worrying me. One at least (which would then have to be rather large) is absolutely essential. I think three are needed: 1. Of the Shire; 2. Of Gondor; and 3. A general small-scale map of the whole field of action. They exist, of course; though not in any form fit for reproduction – for of course in such a story one cannot make a map for the narrative, but must first make a map and make the narrative agree. 3 is needed throughout. 1 is needed in the first volume and the last. 2 is essential in vols II and III. Shall I try and draw them in suitable form as soon as ever I can, and let you have them for the consideration of the Production Department?

Well, now I must, as usual, forcibly break my concentration for a while and turn to something else: in this case the *moralitas* of *Sir Gawain and the Green Knight*.[4]

But I see I have forgotten the matter of Publicity. To save me a separate letter would you be so kind as to apologize to the Department, if I seemed rather rude? I was much bothered when I received their letter. I tried to do something, without much success, even though I took about 300 words. The result, such as it is, I now send. If it is legible, it might be of some use.

I also applied to my friend George Sayer, English Master at Malvern, as the most normal reader and liker of the work that I could think of; and he sent in a blurb of 95 words. I send you his letter and the blurb – not that it will do, but perhaps a phrase or two might serve, and it may give a hint of what such folk as like this sort of thing like in *The Lord of the Rings*. He surprised me. I did not think he would be overheated! But though 'greatest living poet' is absurd, at least I am comforted in the thought that the verses are up to standard, and are (as I think) adequate and in place; though C. S. Lewis regards them as on the whole poor, regrettable, and out of place. When I tried once to explain briefly to a friend what it was all about, I found that with the exercise of severe economy I took 41 pages and 10,000 words.[5] He was sufficiently interested to get the thing typed. You might like to see it sometime; and den again you moutn't.

> With many thanks, and best wishes,
> Yours sincerely,
> J. R. R. Tolkien.

138 From a letter to Christopher Tolkien   4 August 1953

[Galley-proofs of the first volume of *The Lord of the Rings* were sent to Tolkien in mid-July.]

The galleys are proving rather a bore! There seem such an endless lot of them; and they have put me very much out of conceit with parts of the Great Work, which seems, I must confess, in print very long-winded in parts. But the printing is very good, as it ought to be from an almost faultless copy; except that the impertinent compositors have taken it upon themselves to correct, as they suppose, my spelling and grammar: altering throughout *dwarves* to *dwarfs*; *elvish* to *elfish*; *further* to *farther*; and worst of all, *elven-* to *elfin*. I let off my irritation in a snorter to A. and U. which produced a grovel.

139 From a letter to Rayner Unwin   8 August 1953

[Rayner Unwin told Tolkien that it would be desirable to have a separate title for each of the three volumes of *The Lord of the Rings*, and referred Tolkien to his own letter of 24 March, which made suggestions for sub-titles for the various parts.]

I wrote in rather a hurry in the Spring, and did not take a copy of my letter of 24 March. If I could have it back, or a copy, it would help me. I am, however, opposed to having separate titles for each of the volumes, and no over-all title. *The Lord of the Rings* is a good over-all title, I think, but it is not applicable specially to Volume I, indeed it is probably least suited to that volume. Except possibly in the matter of cost, I cannot see the objection to:

It is, surely, only by the use of a single over-all title that the confusion that you speak of can be certainly avoided.

I am not wedded to any of the suggested sub-titles; and wish they could be avoided. For it is really impossible to devise ones that correspond to the contents; since the division into two 'books' per volume is purely a matter of convenience with regard to length, and has no relation to the rhythm or ordering of the narrative. . . . .

What is the position about the reproduction of the burned pages of the 'Book of Mazarbul' belonging to the opening of Chapter V of the second book? The text as it stands is rather pointless without them. I still hold the original 'facsimiles'. I also hold the drawing of the secret door, which is required to face, or to be included in the text, corresponding to the bottom of Galley 98, towards the end of Chapter IV of the second book. I shall attempt to re-draw and improve that and send it along as soon as possible, as I have now finished the correction of the galleys on the rough sheets.

I am sorry I have delayed the re-drawing of the essential maps; but I really have not had a day off from drudgery. I am turning to them at once.

140   From a letter to Rayner Unwin   17 August 1953

[This letter, typed with a red ribbon, was sent immediately after Rayner Unwin had visited Tolkien.]

It was extremely kind of you to come and see me and clear things up. It was only after I had seen you on to the bus that I recollected that you had in the end never had any beer or other refreshment. I am sorry. Very much below hobbit standards, my behaviour, I am afraid.

I now suggest as titles of the *volumes*, under the over-all title *The Lord of the Rings*: Vol. I The Fellowship of the Ring. Vol. II The Two Towers. Vol. III The War of the Ring (or, if you still prefer that: The Return of the King).

The Fellowship of the Ring will do, I think; and fits well with the fact that the last chapter of the Volume is The Breaking of the Fellowship. The Two Towers gets as near as possible to finding a title to cover the widely divergent Books 3 and 4; and can be left ambiguous – it might refer to Isengard and Barad-dûr, or to Minas Tirith and B; or Isengard and Cirith Ungol.[1] On reflection I prefer for Vol. III The War of the Ring, since it gets in the Ring again; and also is more non-committal, and gives less hint about the turn of the story: the chapter titles have been chosen also to give away as little as possible in advance. But I am not set in my choice.

Reconsidering our conversation: I doubt if *red* letters are now sufficiently important for the fire-letters of the Ring in Book I ch. 2 (Galley 15) to be worth the expense of alteration. I think it would be a good thing to have the last Runic page of the Book of Mazarbul (Book II ch. 5) reproduced, as a frontispiece (?). The last page because, though less well forged, perhaps, it closely concerns the actual narrative.

I will bring in person the Copy for Vol. II on September the 1st. It already seems pretty well in order. I am now turning to the Maps – and the Foreword.

Excuse red: it does not represent any fiery emotion. Mere economy. I now type such a lot for my hand's sake that type-reels are a consideration; and the red on this one is hardly used!

141   From a letter to Allen & Unwin   9 October 1953

The Maps. I am stumped. Indeed in a panic. They are essential; and urgent; but I just cannot get them done. I have spent an enormous amount of time on them without profitable result. Lack of skill combined with being harried. Also the shape and proportions of 'The Shire' as described in the tale cannot (by me) be made to fit into shape of a page; nor at that size be contrived to be informative. . . . .

I feel that the maps ought to be done properly. The 'burned manuscripts', which readers had found engaging, have disappeared, – making the text of Book ii, Ch. 5 at the beginning rather absurd, and losing the Runes which seem a great attraction to readers of all ages (such as are foolish enough to read this kind of thing at all). Even at a little cost there should be picturesque maps, providing more than a mere index to what is said in the text. I could do maps suitable to the text. It is the attempt to cut them down and omitting all their colour (verbal and otherwise) to reduce them to black and white bareness, on a scale so small that hardly any names can appear, that has stumped me.

142   To Robert Murray, S.J.

[Father Robert Murray, grandson of Sir James Murray (the founder of the *Oxford English Dictionary*) and a close friend of the Tolkien family, had read part of *The Lord of the Rings* in galley-proofs and typescript, and had, at Tolkien's instigation, sent comments and criticism. He wrote that the book left him with a strong sense of 'a positive compatibility with the

2 December 1953   76 Sandfield Road, Headington, Oxford

My dear Rob,

It was wonderful to get a long letter from you this morning. . . . . I am
sorry if casual words of mine have made you labour to criticize my
work. But, to tell you the truth, though praise (or what is not quite the
same thing, and better, expressions of pleasure) is pleasant, I have been
cheered specially by what you have said, this time and before, because
you are more perceptive, especially in some directions, than any one
else, and have even revealed to me more clearly some things about my
work. I think I know exactly what you mean by the order of Grace; and
of course by your references to Our Lady, upon which all my own small
perception of beauty both in majesty and simplicity is founded. *The
Lord of the Rings* is of course a fundamentally religious and Catholic
work; unconsciously so at first, but consciously in the revision. That is
why I have not put in, or have cut out, practically all references to
anything like 'religion', to cults or practices, in the imaginary world.
For the religious element is absorbed into the story and the symbolism.
However that is very clumsily put, and sounds more self-important
than I feel. For as a matter of fact, I have consciously planned very little;
and should chiefly be grateful for having been brought up (since I was
eight) in a Faith that has nourished me and taught me all the little that I
know; and that I owe to my mother, who clung to her conversion and
died young, largely through the hardships of poverty resulting from it.

Certainly I have not been nourished by English Literature, in which I
do not suppose I am better read than you; for the simple reason that I
have never found much there in which to rest my heart (or heart and
head together). I was brought up in the Classics, and first discovered the
sensation of literary pleasure in Homer. Also being a philologist, getting
a large part of any aesthetic pleasure that I am capable of from the *form*
of words (and especially from the *fresh* association of word-form with
word-sense), I have always best enjoyed things in a foreign language, or
one so remote as to feel like it (such as Anglo-Saxon). But that is enough
about me.

I am afraid it is only too likely to be true: what you say about the
critics and the public. I am dreading the publication, for it will be
impossible not to mind what is said. I have exposed my heart to be shot
at. I think the publishers are very anxious too; and they are very keen
that as many people as possible should read advance copies, and form a
sort of opinion before the hack critics get busy. . . . .

I was sorry to hear that you are now without a 'cello, after having got some way (I am told) with that lovely and difficult instrument. Anyone who can play a stringed instrument seems to me a wizard worthy of deep respect. I love music, but have no aptitude for it; and the efforts spent on trying to teach me the fiddle in youth, have left me only with a feeling of awe in the presence of fiddlers. Slavonic languages are for me almost in the same category. I have had a go at many tongues in my time, but I am in no ordinary sense a 'linguist'; and the time I once spent on trying to learn Serbian and Russian have left me with no practical results, only a strong impression of the structure and word-aesthetic. . . . .

Please forgive the apparent unfriendliness of type! My typing does not improve. Except in speed. I am now much faster than with my laborious hand, which has to be spared as it quickly gets tired and painful. I have no doubt that you will also be hearing shortly from Edith.

With much love to you

Ronald Tolkien.

143 From a letter to Rayner Unwin 22 January 1954

I am sending now Book III, first half of Vol. II, carefully corrected. Book IV is nearly done and shall follow on Monday.

I have also revised Vol. III and can let you have the MS. of that (as far as the end of the story) as soon as you wish. The matter for the extra 50 pages[1] I shall not be able to do just yet.

I am not at all happy about the title 'the Two Towers'. It must if there is any real reference in it to Vol II refer to *Orthanc* and the *Tower of Cirith Ungol*. But since there is so much made of the basic opposition of the Dark Tower and Minas Tirith, that seems very misleading. There is, of course, actually no real connecting link between Books III and IV, when cut off and presented separately as a volume.

144 To Naomi Mitchison

[Mrs Mitchison had been reading page-proofs of the first two volumes of *The Lord of the Rings,* and wrote to Tolkien with a number of questions about the book.]

25 April 1954   76 Sandfield Road, Headington, Oxford

Dear Mrs. Mitchison,

It has been both rude and ungrateful of me not to have acknowledged, or to have thanked you for past letters, gifts, and remembrances – all the more so, since your interest has, in fact, been a great comfort to me, and encouragement in the despondency that not unnaturally accompanies the labours of actually publishing such a work as *The Lord of the Rings.*

173

But it is most unfortunate that this has coincided with a period of exceptionally heavy labours and duties in other functions, so that I have been at times almost distracted.

I will try and answer your questions. I may say that they are very welcome. I like things worked out in detail myself, and answers provided to all reasonable questions. Your letter will, I hope, guide me in choosing the kind of information to be provided (as promised) in an appendix, and strengthen my hand with the publishers. Since the third volume will be rather slimmer than the second (events move quicker, and less explanations are needed), there will, I believe be a certain amount of room for such matter. My problem is not the difficulty of providing it, but of choosing from the mass of material I have already composed.

There is of course a clash between 'literary' technique, and the fascination of elaborating in detail an imaginary mythical Age (mythical, not allegorical: my mind does not work allegorically). As a story, I think it is good that there should be a lot of things unexplained (especially if an explanation actually exists); and I have perhaps from this point of view erred in trying to explain too much, and give too much past history. Many readers have, for instance, rather stuck at the *Council of Elrond*. And even in a mythical Age there must be some enigmas, as there always are. Tom Bombadil is one (intentionally).

But as much further history (backwards) as anyone could desire actually exists in the *Silmarillion* and related stories and poems, composing the *History of the Eldar* (Elves). I believe that in the event (which seems much to hope) of sufficient people being interested in the *Lord of the Rings* to pay for the cost of its publication, the gallant publishers may consider printing some of that. It was actually written first, and I wished to have the matter issued in historical order, which would have saved a lot of allusion and explanation in the present book. But I could not get it accepted.

The third volume was of course completed years ago, as far as the tale goes. I have finished such revision, as seemed necessary, and it will go to be set up almost at once. In the meanwhile I am giving what fragments of time I have to making compressed versions of such historical, ethnographical, and linguistic matter as can go in the Appendix. If it will interest you, I will send you a copy (rather rough) of the matter dealing with Languages (and Writing), Peoples and Translation.

The latter has given me much thought. It seems seldom regarded by other creators of imaginary worlds, however gifted as narrators (such as Eddison). But then I am a philologist, and much though I should like to be more precise on other cultural aspects and features, that is not within my competence. Anyway 'language' is the most important. for the story has to be told, and the dialogue conducted in a language; but English cannot have been the language of any people at that time. What I have, in fact done, is to equate the Westron or wide-spread Common Speech of the Third Age with English; and translate everything, including names such as *The Shire*, that was in the Westron into English terms, with some differentiation of style to represent dialectal differences. Languages quite alien to the C.S. have been left alone. Except for a few scraps in the Black Speech of Mordor, and a few names and a battle-cry in Dwarvish, these are almost entirely Elvish (*Eldarin*).

Languages, however, that were related to the Westron presented a special problem. I turned them into forms of speech related to English. Since the *Rohirrim* are represented as recent comers out of the North, and users of an archaic Mannish language relatively untouched by the influence of *Eldarin*, I have turned their names into forms like (but not identical with) Old English. The language of Dale and the Long Lake would, if it appeared, be represented as more or less Scandinavian in character; but it is only represented by a few names, especially those of the Dwarves that came from that region. These are all Old Norse Dwarf-names.

(Dwarves are represented as keeping their own native tongue more or less secret, and using for all 'outer' purposes the language of the people they dwelt near; they never reveal their own 'true' personal names in their own tongue.)

The Westron or C.S. is supposed to be derived from the Mannish *Adunaic* language of the Númenóreans, spreading from the Númenórean Kingdoms in the days of the Kings, and especially from *Gondor*, where it remains spoken in nobler and rather more antique style (a style also usually adopted by the Elves when they use this language). But all the names in *Gondor*, except for a few of supposedly prehistoric origin, are of Elvish form, since the Númenórean nobility still used an Elvish language, or could. This was because they had been allies of the Elves in the First Age, and had for that reason been granted the Atlantis isle of Númenor.

Two of the Elvish tongues appear in this book. They have some sort of existence, since I have composed them in some completeness, as well as their history and account of their relationship. They are intended (a) to be definitely of a European kind in style and structure (not in detail); and (b) to be specially pleasant. The former is not difficult to achieve; but the latter is more difficult, since individuals' personal predilections, especially in the phonetic structure of languages, varies widely, even when modified by the imposed languages (including their so-called 'native' tongue).

I have therefore pleased myself. The archaic language of lore is meant to be a kind of 'Elven-latin', and by transcribing it into a spelling closely resembling that of Latin (except that *y* is only used as a consonant, as *y* in E. *Yes*) the similarity to Latin has been increased ocularly. Actually it might be said to be composed on a Latin basis with two other (main) ingredients that happen to give me 'phonaesthetic' pleasure: Finnish and Greek. It is however less consonantal than any of the three. This language is High-elven or in its own terms *Quenya* (Elvish).

The living language of the Western Elves (*Sindarin* or Grey-elven) is the one usually met, especially in names. This is derived from an origin common to it and *Quenya*; but the changes have been deliberately devised to give it a linguistic character very like (though not identical with) British-Welsh: because that character is one that I find, in some linguistic moods, very attractive; and because it seems to fit the rather 'Celtic' type of legends and stories told of its speakers.

'Elves' is a translation, not perhaps now very suitable, but originally good enough, of *Quendi*. They are represented as a race similar in appearance (and more so the further back) to Men, and in former days of the same stature. I will not here go into their differences from Men! But I suppose that the *Quendi* are in fact in these histories very little akin to the Elves and Fairies of Europe; and if I were pressed to rationalize, I should say that they represent really Men with greatly enhanced aesthetic and creative faculties, greater beauty and longer life, and nobility – the Elder Children, doomed to fade before the Followers (Men), and to live ultimately only by the thin line of their blood that was mingled with that of Men, among whom it was the only real claim to 'nobility'.

They are represented as having become early divided in to two, or three, varieties. 1. The *Eldar* who heard the summons of the Valar or Powers to pass from Middle-earth over the Sea to the West; and 2. the Lesser Elves who did not answer it. Most of the *Eldar* after a great march reached the Western Shores and passed over Sea; these were the High Elves, who became immensely enhanced in powers and knowledge. But part of them in the event remained in the coast-lands of the North-west: these were the *Sindar* or Grey-elves. The lesser Elves hardly appear, except as part of the people of The Elf-realm; of Northern Mirkwood, and of Lórien, ruled by *Eldar*; their languages do not appear.

The High Elves met in this book are Exiles, returned back over Sea to Middle-earth, after events which are the main matter of the *Silmarillion*, part of one of the main kindreds of the *Eldar*: the Noldor* (Masters of Lore). Or rather a last remnant of these. For the *Silmarillion* proper and the First Age ended with the destruction of the primeval Dark Power (of whom Sauron was a mere lieutenant), and the rehabilitation of the

*N = ng as in *ding*.

Exiles, who returned again over Sea. Those who lingered were those who were enamoured of Middle-earth and yet desired the unchanging beauty of the Land of the Valar. Hence the making of the Rings; for the Three Rings were precisely endowed with the power of preservation, not of birth. Though unsullied, because they were not made by Sauron nor touched by him, they were nonetheless partly products of his instruction, and ultimately under the control of the One. Thus, as you will see, when the One goes, the last defenders of High-elven lore and beauty are shorn of power to hold back time, and depart.

I am sorry about the Geography. It must have been dreadfully difficult without a map or maps. There will be in volume I a map of part of the Shire, and a small-scale general map of the whole scene of action and reference (of which the map at the end of *The Hobbit* is the N.E. corner). These have been drawn from my less elegant maps by my son Christopher, who is learned in this lore. But I have only had one proof and that had to go back. I wisely started with a map, and made the story fit (generally with meticulous care for distances). The other way about lands one in confusions and impossibilities, and in any case it is weary work to compose a map from a story — as I fear you have found.

I cannot send you my own working maps; but perhaps these very rough and not entirely accurate drafts, made hurriedly at various times for readers, would be of some assistance. . . . . Perhaps when you have done with these MS. maps or made some notes you would not mind sending them back. I shall find them useful in making some more; but I cannot get to that yet. I may say that my son's maps are beautifully clear, as far as reduction in reproduction allows; but they do not contain everything, alas!

Some stray answers. *Dragons.* They had not stopped; since they were active in far later times, close to our own. Have I said anything to suggest the final ending of dragons? If so it should be altered. The only passage I can think of is Vol. I p. 70: 'there is not now any dragon left on earth in which the old fire is hot enough'. But that implies, I think, that there are still dragons, if not of full primeval stature. I have a long historical table of events from the Beginning to the End of the Third Age. It is rather full; but I agree that a short form, containing events important for this tale would be useful. If you would care for typed copies of some of this material: eg. The Rings of Power; The Downfall of Númenor; the Lists of the Heirs of Elendil; the House of Eorl (Genealogy); Genealogy of Durin and the Dwarf-lords of *Moria*; and The Tale of the Years (esp. those of the Second and Third Ages), I will try and get copies made soon. . . . .

Orcs (the word is as far as I am concerned actually derived from Old

English *orc* 'demon', but only because of its phonetic suitability) are nowhere clearly stated to be of any particular origin. But since they are servants of the Dark Power, and later of Sauron, neither of whom could, or would, produce living things, they must be 'corruptions'. They are not based on direct experience of mine; but owe, I suppose, a good deal to the goblin tradition (*goblin* is used as a translation in *The Hobbit*, where *orc* only occurs once, I think), especially as it appears in George MacDonald, except for the soft feet which I never believed in. The name has the form *orch* (pl. *yrch*) in Sindarin and *uruk* in the Black Speech.

The Black Speech was only used in Mordor; it only occurs in the Ring inscription, and a sentence uttered by the Orcs of *Barad-dûr* (Vol. II p. 48)[1] and in the word *Nazgûl* (cf. *nazg* in the Ring inscription). It was never used willingly by any other people, and consequently even the names of places in Mordor are in English (for the C.S.) or Elvish. *Morannon* is just the Elvish for Black Gate; cf. *Mordor* Black Land, *Mor-ia* Black Chasm, *Mor-thond* Black-root (river-name). *Rohir-rim* is the Elvish (Gondorian) name for the people that called themselves Riders of the Mark or Eorlings. The formation is not meant to resemble Hebrew. The Eldarin languages distinguish in forms and use between a 'partitive' or 'particular' plural, and the general or total plural. Thus *yrch* 'orcs, some orcs, des orques' occurs in vol I pp. 359, 402; the Orcs, as a race, or the whole of a group previously mentioned would have been *orchoth*. In Grey-elven the general plurals were very frequently made by adding to a name (or a place-name) some word meaning 'tribe, host, horde, people'. So *Haradrim* the Southrons: Q. *rimbe*, S. *rim*, host; *Onod-rim* the Ents. The *Rohirrim* is derived from *roch* (Q. *rokko*) horse, and the Elvish stem *kher-* 'possess'; whence Sindarin *Rochir* 'horse-lord', and *Rochir-rim* 'the host of the Horse-lords'. In the pronunciation of Gondor the *ch* (as in German, Welsh, etc) had been softened to a sounded *h*; so in *Rochann* 'Hippia' to *Rohan*.

Beorn is dead; see vol. I p. 241. He appeared in *The Hobbit*. It was then the year Third Age 2940 (Shire-reckoning 1340). We are now in the years 3018–19 (1418–19). Though a skin-changer and no doubt a bit of a magician, Beorn was a Man.

Tom Bombadil is not an important person – to the narrative. I suppose he has some importance as a 'comment'. I mean, I do not really write like that: he is just an invention (who first appeared in the *Oxford Magazine* about 1933), and he represents something that I feel important, though I would not be prepared to analyze the feeling precisely. I would not, however, have left him in, if he did not have some kind of function. I might put it this way. The story is cast in terms of a good side, and a bad side, beauty against ruthless ugliness, tyranny against kingship, moderated freedom with consent against compulsion that has long lost any object save mere power, and so on; but both sides in some degree, conservative or destructive, want a measure of control. but if you have, as it were taken 'a vow of poverty', renounced control, and take your delight in things for themselves without reference to yourself, watching, observing, and to some extent knowing, then the question of the rights and wrongs of power and control might become utterly meaningless to you, and the means of power quite valueless. It is a natural pacifist view, which always arises in the mind when there is a war. But the view of Rivendell seems to be that it is an excellent thing to have represented, but that there are in fact things with which it cannot cope; and upon which its existence nonetheless depends. Ultimately only the victory of the West will allow Bombadil to continue, or even to survive. Nothing would be left for him in the world of Sauron.

He has no connexion in my mind with the Entwives. What had happened to them is not resolved in this book. He is in a way the answer to them in the sense that he is almost the opposite, being say, Botany and Zoology (as sciences) and Poetry as opposed to Cattle-breeding and Agriculture and practicality.

I think that in fact the Entwives had disappeared for good, being destroyed with their gardens in the War of the Last Alliance (Second Age 3429–3441) when Sauron pursued a scorched earth policy and burned their land against the advance of the Allies down the Anduin (vol. II p. 79 refers to it[2]). They survived only in the 'agriculture' transmitted to Men (and Hobbits). Some, of course, may have fled east, or even have become enslaved: tyrants even in such tales must have an economic and agricultural background to their soldiers and metal-workers. If any survived so, they would indeed be far estranged from the Ents, and any rapprochement would be difficult – unless experience of industrialized and militarized agriculture had made them a little more anarchic. I hope so. I don't know.

Hobbit-children were delightful, but I am afraid that the only glimpses of them in this book are found at the beginning of vol. I. An epilogue giving a further glimpse (though of a rather exceptional family) has been so universally condemned that I shall not insert it. One must stop somewhere.

Yes, *Sam Gamgee* is in a sense a relation of *Dr. Gamgee*, in that his name would not have taken that form, if I had not heard of 'Gamgee tissue'; there was I believe a Dr. Gamgee (no doubt of the kin) in Birmingham when I was a child. The name was any way always familiar to me. Gaffer Gamgee arose first: he was a legendary character to my children (based on a real-life gaffer, not of that name). But, as you will find explained, in this tale the name is a 'translation' of the real Hobbit name, derived from a village (devoted to rope-making) anglicized as

Gamwich (pron. Gammidge), near Tighfield (see vol. II p. 217).[3] Since Sam was close friends of the family of Cotton (another village-name), I was led astray into the Hobbit-like joke of spelling Gamwichy Gamgee, though I do not think that in actual Hobbit-dialect the joke really arose.

There are no precise opposites to the Wizards – a translation (perhaps not suitable, but throughout distinguished from other 'magician' terms) of Q. Elvish *Istari*. Their origin was not known to any but a few (such as Elrond and Galadriel) in the Third Age. They are said to have first appeared about the year 1000 of the Third Age, when the shadow of Sauron began first to grow again to new shape. They always appeared old, but grew older with their labours, slowly, and disappeared with the end of the Rings. They were thought to be Emissaries (in the terms of this tale from the Far West beyond the Sea), and their proper function, maintained by Gandalf, and perverted by Saruman, was to encourage and bring out the native powers of the Enemies of Sauron. Gandalf's opposite was, strictly, Sauron, in one part of Sauron's operations; as Aragorn was in another.

The *Balrog* is a survivor from the *Silmarillion* and the legends of the First Age. So is *Shelob*. The *Balrogs*, of whom the whips were the chief weapons, were primeval spirits of destroying fire, chief servants of the primeval Dark Power of the First Age. They were supposed to have been all destroyed in the overthrow of *Thangorodrim*, his fortress in the North. But it is here found (there is usually a hang-over especially of evil from one age to another) that one had escaped and taken refuge under the mountains of Hithaeglin (the Misty Mountains). It is observable that only the Elf knows what the thing is – and doubtless Gandalf.

Shelob (English representing C.S 'she-lob' = female spider) is a translation of Elvish *Ungol* 'spider'. She is represented in vol. II p. 332 as descendant of the giant spiders of the glens of *Nandungorthin*, which come into the legends of the First Age, especially into the chief of them, the tale of Beren and Lúthien. This is constantly referred to, since as Sam points out (vol. II p. 321)[4] this history is in a sense only a further continuation of it. Both Elrond (and his daughter Arwen Undómiel, who resembles Lúthien closely in looks and fate) are descendants of Beren and Lúthien; and so at very many more removes is Aragorn. The giant spiders were themselves only the offspring of Ungoliante the primeval devourer of light, that in spider-form assisted the Dark Power, but ultimately quarrelled with him. There is thus no alliance between Shelob and Sauron, the Dark Power's deputy; only a common hatred.

Galadriel is as old, or older than Shelob. She is the last remaining of the Great among the High Elves, and 'awoke' in Eldamar beyond the Sea, long before Ungoliante came to Middle-earth and produced her broods there. . . . .

Well, after a long silence you have evoked a fairly long reply. Not too long, I hope, even for such delightful and encouraging interest. I am deeply grateful for it; and I hope all staying at Carradale⁵ will accept my thanks.

Yours sincerely,

J. R. R. Tolkien.

145 From a letter to Rayner Unwin 13 May 1954

[Tolkien had been sent the Houghton Mifflin Co.'s draft for the 'blurbs' on the dust-jackets of the American edition of *The Lord of the Rings*. He was also shown a set of opinions of the book which Allen & Unwin proposed to cite on the jacket of the British edition. In these, C. S. Lewis was quoted as comparing the book favourably with Ariosto, Richard Hughes remarked that nothing had been attempted on the same scale since *The Faerie Queene*, and Naomi Mitchison called Tolkien's story 'super science fiction'. Rayner Unwin also gave Tolkien news of the birth of his son, Merlin – a name that he suggested was more appropriate for a child than 'Gandalf'.]

Thank you for sending me the projected 'blurbs', which I return. The Americans are not as a rule at all amenable to criticism or correction; but I think their effort is so poor that I feel constrained to make some effort to improve it, though without much more hope of effect than in the case of the appalling jacket they produced for The Hobbit. I enclose a page of suggestions, which you might perhaps send on to Houghton Mifflin. . . . .

May I beg of you earnestly to try and make the publication July? I think it would be a pity to let the enthusiasm go off the boil. I also think that July is much the better date for many, especially scholastics and academics, who in July begin to lift up their heads and in September begin to bow them again under a load of cares. But I have some cogent private reasons. One of them is that I am *particularly anxious* that Vol. I should be in public existence before I arrive in Dublin to take the degree of D. Litt. on July 20 at the centenary celebrations. (Though the Irish have not much money for such expensive books, you might get Dublin to take a copy or two on the strength of the celebrations!)

It never rains but it pours (as I am sure Mr Butterbur must have said), and I am going to get a doctorate at Liége on October 2nd; but I suppose that Vol. I will be out at least before then. . . . .

I am pleased to find that the preliminary opinions are so good, though I feel that comparisons with Spenser, Malory, and Ariosto (not to mention super Science Fiction) are too much for my vanity! I showed your draft to Geoffrey Mure (Warden), who was being tiresome this morning and threatening to eject me from my room in favour of a mere tutor. He was visibly shaken, and evidently did not know before what the college had been harbouring. He went so far as to say that Merton seemed to be doing well, though he doubted if I should get quite into the Roger Bannister class. [1] Anyway my stock went up sufficiently to obtain me an even better room, even at the cost of ejecting one so magnificent as the Steward. So if you have any more appreciations which I have not seen, please let me have a look at them. I promise not to become like Mr Toad. . . . .

I am delighted to hear that all is going well. This is the second Merlin with whom I am acquainted. Professor Turville Petre's second son bears the names Merlin Oswald (not an Anglo-Welsh rapprochement; I think the Oswald is parental and grand-parental). I am sure you are right: Gandalf was of course always old. He was an Emissary, who had that shape from the first; but all things wear in Middle-Earth, so that he got older before his task was done. Not a name for a child of Men!

146 From a letter to Allen & Unwin 3 June 1954

[The Production Department had asked Tolkien to approve the design of the dust-jacket for *The Lord of the Rings*.]

I wish that I could say that I approve of the proofs of the jacket, herewith returned. I do not. I think they are very ugly indeed. But to be effective I should have been given an opportunity of criticism at an earlier stage.

What the jacket looks like is, I think, of much less importance now than issuing the book as soon as possible; and if I had had nothing to do with it, I should not much mind. But as the Ring-motif remains obviously mine (though made rather clumsier), I am likely to be suspected by the few who concern me of having planned the whole. . . . .

I tell you what I think, since I am asked: tasteless and depressing. But surely asking my opinion is a formality. I do not suppose that any of my criticisms could be met without serious delay. *I would rather have the things as they are than cause any more delay*. But *if this can be done without delay*, I would like a different type for the title-lettering at least (on the page; the spine is passable).

147 From a letter to Allen & Unwin 15 June 1954

[The jacket of *The Lord of the Rings* was altered by the publishers in the light of Tolkien's comments in the previous letter.]

It was a great moment yesterday when I received the advance copy of *The Fellowship of the Ring*. The book itself is very presentable indeed.

I think the jacket is now much improved, and is rather striking. I like the grey paper used, and much prefer it to the other colours. But the specimens of the jackets for II and III do bring home to me the point, which I had not fully appreciated: the need for differentiation. Since the same device is, for economy, to be used throughout, they do look too much alike; and choice of colour is perhaps less important than distinction. But this could perhaps better be achieved by varying the colour of the major lettering? Title and author in red?

I do not really myself mind at all, and leave it to you.

148   From a letter to Katherine Farrer   7 August 1954

[The first volume of *The Lord of the Rings*, *The Fellowship of the Ring*, was published on 29 July 1954.]

I am afraid there are still a number of 'misprints' in Vol. I! Including the one on p. 166. But *nasturtians* is deliberate, and represents a final triumph over the high-handed printers. Jarrold's appear to have a highly educated pedant as a chief proof-reader, and they started correcting my English without reference to me: *elfin* for *elven*; *farther* for *further*; *try to say* for *try and say* and so on. I was put to the trouble of proving to him his own ignorance, as well as rebuking his impertinence. So, though I do not much care, I dug my toes in about *nasturtians*. I have always said this. It seems to be a natural anglicization that started soon after the 'Indian Cress' was naturalized (from Peru, I think) in the 18th century; but it remains a minority usage. I prefer it because *nasturtium* is, as it were, bogusly botanical, and falsely learned.

I consulted the college gardener to this effect: 'What do you call these things, gardener?'

'I calls them *tropaeolum*, sir.'

'But, when you're just talking to dons?'

'I says *nasturtians*, sir.'

'Not *nasturtium*?'

'No, sir; that's watercress.'

And that seems to be the fact of botanical nomenclature. . . . .

It has been (and continues to be) a crushingly laborious year! So many things at once, each needing exclusive attention. They are clamouring for *Gawain*.[1] (It is being repeated next month.) And I am struggling to select from all the mass of private stuff about the languages, scripts, calendars and history of the Third Age, what may prove interesting to those who like that sort of thing, and will go into the space (about 40 pages). Time runs on; for I have to go to Ireland again about mid-Sept. and then on to Belgium, and then it will be term. . . . .

149 From a letter to Rayner Unwin   9 September 1954

[Reviews of *The Fellowship of the Ring* began to appear during August.]

As for the reviews they were a great deal better than I feared, and I think might have been better still, if we had not quoted the Ariosto remark, or indeed got involved at all with the extraordinary animosity that C.S.L. seems to excite in certain quarters. He warned me long ago that his support might do me as much harm as good. I did not take it seriously, though in any case I should not have wished other than to be associated with him – since only by his support and friendship did I ever struggle to the end of the labour. All the same many commentators seem to have preferred lampooning his remarks or his review to reading the book.

The (unavoidable) disadvantage of issuing in three parts has been shown in the 'shapelessness' that several readers have found, since that is true if one volume is supposed to stand alone. 'Trilogy', which is not really accurate, is partly to blame. There is too much 'hobbitry' in Vol. I taken by itself; and several critics have obviously not got far beyond Chapter I.

I must say that I was unfortunate in coming into the hands of the D. Telegraph, during the absence of Betjeman. My work is not in his line, but he at any rate is neither ignorant nor a gutter-boy. Peter Green seems to be both. I do not know him or of him, but he is so rude as to make one suspect malice.[1] Though actually I think 'the cold in his head' made it more convenient for him to use Edwin Muir in the Observer[2] and Lambert in the S. Times,[3] with a slight hotting up of the above.

I am most puzzled by the remarks on the style. I do not expect, and did not expect, many to be amused by hobbits, or interested in the general story and its modes, but the discrepancy in the judgements on the style (which one would have thought referable to standards independent of personal liking) are very odd – from laudatory quotation to 'Boys Own Paper' (which has no one style)!

I gather that you are not wholly dissatisfied. But there have been some very appreciative notices apart from C.S.L. (who had the advantage of knowing the whole), though not usually in the high places. Cherryman in *Truth*[4] and Howard Spring in *C. Life*[5] were pleasing to one's vanity, and also Cherryman's ending: that he would turn eagerly to the second and third volumes! May others feel the same!

Fawcett in the *M. Guardian*[6] was complimentary in brief; and I was specially interested by a long notice in the *Oxford Times* (by the editor himself)[7] in being by one quite outside the ring, and he seemed to have enjoyed himself. He sent an interviewer up, but what he will churn out for the O. Mail this week I do not know. . . . .

Well, this letter is already inordinately long. In the midst of it Professor d'Ardenne of Liège has arrived to harass me with philological work on which we are supposed to be engaged.

150   From a letter to Allen & Unwin   18 September 1954

I regret that I have not yet any copy to send in for the Appendices. All I can say is that I will do my best to produce this before the end of the month. My trouble is indecision (and conflicting advice) in selection from the too abundant matter. I have spent much ineffectual time on the attempt to satisfy the unfortunate promises of Vol. I p. 8.[1]

The Index has proceeded in rough form as far as the middle of Vol. II. The 'alphabets' reduced to simplest form will need blocks. . . . .

A map of the Gondor area is perhaps the most urgent. I am hoping to get my son Christopher to produce one from my drafts, as soon as possible.

151   From a letter to Hugh Brogan   18 September 1954

If you want my opinion, a part of the 'fascination' [of *The Lord of the Rings*] consists in the vistas of yet more legend and history, to which this work does not contain a full clue. For the present we had better leave it at that. If there is a fault in the work which I myself clearly perceive, it is that I have perhaps overweighted Part I too much with attempts to depict the setting and historical background in the course of the narrative. Of course, in actual fact, this background already 'exists', that is, is written, and was written first. But I could not get it published, in chronological order, until and unless a public could be found for the mixture of Elvish and Númenórean legend with the Hobbits. . . . .

Your preference of *goblins* to *orcs* involves a large question and a matter of taste, and perhaps historical pedantry on my part. Personally I prefer Orcs (since these creatures are not 'goblins', not even the goblins of George MacDonald, which they do to some extent resemble). Also I now deeply regret having used Elves, though this is a word in ancestry and original meaning suitable enough. But the disastrous debasement of this word, in which Shakespeare played an unforgiveable part, has really overloaded it with regrettable tones, which are too much to overcome. I hope in the Appendices to Vol. III to be able to include a note 'On translation' in which the matter of equivalences and my uses may be made clearly. My difficulty has been that, since I have tried to present a kind of legendary and history of a 'forgotten epoch', all the specific terms were in a foreign language, and no *precise* equivalents exist in English. . . . .

I am more than grateful to you for one thing: apart from one line in the Manchester Guardian no one else has yet even referred to the fact that there are any *verses* in the book – or I think not. . . . .

Frodo is not intended to be another Bilbo. Though his opening style is not wholly un-kin. But he is rather a study of a hobbit broken by a burden of fear and horror – broken down, and in the end made into something quite different. None of the hobbits come out of it in pure Shire-fashion. They wouldn't. But you have got Samwise Gamwichy (or Gamgee).

Middle-earth is just archaic English for ἡ οἰκουμένη, the inhabited world of men. It lay then as it does. In fact just as it does, round and inescapable. That is partly the point. The new situation, established at the beginning of the Third Age, leads on eventually and inevitably to ordinary History, and we here see the process culminating. If you or I or any of the mortal men (or hobbits) of Frodo's day had set out over sea, west, we should, as now, eventually have come back (as now) to our starting point. Gone was the 'mythological' time when Valinor (or Valimar), the Land of the Valar (gods if you will) existed physically in the Uttermost West, or the Eldaic (Elvish) immortal Isle of Eressëa; or the Great Isle of Westernesse (Númenor-Atlantis). After the Downfall of Númenor, and its destruction, all this was removed from the 'physical' world, and not reachable by material means. Only the Eldar (or High-Elves) could still sail thither, forsaking time and mortality, but never returning.

Very many thanks for remembering the ageing Professor, and bracing him up with your letter. I know 21/- is a frightful price, but don't forget that I have to sell an awful lot before the ghastly expenses are paid off. The fact that I get not a halfpenny until that is done, does not matter so much, as this: if enough are sold I may be able to *publish more*. So add to your great kindness in inducing such as you can to beg borrow or steal a guinea rather than a copy!

Pictures are far too expensive, even if I had sufficent skill to do them and cut out artist's fees. I tried, but alas! can only draw v. imperfectly what I can, and not what I see. The wrapper is all that survived of three separate designs I made, one for each part. Part I was to have been all black with red and gold letters, and the three opposing rings: Narya (red), Vilya (blue), Nenya (white). . . . .[1] But it was reduced; and the lovely (I thought) facsimiles of the 3 burned pages of the Book of Mazarbul also vanished – so that folk could have the thing at the trifling cost of 21/-!

[Tolkien's dramatic dialogue, *The Homecoming of Beorhtnoth*, was broadcast on the BBC Third Programme on 3 December 1954. Rayner Heppenstall, the producer, had asked Tolkien what 'dialect' the speakers should adopt.]

As for the English dialogue no 'dialect' tone or rural quality is required at all. There is not intended to be what we should call a difference of social standing between the two speakers. One requires a younger lighter voice, and the other an older and deeper. The difference between them is rather one of temper, and matter, than 'class'. The young minstrel bursts into formal verse, and so uses an archaic style – as anyone would capable of verse at the time, and as Tidwald himself does when he mocks Torhthelm.

It is not indicated what part of the country either came from. Torhthelm is in fact much more likely to have come from the West Midlands, as did many who fell at Maldon. But in a period when 'dialect' merely marked place and not rank or function, and at any rate details of grammar and vowels had no social implications, it would be best to avoid any modern rusticity. In any case any modern East Anglian characteristics would be anachronistic, since they did not then exist – the fusion of the Danish and English elements that eventually produced them was not yet accomplished. And Essex of the East Saxons was (and is) a very different affair from the Northfolk and Southfolk.

153   To Peter Hastings (draft)

[Peter Hastings, manager of the Newman Bookshop (a Catholic bookshop in Oxford), wrote expressing enthusiasm for *The Lord of the Rings*, but asked if Tolkien had not 'over-stepped the mark in metaphysical matters'. He gave several examples: first, 'Treebeard's statement that the Dark Lord created the Trolls and the Orcs'. Hastings suggested that evil was incapable of creating anything, and argued that even if it could create, its creatures 'could not have a tendency to good, even a very small one'; whereas, he argued, one of the Trolls in *The Hobbit*, William, does have a feeling of pity for Bilbo. He also cited the description of Bombadil by Goldberry: 'He is.' Hastings said that this seemed to imply that Bombadil was God. Hastings was most of all concerned with the reincarnation of the Elves, which Tolkien had mentioned to him in a conversation. He wrote of this: 'God has not used that device in any of the creations of which we have knowledge, and it seems to me to be stepping beyond the position of a sub-creator to produce it as an actual working thing, because a sub-creator, when dealing with the relations between creator and created, should use those channels which he knows the creator to have used already. . . . . "The Ring" is so good that it is a pity to deprive it of its reality by over-stepping the bounds of a writer's job.' He also asked if the reincarnation of the Elves did not produce practical problems: 'What happens to the descendants of a human and an elf who marry?' And, on another matter, he asked how Sauron, given his extreme evil, could 'keep the co-operation of the elves' until the time when the Rings of Power were forged.]

September 1954
Dear Mr Hastings,

Thank you very much for your long letter. I am sorry that I have not the time to answer it, as fully as it deserves. You have at any rate paid me the compliment of taking me seriously; though I cannot avoid wondering whether it is not 'too seriously', or in the wrong directions. The tale is after all in the ultimate analysis a tale, a piece of literature, intended to have literary effect, and not real history. That the device adopted, that of giving its setting an historical air or feeling, and (an illusion of ?) three dimensions, is successful, seems shown by the fact that several correspondents have treated it in the same way – according to their different points of interest or knowledge: i.e. as if it were a report of 'real' times and places, which my ignorance or carelessness had misrepresented in places or failed to describe properly in others. Its economics, science, artefacts, religion, and philosophy are defective, or at least sketchy.

I have, of course, already considered all the points that you raise. But to present my reflexions to you (in other form) would take a book,* and any kind of real answer to your more profound queries must at least wait till you have more in hand: Vol. III, for instance, not to mention the more mythical histories of the Cosmogony, First, and Second Ages. Since the whole matter from beginning to end is mainly concerned with the relation of Creation to making and sub-creation (and subsidiarily with the related matter of 'mortality'), it must be clear that references to these things are not casual, but fundamental: they may well be fundamentally 'wrong' from the point of view of Reality (external reality). But they cannot be wrong inside this imaginary world, since that is how it is made.

We differ entirely about the nature of the relation of sub-creation to Creation. I should have said that liberation 'from the channels the creator is known to have used already' is the fundamental function of 'sub-creation', a tribute to the infinity of His potential variety, one of the ways in which indeed it is exhibited, as indeed I said in the Essay. I am not a metaphysician; but I should have thought it a curious metaphysic – there is not one but many, indeed potentially innumerable ones

*It nearly has, even in hasty sketch!

– that declared the channels known (in such a finite corner as we have any inkling of) to have been used, are the only possible ones, or efficacious, or possibly acceptable to and by Him!

'Reincarnation' may be bad *theology* (that surely, rather than metaphysics) as applied to Humanity; and my *legendarium*, especially the 'Downfall of Númenor' which lies immediately behind *The Lord of the Rings*, is based on my view: that Men are essentially mortal and must not try to become 'immortal' in the flesh.* But I do not see how even in the Primary World any theologian or philosopher, unless very much better informed about the relation of spirit and body than I believe anyone to be, could deny the *possibility* of re-incarnation as a mode of existence, prescribed for certain kinds of rational incarnate creatures.

I suppose that actually the chief difficulties I have involved myself in are scientific and biological – which worry me just as much as the theological and metaphysical (though you do not seem to mind them so much). Elves and Men are evidently in biological terms one race, or they could not breed and produce fertile offspring – even as a rare event: there are 2 cases only in my legends of such unions, and they are merged in the descendants of *Eärendil*.[1] But since some have held that the rate of longevity is a biological characteristic, within limits of variation, you could not have Elves in a sense 'immortal' – not eternal, but not dying by 'old age'– and Men mortal, more or less as they now seem to be in the Primary World – and yet sufficiently akin. I might answer that this 'biology' is only a theory, that modern 'gerontology', or whatever they call it, finds 'ageing' rather more mysterious, and less clearly inevitable in bodies of human structure. But I should actually answer: I do not care. This is a biological dictum in my imaginary world. It is only (as yet) an incompletely imagined world, a rudimentary 'secondary'; but if it pleased the Creator to give it (in a corrected form) Reality on any plane, then you would just have to enter it and begin studying its different biology, that is all.

But as it is – though it seems to have grown out of hand, so that parts seem (to me) rather revealed through me than by me – its purpose is still largely literary (and, if you don't boggle at the term, didactic). Elves and Men are represented as biologically akin in this 'history', because Elves are certain aspects of Men and their talents and desires, incarnated in my little world. They have certain freedoms and powers we should like to have, and the beauty and peril and sorrow of the possession of these things is exhibited in them. . . . .

*Since 'mortality' is thus represented as a special gift of God to the Second Race of the Children (the *Eruhíni*, the Children of the One God) and not a punishment for a Fall, you may call that 'bad theology'. So it may be, in the primary world, but it is an imagination capable of elucidating truth, and a legitimate basis of legends.

Sauron was of course not 'evil' in origin. He was a 'spirit' corrupted by the Prime Dark Lord (the Prime sub-creative Rebel) Morgoth. He was given an opportunity of repentance, when Morgoth was overcome, but could not face the humiliation of recantation, and suing for pardon; and so his temporary turn to good and 'benevolence' ended in a greater relapse, until he became the main representative of Evil of later ages. But at the beginning of the Second Age he was still beautiful to look at, or could still assume a beautiful visible shape – and was not indeed wholly evil, not unless all 'reformers' who want to hurry up with 'reconstruction' and 'reorganization' are wholly evil, even before pride and the lust to exert their will eat them up. The particular branch of the High-Elves concerned, the Noldor or Loremasters, were always on the side of 'science and technology', as we should call it: they wanted to have the knowledge that Sauron genuinely had, and those of Eregion refused the warnings of Gilgalad and Elrond. The particular 'desire' of the Eregion Elves – an 'allegory' if you like of a love of machinery, and technical devices – is also symbolised by their special friendship with the Dwarves of Moria.

I should regard them as no more wicked or foolish (but in much the same peril) as Catholics engaged in certain kinds of physical research (e.g. those producing, if only as by-products, poisonous gases and explosives): things not necessarily evil, but which, things being as they are, and the nature and motives of the economic masters who provide all the means for their work being as they are, are pretty certain to serve evil ends. For which they will not necessarily be to blame, even if aware of them.

As for other points. I think I agree about the 'creation by evil'. But you are more free with the word 'creation' than I am.* Treebeard does not say that the Dark Lord 'created' Trolls and Orcs. He says he 'made' them in *counterfeit* of certain creatures pre-existing. There is, to me, a wide gulf between the two statements, so wide that Treebeard's statement could (in my world) have possibly been true. It is *not* true actually of the Orcs – who are fundamentally a race of 'rational incarnate' creatures, though horribly corrupted, if no more so than many Men to be met today. Treebeard is a *character* in my story, not me; and though he has a great memory and some earthy wisdom, he is not one of the Wise, and there is quite a lot he does not know or understand. He does not know what 'wizards' are, or whence they came (though I do, even if exercising my subcreator's right I have thought it best in this Tale to leave the question a 'mystery', not without pointers to the solution).

*Inside this mythical history (as its metaphysic is, not necessarily as a metaphysic of the real World) Creation, the act of Will of Eru the One that gives Reality to conceptions, is distinguished from Making, which is permissive.

Suffering and experience (and possibly the Ring itself) gave Frodo more insight; and you will read in Ch. I of Book VI the words to Sam. 'The Shadow that bred them can only mock, it cannot make real new things of its own. I don't think it gave life to the Orcs, it only ruined them and twisted them.' In the legends of the Elder Days it is suggested that the Diabolus subjugated and corrupted some of the earliest Elves, before they had ever heard of the 'gods', let alone of God.

I am not sure about Trolls. I think they are mere 'counterfeits', and hence (though here I am of course only using elements of old barbarous mythmaking that had no 'aware' metaphysic) they return to mere stone images when not in the dark. But there are other sorts of Trolls beside these rather ridiculous, if brutal, Stone-trolls, for which other origins are suggested. Of course (since inevitably my world is highly imperfect even on its own plane nor made wholly coherent – our Real World does not *appear* to be wholly coherent either; and I am actually not myself convinced that, though in every world on every plane all must ultimately be under the Will of God, even in ours there are not some 'tolerated' sub-creational counterfeits!) when you make Trolls *speak* you are giving them a power, which in our world (probably) connotes the possession of a 'soul'. But I do not agree (if you admit that fairy-story element) that my trolls show any sign of 'good', strictly and unsentimentally viewed. I do not say William felt *pity* – a word to me of moral and imaginative worth: it is the Pity of Bilbo and later Frodo that ultimately allows the Quest to be achieved – and I do not think he showed Pity. I might not (if *The Hobbit* had been more carefully written, and my world so much thought about 20 years ago) have used the expression 'poor little blighter', just as I should not have called the troll *William*. But I discerned no pity even then, and put in a plain caveat. Pity must restrain one from doing something immediately desirable and seemingly advantageous. There is no more 'pity' here than in a beast of prey yawning, or lazily patting a creature it could eat, but does not want to, since it is not hungry. Or indeed than there is in many of men's actions, whose real roots are in satiety, sloth, or a purely non-moral natural softness, though they may dignify them by 'pity's' name.

As for Tom Bombadil, I really do think you are being too serious, besides missing the point. (Again the words used are by Goldberry and Tom not me as a commentator). You rather remind me of a Protestant relation who to me objected to the (modern) Catholic habit of calling priests Father, because the name father belonged only to the First Person, citing last Sunday's Epistle – inappositely since that says *ex quo*. Lots of other characters are called Master; and if 'in time' Tom was primeval he was Eldest in Time. But Goldberry and Tom are referring to the mystery of *names*. See and ponder Tom's words in Vol. I p. 142.[2]

You may be able to conceive of your unique relation to the Creator without a name – can you: for in such a relation pronouns become proper nouns? But as soon as you are in a world of other finites with a similar, if each unique and different, relation to Prime Being, who are you? Frodo has asked not 'what is Tom Bombadil' but 'Who is he'. We and he no doubt often laxly confuse the questions. Goldberry gives what I think is the correct answer. We need not go into the sublimities of 'I am that am' – which is quite different from *he is*.* She adds as a concession a statement of part of the 'what'. He is *master* in a peculiar way: he has no fear, and no desire of possession or domination at all. He merely knows and understands about such things as concern him in his natural little realm. He hardly even judges, and as far as can be seen makes no effort to reform or remove even the Willow.

I don't think Tom needs philosophizing about, and is not improved by it. But many have found him an odd or indeed discordant ingredient. In historical fact I put him in because I had already 'invented' him independently (he first appeared in the Oxford Magazine)[3] and wanted an 'adventure' on the way. But I kept him in, and as he was, because he represents certain things otherwise left out. I do not mean him to be an allegory – or I should not have given him so particular, individual, and ridiculous a name – but 'allegory' is the only mode of exhibiting certain functions: he is then an 'allegory', or an exemplar, a particular embodying of pure (real) natural science: the spirit that desires knowledge of other things, their history and nature, *because they are 'other'* and wholly independent of the enquiring mind, a spirit coeval with the rational mind, and entirely unconcerned with 'doing' anything with the knowledge: Zoology and Botany not Cattle-breeding or Agriculture. Even the Elves hardly show this: they are primarily artists. Also T.B. exhibits another point in his attitude to the Ring, and its failure to affect him. You must concentrate on some part, probably relatively small, of the World (Universe), whether to tell a tale, however long, or to learn anything however fundamental – and therefore much will from that 'point of view' be left out, distorted on the circumference, or seem a discordant oddity. The power of the Ring over all concerned, even the Wizards or Emissaries, is not a delusion – but it is not the whole picture, even of the then state and content of that part of the Universe.

I have already dealt with the biological difficulty of Elf-Human marriage. It occurs of course in 'fairy-story' and folk-lore, though not all cases have the same notions behind them. But I have made it far more exceptional. I do not see that 'reincarnation' affects the resulting

*Only the *first* person (of worlds or anything) can be unique. If you say *he is* there must be more than one, and created (sub) existence is implied. I can say 'he is' of Winston Churchill as well as of Tom Bombadil, surely?

192

problems at all. But 'immortality' (in my world only within the limited longevity of the Earth) does, of course. As many fairy-stories perceive.

In the primary story of *Lúthien* and *Beren*, Lúthien is allowed as an absolute exception to divest herself of 'immortality' and become 'mortal' – but when Beren is slain by the Wolf-warden of the Gates of Hell, Lúthien obtains a brief respite in which they both return to Middle-earth 'alive' – though not mingling with other people: a kind of Orpheus-legend in reverse, but one of Pity not of Inexorability. Túor weds Idril the daughter of Turgon King of Gondolin; and 'it is supposed' (not stated) that he as an unique exception receives the Elvish limited 'immortality': an exception either way. Eärendil is Túor's son & father of Elros (First King of Númenor) and Elrond, their mother being Elwing daughter of Dior, son of Beren and Lúthien: so the problem of the Half-elven becomes united in one line. The view is that the Half-elven have a power of (irrevocable) choice, which may be delayed but not permanently, which kin's fate they will share. Elros chose to be a King and 'longaevus' but mortal, so all his descendants are mortal, and of a specially noble race, but with dwindling longevity: so Aragorn (who, however, has a greater life-span than his contemporaries, double, though not the original Númenórean treble, that of Men). Elrond chose to be among the Elves. His children – with a renewed Elvish strain, since their mother was Celebrían dtr. of Galadriel – have to make their choices. Arwen is not a 're-incarnation' of Lúthien (that in the view of this mythical history would be impossible, since Lúthien has died like a mortal and left the world of time) but a descendant very like her in looks, character, and fate. When she weds Aragorn (whose love-story elsewhere recounted is not here central and only occasionally referred to) she 'makes the choice of Lúthien', so the grief at her parting from Elrond is specially poignant. Elrond passes Over Sea. The end of his sons, Elladan and Elrohir, is not told: they delay their choice, and remain for a while.

As for 'whose authority decides these things?' The immediate 'authorities' are the Valar (the Powers or Authorities): the 'gods'. But they are only created spirits – of high angelic order we should say, with their attendant lesser angels – reverend, therefore, but not worshipful*;

*There are thus no temples or 'churches' or fanes in this 'world' among 'good' peoples. They had little or no 'religion' in the sense of worship. For help they may call on a *Vala* (as *Elbereth*), as a Catholic might on a Saint, though no doubt knowing in theory as well as he that the power of the Vala was limited and derivative. But this is a 'primitive age': and these folk may be said to view the Valar as children view their parents or immediate adult superiors, and though they know they are subjects of the King he does not live in their country nor have there any dwelling. I do not think Hobbits practised any form of worship or prayer (unless through exceptional contact with Elves). The Númenóreans and though potently 'subcreative', and resident on Earth to which they are bound by love, having assisted in its making and ordering, they cannot by their own will alter any fundamental provision. They called upon the One in the crisis of the rebellion of Númenor – when the Númenóreans attempted to take the Undying Land by force of a great armada in their lust for corporal immortality – which necessitated a catastrophic change in the shape of Earth. Immortality and Mortality being the special gifts of God to the *Eruhíni* (in whose conception and creation the Valar had no part at all) it must be assumed that no alteration of their fundamental kind could be effected by the Valar even in one case: the cases of Lúthien (and Túor) and the position of their descendants was a direct act of God. The entering into Men of the Elven-strain is indeed represented as part of a Divine Plan for the ennoblement of the Human Race, from the beginning destined to replace the Elves.

Are there any 'bounds to a writer's job' except those imposed by his own finiteness? No bounds, but the laws of contradiction, I should think. But, of course, humility and an awareness of peril is required. A writer may be basically 'benevolent' according to his lights (as I hope I am) and yet not be 'beneficent' owing to error and stupidity. I would claim, if I did not think it presumptuous in one so ill-instructed, to have as one object the elucidation of truth, and the encouragement of good morals in this real world, by the ancient device of exemplifying them in unfamiliar embodiments, that may tend to 'bring them home'. But, of course, I may be in error (at some or all points): my truths may not be true, or they may be distorted: and the mirror I have made may be dim and cracked. But I should need to be fully convinced that anything I have 'feigned' is actually harmful, *per se* and not merely because misunderstood, before I should recant or rewrite anything.

Great harm can be done, of course, by this potent mode of 'myth' – especially wilfully. The right to 'freedom' of the sub-creator is no guarantee among fallen men that it will not be used as wickedly as is Free Will. I am comforted by the fact that some, more pious and learned

---

(and others of that branch of Humanity, that fought against Morgoth, even if they elected to remain in Middle-earth and did not go to Númenor: such as the Rohirrim) were pure monotheists. But there was no temple in Númenor (until Sauron introduced the cult of Morgoth). The top of the Mountain, the Meneltarma or Pillar of Heaven, was dedicated to Eru, the One, and there at any time privately, and at certain times publicly, God was invoked, praised, and adored: an imitation of the Valar and the Mountain of Aman. But Númenor fell and was destroyed and the Mountain engulfed, and there was no substitute. Among the exiles, remnants of the Faithful who had not adopted the false religion nor taken part in the rebellion, religion as divine worship (though perhaps not as philosophy and metaphysics) seems to have played a small part; though a glimpse of it is caught in Faramir's remark on 'grace at meat', Vol. II p. 285.[4]

than I, have found nothing harmful in this Tale or its feignings as a 'myth'. . . . .

To conclude: having mentioned Free Will, I might say that in my myth I have used 'subcreation' in a special way (not the same as 'subcreation' as a term in criticism of art, though I tried to show allegorically how that might come to be taken up into Creation in some plane in my 'purgatorial' story *Leaf by Niggle* (Dublin Review 1945)) to make visible and physical the effects of Sin or misused Free Will by men. Free Will is derivative, and is ∴ only operative within provided circumstances; but in order that it may exist, it is necessary that the Author should guarantee it, whatever betides: sc. when it is 'against His Will', as we say, at any rate as it appears on a finite view. He does not stop or make 'unreal' sinful acts and their consequences. So in this myth, it is 'feigned' (legitimately whether that is a feature of the real world or not) that He gave special 'sub-creative' powers to certain of His highest created beings: that is a guarantee that what they devised and made should be given the reality of Creation. Of course within limits, and of course subject to certain commands or prohibitions. But if they 'fell', as the Diabolus Morgoth did, and started making things 'for himself, to be their Lord', these would then 'be', even if Morgoth broke the supreme ban against making other 'rational' creatures like Elves or Men. They would at least 'be' real physical realities in the physical world, however evil they might prove, even 'mocking' the Children of God. They would be Morgoth's greatest Sins, abuses of his highest privilege, and would be creatures begotten of Sin, and naturally bad. (I nearly wrote 'irredeemably bad'; but that would be going too far. Because by accepting or tolerating their making – necessary to their actual existence – even Orcs would become part of the World, which is God's and ultimately good.) But whether they could have 'souls' or 'spirits' seems a different question; and since in my myth at any rate I do not conceive of the making of souls or spirits, things of an equal order if not an equal power to the Valar, as a possible 'delegation', I have represented at least the Orcs as pre-existing real beings on whom the Dark Lord has exerted the fullness of his power in remodelling and corrupting them, not making them. That God would 'tolerate' that, seems no worse theology than the toleration of the calculated dehumanizing of Men by tyrants that goes on today. There might be other 'makings' all the same which were more like puppets filled (only at a distance) with their maker's mind and will, or ant-like operating under direction of a queen-centre.

Now (you will reasonably say) I am taking myself even more seriously than you did, and making a great song and oration about a good tale, which admittedly owes its similitude to mere craft. It is so. But the things I have scribbled about, arise in some form or another from all

195

writing (or art) that is not careful to dwell within the walls of 'observed fact'.

[The draft ends here. At the top, Tolkien has written: 'Not sent', and has added: 'It seemed to be taking myself too importantly.']

154 To Naomi Mitchison

25 September 1954   76 Sandfield Road, Headington, Oxford
Dear Mrs Mitchison,

I have been plagued by business, troubles, illness, and journeys, or I should have written long before, and especially after your kind letter of last month: temporarily mislaid in a broil of exam-papers, galleys, and what not: after reading to the end of *The Lord* &c.

You have been most kind and encouraging to me, and your generous and perceptive review[1] puts me in your debt. Yours is the only comment that I have seen that, besides treating the book as 'literature', at least in intent, and even taking it seriously (and praising or ridiculing it accordingly), also sees it as an elaborate form of the *game* of inventing a country – an endless one, because even a committee of experts in different branches could not complete the overall picture. I am more conscious of my sketchiness in the archaeology and *realien*[2] than in the economics: clothes, agricultural implements, metal-working, pottery, architecture and the like. Not to mention music and its apparatus. I am not incapable of or unaware of economic thought; and I think as far as the 'mortals' go, Men, Hobbits, and Dwarfs,[3] that the situations are so devised that economic likelihood is there and could be worked out: Gondor has sufficient 'townlands' and fiefs with a good water and road approach to provide for its population; and clearly has many industries though these are hardly alluded to. The Shire is placed in a water and mountain situation and a distance from the sea and a latitude that would give it a natural fertility, quite apart from the stated fact that it was a well-tended region when they took it over (no doubt with a good deal of older arts and crafts). The Shire-hobbits have no very great need of metals, but the Dwarfs are agents; and in the east of the Mountains of Lune are some of their mines (as shown in the earlier legends): no doubt, the reason, or one of them, for their often crossing the Shire. Some of the modernities found among them (I think especially of *umbrellas*) are probably, I think certainly, a mistake, of the same order as their silly names, and tolerable with them only as a deliberate 'anglicization' to point the contrast between them and other peoples in the most familiar terms. I do not think people of that sort and stage of life and development can be both peaceable and very brave and tough 'at a pinch'.* Experience in two wars has confirmed me in that view. But *hobbits* are not a Utopian vision, or recommended as an ideal in their own or any age. They, as all peoples and their situations, are an historical accident – as the Elves point out to Frodo – and an impermanent one in the long view. I am not a reformer nor an 'embalmer'! I am not a 'reformer' (by exercise of power) since it seems doomed to Sarumanism. But 'embalming' has its own punishments.

Some reviewers have called the whole thing simple-minded, just a plain fight between Good and Evil, with all the good just good, and the bad just bad. Pardonable, perhaps (though at least Boromir has been overlooked) in people in a hurry, and with only a fragment to read, and, of course, without the earlier written but unpublished Elvish histories. But the Elves are *not* wholly good or in the right. Not so much because they had flirted with Sauron; as because with or without his assistance they were 'embalmers'. They wanted to have their cake and eat it: to live in the mortal historical Middle-earth because they had become fond of it (and perhaps because they there had the advantages of a superior caste), and so tried to stop its change and history, stop its growth, keep it as a pleasaunce, even largely a desert, where they could be 'artists' – and they were overburdened with sadness and nostalgic regret. In their way the Men of Gondor were similar: a withering people whose only 'hallows' were their tombs. But in any case this is a tale about a war, and if war is allowed (at least as a topic and a setting) it is not much good complaining that all the people on one side are against those on the other. Not that I have made even this issue quite so simple: there are Saruman, and Denethor, and Boromir; and there are treacheries and strife even among the Orcs.

Actually in the imagination of this story we are now living on a physically round Earth. But the whole 'legendarium' contains a transition from a flat world (or at least an οἰκουμένη with borders all about it) to a globe: an inevitable transition, I suppose, to a modern 'myth-maker' with a mind subjected to the same 'appearances' as ancient men, and partly fed on their myths, but taught that the Earth was round from the earliest years. So deep was the impression made by 'astronomy' on me that I do not think I could deal with or imaginatively conceive a flat world, though a world of static Earth with a Sun going round it seems easier (to fancy if not to reason).

The particular 'myth' which lies behind this tale, and the mood both of Men and Elves at this time, is the Downfall of Númenor: a special

*The chief way in which *Hobbits* differ from experience is that they are not cruel, and have no blood-sports, and have by implication a feeling for 'wild creatures' that are not alas! very commonly found among the nearest contemporary parallels.

variety of the Atlantis tradition. That seems to me so fundamental to 'mythical history' – whether it has any kind of basis in real history, *pace* Saurat and others, is not relevant – that some version of it would have to come in.

I have written an account of the Downfall, which you might be interested to see. But the immediate point is that before the Downfall there lay beyond the sea and the west-shores of Middle-earth an *earthly* Elvish paradise Eressëa, and *Valinor* the land of the *Valar* (the Powers, the Lords of the West*), places that could be reached physically by ordinary sailing-ships, though the Seas were perilous. But after the rebellion of the Númenóreans, the Kings of Men, who dwelt in a land most westerly of all mortal lands, and eventually in the height of their pride attempted to occupy Eressëa and Valinor by force, Númenor was destroyed, and Eressëa and Valinor removed from the physically attainable Earth: the way west was open, but led nowhere but back again – for mortals.

Elendil and his sons were the chiefs of the small 'faithful' party that took no part in the attempt to seize world-power and immortality by force, and they escaped the drowning of Númenor, and were borne east on a great storm, and cast up on the west-shores of Middle-earth, where they established their realms. But there was no going back for them or any mortal men; hence their nostalgic mood.

But the promise made to the Eldar (the High Elves – not to other varieties, they had long before made their irrevocable choice, preferring Middle-earth to paradise) for their sufferings in the struggle with the prime Dark Lord had still to be fulfilled: that they should always be able to leave Middle-earth, if they wished, and pass over Sea to the True West, by the Straight Road, and so come to Eressëa – but so pass out of time and history, never to return. The Half-elven, such as Elrond and Arwen, can choose to which kind and fate they shall belong: choose once and for all. Hence the grief at the parting of Elrond and Arwen.

But in this story it is supposed that there may be certain rare exceptions or accommodations (legitimately supposed? there always seem to be exceptions); and so certain 'mortals', who have played some great part in Elvish affairs, may pass with the Elves to Elvenhome. Thus Frodo (by the express gift of Arwen) and Bilbo, and eventually Sam (as adumbrated by Frodo); and as a unique exception Gimli the Dwarf, as friend of Legolas and 'servant' of Galadriel.

I have said nothing about it in this book, but the mythical idea underlying is that for mortals, since their 'kind' cannot be changed for ever, this is strictly only a temporary reward: a healing and redress of suffering. They cannot abide for ever, and though they cannot return to

*'gods' is the nearest equivalent, but not strictly accurate.

mortal earth, they can and will 'die' – of free will, and leave the world. (In this setting the return of Arthur would be quite impossible, a vain imagining.)

I am sorry that the Ice-bay of Forochel[4] has not (so far) been cast for any significant part. It is just 'Elvish' for Northern Ice; and is a mere remnant of the colds of the North, the realm of the prime Dark Lord of earlier Ages. Arvedui, the last king of Arnor, is said, indeed, to have fled thither, and attempted to escape thence by ship, but to have been destroyed in the ice; and with him perished the last of the *palantíri* of the North Kingdom.

I am afraid this is a preposterously long letter; and perhaps presumptuous in its length, though your kindness and interest offer some excuse.

Soon after your visit, as pleasant as unexpected, I had a copy made of the chronology of the Second and Third Ages, for your perusal – purely annalistic and unmotivated. If it would still interest you, I will send it.

I was sorry to find, when it was returned, that the screed on 'languages' etc. had been sent uncorrected, and with lots of words and phrases unerased, so that parts were hardly intelligible.

You may be interested to hear that a reprint of *The Fellowship* seems already to be needed. But I do not suppose the first printing was very large.

Yours sincerely
J. R. R. Tolkien.

155 To Naomi Mitchison (draft)

[A passage from a draft of the above letter, which was not included in the version actually sent.]

I am afraid I have been far too casual about 'magic' and especially the use of the word; though Galadriel and others show by the criticism of the 'mortal' use of the word, that the thought about it is not altogether casual. But it is a v. large question, and difficult; and a story which, as you so rightly say, is largely about motives (choice, temptations etc.) and the intentions for using whatever is found in the world, could hardly be burdened with a pseudo-philosophic disquisition! I do not intend to involve myself in any debate whether 'magic' in any sense is real or really possible in the world. But I suppose that, for the purposes of the tale, some would say that there is a latent distinction such as once was called the distinction between *magia* and *goeteia*.[1] Galadriel speaks of the 'deceits of the Enemy'. Well enough, but *magia* could be, was, held good (per se), and *goeteia* bad. Neither is, in this tale, good or bad (per se), but only by motive or purpose or use. Both sides use both, but

199

with different motives. The supremely bad motive is (for this tale, since it is specially about it) domination of other 'free' wills. The Enemy's operations are by no means all goetic deceits, but 'magic' that produces real effects in the physical world. But his *magia* he uses to bulldoze both people and things, and his *goeteia* to terrify and subjugate. Their *magia* the Elves and Gandalf use (sparingly): a *magia*, producing real results (like fire in a wet faggot) for specific beneficent purposes. Their goetic effects are entirely *artistic* and not intended to deceive: they never deceive Elves (but may deceive or bewilder unaware Men) since the difference is to them as clear as the difference to us between fiction, painting, and sculpture, and 'life'.

Both sides live mainly by 'ordinary' means. The Enemy, or those who have become like him, go in for 'machinery' – with destructive and evil effects – because 'magicians', who have become chiefly concerned to use *magia* for their own power, would do so (do do so). The basic motive for *magia* – quite apart from any philosophic consideration of how it would work – is immediacy: speed, reduction of labour, and reduction also to a minimum (or vanishing point) of the gap between the idea or desire and the result or effect. But the *magia* may not be easy to come by, and at any rate if you have command of abundant slave-labour or machinery (often only the same thing concealed), it may be as quick or quick enough to push mountains over, wreck forests, or build pyramids by such means. Of course another factor then comes in, a moral or pathological one: the tyrants lose sight of objects, become cruel, and like smashing, hurting, and defiling as such. It would no doubt be possible to defend poor Lotho's introduction of more efficient mills; but not of Sharkey and Sandyman's use of them.

Anyway, a difference in the use of 'magic' in this story is that it is not to be come by by 'lore' or spells; but is in an inherent power not possessed or attainable by Men as such. Aragorn's 'healing' might be regarded as 'magical', or at least a blend of magic with pharmacy and 'hypnotic' processes. But it is (in theory) reported by hobbits who have very little notions of philosophy and science; while A. is not a pure 'Man', but at long remove one of the 'children of Lúthien'.[2]

156 To Robert Murray, S.J. (draft)

[An answer to further comments on *The Lord of the Rings*.]

4 November 1954   76 Sandfield Road, Headington, Oxford
My dear Rob,

It is remarkably kind of you to write at such length amid, I fear, weariness. I am answering at once, because I am grateful, and because only letters that I do treat so ever get answered, and most of all because your parcel has arrived when having done all my 'prep' – ordering all the minutes and resolutions of a long and argumentative College-meeting yesterday (there being no fellow of ill-will, and only 24 persons of the usual human absurdity. I felt rather like an observer at the meeting of Hobbit-notables to advise the Mayor on the precedence and choice of dishes at a Shire-banquet) – I have half an hour to spare before going down hill for a session with the College secretary. That is the kind of sentence I naturally write. . . . .

No, 'Sméagol' was not, of course, fully envisaged at first, but I believe his character was implicit, and merely needed attention. As for Gandalf: surely it is not to join P. H.[1] to voice *any* criticism! I could be much more destructive myself. There are, I suppose, always defects in any large-scale work of art; and especially in those of literary form that are founded on an earlier matter which is put to new uses – like Homer, or Beowulf, or Virgil, or Greek or Shakespearean tragedy! In which class, as a class not as a competitor, *The Lord of the Rings* really falls though it is only founded on the author's own first draft! I think the way in which Gandalf's return is presented is a defect, and one other critic, as much under the spell as yourself, curiously used the same expression: 'cheating'. That is partly due to the ever-present compulsions of narrative technique. He must return at that point, and such explanations of his survival as are explicitly set out must be given there – but the narrative is urgent, and must not be held up for elaborate discussions involving the whole 'mythological' setting. It is a little impeded even so, though I have severely cut G's account of himself. I might perhaps have made more clear the later remarks in Vol. II (and Vol. III) which refer to or are made by Gandalf, but I have purposely kept all allusions to the highest matters down to mere hints, perceptible only by the most attentive, or kept them under unexplained symbolic forms. So God and the 'angelic' gods, the Lords or Powers of the West, only peep through in such places as Gandalf's conversation with Frodo: 'behind that there was something else at work, beyond any design of the Ring-maker's'; or in Faramir's Númenórean grace at dinner.

Gandalf really 'died', and was changed: for that seems to me the only real cheating, to represent anything that can be called 'death' as making no difference. 'I am G. the *White*, who has returned from death'. Probably he should rather have said to Wormtongue: 'I have not passed through death (*not* 'fire and flood') to bandy crooked words with a serving-man'. And so on. I might say much more, but it would only be in (perhaps tedious) elucidation of the 'mythological' ideas in my mind; it would not, I fear, get rid of the fact that the return of G. is as presented in this book a 'defect', and one I was aware of, and probably did not work hard enough to mend. But G. is not, of course, a human being (Man or Hobbit). There are naturally no precise modern terms to say what he was. I wd. venture to say that he was an *incarnate* 'angel'–strictly an ἄγγελος:[2] that is, with the other *Istari*, wizards, 'those who know', an emissary from the Lords of the West, sent to Middle-earth, as the great crisis of Sauron loomed on the horizon. By 'incarnate' I mean they were embodied in physical bodies capable of pain, and weariness, and of afflicting the spirit with physical fear, and of being 'killed', though supported by the angelic spirit they might endure long, and only show slowly the wearing of care and labour.

Why they should take such a form is bound up with the 'mythology' of the 'angelic' Powers of the world of this fable. At this point in the fabulous history the purpose was precisely to limit and hinder their exhibition of 'power' on the physical plane, and so that they should do what they were primarily sent for: train, advise, instruct, arouse the hearts and minds of those threatened by Sauron to a resistance with their own strengths; and not just to do the job for them. They thus appeared as 'old' sage figures. But in this 'mythology' all the 'angelic' powers concerned with this world were capable of many degrees of error and failing between the absolute Satanic rebellion and evil of Morgoth and his satellite Sauron, and the fainéance of some of the other higher powers or 'gods'. The 'wizards' were not exempt, indeed being incarnate were more likely to stray, or err. Gandalf alone fully passes the tests, on a moral plane anyway (he makes mistakes of judgement). For in his condition it was for him a *sacrifice* to perish on the Bridge in defence of his companions, less perhaps than for a mortal Man or Hobbit, since he had a far greater inner power than they; but also more, since it was a humbling and abnegation of himself in conformity to 'the Rules': for all he could know at that moment he was the *only* person who could direct the resistance to Sauron successfully, and all *his* mission was vain. He was handing over to the Authority that ordained the Rules, and giving up personal hope of success.

That I should say is what the Authority wished, as a set-off to Saruman. The 'wizards', as such, had failed; or if you like: the crisis had become too grave and needed an enhancement of power. So Gandalf sacrificed himself, was accepted, and enhanced, and returned. 'Yes, that was the name. I was Gandalf.' Of course he remains similar in personality and idiosyncrasy, but both his wisdom and power are much greater. When he speaks he commands attention; the old Gandalf could not have dealt so with Théoden, nor with Saruman. He is still under the obligation of concealing his power and of teaching rather than forcing or dominating wills, but where the physical powers of the Enemy are too great for the good will of the opposers to be effective he can act in emergency as an 'angel' – no more violently than the release of St Peter from prison. He seldom does so, operating rather through others, but in one or two cases in the War (in Vol. III) he does reveal a sudden power: he twice rescues Faramir. He alone is left to forbid the entrance of the Lord of Nazgûl to Minas Tirith, when the City has been overthrown and its Gates destroyed – and yet so powerful is the whole train of human resistance, that he himself has kindled and organized, that in fact no battle between the two occurs: it passes to other mortal hands. In the end before he departs for ever he sums himself up: 'I was the enemy of Sauron'. He might have added: 'for that purpose I was sent to Middle-earth'. But by that he would at the end have meant more than at the beginning. He was sent by a mere prudent plan of the angelic Valar or governors; but Authority had taken up this plan and enlarged it, at the moment of its failure. 'Naked I was sent back – for a brief time, until my task is done'. Sent back by whom, and whence? Not by the 'gods' whose business is only with this embodied world and its time; for he passed 'out of thought and time'. Naked is alas! unclear. It was meant just literally, 'unclothed like a child' (not discarnate), and so ready to receive the white robes of the highest. Galadriel's power is not divine, and his healing in Lórien is meant to be no more than physical healing and refreshment.

But if it is 'cheating' to treat 'death' as making no difference, embodiment must not be ignored. Gandalf may be enhanced in power (that is, under the forms of this fable, in sanctity), but if still embodied he must still suffer care and anxiety, and the needs of flesh. He has no more (if no less) certitudes, or freedoms, than say a living theologian. In any case none of my 'angelic' persons are represented as knowing the future completely, or indeed at all where other *wills* are concerned. Hence their constant temptation to do, or try to do, what is for them *wrong* (and disastrous): to force lesser wills by power: by awe if not by actual fear, or physical constraint. But the nature of the gods' knowledge of the history of the World, and their part in making it (before it was embodied or made 'real') – whence they drew their knowledge of the future, such as they had, is part of the major mythology. It is at least there represented that the intrusion of Elves and Men into that story was not any part of theirs at all, but reserved: hence Elves and Men were called the Children of God; and hence the gods either loved (or hated) them specially: as having a relation to the Creator equal to their own, if of different stature. This is the mythological-theological situation at this moment in History, which has been made explicit but has not yet been published.

Men have 'fallen' – any legends put in the form of supposed ancient history of this actual world of ours must accept that – but the peoples of the West, the good side are Re-formed. That is they are the descendants of Men that tried to repent and fled Westward from the domination of the Prime Dark Lord, and his false worship, and by contrast with the Elves renewed (and enlarged) their knowledge of the truth and the nature of the World. They thus escaped from 'religion' in a pagan sense, into a pure monotheist world, in which all things and beings and powers that might seem worshipful were not to be worshipped, not even the gods (the Valar), being only creatures of the One. And He was immensely remote.

The High Elves were exiles from the Blessed Realm of the Gods (after their own particular Elvish fall) and they had no 'religion' (or religious practices, rather) for those had been in the hands of the gods, praising and adoring *Eru* 'the One', *Ilúvatar* the Father of All on the Mt. of Aman.

The highest kind of Men, those of the Three Houses, who aided the Elves in the primal War against the Dark Lord, were rewarded by the gift of the Land of the Star, or Westernesse (= Númenor) which was most westerly of all mortal lands, and almost in sight of Elvenhome (Eldamar) on the shores of the Blessed Realm. There they became the Númenóreans, the Kings of Men. They were given a triple span of life – but not elvish 'immortality' (which is not eternal, but measured by the duration in time of Earth); for the point of view of this mythology is that 'mortality' or a short span, and 'immortality' or an indefinite span was part of what we might call the biological and spiritual *nature* of the Children of God, Men and Elves (the firstborn) respectively, and could *not* be altered by anyone (even a Power or god), and would not be altered by the One, except perhaps by one of those strange exceptions to all rules and ordinances which seem to crop up in the history of the Universe, and show the Finger of God, as the one wholly free Will and Agent.*

The Númenóreans thus began a great new good, and as monotheists; but like the Jews (only more so) with only one physical centre of 'worship': the summit of the mountain Meneltarma 'Pillar of Heaven' – literally, for they did not conceive of the sky as a divine residence – in the centre of Númenor; but it had no building and no temple, as all such things had evil associations. But they 'fell' again – because of a Ban or prohibition, inevitably. They were forbidden to sail *west* beyond their own land because they were not allowed to be or try to be 'immortal'; and in this myth the Blessed Realm is represented as still having an actual physical existence as a region of the real world, one which they could have reached by ship, being very great mariners. While obedient, people

---

*The story of Beren and Lúthien is the one great exception, as it is the way by which 'Elvishness' becomes wound in as a thread in human history.

from the Blessed Realm often visited them, and so their knowledge and arts reached almost an Elvish height.

But the proximity of the Blessed Realm, the very length of their life-span given as a reward, and the increasing delight of life, made them begin to hanker after 'immortality'. They did not break the ban but they begrudged it. And forced east they turned from beneficence in their appearances on the coasts of Middle-earth, to pride, desire of power and wealth. So they came into conflict with Sauron, the lieutenant of the Prime Dark Lord, who had fallen back into evil and was claiming both kingship and godship over Men of Middle-earth. It was on the *kingship* question that Ar-pharazôn the 13th[3] and mightiest King of Númenor challenged him primarily. His armada that took haven at Umbar was so great, and the Númenóreans at their height so terrible and resplendent, that Sauron's servants deserted him.

So Sauron had recourse to guile. He submitted, and was carried off to Númenor as a prisoner-hostage. But he was of course a 'divine' person (in the terms of this mythology; a lesser member of the race of Valar) and thus far too powerful to be controlled in this way. He steadily got Arpharazôn's mind under his own control, and in the event corrupted many of the Númenóreans, destroyed the conception of Eru, now represented as a mere figment of the Valar or Lords of the West (a fictitious sanction to which they appealed if anyone questioned their rulings), and substituted a Satanist religion with a large temple, the worship of the dispossessed eldest of the Valar (the rebellious Dark Lord of the First Age).* He finally induces Arpharazôn, frightened by the approach of old age, to make the greatest of all armadas, and go up with war against the Blessed Realm itself, and wrest it and its 'immortality' into his own hands.†

---

*There is only one 'god': God, *Eru Ilúvatar*. There are the first creations, angelic beings, of which those most concerned in the Cosmogony reside (of love and choice) inside the World, as Valar or gods, or governors; and there are incarnate rational creatures, Elves and Men, of similar but different status and natures.

†This was a delusion of course, a Satanic lie. For as emissaries from the Valar clearly inform him, the Blessed Realm does not confer immortality. The land is blessed because the Blessed dwell there, not vice versa, and the Valar are immortal by right and nature, while Men are mortal by right and nature. But cozened by Sauron he dismisses all this as a diplomatic argument to ward off the power of the King of Kings. It might or might not be 'heretical', if these myths were regarded as statements about the actual nature of Man in the real world: I do not know. But the view of the myth is that Death – the mere shortness of human life-span – is not a punishment for the Fall, but a biologically (and therefore also spiritually, since body and spirit are integrated) inherent part of Man's nature. The attempt to escape it is wicked because 'unnatural', and silly because Death in that sense is the Gift of God (envied by the Elves), release from the weariness of Time. Death, in the penal sense, is viewed as a change in attitude to it: fear, reluctance. A good Númenórean died of free will when he felt it to be time to do so.

The Valar had no real answer to this monstrous rebellion — for the Children of God were not under their ultimate jurisdiction: they were not allowed to destroy them, or coerce them with any 'divine' display of the powers they held over the physical world. They appealed to God; and a catastrophic 'change of plan' occurred. At the moment that Arpharazôn set foot on the forbidden shore, a rift appeared: Númenor foundered and was utterly overwhelmed; the armada was swallowed up; and the Blessed Realm removed for ever from the circles of the physical world. Thereafter one could sail right round the world and never find it.

So ended Númenor-Atlantis and all its glory. But in a kind of Noachian situation the small party of the Faithful in Númenor, who had refused to take part in the rebellion (though many of them had been sacrificed in the Temple by the Sauronians) escaped in Nine Ships (Vol. I. 379, II. 202) under the leadership of *Elendil* (= Ælfwine, Elf-friend) and his sons *Isildur* and *Anárion,* and established a kind of diminished memory of Númenor in Exile on the coasts of Middle-earth – inheriting the hatred of Sauron, the friendship of the Elves, the knowledge of the True God, and (less happily) the yearning for longevity, and the habit of embalming and the building of splendid tombs – their only 'hallows': or almost so. But the 'hallow' of God and the Mountain had perished, and there was no real substitute. Also when the 'Kings' came to an end there was no equivalent to a 'priesthood': the two being identical in Númenórean ideas. So while God (Eru) was a datum of good* Númenórean philosophy, and a prime fact in their conception of history, He had at the time of the War of the Ring no worship and no hallowed place. And that kind of negative truth was characteristic of the West, and all the area under Númenórean influence: the refusal to worship any 'creature', and above all no 'dark lord' or satanic demon, Sauron, or any other, was almost as far as they got. They had (I imagine) no petitionary prayers to God; but preserved the vestige of thanksgiving. (Those under special Elvish influence might call on the angelic powers for help in immediate peril or fear of evil enemies.†) It later appears that there had been a 'hallow' on Mindolluin, only approachable by the King, where he had anciently offered thanks and praise on behalf of his people; but it had been forgotten. It was re-entered by Aragorn, and there he found a sapling of the White Tree, and replanted it in the Court of the Fountain. It is to be presumed that with the reemergence of the lineal priest kings (of whom Lúthien the Blessed Elf-maiden was a

*There were evil Númenóreans: Sauronians, but they do not come into this story, except remotely; as the wicked Kings who had become Nazgûl or Ringwraiths.

†The Elves often called on Varda-Elbereth, the Queen of the Blessed Realm, their especial friend; and so does Frodo.

foremother) the worship of God would be renewed, and His Name (or title) be again more often heard. But there would be no *temple* of the True God while Númenórean influence lasted.

But they were still living on the borders of myth – or rather this story exhibits 'myth' passing into History or the Dominion of Men; for of course the Shadow will arise again in a sense (as is clearly foretold by Gandalf), but never again (unless it be before the great End) will an evil daemon be incarnate as a physical enemy; he will direct Men and all the complications of half-evils, and defective-goods, and the twilights of doubt as to sides, such situations as he most loves (you can see them already arising in the War of the Ring, which is by no means so clear cut an issue as some critics have averred): those will be and are our more difficult fate. But if you imagine people in such a mythical state, in which Evil is largely incarnate, and in which physical resistance to it is a major act of loyalty to God, I think you would have the 'good people' in just such a state: concentrated on the negative: the resistance to the false, while 'truth' remained more historical and philosophical than religious.

But 'wizards' are not in any sense or degree 'shady'. Not mine. I am under the difficulty of finding English names for mythological creatures with other names, since people would not 'take' a string of Elvish names, and I would rather they took my legendary creatures even with the false associations of the 'translation' than not at all.

Even the dwarfs are not really Germanic 'dwarfs' (*Zwerge, dweorgas, dvergar*), and I call them 'dwarves' to mark that. They are not naturally evil, not necessarily hostile, and not a kind of maggot-folk bred in stone; but a variety of incarnate rational creature. The *istari* are translated 'wizards' because of the connexion of 'wizard' with *wise* and so with 'witting' and knowing. They are actually emissaries from the True West, and so mediately from God, sent precisely to strengthen the resistance of the 'good', when the Valar become aware that the shadow of Sauron is taking shape again.

[The draft ends with a discussion of the nature of the *istari* and the death and reincarnation of Gandalf which resembles the passage on this subject earlier in the letter.]

157 From a letter to Katherine Farrer 27 November 1954

[The second volume of *The Lord of the Rings* was published, under the title *The Two Towers*, on 11 November.]

I have felt very mean indeed, since I have known that you have both been ill and troubled, and I have never written, or called, or made any offer of help (or even sympathy). Always meaning to, of course! To any eyes but those of your charity I shd. have appeared the sort of 'friend' that dumps his works on you when you are already overloaded, sucks up praise and encouragement, expects reviews, and then departs when you begin to break down. . . . .

Of course I understand the financial difficulties. For a real holiday it shd. be not only 'with pay' but 'with more than pay'. I am sure there must be funds somewhere that are meant for such a purpose. If they cannot be found or tapped, *nothing* would give me more pleasure than to become one. I could for instance *well* spare £50 (and *more* if this rise in my wages occurs). But perhaps this will seem rather impertinent. Forget it, if it does. (I can only say that Trinity was very kind to me when I was in a dreadful pinch in the early war years,[1] and I should prefer this way of being grateful – by helping far its most distinguished member and wife 'towards the sun'.) Bless you both. . . . .

I return a copy of *Lewis*.[2] Also I send a copy of 'Encounter' in which one of Auden's volleys occurred: much the same but longer than the N.Y.S. Times.[3] I got 'Encounter' for you, so you need not return it. The Ents seem to have been a success generally (even with Muir);[4] but A. is a better critic. As usually with me they grew rather out of their name, than the other way about. I always felt that something ought to be done about the peculiar A. Saxon word *ent* for a 'giant' or mighty person of long ago – to whom all old works were ascribed. If it had a slightly philosophical tone (though in ordinary philology it is 'quite unconnected with any present participle of the verb to be') that also interested me.

I am hopelessly behind with the 'Appendices' to Vol. III; but I have been be-bothered with many things; and Chris. too overwhelmed to help with maps. It just can't be helped. I am at it.

158 From a letter to Rayner Unwin 2 December 1954

[A comment on the 'blurb' on the dust-jacket of Houghton Mifflin's edition of *The Two Towers*.]

I have only just had time to glance at the H.M. 'jacket' stuff. . . . . This account must have been written by someone who has not read the book, but relied on hearsay inaccurately remembered. The 'giving away of the plot' is, of course, a silly (and unnecessary) procedure; but at least the plot given away might be that of the book described. Or is that part of the game?

[A reply to a letter from a reader of *The Lord of the Rings*.]

I had great difficulty (it took several years) to get my story published, and it is not easy to say who is most surprised at the result: myself or the publishers! But it remains an unfailing delight to me to find my own belief justified: that the 'fairy-story' is really an adult genre, and one for which a starving audience exists. I said so, more or less, in my essay on the fairy-story in the collection dedicated to the memory of Charles Williams. But it was a mere proposition – which awaited proof. As C. S. Lewis said to me long ago, more or less – (I do not suppose my memory of his *dicta* is any more precisely accurate than his of mine: I often find strange things attributed to me in his works) – 'if they won't write the kind of books we want to read, we shall have to write them ourselves; but it is very laborious'. Being a man of immense power and industry, his 'trilogy' was finished much sooner amidst much other work; but at last my slower and more meticulous (as well as more indolent and less organized) machine has produced its effort. The labour! I have typed myself nearly all of it *twice*, and parts more often; not to mention the written stages! But I am amply rewarded and encouraged to find that the labour was not wasted. One such letter as yours is sufficient – and 'furnishes more than any author ought to ask'.

I knew Charles Williams well in his last few years: partly because of Lewis's good habit of writing to authors who pleased him (which put us both in touch with Williams); and still more because of the good fortune amid disaster that transferred Williams to Oxford during the War. But I do not think we influenced one another at all! Too 'set', and too different. We both listened (in C.S.L.'s rooms) to large and largely unintelligible fragments of one another's works read aloud; because C.S.L. (marvellous man) seemed able to enjoy us both. But I think we both found the other's mind (or rather mode of expression, and climate) as impenetrable when cast into 'literature', as we found the other's presence and conversation delightful.

160   **From a letter to Rayner Unwin**   6 March 1955

[Tolkien had handed over some of the material for the Appendices to Volume III of *The Lord of the Rings*, and Allen & Unwin were pressing him for the remainder. On 2 March, Rayner Unwin wrote to plead for it to be delivered, saying that otherwise the publishers would have to 'yield to the intense pressure that is accumulating and publish [the third volume] without all the additional material'.]

I must accept your challenge. We must make do with what material I can produce by your return. I hope the Map, which is really the most necessary, will be included.

I now wish that no appendices had been promised! For I think their appearance in truncated and compressed form will satisfy nobody: certainly not me; clearly from the (appalling mass of) letters I receive not those people who like that kind of thing – astonishingly many; while those who enjoy the book as an 'heroic romance' only, and find 'unexplained vistas' part of the literary effect, will neglect the appendices, very properly.

I am not now at all sure that the tendency to treat the whole thing as a kind of vast game is really good – cert. not for me, who find that kind of thing only too fatally attractive. It is, I suppose, a tribute to the curious effect that story has, when based on very elaborate and detailed workings of geography, chronology, and language, that so many should clamour for sheer 'information', or 'lore'. But the demands such people make would again require a book, at least the size of Vol. I.

In any case the 'background' matter is very intricate, useless unless exact, and compression within the limits available leaves it unsatisfactory. It needs great concentration (and leisure), and being completely interlocked cannot be dealt with piecemeal. I have found that out, since I let part of it go.

161   From a letter to Rayner Unwin   14 April 1955

The map is hell! I have not been as careful as I should in keeping track of distances. I think a large scale map simply reveals all the chinks in the armour – besides being obliged to differ somewhat from the printed small scale version, which was semi-pictorial. May have to abandon it for this trip!

162   From a letter to Rayner Unwin   18 April 1955

I have sent, registered under separate cover, Christopher's beautiful re-drawing of the large scale draft-map I made of the area with which Vol. III is mainly concerned.

I hope it will be approved. . . . . The scale (which I noticed he had not inserted) is 5 times enlarged exactly from that of the general map.

[Auden, who had reviewed *The Fellowship of the Ring* in the *New York Times Book Review* and *Encounter,* had been sent proofs of the third volume, *The Return of the King.* He wrote to Tolkien in April 1955 to ask various questions arising from the book. Tolkien's reply does not survive (Auden usually threw away letters after reading them). Auden wrote again on 3 June to say that he had been asked to give a talk about *The Lord of the Rings* on the BBC Third Programme in October. He asked Tolkien if there were any points he would like to hear made in the broadcast, and whether he would supply a few 'human touches' in the form of information about how the book came to be written. Tolkien's reply survives because on this occasion – and when he subsequently wrote to Auden – he kept a carbon copy, from which this text is taken.]

7 June 1955   76 Sandfield Road, Headington, Oxford

Dear Auden,

I was very pleased to hear from you, and glad to feel that you were not bored. I am afraid that you may be in for rather a long letter again; but you can do what you like with it. I type it so that it may at any rate be quickly readable. I do not really think that I am frightfully important. I wrote the Trilogy[1] as a personal satisfaction, driven to it by the scarcity of literature of the sort that I wanted to read (and what there was was often heavily alloyed). A great labour; and as the author of the *Ancrene Wisse* says at the end of his work: 'I would rather, God be my witness, set out on foot for Rome than begin the work over again!' But unlike him I would not have said: 'Read some of this book at your leisure every day; and I hope that if you read it often it will prove very profitable to you; otherwise I shall have spent my long hours very ill.' I was not thinking much of the profit or delight of others; though no one can really write or make anything purely privately.

However, when the BBC employs any one so important as yourself to talk publicly about the Trilogy, not without reference to the author, the most modest (or at any rate retiring) of men, whose instinct is to cloak such self-knowledge as he has, and such criticisms of life as he knows it, under mythical and legendary dress, cannot help thinking about it in personal terms – and finding it interesting, and difficult, too, to express both briefly and accurately.

The Lord of the Rings as a story was finished so long ago now that I can take a largely impersonal view of it, and find 'interpretations' quite amusing; even those that I might make myself, which are mostly *post scriptum*: I had very little particular, conscious, intellectual, intention in mind at any point.* Except for a few deliberately disparaging reviews –

---

*Take the Ents, for instance. I did not consciously invent them at all. The chapter called 'Treebeard', from Treebeard's first remark on p. 66, was written off more or less as it

such as that of Vol. II in the *New Statesman*,[3] in which you and I were both scourged with such terms as 'pubescent' and 'infantilism' – what appreciative readers have got out of the work or seen in it has seemed fair enough, even when I do not agree with it. Always excepting, of course, any 'interpretations' in the mode of simple allegory: that is, the particular and topical. In a larger sense, it is I suppose impossible to write any 'story' that is not allegorical in proportion as it 'comes to life'; since each of us is an allegory, embodying in a particular tale and clothed in the garments of time and place, universal truth and everlasting life. Anyway most people that have enjoyed *The Lord of the Rings* have been affected primarily by it as an exciting story; and that is how it was written. Though one does not, of course, escape from the question 'what is it about?' by that back door. That would be like answering an aesthetic question by talking of a point of technique. I suppose that if one makes a good choice in what is 'good narrative' (or 'good theatre') at a given point, it will also be found to be the case that the event described will be the most 'significant'.

To turn, if I may, to the 'human Touches' and the matter of when I started. That is rather like asking of Man when language started. It was an inevitable, though conditionable, evolvement of the birth-given. It has been always with me: the sensibility to linguistic pattern which affects me emotionally like colour or music; and the passionate love of growing things; and the deep response to legends (for lack of a better word) that have what I would call the North-western temper and temperature. In any case if you want to write a tale of this sort you must consult your roots, and a man of the North-west of the Old World will set his heart and the action of his tale in an imaginary world of that air, and that situation: with the Shoreless Sea of his innumerable ancestors to the West, and the endless lands (out of which enemies mostly come) to the East. Though, in addition, his heart may remember, even if he has been cut off from all oral tradition, the rumour all along the coasts of the Men out of the Sea.

---

stands, with an effect on my self (except for labour pains) almost like reading some one else's work. And I like Ents now because they do not seem to have anything to do with me. I daresay something had been going on in the 'unconscious' for some time, and that accounts for my feeling throughout, especially when stuck, that I was not inventing but reporting (imperfectly) and had at times to wait till 'what really happened' came through. But looking back analytically I should say that Ents are composed of philology, literature, and life. They owe their name to the *eald enta geweorc*[2] of Anglo-Saxon, and their connexion with stone. Their part in the story is due, I think, to my bitter disappointment and disgust from schooldays with the shabby use made in Shakespeare of the coming of 'Great Birnam wood to high Dunsinane hill': I longed to devise a setting in which the trees might really march to war. And into this has crept a mere piece of experience, the difference of the 'male' and 'female' attitude to wild things, the difference between unpossessive love and gardening.

I say this about the 'heart', for I have what some might call an Atlantis complex. Possibly inherited, though my parents died too young for me to know such things about them, and too young to transfer such things by words. Inherited from me (I suppose) by one only of my children,[4] though I did not know that about my son until recently, and he did not know it about me. I mean the terrible recurrent dream (beginning with memory) of the Great Wave, towering up, and coming in ineluctably over the trees and green fields. (I bequeathed it to Faramir.) I don't think I have had it since I wrote the 'Downfall of Númenor' as the last of the legends of the First and Second Age.

I am a West-midlander by blood (and took to early west-midland Middle English as a known tongue as soon as I set eyes on it), but perhaps a fact of my personal history may partly explain why the 'North-western air' appeals to me both as 'home' and as something discovered. I was actually born in Bloemfontein, and so those deeply implanted impressions, underlying memories that are still pictorially available for inspection, of first childhood are for me those of a hot parched country. My first Christmas memory is of blazing sun, drawn curtains and a drooping eucalyptus.

I am afraid this is becoming a dreadful bore, and going on too long, at any rate longer than 'this contemptible person before you' merits. But it is difficult to stop once roused on such an absorbing topic to oneself as oneself. As for the conditioning: I am chiefly aware of the linguistic conditioning. I went to King Edward's School and spent most of my time learning Latin and Greek; but I also learned English. Not English Literature! Except Shakespeare (which I disliked cordially), the chief contacts with poetry were when one was made to try and translate it into Latin. Not a bad mode of introduction, if a bit casual. I mean something of the English language and its history. I learned Anglo-Saxon at school (also Gothic, but that was an accident quite unconnected with the curriculum though decisive – I discovered in it not only modern historical philology, which appealed to the historical and scientific side, but for the first time the study of a language out of mere love: I mean for the acute aesthetic pleasure derived from a language for its own sake, not only free from being useful but free even from being the 'vehicle of a literature').

There are two strands, or three. A fascination that Welsh names had for me, even if only seen on coal-trucks, from childhood is another; though people only gave me books that were incomprehensible to a child when I asked for information. I did not learn any Welsh till I was an undergraduate, and found in it an abiding linguistic-aesthetic satisfaction. Spanish was another: my guardian was half Spanish, and in my early teens I used to pinch his books and try to learn it: the only Romance

213

language that gives me the particular pleasure of which I am speaking – it is not quite the same as the mere perception of beauty: I feel the beauty of say Italian or for that matter of modern English (which is very remote from my personal taste): it is more like the appetite for a needed food. Most important, perhaps, after Gothic was the discovery in Exeter College library, when I was supposed to be reading for Honour Mods, of a Finnish Grammar. It was like discovering a complete wine-cellar filled with bottles of an amazing wine of a kind and flavour never tasted before. It quite intoxicated me; and I gave up the attempt to invent an 'unrecorded' Germanic language, and my 'own language' – or series of invented languages – became heavily Finnicized in phonetic pattern and structure.

That is of course long past now. Linguistic taste changes like everything else, as time goes on; or oscillates between poles. Latin and the British type of Celtic have it now, with the beautifully co-ordinated and patterned (if simply patterned) Anglo-Saxon near at hand and further off the Old Norse with the neighbouring but alien Finnish. Roman-British might not one say? With a strong but more recent infusion from Scandinavia and the Baltic. Well, I daresay such linguistic tastes, with due allowance for school-overlay, are as good or better a test of ancestry as blood-groups.

All this only as background to the stories, though languages and names are for me inextricable from the stories. They are and were so to speak an attempt to give a background or a world in which my expressions of linguistic taste could have a function. The stories were comparatively late in coming.

I first tried to write a story when I was about seven. It was about a dragon. I remember nothing about it except a philological fact. My mother said nothing about the dragon, but pointed out that one could not say 'a green great dragon', but had to say 'a great green dragon'. I wondered why, and still do. The fact that I remember this is possibly significant, as I do not think I ever tried to write a story again for many years, and was taken up with language.

I mentioned Finnish, because that set the rocket off in story. I was immensely attracted by something in the air of the Kalevala, even in Kirby's poor translation. I never learned Finnish well enough to do more than plod through a bit of the original, like a schoolboy with Ovid; being mostly taken up with its effect on 'my language'. But the beginning of the legendarium, of which the Trilogy is part (the conclusion), was in an attempt to reorganize some of the Kalevala, especially the tale of Kullervo the hapless, into a form of my own. That began, as I say, in the Honour Mods period; nearly disastrously as I came very near having my exhibition taken off me if not being sent down. Say 1912 to 1913. As the thing went on I actually wrote in verse. Though the first real story of this imaginary world almost fully formed as it now appears was written in prose during sick-leave at the end of 1916: The Fall of Gondolin, which I had the cheek to read to the Exeter College Essay Club in 1918.[5] I wrote a lot else in hospitals before the end of the First Great War.

I went on after return; but when I attempted to get any of this stuff published I was not successful. *The Hobbit* was originally quite unconnected, though it inevitably got drawn in to the circumference of the greater construction; and in the event modified it. It was unhappily really meant, as far as I was conscious, as a 'children's story', and as I had not learned sense then, and my children were not quite old enough to correct me, it has some of the sillinesses of manner caught unthinkingly from the kind of stuff I had had served to me, as Chaucer may catch a minstrel tag. I deeply regret them. So do intelligent children.

All I remember about the start of *The Hobbit* is sitting correcting School Certificate papers in the everlasting weariness of that annual task forced on impecunious academics with children. On a blank leaf I scrawled: 'In a hole in the ground there lived a hobbit.' I did not and do not know why. I did nothing about it, for a long time, and for some years I got no further than the production of Thror's Map. But it became *The Hobbit* in the early 1930s, and was eventually published not because of my own children's enthusiasm (though they liked it well enough[*]), but because I lent it to the then Rev. Mother of Cherwell Edge when she had flu, and it was seen by a former student who was at that time in the office of Allen and Unwin. It was I believe tried out on Rayner Unwin; but for whom when grown up I think I should never have got the Trilogy published.

Since *The Hobbit* was a success, a sequel was called for; and the remote Elvish Legends were turned down. A publisher's reader said they were too full of the kind of Celtic beauty that maddened Anglo-Saxons in a large dose. Very likely quite right. Anyway I myself saw the value of Hobbits, in putting earth under the feet of 'romance', and in providing subjects for 'ennoblement' and heroes more praiseworthy than the professionals: *nolo heroizari* is of course as good a start for a hero, as *nolo episcopari* for a bishop. Not that I am a 'democrat' in any of its current uses; except that I suppose, to speak in literary terms, we are all equal before the Great Author, *qui deposuit potentes de sede et exaltavit humiles.*[6]

---

[*]Not any better I think than *The Marvellous Land of Snergs*, Wyke-Smith, Ernest Benn 1927. Seeing the date, I should say that this was probably an unconscious source-book! for the Hobbits, not of anything else.

All the same, I was not prepared to write a 'sequel', in the sense of another children's story. I had been thinking about 'Fairy Stories' and their relation to children – some of the results I put into a lecture at St Andrews and eventually enlarged and published in an Essay (among those listed in the O.U.P. as *Essays Presented to Charles Williams* and now most scurvily allowed to go out of print). As I had expressed the view that the connexion in the modern mind between children and 'fairy stories' is false and accidental, and spoils the stories in themselves and for children, I wanted to try and write one that was not addressed to children at all (as such); also I wanted a large canvas.

A lot of labour was naturally involved, since I had to make a linkage with *The Hobbit*; but still more with the background mythology. That had to be re-written as well. *The Lord of the Rings* is only the end part of a work nearly twice as long[7] which I worked at between 1936 and 53. (I wanted to get it all published in chronological order, but that proved impossible.) And the languages had to be attended to! If I had considered my own pleasure more than the stomachs of a possible audience, there would have been a great deal more Elvish in the book. But even the snatches that there are required, if they were to have a meaning, two organized phonologies and grammars and a large number of words.

It would have been a big task without anything else; but I have been a moderately conscientious administrator and teacher, and I changed professorships in 1945 (scrapping all my old lectures). And of course during the War there was often no time for anything rational. I stuck for ages at the end of Book Three. Book Four was written as a serial and sent out to my son serving in Africa in 1944. The last two books were written between 1944 and 48. That of course does not mean that the main idea of the story was a war-product. That was arrived at in one of the earliest chapters still surviving (Book I, 2). It is really given, and present in germ, from the beginning, though I had no conscious notion of what the Necromancer stood for (except ever-recurrent evil) in *The Hobbit*, nor of his connexion with the Ring. But if you wanted to go on from the end of *The Hobbit* I think the ring would be your inevitable choice as the link. If then you wanted a large tale, the Ring would at once acquire a capital letter; and the Dark Lord would immediately appear. As he did, unasked, on the hearth at Bag End as soon as I came to that point. So the essential Quest started at once. But I met a lot of things on the way that astonished me. Tom Bombadil I knew already; but I had never been to Bree. Strider sitting in the corner at the inn was a shock, and I had no more idea who he was than had Frodo. The Mines of Moria had been a mere name; and of Lothlórien no word had reached my mortal ears till I came there. Far away I knew there were the Horse-lords on the confines of an ancient Kingdom of Men, but Fangorn Forest was an unforeseen adventure. I had never heard of the House of Eorl nor of the Stewards of Gondor. Most disquieting of all, Saruman had never been revealed to me, and I was as mystified as Frodo at Gandalf's failure to appear on September 22. I knew nothing of the *Palantíri*, though the moment the Orthanc-stone was cast from the window, I recognized it, and knew the meaning of the 'rhyme of lore' that had been running in my mind: *seven stars and seven stones and one white tree*. These rhymes and names will crop up; but they do not always explain themselves. I have yet to discover anything about the cats of Queen Berúthiel.[8] But I did know more or less all about Gollum and his part, and Sam, and I knew that the way was guarded by a Spider. And if that has anything to do with my being stung by a tarantula when a small child,[9] people are welcome to the notion (supposing the improbable, that any one is interested). I can only say that I remember nothing about it, should not know it if I had not been told; and I do not dislike spiders particularly, and have no urge to kill them. I usually rescue those whom I find in the bath!

Well now I am really getting garrulous. I do hope you will not be frightfully bored. I hope also to see you again some time. In which case we may perhaps talk about you and your work and not mine. Any way your interest in mine is a considerable encouragement.

With very best wishes. Yours sincerely,

J. R. R. Tolkien.

164   From a letter to Naomi Mitchison   29 June 1955

I have had a very gruelling time, with far more work than I could really cope with, *plus* Vol. III. I am feeling as flat as a burst tyre; but may revive when (or if, as promised) the final proofs of Vol. III arrive tomorrow.

The booksellers – among them Mr Wilson of Bumpus – say that, having delayed so long, late in September is now the proper time for publication. . . . .

I think 'A and U' may now take the 'earlier history' in some form. When I was in town last Friday they seemed willing to envisage a book about as long as Vol. I.

165   To the Houghton Mifflin Co.

[On 5 June 1955 in the *New York Times Book Review*, the columnist Harvey Breit devoted part of his weekly article 'In and Out of Books' to an account of Tolkien and his writings. It included this passage: 'What, we asked Dr [sic] Tolkien, makes you tick? Dr T., who teaches at Oxford when he isn't writing novels, has this brisk reply: "I don't tick. I am not a machine. (If I did tick, I should have no views on it, and you had better ask the winder.) My work did not 'evolve' into a serious work. It started like that. The so-called 'children's story' [*The Hobbit*] was a fragment, torn out of an already existing mythology. In so far as it was dressed up as 'for children', in style or manner, I regret it. So do the children. I am a philologist, and all my work is philological. I avoid hobbies because I am a very serious person and cannot distinguish between private amusement and duty. I am affable, but unsociable. I only work for private amusement, since I find my duties privately amusing." '

These remarks were apparently taken from a letter written by Tolkien in answer to enquiries by a representative of the *New York Times*. On 30 June 1955, Tolkien wrote to the Houghton Mifflin Co., his American publishers: 'Please do not blame me for what Breit made of my letter! . . . . The original made sense: not a quality, however, of which Harvey B. seems perceptive. I was asked a series of questions, with a request to answer briefly, brightly, and quotably. . . . . Out of sheer pity [for another enquirer wanting information] . . . . I do enclose a few notes on points other than mere facts of my "curriculum vitae" (which can be got from reference books).' What follows is these 'few notes'. The text is taken from a typescript apparently made by the Houghton Mifflin Co. from Tolkien's original; this typescript was sent to a number of enquirers at different times, some of whom quoted from it in articles about Tolkien. Tolkien himself was given a copy of the typescript, and he made a number of annotations and corrections to it, which are incorporated into the text which is here printed.]

My name is TOLKIEN (*not -kein*). It is a German name (from Saxony), an anglicization of *Tollkiehn*, i.e. *tollkühn*. But, except as a guide to spelling, this fact is as fallacious as all facts in the raw. For I am neither 'foolhardy'[1] nor German, whatever some remote ancestors may have been. They migrated to England more than 200 years ago, and became quickly intensely English (not British), though remaining musical – a talent that unfortunately did not descend to me.*

I am in fact far more of a Suffield[2] (a family deriving from Evesham in Worcestershire), and it is to my mother who taught me (until I obtained a scholarship at the ancient Grammar School in Birmingham) that I owe my tastes for philology, especially of Germanic languages, and for romance. I am indeed in English terms a West-midlander at home only in the counties upon the Welsh Marches; and it is, I believe, as much due to descent as to opportunity that Anglo-Saxon and Western Middle English and alliterative verse have been both a childhood attraction and my main professional sphere. (I also find the Welsh language specially

*The name, spelt this way, also entered the United States, 2 or 3 generations ago, from Canada. I recently had some correspondence with a family in Texas.

218

attractive.*) I write alliterative verse with pleasure, though I have published little beyond the fragments in *The Lord of the Rings*, except 'The Homecoming of Beorhtnoth' (in *Essays and Studies of the English Association*, 1953, London, John Murray) recently twice broadcast by the BBC: a dramatic dialogue on the nature of the 'heroic' and the 'chivalrous'. I still hope to finish a long poem on *The Fall of Arthur* in the same measure.[3]

All the same, I was born in Bloemfontein, Orange River Free State – another fallacious fact (though my earliest memories are of a hot country) since I was shipped home in 1895, and have spent most of 60 years since in Birmingham and Oxford, except for 5 or 6 years in Leeds: my first post after the 1914–18 War was in the university there. I am very untravelled, though I know Wales, and have often been in Scotland (never north of the Tay), and know something of France, Belgium, and Ireland. I have spent a good deal of time in Ireland, and am since last July actually a D. Litt. of University College Dublin; but be it noted I first set foot in 'Eire' in 1949 after *The Lord of the Rings* was finished, and find both Gaelic and the air of Ireland wholly alien – though the latter (not the language) is attractive.

I might add that in October I received a degree (Doct. en Lettres et Phil.) at Liège (Belgium) – if only to record the fact that it astonished me to be welcomed in French as 'le createur de M. Bilbo Baggins' and still more to be told in explanation of applause that I was a 'set book' ?????? Alas!

If I might elucidate what H. Breit has left of my letter: the remark about 'philology' was intended to allude to what is I think a primary 'fact' about my work, that it is all of a piece, and *fundamentally linguistic* in inspiration. The authorities of the university might well consider it an aberration of an elderly professor of philology to write and publish fairy stories and romances, and call it a 'hobby', pardonable because it has been (surprisingly to me as much as to anyone) successful. But it is not a 'hobby', in the sense of something quite different from one's work, taken up as a relief-outlet. The invention of languages is the foundation. The 'stories' were made rather to provide a world for the languages than the reverse. To me a name comes first and the story follows.† I should have preferred to write in 'Elvish'. But, of course, such a work as *The Lord of the Rings* has been edited and only as much 'language' has been left in as

---

*The 'Sindarin', a Grey-elven language, is in fact constructed deliberately to resemble Welsh phonologically and to have a relation to High-elven similar to that existing between British (properly so-called, sc. the Celtic languages spoken in this island at the time of the Roman Invasion) and Latin. All the names in the book, and the languages, are of course constructed, and not at random.

†I once scribbled 'hobbit' on a blank page of some boring school exam. paper in the early 1930's. It was some time before I discovered what it referred to!

I thought would be stomached by readers. (I now find that many would have liked more.) But there is a great deal of linguistic matter (other than actually 'elvish' names and words) included or mythologically expressed in the book. It is to me, anyway, largely an essay in 'linguistic aesthetic', as I sometimes say to people who ask me 'what is it all about?'

It is not 'about' anything but itself. Certainly it has *no* allegorical intentions, general, particular, or topical, moral, religious, or political. The only criticism that annoyed me was one that it 'contained no religion' (and 'no Women', but that does not matter, and is not true anyway). It is a monotheistic world of 'natural theology'. The odd fact that there are no churches, temples, or religious rites and ceremonies, is simply part of the historical climate depicted. It will be sufficiently explained, if (as now seems likely) the *Silmarillion* and other legends of the First and Second Ages are published. I am in any case myself a Christian; but the 'Third Age' was not a Christian world.

'Middle-earth', by the way, is not a name of a never-never land without relation to the world we live in (like the Mercury of Eddison).[4] It is just a use of Middle English *middel-erde* (or *erthe*), altered from Old English *Middangeard*: the name for the inhabited lands of Men 'between the seas'. And though I have not attempted to relate the shape of the mountains and land-masses to what geologists may say or surmise about the nearer past, imaginatively this 'history' is supposed to take place in a period of the actual Old World of this planet.

There are of course certain things and themes that move me specially. The inter-relations between the 'noble' and the 'simple' (or common, vulgar) for instance. The ennoblement of the ignoble I find specially moving. I am (obviously) much in love with plants and above all trees, and always have been; and I find human maltreatment of them as hard to bear as some find ill-treatment of animals.

I think the so-called 'fairy story' one of the highest forms of literature, and quite erroneously associated with children (as such). But my views on that I set out in a lecture delivered at St Andrew's (on the Andrew Lang foundation, eventually published in *Essays Presented to Charles Williams* by Oxford University Press, as 'On Fairy Stories'). I think it is quite an important work, at least for anyone who thinks me worth considering at all; but the O.U.P. have infuriatingly let it go out of print, though it is now in demand – and my only copy has been stolen. Still it might be found in a library, or I might get hold of a copy.

If all this is obscure, wordy, and self-regarding and neither 'bright, brief, nor quotable' forgive me. Is there anything else you would like me to say?

Yours sincerely,
J(ohn) R(onald) R(euel) Tolkien.

P.S. The book is *not* of course a 'trilogy'. That and the titles of the volumes was a fudge thought necessary for publication, owing to length and cost. There is no real division into 3, nor is any one part intelligible alone. The story was conceived and written as a whole and the only natural divisions are the 'books' I–VI (which originally had titles).

[Most of the central portion of this autobiographical statement was incorporated into an article, 'Tolkien on Tolkien', in the October 1966 issue of the magazine *Diplomat*. This article included three paragraphs not in the text quoted above, which were presumably written *circa* 1966:]

This business began so far back that it might be said to have begun at birth. Somewhere about six years old I tried to write some verses on a *dragon* about which I now remember nothing except that it contained the expression a *green great dragon* and that I remained puzzled for a very long time at being told that this should be *great green*. But the mythology (and associated languages) first began to take shape during the 1914–18 war. *The Fall of Gondolin* (and the birth of Eärendil) was written in hospital and on leave after surviving the Battle of the Somme in 1916. The kernel of the mythology, the matter of *Lúthien Tinúviel* and *Beren*, arose from a small woodland glade filled with 'hemlocks' (or other white umbellifers) near Roos on the Holderness peninsula – to which I occasionally went when free from regimental duties while in the Humber Garrison in 1918.

I came eventually and by slow degrees to write *The Lord of the Rings* to satisfy myself: of course without success, at any rate not above 75 percent. But now (when the work is no longer hot, immediate or so personal) certain features of it, and especially certain places, still move me very powerfully. The heart remains in the description of Cerin Amroth (end of Vol. I, Bk. ii, ch. 6), but I am most stirred by the sound of the horses of the Rohirrim at cockcrow; and most grieved by Gollum's failure (just) to repent when interrupted by Sam: this seems to me really like the *real* world in which the instruments of just retribution are seldom themselves just or holy; and the good are often stumbling blocks. . . . .

Nothing has astonished me more (and I think my publishers) than the welcome given to *The Lord of the Rings*. But it is, of course, a constant source of consolation and pleasure to me. And, I may say, a piece of singular good fortune, much envied by some of my contemporaries. Wonderful people still *buy* the book, and to a man 'retired' that is both grateful and comforting.

[The proofs of the Appendices to the third volume, *The Return of the King*, caused Tolkien much worry. They arrived late from the printers, and he found that the page intended to carry a phonetic 'key' to the *Angerthas* or Dwarf-runes had been printed without the phonetic symbols it was supposed to contain. He sent back this page with the symbols drawn in by hand, whereupon the printers reproduced this rough drawing in facsimile, which was not what he had intended; his wish was that they should set up the phonetic symbols in type. He was also anxious because he had not received page proofs of the narrative of *The Return of the King* incorporating revisions that he had sent to the printers some time earlier. The following letter, dealing with these matters, is typical of many harassed letters he wrote during these weeks.]

I return in separate parcel the material sent to me (arrived mid-day Wednesday). I have done my best and quickest with it; but I fear I have missed today's post and this will not go until tomorrow. Time is short, and the material rather intricate!

I am still puzzled and dissatisfied with the procedure – at any rate it makes my part much more laborious, and greatly increases the chances of errors and discrepancies still appearing in the published volume.

I know that I sent in corrections after the revised page proofs had been returned. But that is now a very long time back and I do not yet understand why I should now receive Queries, raised by the head reader in the course of his *'final reading of the main text'* that are not based on the final text, but on one that does not incorporate numerous (and some extensive) revisions. Errors are almost certain to occur, or to have occurred, at some of these points. The compositors always make mistakes in setting from my handwriting!

I am also a little disturbed because though the selected pages of Queries are presented 'for Queries only', and contain corrections of small details (as well as Queries) throughout, there remain *errors* in these pages that are neither queried nor corrected. For instance the heading House of Healing throughout Bk. V Ch. 8 in spite of the chapter title.

I have, however, v. little time left now, and could not deal with anything that arrived after Wed. morning next. Not being satisfied nor indeed (frankly) wholly reassured, I have made out a list of all the emendations, insertions, and corrections of the main text which do *not* yet appear in the proofs. I have made this list as clear as I can, and I hope it will be carefully checked with the text. . . . .

I can only hope that the *Angerthas* will come out all right in the wash! But I am rather anxious. Jarrolds appear to have adopted my suggestion and now propose to use the phonetic letter ŋ instead of my ṅg. But the

Table in printable form that I sent in, & which you reported (on 'phone) was being adopted, used ṅg.

☞ I hope care will be taken to use either ṅg or ŋ throughout. *And also, please, NOT to replace* ng *by* ŋ. I am alarmed by the Reader's query of *ng* at the end of (p. 404) line 23. This reveals that, for all his eagle eye, he has not understood the simple distinction that is being made; or so it would seem. . . . .

I hope some of this is legible. I am v. tired.

167   From a letter to Christopher and Faith Tolkien   15 August 1955

[Tolkien, with his daughter Priscilla, visited Italy from late July to mid-August.]

I am still staggered by the frescoes of Assisi. You must visit it. We came in for the great feast of Santa Chiara and the eve Aug. 11–12. High Mass sung by Cardinal Micara with silver trumpets at the elevation!

I am typing out a diary. I remain in love with Italian, and feel quite lorn without a chance of trying to speak it! We must keep it up. . . . .

On the whole for pure fun and pleasure, I enjoyed the first days at Venice most. But we lived v. cheap in Assisi, and I have brought about £50 back. Our opera was washed out by torrents all Thursday evening; but they put on a special extra on Friday (our last day in Venice) at which our tickets were good. So we had our *Rigoletto*. Perfectly astounding.

168   To Richard Jeffery

[A reply to a reader who had asked for a translation of the opening words of one of Treebeard's songs (Book III, chapter 4), and for an explanation of several names, including 'Onodrim', the Sindarin Elvish name for the Ents.]

7 September 1955   76 Sandfield Road, Headington, Oxford
Dear Mr Jeffery,

Thank you very much for your letter. . . . It came while I was away, in Gondor (sc. Venice), as a change from the North Kingdom, or I would have answered before.

At any rate your command of Elvish script (not Runes) is quite good enough to read. But there are, of course, no rules for the application to English, so it is impossible to make mistakes, unless according to your own system – so I suppose your name is Richard, though you wrote ℘ ⲥⲥⲩⲣⲟ, which on your system should be Rijard (ᴄᴄᵳ for ᴄᵳ). However, there will be sufficient description of the 'letters' (*tengwar*) and of the 'runes' (*certar*) in Vol. III Appendices for anyone who is interested. . . . .

It has unfortunately not proved possible, as I had hoped, to give an index of Names (with meanings), which would have provided also a fair vocabulary of Elvish words. There were far too many and the space and cost were prohibitive. But I spent a long time trying to make a list, and that is one reason for the delay of Vol. III. . . . .

Most of the questions you ask will be answered in Vol. III, I think. . . . . *Orofarne, lassemista, carnemírie* is High-elven (the language preferred by Ents) for 'mountain-dwelling, leaf-grey, with adornment of red jewels'.

The 'correct' plural of *onod* was *enyd*, or general plural *onodrim*; though *ened* might be a form used in Gondor. But *en, ened* = middle, centre as in *Endor, Endóre* Middle-earth (S. *ennorath*); and *enedwaith* = middle-people/ or region, as *Forodwaith* = north-region, &c. It was not a desert when the name was given; but became so during the Third Age.[1] See the Chronology of the Second and Third Ages in Appendices to Vol. III. Peregrin is, of course, a real modern name, though it means 'traveller in strange countries'. Frodo is a real name from the Germanic tradition. Its Old English form was *Fróda*. Its obvious connexion is with the old word *fród* meaning etymologically 'wise by experience', but it had mythological connexions with legends of the Golden Age in the North. . . . .

Yours sincerely,
J. R. R. Tolkien

ᚱᚾᚫᛡᚣᛖ

169 From a letter to Hugh Brogan   11 September 1955

Your discovery of 'Numinor' in C.S.L.'s *That Hideous Strength* is discovery of a plagiarism: well, not that, since he used the word, taken from my legends of the First and Second Ages, in the belief that they would soon appear. They have not, but I suppose now they may. The spelling *Numinor* is due to his hearing it and not seeing it. *Númenóre* or *Númenor* means in High-elven simply West-land. As for the shape of the world of the Third Age, I am afraid that was devised 'dramatically' rather than geologically, or paleontologically. I do sometimes wish that I had made some sort of agreement between the imaginations or theories of the geologists and my map a little more possible. But that would only have made more trouble with human history.

170 From a letter to Allen & Unwin   30 September 1955

When is Vol. III likely now to appear? I shall be murdered if something does not happen soon.

[In December 1954, Brogan wrote to Tolkien criticising the archaic narrative style of parts of *The Two Towers*, especially the chapter 'The King of the Golden Hall'; he called this style 'Ossianic', and said he agreed with a critic's description of it as 'tushery'. At the time, Tolkien made no reply to this; but when on 18 September 1955 Brogan wrote again, apologising for being 'impertinent, stupid, or sycophantic', Tolkien began to draft what follows. In the event he did not send it, but instead wrote a brief note saying that the matter of archaism 'would take too long to debate' in a letter and must wait until their next meeting.]

[September 1955]
Dear Hugh,

. . . . Don't be disturbed: I have not noticed any impertinence (or sycophancy) in your letters; and anyone so appreciative and so perceptive is entitled to criticism. Anyway, I do not naturally breathe an air of undiluted incense! It was not what you said (last letter but one, not the one that I answered) or your right to say it, that might have called for a reply, if I had the time for it; but the pain that I always feel when anyone – in an age when almost all auctorial manhandling of English is permitted (especially if disruptive) in the name of art or 'personal expression' – immediately dismisses out of court deliberate 'archaism'. The proper use of 'tushery' is to apply it to the kind of bogus 'medieval' stuff which attempts (without knowledge) to give a supposed temporal colour with expletives, such as *tush, pish, zounds, marry*, and the like. But a real archaic English is far more *terse* than modern; also many of things said could not be said in our slack and often frivolous idiom. Of course, not being specially well read in modern English, and far more familiar with works in the ancient and 'middle' idioms, my own ear is to some extent affected; so that though I could easily recollect how a modern would put this or that, what comes easiest to mind or pen is not quite that. But take an example from the chapter that you specially singled out (and called terrible): Book iii, 'The King of the Golden Hall'. 'Nay, Gandalf!' said the King. 'You do not know your own skill in healing. It shall not be so. I myself will go to war, to fall in the front of the battle, if it must be. Thus shall I sleep better.'

This is a fair sample – moderated or watered archaism. Using only words that still are used or known to the educated, the King would really have said: 'Nay, thou (n')wost[1] not thine own skill in healing. It shall not be so. I myself will go to war, to fall . . .' etc. I know well enough what a modern would say. 'Not at all my dear G. You don't know your own skill as a doctor. Things aren't going to be like that. I shall go to the war in person, even if I have to be one of the first casualties' – and then what? Theoden would certainly think, and probably say 'thus shall

I sleep better'! But people who think like that just do not talk a modern idiom. You can have 'I shall lie easier in my grave', or 'I should sleep sounder in my grave like that rather than if I stayed at home' – if you like. But there would be an insincerity of thought, a disunion of word and meaning. For a King who spoke in a modern style would not really think in such terms at all, and any reference to sleeping quietly in the grave would be a deliberate archaism of expression on his part (however worded) far more bogus than the actual 'archaic' English that I have used. Like some non-Christian making a reference to some Christian belief which did not in fact move him at all.

Or p. 127, as an example of 'archaism' that cannot be defended as 'dramatic', since it is not in dialogue, but the author's description of the arming of the guests – which seemed specially to upset you. But such 'heroic' scenes do not occur in a modern setting to which a modern idiom belongs. Why deliberately ignore, refuse to use the wealth of English which leaves us a choice of styles – without any possibility of unintelligibility.

I can see no more reason for not using the much *terser* and more vivid ancient *style*, than for changing the obsolete weapons, helms, shields, hauberks into modern uniforms.

'Helms too they chose' is archaic. Some (wrongly) class it as an 'inversion', since normal order is 'They also chose helmets' or 'they chose helmets too'. (Real mod. E. 'They also picked out some helmets and round shields'.) But this is not normal order, and if mod. E. has lost the trick of putting a word desired to emphasize (for pictorial, emotional or logical reasons) into prominent first place, without addition of a lot of little 'empty' words (as the Chinese say), so much the worse for it. And so much the better for it the sooner it learns the trick again. And *some* one must begin the teaching, by example.

I am sorry to find *you* affected by the extraordinary 20th.C. delusion that its usages *per se* and simply as 'contemporary' – irrespective of whether they are terser, more vivid (or even nobler!) – have some peculiar validity, above those of all other times, so that not to use them (even when quite unsuitable in tone) is a solecism, a gaffe, a thing at which one's friends shudder or feel hot in the collar. Shake yourself out of this parochialism of time! Also (not to be too donnish) learn to discriminate between the bogus and genuine antique – as you would if you hoped not to be cheated by a dealer!

[The draft ends here.]

172 From a letter to Allen & Unwin 12 October 1955

[Allen & Unwin proposed to publish *The Return of the King* on 20 October 1955.]

Don't fail of 20 October! The last possible day. On the 21st. I have to give the first 'O'Donnell Lecture' (overdue), & I must hope that a large part of my audience will be so bemused by sitting up late the night before that they will not so closely observe my grave lack of equipment as a lecturer on a Celtic subject.[1] Anyway, I want to tactfully allude to the book, since a part of what I wish to say is about 'Celticness' and in what that consists as a linguistic pattern.

173 From a letter to Katherine Farrer 24 October 1955

[*The Return of the King* was duly published on 20 October.]

Since (in spite of being laid up with a throat that made lecturing impossible until last Friday) I have actually managed to deliver the O'Donnell Lecture on English and Welsh (Friday), and am no longer a college official, and the Book is complete – except for an errata slip for the reprint already required for Vol. III, to cover the important errors of the whole: I shall be a great deal freer after this week. . . . .

I am indeed surprised at the reception of the 'Ring', and immensely pleased. But I don't think I have started any tide. I don't think such a small hobbitlike creature, or even a Man of any size, does that. If there is a tide (I think there is) then I am just lucky enough to have caught it, being just a bit of it. . . . .

I still feel the picture incomplete without something on Samwise and Elanor, but I could not devise anything that would not have destroyed the ending, more than the hints (possibly sufficient) in the appendices.

174 To Lord Halsbury

[Lord Halsbury, at that time Managing Director of the National Research Development Corporation, wrote to suggest that *The Silmarillion* might be published by subscription, if Allen & Unwin were unwilling to undertake it on a commercial basis.]

10 November 1955   Merton College, Oxford
Dear Lord Halsbury,

It was kind of you to write, & I was pleased to have your approval and interest. I was also grateful for your suggestion of an edition by subscription.

However, the surprising welcome given to *The Lord of the Rings* will probably make this procedure unnecessary; and has justified the publishers' firm resolve to issue the present work first; though I wanted to present the matter in 'chronological order'. For one thing, it would have lightened and quickened the narrative of the Third Age!

I do not think that anything is referred to in *The L. of the R.* which does not actually exist in legends written before it was begun, or at least belonging to an earlier period – except only the 'cats of Queen Berúthiel'.[1] But I am afraid that all the matter of the First and Second Ages is very 'high-mythical' or Elvish and heroic, and there is no 'hobbitry' at all: an ingredient that seems to have made the present mixture more generally palatable.

Since the publishers are now pressing for the *Silmarillion* &c. (which was long ago turned down), I do intend as soon as I can find time to try to set the material in order for publication. Though I am rather tired, and no longer young enough to pillage the night to make up for the deficit of hours in the day. . . .

It might conceivably interest you to see some of this [*The Silmarillion*] before it is properly shaped or revised, bearing in mind that it is likely to be much altered in detail & presentation – and certainly in style.

Thanking you again for your encouragement.

Yours sincerely

J. R. R. Tolkien.

175 From a letter to Mrs Molly Waldron 30 November 1955

[*The Lord of the Rings* was broadcast on the BBC Third Programme during 1955 and 1956. Among the large cast, the parts of Gandalf and Tom Bombadil were played by the actor Norman Shelley.]

I think the book quite unsuitable for 'dramatization', and have not enjoyed the broadcasts – though they have improved. I thought Tom Bombadil dreadful – but worse still was the announcer's preliminary remarks that Goldberry was his daughter (!), and that Willowman was an ally of Mordor (!!). Cannot people imagine things hostile to men and hobbits who prey on them without being in league with the Devil!

176 From a letter to Naomi Mitchison 8 December 1955

I had to deliver the opening lecture of the newly-founded O'Donnell Lectures in Celtic Studies – already overdue: and I composed it with 'all the woe in the world', as the Gawain-poet says of the wretched fox with the hounds on his tail. All the more woe, since I am the merest amateur in such matters, and Celtic scholars are critical and litigious; and more woe since I was smitten with laryngitis.

I think poorly of the broadcast adaptations. Except for a few details I think they are not well done, even granted the script and the legitimacy of the enterprise (which I do not grant). But they took some trouble with the names. I thought that the Dwarf (Glóin not Gimli, but I suppose Gimli will look like his father – apparently someone's idea of a German) was not too bad, if a bit exaggerated. I do think of the 'Dwarves' like Jews: at once native and alien in their habitations, speaking the languages of the country, but with an accent due to their own private tongue. . . . .

I have now got a pestilent doctorate thesis to explore, when I would rather be doing something less useful. . . . .

I am sorry about my childish amusement with arithmetic; but there it is: the Númenórean calendar was just a bit better than the Gregorian: the latter being on average 26 secs fast p. a., and the N[úmenórean] 17.2 secs slow.

177   From a letter to Rayner Unwin   8 December 1955

[The radio adaptation of *The Lord of the Rings* was discussed on the BBC programme 'The Critics'; and on 16 November, W. H. Auden gave a radio talk about the book in which he said: 'If someone dislikes it, I shall never trust their literary judgement about anything again.' Meanwhile Edwin Muir, reviewing *The Return of the King* in the *Observer* on 27 November, wrote: 'All the characters are boys masquerading as adult heroes . . . . and will never come to puberty. . . . . Hardly one of them knows anything about women.']

I agreed with the 'critics' view of the radio adaptation; but I was annoyed that after confessing that none of them had read the book they should turn their attention to it and me – including surmises on my religion. I also thought Auden rather bad – he cannot at any rate read verse, having a poor rhythmical sense; and deplored his making the book 'a test of literary taste'. You cannot do that with any work – and if you could you only infuriate. I was fully prepared for Robert Robinson's rejoinder 'fair-ground barker'. But I suppose all this is good for sales. My correspondence is now increased by letters of fury against the critics and the broadcast. One elderly lady – in part the model for 'Lobelia' indeed, though she does not suspect it – would I think certainly have set about Auden (and others) had they been in range of her umbrella. . . . .

I hope in this vacation to begin surveying the *Silmarillion*; though evil fate has plumped a doctorate thesis on me. . . . .

Blast Edwin Muir and his delayed adolescence. He is old enough to know better. It might do him good to hear what women think of his 'knowing about women', especially as a test of being mentally adult. If he had an M.A. I should nominate him for the professorship of poetry[1] – a sweet revenge.

178 From a letter to Allen & Unwin   12 December 1955

[Containing a reference to Sarehole, the hamlet where Tolkien spent part of his childhood.]

By the way, there is no need to alter 'Mr' to Professor. In proper Oxford tradition professor is not a title of address – or was not, though the habit has drifted in from places where 'professors' are powerful little domestic potentates. I am sure that without 'professor' I should have heard less about my donnishness, and no one would have said 'The Shire is not far from North Oxford'. It is in fact more or less a Warwickshire village of about the period of the Diamond Jubilee – that is as far away as the Third Age from that depressing and perfectly characterless straggle of houses north of old Oxford, which has not even a postal existence.

179 From a letter to Hugh Brogan   14 December 1955

[Brogan wrote on 4 December to say that he had 'recurrent nightmares' that he might have been stupid or tactless, or given a wrong impression of 'my real admiration for your great book'.]

Dismiss the nightmare! I can stand criticism – not being unduly puffed up by the success (v. unexpected) of 'The Lord of the Rings' – even when stupid, or unfair, or even (as I occasionally suspect) a little malicious. Otherwise I should be in a fine taking, what with 'emasculate' and other kind adjectives. But you are welcome to let your pen run as it will (it is horrible writing letters to people with whom you have to be 'careful'), since you give me such close attention, and sensitive perception.

180 To 'Mr Thompson' [draft]

[A letter to an unidentified reader.]

14 January 1956   Merton College, Oxford
Dear Mr Thompson,
    Thank you very much for your kind and encouraging letter. Having set myself a task, the arrogance of which I fully recognized and trembled

at: being precisely to restore to the English an epic tradition and present them with a mythology of their own: it is a wonderful thing to be told that I have succeeded, at least with those who have still the undarkened heart and mind.

It has been a considerable labour, beginning really as soon as I was able to begin anything, but effectively beginning when I was an under-graduate and began to explore my own linguistic aesthetic in language-composition. It was just as the 1914 War burst on me that I made the discovery that 'legends' depend on the language to which they belong; but a living language depends equally on the 'legends' which it conveys by tradition. (For example, that the Greek mythology depends far more on the marvellous aesthetic of its language and so of its nomenclature of persons and places and less on its content than people realize, though of course it depends on both. And *vice versa*. Volapük, Esperanto, Ido, Novial,[1] &c &c are dead, far deader than ancient unused languages, because their authors never invented any Esperanto legends.) So though being a philologist by nature and trade (yet one always primarily interested in the aesthetic rather than the functional aspects of language) I began with language, I found myself involved in inventing 'legends' of the same 'taste'. The early work was mostly done in camps and hospitals between 1915 and 1918 – when time allowed. But I think a lot of this kind of work goes on at other (to say lower, deeper, or higher introduces a false gradation) levels, when one is saying how-do-you-do, or even 'sleeping'. I have long ceased to *invent* (though even patronizing or sneering critics on the side praise my 'invention'): I wait till I seem to know what really happened. Or till it writes itself. Thus, though I knew for years that Frodo would run into a tree-adventure somewhere far down the Great River, I have no recollection of inventing Ents. I came at last to the point, and wrote the 'Treebeard' chapter without any recol-lection of any previous thought: just as it now is. And then I saw that, of course, it had not happened to Frodo at all.

All this is boring, I am sure, because it is apparently self-centred; but I am old enough (alas!) to take a dispassionate and scientific, properly so-called, interest in these matters, and cite myself simply because I am interested in mythological 'invention', and the mystery of literary creation (or sub-creation as I have elsewhere called it) and I am the most readily available *corpus vile* for experiment or observation.

My chief reason for talking so, is to say that, of course, all these things are more or less written. There is hardly any reference in *The Lord of the Rings* to things that do not actually *exist** on its own plane (of secondary or sub-creational reality): sc. have been written. *The Silmarillion* was

---

*The cats of Queen Berúthiel and the names and adventures of the other 2 wizards[2] (5 minus Saruman, Gandalf, Radagast) are all that I recollect.

offered for publication years ago, and turned down. Good may come of such blows. *The Lord of the Rings* was the result. The hobbits had been welcomed. I loved them myself, since I love the vulgar and simple as dearly as the noble, and nothing moves my heart (beyond all the passions and heartbreaks of the world) so much as 'ennoblement' (from the Ugly Duckling to Frodo). I would build on the hobbits. And I saw that I was *meant* to do it (as Gandalf* would say), since without thought, in a 'blurb' I wrote for *The Hobbit*, I spoke of the time between the Elder Days and the Dominion of Men. Out of that came the 'missing link': the 'Downfall of Númenor', releasing some hidden 'complex'. For when Faramir speaks of his private vision of the Great Wave, he speaks for me. That vision and dream has been ever with me – and has been inherited (as I only discovered recently) by one of my children.[3]

However, such has been the success – not financial: costs were enormous, and nobody nowadays buys a book that they can borrow: I have not yet received a farthing – of *The Lord of the Rings* that the ugly duckling has become a publisher's swan, and I am being positively *bullied* to put *The Silmarillion* into form, and anything else!

[The draft is incomplete.]

181 To Michael Straight [drafts]

[Before writing a review of *The Lord of the Rings*, Michael Straight, the editor of *New Republic*, wrote to Tolkien asking a number of questions: first, whether there was a 'meaning' in Gollum's rôle in the story and in Frodo's moral failure at the climax; second, whether the 'Scouring of the Shire' chapter was directed especially to contemporary England; and third, why the other voyagers should depart from the Grey Havens with Frodo at the end of the book – 'Is it for the same reason that there are those who gain in the victory but cannot enjoy it?']

[Not dated; probably January or February 1956.]
Dear Mr Straight,

Thank you for your letter. I hope that you have *enjoyed The Lord of the Rings*? *Enjoyed* is the key-word. For it was written to *amuse* (in the highest sense): to be readable. There is *no* 'allegory', moral, political, or contemporary in the work at all.

It is a 'fairy-story', but one written – according to the belief I once expressed in an extended essay 'On Fairy-stories' that they are the

---

*I am *not* Gandalf, being a transcendent Sub-creator in this little world. As far as any character is 'like me' it is Faramir – except that I lack what all my characters possess (let the psychoanalysts note!) *Courage*.

proper audience – for adults. Because I think that fairy story has its own mode of reflecting 'truth', different from allegory, or (sustained) satire, or 'realism', and in some ways more powerful. But first of all it must succeed just as a tale, excite, please, and even on occasion move, and within its own imagined world be accorded (literary) belief. To succeed in that was my primary object.

But, of course, if one sets out to address 'adults' (mentally adult people anyway), they will not be pleased, excited, or moved unless the whole, or the incidents, seem to be about something worth considering, more e.g. than mere danger and escape: there must be some relevance to the 'human situation' (of all periods). So something of the teller's own reflections and 'values' will inevitably get worked in. This is not the same as allegory. We all, in groups or as individuals, *exemplify* general principles; but we do not *represent* them. The Hobbits are no more an 'allegory' than are (say) the pygmies of the African forest. Gollum is to me just a 'character' – an imagined person – who granted the situation acted so and so under opposing strains, as it appears to be *probable* that he would (there is always an incalculable element in any individual real or imagined: otherwise he/she would not be an individual but a 'type'.)

I will try and answer your specific questions. The final scene of the Quest was so shaped simply because having regard to the situation, and to the 'characters' of Frodo, Sam, and Gollum, those events seemed to me mechanically, morally, and psychologically credible. But, of course, if you wish for more reflection, I should say that within the mode of the story the 'catastrophe' *exemplifies* (an aspect of) the familiar words: 'Forgive us our trespasses as we forgive them that trespass against us. Lead us not into temptation, but deliver us from evil.'

'Lead us not into temptation &c' is the harder and the less often considered petition. The view, in the terms of my story, is that though every event or situation has (at least) two aspects: the history and development of the individual (it is something out of which he can get good, ultimate good, for himself, or fail to do so), and the history of the world (which depends on his action for its own sake) – still there are abnormal situations in which one may be placed. 'Sacrificial' situations, I should call them: sc. positions in which the 'good' of the world depends on the behaviour of an individual in circumstances which demand of him suffering and endurance far beyond the normal – even, it may happen (or seem, humanly speaking), demand a strength of body and mind which he does not possess: he is in a sense doomed to failure, doomed to fall to temptation or be broken by pressure against his 'will': that is against any choice he could make or would make unfettered, not under the duress.

Frodo was in such a position: an apparently complete trap: a person of greater native power could probably never have resisted the Ring's lure to power so long; a person of less power could not hope to resist it in the final decision. (Already Frodo had been unwilling to harm the Ring before he set out, and was incapable of surrendering it to Sam.)

The Quest ∴ was bound to fail as a piece of world-plan, and also was bound to end in disaster as the story of humble Frodo's development to the 'noble', his sanctification. Fail it would and did as far as Frodo considered alone was concerned. He 'apostatized' – and I have had one savage letter, crying out that he shd. have been executed as a traitor, not honoured. Believe me, it was not until I read this that I had myself any idea how 'topical' such a situation might appear. It arose naturally from my 'plot' conceived in main outline in 1936.[1] I did not foresee that before the tale was published we should enter a dark age in which the technique of torture and disruption of personality would rival that of Mordor and the Ring and present us with the practical problem of honest men of good will broken down into apostates and traitors.

But at this point the 'salvation' of the world and Frodo's own 'salvation' is achieved by his previous *pity* and forgiveness of injury. At any point any prudent person would have told Frodo that Gollum would certainly* betray him, and could rob him in the end. To 'pity' him, to forbear to kill him, was a piece of folly, or a mystical belief in the ultimate value-in-itself of pity and generosity even if disastrous in the world of time. He did rob him and injure him in the end – but by a 'grace', that last betrayal was at a precise juncture when the final evil deed was the most beneficial thing any one cd. have done for Frodo! By a situation created by his 'forgiveness', he was saved himself, and relieved of his burden. He was very justly accorded the highest honours – since it is clear that he & Sam never concealed the precise course of events. Into the ultimate judgement upon Gollum I would not care to enquire. This would be to investigate 'Goddes privitee', as the Medievals said. Gollum was pitiable, but he ended in persistent wickedness, and the fact that this worked good was no credit to him. His marvellous courage and endurance, as great as Frodo and Sam's or greater, being devoted to evil was portentous, but not honourable. I am afraid, whatever our beliefs, we have to face the fact that there are persons who yield to temptation, reject their chances of nobility or salvation, and appear to be 'damnable'. Their 'damnability' is *not* measurable in the terms of the macrocosm (where it may work good). But we who are all 'in the same boat' must not usurp the Judge. The domination of the Ring was much too strong for the mean soul of Sméagol. But he would have never had to endure it if he had not become a mean sort of thief before it

*Not quite 'certainly'. The clumsiness in fidelity of Sam was what finally pushed Gollum over the brink, when about to repent.

crossed his path. Need it ever have crossed his path? Need anything dangerous ever cross any of our paths? A kind of answer cd. be found in trying to imagine Gollum overcoming temptation. The story would have been quite different! By temporizing, not fixing the still not wholly corrupt Sméagol-will towards good in the debate in the slag hole, he weakened himself for the final chance when dawning love of Frodo was too easily withered by the jealousy of Sam before Shelob's lair. After that he was lost.

There is no special reference to England in the 'Shire' – except of course that as an Englishman brought up in an 'almost rural' village of Warwickshire on the edge of the prosperous bourgeoisie of Birmingham (about the time of the Diamond Jubilee!) I take my models like anyone else – from such 'life' as I know. But there is no post-war reference. I am not a 'socialist' in any sense – being averse to 'planning' (as must be plain) most of all because the 'planners', when they acquire power, become so bad – but I would not say that we had to suffer the malice of Sharkey and his Ruffians here. Though the spirit of 'Isengard', if not of Mordor, is of course always cropping up. The present design of destroying Oxford in order to accommodate motor-cars is a case.[2] But our chief adversary is a member of a 'Tory' Government. But you could apply it anywhere in these days.

Yes: I think that 'victors' never can enjoy 'victory' – not in the terms that they envisaged; and in so far as they fought for something *to be enjoyed by themselves* (whether acquisition or mere preservation) the less satisfactory will 'victory' seem. But the departure of the Ringbearers has quite another side, as far as the Three are concerned. There is, of course, a mythological structure behind this story. It was actually written first, and may now perhaps be in part published. It is, I should say, a 'monotheistic but "sub-creational" mythology'. There is no embodiment of the One, of God, who indeed remains remote, outside the World, and only directly accessible to the Valar or Rulers. These take the place of the 'gods', but are created spirits, or those of the primary creation who by their own will have entered into the world.*
But the One retains all ultimate authority, and (or so it seems as viewed in serial time) reserves the right to intrude the finger of God into the story: that is to produce realities which could not be deduced even from a complete knowledge of the previous past, but which being real become part of the effective past for all subsequent time (a possible definition of a 'miracle'). According to the fable Elves and Men were the first of these intrusions, made indeed while the 'story' was still only a story and not

*They shared in its 'making' – but only on the same terms as we 'make' a work of art or story. The realization of it, the gift to it of a created reality of the same grade as their own, was the act of the One God.

'realized'; they were not therefore in any sense conceived or made by the gods, the Valar, and were called the Eruhíni or 'Children of God', and were for the Valar an incalculable element: that is they were rational creatures of free will in regard to God, of the same historical rank as the Valar, though of far smaller spiritual and intellectual power and status.

Of course, in fact exterior to my story, Elves and Men are just different aspects of the Humane, and represent the problem of Death as seen by a finite but willing and self-conscious person. In this mythological world the Elves and Men are in their incarnate forms kindred, but in the relation of their 'spirits' to the world in time represent different 'experiments', each of which has its own natural trend, and weakness. The Elves represent, as it were, the artistic, aesthetic, and purely scientific aspects of the Humane nature raised to a higher level than is actually seen in Men. That is: they have a devoted love of the physical world, and a desire to observe and understand it for its own sake and as 'other' – sc. as a reality derived from God in the same degree as themselves – not as a material for use or as a power-platform. They also possess a 'subcreational' or artistic faculty of great excellence. They are therefore 'immortal'. *Not* 'eternally', but to endure with and within the created world, while its story lasts. When 'killed', by the injury or destruction of their incarnate form, they do not escape from time, but remain *in* the world, either discarnate, or being re-born. This becomes a great burden as the ages lengthen, especially in a world in which there is malice and destruction (I have left out the mythological form which Malice or the Fall of the Angels takes in this fable). Mere *change* as such is not represented as 'evil': it is the unfolding of the story and to refuse this is of course against the design of God. But the Elvish weakness is in these terms naturally to regret the past, and to become unwilling to face change: as if a man were to hate a very long book still going on, and wished to settle down in a favourite chapter. Hence they fell in a measure to Sauron's deceits: they desired some 'power' over things as they are (which is quite distinct from art), to make their particular will to preservation effective: to arrest change, and keep things always fresh and fair. The 'Three Rings' were 'unsullied', because this object was in a limited way good, it included the healing of the real damages of malice, as well as the mere arrest of change; and the Elves did not desire to dominate other wills, nor to usurp all the world to their particular pleasure. But with the downfall of 'Power' their little efforts at preserving the past fell to bits. There was nothing more in Middle-earth for them, but weariness. So Elrond and Galadriel depart. Gandalf is a special case. He was not the maker or original holder of the Ring – but it was surrendered to him by Círdan, to assist him in his task. Gandalf was returning, his labour and errand finished, to his home, the land of the Valar.

The passage over Sea is not Death. The 'mythology' is Elf-centred. According to it there was at first an actual Earthly Paradise, home and realm of the Valar, as a physical part of the earth.

There is no 'embodiment' of the Creator anywhere in this story or mythology. Gandalf is a 'created' person; though possibly a spirit that existed before in the physical world. His function as a 'wizard' is an angelos or messenger from the Valar or Rulers: to assist the rational creatures of Middle-earth to resist Sauron, a power too great for them unaided. But since in the view of this tale & mythology Power – when it dominates or seeks to dominate other wills and minds (except by the assent of their reason) – is evil, these 'wizards' were incarnated in the life-forms of Middle-earth, and so suffered the pains both of mind and body. They were also, for the same reason, thus involved in the peril of the incarnate: the possibility of 'fall', of sin, if you will. The chief form this would take with them would be impatience, leading to the desire to force others to their own good ends, and so inevitably at last to mere desire to make their own wills effective by any means. To this evil Saruman succumbed. Gandalf did not. But the situation became so much the worse by the fall of Saruman, that the 'good' were obliged to greater effort and sacrifice. Thus Gandalf faced and suffered death; and came back or was sent back, as he says, with enhanced power. But though one may be in this reminded of the Gospels, it is not really the same thing at all. The Incarnation of God is an *infinitely* greater thing than anything I would dare to write. Here I am only concerned with Death as part of the nature, physical and spiritual, of Man, and with Hope without guarantees. That is why I regard the tale of Arwen and Aragorn as the most important of the Appendices; it is part of the essential story, and is only placed so, because it could not be worked into the main narrative without destroying its structure: which is planned to be 'hobbito-centric', that is, primarily a study of the ennoblement (or sanctification) of the humble.

[None of the drafts from which this text has been assembled was completed.]

182 From a letter to Anne Barrett, Houghton Mifflin Co.
[Not dated; 1956]

I shall certainly now, if I am allowed, publish the parts of the great history that was written first – and rejected. But the (to me v. surprising) success of *The Lord of the Rings* will probably cause that rejection to be reconsidered. Though I do not think it would have the appeal of the L.R. – no hobbits! Full of mythology, and elvishness, and all that 'heigh stile' (as Chaucer might say), which has been so little to the taste of many reviewers. But I am not allowed to get at it. I am not only submerged (sans secretary) under business of the L.R., but also under professional business – one of the ways of making us professors 'go quietly' with practically no pension, is to make our last two or three years of office intolerably laborious – ; while the appearance of the L.R. has landed me in the pincers. Most of my philological colleagues* are shocked (cert. behind my back, sometimes to my face) at the fall of a philological into 'Trivial literature'; and anyway the cry is: 'now we know how you have been wasting your time for 20 years'. So the screw is on for many things of a more professional kind long overdue. Alas! I like them both, but have only one man's time. Also I am getting rather ripe, if not actually decrepit! With the retirement this summer of Sir John Beasly, and Lord Cherwell, I am left the senior professor of this ancient institution, having sat in a chair here since 1925 – or 31 years, though no one seems to observe the fact. Except for one or two who cry: 'How long, O Lord, how long?', yearning for the padded seat (actually stuffed with thistle, as one of them will discover).

183 Notes on W. H. Auden's review of *The Return of the King*

[A comment, apparently written for Tolkien's own satisfaction and not sent or shown to anyone else, on 'At the End of the Quest, Victory', a review of *The Return of the King* by W. H. Auden in the *New York Times Book Review*, 22 January 1956. The text given here is a rewriting at some later date of an earlier version, now lost, which was in all probability written in 1956. In the review, Auden wrote: 'Life, as I experience it in my own person, is primarily a continuous succession of choices between alternatives. . . . . For objectifying this experience, the natural image is that of a journey with a purpose, beset by dangerous hazards and obstacles. . . . . But when I observe my fellow-men, such an image seems false. I can see, for example, that only the rich and those on vacation can take journeys; most men, most of the time, must work in one place. I cannot observe them making choices, only the actions they take and, if I know someone well, I can usually predict how he will act in a given situation. . . . . If, then, I try to describe what I see as if I were an impersonal camera, I shall produce, not a Quest, but a "naturalistic" document. . . . . Both extremes, of course, falsify life. There are medieval Quests which justify the criticism made by Erich Auerbach in his book *Mimesis*: "The world of knightly proving is a world of adventure. . . . . [The knight's] exploits . . . . are feats accomplished at random which do

*Notably C. L. Wrenn who succeeded me as professor of Anglo-Saxon and who is, I believe, coming to the U.S.A. this autumn for a year, if you (i.e. U.S.A. officials) let him in.

238

not fit into any politically purposive pattern." . . . . Mr Tolkien has succeeded more completely than any previous writer in this genre in using the traditional properties of the Quest.']

I am very grateful for this review. Most encouraging, as coming from a man who is both a poet and a critic of distinction. Yet not (I think) one who has much practised the telling of tales. In any case I am a little surprised by it, for in spite of its praise it seems to me a critic's way of talking rather than an author's. It is not, to my feeling, the right way of considering either Quests in general or my story in particular. I believe that it is precisely because I did *not* try, and have never thought of trying to 'objectify' my personal experience of life that the account of the Quest of the Ring is successful in giving pleasure to Auden (and others). Probably it is also the reason, in many cases, why it has failed to please some readers and critics. The story is not about JRRT at all, and is at no point an attempt to allegorize his experience of life – for that is what the objectifying of his subjective experience in a tale must mean, if anything.

I am historically minded. Middle-earth is not an imaginary world. The name is the modern form (appearing in the 13th century and still in use) of *midden-erd > middel-erd*, an ancient name for the *oikoumenē*, the abiding place of Men, the objectively real world, in use specifically opposed to imaginary worlds (as Fairyland) or unseen worlds (as Heaven or Hell). The theatre of my tale is this earth, the one in which we now live, but the historical period is imaginary. The essentials of that abiding place are all there (at any rate for inhabitants of N.W. Europe), so naturally it feels familiar, even if a little glorified by the enchantment of distance in time.

Men do go, and have in history gone on journeys and quests, without any intention of acting out allegories of life. It is not true of the past or the present to say that 'only the rich or those on vacation can take journeys'. Most men make some journeys. Whether long or short, with an errand or simply to go 'there and back again', is not of primary importance. As I tried to express it in Bilbo's Walking Song, even an afternoon-to-evening walk may have important effects. When Sam had got no further than the Woody End he had already had an 'eye-opener'. For if there is anything in a journey of any length, for me it is this: a deliverance from the plantlike state of helpless passive sufferer, an exercise however small of will, and mobility – and of curiosity, without which a rational mind becomes stultified. (Though of course all this is an afterthought, and misses the major point. To a story-teller a journey is a marvellous device. It provides a strong thread on which a multitude of things that he has in mind may be strung to make a new thing, various, unpredictable, and yet coherent. My chief reason for using this form was simply technical.)

In any case I do not look on those of my fellow men that I have observed in the way described. I am old enough now to have observed some of them long enough to have a notion of what, I suppose, Auden would call their basic or innate character, while noting changes (often considerable) in their modes of behaviour. I do not feel that a journey in space is a useful comparison for understanding these processes. I think that comparison with a seed is more illuminating: a seed with its innate vitality and heredity, its capacity to grow and develop. A great part of the 'changes' in a man are no doubt unfoldings of the patterns hidden in the seed; though these are of course modified by the situation (geographical or climatic) into which it is thrown, and may be damaged by terrestrial accidents. But this comparison leaves out inevitably an important point. A man is not only a seed, developing in a defined pattern, well or ill according to its situation or its defects as an example of its species; a man is both a seed and in some degree also a gardener, for good or ill. I am impressed by the degree in which the development of 'character' *can* be a product of conscious intention, the will to modify innate tendencies in desired directions; in some cases the change can be great and permanent. I have known one or two men and women who could be described as 'self-made' in this respect with at least as much partial truth as 'self-made' can be applied to those whose affluence or position can be said to have been achieved largely by their own will and efforts with little or no help from inherited wealth or social position.

In any case, I personally find most people *in*calculable in any particular situation or emergency. Perhaps because I am not a good judge of character. But even Auden says only that he can 'usually predict' how they will act; and by the insertion of 'usually' an element of incompatibility is admitted that, however small, is damaging to his point.

Some persons are, or seem to be, more calculable than others. But that is due rather to their fortune than to their nature (as individuals). The calculable people reside in relatively fixed circumstances, and it is difficult to catch and observe them in situations that are (to them) strange. That is another good reason for sending 'hobbits' – a vision of a simple and calculable people in simple and long-settled circumstances – on a *journey* far from settled home into strange lands and dangers. Especially if they are provided with some strong motive for endurance and adaptation. Though without any high motive people do change (or rather reveal the latent) on journeys: that is a fact of ordinary observation without any need of symbolical explanation. On a journey of a length sufficient to provide the untoward in any degree from discomfort to fear the change in companions well-known in 'ordinary life' (and in oneself) is often startling.

I dislike the use of 'political' in such a context; it seems to me false. It seems clear to me that Frodo's duty was 'humane' not political. He naturally thought first of the Shire, since his roots were there, but the quest had as its object not the preserving of this or that polity, such as the half republic half aristocracy of the Shire, but the liberation from an evil tyranny of all the 'humane'* – including those, such as 'easterlings' and Haradrim, that were still servants of the tyranny.

Denethor *was* tainted with mere politics: hence his failure, and his mistrust of Faramir. It had become for him a prime motive to preserve the polity of Gondor, as it was, against another potentate, who had made himself stronger and was to be feared and opposed for that reason rather than because he was ruthless and wicked. Denethor despised lesser men, and one may be sure did not distinguish between orcs and the allies of Mordor. If he had survived as victor, even without use of the Ring, he would have taken a long stride towards becoming himself a tyrant, and the terms and treatment he accorded to the deluded peoples of east and south would have been cruel and vengeful. He had become a 'political' leader: sc. Gondor against the rest.

But that was not the policy or duty set out by the Council of Elrond. Only after hearing the debate and realizing the nature of the quest did Frodo accept the burden of his mission. Indeed the Elves destroyed their own polity in pursuit of a 'humane' duty. This did not happen merely as an unfortunate damage of War; it was known by them to be an inevitable result of victory, which could in no way be advantageous to Elves. Elrond cannot be said to have a political duty or purpose.

Auerbach's use of 'political' may at first sight seem more justified; but it is not, I think, really admissible – not even if we acknowledge the weariness to which mere 'errantry' was reduced as the pastime reading of a class chiefly interested in feats of arms and love.† About as amusing to us (or to me) as are stories about cricket, or yarns about a touring team, to those who (like me) find cricket (as it now is) a ridiculous bore. But the feats of arms in (say) Arthurian Romance, or romances attached to that great centre of imagination, do not need to 'fit into a politically purposive pattern'.‡ So it was in the earlier Arthurian traditions. Or at least this thread of primitive but powerful imagination was an important element in them. As also in *Beowulf*. Auerbach should approve of *Beowulf*, for in it an author tried to fit a deed of 'errantry' into a complex political field:

*humane: this (being in a fairy-story) includes of course Elves, and indeed all 'speaking creatures'.

†chiefly interested: that is as themes of 'literature', as an amusement. Actually most of them were primarily interested in the acquisition of land and the use of marriage-alliances in furthering their aims.

‡Not unless 'political' is narrowed (or enlarged), so that we are considering imaginatively only one centre or fortress of order and grace surrounded by enemies: the untilled woods and mountains, hostile and barbarous men, wild beasts and monsters, and the Unknown. The defence of the realm may then indeed become symbolic of the human situation.

241

the English traditions of the international relations of Denmark, Gotland, and Sweden in ancient days. But that is not the strength of the story, rather its weakness. Beowulf's personal objects in his journey to Denmark are precisely those of a later Knight: his own renown, and above that the glory of his lord and king; but all the time we glimpse something deeper. Grendel is an enemy who has attacked the centre of the realm, and brought into the royal hall the outer darkness, so that only in daylight can the king sit upon the throne. This is something quite different and more horrible than a 'political' invasion of equals – men of another similar realm, such as Ingeld's later assault upon Heorot.

The overthrow of Grendel makes a good wonder-tale, because he is too strong and dangerous for any ordinary man to defeat, but it is a victory in which all men can rejoice because he was a monster, hostile to all men and to all humane fellowship and joy. Compared with him even the long politically hostile Danes and Geats were Friends, on the same side. It is the monstrosity and fairy-tale quality of Grendel that really makes the tale important, surviving still when the politics have become dim and the healing of Danish-Geatish relations in an 'entente cordiale' between two ruling houses a minor matter of obscure history. In that political world Grendel looks silly, though he certainly is not silly, however naif may be the poet's imagination and description of him.

Of course in 'real life' causes are not clear cut – if only because human tyrants are seldom utterly corrupted into pure manifestations of evil will. As far as I can judge some seem to have been so corrupt, but even they must rule subjects only part of whom are equally corrupt, while many still need to have 'good motives', real or feigned, presented to them. As we see today. Still there are clear cases: e.g. acts of sheer cruel aggression, in which therefore *right* is from the beginning wholly on one side, whatever evil the *resentful* suffering of evil may eventually generate in members of the right side. There are also conflicts about important things or ideas. In such cases I am more impressed by the extreme importance of being on the right side, than I am disturbed by the revelation of the jungle of confused motives, private purposes, and individual actions (noble or base) in which the *right* and the *wrong* in actual human conflicts are commonly involved. If the conflict really is about things properly called *right* and *wrong*, or *good* and *evil*, then the rightness or goodness of one side is not proved or established by the claims of either side; it must depend on values and beliefs above and independent of the particular conflict. A judge must assign *right* and *wrong* according to principles which he holds valid in all cases. That being so, the *right* will remain an inalienable possession of the right side and justify its cause throughout.

(I speak of causes, not of individuals. Of course to a judge whose moral ideas have a religious or philosophical basis, or indeed to anyone not blinded by partisan fanaticism, the rightness of the cause will not justify the actions of its supporters, as individuals, that are morally wicked. But though 'propaganda' may seize on them as proofs that their cause was not in fact 'right', that is not valid. The aggressors are themselves primarily to blame for the evil deeds that proceed from their original violation of justice and the passions that their own wickedness must naturally (by their standards) have been expected to arouse. They at any rate have no right to demand that their victims when assaulted should not demand an eye for an eye or a tooth for a tooth.)

Similarly, good actions by those on the wrong side will not justify their cause. There may be deeds on the wrong side of heroic courage, or some of a higher moral level: deeds of mercy and forbearance. A judge may accord them honour and rejoice to see how some men can rise above the hate and anger of a conflict; even as he may deplore the evil deeds on the right side and be grieved to see how hatred once provoked can drag them down. But this will not alter his judgement as to which side was in the right, nor his assignment of the primary blame for all the evil that followed to the other side.

In my story I do not deal in Absolute Evil. I do not think there is such a thing, since that is Zero. I do not think that at any rate any 'rational being' is wholly evil. Satan fell. In my myth Morgoth fell before Creation of the physical world. In my story Sauron represents as near an approach to the wholly evil will as is possible. He had gone the way of all tyrants: beginning well, at least on the level that while desiring to order all things according to his own wisdom he still at first considered the (economic) well-being of other inhabitants of the Earth. But he went further than human tyrants in pride and the lust for domination, being in origin an immortal (angelic) spirit.* In *The Lord of the Rings* the conflict is not basically about 'freedom', though that is naturally involved. It is about God, and His sole right to divine honour. The Eldar and the Númenóreans believed in The One, the true God, and held worship of any other person an abomination. Sauron desired to be a God-King, and was held to be this by his servants;† if he had been

---

*Of the same kind as Gandalf and Saruman, but of a far higher order.

†By a triple treachery: 1. Because of his admiration of Strength he had become a follower of Morgoth and fell with him down into the depths of evil, becoming his chief agent in Middle Earth. 2. When Morgoth was defeated by the Valar finally he forsook his allegiance; but out of fear only; he did not present himself to the Valar or sue for pardon, and remained in Middle Earth. 3. When he found how greatly his knowledge was admired by all other rational creatures and how easy it was to influence them, his pride became boundless. By the end of the Second Age he assumed the position of Morgoth's representative. By the end of the Third Age (though actually much weaker than before) he claimed to be Morgoth returned.

victorious he would have demanded divine honour from all rational creatures and absolute temporal power over the whole world. So even if in desperation 'the West' had bred or hired hordes of orcs and had cruelly ravaged the lands of other Men as allies of Sauron, or merely to prevent them from aiding him, their Cause would have remained indefeasibly right. As does the Cause of those who oppose now the State-God and Marshal This or That as its High Priest, even if it is true (as it unfortunately is) that many of their deeds are wrong, even if it were true (as it is not) that the inhabitants of 'The West', except for a minority of wealthy bosses, live in fear and squalor, while the worshippers of the State-God live in peace and abundance and in mutual esteem and trust.

So I feel that the fiddle-faddle in reviews, and correspondence about them, as to whether my 'good people' were kind and merciful and gave quarter (in fact they do), or not, is quite beside the point. Some critics seem determined to represent me as a simple-minded adolescent, inspired with, say, a With-the-flag-to-Pretoria spirit, and wilfully distort what is said in my tale. I have not that spirit, and it does not appear in the story. The figure of Denethor alone is enough to show this; but I have not made any of the peoples on the 'right' side, Hobbits, Rohirrim, Men of Dale or of Gondor, any better than men have been or are, or can be. Mine is not an 'imaginary' world, but an imaginary historical moment on 'Middle-earth' – which is our habitation.

184 To Sam Gamgee

[On 13 March, a letter was written to Tolkien by a Mr Sam Gamgee of Brixton Road, London S.W.9: 'I hope you do not mind my writing to you, but with reference to your story "Lord of the Rings" running as a serial on the radio . . . . I was rather interested at how you arrived at the name of one of the characters named Sam Gamgee because that happens to be my name. I haven't heard the story myself not having a wireless but I know some who have. . . . . I know it's fiction, but it is rather a coincidence as the name is very uncommon, but well known in the medical profession.']

18 March 1956   As from 76 Sandfield Road, Headington, Oxford
Dear Mr Gamgee,

It was very kind of you to write. You can imagine my astonishment, when I saw your signature! I can only say, for your comfort I hope, that the 'Sam Gamgee' of my story is a most heroic character, now widely beloved by many readers, even though his origins are rustic. So that perhaps you will not be displeased by the coincidence of the name of this imaginary character (of supposedly many centuries ago) being the same as yours. The reason of my use of the name is this. I lived near Birmingham as a child, and we used 'gamgee' as a word for 'cotton-wool'; so in my story the families of Cotton and Gamgee are connected. I did not know as a child, though I know now, that 'Gamgee' was shortened from 'gamgee-tissue', and that [it was] named after its inventor (a surgeon I think) who lived between 1828 and 1886. It was probably (I think) his son who died this year, on 1 March, aged 88, after being for many years Professor of Surgery at Birmingham University. Evidently 'Sam' or something like it,* is associated with the family – though I never knew this until a few days ago, when I saw Professor Gamgee's obituary notice, and saw that he was son of *Sampson Gamgee* – and looked in a dictionary and found that the inventor was *S. Gamgee* (1828–86), & ∴ probably the same.

Have you any tradition as to the real origin of your distinguished and rare name? Having a rare name myself (often troublesome) I am specially interested.

The 'etymology' given in my book is of course quite fictitious, and made up simply for the purposes of my story. I do not suppose you could be bothered to *read* so long and fantastic a work, especially if you do not care for stories about a mythical world, but if you could be bothered, I know that the work (which has been astonishingly successful) is in most public libraries. It is alas! very expensive to buy – £3/3/0. But if you or any of your family try it, and find it interesting enough, I can only say that I shall be happy and proud to send you a signed copy of all 3 vols. as a tribute from the author to the distinguished family of Gamgee.

Yrs sincerely
J. R. R. Tolkien.

[Mr Gamgee replied on 30 March with more information about his family. He expressed himself delighted at Tolkien's offer of signed volumes. Tolkien sent them, and Mr Gamgee acknowledged their arrival, adding: 'I can assure you that I have every intention of reading them.']

185 From a letter to Christopher and Faith Tolkien 19 March 1956

I have had a letter from a real *Sam Gamgee,* from Tooting! He could not have chosen a more Hobbit-*sounding* place, could he? – though un-Shirelike, I fear, in reality.

Also A. & Unwin send extremely good news or prophecies of probable financial results to come later.

---

*My Sam Gamgee is *Samwise* not Sam(p)son or Samuel.

Of course my story is not an allegory of Atomic power, but of *Power* (exerted for Domination). Nuclear physics can be used for that purpose. But they need not be. They need not be used at all. If there is any contemporary reference in my story at all it is to what seems to me the most widespread assumption of our time: that if a thing can be done, it must be done. This seems to me wholly false. The greatest examples of the action of the spirit and of reason are in *abnegation*. When you say A[tomic] P[ower] is 'here to stay' you remind me that Chesterton said that whenever he heard that, he knew that whatever it referred to would soon be replaced, and thought pitifully shabby and old-fashioned. So-called 'atomic' power is rather bigger than anything he was thinking of (I have heard it of trams, gas-light, steam-trains). But it surely is clear that there will have to be some 'abnegation' in its use, a deliberate refusal to do some of the things it is possible to do with it, or nothing will stay! However, that is simple stuff, a contemporary & possibly passing and ephemeral problem. I do not think that even Power or Domination is the real centre of my story. It provides the theme of a War, about something dark and threatening enough to seem at that time of supreme importance, but that is mainly 'a setting' for characters to show themselves. The real theme for me is about something much more permanent and difficult: Death and Immortality: the mystery of the love of the world in the hearts of a race 'doomed' to leave and seemingly lose it; the anguish in the hearts of a race 'doomed' not to leave it, until its whole evil-aroused story is complete. But if you have now read Vol. III and the story of Aragorn, you will have perceived that. (This story is placed in an appendix, because I have told the whole tale more or less through 'hobbits'; and that is because another main point in the story for me is the remark of Elrond in Vol. I: 'Such is oft the course of deeds that move the wheels of the world: small hands do them because they must, while the eyes of the great are elsewhere.' Though equally important is Merry's remark (Vol. III p. 146): 'the soil of the Shire is deep. Still there are things deeper and higher; and not a gaffer could tend his garden in what he calls peace, but for them.') I am *not* a 'democrat' only because 'humility' and equality are spiritual principles corrupted by the attempt to mechanize and formalize them, with the result that we get not universal smallness and humility, but universal greatness and pride, till some Orc gets hold of a ring of power – and then we get and are getting slavery. But all that is rather 'after-thought'. The story is really a story of what happened in B.C. year X, and it just happened to people who were like that! . . . .

I hope you have now 'come by' Vol. III! I am afraid I am always rather pleased when I hear of somebody being obliged to *buy* the book! An author cannot live on library-subscriptions.

I received a letter the other day from a well known, and certainly not impoverished, man, who informed me as a high compliment that he had become so enthralled that he got out the book several times, and paid heavy fines for keeping it out too long. Words failed me in reply. The *L of the R* cost some £4000 to produce to begin with, after it left my hands. Before that apart from any other labour I typed it out twice (in places several times). A professional would have charged about £200. There is a laborious practical side even to high Romance – not that hobbits ever forget that.

187   From a letter to H. Cotton Minchin (draft)

[Not dated; April 1956. Tolkien has written at the top: 'More or less as sent 16 April (with some reduction).']

As 'research students' always discover, however long they are allowed, and careful their work and notes, there is always a rush at the end, when the last date suddenly approaches on which their thesis must be presented. So it was with this book, and the maps. I had to call in the help of my son – the C.T. or C.J.R.T. of the modest initials on the maps – an accredited student of hobbit-lore. And neither of us had an entirely free hand. I remember that when it became apparent that the 'general map' would not suffice for the final Book, or sufficiently reveal the courses of Frodo, the Rohirrim, and Aragorn, I had to devote many days, the last three virtually without food or bed, to drawing re-scaling and adjusting a large map, at which he then worked for 24 hours (6 a.m. to 6 a.m. without bed) in re-drawing just in time. Inconsistencies of spelling are due to me. It was only in the last stages that (in spite of my son's protests: he still holds that no one will ever pronounce *Cirith* right, it appears as *Kirith* in his map, as formerly also in the text) I decided to be 'consistent' and spell Elvish names and words throughout without *k*. There are no doubt other variations. . . . .

I am, however, primarily a philologist and to some extent a calligrapher (though this letter may make that difficult to believe). And my son after me. To us far and away the most absorbing interest is the Elvish tongues, and the nomenclature based on them; and the alphabets. My plans for the 'specialist volume' were largely linguistic. An index of names was to be produced, which by etymological interpretation would also provide quite a large Elvish vocabulary; this is of course a first requirement. I worked at it for months, and indexed the first two vols.

(it was the chief cause of the delay of Vol iii) until it became clear that size and cost were ruinous. Reluctantly also I had to abandon, under pressure from the 'production department', the 'facsimiles' of the three pages of the *Book of Mazarbul*, burned tattered and blood-stained, which I had spent much time on producing or forging. Without them the opening of Book Two, ch. 5 (which was meant to have the facsimiles and a transcript alongside) is defective, and the Runes of the Appendices unnecessary.

But the problems (delightful if I had time) which the extra volume will set, will seem clear if I tell you that while many like you demand *maps*, others wish for *geological** indications rather than places; many want Elvish grammars, phonologies, and specimens; some want metrics and prosodies — not only of the brief Elvish specimens, but of the 'translated' verses in less familiar modes, such as those written in the strictest form of Anglo-Saxon alliterative verse (e.g. the fragment at the end of the *Battle of the Pelennor*, V vi 124). Musicians want tunes, and musical notation; archaeologists want ceramics and metallurgy. Botanists want a more accurate description of the *mallorn*, of *elanor*, *niphredil*, *alfirin*, *mallos*, and *symbelmynë*; and historians want more details about the social and political structure of Gondor; general enquirers want information about the Wainriders, the Harad, Dwarvish origins, the Dead Men, the Beornings, and the missing two wizards (out of five). It will be a big volume, even if I attend only to the things revealed to my limited understanding!

188 From a letter to Allen & Unwin 3 April 1956

[In March, Allen & Unwin told Tolkien that they had signed an agree-ment for a Dutch edition of *The Lord of the Rings*. Tolkien replied that this was the first he had heard of such a proposal, and asked to be told more. The publishers answered that they were making 'all possible efforts' to sell foreign rights, and asked for confirmation that Tolkien wanted them to do so.]

Of course, I wish you to pursue your efforts with regard to foreign editions. . . . . It is however surely intelligible that an author, while still alive, should feel a deep and immediate concern in *translation*. And this one is, unfortunately, also a professional linguist, a pedantic don, who has wide personal connexions and friendships with the chief English scholars of the continent. . . . . The translation of *The Lord of the Rings* will prove a formidable task, and I do not see how it can be performed

---

*Having geological interests, and a very little knowledge, I have not wholly neglected this aspect, but its indication is rather more difficult – and perilous!

satisfactorily without the assistance of the author.* That assistance I am prepared to give, promptly, if I am consulted.

I wish to avoid a repetition of my experience with the Swedish translation of *The Hobbit*.[1] I discovered that this had taken unwarranted liberties with the text and other details, without consultation or approval; it was also unfavourably criticized in general by a Swedish expert, familiar with the original, to whom I submitted it. I regard the text (in all its details) of *The Lord of the Rings* far more jealously. No alterations, major or minor, re-arrangements, or abridgements of this text will be approved by me – unless they proceed from myself or from direct consultation. I earnestly hope that this concern of mine will be taken account of.

189   From a letter to Mrs M. Wilson   11 April 1956

I find that many children become interested, even engrossed, in *The Lord of the Rings*, from about 10 onwards. I think it rather a pity, really. It was not written for them. But then I am a very 'unvoracious' reader, and since I can seldom bring myself to read a work twice I think of the many things that I read – too soon! Nothing, not even a (possible) deeper appreciation, for me replaces the bloom on a book, the freshness of the unread. Still what we read and when goes, like the people we meet, by 'fate.'

190   From a letter to Rayner Unwin   3 July 1956

[In June, the Foreign Rights Department of Allen & Unwin sent Tolkien a list of Dutch versions of place-names in *The Lord of the Rings* that had been made by the book's Dutch translator, with the request: 'Will you please send them back with, we trust, your approval?']

I hope you, & the Foreign Rights Dept., will forgive my now at length writing to *you* about the Dutch translation. The matter is (to me) important; it has disturbed and annoyed me greatly, and given me a good deal of unnecessary work at a most awkward season. . . . .

In principle I object as strongly as is possible to the 'translation' of the

---

*By 'assistance' I do not, of course, mean interference, though the opportunity to consider specimens would be desirable. My linguistic knowledge seldom extends, beyond the detection of obvious errors and liberties, to the criticism of the niceties that would be required. But there are many special difficulties in this text. To mention one: there are a number of words not to be found in the dictionaries, or which require a knowledge of older English. On points such as these, and others that would inevitably arise, the author would be the most satisfactory, and the quickest, source of information.

nomenclature at all (even by a competent person). I wonder why a translator should think himself called on or entitled to do any such thing. That this is an 'imaginary' world does not give him any right to remodel it according to his fancy, even if he could in a few months create a new coherent structure which it took me years to work out.

I presume that if I had presented the Hobbits as speaking Italian, Russian, Chinese, or what you will, he would have left the names alone. Or, if I had pretended that 'the Shire' was some fictitious Loamshire[1] of actual England. Yet actually in an imaginary country and period, as this one, coherently made, the nomenclature is a more important element than in an 'historical' novel. But, of course, if we drop the 'fiction' of long ago, 'The Shire' is based on rural England and not any other country in the world – least perhaps of any in Europe on Holland, which is topographically wholly dissimilar. (In fact so different is it, that in spite of the affinity of its language, and in many respects of its idiom, which should ease some part of the translator's labour, its *toponymy* is specially unsuitable for the purpose.) The toponymy of *The Shire*, to take the first list, is a 'parody' of that of rural England, in much the same sense as are its inhabitants: they go together and are meant to. After all the book is English, and by an Englishman, and presumably even those who wish its narrative and dialogue turned into an idiom that they understand, will not ask of a translator that he should deliberately attempt to destroy the local colour. I do not ask that of a translator, though I might be glad of a glossary where (seldom) the meaning of the place-name is essential. I would not wish, in a book starting from an imaginary mirror of Holland, to meet *Hedge, Duke'sbush, Eaglehome,* or *Applethorn* even *if* these were 'translations' of 'sGravenHage, Hertogenbosch, Arnhem, or Apeldoorn! These 'translations' are not English, they are just homeless.

Actually the Shire Map plays a very small part in the narrative, and most of its purpose is a descriptive build-up. It is, of course, based on some acquaintance with English toponymical history, which the translator would appear not to possess (nor I guess does he know much of that of the Netherlands). But he *need not,* if he would leave it alone. The proper way to treat the first map is to change its title to *Een Deel von 'The Shire'* and no more; though I suppose *naar* for 'to' in such directions as *'To Little Delving'* wd. do no harm.

The Translator has (on internal evidence) glanced at but not used the Appendices. He seems incidentally quite unaware of difficulties he is creating for himself later. The 'Anglo-Saxon' of the Rohirrim is not much like Dutch. In fact he is pulling to bits with very clumsy fingers a web that he has made only a slight attempt to understand. . . . .

The essential point missed, of course, is: even where a place-name is fully analysable by speakers of the language (usually not the case) this is not as a rule done. If in an imaginary land *real* place-names are used, or ones that are carefully constructed to fall into familiar patterns, these become integral names, 'sound real', and translating them by their analysed senses is quite insufficient. This Dutchman's Dutch names should sound real Dutch. Well, actually I am no Dutch scholar at all, and know little of the peculiar history of Dutch toponymy, but I do not believe that as a rule they do. Anyway lots of them are *nonsense* anyway or wholly erroneous, which I can only equal by supposing that you met Blooming, Newtown, Lake How, Documents, Baconbury, Blushing and then discovered the author had written Florence, Naples, (Lake or Lago di) Como, Chartres, Hamburg, and Flushing=Vlissingen!

I enclose in justification of my strictures a detailed commentary on the lists. . . . . I am sure the correct (as well as for publisher and translator the more economical?) way is to leave the maps and nomenclature alone as far as possible, but to substitute for some of the least-wanted Appendices a glossary of names (with meanings but no refs.). I could supply one for translation.

May I say now at once that I will *not* tolerate any similar tinkering with the *personal nomenclature*. Nor with the name/word *Hobbit*. I will not have any more *Hompen* (in which I was not consulted), nor any *Hobbel* or what not. Elves, Dwarfs/ves, Trolls, yes: they are mere modern equivalents of the correct terms. But *hobbit* (and *orc*) are of that world, and they must stay, whether they sound Dutch or not. . . . .

If you think I am being absurd, then I shall be greatly distressed; but I fear not altered in my opinions. The few people I have been able to consult, I must say, express themselves equally strongly. Anyway I'm not going to be treated à la Mrs Tiggywinkle = Poupette à l'épingle.* Not that B[eatrix] P[otter] did not give translators hell. Though possibly from securer grounds than I have. I am no linguist, but I do know something about *nomenclature*, and have specially studied it, and I am actually very angry indeed.

191   **From a letter to Miss J. Burn (draft)**   26 July 1956

If you re-read all the passages dealing with Frodo and the Ring, I think you will see that not only was it *quite impossible* for him to surrender the Ring, in act or will, especially at its point of maximum power, but that this failure was adumbrated from far back. He was honoured because he had accepted the burden voluntarily, and had then done all that was within his utmost physical and mental strength to do. He (and the

---

*Anyway Canétang=Puddleduck[2] is several classes above this performer!

Cause) were saved – by Mercy: by the supreme value and efficacy of Pity and forgiveness of injury.

Corinthians I x. 12-13[1] may not at first sight seem to fit – unless 'bearing temptation' is taken to mean resisting it while still a free agent in normal command of the will. I think rather of the mysterious last petitions of the Lord's Prayer: Lead us not into temptation, but deliver us from evil. A petition against something that cannot happen is unmeaning. There exists the possibility of being placed in positions beyond one's power. In which case (as I believe) salvation from ruin will depend on something apparently unconnected: the general sanctity (and humility and mercy) of the sacrificial person. I did not 'arrange' the deliverance in this case: it again follows the logic of the story. (Gollum had had his chance of repentance, and of returning generosity with love; and had fallen off the knife-edge.) In the case of those who now issue from prison 'brainwashed', broken, or insane, praising their torturers, no such immediate deliverance is as a rule to be seen. But we can at least judge them by the will and intentions with which they entered the *Sammath Naur*; and not demand impossible feats of will, which could only happen in stories unconcerned with real moral and mental probability.

No, Frodo 'failed'. It is possible that once the ring was destroyed he had little recollection of the last scene. But one must face the fact: the power of Evil in the world is *not* finally resistible by incarnate creatures, however 'good'; and the Writer of the Story is not one of us.

I am afraid I have the same feeling – I have been forced to publish up-side-down or backwards; and after the grand crash (and the end of visibly incarnate Evil) before the Dominion of Men (or simple History) to which it all led up the mythological and elvish legends of the Elder Days will not be quite the same. But perhaps read, eventually, from beginning to end in the right order, both parts may gain. I am not writing the *Silmarillion*, which was long ago written; but trying to find a way and order in which to make the legends and annals publishable. And I have a dreadful lot of other work to do as well.

192 From a letter to Amy Ronald 27 July 1956

By chance, I have just had another letter regarding the failure of Frodo. Very few seem even to have observed it. But following the logic of the plot, it was clearly inevitable, as an event. And surely it is a more significant and real event than a mere 'fairy-story' ending in which the hero is indomitable? It is possible for the good, even the saintly, to be subjected to a power of evil which is too great for them to overcome – in themselves. In this case the cause (not the 'hero') was triumphant, because by the exercise of pity, mercy, and forgiveness of injury, a situation was produced in which all was redressed and disaster averted. Gandalf certainly foresaw this. See Vol. I p. 68–9.[1] Of course, he did not mean to say that one must be merciful, for it may prove useful later – it would not then be mercy or pity, which are only truly present when contrary to prudence. Not ours to plan! But we are assured that we must be ourselves extravagantly generous, if we are to hope for the extravagant generosity which the slightest easing of, or escape from, the consequences of our own follies and errors represents. And that mercy does sometimes occur in this life.

Frodo deserved all honour because he spent every drop of his power of will and body, and that was just sufficient to bring him to the destined point, and no further. Few others, possibly no others of his time, would have got so far. The Other Power then took over: the Writer of the Story (by which I do not mean myself), 'that one ever-present Person who is never absent and never named'* (as one critic has said). See Vol. I p. 65.[2] A third (the only other) commentator on the point some months ago reviled Frodo as a scoundrel (who should have been hung and not honoured), and me too. It seems sad and strange that, in this evil time when daily people of good will are tortured, 'brainwashed', and broken, anyone could be so fiercely simpleminded and selfrighteous.

I do not think Walter de la Mare walked in my country, whether you mean: read my work before he died, or inhabited a similar world, or both. I only met him once, many years ago, and we had little to say; but as far as my feelings for and understanding of his work goes, I should guess that he inhabited a much darker and more hopeless world: one anyway that alarms me profoundly.

193   From a letter to Terence Tiller   2 November 1956

[Tiller, the adapter and producer of the BBC Third Programme version of *The Lord of the Rings* (see no. 175), had asked for Tolkien's advice on 'accents' for the second series of six episodes of the book, which were based on *The Two Towers* and *The Return of the King*.]

Taking 'accent' to mean, as it usually does in non-technical language: 'more or less consistent alterations of the vowels/consonants of "received" English': I should say that, in the cases you query, *no* accent-differentiation is needed or desirable. For instance, it would probably be better to avoid certain, actual or conventional, features of

*Actually referred to as 'the One' in App. A III p. 317 1. 20. The Númenóreans (and Elves) were absolute monotheists.

modern 'vulgar' English in representing Orcs, such as the dropping of aitches (these are, I think, *not* dropped in the text, and that is deliberate).

But, of course, for most people, 'accent' as defined above is confused with impressions of different intonation, articulation, and tempo. You will, I suppose, have to use such means to make Orcs sound nasty!

I have no doubt that, if this 'history' were real, all users of the C[ommon] Speech would reveal themselves by their accent, differing in place, people, and rank, but that cannot be represented when C. S. is turned into English – and is not (I think) necessary. I paid great attention to such linguistic differentiation as was possible: in diction, idiom, and so on; and I doubt if much more can be imported, except in so far as the individual actor represents his feeling for the character in tone and style.

As Minas Tirith is at the source of C. Speech it is to C.S. as London is to modern English, and the standard of comparison! None of its inhabitants should have an 'accent' in terms of vowels &c.

The Rohirrim no doubt (as our ancient English ancestors in a similar state of culture and society) spoke, at least their own tongue, with a slower tempo and more sonorous articulation, than modern 'urbans'. But I think it is safe to represent them when using C. S., as they practically always do (for obvious reasons) as speaking the best M[inas] T[irith]. Possibly a little too good, as it would be a learned language, somewhat slower and more careful than a native's. But that is a nicety safely neglected, and not always true: *Théoden* was born in Gondor and C.S. was the domestic language of the Golden Hall in his father's day (*Return of the King* p. 350).[1]

194 To Terence Tiller

6 November 1956   76 Sandfield Road, Headington, Oxford
Dear Tiller,

Lord of the Rings

I have not had time for more than two rapid readings of the 3 episodes that you sent me; but I suppose it is 'now or never', if any comment is to be of practical use.

I am not offering any criticism of detail. The objects you had in making this version seem fairly clear, and (granted their value or legitimacy) I do not think that they could have been much better achieved. I wish your efforts all success.

But, as a private conversation between you and me, I could wish you had perhaps time to spare to tell me *why* this sort of treatment is accorded to the book, and what value it has – on Third. For myself, I do not believe that many, if any, listeners who do not know the book will thread the plot or grasp at all what is going on. And the text is (necessarily in the space) reduced to such simple, even simple-minded, terms that I find it hard to believe it would hold the attention of the Third.

Here is a book very unsuitable for dramatic or semi-dramatic representation. If that is attempted it needs more space, a lot of space. It is sheerly impossible to pot the two books in the allotted time – whether the object be to provide something in itself entertaining in the medium; or to indicate the nature of the original (or both). Why not then turn it down as unsuitable, if more space is not available?

I remain, of course, flattered and pleased that my book should receive this attention; but I still cannot help wondering: why this form? Personally, I think it requires rather the older art of the reading 'mime', than the more nearly dramatic, which results in too great an emphasis on dialogue (mostly with its setting removed). To take two points: (1) the episode of the corpse-candles is cut down to ineffectiveness; (2) the crucial moment when Gollum nearly repents disappears in a mere '*and so Gollum found them. . . &c.*' III/12. In this way both the 'scenery' and the 'characters' become flat: without precision and colour; and without motives or conflicts. I cannot help thinking that longer actual passages read, as a necklace upon a thread of narration (in which the narrator might occasionally venture an interpretation of more than mere plot-events) would, or might, prove both more interesting to listeners, and fairer to the author. But, as I have said, I lack experience in the medium, & this is in any case no criticism of your text, but a sighing for something quite different – a moon no doubt. Final query: can a tale not conceived dramatically but (for lack of a more precise term) epically, be dramatized – unless the dramatizer is given or takes liberties, as an independent person? I feel you have had a very hard task.

Yours sincerely

J. R. R. Tolkien.

195 From a letter to Amy Ronald 15 December 1956

One point: Frodo's attitude to weapons was personal. He was not in modern terms a 'pacifist'. Of course, he was mainly horrified at the prospect of civil war among Hobbits;[1] but he had (I suppose) also reached the conclusion that physical fighting is actually less ultimately effective than most (good) men think it! Actually I am a Christian, and indeed a Roman Catholic, so that I do not expect 'history' to be anything but a 'long defeat' – though it contains (and in a legend may contain more clearly and movingly) some samples or glimpses of final victory.

196 From a letter to Katherine Farrer 21 March 1957

[Written, though Tolkien did not know it, on the day that C. S. Lewis was married, in a Church of England ceremony at her hospital bedside, to Joy Davidman, who was believed to be dying.]

I believe you have been much concerned with the troubles of poor Jack Lewis. Of these I know little beyond the cautious hints of the extremely discreet Havard. When I see Jack he naturally takes refuge in 'literary' talk (for which no domestic griefs and anxieties have yet dimmed his enthusiasm).

197 From a letter to Rayner Unwin 9 May 1957

[Allen & Unwin had sent a substantial cheque for Tolkien's earnings from *The Lord of the Rings*. Rayner Unwin reported excellent sales, and prophesied continuing success.]

Your 'bombshell' arrived at a moment of rush. . . . . Otherwise I would have thanked you for your kind letter sooner.

If I had had any notion of this, I should have thought seriously of retiring at the proper time (this July) and refusing the extra two years, which will not make sufficient difference to my superannuation pittance to be worth bothering about. As it is, I am merely going to be fined for going on 'working', about to the equivalent of my salary, unless my I[ncome] T[ax] agent is unduly gloomy about this remarkable second instalment. Also it is practically impossible to get any connected time to spend on *The Silmarillion* while I remain in office. I have had to lay it aside since last autumn; though I hope to resume it at the end of next month. I have not been very well lately, and am beginning to be affected by arthritis which often makes long sitting painful.

Aggrieved as I am at being deprived of the fruits of so many years labour (which meant not only the sacrifice of leisure but also of other occupations of immediate annual profit), I must say I am very much enheartened by your sales-report and hopes for the immediate future, not only on my own account, but on yours (and A. & U.'s) too. You have been so kind and patient to me; and without your encouragement, and generous 'adventure', I expect the *L. of the R.* would still be a heap of MS. I am afraid I cannot help feeling that there is a lot to be said for 'the grosser forms of literary success' as a sneering critic recently called it (not mine but a 'grosser' case).

198 From a letter to Rayner Unwin   19 June 1957

[An American film-maker had enquired about the possibility of making a cartoon film of *The Lord of the Rings*.]

As far as I am concerned personally, I should welcome the idea of an animated motion picture, with all the risk of vulgarization; and that quite apart from the glint of money, though on the brink of retirement that is not an unpleasant possibility. I think I should find vulgarization less painful than the sillification achieved by the B.B.C.

199   From a letter to Caroline Everett   24 June 1957

Though it is a great compliment, I am really rather sorry to find myself the subject of a thesis. I do not feel inclined to go into biographical detail. I doubt its relevance to criticism. Certainly in any form less than a complete biography, interior and exterior, which I alone could write, and which I do not intend to write. The chief biographical fact to me is the completion of *The Lord of the Rings*, which still astonishes me. A notorious beginner of enterprises and non-finisher, partly through lack of time, partly through lack of single-minded concentration, I still wonder how and why I managed to peg away at this thing year after year, often under real difficulties, and bring it to a conclusion. I suppose, because from the beginning it began to catch up in its narrative folds visions of most of the things that I have most loved or hated.

I did not go to a 'public' school in the sense of a residential school; but to a great 'grammar school', of ultimately medieval foundation. My experience had therefore nothing whatever in common with that of Mr. Lewis. I was at the one school from 1900 to 1911, with one short interval. I was as happy or the reverse at school as anywhere else, the faults being my own. I ended up anyway as a perfectly respectable and tolerably successful senior. I did not dislike games. They were not compulsory, fortunately, as I have always found cricket a bore: chiefly, though, because I was not good at it. . . . .

I have not published any other short story but *Leaf by Niggle*. They do not arise in my mind. *Leaf by Niggle* arose suddenly and almost complete. It was written down almost at a sitting, and very nearly in the form in which it now appears. Looking at it myself now from a distance I should say that, in addition to my tree-love (it was originally called *The Tree*), it arose from my own pre-occupation with *The Lord of the Rings*, the knowledge that it would be finished in great detail or not at all, and the fear (near certainty) that it would be 'not at all'. The war had arisen to darken all horizons. But no such analyses are a complete explanation even of a short story. . . . .

I read the works of [E.R.] Eddison, long after they appeared; and I once met him. I heard him in Mr. Lewis's room in Magdalen College read aloud some parts of his own works – from the *Mistress of Mistresses*, as far as I remember.[1] He did it extremely well. I read his works with great enjoyment for their sheer literary merit. My opinion of them is almost the same as that expressed by Mr. Lewis on p. 104 of the *Essays presented to Charles Williams*.[2] Except that I disliked his characters (always excepting the Lord Gro) and despised what he appeared to admire more intensely than Mr. Lewis at any rate saw fit to say of himself. Eddison thought what I admire 'soft' (his word: one of complete condemnation, I gathered); I thought that, corrupted by an evil and indeed silly 'philosophy', he was coming to admire, more and more, arrogance and cruelty. Incidentally, I thought his nomenclature slipshod and often inept. In spite of all of which, I still think of him as the greatest and most convincing writer of 'invented worlds' that I have read. But he was certainly not an 'influence'.

The general idea of the *Lord of the Rings* was certainly in my mind from an early stage: that is from the first draft of Book I Chapter 2, written in the 1930s. From time to time I made rough sketches or synopses of what was to follow, immediately or far ahead; but these were seldom of much use: the story unfolded itself as it were. The tying-up was achieved, so far as it is achieved, by constant re-writing backwards. I had a many-columned calendar with dates and a brief statement of where all the major actors or groups were on each day and what they were doing.

The last volume was naturally the most difficult, since by that time I had accumulated a large number of narrative debts, and set some awkward problems of presentation in drawing together the separated threads. But the problem was not so much 'what happened?', about which I was only occasionally in doubt – though praised for 'invention' I have not in fact any conscious memory of sitting down and deliberately thinking out any episode – as how to order the account of it. The solution is imperfect. Inevitably.

Obviously the chief problem of this sort, is how to bring up Aragorn unexpectedly to the raising of the Siege, and yet inform readers of what he had been up to. Told in full in its proper place (Vol III, ch.2), though it would have been better for the episode, it would have destroyed Chapter 6. Told in full, or indeed in part, in retrospect it would be out of date and hold up the action (as it does in Chapter 9).

The solution, imperfect, was to cut down the whole episode (which in full would belong rather to a *Saga of Aragorn Arathorn's son* than to my story) and tell the ending of it briefly during the inevitable pause after the Battle of the Pelennor.

I was in fact longest held up – by exterior circumstances as well as interior – at the point now represented by the last words of Book iii (reached about 1942 or 3). After that Chapter 1 of Book v remained very long as a mere opening (as far as the arrival in Gondor); Chapter 2 did not exist; and Chapter 3, Muster of Rohan, had got no further than the arrival at Harrowdale. Chapter 1 of Book iv had hardly got beyond Sam's opening words (Vol II p. 209). Some parts of the adventures of Frodo and Sam on the confines of Mordor and in it had been written (but were eventually abandoned).

200 From a letter to Major R. Bowen 25 June 1957

I note your remarks about Sauron. He was always de-bodied when vanquished. The theory, if one can dignify the modes of the story with such a term, is that he was a spirit, a minor one but still an 'angelic' spirit. According to the mythology of these things that means that, though of course a creature, he belonged to the race of intelligent beings that were made before the physical world, and were permitted to assist in their measure in the making of it. Those who became most involved in this work of Art, as it was in the first instance, became so engrossed with it, that when the Creator made it real (that is, gave it the secondary reality, subordinate to his own, which we call primary reality, and so in that hierarchy on the same plane with themselves) they desired to enter into it, from the beginning of its 'realization'.

They were allowed to do so, and the great among them became the equivalent of the 'gods' of traditional mythologies; but a condition was that they would remain 'in it' until the Story was finished. They were thus in the world, but not of a kind whose essential nature is to be physically incarnate. They were self-incarnated, if they wished; but their incarnate forms were more analogous to our clothes than to our bodies, except that they were more than are clothes the expression of their desires, moods, wills and functions. Knowledge of the Story as it was when composed, before realization, gave them their measure of fore-knowledge; the amount varied very much, from the fairly complete knowledge of the mind of the Creator in this matter possessed by Manwë, the 'Elder King', to that of lesser spirits who might have been interested only in some subsidiary matter (such as trees or birds). Some had attached themselves to such major artists and knew things chiefly indirectly through their knowledge of the minds of these masters. Sauron had been attached to the greatest, Melkor, who ultimately became the inevitable Rebel and self-worshipper of mythologies that begin with a transcendent unique Creator. Olórin (Vol II p. 279) had been attached to Manwë.[1]

The Creator did not hold himself aloof. He introduced new themes into the original design, which might therefore be unforeseen by many of the spirits in realization; there were also unforeseeable events (that is happenings which not even a complete knowledge of the past could predict).

Of the first kind and the chief was the theme of the incarnate intelligence, Elves and Men, which was not thought of nor treated by any of the Spirits. They were therefore called the Children of God. Being other than the Spirits, of less 'stature', and yet of the same order, they were the object of hope and desire to the greater spirits, who knew something of their form and nature and the mode and approximate time of their appearance in the realization. But they also realized that the Children of God must not be 'dominated', though they would be specially susceptible to it.

It was because of this pre-occupation with the Children of God that the spirits so often took the form and likeness of the Children, especially after their appearance. It was thus that Sauron appeared in this shape. It is mythologically supposed that when this shape was 'real', that is a physical actuality in the physical world and not a vision transferred from mind to mind, it took some time to build up. It was then destructible like other physical organisms. But that of course did not destroy the spirit, nor dismiss it from the world to which it was bound until the end. After the battle with Gilgalad and Elendil, Sauron took a long while to re-build, longer than he had done after the Downfall of Númenor (I suppose because each building-up used up some of the inherent energy of the spirit, which might be called the 'will' or the effective link between the indestructible mind and being and the realization of its imagination). The impossibility of re-building after the destruction of the Ring, is sufficiently clear 'mythologically' in the present book.

I am sorry if this all seems dreary and 'pompose'. But so do all attempts to 'explain' the images and events of a mythology. Naturally the stories come first. But it is, I suppose, some test of the consistency of a mythology as such, if it is capable of some sort of rational or rationalized explanation.

201 From a letter to Rayner Unwin 7 September 1957

[On 4 September, Tolkien was visited by representatives of the American company which was interested in making an animated film of *The Lord of the Rings*. He was given a copy of the synopsis of the film, which he agreed to read.]

You will receive on Monday the copy of the 'Story Line' or synopsis of the proposed film version of *The Lord of the Rings*. I could not get it off yesterday. . . . .

An *abridgement* by selection with some good picture-work would be pleasant, & perhaps worth a good deal in publicity; but the present script is rather a *compression* with resultant over-crowding and confusion, blurring of climaxes, and general degradation: a pull-back towards more conventional 'fairy-stories'. People gallop about on Eagles at the least provocation; Lórien becomes a fairy-castle with 'delicate minarets', and all that sort of thing.

But I am quite prepared to play ball, if they are open to advice – and if you decide that the thing is genuine, and worthwhile.

202   From a letter to Christopher and Faith Tolkien
11 September 1957

My heart and mind is in the *Silmarillion*, but I have not had much time for it. . . . .

It may amuse you to hear that (unsolicited) I suddenly found myself the winner of the International Fantasy Award, presented (as it says) 'as a fitting climax to the Fifteenth World Science Fiction Convention'. What it boiled down to was a lunch at the Criterion yesterday with speeches, and the handing over of an absurd 'trophy'. A massive metal 'model' of an upended Space-rocket (combined with a Ronson lighter). But the speeches were far more intelligent, especially that of the introducer: Clemence Dane, a massive woman of almost Sitwellian presence. Sir Stanley himself was present. Not having any immediate use for the trophy (save publicity=sales=cash) I deposited it in the window of 40 Museum Street. A back-wash from the Convention was a visit from an American film-agent (one of the adjudicating panel) who drove out all the way in a taxi from London to see me last week, filling 76 S[andfield] with strange men and stranger women – I thought the taxi would never stop disgorging. But this Mr Ackerman brought some really astonishingly good pictures (Rackham rather than Disney) and some remarkable colour photographs. They have apparently toured America shooting mountain and desert scenes that seem to fit the story. The Story Line or Scenario was, however, on a lower level. In fact bad. But it looks as if business might be done. Stanley U. & I have agreed on our policy: *Art or Cash*. Either very profitable terms indeed; or absolute author's veto on objectionable features or alterations.

203 From a letter to Herbert Schiro[1]   17 November 1957

There is *no* 'symbolism' or conscious allegory in my story. Allegory of the sort 'five wizards=five senses' is wholly foreign to my way of thinking. There were five wizards and that is just a unique part of history. To ask if the Orcs 'are' Communists is to me as sensible as asking if Communists are Orcs.

That there is no allegory does not, of course, say there is no applicability. There always is. And since I have not made the struggle wholly unequivocal: sloth and stupidity among hobbits, pride and [illegible] among Elves, grudge and greed in Dwarf-hearts, and folly and wickedness among the 'Kings of Men', and treachery and power-lust even among the 'Wizards', there is I suppose applicability in my story to present times. But I should say, if asked, the tale is not really about Power and Dominion: that only sets the wheels going; it is about Death and the desire for deathlessness. Which is hardly more than to say it is a tale written by a Man!

204 From a letter to Rayner Unwin   7 December 1957

[Lord Halsbury (see no. 174) was invited by Tolkien to read several parts of *The Silmarillion* in manuscript during the latter part of 1957. In December, Rayner Unwin visited Tolkien to discuss that book and borrow portions of it, and to bring information about the Swedish translation of *The Lord of the Rings*.]

As soon as you had gone, I found Halsbury's letter in full view. . . . . Though his commentary and criticism (I have now received another 14 pages) is very interesting to me, and in some points useful, the covering letter is chiefly of interest as an indication that, surprising as it may seem, this Silmarillion stuff would have at least some audience. He saw what I handed to you. He wrote: 'Thank you for the privilege of seeing this wonderful mythology. I have never read anything like it and can hardly wait for its publication. You *must* get it published while your sales of *The Lord of the Rings* are still actively developing. . . . I can quite see that there is a struggle ahead to re-mould it into the requisite form for publication and wish you luck.' . . . .

I now see quite clearly that I must, as a necessary preliminary to 're-moulding', get copies made of all copyable material. And I shall put that in hand as soon as possible. But I think the best way of dealing with this (at this stage, in which much of the stuff is in irreplaceable sole copies) is to install a typist in my room in college, and not let any material out of my keeping, until it is multiplied. I hope that, perhaps, then your interest will be sufficient for you to want at least a sketch of the remaining part.

Sweden. The enclosure that you brought from Almqvist &c.[1] was both puzzling and irritating. A letter in Swedish from fil. dr. Åke Ohlmarks,[2] and a huge list (9 pages foolscap) of names in the *L.R.* which he had altered. I hope that my inadequate knowledge of Swedish – no better than my kn. of Dutch, but I possess a v. much better Dutch dictionary! – tends to exaggerate the impression I received. The impression remains, nonetheless, that Dr Ohlmarks is a conceited person, less competent than charming Max Schuchart,[3] though he thinks much better of himself. In the course of his letter he lectures me on the character of the Swedish language and its antipathy to borrowing foreign words (a matter which seems beside the point), a procedure made all the more ridiculous by the language of his letter, more than ⅓ of which consists of 'loan-words' from German, French and Latin: *thriller-genre* being a good specimen of good old pure Swedish.

I find this procedure puzzling, because the letter and the list seem totally pointless unless my opinion and criticism is invited. But if this is its object, then surely the timing is both unpractical and impolite, presented together with a pistol: 'we are going to start the composition now'. Neither is my convenience consulted: the communication comes out of the blue in the second most busy academic week of the year. I have had to sit up far into the night even to survey the list. Conceding the legitimacy or necessity of translation (which I do not, except in a limited degree), the translation does not seem to me to exhibit much skill, and contains a fair number of positive errors.* Even if excusable, in view of the difficulty of the material, I think this regrettable, & they could have been avoided by earlier consultation. It seems to me fairly evident that Dr. O. has stumbled along dealing with things as he came to them, without much care for the future or co-ordination, and that he has not read the Appendices† at all, in which he would have found many answers. . . . .

I do hope that it can be arranged, if and when any further translations are negotiated, *that I should be consulted at an early stage* – without frightening a shy bird off the eggs. After all, I charge nothing, and can save a translator a good deal of time and puzzling; and if *consulted* at an early stage my remarks will appear far less in the light of peevish criticisms.

I see now that the lack of an 'index of names' is a serious handicap in dealing with these matters. If I had an index of names (even one with only reference to Vol. and chapter, not page) it would be a comparatively

---

*For example: *Ford of Bruinen* = Björnavad! *Archet* = Gamleby (a mere guess, I suppose, from 'archaic'?) *Mountains of Lune* (Ered Luin) = Månbergen; *Gladden Fields* (in spite of descr. in I. 62) = *Ljusa slätterna,* & so on.[4]

†Or (I surmise) the nomenclature of later volumes.

easy matter to indicate at once all names suitable for translation (as being themselves according to the fiction 'translated' into English), and to add a few notes on points where (I know now) translators are likely to trip. . . . .

This 'handlist' would be of *great use* to me in future corrections and in composing an index (which I think should replace some of the present appendices); also in dealing with *The Silmarillion* (into which some of the L.R. has to be written backwards to make the two coherent). Do you think you could do anything about this?

205 From a letter to Christopher Tolkien 21 February 1958

[Christopher Tolkien, now a university lecturer at Oxford, gave a paper to a society at St Anne's College on 'Barbarians and Citizens', his subject being the heroes of northern legend as seen in different fashion by Germanic poets and Roman writers. His father was present at the reading of the paper.]

I think it was a very excellent performance. It filled me with great delight: first of all because it was so interesting that, after a day (for me) of unceasing labour & movement, I never desired to close my eyes or abstract my mind for a second – and I felt that all round me; and secondly because of parental pride. (Not that I think that this sensation is really one of the *hwelpes of þe liun* at all: it is a legitimate satisfaction with the least possible of egotism in it (there is never none) to feel that one has not wholly failed in one's appointed part, and has paid forward at least a part of the debt one owes backward.)

It was enormously successful, and I realize now why you hold audiences. There was, of course, life and vividness in your phrases, but you are clear, generally unemphatic and let your stuff speak for itself by sheer placing and shaping. All the same, I suddenly realized that I am a *pure* philologist. I like history, and am moved by it, but its finest moments for me are those in which it throws light on words and names! Several people (and I agree) spoke to me of the art with which you made the beady-eyed Attila on his couch almost vividly present. Yet oddly, I find the thing that really thrills my nerves is the one you mentioned casually: *atta, attila*.[1] Without those syllables the whole great drama both of history and legend loses savour for me – or would.

I do not know what I mean, because 'aesthetic' is always impossible to catch in a net of words. Nobody believes me when I say that my long book is an attempt to create a world in which a form of language agreeable to my personal aesthetic might seem real. But it is true. An enquirer (among many) asked what the L.R. was all about, and whether it was an 'allegory'. And I said it was an effort to create a situation in which a common greeting would be *elen síla lúmenn' omentielmo*,[2] and that the phase long antedated the book. I never heard any more. But I enjoyed myself immensely and retire to bed really happy. It was obvious that the ball is right at your toes, so far as the *total sphere* of the academic world is concerned. (Actually I think it of vast nobility and importance.)

206 From a letter to Rayner Unwin 8 April 1958

[At the end of March 1958, Tolkien visited Holland at the invitation of the Rotterdam booksellers Voorhoeve en Dietrich; his travelling expenses were paid by Allen & Unwin. He attended a 'Hobbit Dinner' at which he gave a speech. One item on the menu was 'Maggot Soup', an intended allusion to Farmer Maggot's mushrooms in *The Lord of the Rings*.]

Since I had the remarkable, and in the event extremely enjoyable, experience in Holland by the generosity of 'A. and U.', I think some kind of report would be proper. I have had time to simmer down a bit, and recover some sense of proportion. The incense was thick and very heady; and the kindness overwhelming. My journey was very comfortable, and the reservations magnificent: the outward boat was packed, and the train from L[iverpool] Street went in two parts. I arrived in cold mist and drizzle, but by the time I had found my way to Rotterdam the sun was shining, and it remained so for two days. Ouboter of V[oorhoeve] and D[ietrich] was waving a *Lord of the Rings* and so easy to pick out of the crowd, but I did not fit his expectations, as he confessed (after dinner); my 'build-up' by letter had been too successful, and he was looking for something much smaller and more shy and hobbit-like.

(I thought he was charming and intelligent; but he was still a little upset about the hilarity caused by 'maggot-soup' on the Menu. It was, of course, mushroom soup; but he said he would not have chosen the name if he had known 'all the names of the English vermins'.) I met a representative of *Het Spectrum*,[1] and saw a good deal of the depressing world of ruined and half-rebuilt Rotterdam. I think it is largely the breach between this comfortless world, with its gigantic and largely dehumanised reconstruction, and the natural and ancestral tastes of the Dutch, that has (as it seems) made them, in R[otterdam] especially, almost intoxicated with *hobbits*! It was almost entirely of hobbits that they spoke.

At 5.30 on Friday I faced quite a large concourse in an assembly hall. Apparently over 200 (largely ordinary people) had paid to be present, and many had been turned away. Professor Harting[2] was even more astonished than I was. The dinner was certainly 'abundant and prolonged': the latter, because the speeches were interleaved between the courses. In the event they were all in English; and all but one quite sensible (if one deducts the high pitch of the eulogy, which was rather embarrassing). The exception was a lunatic *phycholog*, but the able chairman held him to five minutes. My final reply was I hope adequate, and was I believe audible; but I need not dwell on it. It was partly a parody of Bilbo's speech in Chapter I.[3]

In this home of 'smoking', *pipe-weed* seems specially to have caught on. There were clay pipes on the table and large jars of tobacco – provided, I believe, by the firm of Van Rossem. The walls were decorated with Van Rossem posters over-printed Pipe-weed for Hobbits: In 3 qualities: *Longbottom Leaf, Old Toby, and Southern Star.* V. Rossem has since sent me pipes and tobacco! I carried off one of the posters. You might like to see it. . . . .

I cannot thank you enough for providing me with this short but memorable expedition – the only one I am likely to get after all out of my 'leave' – and for gently pressing me to go.

207 **From a letter to Rayner Unwin** 8 April 1958

[Negotiations were proceeding with the American film company. The synopsis of the proposed film of *The Lord of the Rings* was the work of Morton Grady Zimmerman.]

Zimmerman – 'Story-Line'

Of course, I will get busy on this at once, now that Easter is over, and the Dutch incense is dissipated. Thank you for the copy of the *Story-line*, which I will go through again.

I am entirely ignorant of the process of producing an 'animated picture' from a book, and of the jargon connected with it. Could you let me know exactly what is a 'story-line', and its function in the process?

It is not necessary (or advisable) for me to waste time on mere expressions if these are simply directions to picture-producers. But this document, as it stands, is sufficient to give me grave anxiety about the actual *dialogue* that (I suppose) will be used. I should say Zimmerman, the constructor of this s-l, is quite incapable of excerpting or adapting the 'spoken words' of the book. He is hasty, insensitive, and impertinent.

He does not *read* books. It seems to me evident that he has skimmed through the L.R. at a great pace, and then constructed his s.l. from partly confused memories, and with the minimum of references back to the original. Thus he gets most of the names wrong in form – not occasionally by casual error but fixedly (always *Borimor* for *Boromir*); or he misapplies them: *Radagast* becomes an Eagle. The introduction of

266

characters and the indications of what they are to say have little or no reference to the book. Bombadil comes in with 'a gentle laugh'! . . . .

I feel very unhappy about the extreme silliness and incompetence of Z and his complete lack of respect for the original (it seems wilfully wrong without discernible technical reasons at nearly every point). But I need, and shall soon need very much indeed, money, and I am conscious of your rights and interests; so that I shall endeavour to restrain myself, and avoid all avoidable offence. I will send you my remarks, particular and general, as soon as I can; and of course nothing will go to Ackerman[1] except through you and with at least your assent.

208   From a letter to C. Ouboter, Voorhoeve en Dietrich, Rotterdam   10 April 1958

As for 'message': I have none really, if by that is meant the conscious purpose in writing *The Lord of the Rings*, of preaching, or of delivering myself of a vision of truth specially revealed to me! I was primarily writing an exciting story in an atmosphere and background such as I find personally attractive. But in such a process inevitably one's own taste, ideas, and beliefs get taken up. Though it is only in reading the work myself (with criticisms in mind) that I become aware of the dominance of the theme of Death. (Not that there is any original 'message' in that: most of human art & thought is similarly preoccupied.) But certainly Death is not an Enemy! I said, or meant to say, that the 'message' was the hideous peril of confusing true 'immortality' with limitless serial longevity. Freedom from Time, and clinging to Time. The *confusion* is the work of the Enemy, and one of the chief causes of human disaster. Compare the death of Aragorn with a Ringwraith. The Elves call 'death' the Gift of God (to Men). Their temptation is different: towards a fainéant melancholy, burdened with Memory, leading to an attempt to halt Time.

209   From a letter to Robert Murray, S.J.   4 May 1958

[Murray wrote to Tolkien asking if 'I could pick your brains about "holy" words'. He wanted to know Tolkien's views on the original meaning of, and relationships between, the various words for 'holy' in the Indo-European languages.]

These problems concerning the 'original' meanings of words (or families of formally connected words) are fascinating: strictly – that is: alluring, but not necessarily by a wholesome attraction! I often wonder what use (except *historical*: knowledge or glimpses of what words *have* meant and how they have changed in fact so far as ascertainable) we gain by such investigations. It is practically impossible to avoid the vicious circle of discovering from word-histories, or supposed histories, 'primitive' meanings and associations, and then using these for tracing histories of meaning. Is it not possible to discuss the 'meaning' *now* of 'sanctity' (for instance) without reference to the history of the meaning of the word-forms now employed in that meaning? The other way round seems rather like describing a place (or stage in a journey) in terms of the different routes by which people have arrived there, though the place has a location and existence quite independent of these routes, direct or more circuitous.

In any case in an historical enquiry we are obliged to deal simultaneously with two variables each in motions that are independent fundamentally, even when affecting one another 'accidentally': the meanings and associations of meaning are one, and the word-forms another, and their changes are independent. The word-form can go through a whole cycle of change, until it is phonetically unrecognizable without measurable change of meaning; and at any moment without any change in phonetics 'the meaning' of a 'word' may change. Quite suddenly* (as far as the evidence goes) *yelp* which meant 'to speak proudly', and was especially used of proud vows (such as a knight vowing to do some dangerous deed) stopped meaning that and became used of the noise of foxes or dogs! Why? At any rate, *not* because of any change in ideas about vaunts or animals! It is a long way from ὀδοντ- to *tooth*, but the changes of form have not much affected the meaning (nor has *tine* the equivalent of *dent-* moved very far).†

We do not know the 'original' meaning of any word, still less the meaning of its basic element (sc. the part it shares with or seems to share with other related words: once called its 'root'): there is always a lost past. Thus we do not know the original meaning of θέος or *deus* or *god*. We can, of course, make some guesses about the formation of these three quite distinct words, and then try to generalize a basic meaning from the senses shown by their relatives – *but* I do not think we shall necessarily by that way get any nearer to the idea 'god' at any actual moment in any language using one of these words. It is an odd fact that English *dizzy* (olim *dysig*) and *giddy* (olim *gydig*) seem related to θέος and *god* respectively. In English they once meant 'irrational', and now 'vertiginous', but that does not help much (except to cause us to reflect that there was a long past before θέος or *god* reached their forms or

*Soon after AD 1400.

†But even so we do not know the original meaning of *tooth*. Did it mean 'spike, sharp point' or was it (as some guess) really the participial agent to ED 'eat', sc. a functional and non-pictorial name?

senses and equally queer changes may have gone on in unrecorded ages).
We may, of course, guess that we have a remote effect of primitive ideas
of 'inspiration' (to the 18th C[entury] an *enthusiast* was much what an
Anglo-Saxon would have called a *dysiga*!). But that is not of much
theological use? *We are faced by endless minute parallels to the mystery
of incarnation.* Is not the idea of *god* ultimately independent of the ways
by which a word for it has come to be?* whether through √*dh(e)wes*
(which *seems* to refer basically to stirring and excitement); or √*d(e)jew*
(which *seems* to refer basically to brightness (esp. of the sky)); or
possibly (it is a mere guess) √*ghew* cry, – *god* is originally neuter and is
supposed to 'mean' *that which is invoked*: an old past participle.
Possibly a taboo-word. The old *deiwos* word (which produced *dīvus*,
deus) survives only in *Tuesday*.†

If he has to tackle such a word as *holy*, the old-fashioned philologist
(such as I am) looks first at the history of the *form*. According to rules
laboriously elaborated (and I think certainly valid within limits‡) he will
say what it is *probably* formally related to. But he cannot wholly escape
the quicksand of *semantics*. Before he proposes a relationship (that is an
actual historical nexus of change) between *holy* and other words in the
same language (or in other believed to be related to English) he will want
both a phonologically possible kinship, and some 'possible kinship' in
sense. All the time he will be uneasily aware of two things found in
linguistic experience: (1) that there seem always to have been
'homophones', or 2 (or more) phonetically indistinguishable elements
that possessed *distinct* senses and are therefore 'different words',§ like
I[ndo]-E[uropean] stems *men* 'stick out', and *men* 'think'; and (2) that
semantic change is sometimes violent, and in the dark past may have
operated without leaving evidence of its occurrence. For instance the
formal equivalence of √*sequ* in Greek ἕπομαι and Latin *sequor* (and
other languages) meaning 'follow' is exact with Germanic *sekʷ* – stem of
a verb: but this means 'to see'. Which is to have most weight: the form or
the sense? He cannot decide finally on the evidence; though fiddling in

*Because a single word in human language (unlike Entish!) is a short-hand sign, &
conventional. The fact that it is derived from a single facet, even if proved, does not prove
that other facets were not equally present to the mind of the users of this conventional
sign. The λόγος is ultimately independent of the *verbum*.

†But we do not know how *Tīw* (=dívus) became a 'name' equated in the interpretatio
romana with Mars. Perhaps another substitution of a general term (divinity) for a 'true
name'. The plural *tívar* in O. Norse verse still means 'gods'.

‡That is: they refer to undisturbed norms of habitual change (like simple statements of
the action of frost), but the norms may be interfered with – the patterns on a given window
are practically unpredictable, though one believes that if one knew *all* the circumstances, it
would not be so.

§By which he means that they are *not* connected by lost semantic change; but how can
he be sure of that?

an amateur way with 'semantics' he can make the sense-jump seems less impossible than it looks at first, by referring to the uses of 'follow'= 'understand', and to the fact that I-E words for *see* (as indeed our *see*) often mean, or the same 'bases' may mean, 'know', 'understand'. (This is particularly true of the $\sqrt{\text{WID}}$ base: Latin *video* has its exact equivalent in O.E. *witian* 'watch, guard'; but *Fοῖδα* (=Latin *vīdī*) in O.E. *wāt* 'wot', 'I know'.) But probably, if he finds Germanic *salwo-* (our *sallow*) and Latin *salvus* (*saluos*), he will decide that there is no bridge between 'dirty yellow' and 'safe and sound'; so that either some thing is wrong with the phonological equation, or that he is dealing with 'homophones'. (There is always also the possibility that either *sallow* or *salvus* did not descend from a common antiquity – words can be *invented*, or borrowed and may closely resemble older words in either case.) The formal equivalent (the only known one) of our *harp* is Latin *corbis*. (The Romance *arpa* etc. are borrowed from Germanic.) But the poor philologist will have to call on some archaeological expert before he can decide whether any relationship between 'harps' and 'baskets' is possible – supposing Gmc. *harpō* always meant 'harp' or *corbi-s* always meant 'wicker basket'! *corbīta* means a fat-bellied ship.

210 From a letter to Forrest J. Ackerman [Not dated; June 1958]

[Tolkien's comments on the film 'treatment' of *The Lord of the Rings*.]

I have at last finished my commentary on the Story-line. Its length and detail will, I hope, give evidence of my interest in the matter. Some at least of the things that I have said or suggested may be acceptable, even useful, or at least interesting. The commentary goes along page by page, according to the copy of Mr Zimmerman's work, which was left with me, and which I now return. I earnestly hope that someone will take the trouble to read it.

If Z and/or others do so, they may be irritated or aggrieved by the tone of many of my criticisms. If so, I am sorry (though not surprised). But I would ask them to make an effort of imagination sufficient to understand the irritation (and on occasion the resentment) of an author, who finds, increasingly as he proceeds, his work treated as it would seem carelessly in general, in places recklessly, and with no evident signs of any appreciation of what it is all about. . . . .

The canons of narrative art in any medium cannot be wholly different; and the failure of poor films is often precisely in exaggeration, and in the intrusion of unwarranted matter owing to not perceiving where the core of the original lies.

Z . . . . has intruded a 'fairy castle' and a great many Eagles, not to mention incantations, blue lights, and some irrelevant magic (such as the floating body of Faramir). He has cut the parts of the story upon which its characteristic and peculiar tone principally depends, showing a preference for fights; and he has made no serious attempt to represent the heart of the tale adequately: the journey of the Ringbearers. The last and most important part of this has, and it is not too strong a word, simply been murdered.

[Some extracts from Tolkien's lengthy commentary on the Story Line:]

Z is used as an abbreviation for (the writer of) the synopsis. References to this are by page (and line where required); references to the original story are by Volume and page.

2. Why should the firework display include *flags* and *hobbits*? They are not in the book. 'Flags' of what? I prefer my own choice of fireworks.

Gandalf, please, should not 'splutter'. Though he may seem testy at times, has a sense of humour, and adopts a somewhat avuncular attitude to hobbits, he is a person of high and noble authority, and great dignity. The description on I p. 239[1] should never be forgotten.

4. Here we meet the first intrusion of the Eagles. I think they are a major mistake of Z, and without warrant.
    The Eagles are a dangerous 'machine'. I have used them sparingly, and that is the absolute limit of their credibility or usefulness. The alighting of a Great Eagle of the Misty Mountains in the Shire is absurd; it also makes the later capture of G. by Saruman incredible, and spoils the account of his escape. (One of Z's chief faults is his tendency to anticipate scenes or devices used later, thereby flattening the tale out.) *Radagast* is not an Eagle-name, but a wizard's name; several eagle-names are supplied in the book. These points are to me important.
    Here I may say that I fail to see why the time-scheme should be deliberately *contracted*. It is already rather packed in the original, the main action occurring between Sept. 22 and March 25 of the following year. The many impossibilities and absurdities which further hurrying produces might, I suppose, be unobserved by an uncritical viewer; but I do not see why they should be unnecessarily introduced. Time must naturally be left vaguer in a picture than in a book; but I cannot see why *definite* time-statements, contrary to the book and to probability, should be made. . . . .
    Seasons are carefully regarded in the original. They are pictorial, and should be, and easily could be, made the main means by which the

artists indicate time-passage. The main action begins in autumn and passes through winter to a brilliant spring: this is basic to the purport and tone of the tale. The contraction of time and space in Z destroys that. His arrangements would, for instance, land us in a snowstorm while summer was still in. *The Lord of the Rings* may be a 'fairy-story', but it takes place in the Northern hemisphere of this earth: miles are miles, days are days, and weather is weather.

Contraction of this kind is not the same thing as the necessary reduction or selection of the scenes and events that are to be visually represented.

7. The first paragraph misrepresents Tom Bombadil. He is *not* the owner of the woods; and he would never make any such threat.

'Old scamp!' This is a good example of the general tendency that I find in Z to reduce and lower the tone towards that of a more childish fairy-tale. The expression does not agree with the tone of Bombadil's long later talk; and though that is cut, there is no need for its indications to be disregarded.

I am sorry, but I think the manner of the introduction of Goldberry is silly, and on a par with 'old scamp'. It also has no warrant in my tale. We are not in 'fairy-land', but in real river-lands in autumn. Goldberry represents the actual seasonal changes in such lands. Personally I think she had far better disappear than make a meaningless appearance.

8 line 24. The landlord does *not* ask Frodo to 'register'![2] Why should he? There are no police and no government. (Neither do I make him number his rooms.) *If details are to be added to an already crowded picture, they should at least fit the world described.*

9. Leaving the inn at *night* and running off into the dark is an impossible solution of the difficulties of presentation here (which I can see). It is the last thing that Aragorn would have done. It is based on a misconception of the Black Riders throughout, which I beg Z to reconsider. Their peril is almost entirely due to the unreasoning *fear* which they inspire (like ghosts). They have no great physical power against the fearless; but what they have, and the fear that they inspire, is enormously increased in *darkness*. The Witch-king, their leader, is more powerful in all ways than the others; but he must not yet be raised to the stature of Vol. III. There, put in command by Sauron, he is given an added demonic force. But even in the Battle of the Pelennor, the darkness had only just broken. See III 114.[3]

10. Rivendell was *not* 'a shimmering forest'. This is an unhappy antici-

pation of Lórien (which it in no way resembled). It could not be seen from Weathertop: it was 200 miles away and hidden in a ravine. I can see no pictorial or story-making gain in needlessly contracting the geography.

Strider does not 'Whip out a sword' in the book. Naturally not: his sword was broken. (Its elvish light is another false anticipation of the reforged Anduril. Anticipation is one of Z's chief faults.) Why then make him do so here, in a contest that was explicitly not fought with weapons?

11. Aragorn did not 'sing the song of Gil-galad'. Naturally: it was quite inappropriate, since it told of the *defeat* of the Elven-king by the Enemy. The Black Riders do not scream, but keep a more terrifying silence. Aragorn does not blanch. The riders draw slowly in on foot in darkness, and do not 'spur'. There is no fight. Sam does not 'sink his blade into the Ringwraith's thigh', nor does his thrust save Frodo's life. (If he had, the result would have been much the same as in III 117–20:[4] the Wraith would have fallen down and the sword would have been destroyed.)

Why has my account been entirely rewritten here, with disregard for the rest of the tale? I can see that there are certain difficulties in representing a dark scene; but they are not insuperable. A scene of gloom lit by a small red fire, with the Wraiths slowly approaching as darker shadows – until the moment when Frodo puts on the Ring, and the King steps forward revealed – would seem to me far more impressive than yet one more scene of screams and rather meaningless slashings. . . . .

I have spent some time on this passage, as an example of what I find too frequent to give me 'pleasure or satisfaction': deliberate alteration of the story, in fact and significance, without any practical or artistic object (that I can see); and of the flattening effect that assimilation of one incident to another must have.

15. Time is again contracted and hurried, with the effect of reducing the importance of the Quest. Gandalf does not say they will leave as soon as they can pack! Two months elapse. There is no need to say anything with a time-purport. The lapse of time should be indicated, if by no more than the change to winter in the scenery and trees.

At the bottom of the page, the Eagles are again introduced. *I feel this to be a wholly unacceptable tampering with the tale.* 'Nine Walkers' and they immediately go up in the air! The intrusion achieves nothing but incredibility, and the staling of the device of the Eagles when at last they are really needed. It is well within the powers of pictures to suggest, relatively briefly, a long and arduous journey, *in secrecy*, on foot, with the three ominous mountains getting nearer.

Z does not seem much interested in seasons or scenery, though from what I saw I should say that in the representation of these the chief virtue and attraction of the film is likely to be found. But would Z think that he had improved the effect of a film of, say, the ascent of Everest by introducing helicopters to take the climbers half way up (in defiance of probability)? It would be *far better* to cut the Snow-storm and the Wolves than to make a farce of the arduous journey.

19. Why does Z put beaks and feathers on *Orcs*!? (*Orcs* is not a form of *Auks*.) The Orcs are definitely stated to be corruptions of the 'human' form seen in Elves and Men. They are (or were) squat, broad, flat-nosed, sallow-skinned, with wide mouths and slant eyes: in fact degraded and repulsive versions of the (to Europeans) least lovely Mongol-types.

20. The Balrog *never speaks or makes any vocal sound* at all. Above all he *does not* laugh or sneer. . . . . Z may think that he knows more about Balrogs than I do, but he cannot expect me to agree with him.

21 ff. '*A splendid sight. It is the home of Galadriel . . . an Elvenqueen.*' (She is not in fact one.) '*Delicate spires and tiny minarets of Elven-color are cleverly woven into a beautiful[ly] designed castle.*' I think this deplorable in itself, and in places impertinent. Will Z please pay my text some respect, at least in descriptions that are obviously central to the general tone and style of the book! I will in no circumstances accept this treatment of Lórien, even if Z personally prefers 'tiny' fairies and the gimcrack of conventional modern fairy-tales.

The disappearance of the temptation of Galadriel is significant. Practically everything having moral import has vanished from the synopsis.

22. *Lembas*, 'waybread', is called a 'food concentrate'. As I have shown I dislike strongly any pulling of my tale towards the style and feature of 'contes des fées', or French fairy-stories. I dislike equally any pull towards 'scientification', of which this expression is an example. Both modes are alien to my story.

We are not exploring the Moon or any other more improbable region. No analysis in any laboratory would discover chemical properties of *lembas* that made it superior to other cakes of wheat-meal.

I only comment on the expression here as an indication of attitude. It is no doubt casual; and nothing of this kind or style will (I hope) escape into the actual dialogue.

In the book *lembas* has two functions. It is a 'machine' or device for making credible the long marches with little provision, in a world in which as I have said 'miles are miles'. But that is relatively unimportant. It also has a much larger significance, of what one might hesitatingly call a 'religious' kind. This becomes later apparent, especially in the chapter 'Mount Doom' (III 213^5 and subsequently). I cannot find that Z has made any particular use of *lembas* even as a device; and the whole of 'Mount Doom' has disappeared in the distorted confusion that Z has made of the ending. As far as I can see *lembas* might as well disappear altogether.

I do earnestly hope that in the assignment of actual speeches to the characters they will be represented as I have presented them: in style and sentiment. I should resent perversion of the characters (and do resent it, so far as it appears in this sketch) even more than the spoiling of the plot and scenery.

Parts II & III. I have spent much space on criticizing even details in Part I. It has been easier, because Part I in general respects the line of narrative in the book, and retains some of its original coherence. Part II exemplifies all the faults of Part I; but it is far more unsatisfactory, & still more so Part III, in more serious respects. It almost seems as if Z, having spent much time and work on Part I, now found himself short not only of space but of patience to deal with the two more difficult volumes in which the action becomes more fast and complicated. He has in any case elected to treat them in a way that produces a confusion that mounts at last almost to a delirium. . . . .

The narrative now divides into two main branches: 1. Prime Action, the Ringbearers. 2. Subsidiary Action, the rest of the Company leading to the 'heroic' matter. *It is essential that these two branches should each be treated in coherent sequence.* Both to render them intelligible as a story, and because they are totally different in tone and scenery. Jumbling them together entirely destroys these things.

31. I deeply regret this handling of the 'Treebeard' chapter, whether necessary or not. I have already suspected Z of not being interested in trees: unfortunate, since the story is so largely concerned with them. But surely what we have here is in any case a quite unintelligible glimpse? What are Ents?

31 to 32. We pass now to a dwelling of Men in an 'heroic age'. Z does not

seem to appreciate this. *I hope the artists do.* But he and they have really only to follow what is said, and not alter it to suit their fancy (out of place).

In such a time private 'chambers' played no part. Théoden probably had none, unless he had a sleeping 'bower' in a separate small 'outhouse'. He received guests or emissaries, seated on the dais in his royal hall. This is quite clear in the book; and the scene should be much more effective to illustrate.

31 to 32. Why do not Théoden and Gandalf go into the open before the doors, as I have told? Though I have somewhat enriched the culture of the 'heroic' Rohirrim, it did *not* run to glass windows that could be thrown open!! We might be in a hotel. (The 'east windows' of the hall, II 116, 119,[6] were slits under the eaves, unglazed.)

Even if the king of such a people had a 'bower', it could not become 'a beehive of bustling activity'!! The bustle takes place outside and in the town. What is showable of it should occur on the wide pavement before the great doors.

33. I am afraid that I do not find the glimpse of the 'defence of the Hornburg' – this would be a better title, since Helm's Deep, the ravine behind, is not shown – entirely satisfactory. It would, I guess, be a fairly meaningless scene in a picture, stuck in in this way. Actually I myself should be inclined to cut it right out, if it cannot be made more coherent and a more significant part of the story. . . . . If both the Ents and the Hornburg cannot be treated at sufficient length to make sense, then one should go. It should be the Hornburg, which is incidental to the main story; and there would be this additional gain that we are going to have a big battle (of which as much should be made as possible), but battles tend to be too similar: the big one would gain by having no competitor.

34. Why on earth should Z say that the hobbits 'were munching ridiculously long sandwiches'? Ridiculous indeed. I do not see how any author could be expected to be 'pleased' by such silly alterations. One hobbit was sleeping, the other smoking.

The spiral staircase 'weaving' round the Tower [Orthanc] comes from Z's fancy not my tale. I prefer the latter. The tower was 500 feet high. There was a flight of 27 steps leading to the great door; above which was a window and a balcony.

Z is altogether too fond of the words *hypnosis* and *hypnotic*. Neither genuine hypnosis, nor scientifictitious variants, occur in my tale. Saruman's voice was not hypnotic but persuasive. Those who listened to him were not in danger of falling into a trance, but of agreeing with his arguments, while fully awake. It was always open to one to reject, *by free will and reason*, both his voice while speaking and its after-impressions. Saruman corrupted the reasoning powers.

Z has cut out the end of the book, including Saruman's proper death. In that case I can see no good reason for making him die. Saruman would never have committed suicide: to cling to life to its basest dregs is the way of the sort of person he had become. If Z wants Saruman tidied up (I cannot see why, where so many threads are left loose) Gandalf should say something to this effect: as Saruman collapses under the excommunication: 'Since you will not come out and aid us, here in Orthanc you shall stay till you rot, Saruman. Let the Ents look to it!'

Part III . . . . *is totally unacceptable to me, as a whole and in detail.* If it is meant as notes only for a section of something like the pictorial length of I and II, then in the filling out it must be brought into relation with the book, and its gross alterations of that corrected. If it is meant to represent only a kind of short finale, then all I can say is: *The Lord of the Rings* cannot be garbled like that.

211 To Rhona Beare

[Rhona Beare wrote, asking a number of questions, so that she could pass on Tolkien's answers to a meeting of fellow-enthusiasts for *The Lord of the Rings*. Why, she asked, does Sam speak the Elvish invocation as 'O Elbereth Gilthoniel' in the chapter 'The Choices of Master Samwise' when elsewhere the form used is 'A Elbereth Gilthoniel'? (This was the reading used in the first edition of the book.) What is the meaning of this invocation, and of Frodo's words in the previous chapter, 'Aiya Eärendil Elenion Ancalima!'? Miss Beare then asked a series of numbered questions. 'Question 1': Why (in the first edition, I. 221) is Glorfindel's horse described as having a 'bridle and bit' when Elves ride without bit, bridle or saddle? 'Question 2': How could Ar-Pharazôn defeat Sauron when Sauron had the One Ring? 'Question 3': What were the colours of the two wizards mentioned but not named in the book? 'Question 4': What clothes did the peoples of Middle-earth wear? Was the winged crown of Gondor like that of a Valkyrie, or as depicted on a Gauloise cigarette packet? Explain the meaning of *El*- in Elrond, Elladan, Elrohir; when does *El*- mean 'elf' and when 'star'? Explain the meaning of the name Legolas. Did the Witch-king ride a pterodactyl at the siege of Gondor? 'Question 5': Who is the Elder King mentioned by Bilbo in his song of Eärendil? Is he the One?]

14 October 1958   Merton College, Oxford
Dear Miss Beare,

I am afraid that this reply is too late to be useful for the event; but it was not possible to write before. I have only just returned from a year's leave, one object of which was to enable me to complete some of the 'learned' works neglected during my preoccupation with unprofessional trifles (such as *The Lord of the Rings*): I record the tone of many of my colleagues. Actually the time has mainly been occupied with grave troubles, including the illness of my wife; but I was all through August working long hours, seven days a week, against time, to finish a piece of work before going to Ireland on official business. I arrived back a few days ago, just in time for our Michaelmas Term.

In a momentary lull I will try and answer your questions briefly. I do not 'know all the answers'. Much of my own book puzzles me; & in any case much of it was written so long ago (anything up to 20 years) that I read it now as if it were from a strange hand.

The use of *O* on II p. 339 is an error. Mine in fact, taken over from p. 338, where *Gilthoniel O Elbereth* is, of course, a quotation of I p. 88, which was a 'translation', English in all but proper names. Sam's invocation is, however, in pure Elvish and should have had *A* as in I p. 250. Since hobbit-language is represented as English, *O* could be defended as an inaccuracy of his own; but I do not propose to defend it. He was 'inspired' to make this invocation in a language he did not know (II 338). Though it is, of course, in the style and metre of the hymn-fragment, I think it is composed or inspired for his particular situation.

It means, more or less: '*O Elbereth Starkindler* (in the past tense: the title belongs to mythical pre-history and does not refer to a permanent function) *from heaven gazing-afar, to thee I cry now in the shadow of (the fear of) death. O look towards me, Everwhite!*' *Everwhite* is an inadequate translation; as is equally the *snow-white* of I 88. The element *ui* (Primitive Elvish *oio*) means *ever*; both *fan-* and *los(s)* convey *white*, but *fan* connotes the whiteness of clouds (in the sun); *loss* refers to *snow*.

Amon Uilos, in High-elven *Oiolosse*,* was one of the names of the highest peak of the Mountains of Valinor, upon which Manwe and Varda dwelt. So that an Elf using or hearing the name *Fanuilos*, would not think of (or picture) only a majestic figure robed in white, standing in a high place and gazing eastward to mortal lands, he would at the same time picture an immense peak, snow-capped, crowned with a piercing or dazzling white cloud.

Ancalima = 'exceedingly bright'. Element *kal†* the usual stem for

*(See the lament of Galadriel I 394) *oiolossëo* = from *Mt. Uilos*.

†In High-elven. There was also a more or less synonymous stem *gal* (corresponding to *gil* which only applied to white or silver light). This variation g/k is not to be confused

words referring to light; *kălĭma*, 'shining brilliant'; *an-* superlative or intensive prefix.

Question 1. I could, I suppose, answer: 'a trick-cyclist can ride a bicycle with handle-bars!' But actually *bridle* was casually and carelessly used for what I suppose should have been called a *headstall*.[1] Or rather, since *bit* was added (I 221) long ago (Chapter I 12 was written very early) I had not considered the natural ways of elves with animals. Glorfindel's horse would have an ornamental *headstall*, carrying a plume, and with the straps studded with jewels and small bells; but Glor. would certainly not use a *bit*. I will change *bridle and bit* to *headstall*.

Question 2. This question, & its implications, are answered in the 'Downfall of Númenor', which is not yet published, but which I cannot set out now. You cannot press the One Ring too hard, for it is of course a mythical feature, even though the world of the tales is conceived in more or less historical terms. The Ring of Sauron is only one of the various mythical treatments of the placing of one's life, or power, in some external object, which is thus exposed to capture or destruction with disastrous results to oneself. If I were to 'philosophize' this myth, or at least the Ring of Sauron, I should say it was a mythical way of representing the truth that *potency* (or perhaps rather *potentiality*) if it is to be exercised, and produce results, has to be externalized and so as it were passes, to a greater or less degree, out of one's direct control. A man who wishes to exert 'power' must have subjects, who are not himself. But he then depends on them.

Ar-Pharazôn, as is told in the 'Downfall' or *Akallabêth*, conquered a terrified Sauron's *subjects*, not Sauron. Sauron's personal 'surrender' was voluntary and cunning*: he got free transport to Númenor! He naturally had the One Ring, and so very soon dominated the minds and wills of most of the Númenóreans. (I do not think Ar-Pharazôn knew anything about the One Ring. The Elves kept the matter of the Rings very secret, as long as they could. In any case Ar-Pharazôn was not in communication with them. In the *Tale of Years* III p. 364 you will find hints of the trouble: 'the Shadow falls on Númenor'. After *Tar-Atanamir* (an Elvish name) the next name is *Ar-Adûnakhôr* a Númen-órean name. See p. 315.[2] The change of names went with a complete rejection of the Elf-friendship, and of the 'theological' teaching the Númenóreans had received from them.)

Sauron was first defeated by a 'miracle': a direct action of God the Creator, changing the fashion of the world, when appealed to by

---

with the *grammatical* change or k, c > g in Grey-elven, seen in the initials of words in composition or after closely connected particles (like the article). So *Gil-galad* 'star-light'. Cf. *palan-díriel* compared with *a tíro niu*.

*Note the expression III p. 364 [2nd edition p. 365] 'taken *as* prisoner'.

Manwë: see III p. 317. Though reduced to 'a spirit of hatred borne on a dark wind', I do not think one need boggle at this spirit carrying off the One Ring, upon which his power of dominating minds now largely depended. That Sauron was not himself destroyed in the anger of the One is not my fault: the problem of evil, and its apparent toleration, is a permanent one for all who concern themselves with our world. The indestructibility of *spirits* with free wills, even by the Creator of them, is also an inevitable feature, if one either believes in their existence, or feigns it in a story.

Sauron was, of course, 'confounded' by the disaster, and diminished (having expended enormous energy in the corruption of Númenor). He needed time for his own bodily rehabilitation, and for gaining control over his former subjects. He was attacked by Gil-galad and Elendil before his new domination was fully established.

Question 3. I have not named the colours, because I do not know them.[3] I doubt if they had distinctive colours. Distinction was only required in the case of the three who remained in the relatively small area of the North-west. (On the *names* see Q[uestion]5.) I really do not know anything clearly about the other two – since they do not concern the history of the N.W. I think they went as emissaries to distant regions, East and South, far out of Númenórean range: missionaries to 'enemy-occupied' lands, as it were. What success they had I do not know; but I fear that they failed, as Saruman did, though doubtless in different ways; and I suspect they were founders or beginners of secret cults and 'magic' traditions that outlasted the fall of Sauron.

Question 4. I do not know the detail of clothing. I visualize with great clarity and detail scenery and 'natural' objects, but not artefacts. Pauline Baynes drew her inspiration for *F. Giles* largely from mediæval MS. drawings – except for the knights (who are a bit 'King-Arthurish')* the style seems to fit well enough. Except that males, especially in northern parts such as the Shire, would wear breeches, whether hidden by a cloak or long mantle, or merely accompanied by a tunic.

I have no doubt that in the area envisaged by my story (which is large) the 'dress' of various peoples, Men and others, was much diversified in the Third Age, according to climate, and inherited custom. As was our world, even if we only consider Europe and the Mediterranean and the very near 'East' (or South), before the victory in our time of the least lovely style of dress (especially for males and 'neuters') which recorded history reveals – a victory that is still going on, even among those who most hate the lands of its origin. The Rohirrim were not 'mediaeval', in

---

*Sc. belong to our 'mythological' Middle-Ages which blends unhistorically styles and details ranging over 500 years, and most of which did not of course exist in the Dark Ages of c. 500 A.D.

our sense. The styles of the Bayeux Tapestry (made in England) fit them well enough, if one remembers that the kind of tennis-nets [the] soldiers seem to have on are only a clumsy conventional sign for chain-mail of small rings.

The Númenóreans of Gondor were proud, peculiar, and archaic, and I think are best pictured in (say) Egyptian terms. In many ways they resembled 'Egyptians' – the love of, and power to construct, the gigantic and massive. And in their great interest in ancestry and in tombs. (But not of course in 'theology': in which respect they were Hebraic and even more puritan – but this would take long to set out: to explain indeed why there is practically no overt 'religion',* or rather religious acts or places or ceremonies among the 'good' or anti-Sauron peoples in *The Lord of the Rings*.) I think the crown of Gondor (the S. Kingdom) was very tall, like that of Egypt, but with wings attached, not set straight back but at an angle.

The N. Kingdom had only a *diadem* (III 323). Cf. the difference between the N. and S. kingdoms of Egypt.

El. Difficult to distinguish 'star' and 'elf', since they are derivatives of the same basic element EL 'star'; as the first element in compounds *el-* may mean (or at least symbolize) either. As a separate word 'star' was **ĕlĕn*, plural **elenī* in primitive Elvish. The Elves were called *eledā/elenā* 'an Elf' (High-elven *Elda*) because they were found by the Vala *Oromë* in a valley under the star-light; and they remained always lovers of the stars. But this name became specially attached to those that eventually marched West guided by Oromë (and mostly passed Oversea).

The Grey-elven (Sindarin) forms should have been *êl*, pl. *elin*; and *eledh* (pl. *elidh*). But the latter term passed out of use among the Grey-elves (Sindar) who did not go over Sea; though it remained in some proper-names as *Eledhwen*, 'Elven-fair'. After the return in exile of the Noldor (part of the High-elves), the High-elven *elda* was taken over again by the Grey-elves as *eld>ell*, and referred to the High-elven exiles. This is, no doubt, the origin of *el, ell-* in such names as *Elrond, Elros, Elladan, Elrohir*.

*Almost the only vestige of 'religion' is seen on II pp. 284–5 in the 'Grace before Meat'. This is indeed mainly as it were a commemoration of the Departed, and theology is reduced to 'that which is beyond Elvenhome and ever will be', sc. is beyond the mortal lands, beyond the memory of unfallen Bliss, beyond the physical world.

Elrond, Elros. *rondō was a prim[itive] Elvish word for 'cavern'. Cf. *Nargothrond* (fortified cavern by the R. Narog), *Aglarond*, etc. *rossē meant 'dew, spray (of fall or fountain)'. *Elrond* and *Elros*, children of *Eärendil* (sea-lover) and *Elwing* (Elf-foam), were so called, because they were carried off by the sons of Fëanor, in the last act of the feud between the high-elven houses of the Noldorin princes concerning the Silmarils; the Silmaril rescued from Morgoth by Beren and Lúthien, and given to King Thingol Lúthien's father, had descended to Elwing dtr. of Dior, son of Lúthien. The infants were not slain, but left like 'babes in the wood', in a cave with a fall of water over the entrance. There they were found: Elrond within the cave, and Elros dabbling in the water.[4]

Elrohir, Elladan: these names, given to his sons by Elrond, refer to the fact that they were 'half-elven' (III 314): they had mortal as well as Elvish ancestors on *both* sides; Tuor on their father's side, Beren on their mother's. Both signify *elf+man. Elrohir* might be translated 'Elf-knight'; *rohir* being a later form (III 391) of *rochir* 'horse-lord' from *roch* 'horse'+*hir* 'master': Prim. Elvish *rokkō* and *khēr* or *kherū*: High-elven *rocco, hēr (hērū). Elladan* might be translated 'Elf-Númenórean'. *Adan* (pl. *Edair.*) was the Sindarin form of the name given to the 'fathers of men', the members of the Three Houses of Elf-friends, whose survivors afterwards became the Númenóreans, or *Dún-edain.*

Legolas means 'green-leaves', a woodland name – dialectal form of pure Sindarin *laegolas*: *lassē (High-elven *lasse*, S. *las(s)*) 'leaf'; *gwa-lassa/*gwa-lassiē 'collection of leaves, foliage' (H.E. *olassiē*, S. *golas*, *-olas*); *laikā 'green' – basis LAY as in *laire* 'summer' (H.E. *laica*, S. *laeg* (seldom used, usually replaced by *calen*), woodland *leg*).

Pterodactyl. Yes and no. I did not intend the steed of the Witch-King to be what is now called a 'pterodactyl', and often is drawn (with rather less shadowy evidence than lies behind many monsters of the new and fascinating semi-scientific mythology of the 'Prehistoric'). But obviously it is *pterodactylic* and owes much to the new mythology, and its description even provides a sort of way in which it could be a last survivor of older geological eras.[5]

Question 5. Manwë, husband of Varda; or in Grey-elven Manwë and Elbereth. Since the Valar had no language of their own, not needing one, they had no 'true' names, only identities, and their names were conferred on them by the Elves, being in origin therefore all, as it were, 'nicknames', referring to some striking peculiarity, function, or deed. (The same is true of the 'Istari' or Wizards who were emissaries of the Valar, and of their kind.) In consequence each identity had several 'nicknames'; and the names of the Valar were not necessarily related in different Elvish languages (or languages of Men deriving their knowledge from Elves). (*Elbereth* and *Varda* 'Star-lady' and 'Lofty' are not related words, but refer to the same person.) Manwë (Blessed Being) was Lord of the Valar, and therefore the high or Elder King of Arda. *Arda* 'realm' was the name given to our world or earth, as being the place, within the immensity of Eä, selected to be the seat and special domain of the King – because of his knowledge that the Children of God would appear there. In the cosmogonic myth Manwë is said to be 'brother' of Melkor, that is they were coëval and equipotent in the mind of the Creator. Melkor became the rebel, and the Diabolos of these tales, who disputed the kingdom of Arda with Manwë. (He was usually called *Morgoth* in Grey-elven.)

The One does not physically inhabit any part of Eä.

May I say that all this is 'mythical', and not any kind of new religion or vision. As far as I know it is merely an imaginative invention, to express, in the only way I can, some of my (dim) apprehensions of the world. All I can say is that, if it were 'history', it would be difficult to fit the lands and events (or 'cultures') into such evidence as we possess, archaeological or geological, concerning the nearer or remoter part of what is now called Europe; though the Shire, for instance, is expressly stated to have been in this region (I p. 12).[6] I could have fitted things in with greater versimilitude, if the story had not become too far developed, before the question ever occurred to me. I doubt if there would have been much gain; and I hope the, evidently long but undefined, gap* in time between the Fall of Barad-dûr and our Days is sufficient for 'literary credibility', even for readers acquainted with what is known or surmised of 'pre-history'.

I have, I suppose, constructed an imaginary *time*, but kept my feet on my own mother-earth for *place*. I prefer that to the contemporary mode of seeking remote globes in 'space'. However curious, they are alien, and not lovable with the love of blood-kin. *Middle-earth* is (by the way & if such a note is necessary) not my own invention. It is a modernization or alteration (N[ew] E[nglish] D[ictionary] 'a perversion') of an old word for the inhabited world of Men, the *oikoumenē*: middle because thought of vaguely as set amidst the encircling Seas and (in the northern-imagination) between ice of the North and the fire of the South. O.English *middan-geard*, mediæval E. *midden-erd, middle-erd*. Many reviewers seem to assume that Middle-earth is another planet!

Theologically (if the term is not too grandiose) I imagine the picture to be less dissonant from what some (including myself) believe to be the truth. But since I have deliberately written a tale, which is built on or out of certain 'religious' ideas, but is *not* an allegory of them (or anything

---

*I imagine the gap to be about 6000 years: that is we are now at the end of the Fifth Age, if the Ages were of about the same length as S.A. and T.A. But they have, I think, quickened; and I imagine we are actually at the end of the Sixth Age, or in the Seventh.

else), and does not mention them overtly, still less preach them, I will not now depart from that mode, and venture on theological disquisition for which I am not fitted. But I might say that if the tale is 'about' anything (other than itself), it is not as seems widely supposed about 'power'. Power-seeking is only the motive-power that sets events going, and is relatively unimportant, I think. It is mainly concerned with Death, and Immortality; and the 'escapes': serial longevity, and hoarding memory.

Yours sincerely

J. R. R. Tolkien.

212 Draft of a continuation of the above letter (not sent)

Since I have written so much (I hope not too much) I might as well add a few lines on the Myth on which all is founded, since it may make clearer the relations of Valar, Elves, Men, Sauron, Wizards &c.

The Valar or 'powers, rulers' were the first 'creation': rational spirits or minds without incarnation, created *before* the physical world. (Strictly these *spirits* were called *Ainur*, the *Valar* being only those from among them who entered the world after its making, and the name is properly applied only to the great among them, who take the imaginative but not the theological place of 'gods'.) The Ainur took part in the making of the world as 'sub-creators': in various degrees, after this fashion. They interpreted according to their powers, and completed in detail, the Design propounded to them by the One. This was propounded first in musical or abstract form, and then in an 'historical vision'. In the first interpretation, the vast Music of the Ainur, Melkor introduced alterations, not interpretations of the mind of the One, and great discord arose. The One then presented this 'Music', including the apparent discords, as a visible 'history'.

At this stage it had still only a validity, to which the validity of a 'story' among ourselves may be compared: it 'exists' *in* the mind of the teller, and derivatively in the minds of hearers, but not on the same plane as teller or hearers. When the One (the Teller) said *Let it Be*,* then the Tale became History, on the same plane as the hearers; and these could, if they desired, *enter into it*. Many of the Ainur did enter into it, and must bide in it till the End, being involved in Time, the series of events that complete it. These were the Valar, and their lesser attendants. They were those who had 'fallen in love' with the vision, and no doubt, were those who had played the most 'sub-creative' (or as we might say 'artistic') part in the Music.

*Hence the Elves called the World, the Universe, Eä – It Is.

It was because of their love of Eä, and because of the part they had played in its making, that they *wished* to, and *could,* incarnate themselves in visible physical forms, though these were comparable to our *clothes* (in so far as our clothes are a personal expression) not to our bodies. Their forms were thus expressions of their persons, powers, and loves. They need not be anthropomorphic (*Yavanna* wife* of Aulë would, for instance, appear in the form of a great Tree.) But the 'habitual' shapes of the Valar, when visible or clothed, were anthropomorphic, because of their intense concern with Elves and Men.

Elves and Men were called the 'children of God', because they were, so to speak, a private addition to the Design, by the Creator, and one in which the Valar had no part. (Their 'themes' were introduced into the Music by the One, when the discords of Melkor arose.) The Valar knew that they would appear, and the great ones knew when and how (though not precisely), but they knew little of their nature, and their foresight, derived from their pre-knowledge of the Design, was imperfect or failed in the matter of the deeds of the Children. The uncorrupted Valar, therefore, yearned for the Children before they came and loved them afterwards, as creatures 'other' than themselves, independent of them and their artistry, 'children' as being weaker and more ignorant than the Valar, but of equal lineage (deriving being direct from the One); even though under their authority as rulers of Arda. The corrupted, as was Melkor/Morgoth and his followers (of whom Sauron was one of the chief) saw in them the ideal material for subjects and slaves, to whom they could become masters and 'gods', envying the Children, and secretly hating them, in proportion as they became rebels against the One (and Manwë his Lieutenant in Eä).

In this mythical 'prehistory' *immortality*, strictly longevity co-extensive with the life of Arda, was part of the given nature of the Elves; beyond the End nothing was revealed. *Mortality*, that is a short life-span having no relation to the life of Arda, is spoken of as the given nature of Men: the Elves called it the *Gift of Ilúvatar* (God). But it must be remembered that *mythically* these tales are Elf-centred,† not anthropocentric, and Men only appear in them, at what must be a point long after their Coming. This is therefore an 'Elvish' view, and does not necessarily have anything to say for or against such beliefs as the Christian that 'death' is not part of human nature, but a punishment for sin (rebellion),

*It is the view of the Myth that in (say) Elves and Men 'sex' is only an expression in physical or biological terms of a difference of nature in the 'spirit', not the *ultimate* cause of the difference between femininity and masculinity.

†In *narrative*, as soon as the matter becomes 'storial' and not mythical, being in fact *human* literature, the centre of interest *must* shift to Men (and their relations with Elves or other creatures). We cannot write stories *about* Elves, whom we do not know inwardly; and if we try we simply turn Elves into men.

285

a result of the 'Fall'. It should be regarded as an Elvish perception of what *death* – not being tied to the 'circles of the world' – should now become for Men, however it arose. A divine 'punishment' is also a divine 'gift', if accepted, since its object is ultimate blessing, and the supreme inventiveness of the Creator will make 'punishments' (that is changes of design) produce a good not otherwise to be attained: a 'mortal' Man has probably (an Elf would say) a higher if unrevealed destiny than a longeval one. To attempt by device or 'magic' to recover longevity is thus a supreme folly and wickedness of 'mortals'. Longevity or counterfeit 'immortality' (true immortality is beyond Eä) is the chief bait of Sauron – it leads the small to a Gollum, and the great to a Ringwraith.

In the Elvish legends there is record of a strange case of an Elf (Míriel mother of Fëanor) that tried to *die*, which had disastrous results, leading to the 'Fall' of the High-elves. The Elves were not subject to disease, but they could be 'slain': that is their bodies could be destroyed, or muti-lated so as to be unfit to sustain life. But this did not lead naturally to 'death': they were rehabilitated and reborn and eventually recovered memory of all their past: they remained 'identical'. But Míriel wished to abandon being, and refused rebirth.*

I suppose a difference between this Myth and what may be perhaps called Christian mythology is this. In the latter the Fall of Man is subsequent to and a consequence (though not a necessary consequence) of the 'Fall of the Angels': a rebellion of created free-will at a higher level than Man; but it is not clearly held (and in many versions is not held at all) that this affected the 'World' in its nature: evil was brought in from outside, by Satan. In this Myth the rebellion of created free-will pre-cedes creation of the World (Eä); and Eä has in it, subcreatively introduced, evil, rebellions, discordant elements of its own nature already when the *Let it Be* was spoken. The Fall or corruption, there-

---

*[A note apparently added later:] It was also the Elvish (and uncorrupted Númenórean) view that a 'good' Man would or should *die* voluntarily by surrender with trust *before being compelled* (as did Aragorn). This may have been the nature of *unfallen* Man; though *compulsion* would not threaten him: he would desire and ask to be allowed to 'go on' to a higher state. The Assumption of Mary, the only *unfallen* person, may be regarded as in some ways a simple regaining of unfallen grace and liberty: she asked to be received, and was, having no further function on Earth. Though, of course, even if *unfallen* she was not 'pre-Fall'. Her destiny (in which she had cooperated) was far higher than that of any 'Man' would have been, had the Fall not occurred. It was also unthinkable that her body, the immediate source of Our Lord's (without other physical intermediary) should have been disintegrated, or 'corrupted', nor could it surely be long separated from Him after the Ascension. There is of course no suggestion that Mary did not 'age' at the normal rate of her race; but certainly this process cannot have proceeded or been allowed to proceed to decrepitude or loss of vitality and comeliness. The Assumption was in any case as distinct from the Ascension as the raising of Lazarus from the (self) Resurrection.

fore, of all things in it and all inhabitants of it, was a possibility if not inevitable. Trees may 'go bad' as in the Old Forest; Elves may turn into Orcs, and if this required the special perversive malice of Morgoth, still Elves themselves could do evil deeds. Even the 'good' Valar as inhabiting the World could at least err; as the Great Valar did in their dealings with the Elves; or as the lesser of their kind (as the Istari or wizards) could in various ways become self-seeking. Aulë, for instance, one of the Great, in a sense 'fell'; for he so desired to see the Children, that he became impatient and tried to anticipate the will of the Creator. Being the greatest of all craftsmen he tried to *make* children according to his imperfect knowledge of their kind. When he had made thirteen,* God spoke to him in anger, but not without pity: for Aulë had done this thing *not* out of evil desire to have slaves and subjects of his own, but out of impatient love, desiring children to talk to and teach, sharing with them the praise of Ilúvatar and his great love of the *materials* of which the world is made.

The One rebuked Aulë, saying that he had tried to usurp the Creator's power; but he could not give independent *life* to his makings. He had only one life, his own derived from the One, and could at most only distribute it. 'Behold' said the One: 'these creatures of thine have only thy will, and thy movement. Though you have devised a language for them, they can only report to thee thine own thought. This is a mockery of me.'

Then Aulë in grief and repentance humbled himself and asked for pardon. And he said: 'I will destroy these images of my presumption, and wait upon thy will.' And he took a great hammer, raising it to smite the eldest of his images; but it flinched and cowered from him. And as he withheld his stroke, astonished, he heard the laughter of Ilúvatar.

'Do you wonder at this?' he said. 'Behold! thy creatures now live, free from thy will! For I have seen thy humility, and taken pity on your impatience. Thy making I have taken up into my design.'

This is the Elvish legend of the making of the Dwarves; but the Elves report that Ilúvatar said thus also: 'Nonetheless I will not suffer my design to be forestalled: thy children shall not awake before mine own.' And he commanded Aulë to lay the fathers of the Dwarves severally in deep places, each with his mate, save Dúrin the eldest who had none. There they should sleep long, until Ilúvatar bade them awake. Nonetheless there has been for the most part little love between the Dwarves and the children of Ilúvatar. And of the fate that Ilúvatar has set upon the children of Aulë beyond the Circles of the world Elves and men know nothing, and if Dwarves know they do not speak of it.

*One, the eldest, alone, and six more with six mates.[1]

I do not like giving 'facts' about myself other than 'dry' ones (which anyway are quite as relevant to my books as any other more juicy details). Not simply for personal reasons; but also because I object to the contemporary trend in criticism, with its excessive interest in the details of the lives of authors and artists. They only distract attention from an author's works (if the works are in fact worthy of attention), and end, as one now often sees, in becoming the main interest. But only one's guardian Angel, or indeed God Himself, could unravel the real relationship between personal facts and an author's works. Not the author himself (though he knows more than any investigator), and certainly not so-called 'psychologists'.

But, of course, there is a scale of significance in 'facts' of this sort. There are insignificant facts (those particularly dear to analysts and writers about writers): such as drunkenness, wife-beating, and suchlike disorders. I do not happen to be guilty of these particular sins. But if I were, I should not suppose that artistic work proceeded from the weaknesses that produced them, but from other and still uncorrupted regions of my being. Modern 'researchers' inform me that Beethoven cheated his publishers, and abominably ill-treated his nephew; but I do not believe that has anything to do with his music. Then there are more significant facts, which *have* some relation to an author's works; though knowledge of them does not really explain the works, even if examined at length. For instance I dislike French, and prefer Spanish to Italian – but the relation of these facts to my taste in languages (which is obviously a large ingredient in *The Lord of the Rings*) would take a long time to unravel, and leave you liking (or disliking) the names and bits of language in my books, just as before. And there are a few basic facts, which however drily expressed, are really significant. For instance I was born in 1892 and lived for my early years in 'the Shire' in a pre-mechanical age. Or more important, I am a Christian (which can be deduced from my stories), and in fact a Roman Catholic. The latter 'fact' perhaps cannot be deduced; though one critic (by letter) asserted that the invocations of Elbereth, and the character of Galadriel as directly described (or through the words of Gimli and Sam) were clearly related to Catholic devotion to Mary. Another saw in waybread (lembas)= viaticum and the reference to its feeding the *will* (vol. III, p. 213) and being more potent when fasting, a derivation from the Eucharist. (That is: far greater things may colour the mind in dealing with the lesser things of a fairy-story.)

I am in fact a *Hobbit* (in all but size). I like gardens, trees and unmechanized farmlands; I smoke a pipe, and like good plain food (unrefrigerated), but detest French cooking; I like, and even dare to wear in these dull days, ornamental waistcoats. I am fond of mushrooms (out of a field); have a very simple sense of humour (which even my appreciative critics find tiresome); I go to bed late and get up late (when possible). I do not travel much. I love Wales (what is left of it, when mines, and the even more ghastly sea-side resorts, have done their worst), and especially the Welsh language. But I have not in fact been in W. for a long time (except for crossing it on the way to Ireland). I go frequently to Ireland (Eire: Southern Ireland) being fond of it and of (most of) its people; but the Irish language I find wholly unattractive. I hope that is enough to go on with.

214 To A. C. Nunn (draft)

[A reply to a reader who pointed out an apparent contradiction in *The Lord of the Rings*: that in the chapter 'A Long-expected Party' it is stated that 'Hobbits give presents to other people on their own birthdays'; yet Gollum refers to the Ring as his 'birthday present', and the account of how he acquired it, in the chapter 'The Shadow of the Past', indicates that his people *received* presents on their birthdays. Mr Nunn's letter continued: 'Therefore, one of the following must be true: (1) Sméagol's people were *not* "of hobbit-kind" as suggested by Gandalf (I p. 62); (2) the Hobbit custom of giving presents was only a recent growth; (3) the customs of the Stoors [Sméagol-Gollum's people] differed from those of other Hobbits; or (5) [sic] there is an error in the text. I shall be most grateful if you can spare the time to undertake some research into this important matter.]

[Not dated; probably late 1958-early 1959.]
Dear Mr Nunn,
  I am not a model of scholarship;[1] but in the matter of the Third Age I regard myself as a 'recorder' only. The faults that may appear in my record are, I believe, in no case due to errors, that is statements of what is not true, but omissions, and incompleteness of information, mostly due to the necessity of compression, and to the attempt to introduce information *en passant* in the course of narrative which naturally tended to cut out many things not immediately bearing on the tale.
  In the matter of birthday-customs and the apparent discrepancies that you note, we can therefore, I think, dismiss your alternatives (1) and (5). You omit (4).
  With regard to (1) Gandalf certainly says at first 'I guess' p. 62; but that is in accordance with his character and wisdom. In more modern

language he would have said 'I deduce', referring to matters that had not come under his direct observation, but on which he had formed a conclusion based on study. (You will observe in the Appendix B that the Wizards did not come until shortly before the first appearance of Hobbits in any records, at which time they were already divided into three marked branches.) But he did not in fact doubt his conclusion 'It is true all the same, etc.' p. 63.

Your alternative (2) would be possible; but since the recorder says on p. 35 *Hobbits* (which he uses whatever its origin, as the name for the whole race), and not *the Hobbits of the Shire,* or *Shire-folk,* it must be supposed that he means that the custom of *giving presents* was in some form common to all varieties, including Stoors. But since your (3) is naturally true, we might expect even so deep-rooted a custom to be exhibited in rather different ways in different branches. With the remigration of the Stoors back to Wilderland in TA 1356, all contact between this retrograde group and the ancestors of the Shirefolk was broken. More than 1100 years elapsed before the Déagol-Sméagol incident (c. 2463). At the time of the Party in TA 3001, when the customs of the Shire-folk are cursorily alluded to insofar as they affect the story, the gap of time was nearly 1650 years.

All Hobbits were slow to change, but the remigrant Stoors were going back to a wilder and more primitive life of small and dwindling* communities; while the Shire-folk in the 1400 years of their occupation had developed a more settled and elaborate social life, in which the importance of kinship to their sentiment and customs was assisted by detailed traditions, written and oral.

Though I omitted any discourse on this curious but characteristic fact of their behaviour, the facts concerning the Shire could be set out in some detail. The riverside Stoors must, naturally, remain more conjectural.

'Birthdays' had a considerable social importance. A person celebrating his/her birthday was called a *ribadyan* (which may be rendered according to the system described[2] and adopted a *byrding*[3]). The customs connected with birthdays had, though deeply rooted, become regulated by fairly strict etiquette; and so in consequence were in many cases reduced to formalities: as indeed suggested by 'not very expensive ones as a rule' p. 35; and especially by p. 46 ll. 20-26. With regard to *presents*: on his birthday the 'byrding' both *gave* and *received* presents; but the processes were different in origin, function, and etiquette. The *reception* was omitted by the narrator (since it does not concern the

*Between 2463 and the beginning of Gandalf's special enquiries concerning the Ring (nearly 500 years later) they appear indeed to have died out altogether (except, of course, for Sméagol); or to have fled from the shadow of Dol Guldur.

Party) but it was in fact the older custom, and therefore the one most formalized. (It does concern the Sméagol-Déagol incident, but the narrator, being obliged to reduce this to its most significant elements, and to put it into the mouth of Gandalf talking to a hobbit, naturally made no comment on a custom which the hobbit (and we) should regard as natural in connexion with birthdays.)

Receiving of gifts: this was an ancient ritual connected with *kinship*. It was in origin a recognition of the *byrding's* membership of a family or clan, and a commemoration of his formal 'incorporation'.* *No* present was given by father or mother to their children on their (the children's) birthdays (except in the rare cases of *adoption*); but the reputed head of the family was supposed to give something, if only in 'token'.

Giving gifts: was a personal matter, not limited to kinship. It was a form of 'thanksgiving', and taken as a recognition of services, benefits, and friendship shown, especially in the past year.

It may be noted that Hobbits, as soon as they became 'faunts' (that is talkers and walkers: formally taken to be on their third birthday-anniversary) *gave presents* to their parents. These were supposed to be things 'produced' by the giver (that is found, grown, or made by the 'byrding'), beginning in small children with bunches of wild flowers. This may have been the origin of the 'thanksgiving' presents of wider distribution, and the reason why it remained 'correct' even in the Shire for such presents to be things belonging to or produced by the giver. Samples of the produce of their gardens fields or workshops remained the usual 'gifts given', especially among the poorer Hobbits.

In the Shire etiquette, at the date of the Party, 'expectation of receiving' was limited to second cousins or nearer kin, and to residence *within* 12 miles.† Even close friends (if unrelated) were not 'expected' to give, though they might. The Shire residence-limit was obviously a fairly recent result of the gradual break-up of kinship communities and families and dispersal of relatives, under long-settled conditions. For the received birthday presents (no doubt as a relic of the customs of small ancient families) must be delivered in person, properly on the eve of the Day, and at latest before nuncheon on the Day. They were received privately by the 'byrding'; and it was very improper to exhibit them separately or as a collection – precisely to avoid such embarrassments as may occur in our wedding-exhibitions (which would have

*Anciently this apparently took place, shortly after birth, by the announcement of the *name* of the child to the family assembled, or in larger more elaborate communities to the titular 'head' of the clan or family. See note at end.

†Hence the Hobbit expression 'a twelve-mile cousin' for a person who stickled for the law, and recognized no obligations beyond its precise interpretation: one who would give you no present if the distance from his doorstep to yours was not *under* 12 miles (according to his own measurement).

horrified the Shirefolk).* The giver could thus accommodate his gift to his purse and his affections without incurring public comment or offending (if anyone) any other than the recipient. But custom did not demand costly presents, and a Hobbit was more readily flattered and delighted by an unexpectedly 'good' or desirable present than offended by a customary token of family good-will.

A trace of this can be seen in the account of Sméagol and Déagol – modified by the individual characters of these rather miserable specimens. Déagol, evidently a relative (as no doubt all the members of the small community were), had already given his customary present to Sméagol, although they probably set out on their expedition v. early in the morning. Being a mean little soul he grudged it. Sméagol, being meaner and greedier, tried to use the 'birthday' as an excuse for an act of tyranny. 'Because I wants it' was his frank statement of his chief claim. But he also implied that D's gift was a poor and insufficient token: hence D's retort that on the contrary it was more than he could afford.

The *giving of presents* by the 'byrding' – leaving out of account the gifts to parents,† mentioned above – being personal and a form of thanks, varied much more in form in different times and places, and according to the *age* and *status* of the 'byrding'. The master and mistress of a house or hole, in the Shire, would give gifts to all under their roof, or in their service, and usually also to near neighbours. And they might extend the list as they pleased, remembering any special favours in the past year. It was understood that the giving of presents was not fixed by rule; though the withholding of a usual gift (as e.g. to a child, a servant, or a next door neighbour) was taken as a rebuke and mark of severe displeasure. Juniors & Inmates (those having no house of their own) were under no such obligations as rested on householders; but they usually gave presents according to their means or affections. 'Not very expensive as a rule' – applied to all the gifts. Bilbo was in this as in other ways an exceptional person, and his Party was a riot of generosity even for a wealthy Hobbit. But one of the commonest birthday ceremonies was the giving of a 'party' – in the evening of the Day. All those invited were given presents by the host, and expected them, as part of the

---

*No presents were given at or during the celebration of Hobbit weddings, except flowers (weddings were mostly in Spring or early Summer). Assistance in furnishing a home (if the couple were to have a separate one, or private apartments in a Smial) was given long before by the parents on either side.

†In more primitive communities, as those still living in clan-smials, the *byrding* also made a gift to the 'head of the family'. There is no mention of Sméagol's presents. I imagine that he was an orphan; and do not suppose that he *gave* any present on his birthday, save (grudgingly) the tribute to his 'grandmother'. Fish probably. One of the reasons, maybe, for the expedition. It would have been just like Sméagol to give fish, actually caught by Déagol!

entertainment (if secondary to the fare provided). But they did *not* bring presents with them. Shire-folk would have thought that very improper. If the guests had not already given a gift (being one of those required to do so by kinship), it was too late. For other guests it was a thing 'not done' – it looked like paying for the party or matching the party-gift, and was most embarrassing. Sometimes, in the case of a very dear friend unable to come to a party (because of distance or other causes) a token invitation would be sent, with a present. In that case the present was always something to eat or drink, purporting to be a sample of the party-fare.

I think it will be seen that all the details recorded as 'facts' do actually fit into a definite picture of sentiment and custom, though this picture is not sketched even in the incomplete fashion of this note. It *could*, of course, have appeared in the Prologue: e.g. in the middle of p. 12. But though I cut out a great deal, that Prologue is still too long and over-loaded according even to those critics who allow that it has some use, and do not (as some) advise readers to forget it or skip it.

Incomplete as it is, this note may seem to you much too long; and though you asked for it, more than you asked for. But I do not see how I could have answered your queries more shortly in a way suitable to the compliment you pay me by taking an interest in Hobbits sufficient to mark the lacuna in the information provided.

However, the giving of information always opens still further vistas; and you will no doubt see that the brief account of 'presents' opens yet more anthropological matters implicit to such terms as kinship, family, clan, and so on. I venture to add a further note on this point, lest, in considering the text in the light of my reply, you should feel inclined to enquire further about Sméagol's 'grandmother', whom Gandalf represents as a ruler (of a family of high repute, large and wealthier than most, p. 62) and even calls a 'matriarch' (p. 66).

As far as I know Hobbits were universally monogamous (indeed they very seldom married a second time, even if wife or husband died very young); and I should say that their family arrangements were 'patrilinear' rather than patriarchal. That is, their family names descended in the male-line (and women were adopted into their husband's name); also the titular head of the family was usually the eldest male. In the case of large powerful families (such as the Tooks), still cohesive even when they had become very numerous, and more what we might call clans, the head was properly the eldest male of what was considered the most direct line of descent. But the government of a 'family', as of the real unit: the 'household', was not a monarchy (except by accident). It was a 'dyarchy', in which master and mistress had equal status, if different functions. Either was held to be the proper representative of the other in the case of absence (including death). There were no 'dowagers'. If the master died first, his place was taken by his wife, and this included (if he had held that position) the titular headship of a large family or clan. This title thus did not descend to the son, or other heir, while she lived, unless she voluntarily resigned.* It could, therefore, happen in various circumstances that a long-lived woman of forceful character remained 'head of the family', until she had full-grown grandchildren.

Laura Baggins (née Grubb) remained 'head' of the family of 'Baggins of Hobbiton', until she was 102. As she was 7 years younger than her husband (who died at the age of 93 in SY 1300), she held this position for 16 years, until SY 1316; and her son Bungo did not become 'head', until he was 70, ten years before he died at the early age of 80. Bilbo did not succeed, until the death of his Took mother, Belladonna, in 1334, when he was 44.

The Baggins headship then, owing to the strange events, fell into doubt. Otho Sackville-Baggins was heir to this title – quite apart from questions of property that would have arisen if his cousin Bilbo had died intestate; but after the legal fiasco of 1342 (when Bilbo returned alive after being 'presumed dead') no one dared to presume his death again. Otho died in 1412, his son Lotho was murdered in 1419, and his wife Lobelia died in 1420. When Master Samwise reported the 'departure over Sea' of Bilbo (and Frodo) in 1421, it was still held impossible to presume death; and when Master Samwise became Mayor in 1427, a rule was made that: 'if any inhabitant of the Shire shall pass over Sea in the presence of a reliable witness, with the expressed intention not to return, or in circumstances plainly implying such an intention, he or she shall be deemed to have relinquished all titles rights or properties previously held or occupied, and the heir or heirs thereof shall forthwith enter into possession of these titles, rights, or properties, as is directed by established custom, or by the will and disposition of the departed, as the case may require.' Presumably the title of 'head' then passed to the descendants of *Ponto* Baggins – probably *Ponto* (II).[4]

A well-known case, also, was that of *Lalia the Great*[5] (or less courteously the Fat). *Fortinbras II*, one time head of the Tooks and Thain, married *Lalia* of the Clayhangers in 1314, when he was 36 and she was 31. He died in 1380 at the age of 102, but she long outlived him, coming to an unfortunate end in 1402 at the age of 119. So she ruled the

---

*We are here dealing only with titular 'headship' not with ownership of property, and its management. These were distinct matters; though in the case of the surviving 'great households', such as *Great Smials* or *Brandy Hall*, they might overlap. In other cases, headship, being a mere title, and a matter of courtesy, was naturally seldom relinquished by the living.

Tooks and the Great Smials for 22 years, a great and memorable, if not universally beloved, 'matriarch'. She was not at the famous Party (SY 1401), but was prevented from attending rather by her great size and immobility than by her age. Her son, *Ferumbras*, had no wife, being unable (it was alleged) to find anyone willing to occupy apartments in the Great Smials, under the rule of Lalia. Lalia, in her last and fattest years, had the custom of being wheeled to the Great Door, to take the air on a fine morning. In the spring of SY 1402 her clumsy attendant let the heavy chair run over the threshold and tipped Lalia down the flight of steps into the garden. So ended a reign and life that might well have rivalled that of the Great Took.

It was widely rumoured that the attendant was Pearl (Pippin's sister), though the Tooks tried to keep the matter within the family. At the celebration of Ferumbras' accession the displeasure and regret of the family was formally expressed by the exclusion of Pearl from the ceremony and feast; but it did not escape notice that later (after a decent interval) she appeared in a splendid necklace of her name-jewels that had long lain in the hoard of the Thains.

Customs differed in cases where the 'head' died leaving no son. In the Took-family, since the headship was also connected with the title and (originally military) office of Thain,* descent was strictly through the male line. In other great families the headship might pass through a *daughter of the deceased* to his *eldest* grandson (irrespective of the daughter's age). This latter custom was usual in families of more recent origin, without ancient records or ancestral mansions. In such cases the heir (if he accepted the courtesy title) took the name of his mother's family – though he often retained that of his father's family also (placed second). This was the case with *Otho Sackville-Baggins*. For the nominal headship of the *Sackvilles* had come to him through his mother *Camellia*. It was his rather absurd ambition to achieve the rare distinction of being 'head' of two families (he would probably then have called himself *Baggins-Sackville-Baggins*): a situation which will explain his exasperation with the adventures and disappearances of Bilbo, quite apart from any loss of property involved in the adoption of Frodo.

I believe it was a moot-point in Hobbit lore (which the ruling of Mayor Samwise prevented from being argued in this particular case) whether 'adoption' by a childless 'head' could affect the descent of the headship. It was agreed that the adoption of a member of a different family could not affect the headship, that being a matter of blood and kinship; but there was an opinion that adoption of a close relative of the

*This title and office descended immediately, and was not held by a widow. But Ferumbras, though he became Thain Ferumbras III in 1380, still occupied no more than a small bachelor-son's apartment in the Great Smials, until 1402.

same name* before he was of age entitled him to all privileges of a son. This opinion (held by Bilbo) was naturally contested by Otho.

There is no reason to suppose that the Stoors of Wilderland had developed a strictly 'matriarchal' system, properly so called. No trace of any such thing was to be found among the Stoor-element in the East-farthing and Buckland, though they maintained various differences of custom and law. Gandalf's use (or rather his reporter and translator's use) of the word 'matriarch' was not 'anthropological', but meant simply a woman who in fact ruled the clan. No doubt because she had outlived her husband, and was a woman of dominant character.

It is likely enough that, in the recessive and decadent Stoor-country of Wilderland, the women-folk (as is often to be observed in such conditions) tended to preserve better the physical and mental character of the past, and so became of special importance. But it is not (I think) to be supposed that any fundamental change in their marriage-customs had taken place, or any sort of matriarchal or polyandrous society developed (even though this might explain the absence of any reference whatever to Sméagol-Gollum's father). 'Monogamy' was at this period in the West universally practised, and other systems were regarded with repugnance, as things only done 'under the Shadow'.

I actually started this letter nearly four months ago; but it never got finished. Shortly after I received your enquiries my wife, who had been ill most of 1958, celebrated the return of health by a fall in the garden, smashing up her left arm so badly that she is still crippled and in plaster. So 1958 was an almost completely frustrated year, and with other troubles, and the imminence of my retirement involving many re-arrangements, I have had no time at all to deal with the *Silmarillion*. Much though I wish to do so (and, happily, Allen and Unwin also seem to wish me to do).

[The draft ends here.]

215 To Walter Allen, *New Statesman* (drafts)

[Tolkien was asked to contribute to a symposium to be published in a Children's Book Supplement of the *New Statesman*. He was told: 'The kind of questions we should hope you would consider are: how far do you write with a specific audience in mind, i.e. how do you feel writing for children differs from writing for adult readers? To what extent do you feel that writing for children satisfies a need in yourself, for example, by

*descendants of a common great-grandfather of the same name.

expressing a side of you repressed in ordinary life or by the exigencies of writing for adults? How do you see the relation between *The Hobbit* and *The Fellowship of the Ring* [sic]? Are you conscious of a didactic purpose, and if so, how do you construe it?']

[Not dated; April 1959.]

Dear Mr Allen,

I am very sorry, but I shall not be able to take part in the symposium. I have only recently returned from convalescence after an operation, and am faced with much neglected work. Term begins on April 24.

I have said all that I have to say about writing for children in my contribution: 'On Fairy-Stories': to *Essays Presented to Charles Williams* (O.U.P. 1947). It has no special interest to me.

When I published *The Hobbit* – hurriedly and without due consideration – I was still influenced by the convention that 'fairy-stories' are naturally directed to children (with or without the silly added waggery 'from seven to seventy'). And I had children of my own. But the desire to address children, as such, had nothing to do with the story as such in itself or the urge to write it. But it had some unfortunate effects on the mode of expression and narrative method, which if I had not been rushed, I should have corrected. Intelligent children of good taste (of which there seem quite a number) have always, I am glad to say, singled out the points in manner where the address is to children as blemishes.

I had given a great deal more thought to the matter before beginning the composition of *The Lord of the Rings*; and that work was not specially addressed to children or to any other class of people. But to any one who enjoyed a long exciting story, of the sort that I myself naturally enjoy. . . . .

I am not specially interested in children, and certainly not in writing for them: i.e. in addressing directly and expressly those who cannot understand adult language.

I write things that might be classified as fairy-stories not because I wish to address children (who qua children I do not believe to be specially interested in this kind of fiction) but because I wish to write this kind of story and no other.

I do this because if I do not apply too grandiloquent a title to it I find that my comment on the world is most easily and naturally expressed in this way. I am not conscious of any repression exerted upon me by 'ordinary life'. Since large numbers of adults seem to enjoy what I write – quite enough to keep me happy – I have no need to seek escape to another and (possibly) less exigent audience.

I hope 'comment on the world' does not sound too solemn. I have no didactic purpose, and no allegorical intent. (I do not like allegory (properly so called: most readers appear to confuse it with significance or applicability) but that is a matter too long to deal with here.) But long narratives cannot be made out of nothing; and one cannot rearrange the primary matter in secondary patterns without indicating feelings and opinions about one's material. . . . .

The relation between *The Hobbit* and its sequel is I think this. *The Hobbit* is a first essay or introduction (consideration will admit I think that it is a very just point at which to begin the narration of the subsequent events) to a complex narrative which had been brewing in my mind for years. It was overtly addressed to children for two reasons: I had at that time children of my own and was accustomed to making up (ephemeral) stories for them; I had been brought up to believe that there was a real and special connexion between children and fairy-stories. Or rather to believe that this was a received opinion of my world and of publishers. I doubted it, since it did not accord with my personal experience of my own taste, nor with my observation of children (notably my own). But the convention was strong.

I think that *The Hobbit* can be seen to begin in what might be called a more 'whimsy' mode, and in places even more facetious, and move steadily to a more serious or significant, and more consistent and historical. . . . . But I regret much of it all the same. . . . .

The first question, it seems to me, to ask in any discussion of this kind is: What are 'Children'? Do you limit your enquiry, as may be supposed, to (North) European children? Then in what ages between the cradle and the end of legal infancy? To what grades of intelligence? Or literary talent and perceptiveness? Some intelligent children may have little of this. Children's tastes and talents differ as widely as those of adults, as soon as they are old enough to be differentiated clearly, and therefore to be the target of any thing that can bear the name of literature. It would be useless to offer to many children of 14 or even of 12 the trash that is good enough for many respectable adults of twice or three times the age, but less gifts natural.

Life is rather above the measure of us all (save for a very few perhaps). We all need literature that is above our measure – though we may not have sufficient energy for it all the time. But the energy of youth is usually greater. Youth needs then less than adulthood or Age what is down to its (supposed) measure. But even in Age I think we only are really moved by what is at least in some point or aspect above us, above our measure, at any rate before we have read it and 'taken it in'. Therefore do not write down to Children or to anybody. Not even in language. Though it would be a good thing if that great reverence which is due to children took the form of eschewing the tired and flabby cliches of adult life. But an honest word is an honest word, and its acquaintance can only be made by meeting it in a right context. A good vocabulary is not acquired by reading books written according to some notion of the vocabulary of one's age-group. It comes from reading books above one.

[The draft ends here. The following is the letter that Tolkien actually sent to the *New Statesman* on 17 April:]

Dear Mr Allen,

I very much regret that it seems impossible for me to take part in this symposium that you propose. I have only recently returned from convalescence after an operation and I am faced with much neglected work. Term begins next week and I shall not have time to produce any copy before April 19th.

Yours sincerely,
J. R. R. Tolkien.

216 From a letter to the Deputy Registrar, University of Madras
12 August 1959

I have to thank you for the honour of appointing me a member of your Board of Examiners. May I respectfully suggest, nonetheless, that it is inadvisable to do this without first consulting the persons appointed? I am unable to accept this examinership. I am fully occupied with other affairs, and I have in any case retired, and do not propose to take any further part in teaching and examining.

217 From a letter to Allen & Unwin   11 September 1959

[Concerning the Polish translation of *The Lord of the Rings*.]

I am sorry that owing to domestic troubles and turmoil I have neglected Mrs Skibniewska's letter.

It is quite impossible for me to write a lot of notes for her use. . . . . As a general principle for her guidance, my preference is for as little translation or alteration of any names as possible. As she perceives, this is an English book and its Englishry should not be eradicated. That the Hobbits actually spoke an ancient language of their own is of course a pseudo-historical assertion made necessary by the nature of the narrative. I could provide or invent the original Hobbit language form of all the names that appear in English, like Baggins or Shire, but this would be quite pointless. My own view is that the names of persons should all be left as they stand. I should prefer that the names of places were left untouched also, including Shire. The proper way of treating these I think is for a list of those that have a meaning in English to be given at the end, with glosses or explanations in Polish.

218   To Eric Rogers

[A reply to a letter addressed to 'any Professor of English Language' at Oxford, asking whether it is correct to say 'A number of office walls *has* been damaged' or '*have* been damaged'.]

9 October 1959   76 Sandfield Road, Headington, Oxford

Dear Sir,

Your letter has eventually reached me, though I am not 'any Professor of English Language', since I have now retired. The answer is that you can say what you like. Pedantry insists that since *number* is a singular noun, the verb should be singular, (has). Common sense feels that since the *walls* is plural, and are really concerned, the verb should be plural, (have). You may take your choice.

Yours sincerely

J. R. R. Tolkien.

219   From a letter to Allen & Unwin   14 October 1959

[A Cambridge cat breeder had asked if she could register a litter of Siamese kittens under names taken from *The Lord of the Rings*.]

My only comment is that of Puck upon mortals. I fear that to me Siamese cats belong to the fauna of Mordor, but you need not tell the cat breeder that.

220   From a letter to Naomi Mitchison   15 October 1959

I 'retired' – or rather, since even British generals usually imply a voluntary movement to the rear when they 'retire', I was extruded on the age limit at the end of last term. In many ways a melancholy proceeding, especially financially. Though I have belonged to F.S.S.U.[1] since it began in 1920, it does not provide enough for one to live on one's laurels (old and dusty as Christmas decorations in January). Without the assistance of 'Hobbits and all that' things would be meagre. Nonetheless (not a little encouraged by your letter) I decided to get off the treadmill, and resigned from my appointment in Ireland[2] before I returned. I shall, if I get a chance, turn back to the matter of the Red Book and allied histories soon.

221   From a letter to the First Assistant Registrar, Oxford University   24 November 1959

[Following Tolkien's retirement, the Board of the Faculty of English sent an appreciation of his 'long and invaluable service', and expressed 'its

300

regret that it will not in future have the benefit of your wise advice and unsparing help in its deliberations. It wishes at the same time to express its sense of the distinction which your wide, meticulous, and imaginative scholarship has brought to the faculty and to the University.']

I am deeply grateful to the Board of the Faculty of English for the extremely generous terms in which they have addressed me. My only misgiving is that they present a picture of a professor far superior to the one that has retired. However, conscious merit is no doubt a solace and support, but there is nonetheless a peculiar pleasure in receiving honours and compliments one doesn't deserve. One result of retirement that I never expected is that I actually miss the meetings of the Board. Not, of course, the agenda, but the gathering together of so many dear friends.

222   From a letter to Rayner Unwin   9 December 1959

[Unwin had encouraged Tolkien to prepare his translations of *Sir Gawain and the Green Knight* and *Pearl* for publication.]

My delay in answering your letter of December 3rd is mainly due to the fact that I have become immersed again in work in which you are interested. I am afraid that you may be perturbed rather than surprised (knowing too well the vagaries of authors, or at least of mine), to hear that this is in wrong order. With the help of my secretary I have been charging well ahead with the reconstruction of the *Silmarillion* etc. Your letter comes as a timely if unwelcome jerk on the reins. Quite clearly I must take up *Gawain* immediately. I shall not manage it before Christmas; but I recently ordered and inspected the material and I do not think that the actual text of the translation of *Gawain* and of *Pearl* now need very much work. I shall be able to let you have the text of the two poems soon after Christmas; they can be set up separately. I am still a little uncertain about what other matter to add to them by way of introduction or notes. I think very little, since people who buy the translations will probably belong to one of two classes: those who just want the translation, and those who have access to editions and other full treatments of the problems presented by the poems.

223   From a letter to Rayner Unwin   31 July 1960

I am in fact utterly stuck – lost in a bottomless bog, and anything that would cheer me would be welcome. The crimes of omission that I committed in order to complete the 'L. of the R.' are being avenged. The chief is the *Ancrene Riwle*. My edition of the prime MS. should have

301

been completed *many years* ago! I did at least try to clear it out of the way before retirement, and by a vast effort sent in the text in Sept. *1958*. But then one of the misfortunes that attend on delay occurred; and my MS. disappeared into the confusion of the Printing Strike. The proofs actually arrived at the beginning of *this* June, when I was in full tide of composition for the *Silmarillion*, and had lost the threads of the M[iddle] E[nglish] work. I stalled for a while, but I am now under extreme pressure: 10 hours hard per diem day after day, trying to induce order into a set of confused and desperately tricky proofs, and notes. And then I have to write an introduction. (And then there is *Sir Gawain*.) Until the proofs of the *text* at least have gone back, I cannot lift my head.

224   From a letter to Christopher Tolkien   12 September 1960

[A comment on a book by C. S. Lewis.]

I have just received a copy of C.S.L.'s latest: *Studies in Words*. Alas! His ponderous silliness is becoming a fixed manner. I am deeply relieved to find I am not mentioned.

I wrote for him a long analysis of the semantics and formal history of *BHŪ with special reference to $\phi\acute{v}\sigma\iota\varsigma$. All that remains is the first 9 lines of PHUSIS (pp. 33–34) with the characteristic Lewisian intrusion of 'beards and cucumbers'. The rest is dismissed on p. 36 with 'we have not a shred of evidence'. He remains at best and worst an Oxford 'classical' don – when dealing with words. I think the best bit is the last chapter, and the only really wise remark is on the last page: 'I think we must get it firmly fixed in our minds that the very occasions on which we should most like to write a slashing review are precisely those on which we had much better hold our tongues.' Ergo silebo.[1]

225   From a letter to Rayner Unwin   10 December 1960

[Puffin Books had offered to publish a paperback edition of *The Hobbit*.]

Thank you for your news of the 'Puffin' offer, and your advice. I may safely leave the decision to your own wisdom. The chances of profit or loss, in cash or otherwise, are evidently neatly balanced. If you wish to know my personal feelings: I am no longer able to ignore cash-profit, even to the odd £100, but I do share your reluctance to cheapen the old Hobbit. Unless the profit or advantage is clear, I would much rather leave him to amble along; and he still shows a good walking-pace. And I am not fond of Puffins or Penguins or other soft-shelled fowl: they eat other birds' eggs, and are better left to vacated nests.

The Lord of the Rings was actually begun, as a separate thing, about 1937, and had reached the inn at Bree, before the shadow of the second war. Personally I do not think that either war (and of course not the atomic bomb) had any influence upon either the plot or the manner of its unfolding. Perhaps in landscape. The Dead Marshes and the approaches to the Morannon owe something to Northern France after the Battle of the Somme. They owe more to William Morris and his Huns and Romans, as in *The House of the Wolfings* or *The Roots of the Mountains*.

227 **From a letter to Mrs E. C. Ossen Drijver** 5 January 1961

Númenor, shortened form of *Númenórë*, is my own invention, compounded from *numē–n*, 'going down' ($\sqrt{}$ndū, nu), sunset, West, and *nórë* 'land, country' = *Westernesse*. The legends of *Númenórë* are only in the background of *The Lord of the Rings*, though (of course) they were written first, and are only summarised in Appendix A. They are my own use for my own purposes of the *Atlantis* legend, but not based on special *knowledge*, but on a special personal concern with this tradition of the culture-bearing men of the Sea, which so profoundly affected the imagination of peoples of Europe with westward-shores.

C. S. Lewis is a very old friend and colleague of mine, and indeed I owe to his encouragement the fact that in spite of obstacles (including the 1939 war!) I persevered and eventually finished *The Lord of the Rings*. He heard all of it, bit by bit, read aloud, but never saw it in print till after his trilogy was published. His *Numinor* was derived, by ear, from *Númenor*, and was indeed intended to refer to my work and other legends (not published) of mine, which he had heard.

I am now under contract engaged (among alas! other less congenial tasks) in putting into order for publication the mythology and stories of the First and Second Ages – written long ago, but judged hardly publishable, until (so it seems) the surprising success of *The Lord of the Rings*, which comes at the end, has provided a probable demand for the beginnings. But there are, I fear, no *hobbits* in *The Silmarillion* (or history of the Three Jewels), little fun or earthiness but mostly grief and disaster. Those critics who scoffed at *The Lord* because 'all the good boys came home safe and everyone was happy ever after' (quite untrue) ought to be satisfied. They will not be, of course – even if they deign to notice the book!

[The Swedish publishers of *The Lord of the Rings*, Gebers, were dubious about including the Appendices in their edition of the book. Tolkien's opinion on the matter was sought.]

I have great sympathy with any foreign publisher adventurous enough to embark on a translation of my work. After all, my chief interest in being translated is pecuniary, as long as the basic text is treated with respect; so that even if the touchiness of parenthood is outraged, I should wish to refrain from doing or saying anything that may damage the good business of being published in other countries. And I have also Messrs. Allen and Unwin to consider. But the matter of the Appendices has a pecuniary aspect.

I do not believe that they give the work a 'scholarly' (? read *pedantisk*) look, and they play a major part in producing the total effect: as Messrs. Gebers' translator has himself pointed out (selecting the detail and the *documentation* as two chief ingredients in producing the compelling sense of historical reality). In any case, purchasers of vol. iii will presumably be already involved: vol. iii is not a separate book to be purchased solely on its own merits. Actually, an analysis of many hundreds of letters shows that the Appendices have played a very large part in reader's pleasure, in turning library readers into purchasers (since the Appendices are needed for reference), and in creating the demand for another book. A sharp distinction must be drawn between the tastes of reviewers ('donnish folly' and all that) and of readers! I think I understand the tastes of simple-minded folk (like myself) pretty well. But I do appreciate the question of costs and retail prices. There is a price beyond which simple-minded folk cannot go, even if they would like to. . . . .

I do not know what the situation is with regard to the sale of the English book in countries where a translation has been published. I suppose that no obstacle, direct or indirect, is put in the way of obtaining them, and they can in any case be ordered by a determined purchaser through a bookseller. The demand is no doubt very small . . . . and not of any financial interest. But I am interested in the point. The original is my only protection against the translators. I cannot exercise any control over the translation of such a large text, even into the few languages that I know anything about; yet the translators are guilty of some very strange mistakes. (As I should be, working as they must under pressure in a limited time).

Dr Ohlmarks,[1] for instance, though he is reported to me to be clever and ingenious, can produce such things as this. In translating vol. i p. 12, 'they seldom wore shoes, since their feet had tough leathery soles and were clad in a thick curling hair, much like the hair of their heads', he read the text as '. . . their feet had thick *feathery* soles, and they were clad in a thick curling hair . . .' and so produces in his Introduction a picture of hobbits whose outdoor garb was of matted hair, while under their feet they had solid feather-cushion treads! This is made doubly absurd, since it occurs in a passage where he is suggesting that the hobbits are modelled on the inhabitants of the idyllic suburb of Headington.

I do not object to biographical notice, if it is desirable (the Dutch did without it). But it should be correct, and it should be pertinent. I think I must ask to be allowed to see anything of this kind in future, before it is printed. Or alternatively I will draw up a brief statement which I will submit to you as a possible hand-out in case of any demand for such material.

Who is Who is not a safe source in the hands of foreigners ignorant of England. From it Ohlmarks has woven a ridiculous fantasy. Ohlmarks is a very vain man (as I discovered in our correspondence), preferring his own fancy to facts, and very ready to pretend to knowledge which he does not possess. He does not hesitate to attribute to me sentiments and beliefs which I repudiate. Among them a dislike of the University of Leeds, because it was 'northern' and no older than the Victorian seventies. This is impertinent and entirely untrue. If it should come to the knowledge of Leeds (fortunately unlikely) I should make him apologize.

229 From a letter to Allen & Unwin 23 February 1961

I now enclose a copy and version of Ohlmarks' nonsense. In the hope that you may think it justifies my annoyance. I have not looked at his second outburst. I feel I cannot just now take any more.

[The following are excerpts from Tolkien's commentary on Åke Ohlmarks' introduction to the Swedish translation of *The Lord of the Rings*. Passages in italics are quotations from Tolkien's translation of the introduction.]

It is hard to believe that the deep-rooted native-born hobbit from Middle South England . . . . would feel very much at home [in Leeds]. Inauguration into the Anglo-Saxon chair in Oxford was for him like coming home again from a trial expedition up to the distant 'Fornost'.

This is O[hlmarks]'s first serious piece of presumptuous impertinence. . . . . I was devoted to the University of Leeds, which was very good to me, and to the students, whom I left with regret. The present students are among my most attentive readers, and write to me (especially about the Appendices). If O's nonsense was to come to the notice of the University it would give offence, and O would have to publicly apologize. As for 'Fornost', a glance at the book would show that it is comparable rather to the Kings' mounds at Old Uppsala than to the city of Leeds!

One of his most important writings, published in 1953, also treats of another famous homecoming, 'The Homecoming of Beorhtnot, [sic] Beorhthelm's son.'

Coming home dead without a head (as Beorhtnoth did) is not very delightful. But this is spoof. O. knows nothing about Beorhtnoth, or his homecoming (never mentioned till I wrote a poem about it) and he has not seen the poem. I do not blame him, except for writing as if he knew.

The professor began by telling tales about it [Middle-earth] to his children, then to his grandchildren; and they were fascinated and clamoured for more and still more. One can clearly see before one the fireside evenings in the peaceful villa out at Sandfield Road in Headington near Oxford . . . . with the Barrowdowns or Headington Hills in the rear and the Misty Mountains or the 560 feet high Shotover in the background.

!!This is such outrageous nonsense that I should suspect mockery, if I did not observe that O. is ever ready to assume intimate knowledge that he has not got. I have only two grandchildren. One 18 who first heard of the book 5 years ago. The other is only 2. The book was written before I moved to Headington, which has no hills, but is on a shoulder (as it were) of Shotover.

The Ring is in a certain way 'der Nibelungen Ring' . . . .

Both rings were round, and there the resemblance ceases.

. . . . which was originally forged by Volund the master-smith, and then by way of Vittka-Andvare passed through the hands of the mighty asar [Æsir] into the possession of Hreidmar and the dragon, after the dragon's fall coming to Sigurd the dragonslayer, after his murder by treacherous conspirators coming to the Burgundians, after their death in Atle's snake-pit coming to the Huns, then to the sons of Jonaker, to the Gothic tyrant Ermanrik, etc.

Thank heaven for the *etc.* I began to fear that it would turn up in my pocket. Evidently Dr. O thinks that it is in his. But what is the point of all this? Those who know something about the Old Norse side of the 'Nibelung' traditions (mainly referred to since the name-forms used are Norse) will think this a farrago of nonsense; those who do not, will hardly be interested. But perhaps they are also meant to conclude that Dr. O also has *mästerskap*.[1] It has nothing whatsoever to do with *The Lord of the Rings*. As for Wayland Smith being a Pan-type, or being reflected both in Bombadil and in Gollum: this is sufficient example of the silly methods and nonsensical conclusions of Dr. O. He is welcome to the rubbish, but I do not see that he, as a translator, has any right to unload it here.

Here [in Mordor] rules the personification of satanic might Sauron (read perhaps in the same partial fashion [as other identifications Ohlmarks has made] Stalin).

There is no 'perhaps' about it. I utterly repudiate any such 'reading', which angers me. The situation was conceived long before the Russian revolution. Such allegory is entirely foreign to my thought. The placing of Mordor in the east was due to simple narrative and geographical necessity, within my 'mythology'. The original stronghold of Evil was (as traditionally) in the North; but as that had been destroyed, and was indeed under the sea, there had to be a new stronghold, far removed from the Valar, the Elves, and the sea-power of Númenor.

There are reminiscences of journeys on foot in his own youth up into the Welsh border-regions.

As Bilbo said of the dwarves, he seems to know as much of my private pantries as I do myself. Or pretends to. I never walked in Wales or the marches in my youth. Why should I be made an object of fiction while still alive?

230 **From a letter to Rhona Beare** 8 June 1961

[Answering various questions about *The Lord of the Rings*.]

With regard to Aragorn's boast,[1] I think he was reckoning his ancestry through the paternal line for this purpose; but in any case I imagine that Númenóreans, before their knowledge dwindled, knew more about heredity than other people. To this of course they refer by the common symbol of blood. They recognized the fact that in spite of inter-marriages, some characteristics would appear in pure form in later generations. Aragorn's own longevity was a case in point. Gandalf I think refers to the curious fact that even in the much less well preserved house of the stewards Denethor had come out as almost purely Númenórean.

Vol. II, p. 70.[2] Treebeard was not using Entish sounds on this occasion, but using ancient Elvish words mixed up and run together in

Entish fashion. The elements are *laure*, gold, not the metal but the colour, what we should call golden light; *ndor, nor*, land, country; *lin, lind-*, a musical sound; *malina*, yellow; *orne*, tree; *lor*, dream; *nan, nand-*, valley. So that roughly he means: 'The valley where the trees in a golden light sing musically, a land of music and dreams; there are yellow trees there, it is a tree-yellow land.' The same applies to the last line on that page,[3] where the elements are *taure*, forest; *tumba*, deep valley; *mor*, darkness; *lóme*, night.

Mae govannen[4] means 'well met.'

Treebeard's greeting[5] to Celeborn and Galadriel meant 'O beautiful ones, parents of beautiful children.'

The song of praise in Vol. III, p. 231[6] is not really a song but is represented by a few phrases taken from the languages heard, in which English represents the common speech. The second, fourth and sixth lines are Sindarin or Grey Elvish. The seventh and ninth are High Elvish. Line 2 means 'May the Halflings live long, glory to the Halflings.' The fourth line means 'Frodo and Sam, princes of the west, glorify (them)', the sixth, 'glorify (them)'. The seventh line means 'Bless them, bless them, long we will praise them.' The ninth line means 'The Ring bearers, bless (or praise) them to the height.'

231 From a letter to Jane Neave 4 October 1961

[Tolkien's aunt Jane Neave, then aged ninety, wrote to ask him 'if you wouldn't get out a small book with Tom Bombadil at the heart of it'.]

I think your idea about Tom Bombadil is a good one, not that I feel inclined to write any more about him. But I think that the original poem (which appeared in the *Oxford Magazine* long before *The Lord of the Rings*) might make a pretty booklet of the kind you would like if each verse could be illustrated by Pauline Baynes. If you have not ever seen the original Tom Bombadil poem I will try and find it and have a copy made for you.

232 From a letter to Joyce Reeves 4 November 1961

I always like shrewd sound-hearted maiden aunts. Blessed are those who have them or meet them. Though they are commoner, in my experience, than Saki aunts.[1] The professional aunt is a fairly recent development, perhaps; but I was fortunate in having an early example: one of the first women to take a science degree. She is now ninety, but only a few years ago went botanizing in Switzerland. It was in her company (with a mixed party of about the same size as the company in *The Hobbit*) that I journeyed on foot with a heavy pack through much of Switzerland, and over many high passes. It was approaching the Aletsch that we were nearly destroyed by boulders loosened in the sun rolling down a snow-slope. An enormous rock in fact passed between me and the next in front. That and the 'thunder-battle' – a bad night in which we lost our way and slept in a cattle-shed – appear in *The Hobbit*. It is long ago now......

I have enjoyed the tale;[2] and hope you will forgive my garrulity. My remarks, I fear, must savour a little of the legendary German professor, who wrote a large book on *Das Komische*. After which, whenever anyone told him a funny story, he thought for a moment, and then nodded, saying: 'Yes, there is that joke'.

233 From a letter to Rayner Unwin   15 November 1961

[Allen & Unwin agreed to the suggestion that Tolkien should put together a small book of poems, *The Adventures of Tom Bombadil*.]

I have in fact made a search, as far as time allowed, and had copies made of any poems that might conceivably see the light or (somewhat tidied up) be presented again. The harvest is not rich, for one thing there is not much that really goes together with Tom Bombadil. Besides Tom Bombadil (of which you have a copy) I send Errantry and The Man in the Moon, which might go together. About the others I am altogether doubtful; I do not even know if they have any virtue at all, by themselves or in a series. If, however, you think any of them would make a book and might attract Pauline Baynes to illustrate them I should be delighted.

234 To Jane Neave

[Tolkien had sent his aunt some of the poems he was considering for inclusion in the new book.]

22 November 1961   76 Sandfield Road, Headington, Oxford
My dearest Aunt,

Thank you for returning the poems. Do not worry about giving me trouble. I have enjoyed myself very much digging out these old half-forgotten things and rubbing them up. All the more because there are other and duller things that I ought to have been doing. At any rate they have had you as an audience. Printed publication is, I fear, very unlikely.

Never mind about the young! I am not interested in the 'child' as such, modern or otherwise, and certainly have no intention of meeting him/her half way, or a quarter of the way. It is a mistaken thing to do anyway, either useless (when applied to the stupid) or pernicious (when inflicted on the gifted). I have only once made the mistake of trying to do it, to my lasting regret, and (I am glad to say) with the disapproval of intelligent children: in the earlier part of *The Hobbit*. But I had not then given any serious thought to the matter: I had not freed myself from the contemporary delusions about 'fairy-stories' and children.

I had to think about it, however, before I gave an 'Andrew Lang' lecture at St Andrews on Fairy-stories; and I must say I think the result was entirely beneficial to *The Lord of the Rings*, which was a practical demonstration of the views that I expressed. It was *not* written 'for children', or for any kind of person in particular, but for itself. (If any parts or elements in it appear 'childish', it is because I am childish, and like that kind of thing myself *now*.) I believe children do read it or listen to it eagerly, even quite young ones, and I am very pleased to hear it, though they must fail to understand most of it, and it is in any case stuffed with words that they are unlikely to understand – if by that one means 'recognize as something already known'. I hope it increases their vocabularies.

As for *plenilune* and *argent*,[1] they are beautiful words *before* they are understood – I wish I could have the pleasure of meeting them for the first time again! – and how is one to know them till one does meet them? And surely the first meeting should be in a living context, and not in a dictionary, like dried flowers in a hortus siccus!

Children are not a class or kind, they are a heterogeneous collection of immature persons, varying, as persons do, in their reach, and in their ability to extend it when stimulated. As soon as you limit your vocabulary to what you suppose to be within their reach, you in fact simply cut off the gifted ones from the chance of extending it.

And the meaning of fine words cannot be made 'obvious', for it is not obvious to any one: least of all to adults, who have stopped listening to the sound because they think they know the meaning. They think *argent* 'means' *silver*. But it does not. It and silver have a reference to x or chem. Ag, but in each x is clothed in a totally different phonetic incarnation: $x+y$ or $x+z$; and these do not have the same meaning, not only because they sound different and so arouse different responses, but also because they are not in fact used when talking about Ag. in the same way. It is better, I think, at any rate to begin with, to *hear* 'argent' as a sound only (z without x) in a poetic context, than to think 'it only means silver'. There is some chance then that you may like it for itself, and later learn to appreciate the heraldic overtones it has, in addition to its own peculiar sound, which 'silver' has not.

I think that this writing down, flattening, Bible-in-basic-English attitude is responsible for the fact that so many older children and younger people have little respect and no love for words, and very limited vocabularies – and alas! little desire left (even when they had the gift which has been stultified) to refine or enlarge them.

I am sorry about *The Pied Piper*.[2] I loathe it. God help the children! I would as soon give them crude and vulgar plastic toys. Which of course they will play with, to the ruin of their taste. Terrible presage of the most vulgar elements in Disney. But you cannot say that 'it never fails'. You do not really know what is happening, even in the few cases that have come under your observation. It failed with me, even as a child, when I could not yet distinguish the shallow vulgarity of Browning from the general grown-uppishness of things that I was expected to like. The trouble is one does not really know what is going on, even when a child listens with attention, even when it laughs. Children have one thing (only) in common: a lack of experience and if not of discrimination at least of the language in which to express their perceptions; they are still usually acquiescent (outwardly) in their acceptance of the food presented to them by adults. Though they may mentally or actually throw the stuff over the garden wall, and say demurely how much they have enjoyed it. As my children did (they confess) with their suppers in the garden in summer, giving their parents the permanent delusion that they loved jam-sandwiches. I was of course given Hans Andersen when quite young. At one time I listened with attention which may have looked like rapture to his stories when read to me. I read them myself often. Actually I disliked him intensely; and the vividness of that distaste is the chief thing that I carried down the years in connexion with his name.

Surely I am 'childish' enough, and that ought to be enough for real children or any one 'childish' in the same sort of way, and never mind if the old chap knows a lot of jolly words. I send you a little piece of nonsense that I wrote only the other day,[3] as evidence of my childishness. Though I have alas! picked up enough grown-up jargon to write in imitation of my elders; and I might say 'it is a neatly constructed trifle, an amusing attempt to penetrate the elf-childishness of an elf-child, if any such thing existed!' Excuse type. My scrawly hand won't last out a long letter. Don't bother about the 'opinions'. In fact I write as I do, ill or well, because I cannot write otherwise. If it pleases anybody, large or small, I am as much surprised as delighted. God bless you. Very much love.

R

235 From a letter to Mrs Pauline Gasch (Pauline Baynes)
6 December 1961

[Pauline Baynes, who had illustrated *Farmer Giles of Ham*, had expressed herself willing to provide pictures for *The Adventures of Tom Bombadil*, and had been reading typescripts of the poems.]

If I dare say so, the things sent to you (except the Sea-bell, the poorest, and not one that I shd. really wish to include, at least not with the others) were conceived as a series of very definite, clear and precise, pictures – fantastical, or nonsensical perhaps, but not dreamlike! And I thought of you, because you seem able to produce wonderful pictures with a touch of 'fantasy', but primarily bright and clear visions of things that one might really see. Of course what you say about 'illustrations' in general is very true, and I once (in a long essay on 'Fairy-Stories') ventured at greater length but no more precisely than you, to say much the same.[1] But there is a case for illustration (or decoration!) applied to small things such as these verses, which are light-hearted, and (I think) dexterous in words, but not very profound in intention. I suppose one would also have to except 'The Hoard' from being 'light-hearted', though the woes of the successive (nameless) inheritors are seen merely as pictures in a tapestry of antiquity and do not deeply engage individual pity. I was most interested by your choice of this as your favourite. For it is the least fluid, being written in [a] mode rather resembling the oldest English verse – and was in fact inspired by a single line of ancient verse: *iúmonna gold galdre bewunden,* 'the gold of men of long ago enmeshed in enchantment' (Beowulf 3052). But I do appreciate that it is a tricky task! I hope you may feel inclined to attempt it. Alas! you put your finger unerringly on a main difficulty: they are *not* a unity from any point of view, but made at different times under varying inspiration. I have not much doubt, however, that you would avoid the Scylla of Blyton and the Charybdis of Rackham – though to go to wreck on the latter would be the less evil fate.

236 To Rayner Unwin

[Tolkien received a copy of the Puffin Books edition of *The Hobbit* in September 1961, but did not look at it until December.]

30 December 1961   76 Sandfield Road, Headington, Oxford
Dear Rayner,

.... I wish well-meaning folk who think they know could be restrained! I had occasion a day or two ago to look up a passage in *The Hobbit*, and the 'puffin' lying to hand, I looked it up there. So I discovered that one of this breed had been busy again. *Penguin Books* had, I suppose, no licence to edit my work, and should have reproduced faithfully the printed copy; and at least out of courtesy to Allen and Unwin and myself should have addressed some enquiry before they proceeded to correct the text.

Dwarves, dwarves', dwarvish have been corrected throughout (with one exception on p. 21) to the current dictionary forms *dwarfs, dwarfs', dwarfish. Elvish, elvish* has been changed to *Elfish, elfish* 7 times but left unchanged 3 times. I view this procedure with dudgeon. I deliberately used *dwarves* etc. for a special purpose and effect – that it has an effect can be gauged by comparing the passages with the substitutes *dwarfs,* especially in verse. The point is dealt with in L.R. iii, p. 415.[1] Of course I do not expect compositors or proof-readers to know that, or to know anything about the history of the word 'dwarf'; but I should have thought it might have occurred, if not to a compositor at least to a reader, that the author would not have used consistently getting on for 300 times a particular form, nor would your readers have passed it, if it was a mere casual mistake in 'grammar'.

Dwarfs etc. is of course the only recognized modern form of the plural; but the (inconsistent) correction of *elvish* has not even that excuse. The older and 'historical' form *elvish* is still recognized, and appears even in such popular dictionaries as the 'Pocket Oxford'. I suppose I should be grateful that Cox and Wyman[2] have not inflicted the change from *elven* to *elfin* and *further* to *farther* on me which Jarrolds[3] attempted, but Jarrolds were at least dealing with a MS. that had a good many casual errors in it. I believe there is only one error remaining in the text from which the Puffin was printed: *like* for *likes* (6th imp. p. 85 line 1; Puffin p. 76, line 23). This crept in in the 6th imp. I think. Not that Gollum would miss the chance of a sibilant! Puffin has not emended it. I suppose Gollum was regarded as 'without the law' and immune from the dictates of dictionaries or 'house-rules'. Not so the narrator.

Apart from this the errors appear to be few. I have noted: *waiting* is omitted before *for* (puffin p. 32/11). *ahead* appears as *head* (p. 87/5 from bottom). There is an inverted g in *examining* (p. 225/2 from bottom). And *oubht, bood* appear for *ought* and *good* on p. 228.

I am sorry to inflict such nigglings on you (I am a natural niggler, alas!) which will not seem to anyone else as important as they do to me; and nothing can be done about them now, anyway. Though *Penguin Books* might be informed that they have not passed unobserved. In fact I do not think that I should have signed a copy for Sir Allen Lane,[4] if I had observed them before. I feel inclined to tell him so, and offer to emend the copy in my own fair hand, if he will return it!

This is a Fell Winter indeed, and I am expecting White Wolves to cross the river. At present dead calm reigns, as the only car to appear in my road slid backwards downhill and disappeared. There is small chance of this reaching you tomorrow Jan. 1 to wish you a Happy New Year. I hope you have plenty of food in store! It is my birthday on Jan. 3rd, and I look like spending it in the isolation of a house turned igloo; but the companionship of several bottles of what has turned out a most excellent burgundy (since I helped to select it in its infancy) will no doubt mitigate that: Clos de Tart 1949, just at its top. With that hobbit-like note I will close, wishing you and your wife and children all blessings in 1962.

Yours ever,
Ronald Tolkien.

P.S. Will you please thank Miss M. J. Hill (and yourself) for the copy of *School Magazine* Nov. 1961 (N. S. Wales) containing the *Hobbit* extract and the article 'Something Special'. I thought the latter was well written for its purpose. . . . . But alas! faced with actual stories people are always more ready to believe in learning and arcane knowledge than in invention, especially if they are bemused by the title 'professor'. There are no songs or stories preserved about Elves or Dwarfs in ancient English, and little enough in any other Germanic language. Words, a few names, that is about all. I do not recall any Dwarf or Elf that plays an actual part in any story save Andvari in the Norse versions of the Nibelung matter. There is no story attached to the name Eikinskjaldi, save the one that I invented for Thorin Oakenshield. As far as old English goes 'dwarf' (*dweorg*) is a mere gloss for *nanus,* or the name of convulsions and recurrent fevers; and 'elf' we should suppose to be associated only with rheumatism, toothache and nightmares, if it were not for the occurrence of *ælfsciene* 'elven-fair' applied to Sarah and Judith!, and a few glosses such as *dryades, wuduelfen.* In all Old English poetry 'elves' (ylfe) occurs once only, in *Beowulf,* associated with trolls, giants, and the Undead, as the accursed offspring of Cain. The gap between that and, say, Elrond or Galadriel is not bridged by learning. Now you will feel this letter has become a pamphlet or a new year garland! But you have a w[aste] p[aper] b[asket] I suppose, at least as capacious as mine. JRRT.

237 From a letter to Rayner Unwin   12 April 1962

I have given every moment that I could spare to the 'poems', in spite of the usual obstacles, and some new ones.

I am afraid that I have lost all confidence in these things, and all judgement, and unless Pauline Baynes can be inspired by them, I cannot see them making a 'book'. I do not see why she should be inspired, though I fervently hope that she will be. Some of the things may be good in their way, and all of them privately amuse me; but elderly hobbits are easily pleased.

The various items – all that I now venture to offer, some with misgiving – do not really 'collect'. The only possible link is the fiction that they come from the Shire from about the period of *The Lord of the Rings*. But that fits some uneasily. I have done a good deal of work, trying to make them fit better: if not much to their good, I hope not to their serious detriment. You may note that I have written a new *Bombadil* poem, which I hope is adequate to go with the older one, though for its understanding it requires some knowledge of the *L.R.* At any rate it performs the service of further 'integrating' Tom with the world of the *L.R.* into which he was inserted.* I am afraid it largely tickles my pedantic fancy, because of its echo of the Norse Niblung matter (the otter's whisker);[1] and because one of the lines comes straight, incredible though that may seem, from *The Ancrene Wisse*.[2] ....

Some kind of foreword might possibly be required. The enclosed is not intended for that purpose! Though one or two of its points might be made more simply. But I found it easier, and more amusing (for myself) to represent to you in the form of a ridiculous editorial fiction what I have done to the verses, and what their references now are. Actually, although a fiction, the relative age, order of writing, and references of the items are pretty nearly represented as they really were.

I hope you are not greatly disappointed by my efforts.

238   From a letter to Jane Neave   18 July 1962

[Tolkien's aunt appears to have suggested that she return a cheque he had sent her, so that the money could be spent on buying a wheelchair for Tolkien's wife Edith, who was suffering from arthritis.]

As for your noble and self-sacrificing suggestion. Cash the cheque, please! And spend it. One cannot attach conditions to a gift; but I should be best pleased, if it was spent soon, and on *yourself*. It is a very small sum. Taken only from my present abundance, over and above the needs of Edith and myself, and of my children. Edith happily does not need a chair; and I could give her one if she did. (It is an astonishing situation, and I hope I am sufficiently grateful to God. Only a little while ago I was

*In the original poem he was said to wear a peacock's feather, which (I think you will agree) was entirely unsuitable to his situation in the *L.R.* In it his feather is merely reported as 'blue'. Its origin is now revealed.

wondering if we should be able to go on living here, on my inadequate pension. I have never been able to give before, and I have received unrepayable gifts in the past. . . . . I receive as a septuagenarian a retirement pension, of which I feel it proper to give away at least what the Tax collectors leave in my hands (a National one, I mean: I refused the University pension, and took the lump sum and invested it in a trust managed by my bank). All this, simply to assure you that the little gift was a personal pleasure, hardly worthy of much thanks; also to assure you that I can help more if needed. Saving universal catastrophe, I am not likely to be hard up again in my time. This is the advice of a very shrewd old publisher. Also I gather that he told Edmund Fuller[1] that my books were the most important, and also the most profitable thing that he had published in a long life, and that they would certainly remain so after his time and his sons' time. (This is just for you: it is unwise to advertise still more to boast of good fortune, as all Fairy-stories teach. So say nout. I do not want to wake up one morning and find it all a dream!) . . . .

I am glad to say that we are both rather better this year. . . . . I had some treatment last September, and have been more or less free and easy on the legs since, though my usual lumbago afflicted me in June. Edith is markedly better this year; and we managed a train journey to Bournemouth in July (2nd to 9th). Diet has done much good. We should have to reorganize life altogether if she was reduced to a chair! She does all the cooking, most of the housework, and some of the gardening. I am afraid that this often means rather heroic effort; but of course, within limits, that is beneficial. Still it is hard being attacked in two different ways at once – or three. Great increase in weight due to operations. Arthritis, which is made more painful and acute by the weight; and an internal complaint, small internal lesions (I gather), which cause pain, often incalculably, either by strain, or vibration, or by digestive irritations. Still we accepted this verdict more or less gratefully, after she had spent some time in a nursing home 'for observation' (ominous words).

We lost our 'help', because of ill health, that we had had for about eight years, last autumn. If ever you pray for temporal blessings for us, my dear, ask for the near-miracle of finding some help. Oxford is probably one of the hardest places even in this England, to find such a thing.

The book of poems is going along. Pauline Baynes has accepted the contract and is now beginning on the illustration. The publishers certainly intend it for Christmas. I have done my part.

At the moment I am engaged on putting into order, with notes and brief preface, my translation of *Sir Gawain* and of *Pearl*, before returning to my major work the *Silmarillion*. *The Pearl* is another poem in the same MS as *Sir Gawain*. Neither has any author's name attached; but I believe (as do most others) that they are by the same person. *The Pearl* is much the more difficult to translate, largely for metrical reasons; but being attracted by apparently insoluble metrical problems, I started to render it years ago. Some stanzas were actually broadcast, in the late 1920s.[2] I finished it, more or less, before the war; and it disappeared under the weight of the War, and of *The Lord of the Rings*. The poem is very well-known to mediævalists; but I never agreed to the view of scholars that the metrical form was almost impossibly difficult to write in, and quite impossible to render in modern English. NO scholars (or, nowadays, poets) have any experience in composing themselves in exacting metres. I made up a few stanzas in the metre to show that composition in it was not at any rate 'impossible' (though the result might today be thought bad).[3] The original *Pearl* was more difficult: a translator is not free, and this text is very hard in itself, often obscure, partly from the thought and style, and partly from the corruptions of the only surviving MS.

As these things interest you, I send you the original stanzas of my own – related inevitably as everything was at one time with my own mythology. I will send you a copy of the *Pearl*, as soon as I can get a carbon copy made. It has 101 twelve-line stanzas. It is (I think) evidently inspired by the loss in infancy of a little daughter. It is thus in a sense an elegy; but the author uses the then fashionable (it was contemporary with Chaucer) dream-framework, and uses the occasion to discuss his own theological views about salvation. Though not all acceptable to modern taste, it has moments of poignancy; and though it may in our view be absurdly complex in technical form, the poet surmounts his own obstacles on the whole with success. The stanzas have twelve lines, with only three rhymes: an octet of four couplets rhyming *a b*, and a quartet rhyming *b c*. In addition each line has internal alliteration (it occasionally but rarely fails in the original; the version is inevitably less rich). And if that is not enough, the poem is divided into fives. Within a five-stanza group the chief word of the last line must be echoed in the first line of the following stanza; the last line of the five-group is echoed at the beginning of the next; and the first line of all is to wind up echoed in the last line of all. But oddly enough there are not 100 stanzas, but 101. In group XV there are six stanzas. It has long been supposed that one of these was an uncancelled revision. But there are also 101 stanzas in *Sir Gawain*. The number was evidently aimed at, though what its significance was for the author has not been discovered. The grouping by fives also connects the poem with *Gawain*, where the poet elaborates the significance: the Five Wounds, the Five Joys, the Five virtues, and the Five wits.

Enough of that. I hope you are not bored. I enclose on a separate sheet the opening stanza in the original, and in my version, as a specimen.

239   From a letter to Allen & Unwin   20 July 1962

[With reference to the Spanish translation of *The Hobbit*.]

If *gnomos* is used as a translation of *dwarves*, then it must *not* appear on p. 63 in *the elves that are now called Gnomes*. I need not trouble the translator, or you, with the long explanation needed to account for this aberration; but the word was used as a translation of the real name, according to my mythology, of the High-elven people of the West. Pedantically, associating it with Greek *gnome* 'thought, intelligence'. But I have abandoned it, since it is quite impossible to dissociate the name from the popular associations of the Paracelsan *gnomus = pygmaeus*.[1] Since this word is used – for its aptness in preference to Sp[anish] *enano* I am not able to judge – for 'dwarves', regrettable confusion would be caused, if it is also applied to the High Elves. I earnestly suggest that on p. 63, lines 6–7, the translator should translate *old swords of the High Elves of the West*; and on p. 173, line 14, should delete (*or Gnomes*) altogether. I think these are the only places where *Gnomes* appears in *The Hobbit*.

240   To Mrs Pauline Gasch (Pauline Baynes)

[Pauline Baynes, who was illustrating *The Adventures of Tom Bombadil*, pointed out that the typescript of the title poem described Tom as wearing a peacock's feather in his hat, but the version in the galley-proofs had the reading 'a swan-wing feather'.]

1 August 1962   76 Sandfield Road, Headington, Oxford
Dear Mrs Gasch,

I am sorry that you have been bothered by this detail. There have been a number of minor changes made at various times in the process of assimilating Tom B. to the *Lord of the Rings* world.

The peacock's feather belongs to an old draft. Being unsuitable to the L.R. this becomes in the L.R. (I p. 130)[1] 'a long blue feather'. In the poems as now to be published Tom appears (in line 4 of the first poem) with a 'swan-wing feather': to increase the riverishness, and to allow for the incident in the second poem, the gift of a blue feather by the king's fisher. That incident also explains the blue feather of the L.R. Poem one is evidently, as said in the introduction, a hobbit-version of things long before the days of the L.R. But the second poem refers to the days of growing shadow, before Frodo set out (as the consultation with Maggot shows: cf. L.R. I p. 143).[2] When therefore Tom appears in the L.R. he is wearing a blue feather.

As far as you are concerned peacocks are out. A swan-feather in the first poem; and a blue one after the kingfisher incident.

Thank you for taking so much trouble. I may say that a number of changes were made in the drafts that were originally submitted to you. Only the galleys are reliable.

For instance, in the altercation with the kingfisher, I found that no variety likely to be in our parts of the world has a scarlet crest. (Scarlet *breasts* are more likely though ones I know are pinkish!) Also, more interesting, I found that the bird's name did not mean, as I had supposed, 'a King that fishes'. It was originally *the king's fisher*. That links the swan (traditionally the property of the King) with the fisher-bird; explains both their rivalry, and their special friendship with Tom: they were creatures who looked for the return of their rightful Lord, the true King.

Do not be put off by this sort of thing unless it affects the picture! The inwardly seen picture is to me the most important. I look forward to your interpretation. The donnish detail is just a private pleasure which I do not expect anyone to notice. (E.g. the hanging up of a kingfisher to see the way of the wind, which comes from Sir T. Browne;[3] the otter's whisker sticking out of the gold, from the Norse Nibelung legends;[4] and the three places for gossip, *smithy, mill, and cheaping* (market), from a mediæval instructive work that I have been editing!)[5] With very best wishes

Yours sincerely
Ronald Tolkien.

241 From a letter to Jane Neave   8-9 September 1962

[Tolkien's aunt, who was living in Wales, had been reading a proof copy of his lecture 'English and Welsh', delivered in 1955 and published in 1963 in the volume *Angles and Britons: O'Donnell Lectures.*]

I was so pleased to hear from you again. I was a bit afraid that I had overstepped the mark with that lecture: much of it rather dull except to dons. It is not really 'learned': my task was to thread together items of common (professional) knowledge in an attempt to interest English people. The only 'original' things in it, are the autobiographical bits, and the reference to 'beauty' in language; and the theory that one's 'native language' is not the same as one's 'cradle-tongue'.

319

I should not be surprised to hear that your postman did *not* know *bobi*: *caws bobi*. It seems not to be mentioned in modern dictionaries, and is probably obsolete. It means or meant 'toasted cheese', i.e. *Welsh rabbit*. *pobi* is the Welsh word for 'cook, roast, toast', and (if Andrew Boorde[1] got it right) it has changed p- to b- because *pobi* is used as an adjective, after a noun. London was for a while very Welsh-conscious at the time (as seen in Shakespeare), and bits of Welsh crop up in plays and tales. But the notion that Welsh was the 'language of heaven' was much older. Andrew B. was simply making fun of an often heard Welsh claim. I expect the postman will have heard of it. Postmen are on the whole a good tribe – especially the country ones who still walk. But Welsh postmen seem specially kind, and also learned. Sir John Morris Jones, a famous Welsh scholar (and author of the grammar that I bought with prize-money as related)[2] said, commenting on the work of a learned French scholar (Loth) on Welsh metres: 'I get more learning and sense on the topic out of my postman.'

Which did not mean, of course, that Loth was as ignorant as a mere postman 'passing the time of day'; but that the postman was better read and more learned than a French professor. It may have been true – in Welsh matters. For as a 'poor country' even yet Wales has not learnt to associate art or knowledge solely with certain classes. But the Welsh for all their virtues are contentious and often malicious; and they do not always whet their tongues against 'foreigners', they often turn the sharp edge upon their own kind (who do not readily forgive). All 'scholars' are apt to be quarrelsome, but Welsh scholarship and philology are a faction-fight. My reference on p. 3 to 'entering the litigious lists'[3] was not mere rhetoric, but a necessary disclaimer against belonging to any one of the factions.

It is said that Sir John M. J. built himself a fine house near Bangor overlooking the Menai Straits, to Môn (Anglesey). But the 'friendly' nickname for the inhabitants of that isle is (on the mainland) *moch* 'swine'. Some gentry from Beaumaris paid him a visit, and after admiring his house, asked if he was going to give it a name. 'Yes', said he, 'I shall call it *Gadara View*.' . . . .

I am now sending you 'Leaf by Niggle'. I have had a copy made specially to keep if you wish – from the *Dublin Review* in which it appeared nearly 20 years ago. It was written (I think) just before the War began, though I first read it aloud to my friends early in 1940. I recollect nothing about the writing, except that I woke one morning with it in my head, scribbled it down – and the printed form in the main hardly differs from the first hasty version at all. I find it still quite moving, when I reread it.

It is not really or properly an 'allegory' so much as 'mythical'. For

Niggle is meant to be a real mixed-quality *person* and not an 'allegory' of any single vice or virtue. The name Parish proved convenient, for the Porter's joke, but it was not given with any intention of special significance. I once knew of a gardener called *Parish*. (I see there are six *Parishes* in our telephone book.) Of course some elements are explicable in biographical terms (so obsessively interesting to modern critics that they often value a piece of 'literature' solely in so far as it reveals the author, and especially if that is in a discreditable light). There was a great tree – a huge poplar with vast limbs – visible through my window even as I lay in bed. I loved it, and was anxious about it. It had been savagely mutilated some years before, but had gallantly grown new limbs – though of course not with the unblemished grace of its former natural self; and now a foolish neighbour[4] was agitating to have it felled. Every tree has its enemy, few have an advocate. (Too often the hate is irrational, a fear of anything large and alive, and not easily tamed or destroyed, though it may clothe itself in pseudo-rational terms.) This fool* said that it cut off the sun from her house and garden, and that she feared for her house if it should crash in a high wind. It stood due *east* of her front door, across a wide road, at a distance nearly *thrice* its total height. Thus only about the equinox would it even cast a shadow in her direction, and only in the very early morning one that reached across the road to the pavement outside her front gate. And any wind that could have uprooted it and hurled it on her house, would have demolished her and her house without any assistance from the tree. I believe it still stands where it did. Though many winds have blown since.[5] (The great gale in which the dreadful winter of 46–47 ended (on March 17, 1947) blew down nearly all the mighty trees of the Broadwalk in Christchurch Meadows, and devastated Magdalen deer park – but it did not lose a bough.) Also, of course, I was anxious about my own internal Tree, *The Lord of the Rings*. It was growing out of hand, and revealing endless new vistas – and I wanted to finish it, but the world was threatening. And I was *dead stuck*, somewhere about Ch. 10 (*Voice of Saruman*) in Book III – with fragments ahead some of which eventually fitted into Ch. 1 and 3 of Book V, but most of which proved wrong especially about Mordor – and I did not know how to go on. It was not until Christopher was carried off to S. Africa that I forced myself to write Book IV, which was sent out to him bit by bit. That was 1944. (I did not finish the first rough writing till 1949, when I remember blotting the pages (which now represent the welcome of Frodo and Sam on the Field of Cormallen) with tears as I wrote. I then myself typed the *whole* of that work all VI books out, and then *once again* in revision (in places many times), mostly on my bed in the attic of the tiny terrace-house to which war had

*Only in this respect – hatred of trees. She was a great and gallant lady.

321

exiled us from the house in which my family had grown up.) But none of
that really illuminates 'Leaf by Niggle' much, does it? If it has any
virtues, they remain as such, whether you know all this or do not. I hope
you think it has some virtue. (But for quite different reasons, I think you
may like the personal details. That is because you are a dear, and take an
interest in other people, especially as rightly your kin.)

242 From a letter to Sir Stanley Unwin 28 November 1962

[*The Adventures of Tom Bombadil* was published on 22 November.]

I have so far seen two reviews of 'Tom Bombadil': *T. Litt. Suppl.* and
Listener:[1] I was agreeably surprised: I expected remarks far more snooty
and patronizing. Also I was rather pleased, since it seemed that the
reviewers had both started out not wanting to be amused, but had failed
to maintain their Victorian dignity intact.

Still, I remain puzzled, as before: wondering why if a 'professor'
shows any knowledge of his professional techniques it must be
'waggery', but if a writer shows, say, knowledge of law or law-courts it
is held interesting and creditable.

243 To Michael Tolkien

19 December 1962   76 Sandfield Road, Headington, Oxford
Dearest Mick,

A merry Christmas and God bless you all. I enclose for *you* a little
somewhat that may help, I hope. It is made possible by the unexpected
financial success of my verses (never mind the critics). Almost in 'the
red', I was, as being now practically 'self-employed' I usually have to
wait until May before 'A & U' fork out proceeds for the past year. But
they have made me an advance, since 'T. B.' sold nearly 8,000 copies
before publication (caught on the hop they have had to reprint hastily),
and that, even on a minute initial royalty, means more than is at all usual
for anyone but Betjeman to make on verse! ....

I am extremely weary after returning to term, amidst other labours (of
which *T.B.* for all its slenderness caused quite a lot of sweat). My
Ancrene Wisse also got between covers this week at last, but as it is only a
text (with textual footnotes) in extremely archaic M. English, I do not
think you would be amused by it. But when the translation of *Sir
Gawain* and *Pearl* appears (early next year, I hope) you shall have a
copy. Then ho! for *Númenor* and dark and difficult legends. I have also
been honoured by a 'Festschrift' – a volume of contributions by 22
'Anglists' with a prefatory ode by Auden for my 70th birthday. A plot

hatched and carried out by Rayner Unwin & Norman Davis (my successor) of which I knew nothing until a few weeks ago. . . . .

Well here comes Christmas! That astonishing thing that no 'commercialism' can in fact defile – unless you let it. I hope, my dearest, that it will bring you some rest and refreshment in every way, & I shall remember you in communion (as always but specially) and wish that I had all my family beside me in the ancient patriarchal way!

Your own
Father.

244 From a draft to a reader of *The Lord of the Rings*

[A fragment at the top of which Tolkien has written: 'Comments on a criticism (now lost?) concerning Faramir & Eowyn (c. 1963).']

Eowyn: It is possible to love more than one person (of the other sex) at the same time, but in a different mode and intensity. I do not think that Eowyn's feelings for Aragorn really changed much; and when he was revealed as so lofty a figure, in descent and office, she was able to go on *loving* and admiring him. He was *old*, and that is not only a physical quality: when not accompanied by any physical decay age can be alarming or awe-inspiring. Also she was *not* herself ambitious in the true political sense. Though not a 'dry nurse' in temper, she was also not really a soldier or 'amazon', but like many brave women was capable of great military gallantry at a crisis.

I think you misunderstand *Faramir*. He was daunted by his father: not only in the ordinary way of a family with a stern proud father of great force of character, but as a Númenórean before the chief of the one surviving Númenórean state. He was motherless and sisterless (*Eowyn* was also motherless), and had a 'bossy' brother. He had been accustomed to giving way and not giving his own opinions air, while retaining a power of command among men, such as a man may obtain who is evidently personally courageous and decisive, but also modest, fair-minded and scrupulously just, and very merciful. I think he understood Eowyn very well. Also to be Prince of Ithilien, the greatest noble after Dol Amroth in the revived Númenórean state of Gondor, soon to be of imperial power and prestige, was not a 'market-garden job' as you term it. Until much had been done by the restored King, the P. of Ithilien would be the resident march-warden of Gondor, in its main eastward outpost – and also would have many duties in rehabilitating the lost territory, and clearing it of outlaws and orc-remnants, not to speak of the dreadful vale of Minas Ithil (Morgul). I did not, naturally, go into details about the way in which Aragorn, as King of Gondor, would govern the realm. But it was made clear that there was much fighting, and in the earlier years of A.'s reign expeditions against enemies in the East. The chief commanders, under the King, would be Faramir and Imrahil; and one of these would normally remain a military commander at home in the King's absence. A Númenórean King was *monarch*, with the power of unquestioned decision in debate; but he governed the realm with the frame of ancient law, of which he was administrator (and interpreter) but not the maker. In all debatable matters of importance domestic, or external, however, even Denethor had a Council, and at least listened to what the Lords of the Fiefs and the Captains of the Forces had to say. Aragorn re-established the Great Council of Gondor, and in that Faramir, who remained* by inheritance the *Steward* (or representative of the King during his absence abroad, or sickness, or between his death and the accession of his heir) would [be] the chief counsellor.

Criticism of the speed of the relationship or 'love' of Faramir and Eowyn. In my experience feelings and decisions ripen very quickly (as measured by mere 'clock-time', which is actually not justly applicable) in periods of great stress, and especially under the expectation of imminent death. And I do *not* think that persons of high estate and breeding need all the petty fencing and approaches in matters of 'love'. This tale does not deal with a period of 'Courtly Love' and its pretences; but with a culture more primitive (sc. less corrupt) and nobler.

245   To Rhona Beare

[Answers to the following questions: (1) In the 'English runes' used for Anglo-Saxon inscriptions, the rune ᚷ does not stand for G as it does in *The Lord of the Rings*. Why not? (2) What happened to Elves when they died in battle?]

25 June 1963   76 Sandfield Road, Headington, Oxford
Dear Miss Beare,

The 'cirth' or runes in the 'L.R.' were invented for that story and, within it, have no supposed historical connexion with the Germanic Runic alphabet, to which the English gave its most elaborate development. There is thus nothing to be surprised at if similar signs have different values. The similarity of shapes is inevitable in alphabets devised primarily for cut[ting] or scratching on wood and so made of lines directly or diagonally across the grain. The signs used in the *cirth* are nearly [all] to be extracted from the basic pattern, ᚼ, the possibilities being *decreased* by the avoidance of the juncture of a diagonal with the

*See III p. 245.[1]

324

bottom of an upright (the exceptions are few and limited to cases where as in ß Ⴑ there is also juncture at the top). They are *increased* by the repetition on the opposite side of an upright of any diagonal appendage, & by repeating half the basic pattern: ꝑ hence ↑ ꝗ ⴘ ⴗ etc.

As for the Elves. Even in these legends we see the Elves mainly through the eyes of Men. It is in any case clear that neither side was fully informed about the ultimate destiny of the other. The Elves were sufficiently longeval to be called by Man 'immortal'. But they were not unageing or unwearying. Their own tradition was that they were confined to the limits of this world (in space and time), even if they died, and would continue in some form to exist in it until 'the end of the world'. But what 'the end of the world' portended for it or for themselves they did not know (though they no doubt had theories). Neither had they of course any special information concerning what 'death' portended for Men. They believed that it meant 'liberation from the circles of the world', and was in that respect to them enviable. And they would point out to Men who envied them that a dread of ultimate loss, though it may be indefinitely remote, is not necessarily the easier to bear if it is in the end ineluctably certain: a burden may become heavier the longer it is borne.

I hope you will forgive pencil and a crabbed and not too legible hand. I am (temporarily, I hope) deprived of the use of my right hand and arm, and I am in the early stages of teaching my left hand. Right-handed pens increase the crabbedness, but a pencil accommodates itself.

Yours sincerely
J. R. R. Tolkien.

246   From a letter to Mrs Eileen Elgar (drafts)   September 1963

[A reply to a reader's comments on Frodo's failure to surrender the Ring in the Cracks of Doom.]

Very few (indeed so far as letters go only you and one other) have observed or commented on Frodo's 'failure'. It is a very important point.

From the point of view of the storyteller the events on Mt Doom proceed simply from the logic of the tale up to that time. They were not deliberately worked up to nor foreseen until they occurred.* But, for one thing, it became at last quite clear that Frodo after all that had happened would be incapable of voluntarily destroying the Ring. Reflecting on the solution after it was arrived at (as a mere event) I feel

*Actually, since the events at the Cracks of Doom would obviously be vital to the Tale, I made several sketches or trial versions at various stages in the narrative – but none of them were used, and none of them much resembled what is actually reported in the finished story.

that it is central to the whole 'theory' of true nobility and heroism that is presented.

Frodo indeed 'failed' as a hero, as conceived by simple minds: he did not endure to the end; he gave in, ratted. I do not say 'simple minds' with contempt: they often see with clarity the simple truth and the absolute ideal to which effort must be directed, even if it is unattainable. Their weakness, however, is twofold. They do not perceive the complexity of any given situation in Time, in which an absolute ideal is enmeshed. They tend to forget that strange element in the World that we call Pity or Mercy, which is also an absolute requirement in moral judgement (since it is present in the Divine nature). In its highest exercise it belongs to God. For finite judges of imperfect knowledge it must lead to the use of two different scales of 'morality'. To ourselves we must present the absolute ideal without compromise, for we do not know our own limits of natural strength (+grace), and if we do not aim at the highest we shall certainly fall short of the utmost that we could achieve. To others, in any case of which we know enough to make a judgement, we must apply a scale tempered by 'mercy': that is, since we can with good will do this without the bias inevitable in judgements of ourselves, we must estimate the limits of another's strength and weigh this against the force of particular circumstances.*

I do not think that Frodo's was a *moral* failure. At the last moment the pressure of the Ring would reach its maximum – impossible, I should have said, for any one to resist, certainly after long possession, months of increasing torment, and when starved and exhausted. Frodo had done what he could and spent himself completely (as an instrument of Providence) and had produced a situation in which the object of his quest could be achieved. His humility (with which he began) and his sufferings were justly rewarded by the highest honour; and his exercise of patience and mercy towards Gollum gained him Mercy: his failure was redressed.

We are finite creatures with absolute limitations upon the powers of our soul-body structure in either action or endurance. *Moral* failure can only be asserted, I think, when a man's effort or endurance falls *short* of his limits, and the blame decreases as that limit is closer approached.†

*We frequently see this double scale used by the saints in their judgements upon themselves when suffering great hardships or temptations, and upon others in like trials.

†No account is here taken of 'grace' or the enhancement of our powers as instruments of Providence. Frodo was given 'grace': first to answer the call (at the end of the Council) after long resisting a complete surrender; and later in his resistance to the temptation of the Ring (at times when to claim and so reveal it would have been fatal), and in his endurance of fear and suffering. But grace is not infinite, and for the most part seems in the Divine economy limited to what is sufficient for the accomplishment of the task appointed to one instrument in a pattern of circumstances and other instruments.

Nonetheless, I think it can be observed in history and experience that some individuals seem to be placed in 'sacrificial' positions: situations or tasks that for perfection of solution demand powers beyond their utmost limits, even beyond all possible limits for an incarnate creature in a physical world – in which a body may be destroyed, or so maimed that it affects the mind and will. Judgement upon any such case should then depend on the motives and disposition with which he started out, and should weigh his actions against the utmost possibility of his powers, all along the road to whatever proved the breaking-point.

Frodo undertook his quest out of love – to save the world he knew from disaster at his own expense, if he could; and also in complete humility, acknowledging that he was wholly inadequate to the task. His real contract was only to do what he could, to try to find a way, and to go as far on the road as his strength of mind and body allowed. He did that. I do not myself see that the breaking of his mind and will under demonic pressure after torment was any more a *moral* failure than the breaking of his body would have been – say, by being strangled by Gollum, or crushed by a falling rock.

That appears to have been the judgement of Gandalf and Aragorn and of all who learned the full story of his journey. Certainly nothing would be concealed by Frodo! But what Frodo himself felt about the events is quite another matter.

He appears at first to have had no sense of guilt (III 224–5);[1] he was restored to *sanity* and peace. But then he thought that he had given his life in sacrifice: he expected to die very soon. But he did not, and one can observe the disquiet growing in him. Arwen was the first to observe the signs, and gave him her jewel for comfort, and thought of a way of healing him.* Slowly he fades 'out of the picture', saying and doing less and less. I think it is clear on reflection to an attentive reader that when his dark times came upon him and he was conscious of being 'wounded

---

*It is not made explicit how she could arrange this. She could not of course just transfer her ticket on the boat like that! For any except those of Elvish race 'sailing West' was not permitted, and any exception required 'authority', and she was not in direct communication with the Valar, especially not since her choice to become 'mortal'. What is meant is that it was Arwen who first thought of sending Frodo into the West, and put in a plea for him to Gandalf (direct or through Galadriel, or both), and she used her own renunciation of the right to go West as an argument. Her renunciation and suffering were related to and enmeshed with Frodo's: both were parts of a plan for the regeneration of the state of Men. Her prayer might therefore be specially effective, and her plan have a certain equity of exchange. No doubt it was Gandalf who was the authority that accepted her plea. The Appendices show clearly that he was an emissary of the Valar, and virtually their plenipotentiary in accomplishing the plan against Sauron. He was also in special accord with Cirdan the Ship-master, who had surrendered to him his ring and so placed himself under Gandalf's command. Since Gandalf himself went on the Ship there would be so to speak no trouble either at embarking or at the landing.

by knife sting and tooth and a long burden' (III 268) it was not only nightmare memories of past horrors that afflicted him, but also unreasoning self-reproach: he saw himself and all that he done as a broken failure. 'Though I may come to the Shire, it will not seem the same, for I shall not be the same.' That was actually a temptation out of the Dark, a last flicker of pride: desire to have returned as a 'hero', not content with being a mere instrument of good. And it was mixed with another temptation, blacker and yet (in a sense) more merited, for however that may be explained, he had not in fact cast away the Ring by a voluntary act: he was tempted to regret its destruction, and still to desire it. 'It is gone for ever, and now all is dark and empty', he said as he wakened from his sickness in 1420.

'Alas! there are some wounds that cannot be wholly cured', said Gandalf (III 268) – not in Middle-earth. Frodo was sent or allowed to pass over Sea to heal him – if that could be done, *before he died*. He would have eventually to 'pass away': no mortal could, or can, abide for ever on earth, or within Time. So he went both to a purgatory and to a reward, for a while: a period of reflection and peace and a gaining of a truer understanding of his position in littleness and in greatness, spent still in Time amid the natural beauty of 'Arda Unmarred', the Earth unspoiled by evil.

Bilbo went too. No doubt as a completion of the plan due to Gandalf himself. Gandalf had a very great affection for Bilbo, from the hobbit's childhood onwards. His companionship was really necessary for Frodo's sake – it is difficult to imagine a hobbit, even one who had been through Frodo's experiences, being really happy even in an earthly paradise without a companion of his own kind, and Bilbo was the person that Frodo most loved. (Cf III 252 lines 12 to 21 and 263 lines 1–2.)[2] But he also needed and deserved the favour on his own account. He bore still the mark of the Ring that needed to be finally erased: a trace of pride and personal possessiveness. Of course he was old and confused in mind, but it was still a revelation of the 'black mark' when he said in Rivendell (III 265) 'What's become of *my* ring, Frodo, that you took away?'; and when he was reminded of what had happened, his immediate reply was: 'What a pity! I should have liked to see it again'. As for reward for his part, it is difficult to feel that his life would be complete without an experience of 'pure Elvishness', and the opportunity of hearing the legends and histories in full the fragments of which had so delighted him.

It is clear, of course, that the plan had actually been made and concerted (by Arwen, Gandalf and others) before Arwen spoke. But Frodo did not immediately take it in; the implications would slowly be understood on reflection. Such a journey would at first seem something not necessarily to be feared, even as something to look forward to – so long as undated and postponable. His real desire was hobbitlike (and humanlike) just 'to be himself' again and get back to the old familiar life that had been interrupted. Already on the journey back from Rivendell he suddenly saw that was not for him possible. Hence his cry 'Where shall I find rest?' He knew the answer, and Gandalf did not reply. As for Bilbo, it is probable that Frodo did not at first understand what Arwen meant by 'he will not again make any long journey save one'. At any rate he did not associate it with his own case. When Arwen spoke (in TA 3019) he was still young, not yet 51, and Bilbo 78 years older. But at Rivendell he came to understand things more clearly. The conversations he had there are not reported, but enough is revealed in Elrond's farewell III 267.³ From the onset of the first sickness (Oct. 5, 3019) Frodo must have been thinking about 'sailing', though still resisting a final decision – to go with Bilbo, or to go at all. It was no doubt after his grievous illness in March 3020 that his mind was made up.

Sam is meant to be lovable and laughable. Some readers he irritates and even infuriates. I can well understand it. All hobbits at times affect me in the same way, though I remain very fond of them. But Sam can be very 'trying'. He is a more representative hobbit than any others that we have to see much of; and he has consequently a stronger ingredient of that quality which even some hobbits found at times hard to bear: a vulgarity – by which I do not mean a mere 'down-to-earthiness' – a mental myopia which is proud of itself, a smugness (in varying degrees) and cocksureness, and a readiness to measure and sum up all things from a limited experience, largely enshrined in sententious traditional 'wisdom'. We only meet exceptional hobbits in close companionship – those who had a grace or gift: a vision of beauty, and a reverence for things nobler than themselves, at war with their rustic self-satisfaction. Imagine Sam without his education by Bilbo and his fascination with things Elvish! Not difficult. The Cotton family and the Gaffer, when the 'Travellers' return are a sufficient glimpse.

Sam was cocksure, and deep down a little conceited; but his conceit had been transformed by his devotion to Frodo. He did not think of himself as heroic or even brave, or in any way admirable – except in his service and loyalty to his master. That had an ingredient (probably inevitable) of pride and possessiveness: it is difficult to exclude it from the devotion of those who perform such service. In any case it prevented him from fully understanding the master that he loved, and from following him in his gradual education to the nobility of service to the unlovable and of perception of damaged good in the corrupt. He plainly did not fully understand Frodo's motives or his distress in the incident of the Forbidden Pool. If he had understood better what was going on between Frodo and Gollum, things might have turned out differently in the end. For me perhaps the most tragic moment in the Tale comes in II 323 ff. when Sam fails to note the complete change in Gollum's tone and aspect. 'Nothing, nothing', said Gollum softly. 'Nice master!'. His repentance is blighted and all Frodo's pity is (in a sense*) wasted. Shelob's lair became inevitable.

This is due of course to the 'logic of the story'. Sam could hardly have acted differently. (He did reach the point of pity at last (III 221–222)[4] but for the good of Gollum too late.) If he had, what could then have happened? The course of the entry into Mordor and the struggle to reach Mount Doom would have been different, and so would the ending. The interest would have shifted to Gollum, I think, and the battle that would have gone on between his repentance and his new love on one side and the Ring. Though the love would have been strengthened daily it could not have wrested the mastery from the Ring. I think that in some queer twisted and pitiable way Gollum would have tried (not maybe with conscious design) to satisfy both. Certainly at some point not long before the end he would have stolen the Ring or taken it by violence (as he does in the actual Tale). But 'possession' satisfied, I think he would then have sacrificed himself for Frodo's sake and have *voluntarily* cast himself into the fiery abyss.

I think that an effect of his partial regeneration by love would have been a clearer vision when he claimed the Ring. He would have perceived the evil of Sauron, and suddenly realized that he could not use the Ring and had not the strength or stature to keep it in Sauron's despite: the only way to keep it and hurt Sauron was to destroy it and himself together – and in a flash he may have seen that this would also be the greatest service to Frodo. Frodo in the tale actually takes the Ring and claims it, and certainly he too would have had a clear vision – but he was not given any time: he was immediately attacked by Gollum. When Sauron was aware of the seizure of the Ring his one hope was in its power: that the claimant would be unable to relinquish it until Sauron had time to deal with him. Frodo too would then probably, if not attacked, have had to take the same way: cast himself with the Ring into the abyss. If not he would of course have completely failed. It is an interesting problem: how Sauron would have acted or the claimant have resisted. Sauron sent at once the Ringwraiths. They were naturally fully instructed, and in no way deceived as to the real lordship of the Ring. The wearer would not be invisible to them, but the reverse; and the

*In the sense that 'pity' to be a true virtue must be directed to the good of its object. It is empty if it is exercised *only* to keep oneself 'clean', free from hate or the actual doing of injustice, though this is also a good motive.

more vulnerable to their weapons. But the situation was now different to that under Weathertop, where Frodo acted merely in fear and wished only to use (in vain) the Ring's subsidiary power of conferring invisibility. He had grown since then. Would they have been immune from its power if he claimed it as an instrument of command and domination?

Not wholly. I do not think they could have attacked him with violence, nor laid hold upon him or taken him captive; they would have obeyed or feigned to obey any minor commands of his that did not interfere with their errand – laid upon them by Sauron, who still through their nine rings (which he held) had primary control of their wills. That errand was to remove Frodo from the Crack. Once he lost the power or opportunity to *destroy* the Ring, the end could not be in doubt – saving help from outside, which was hardly even remotely possible.

Frodo had become a considerable person, but of a special kind: in spiritual enlargement rather than in increase of physical or mental power; his will was much stronger than it had been, but so far it had been exercised in resisting not using the Ring and with the object of destroying it. He needed time, much time, before he could control the Ring or (which in such a case is the same) before it could control him; before his will and arrogance could grow to a stature in which he could dominate other major hostile wills. Even so for a long time his acts and commands would still have to seem 'good' to him, to be for the benefit of others beside himself.

The situation as between Frodo with the Ring and the Eight* might be compared to that of a small brave man armed with a devastating weapon, faced by eight savage warriors of great strength and agility armed with poisoned blades. The man's weakness was that he did not know how to use his weapon yet; and he was by temperament and training averse to violence. Their weakness that the man's weapon was a thing that filled them with fear as an object of terror in their religious cult, by which they had been conditioned to treat one who wielded it with servility. I think they would have shown 'servility'. They would have greeted Frodo as 'Lord'. With fair speeches they would have induced him to leave the Sammath Naur – for instance 'to look upon his new kingdom, and behold afar with his new sight the abode of power that he must now claim and turn to his own purposes'. Once outside the chamber while he was gazing some of them would have destroyed the entrance. Frodo would by then probably have been already too enmeshed in great plans of reformed rule – like but far greater and wider than the vision that tempted Sam (III 177)[5] – to heed this. But if he still preserved some sanity and partly understood the significance of it, so that he refused

*The Witch-king had been reduced to impotence.

331

now to go with them to Barad-dûr, they would simply have waited. Until Sauron himself came. In any case a confrontation of Frodo and Sauron would soon have taken place, if the Ring was intact. Its result was inevitable. Frodo would have been utterly overthrown: crushed to dust, or preserved in torment as a gibbering slave. Sauron would not have feared the Ring! It was his own and under his will. Even from afar he had an effect upon it, to make it work for its return to himself. In his actual presence none but very few of equal stature could have hoped to withhold it from him. Of 'mortals' no one, not even Aragorn. In the contest with the Palantír Aragorn was the rightful owner. Also the contest took place at a distance, and in a tale which allows the incarnation of great spirits in a physical and destructible form their power must be far greater when actually physically present. Sauron should be thought of as very terrible. The form that he took was that of a man of more than human stature, but not gigantic. In his earlier incarnation he was able to veil his power (as Gandalf did) and could appear as a commanding figure of great strength of body and supremely royal demeanour and countenance.

Of the others only Gandalf might be expected to master him – being an emissary of the Powers and a creature of the same order, an immortal spirit taking a visible physical form. In the 'Mirror of Galadriel', I 381, it appears that Galadriel conceived of herself as capable of wielding the Ring and supplanting the Dark Lord. If so, so also were the other guardians of the Three, especially Elrond. But this is another matter. It was part of the essential deceit of the Ring to fill minds with imaginations of supreme power. But this the Great had well considered and had rejected, as is seen in Elrond's words at the Council. Galadriel's rejection of the temptation was founded upon previous thought and resolve. In any case Elrond or Galadriel would have proceeded in the policy now adopted by Sauron: they would have built up an empire with great and absolutely subservient generals and armies and engines of war, until they could challenge Sauron and destroy him by force. Confrontation of Sauron alone, unaided, self to self was not contemplated. One can imagine the scene in which Gandalf, say, was placed in such a position. It would be a delicate balance. On one side the true allegiance of the Ring to Sauron; on the other superior strength because Sauron was not actually in possession, and perhaps also because he was weakened by long corruption and expenditure of will in dominating inferiors. If Gandalf proved the victor, the result would have been for Sauron the same as the destruction of the Ring; for him it would have been destroyed, taken from him for ever. But the Ring and all its works would have endured. It would have been the master in the end.

Gandalf as Ring-Lord would have been far worse than Sauron. He would have remained 'righteous', but self-righteous. He would have continued to rule and order things for 'good', and the benefit of his subjects according to his wisdom (which was and would have remained great).

[The draft ends here. In the margin Tolkien wrote: 'Thus while Sauron multiplied [illegible word] evil, he left "good" clearly distinguishable from it. Gandalf would have made good detestable and seem evil.']

247 To Colonel Worskett

[A letter to a reader of The Lord of the Rings.]

20 September 1963   76 Sandfield Road, Headington, Oxford

Dear Colonel Worskett,

Thank you very much for your charming and encouraging letter. It gave me great pleasure. . . . .

I could indeed give you another volume (or many) about the same imaginary world. I am in fact under contract to do so. But I have been held up for some years now, by close and heavy work on professional tasks neglected while seeing The Lord of the Rings into print. That will be over, for the present, when my translation of Sir Gawain and the Green Knight goes to press: soon, I hope. Then I shall return to the task of putting in order all or some of the legends of the earlier ages, referred to in the Appendices (esp. A i.). . . . .

I am afraid all the same that the presentation will need a lot of work, and I work so slowly. The legends have to be worked over (they were written at different times, some many years ago) and made consistent; and they have to be integrated with The L.R.; and they have to be given some progressive shape. No simple device, like a journey and a quest, is available.

I am doubtful myself about the undertaking. Part of the attraction of The L.R. is, I think, due to the glimpses of a large history in the background: an attraction like that of viewing far off an unvisited island, or seeing the towers of a distant city gleaming in a sunlit mist. To go there is to destroy the magic, unless new unattainable vistas are again revealed. Also many of the older legends are purely 'mythological', and nearly all are grim and tragic: a long account of the disasters that destroyed the beauty of the Ancient World, from the darkening of Valinor to the Downfall of Númenor and the flight of Elendil. And there are no hobbits. Nor does Gandalf appear, except in a passing mention; for his time of importance did not begin until the Third Age. The only major characters of the L.R. who appear are Galadriel & Elrond.

There are, of course, quite a lot of links between *The Hobbit* and The L.R. that are not clearly set out. They were mostly written or sketched out, but cut out to lighten the boat: such as Gandalf's exploratory journeys, his relations with Aragorn and Gondor; all the movements of Gollum, until he took refuge in Moria, and so on. I actually wrote in full an account of what really happened before Gandalf's visit to Bilbo and the subsequent 'Unexpected Party', as seen by Gandalf himself. It was to have come in during a looking-back conversation in Minas Tirith; but it had to go, and is only represented in brief in App. A pp. 358 to 360, though the difficulties that Gandalf had with Thorin are omitted. [1]

There are or were no Ents in the older stories – because the Ents in fact only presented themselves to my sight, without premeditation or any previous conscious knowledge, when I came to Chapter IV of Book Three. But since Treebeard shows knowledge of the drowned land of Beleriand (west of the Mountains of Lune) in which the main action of the war against Morgoth took place*, they will have to come in. But as the War in Beleriand was at the time of the hobbits' meeting some 7,000 years ago, no doubt they were not quite the same: less wise, less strong, shyer and more uncommunicable (their own language simpler, but their knowledge of other tongues very small). But I can foresee one action that they took, not without a bearing on The L.R. It was in Ossiriand, a forest country, secret and mysterious before the west feet of the Ered Luin, that Beren and Lúthien dwelt for a while after Beren's return from the Dead (I p. 206). Beren did not show himself among mortals again, except once. He intercepted a dwarf-army that had descended from the mountains, sacked the realm of Doriath and slain King Thingol, Lúthien's father, carrying off a great booty, including Thingol's necklace upon which hung the Silmaril. There was a battle about a ford across one of the Seven Rivers of Ossir, and the Silmaril was recovered, and so came down to Dior Beren's son, and to Elwing Dior's daughter and Earendel her husband (father of Elros and Elrond). It seems clear that Beren, who had no army, received the aid of the Ents – and that would not make for love between Ents and Dwarves.

Forgive me for running on! Also forgive the use of a typewriter. I have been, and still am suffering from rheumatism in the right arm, which seems to object much less to typing than to writing. Thank you again for your letter.

[The draft ends here. At the top, Tolkien has written, not very legibly, a note in pencil:]

---

*Tasarinan, Ossiriand, Neldoreth, Dorthonion were all regions of Beleriand, famous in tales of the War.

No one knew whence they (Ents) came or first appeared. The High Elves said that the Valar did not mention them in the 'Music'. But some (Galadriel) were [of the] opinion that when Yavanna discovered the mercy of Eru to Aulë in the matter of the Dwarves, she besought Eru (through Manwë) asking him to give life to things made of living things not stone, and that the Ents were either souls sent to inhabit trees, or else that slowly took the likeness of trees owing to their inborn love of trees. (Not all were good [words illegible]) The Ents thus had mastery *over stone*. The males were devoted to Oromë, but the Wives to Yavanna.

248 To Sir Stanley Unwin

[Allen & Unwin were to publish a paperback consisting of Tolkien's lecture 'On Fairy-stories' and his short story 'Leaf by Niggle'.]

5 October 1963   76 Sandfield Road, Headington, Oxford
Dear Sir Stanley,
          On Fairy-stories; Leaf by Niggle.
    In Rayner's absence I venture to send you the items required from me for the paper-back just for a glance, perhaps, before they go forward. I should like to have your approval (or censure) especially of the Introductory Note. . . . .
    While I was composing the note it occurred to me that it might be suitable to have a common title, such as I have suggested: *Tree and Leaf*, with reference to the passage at the top of page 73 in the Essay,[1] and to the key-word *effoliation* at the end, p. 84.[2] But this is probably an unnecessary emphasis of what I have said in the note.
    I am afraid that I am falling more and more behind with things that I should do; but it has not been a good year. It was not until the end of August that I got relief from the trouble with my shoulder and right arm. I found not being able to use a pen or pencil as defeating as the loss of her beak would be to a hen.
    With very best wishes,
                    Yours sincerely
                    Ronald Tolkien.

249 From a letter to Michael George Tolkien   16 October 1963

[Written by Tolkien to his grandson from the Hotel Miramar in Bournemouth.]

I have had three rather exhausting experiences since Monday. On Monday I visited an 'admirer' who wrote to me & proved to be living nearly next door to this hotel. But she also proved to be stone-deaf (inoperable & incurable), though highly intelligent & well-read. (Name Elgar, husband distantly related to Edward E.) Conversation by writing pad is defeating. Yesterday in the middle of lunch I had to rescue an old lady (staying with us) who was choking with a whiting-bone, and get her to a doctor. Then in the afternoon entertain another deaf old lady! Almost the last of the children of the great Sir James Augustus Henry Murray of the Dictionary.[1] (His *living* descendants are now more than 100.) She is on mother's side a *Ruthven* and has been researching for years into the Gowrie conspiracy. As my knowledge of Scottish History is v. small I find it difficult to follow who murdered whom, or why – the general trend of Scots history. I hope you can read this! I cannot write decently *without* a proper table or *with* a ball-point.

250 To Michael Tolkien

1 November 1963   76 Sandfield Road, Headington, Oxford
Dearest M.

Thank you for writing – also at length! I do not think you have inherited a dislike of letter-writing from me, but the inability to write briefly. Which inevitably means seldom in your life (and in mine). I think we both like writing letters *ad familiares*; but are obliged to write so much in the way of 'business', that time and energy fail.

I am very sorry that you feel depressed. I hope this is partly due to your ailment. But I am afraid it is mainly an occupational affliction, and also an almost universal human malady (in any occupation) attaching to your age. . . . . I remember clearly enough when I was your age (in 1935). I had returned 10 years before (still dewy-eyed with boyish illusions) to Oxford, and now disliked undergraduates and all their ways, and had begun really to know dons. Years before I had rejected as disgusting cynicism by an old vulgarian the words of warning given me by old Joseph Wright. 'What do you take Oxford for, lad?' 'A university, a place of learning.' 'Nay, lad, it's a factory! And what's it making? I'll tell you. It's making *fees*. Get that in your head, and you'll begin to understand what goes on.'

Alas! by 1935 I now knew that it was perfectly true. At any rate as a key to dons' behaviour. Quite true, but not the whole truth. (The greater part of the truth is always hidden, in regions out of the reach of cynicism.) I was stonewalled and hindered in my efforts (as a schedule B professor on a reduced salary, though with schedule A duties) for the good of my subject and the reform of its teaching, by vested interests in *fees* and fellowships. But at least I did not suffer as you have: I was never obliged to teach anything except what I loved (and do) with an inextinguishable enthusiasm. (Save only for a brief time after my change of Chair in 1945 – that was awful.)

The devotion to 'learning', as such and without reference to one's own repute, is a high and even in a sense spiritual vocation; and since it is 'high' it is inevitably lowered by false brethren, by tired brethren, by the desire of money*, and by pride: the folk who say 'my subject' & do not mean the one I am humbly engaged in, but the subject I adorn, or have 'made my own'. Certainly this devotion is generally degraded and smirched in universities. But it *is still* there. And if you shut them down in disgust, it would perish from the land – until they were re-established, again to fall into corruption in due course. The far higher devotion to religion cannot possibly escape the same process. It is, of course, degraded in some degree by all 'professionals' (and by *all* professing Christians), and by some in different times and places outraged; and since the aim is higher the shortcoming seems (and is) far worse. But you cannot maintain a tradition of learning or true science without schools and universities, and that means schoolmasters and dons. And you cannot maintain a religion without a church and ministers; and that means professionals: priests and bishops – and also monks.† The precious wine must (in this world) have a bottle,‡ or some less worthy substitute. For myself, I find I become less cynical rather than more – remembering my own sins and follies; and realize that men's hearts are not often as bad as their acts, and very seldom as bad as their words. (Especially in our age, which is one of sneer and cynicism. We are freer from hypocrisy, since it does not 'do' to profess holiness or utter high sentiments; but it is one of inverted hypocrisy like the widely current inverted snobbery: men profess to be worse than they are.) . . . .

You speak of 'sagging faith', however. That is quite another matter. In the last resort faith is an act of will, inspired by love. Our love may be chilled and our will eroded by the spectacle of the shortcomings, folly, and even sins of the Church and its ministers, but I do not think that one who has once had faith goes back over the line for these reasons (least of all anyone with any historical knowledge). 'Scandal' at most is an occasion of temptation – as indecency is to lust, which it does not make but arouses. It is convenient because it tends to turn our eyes away from

*Or even the legitimate *need* of money.

†At least they were certainly *once* necessary. And if we are pained or at times scandalized by those we see close to, I think we should remember the enormous debt we owe to the Benedictines, and also remember that (like the Church) they have always been in a state of succumbing to mammon and the world, and never finally overwhelmed. The inner fire has never been extinguished.

‡The unseemly cobwebs & dust, and the stained label, are not always signs of impaired contents, for those who can draw old corks.

ourselves and our own faults to find a scape-goat. But the act of will of faith is not a single moment of final decision: it is a permanent indefinitely repeated act > state which must go on – so we pray for 'final persever-ance'. The temptation to 'unbelief' (which really means rejection of Our Lord and His claims) is always there within us. Part of us longs to find an excuse for it outside us. The stronger the inner temptation the more readily and severely shall we be 'scandalized' by others. I think I am as sensitive as you (or any other Christian) to the 'scandals', both of clergy and laity. I have suffered grievously in my life from stupid, tired, dimmed, and even bad priests; but I now know enough about myself to be aware that I should not leave the Church (which for me would mean leaving the allegiance of Our Lord) for any such reasons: I should leave because I did not believe, and should not believe any more, even if I had never met any one in orders who was not both wise and saintly. I should deny the Blessed Sacrament, that is: call Our Lord a fraud to His face.

If He is a fraud and the Gospels fraudulent – that is: garbled accounts of a demented megalomaniac (which is the only alternative), then of course the spectacle exhibited by the Church (in the sense of clergy) in history and today is simply evidence of a gigantic fraud. If not, however, then this spectacle is alas! only what was to be expected: it began before the first Easter, and it does not affect *faith* at all – except that we may and should be deeply grieved. *But* we should grieve on our Lord's behalf and for Him, associating ourselves with the scandalizers not with the saints, not crying out that we cannot 'take' Judas Iscariot, or even the absurd & cowardly Simon Peter, or the silly women like James' mother, trying to push her sons.

It takes a fantastic will to unbelief to suppose that Jesus never really 'happened', and more to suppose that he did not say the things recorded of him – so incapable of being 'invented' by anyone in the world at that time: such as 'before Abraham came to be *I am*' (John viii). 'He that hath seen me hath seen the Father' (John ix); or the promulgation of the Blessed Sacrament in John v: 'He that eateth my flesh and drinketh my blood hath eternal life'. We must therefore either believe in Him and in what he said and take the consequences; or reject him and take the consequences. I find it for myself difficult to believe that anyone who has ever been to Communion, even once, with at least right intention, can ever again reject Him without grave blame. (However, He alone knows each unique soul and its circumstances.)

The only cure for sagging of fainting faith is Communion. Though always Itself, perfect and complete and inviolate, the Blessed Sacrament does not operate completely and once for all in any of us. Like the act of Faith it must be continuous and grow by exercise. Frequency is of the highest effect. Seven times a week is more nourishing than seven times at intervals. Also I can recommend this as an exercise (alas! only too easy to find opportunity for): make your communion in circumstances that affront your taste. Choose a snuffling or gabbling priest or a proud and vulgar friar; and a church full of the usual bourgeois crowd, ill-behaved children – from those who yell to those products of Catholic schools who the moment the tabernacle is opened sit back and yawn – open necked and dirty youths, women in trousers and often with hair both unkempt and uncovered. Go to Communion *with* them (and pray for them). It will be just the same (or better than that) as a mass said beautifully by a visibly holy man, and shared by a few devout and decorous people. (It could not be worse than the mess of the feeding of the Five Thousand – after which [Our] Lord propounded the feeding that was to come.)

I myself am convinced by the Petrine claims, nor looking around the world does there seem much doubt which (if Christianity is true) is the True Church, the temple of the Spirit* dying but living, corrupt but holy, self-reforming and rearising. But for me that Church of which the Pope is the acknowledged head on earth has as chief claim that it is the one that has (and still does) ever defended the Blessed Sacrament, and given it most honour, and put it (as Christ plainly intended) in the prime place. 'Feed my sheep' was His last charge to St Peter; and since His words are always first to be understood literally, I suppose them to refer primarily to the Bread of Life. It was against this that the W. European revolt (or Reformation) was really launched – 'the blasphemous fable of the Mass' – and faith/works a mere red herring. I suppose the greatest reform of our time was that carried out by St Pius X:[1] surpassing anything, however needed, that the Council[2] will achieve. I wonder what state the Church would now be but for it.

This is rather an alarming and rambling disquisition to write! It is not meant to be a sermon! I have no doubt that you know as much and more. I am an ignorant man, but also a lonely one. And I take the opportunity of a talk, which I am sure I should now never take by word of mouth. But, of course, I live in anxiety concerning my children: who

---

*Not that one should forget the wise words of Charles Williams, that it is our duty to tend the accredited and established altar, though the Holy Spirit may send the fire down somewhere else. God cannot be limited (even by his own Foundations) – of which St Paul is the first & prime example – and may use any channel for His grace. Even to love Our Lord, and certainly to call him Lord, and God, is a grace, and may bring more grace. Nonetheless, speaking institutionally and not of individual souls the channel must eventually run back into the ordained course, or run into the sands and perish. Besides the Sun there may be moonlight (even bright enough to read by); but if the Sun were removed there would be no Moon to see. What would Christianity now be if the Roman Church has in fact been destroyed?

in this harder crueller and more mocking world into which I have survived must suffer more assaults than I have. But I am one who came up out of Egypt, and pray God none of my seed shall return thither. I witnessed (half-comprehending) the heroic sufferings and early death in extreme poverty of my mother who brought me into the Church; and received the astonishing charity of Francis Morgan.[3] But I fell in love with the Blessed Sacrament from the beginning – and by the mercy of God never have fallen out again: but alas! I indeed did not live up to it. I brought you all up ill and talked to you too little. Out of wickedness and sloth I almost ceased to practise my religion – especially at Leeds, and at 22 Northmoor Road.[4] Not for me the Hound of Heaven, but the never-ceasing silent appeal of Tabernacle, and the sense of starving hunger. I regret those days bitterly (and suffer for them with such patience as I can be given); most of all because I failed as a father. Now I pray for you all, unceasingly, that the Healer (the *Hælend* as the Saviour was usually called in Old English) shall heal my defects, and that none of you shall ever cease to cry *Benedictus qui venit in nomine Domini.*[5]

*   *   *

I have got over my complaints for the present and feel as well as my old bones allow. I am getting nearly as unbendable as an Ent. My catarrh is always with me (and will be) – it goes back to a nose broken (and neglected) in schoolboy Rugby. The excellent Doctor Tolhurst[6] urges me to take no drugs or assistants – except those occasionally prescribed specifically by a doctor: sc. when a special infection lodges in the weak areas liable to assault. . . . .

I am interested to hear what you say about M[ichael] G[eorge][7] and 'Anglo-Saxon'. I shall await further news. I cannot (of course) understand why Anglo-Saxon should seem difficult – not to people able to learn any language (other than their own) at all. It is certainly not harder than German, and vastly simpler than say mod. French. And as for Latin or Greek! All the same I can remember old Oliver Elton (once a famous Eng. Lit. scholar but also a 'linguist' who translated Russian) writing to me after a broadcast I made in the 30's,[8] saying that I seemed to understand the language, which he himself found more difficult than Russian. Quite incomprehensible to me; but it does seem that 'A-S' is a kind of 'touchstone' distinguishing the genuine linguists (the students and lovers of Language) from the utilitarians. I hope M.G. is in the former class. But he has enough other talents.

Don't speak to me about 'Income Tax' or I shall boil over. They had *all* my literary earnings until I retired. And now, even with the concession (which I am sure Mr Callaghan[9] would soon revoke) that Earned

Income does not pay Surtax (within my limits of earning), I am being mulcted next January of such a sum as will cripple my desire to distribute some real largesse to each of you. However, I will do something. . . . .

A pity I did not make good and strike my orebearing vein before 39![10] But better late than never. . . . .

251 To Priscilla Tolkien

[Written four days after the death of C. S. Lewis.]

26 November 1963   76 Sandfield Road, Headington, Oxford

Dearest,

Thank you so much for your letter. . . . . So far I have felt the normal feelings of a man of my age – like an old tree that is losing all its leaves one by one: this feels like an axe-blow near the roots. Very sad that we should have been so separated in the last years; but our time of close communion endured in memory for both of us. I had a mass said this morning, and was there, and served; and Havard and Dundas Grant[1] were present. The funeral at Holy Trinity, the Headington Quarry church, which Jack attended, was quiet and attended only by intimates and some Magdalen people including the President. Austin Farrer read the lesson. The grave is under a larch in the corner of the church-yard. Douglas (Gresham)[2] was the only 'family' mourner. Warnie was not present, alas! I saw Owen Barfield, George Sayer and John Lawlor[3] (a good mark to him), among others. Chris. came with us. There will be an official memorial service in Magdalen on Saturday at 2.15 p.m.

It was very sweet of you my dearest to write. . . . .

God bless you.

Daddy.

252 From a letter to Michael Tolkien (draft)

[Not dated; November or December 1963]

I am sorry that I have not answered your letters sooner; but Jack Lewis's death on the 22nd has preoccupied me. It is also involving me in some correspondence, as many people still regard me as one of his intimates. Alas! that ceased to be so some ten years ago. We were separated first by the sudden apparition of Charles Williams, and then by his marriage. Of which he never even told me; I learned of it long after the event.[1] But we owed each a great debt to the other, and that tie with the deep affection that it begot, remains. He was a great man of whom the cold-blooded official obituaries only scraped the surface, in places with injustice. How little truth there may be in literary appraisals one may learn from them – since they were written while he was still alive. Lewis only met Williams in 1939, and W. died early in 1945. The 'space-travel' trilogy ascribed to the influence of Williams was basically foreign to Williams' kind of imagination. It was planned years before, when we decided to divide: he was to do space-travel and I time-travel. My book was never finished,[2] but some of it (the Númenórean-Atlantis theme) got into my trilogy eventually.

Publication dates are not a good guide. *Perelandra* is dated 1943, but does not belong to that period. Williams' influence actually only appeared with his death: *That Hideous Strength,* the end of the trilogy, which (good though it is in itself) I think spoiled it. Also I was wryly amused to be told (*D. Telegraph*) that 'Lewis himself was never very fond of *The Screwtape Letters*'– his best-seller (250,000). He dedicated it to me. I wondered why. Now I know – says they.

253 From a letter to Rayner Unwin   23 December 1963

[It had been agreed that the new paperback (see no. 248) should be given the title *Tree and Leaf*. Rayner Unwin asked if Tolkien could suggest a suitable drawing of a tree for the cover, perhaps taken from a mediæval manuscript.]

I am pleased that *you* approve of the suggested title. Mediæval MSS are not (in my not very extensive experience) good on trees. I have among my 'papers' more than one version of a mythical 'tree', which crops up regularly at those times when I feel driven to pattern-designing. They are elaborated and coloured and more suitable for embroidery than printing; and the tree bears besides various shapes of leaves many flowers small and large signifying poems and major legends.[1] . . . .

Yes – the *Silmarillion* is growing in the mind (I do not mean getting larger, but coming back to leaf & I hope flower) again. But I am still not through with *Gawain* etc. A troublous year, of endless distraction and much weariness, ending with the blow of C.S.L.'s death.

254 To the Rev. Denis Tyndall

[Tyndall, an old boy of King Edward's, Birmingham, had written to Tolkien recalling their schooldays together.]

9 January 1964   76 Sandfield Road, Headington, Oxford

My dear Tyndall,

How delightful to get a card from you, and how kind of you to think of me. . . . .

I do remember very clearly the old IVth class room and Dickie;[1]

indeed I even remember that we read with him a non-classical Greek text furbished up by a German (Willamowitz Möllendorf?) in usum scholarum which bored me extremely. I behaved very badly, together with that later model of rectitude and headmasterly seriousness Christopher Wiseman,[2] as did many of those released from the strict regime of the class below under Heath. Dickie was not an inspiring form-master and made Greek and Roman history as boring as I suspect he felt them to be; but he was immensely interesting as a person. I kept up with him and the Beak (R. C. Gilson)[3] until they died.

My memory is mainly pictorial and vague on dates, but I have a notion that you were a little senior to me and left school first, so that the friends of my later year or two were junior, and mostly younger than myself – I stayed on till I was nearly 20! I was brought up to Oxford by car (then a novelty), together with L. K. Sands, by Dickie: in the October of that astonishing hot year 1911, and we found every one in flannels boating on the river. Punts were then as strange to me as camels; but I later learned to manage them. . . . .

I was 72 on Jan 3, and my eldest grandchild (now at St Andrews) comes of age on Saturday next, but as you say I tick over. . . . .

Yours ever,

[signature not on carbon copy]

255   **From a letter to Mrs Eileen Elgar**   5 March 1964

[Some notes on a poem in *The Adventures of Tom Bombadil*.]

The poem on *Fastitocalon* is not like *Cat* and *Oliphaunt* my own invention entirely but a reduced and rewritten form, to suit hobbit fancy, of an item in old 'bestiaries'. I think it was remarkable that you perceived the Greekness of the name through its corruptions. This I took in fact from a fragment of an Anglo-Saxon bestiary that has survived, thinking that it sounded comic and absurd enough to serve as a hobbit alteration of something more learned and elvish – according to [a] system whereby as English replaces the Shire-speech so Latin and Greek replace the High-elven tongue in names. The learned name in this case seems to have been *Aspido-chelōne* 'turtle with a round shield (of hide)'. Of that *astitocalon* is a corruption no worse than many of the time; but I am afraid the F was put on by the versifier simply to make the name alliterate, as was compulsory for poets in his day, with the other words in his line. Shocking, or charming freedom, according to taste.

He says: *þam is noma cenned/fyrnstreama geflotan Fastitocalon*, 'to him is a name appointed, to the floater in the ancient tides, Fastitocalon'. The notion of the treacherous island that is really a monster seems to derive from the East: the marine turtles enlarged by myth-making fancy; and I left it at that. But in Europe the monster becomes mixed up with whales, and already in the Anglo-Saxon version he is given whale characteristics, such as feeding by trawling with an open mouth. In moralized bestiaries he is, of course, an allegory of the Devil, and is so used by Milton.

256 From a letter to Colin Bailey 13 May 1964

[An account of Tolkien's unfinished story 'The New Shadow'. (See also no. 338.)]

I did begin a story placed about 100 years after the Downfall [of Mordor], but it proved both sinister and depressing. Since we are dealing with *Men* it is inevitable that we should be concerned with the most regrettable feature of their nature: their quick satiety with good. So that the people of Gondor in times of peace, justice and prosperity, would become discontented and restless – while the dynasts descended from Aragorn would become just kings and governors – like Denethor or worse. I found that even so early there was an outcrop of revolutionary plots, about a centre of secret Satanistic religion; while Gondorian boys were playing at being Orcs and going round doing damage. I could have written a 'thriller' about the plot and its discovery and overthrow – but it would be just that. Not worth doing.

257 To Christopher Bretherton

16 July 1964   76 Sandfield Road, Headington, Oxford
Dear Bretherton,
　　Receiving an answer on July 14th to a letter only posted on the 10th was prompt work, even for normal postal conditions. I do not regard typing as a discourtesy. Anyway, I usually type, since my 'hand' tends to start fair and rapidly fall away into picturesque inscrutability. Also I like typewriters; and my dream is of suddenly finding myself rich enough to have an electric typewriter built to my specifications, to type the Fëanorian script. . . . . I typed out *The Hobbit* – and the whole of *The Lord of the Rings* twice (and several sections many times) on my bed in an attic of Manor Road. In the dark days between the loss of my large house in North Oxford, which I could no longer afford, and my brief elevation to the dignity of an old college house in Holywell.
　　That became hellish as soon as petrol restrictions ceased. But Headington is no paradise of peace. Sandfield Road was a cul-de-sac

when I came here, but was soon opened at the bottom end, and became for a time an unofficial lorry by-pass, before Headley Way was completed. Now it is a car-park for the field of 'Oxford United' at the top end. While the actual inhabitants do all that radio, tele, dogs, scooters, buzzbikes, and cars of all sizes but the smallest, can do to produce noise from early morn to about 2 a.m. In addition in a house three doors away dwells a member of a group of young men who are evidently aiming to turn themselves into a Beatle Group. On days when it falls to his turn to have a practice session the noise is indescribable. . . . .

With regard to your question. Not easy to answer, with anything shorter than an autobiography. I began the construction of languages in early boyhood: I am primarily a scientific philologist. My interests were, and remain, largely scientific. But I was also interested in traditional tales (especially those concerning dragons); and writing (not reading) verse and metrical devices. These things began to flow together when I was an undergraduate to the despair of my tutors and near-wrecking of my career. For when officially engaged on 'Classics' I made the acquaintance of languages not usually studied by the modern English, each with a powerfully individual phonetic aesthetic: Welsh, Finnish, and the remnants of fourth-century Gothic. Finnish also provided a glimpse of an entirely different mythological world.

The germ of my attempt to write legends of my own to fit my private languages was the tragic tale of the hapless Kullervo in the Finnish *Kalevala*. It remains a major matter in the legends of the First Age (which I hope to publish as *The Silmarillion*), though as 'The Children of Húrin' it is entirely changed except in the tragic ending. The second point was the writing, 'out of my head', of the 'Fall of Gondolin', the story of Idril and Earendel (III 314), during sickleave from the army in 1917; and by the original version of the 'Tale of Lúthien Tinúviel and Beren' later in the same year. That was founded on a small wood with a great undergrowth of 'hemlock' (no doubt many other related plants were also there) near Roos in Holderness, where I was for a while on the Humber Garrison. I carried on with this construction after escaping from the army: during a short time in Oxford, employed on the staff of the then still incomplete great Dictionary; and then when I went to the University of Leeds, 1920–26. In O. I wrote a cosmogonical myth, 'The Music of the Ainur', defining the relation of The One, the transcendental Creator, to the Valar, the 'Powers', the angelical First-created, and their part in ordering and carrying out the Primeval Design. It was also told how it came about that Eru, the One, made an addition to the Design: introducing the themes of the Eruhîn, the Children of God, The First-born (Elves) and the Successors (Men), whom the Valar were forbidden to try and dominate by fear or force. At that time I also began to invent

345

alphabets. In Leeds I began to try and deal with this matter in high and serious style, and wrote much of it in verse. (The first version of the song of Strider concerning Lúthien, now included in I 204, originally appeared in the Leeds Univ. magazine;[1] but the whole tale, as sketched by Aragorn, was written in a poem of great length, as far as I 206 line 17 'her father'.)[2]

I returned to Oxford in Jan 1926, and by the time *The Hobbit* appeared (1937) this 'matter of the Elder Days' was in coherent form. *The Hobbit* was not intended to have anything to do with it. I had the habit while my children were still young of inventing and telling orally, sometimes of writing down, 'children's stories' for their private amusement – according to the notions I then had, and many still have, of what these should be like in style and attitude. None of these have been published. *The Hobbit* was intended to be one of them. It had no necessary connexion with the 'mythology', but naturally became attracted towards this dominant construction in my mind, causing the tale to become larger and more heroic as it proceeded. Even so it could really stand quite apart, except for the references (unnecessary, though they give an impression of historical depth) to the Fall of Gondolin, Puffin 57 (hardback 63); the branches of the Elfkin, P. 161 (hardback 173 or 178), and the quarrel of King Thingol, Lúthien's father, with the Dwarves, P. 162.

The Hobbit saw the light and made my connexion with A. & U. by an accident. It was not known except to my children and to my friend, C. S. Lewis; but I lent it to the Mother Superior of Cherwell Edge to amuse her while recovering from 'flu. It thus came to the notice of a young woman, a student resident in the house or the friend of one, who worked in A & U's office.[3] Thus it passed to the eyes of Stanley Unwin, who tried it on his younger son Rayner, then a small boy. So it was published. I then offered them the legends of the Elder Days, but their readers turned that down. They wanted a sequel. But I wanted heroic legends and high romance. The result was *The Lord of the Rings.* . . . .

The magic ring was the one obvious thing in *The Hobbit* that could be connected with my mythology. To be the burden of a large story it had to be of supreme importance. I then linked it with the (originally) quite casual reference to the Necromancer, end of Ch. vii and Ch. xix, whose function was hardly more than to provide a reason for Gandalf going away and leaving Bilbo and the Dwarves to fend for themselves, which was necessary for the tale. From *The Hobbit* are also derived the matter of the Dwarves, Durin their prime ancestor, and Moria; and Elrond. The passage in Ch. iii relating him to the Half-elven of the mythology was a fortunate accident, due to the difficulty of constantly inventing good names for new characters. I gave him the name Elrond casually, but as this came from the mythology (Elros and Elrond the two sons of Eärendel) I made him half-elven. Only in *The Lord* was he identified with the son of Eärendel, and so the great-grandson of Lúthien and Beren, a great power and a Ringholder.

Another ingredient, not before mentioned, also came into operation in my need to provide a great function for Strider-Aragorn. What I might call my Atlantis-haunting. This legend or myth or dim memory of some ancient history has always troubled me. In sleep I had the dreadful dream of the ineluctable Wave, either coming out of the quiet sea, or coming in towering over the green inlands. It still occurs occasionally, though now exorcized by writing about it. It always ends by surrender, and I awake gasping out of deep water. I used to draw it or write bad poems about it. When C. S. Lewis and I tossed up, and he was to write on space-travel and I on time-travel, I began an abortive book of time-travel of which the end was to be the presence of my hero in the drowning of Atlantis. This was to be called *Númenor*, the Land in the West. The thread was to be the occurrence time and again in human families (like Durin among the Dwarves) of a father and son called by names that could be interpreted as Bliss-friend and Elf-friend. These no longer understood are found in the end to refer to the Atlantid-Númenórean situation and mean 'one loyal to the Valar, content with the bliss and prosperity within the limits prescribed' and 'one loyal to friendship with the High-elves'. It started with a father-son affinity between Edwin and Elwin of the present, and was supposed to go back into legendary time by way of an Eädwine and Ælfwine of circa A.D. 918, and Audoin and Alboin of Lombardic legend, and so the traditions of the North Sea concerning the coming of corn and culture heroes, ancestors of kingly lines, in boats (and their departure in funeral ships). One such Sheaf, or Shield Sheafing, can actually be made out as one of the remote ancestors of our present Queen. In my tale we were to come at last to Amandil and Elendil leaders of the loyal party in Númenor, when it fell under the domination of Sauron. Elendil 'Elf-friend' was the founder of the Exiled kingdoms in Arnor and Gondor. But I found my real interest was only in the upper end, the *Akallabêth* or *Atalantie**** ('Downfall' in Númenórean and Quenya), so I brought all the stuff I had written on the originally unrelated legends of Númenor into relation with the main mythology.

Well, there you are. I hope it does not bore you. . . . .

[Of his use of the name 'Gamgee':] It started with a holiday about 30 years ago at Lamorna Cove [4] (then wild and fairly inaccessible). There

---

**It is a curious chance that the stem √*talat* used in Q[uenya] for 'slipping, sliding, falling down', of which *atalantie* is a normal (in Q) noun-formation, should so much resemble Atlantis.

347

was a curious local character, an old man who used to go about swapping gossip and weather-wisdom and such like. To amuse my boys I named him Gaffer Gamgee, and the name became part of family lore to fix on old chaps of the kind. At that time I was beginning on *The Hobbit*. The choice of Gamgee was primarily directed by alliteration; but I did not invent it. It was caught out of childhood memory, as a comic word or name. It was in fact the name when I was small (in Birmingham) for 'cotton-wool'. (Hence the association of the Gamgees with the Cottons.) I knew nothing of its origin. . . . .

I hope you are not appalled by these fragments of 'research', or 'auto-research'. It is a terrible temptation, especially to a pedant like myself. I am afraid I have indulged in it almost entirely for private pleasure – in a blessed cessation of letters. (I hasten to say, not of your sort: of them I have too few), which I should have employed in getting on with *Sir Gawain*.

I lived for a while in a rather decayed road (aptly called Duchess) in Edgbaston,[5] B'ham; it ran into a more decayed road called Beaufort. I mention this only because in Beaufort road was a house, occupied in its palmier days, by Mr Shorthouse, a manufacturer of acids, of (I believe) Quaker connexions. He, a mere amateur (like myself) with no status in the literary world, suddenly produced a long book, which was queer, exciting, and debatable – or seemed so then, few now find it possible to read. It slowly took on, and eventually became a best-seller, and the subject of public discussion from the Prime Minister downwards. This was *John Inglesant*. Mr Shorthouse became very queer, and very UnBrummagem[6] not to say UnEnglish. He seemed to fancy himself as a reincarnation of some renaissance Italian, and dressed the part. Also his religious opinions, while never leading him to the final lunacy of Romanism, took on a Catholic tincture. I think he never wrote any more, but wasted the rest of his time trying to explain what he had and what he had not meant in *John Inglesant*. (What happened to the carboys of acid I do not know.) I have always tried to take him as a melancholy warning, and still try to attend to my technical carboys, and to writing some more. But as you see I occasionally fall from wisdom. But not from the sober thought (which this tale of Shorthouse also illustrates) of the fickleness of the Public. It is strange that Sir Stanley, whose *Truth about Publishing* you cite, should be the one most often to make me apprehensive. I am delighted with his approbation*; but I take it as a bit of sunshine on my little hayfield, a special favour and very seasonable; but I follow Gandalf rather, saying: 'we cannot master, nor

---

*In *Time and Tide* of this July 15, in a symposium of publishers telling readers what to take on holiday, he only mentioned *The Lord of the Rings* from all his list, and foretold a long life for it.

foretell, all the tides of the world. What weather is to come we cannot rule or know.'

Yes C.S.L. was my closest friend from about 1927 to 1940, and remained very dear to me. His death was a grievous blow. But in fact we saw less and less of one another after he came under the dominant influence of Charles Williams, and still less after his very strange marriage. . . . . I read *The Pilgrim's Regress* in MS. I have never been able to enjoy *Pickwick*. I now find *The Lord of the Rings* 'good in parts'. I must now end with deep apologies for my garrulity: I hope however that it is interesting 'in parts'.

Yours sincerely
Ronald Tolkien.

258 From a letter to Rayner Unwin 2 August 1964

[During 1964 an Aquastroll hydrofoil, which made a trial crossing from Calais to Dover, was given the name *Shadowfax* (the name of the horse ridden by Gandalf in *The Lord of the Rings*).]

I wish that 'Copyright' could protect *names*, as well as extracts. It is a form of invention that I take a great deal of trouble over, and pleasure in; and really it is quite as difficult (often more so) as, say, lines of verse. I must say I was piqued by the 'christening' of that monstrous 'hydrofoil' *Shadowfax* – without so much as 'by your leave' – to which several correspondents drew my attention (some with indignation). I am getting used to *Rivendells, Lóriens, Imladris* etc. as house-names – though maybe they are more frequent than the letters which say 'by your leave'.

259 From a letter to Anne Barrett, Houghton Mifflin Co. 7 August 1964

I am a man of limited sympathies (but well aware of it), and [Charles] Williams lies almost completely outside them. I came into fairly close contact with him from the end of 1939 to his death – I was in fact a sort of assistant mid-wife at the birth of *All Hallows Eve*, read aloud to us as it was composed, but the very great changes made in it were I think mainly due to C.S.L. – and much enjoyed his company; but our minds remained poles apart. I actively disliked his Arthurian-Byzantine mythology; and still think that it spoiled the trilogy of C.S.L. (a very impressionable, too impressionable, man) in the last part.

In the matter of the proposed blurb to *Tree and Leaf* . . . . I am afraid that difficulty really arises from the juxtaposition of two things that only in fact touch at a corner, so to speak. I do not think I was responsible for the proposed association, and anyway it came up at a time of great troubles and distractions for me. Myself, I had for some time vaguely thought of the reprint together of three things that to my mind really do flow together: *Beowulf: The Monsters and the Critics*; the essay *On Fairy-stories*; and *The Homecoming of Beorhtnoth*. The first deals with the contact of the 'heroic' with fairy-story; the second primarily with fairy-story; and the last with 'heroism and chivalry'.

260 From a letter to Carey Blyton   16 August 1964

[Blyton had asked Tolkien's permission to compose a *Hobbit Overture*.]

You certainly have my permission to compose any work that you wished based on *The Hobbit*. . . . . As an author I am honoured to hear that I have inspired a composer. I have long hoped to do so, and hoped also that I might perhaps find the result intelligible to me, or feel that it was akin to my own inspiration – as much as are, say, some (but not all) of Pauline Baynes' illustrations. . . . .

I have little musical knowledge. Though I come of a musical family, owing to defects of education and opportunity as an orphan, such music as was in me was submerged (until I married a musician), or transformed into linguistic terms. Music gives me great pleasure and sometimes inspiration, but I remain in the position in reverse of one who likes to read or hear poetry but knows little of its technique or tradition, or of linguistic structure.

261 From a letter to Anne Barrett, Houghton Mifflin Co.
30 August 1964

[A comment on an article about C. S. Lewis by one of his former pupils, George Bailey, in *The Reporter*, 23 April 1964.]

C.S.L. of course had some oddities and could sometimes be irritating. He was after all and remained an Irishman of Ulster. But he did nothing for effect; he was not a professional clown, but a natural one, when a clown at all. He was generous-minded, on guard against all prejudices, though a few were too deep-rooted in his native background to be observed by him. That his literary opinions were ever dictated by envy (as in the case of T. S. Eliot) is a grotesque calumny. After all it is possible to dislike Eliot with some intensity even if one has no aspirations to poetic laurels oneself.

Well of course I could say more, but I must draw the line. Still I wish it could be forbidden that after a great man is dead, little men should scribble over him, who have not and must know they have not sufficient knowledge of his life and character to give them any key to the truth. Lewis was not 'cut to the quick' by his defeat in the election to the professorship of poetry: he knew quite well the cause. I remember that we had assembled soon after in our accustomed tavern and found C.S.L. sitting there, looking (and since he was no actor at all probably feeling) much at ease. 'Fill up!' he said, 'and stop looking so glum. The only distressing thing about this affair is that my friends seem to be upset.' And he did not 'readily accept' the chair in Cambridge. It was advertised, and he did not apply. Cambridge of course wanted him, but it took a lot of diplomacy before they got him. His friends thought it would be good for him: he was mortally tired, after nearly 30 years, of the Baileys of this world and even of the Duttons.[1] It proved a good move, and until his health began too soon to fail it gave him a great deal of happiness.

262 To Michael di Capua, Pantheon Books

[Pantheon Books of New York asked Tolkien to write a preface to a new edition of George MacDonald's *The Golden Key*. Although he did not in the event write it, the result of his beginning work on the preface was the composition of *Smith of Wootton Major*, which began as a very short story to be contained within the preface. See further *Biography* pp. 242–3, which quotes part of the intended preface.]

7 September 1964   76 Sandfield Road, Headington, Oxford
Dear Mr di Capua,
    I should like to write a short preface to a separate edition of *The Golden Key*. I am not as warm an admirer of George MacDonald as C. S. Lewis was; but I do think well of this story of his. I mentioned it in my essay *On Fairy-stories*. . . . .
    I am not at all confident that I can produce anything worthy of the honorarium that you offer. I am not naturally attracted (in fact much the reverse) by allegory, mystical or moral. But I will do my best, if there is time. In any case I am grateful to you for your consideration.
                    Yours sincerely,
                    J. R. R. Tolkien.

263 From a letter to the Houghton Mifflin Co.   10 September 1964

I should like to offer criticism on one point, though I do not suppose that it is expected, or will be welcomed. I find the block on p. iii [of *Tree and Leaf*] very distasteful, and wonder if it could not perhaps be reconsidered, or omitted. The lettering is, to my taste, of a bad kind and ill-executed, and though no doubt this is deliberate, I do not like it any the better for that. The fat and apparently pollarded trunk, with no roots, and feeble branches, seems to me quite unfitting as a symbol of Tale-telling, or as a suggestion of anything that Niggle could possibly have drawn! My taste may be at fault. So may the views and sentiments expressed in the text. But if these are thought worthy of reproduction – and I am deeply gratified to find that they are – then I could wish that some design showing more sympathy with them might be produced.

264 From a letter to Allen & Unwin 11 September 1964

As you no doubt know, Houghton Mifflin are now busy re-setting *Tree and Leaf.* On Sept. 8 I received a large parcel containing proofs for my attention. No doubt this was a courtesy; but since it cost me £1. 7. 6 to return in time for their deadline, I am afraid a certain acerbity crept into my comment on the block designed for their p. iii: a ghastly thing, like a cross between a fat sea-anemone and a pollarded spanish chestnut, plastered with lettering of indecent ugliness.

265 From a letter to David Kolb, S.J. 11 November 1964

It is sad that 'Narnia' and all that part of C.S.L.'s work should remain outside the range of my sympathy, as much of my work was outside his. Also, I personally found *Letters to Malcolm* a distressing and in parts horrifying work. I began a commentary on it, but if finished it would not be publishable.

266 From a letter to Michael George Tolkien 6 January 1965

[Tolkien's grandson was studying English at St Andrew's University.]

I am sorry my *Gawain* and *Pearl* will not be in time to assist you (if indeed they would): largely owing, in addition to the natural difficulty of rendering verse into verse, to my discovering many minor points about words, in the course of my work, which lead me off. *Pearl* is, of course, about as difficult a task as any translator could be set. It is impossible to make a version in the same metre close enough to serve as a 'crib'. But I think anyone who reads my version, however learned a Middle English scholar, will get a more direct impression of the poem's impact (on one who knew the language). But truthfully it is I suppose just a private amusement.

My dear old protector, backer, and friend Dr C. T. Onions died on Friday at 91⅓ years. I had not seen him for a long while. He was the last of the people who *were* 'English' at Oxford and at large when I entered the profession. Well not quite: Kenneth Sisam (once my tutor) survives in the Scilly Isles, a mere 76. Incidentally, while on this melancholy subject, T. S. Eliot has gone. But if you want a perfect specimen of bad verse, a ludicrous 'all-time low', about [on the level] of the 'stuffed owl' revived, I could [not] find you a better than poor old John Masefield's 8 lines on Eliot in *The Times* of Friday Jan. 8: 'East Coker'. Almost down/up to Wordsworth's zero-standard. . . . .

I am neither disturbed (nor surprised) at the limitations of my 'fame'. There are lots of people in *Oxford* who have never heard of me, let alone of my books. But I can repay many of them with equal ignorance: neither wilful nor contemptuous, simply accidental. An amusing incident occurred in November, when I went as a courtesy to hear the last lecture of this series of his given by the Professor of Poetry: Robert Graves. (A remarkable creature, entertaining, likeable, odd, bonnet full of wild bees, half-German, half-Irish, very tall, must have looked like Siegfried/Sigurd in his youth, *but* an Ass.) It was the most ludicrously bad lecture I have ever heard. After it he introduced me to a pleasant young woman who had attended it: well but quietly dressed, easy and agreeable, and we got on quite well. But Graves started to laugh; and he said: 'it is obvious neither of you has ever heard of the other before'. Quite true. And I had not supposed that the lady would ever have heard of me. Her name was Ava Gardner, but it still meant nothing, till people more aware of the world informed me that she was a film-star of some magnitude, and that the press of pressmen and storm of flash-bulbs on the steps of the Schools were not directed at Graves (and cert. not at me) but at her. . . . .

Still the old 'ego' gets quite a lot of strong boosts now and again, which surprise me as much as ever. I met Burke Trend on September 29th, at the Merton Septcentenary Dinner – he is a recent honorary Fellow: secretary to the Cabinet then and now: and he declared himself as a 'fan', and added that most of the Cabinet was with him, and as for the House similar views were widely prevalent on both sides of it. Good enough, if they buy the book and don't merely wear out the House of Commons Library copy! No other kind of reward seems in the offing. But I suppose my greatest surprise was 4 days ago to get a warm fan-letter from Iris Murdoch. And if that name is just an 'Ava Gardner' to you, it can't be helped. . . . .

When I think of my mother's death (younger than Prisca) worn out with persecution, poverty, and. largely consequent, disease, in the effort to hand on to us small boys the Faith, and remember the tiny bedroom she shared with us in rented rooms in a postman's cottage at Rednal, where she died alone, too ill for viaticum, I find it very hard and bitter, when my children stray away [from the Church]. Of course Canaan seems different to those who have come into it out of the desert; and the later inhabitants of Jerusalem may often seem fools or knaves, or worse. But *in hac urbe lux solemnis*[1] has seemed to me steadily true. I have met snuffy, stupid, undutiful, conceited, ignorant, hypocritical, lazy, tipsy, hardhearted, cynical, mean, grasping, vulgar, snobbish, and even (at a guess) immoral priests 'in the course of my peregrinations'; but for me one Fr. Francis outweighs them all, and he was an upper-class Welsh-Spaniard Tory, and seemed to some just a pottering old snob and gossip. He was – and he was *not*. I first learned charity and forgiveness from him; and in the light of it pierced even the 'liberal' darkness out of which I came, knowing more about 'Bloody Mary' than the Mother of Jesus – who was never mentioned except as an object of wicked worship by the Romanists.

268 From a letter to Miss A. P. Northey   19 January 1965

I think Shadowfax certainly went with Gandalf [across the Sea], though this is not stated. I feel it is better not to state everything (and indeed it is more realistic, since in chronicles and accounts of 'real' history, many facts that some enquirer would like to know are omitted, and the truth has to be discovered or guessed from such evidence as there is). I should argue so: Shadowfax came of a special race (II 126, 129, III 346)[1] being as it were an Elvish equivalent of ordinary horses: his 'blood' came from 'West over Sea'. It would not be unfitting for him to 'go West'. Gandalf was not 'dying', or going by a special grace to the Western Land, before passing on 'beyond the circles of the world': he was going home, being plainly one of the 'immortals', an angelic emissary of the angelic governors (Valar) of the Earth. He would take or could take what he loved. Gandalf was last seen riding Shadowfax (III 276). He must have ridden to the Havens, and it is inconceivable that he would [have] ridden any beast but Shadowfax; so Shadowfax must have been there. A chronicler winding up a long tale, and for the moment moved principally by the sorrow of those left behind (himself among them!) might omit mention of the horse; but had the great horse also shared in the grief of sundering, he could hardly have been forgotten.

269 From a letter to W. H. Auden   12 May 1965

[Auden had asked Tolkien if the notion of the Orcs, an entire race that was irredeemably wicked, was not heretical.]

With regard to *The Lord of the Rings*, I cannot claim to be a sufficient theologian to say whether my notion of orcs is heretical or not. I don't feel under any obligation to make my story fit with formalized Christian theology, though I actually intended it to be consonant with Christian thought and belief, which is asserted somewhere, Book Five, page 190,[1] where Frodo asserts that the orcs are not evil in origin. We believe that, I suppose, of all human kinds and sorts and breeds, though some appear, both as individuals and groups to be, by us at any rate, unredeemable. . . . .

One of my troubles is that I was just sending into press a revision of my translation of *Gawain* together with one of *Pearl* when a desperate problem of U.S.A. copyright fell on me, and I must now devote all the time I have to produce a revision of both *The Lord of the Rings* and *The Hobbit* that can be copyrighted and, it is hoped, defeat the pirates.

270 To Rayner Unwin

[Tolkien had sent Unwin the typescript of his new story *Smith of Wootton Major*. It seemed to Unwin to need the companionship of other stories to make a sufficiently large book. This suggestion came just as Tolkien was revising *The Lord of the Rings*, so as to produce a new edition that would be protected by U.S.A. copyright. The need for this arose because an American publisher had issued an unauthorised paperback edition of the book, without the consent of Tolkien or Allen & Unwin, and (at first) without paying royalties.]

20 May 1965   76 Sandfield Road, Headington, Oxford
Dear Rayner,

Thank you very much for the return of *Smith of Wootton Major*. I am delighted that it pleased you, as I was quite unable to make my own mind up about it without your assistance. I am afraid there is nothing of similar sort or length deep among my papers. There is a lot of unfinished material there, but everything belongs definitely to the *Silmarillion* or all that world. To which I should now be in only a few days returning, if it was not for this infernal copyright business. I shall be sending you the remainder of the text of *Gawain* and my comments on the specimen pages you sent me, to reach you I hope by Monday next. I cannot produce the prefatory note or the commentary until the revision of *The Lord of the Rings* is finished. I shall have to work hard to get it to Boston[1] by July 1.

                    Yours sincerely,
                    Ronald Tolkien.

PS. I am now inserting in every note of acknowledgement to readers in the U.S.A. a brief note informing them that *Ace Books* is a pirate, and asking them to inform others.

271 From a letter to Rayner Unwin 25 May 1965

I am not relishing the task of 're-editing' *The Lord of the Rings*. I think it will prove very difficult if not impossible to make any substantial changes in the general text. Volume I has now been gone through and the number of necessary or desirable corrections is very small. I am bound to say that my admiration for the tightness of the author's construction is somewhat increased. The poor fellow (who now seems to me only a remote friend) must have put a lot of work into it. I am hoping that alteration of the introductions, considerable modifications of the appendices and the inclusion of an index may prove sufficient for the purpose. Incidentally, I am making a point of including a note in every answer or acknowledgement of 'fan' letters from the U.S.A. to the effect that the paperback edition of Ace Books is piratical and issued without the consent of my publishers or myself and of course without remuneration to us. Do you think that if this were done on a larger scale it might be useful?

272 From a letter to Zillah Sherring 20 July 1965

[In a second-hand bookshop in Salisbury, Wiltshire, Zillah Sherring found and bought a copy of *The Fifth Book of Thucydides* which contained a number of strange inscriptions that had been written in it by a previous owner. Finding Tolkien's name among those on the flyleaf, she wrote to him asking if the inscriptions, particularly a long one at the back, had possibly been his work. She sent him a transcript of it. This is a facsimile of the inscription:]

·IKLAS·þō·WAVRDA·þIZO·
·BOKO·HELENISKAIZOS∴
·JERAMELEINAIS·IN·þAM
MA·MENOþ·SAIHSTIN·þIS·
·JERIS·þŪSUNDI·NIVN·HV
NDAI·TAIHVN·UNSARIS∴

356

·FRAVIINS·OUÞE·IK·BIGETJA·
U·ÞATA·LAVN·GIBAN·ALLIS
·JERIS·ÞAMMA·MAGAV·MAI
ST·KVNNANDIN·BI·ÞŪKYD
IDJA·JAH·HITA·ANAMELID
A·IN·BOKOS·MEINOS·ÞAM
MA·TWALIFTIN·ÞIS·SAIHS
TINS·AFARÞIZEI·IK·JU·FRU
MINS·ÞAIRHLES·JAU·ALLA·Þ
O·WAVRDA·GLAGGWNBA·

⁘ ⁘

The book certainly once belonged to me. . . . . The writing on the back page is in Gothic, or what I thought was Gothic or might be. I had come across this admirable language a year or two before 1910 in Joseph Wright's *Primer of the Gothic Language* (now replaced by *A Grammar of the Gothic Language*). It was sold to me by a school-friend interested in missionary work, who had thought it a Bible Society product and had no use for what it was. I was fascinated by Gothic in itself: a beautiful language, which reached the eminence of liturgical use, but failed owing to the tragic history of the Goths to become one of the liturgical languages of the West. At the time I had only the Primer with its small vocabulary, but I had learned from it some of the technique necessary for converting the words of other Germanic languages into Gothic script. I often put 'Gothic' inscriptions in books, sometimes Gothicizing my Norse name and German surname as Ruginwaldus Dwalakōneis. The inscription you cite is at fault (by accident) in HVNDAI which should be HVNDA. It is also bad Gothic in other respects, but was intended to mean: *I read the words of these books* of Greek history ('year-writing') in the sixth month of this year: thousand, nine hundreds, ten, of Our Lord: in order to gain the prize given every year to the boy knowing most about Thucydides, and this I inscribed in my books† on the twelfth of the sixth* (month) *after I had already ? first read through all the words carefully. Frvmins* is probably an error for *frumist* 'first'.

You probably will not be interested in other 'errors'. The inscription

*an error probably for *þizōs bōkōs*, 'of this book', sg.
†an error probably for *ōka meina*, 'my book', sg.

presented some problems to one having only the vocabulary of short specimens of the fragments of the Gothic versions of the New Testament to go upon. The Gothic word for 'read' was not *lisan, las, galisans,* which still had only its original meaning 'gather' (a sense which its German and Norse equivalents, *lesen* and *lesa,* still retain in addition to the sense 'read' imitated from Latin *lego*). The Gothic word was *us-siggwan* 'recite' (sing out). The art of private reading, silent, and with the use only or chiefly of the eyes, was if practised by the 'ancients' mostly forgotten. I believe it is reported that St Ambrose (in the same century as the Gothic versions were made) astonished observers who saw him reading by only moving his eyes from side to side, without moving his lips or at least murmuring. . . . .

I still feel no compunction in writing in my own books, though I now usually put only notes supposed to be of use – if I can later decipher them.

273 From a letter to Nan C. Scott 21 July 1965

[Mrs Scott was a leading campaigner in the battle to keep the pirate edition of *The Lord of the Rings* out of the American bookshops.]

I am extremely grateful for the information that you have sent me, and still more for your great kindness and energy in attempting to combat the pirates on my behalf. . . . . I have been taken off all my other work and driven nearly over the edge by the attempt to get an *authorized* paperback by Ballantine Books produced as soon as possible.

274 From a letter to the Houghton Mifflin Co. 28 July 1965

[Concerning revisions to *The Lord of the Rings.*]

The *small map* 'Part of the Shire' is most at fault and much needs correction (and some additions), and has caused a number of questions to be asked. The chief fault is that the ferry at Bucklebury and so Brandy Hall and Crickhollow have shifted about 3 miles too far north (about 4 mm.). This cannot be altered at this time, but it is unfortunate that Brandy Hall clearly on the river-bank is placed so that the main road runs in front of it instead of behind. There is also no trace of the wood described at the top of p. 99.[1]

275 From a letter to W. H. Auden   4 August 1965

[Auden had invited Tolkien to contribute to a *festschrift* marking the retirement of Nevill Coghill. He also asked if Tolkien knew that a 'New York Tolkien Society' had been formed, and said he feared that most of the members would be lunatics.]

I still feel grieved that I haven't anything for Neville's [*sic*] festschrift. I hope that perhaps an arrangement will be made in the book for people in my position to register their good wishes. The only thing I have ever written about Neville was:

> Mr Neville Judson Coghill
> Wrote a deal of dangerous doggerill.
> Practical, progressive men
> Called him Little Poison-pen.

That was at a time when under the name of Judson he was writing what I thought very good and funny verses lampooning forward-looking men like Norwood of St John's.[1]

Yes, I have heard about the Tolkien Society. Real lunatics don't join them, I think. But still such things fill me too with alarm and despondency.

276 To Dick Plotz, 'Thain' of the Tolkien Society of America

12 September 1965   76 Sandfield Road, Headington, Oxford

To the T. S. A. First Communiqué from
the Member for Longbottom.

Dear Mr Plotz,

I have been away in Ireland, and have just received your letter (amid a mountain of mail) on my return. I am much interested to hear of the formation of the 'Tolkien Society', and very grateful for the compliment. I do not, however, see how I can become a 'member' of a society inspired by liking for my works and devoted (I suppose) to study and criticism of them, as at least part of their activities.

I should, however, be pleased to be associated with you in some informal capacity. I should, for instance, be willing to offer any advice that you wished to seek, or provide information not yet in print – always with the proviso (especially with regard to 'information') that the plea: *Engaged on the matter of the Eldar and of Númenor*: would be accepted without offence as an adequate excuse for an inadequate answer to enquiries. . . . .

As for the 'Silmarillion' and its appendages; that is written, but it is in a confused state owing to alteration and enlargement at different dates (including 'writing back' to confirm the links between it and *The L. of the Rings*). It lacks a thread on which its diversity can be strung. It also presents in a more acute form than even the difficulties that I found in *The L. of the R.*: the need to acquaint an audience with an unknown mythology without reference to the tales; and to relate a number of long legends dependent on the mythology without holding them up with explanatory digressions. I had hoped by now to be deep in the work necessary to presenting a part of the matter in publishable form. . . . . I think I shall issue it in parts. The first part may, given still the health and vigour, reach the press next year.

There is also a large amount of matter that is not strictly part of the *Silmarillion*: cosmogony and matter concerning the Valar; and later matter concerning Númenor, and the War in Middle-earth (fall of Eregion and death of Celebrimbor, and the history of Celeborn and Galadriel). As for Númenor, the tale of the *Akallabêth* or Downfall is fully written. The rest of its internal history is only in Annal form, and will probably remain so, except for one long Númenórean tale: *The Mariner's Wife*: now nearly complete, concerning the story of Aldarion (the 6th King: L.R. III 315, 316) and his tragic relations with his father and his wife. This is supposed to have been preserved in the Downfall, when most of Númenórean lore was lost except that that dealt with the First Age, because it tells how Númenor became involved in the politics of Middle-earth.

I quite understand the amusement to be got in such a society out of special names for members associated with the story, and of course I see that things are still undecided. But if I might make a suggestion at this stage, I should say that I think it is a mistake to give names of characters (or offices) in the story. Personally I should have liked the society's title to be 'The Shire Society', with perhaps T.S.A. as an explanatory sub-title. But even without any change of title, I think it would be more appropriate and amusing to give members the title of 'Member for Some-place-in-the Shire', or in Bree. Would it not be a good thing to limit the number of persons entitled to a special name in some suitable way: as being earliest members, or later as being those who clearly continue to get some interest or amusement out of membership? There are only about 30 suitable place names in the small section of the Shire printed, but there are more in my map, and if a proper map of the whole Shire were drawn up there could be quite a large number of places entered. The names already entered, even those that seem unlikely (as Nobottle), are in fact devised according to the style, origins, and mode of formation of English (especially Midland) place-names. I should be delighted to construct new names on the same principles as desired and to find them places on the maps of Bree and the Shire. Personally, as an inveterate pipe smoker be happy to accept the title of Member for Longbottom; or if you should wish to accord me mayoral dignity (for which even on Hobbit-scales my years make me just about ripe) the Member for Michel Delving. . . . .

Númínor. C. S. Lewis was one of the only three persons who have so far read all or a considerable part of my 'mythology' of the First and Second Ages,[1] which had already been in the main lines constructed before we met. He had the peculiarity that he liked to be read to. All that he knew of my 'matter' was what his capacious but not infallible memory retained from my reading to him as sole audience. His spelling *numinor* is a hearing error, aided, no doubt, by his association of the name with Latin *nümen, nümina,* and the adjective 'numinous'. Unfortunate, since the name has no such connexions, and has no reference to 'divinity' or sense of its presence. It is a construction from the Eldarin base $\sqrt{\text{NDU}}$ 'below, down; descend'; Q. *núme* 'going down, occident'; *númen* 'the direction or region of the sunset' +*nóre* 'land' as an inhabited area. I have often used *Westernesse* as a translation. This is derived from rare Middle English *Westernesse* (known to me only in MS. C of *King Horn*) where the meaning is vague, but may be taken to mean 'Western lands' as distinct from the East inhabited by the Paynim and Saracens. Lewis took no part in 'research into Númenor'. N. is my personal alteration of the Atlantis myth and/or tradition, and accommodation of it to my general mythology. Of all the mythical or 'archetypal' images this is the one most deeply seated in my imagination, and for many years I had a recurrent Atlantis dream: the stupendous and ineluctable wave advancing from the Sea or over the land, sometimes dark, sometimes green and sunlit.

Lewis was, I think, impressed by 'the Silmarillion and all that', and certainly retained some vague memories of it and of its names in mind. For instance, since he had heard it, before he composed or thought of *Out of the Silent Planet,* I imagine that *Eldil* is an echo of the *Eldar*; in *Perelandra 'Tor and Tinidril'* are certainly an echo, since *Tuor and Idril,* parents of Eärendil, are major characters in 'The Fall of Gondolin', the earliest written of the legends of the First Age. But his own mythology (incipient and never fully realized) was quite different. It was at any rate broken to bits before it became coherent by contact with C. S. Williams and his 'Arthurian' stuff – which happened between *Perelandra* and *That Hideous Strength.* A pity, I think. But then I was and remain wholly unsympathetic to Williams' mind.

I knew Charles Williams only as a friend of C.S.L. whom I met in his company when, owing to the War, he spent much of his time in Oxford. We liked one another and enjoyed talking (mostly in jest) but we had nothing to say to one another at deeper (or higher) levels. I doubt if he had read anything of mine then available; I had read or heard a good deal of his work, but found it wholly alien, and sometimes very distasteful, occasionally ridiculous. (This is perfectly true as a general statement, but is not intended as a criticism of Williams; rather it is an exhibition of my own limits of sympathy. And of course in so large a range of work I found lines, passages, scenes, and thoughts that I found striking.) I remained entirely unmoved. Lewis was bowled over.

But Lewis was a very impressionable man, and this was abetted by his great generosity and capacity for friendship. The unpayable debt that I owe to him was not 'influence' as it is ordinarily understood, but sheer encouragement. He was for long my only audience. Only from him did I ever get the idea that my 'stuff' could be more than a private hobby. But for his interest and unceasing eagerness for more I should never have brought *The L. of the R.* to a conclusion. . . . .

I send you and the T.S.A. my best wishes. If I were not in an interim between secretaries (part-time) for a few days, you might have received a briefer letter, more succinct and better typed.

Yours sincerely,
J. R. R. Tolkien.

277 To Rayner Unwin 12 September 1965

[In August 1965 Ballantine Books produced the first 'authorised' American paperback of *The Hobbit*, without incorporating Tolkien's revisions to the text. The cover picture showed a lion, two emus, and a tree with bulbous fruit. (When the book was reissued by Ballantine the following February, with the revised text, the lion had disappeared beneath yellow-green grass.)]

I wrote to [his American publishers] expressing (with moderation) my dislike of the cover for [the Ballantine edition of] *The Hobbit*. It was a short hasty note by hand, without a copy, but it was to this effect: I think the cover ugly; but I recognize that a main object of a paperback cover is to attract purchasers, and I suppose that you are better judges of what is attractive in USA than I am. I therefore will not enter into a debate about taste – (meaning though I did not say so: horrible colours and foul lettering) – but I must ask this about the vignette: what has it got to do with the story? Where is this place? Why a lion and emus? And what is the thing in the foreground with pink bulbs? I do not understand how anybody who had read the tale (I hope you are one) could think such a picture would please the author.

These points have never been taken up, and are ignored in [their] latest letter. These people seem never to read letters, or have a highly cultivated deafness to anything but 'favorable reactions'.

Mrs. —— [a representative of the paperback publishers] did not find time to visit me. She rang me up. I had a longish conversation; but she seemed to me impermeable. I should judge that all she wanted was that I should recant, be a good boy and react favorably. When I made the above points again, her voice rose several tones and she cried: 'But the man hadn't TIME to read the book!' (As if that settled it. A few minutes conversation with the 'man', and a glance at the American edition's pictures should have been sufficient.) With regard to the pink bulbs she said as if to one of complete obtusity: 'they are meant to suggest a Christmas Tree'. Why is such a woman let loose? I begin to feel that I am shut up in a madhouse. Perhaps with more experience you know of some way out of the lunatic labyrinth. I want to finish off *Gawain* and *Pearl*, and get on with the *Silmarillion* and feel that I cannot deal with H[oughton] M[ifflin] or Ballantine Books any more. Could you suggest that I am now going into purdah (to commune with my creative soul), the veil of which only you have authority to lift – if you think fit?

278 From a letter to Clyde S. Kilby   20 October 1965

I have recently received a copy of *Light on C. S. Lewis*. I hope you have. It is interesting, I think, and does throw a little light on Lewis, though it seems odd to me how they all miss one of the essential points of his temperament. Barfield who knew him longest . . . . gets nearest to the central point. I am afraid I must leave that enigmatic, as I have not time, at the moment, to enlarge upon it.[1]

279 From a letter to Michael George Tolkien   30 October 1965

I think it unlikely that we shall move from Oxford. Anywhere in sight of the sea proves too vastly expensive, while the service problem (our chief trouble) is as bad or worse than here. I am not 'rolling in gold', but by continuing to work I am (so far) continuing to have an income about the same as a professor-in-cathedra, which leaves me with a margin above my needs nowadays. If I had not had singular good fortune with my 'unprofessional' work, I should now be eking out a penurious existence on a perishable annuity of not 'half-pay' but more like ¼ pay. Literary capital is not, however, by its originator realizable. If an author sells any of his rights the proceeds (unlike those of other property) are reckoned to be part of his *income* for the year, and I. tax and Surtax pocket all or nearly all of them. So I certainly cannot provide the *thousands** now asked for a flat or bungalow near the sea. However, on the income-front things still go well. My campaign in U.S.A. has gone well. 'Ace Books' are in quite a spot, and many institutions have banned all their products. They are selling their pirate edition quite well, but it is being discovered to be very badly and erroneously printed; and I am getting such an advt. from the rumpus that I expect my 'authorized' paper-back will in fact sell more copies than it would, if there had been no trouble or competition.

280 From a letter to Rayner Unwin 8 November 1965

Sir Gawain and *Pearl*

I expect you are getting anxious about these. . . . . It was rather disastrous that I had to put them aside, while I had them fully in mind. The work on the 'revision' of *The Lord of the Rings* took me clean away, and I now find work on anything else tiresome.

I am finding the selection of notes, and compressing them, and the introduction difficult. Too much to say, and not sure of my target. The main target is, of course, the general reader of literary bent with no knowledge of Middle English; but it cannot be doubted that the book will be read by students, and by academic folk of 'English Departments'. Some of the latter have their pistols loose in the holsters.

I have, of course, had to do an enormous amount of editorial work, unshown, in order to arrive at a version; and I have, as I think, made important discoveries with regard to certain words, and some passages (as importance in the little world of M[iddle] E[nglish] goes). The exposition of these points, of course, must await articles in the academic journals; but in the meanwhile I think it desirable to indicate to those who possess the original texts where and how my readings differ from the received.

Could you possibly tell me what amount of pages, beyond those absorbed by the two texts, I can be allowed? I can then tailor my trimmings.

281 From a letter to Rayner Unwin 15 December 1965

[Concerning preparations for a British paperback edition of *The Hobbit*.]

The U[nwin Books] cover [of *The Hobbit*]. I do not recollect when the rough sketch of the Death of Smaug[1] was made; but I think it must have

*Yes, even up to £15,000! Or more!

364

been before the first publication, and 1936 must be near the mark. I am in your hands, but I am still not very happy about the use of this scrawl as a cover. It seems too much in the modern mode in which those who can draw try to conceal it. But perhaps there is a distinction between their productions and one by a man who obviously cannot draw what he sees.

The Blurbs. I wrote in haste on the proposed 'blurb' for U[nwin] Books. I do not wish to hurt the feelings of a writer who obviously meant well by me and the book; but I hope you will agree, if you have time to consider it, that this will not do. Apart from its unfortunate style, it misrepresents the story, and the way in which it is presented. Unless you wish to defeat the 'magic', you should NEVER talk like this within the covers of a marvellous tale. The Hobbit saga is presented as *vera historia*, at great pains (which have proved very effective). In that frame the question 'Are you a hobbit?' can only be answered 'No' or 'Yes', according to one's birth. Nobody is a 'hobbit' because he likes a quiet life and abundant food; still less because he has a latent desire for adventure. Hobbits were a breed of which the chief physical mark was their stature; and the chief characteristic of their temper was the almost total eradication of any dormant 'spark', only about one per mil had any trace of it. Bilbo was specially selected by the authority and insight of Gandalf as *abnormal*: he had a good share of hobbit virtues: shrewd sense, generosity, patience and fortitude, and also a strong 'spark' yet unkindled. The story and its sequel are not about 'types' or the cure of bourgeois smugness by wider experience, but about the achievements of specially graced and gifted individuals. I would say, if saying such things did not spoil what it tries to make explicit, 'by ordained individuals, inspired and guided by an Emissary to ends beyond their individual education and enlargement'. This is clear in *The Lord of the Rings*; but it is present, if veiled, in *The Hobbit* from the beginning, and is alluded to in Gandalf's last words.[2]

I do not mean, of course, that anything of this sort should appear in a blurb. Heaven forbid! But I do think that it should not contain words that cannot be reconciled with it and entirely miss the point. . . . .

Very Best Wishes for Christmas and the New Year. Do you think you could mark the New Year by dropping the *Professor*? I belong to a generation which did not use Christian names outside the family, but like the dwarves kept them private, and for even their intimates used surnames (or perversions of them), or nicknames, or (occasionally) Christian names that did not belong to them. Even C. S. Lewis never called me by a Christian name (or I him). So I will be content with a surname. I wish I could be rid of the 'professor' altogether, at any rate when not writing technical matter. It gives a false impression of 'learning', especially in 'folklore' and all that. It also gives a probably truer impression of pedantry; but it is a pity to have my pedantry advertised and underlined, so that people sniff it even when it is not there.

282 From a letter to Clyde S. Kilby 18 December 1965

[Professor Kilby, of Wheaton College, Illinois, had met Tolkien while visiting Oxford in 1964. He now offered to return to England and help Tolkien in any way that might be useful, so as to make it easier for him to finish *The Silmarillion*.]

I have never had much confidence in my own work, and even now when I am assured (still much to my grateful surprise) that it has value for other people, I feel diffident, reluctant as it were to expose my world of imagination to possibly contemptuous eyes and ears. But for the encouragement of C.S.L. I do not think that I should ever have completed or offered for publication *The Lord of the Rings*. *The Silmarillion* is quite different, and if good at all, good in quite another way; & I do not really know what to make of it. It began in hospital and sick-leave (1916–1917) and has been with me ever since, and is now in a confused state having been altered, enlarged, and worked at, at intervals between then and now. If I had the assistance of a scholar at once sympathetic and yet critical, such as yourself, I feel I might make some of it publishable. It needs the actual *presence* of a friend and adviser at one's side, which is just what you offer. As far as I can see, I shall be free soon to return to it, and June, July and August are available.

283 To Benjamin P. Indick

[A reply to a letter from a reader.]

7 January 1966   76 Sandfield Road, Headington, Oxford
Dear Mr Indick,

Thank you very much for your long and interesting letter and comments. They deserve a much fuller answer, but I hope you will forgive me since I am much pressed. Indeed, if I am ever to produce any more of the stories which you ask for, that can only be done by failing to answer letters.

Yours gratefully
J. R. R. Tolkien.

[Auden told Tolkien that he had agreed to write a short book about him, in collaboration with Peter H. Salus, for a seres entitled *Christian Perspectives*; he hoped this did not meet with Tolkien's disapproval. He also mentioned that he and Salus had attended a meeting of the New York Tolkien Society. The meeting, on 27 December 1965, was reported in the *New Yorker* on 15 January 1966, and a quotation from this report was published in the London *Daily Telegraph*, the newspaper that Tolkien read every morning, on 20 January. According to the *Telegraph*, Auden had told the Society: 'He [Tolkien] lives in a hideous house – I can't tell you how awful it is – with hideous pictures on the walls.']

23 February 1966   76 Sandfield Road, Headington, Oxford

Dear Wystan,

I should have replied to your letter of December 28 weeks ago. Nothing is more boring than long explanation of one's neglects, so I will merely say that I have been since Christmas taxed beyond my capacity; and I was also ill (my wife and I were advance victims of the 'flu epidemic here) during the latter half of January.

I regret very much to hear that you have contracted to write a book about me. It does meet with my strong disapproval. I regard such things as premature impertinences; and unless undertaken by an intimate friend, or with consultation of the subject (for which I have at present no time), I cannot believe that they have a usefulness to justify the distaste and irritation given to the victim. I wish at any rate that any book could wait until I produce the *Silmarillion*. I am constantly interrupted in this – but nothing interferes more than the present pother about 'me' and my history.

I was interested to have your note on your visit to the New York Tolkien Society. I have received some other reports of it (including brief extracts in the London press). I cannot say that the (I imagine garbled) notices of your remarks or of Salus' gave me much pleasure.

May I intrude into this letter a note on Ace Books, since I have engaged to inform 'my correspondents' of the situation. They in the event sent me a courteous letter, and I signed an 'amicable agreement' with them to accept their voluntary offer under no legal obligation: to pay a royalty of 4 per cent. on all copies of their edition sold, and not to reprint it when it is exhausted (without my consent). The half of this which I shall retain after taxation will be welcome, but not yet great riches. . . . .

It was most kind and generous of you to send me a copy of *About the House*. I do not pretend that in me (a less generous-minded man than you) your writing arouses the same immediate response. But I can report this. I took the book away (when I took my convalescent wife to the seaside). I took it up to read one night when I was about to get into a warm bed (about midnight). At 2.30 a.m. I found myself, rather cold, still out of bed, reading and re-reading it.

Yours ever,

[carbon copy unsigned]

285 From a letter to W. H. Auden 8 April 1966

If my letter to you of February 23rd was a little tart, I must confess that this was caused by the article in the New Yorker purporting to report the meeting of the Tolkien Society in New York and your remarks about me – not to mention Peter Salus' (as reported) nonsense about the shape of Middle-earth. In case you have missed it I enclose a copy. These remarks, if correctly summarised, seem to me so fantastically wide of the mark that I should have to enter into a long correspondence in order to correct your notions of me sufficiently for the purpose. It is also unfortunate that the general Press, with its usual slant towards sneering, fastened on your remarks about my house and pictures. This was the main item in reports in English papers and exposed my wife and myself to a certain amount of ridicule.

286 From a letter to A. E. Couchman 27 April 1966

[The following is one of many short replies that Tolkien wrote at this period of his life to readers who asked questions about his books. Its characteristic brevity may be compared to the long replies of the years immediately after *The Lord of the Rings* was published.]

There are no 'Gods', properly so-called, in the mythological background in my stories. Their place is taken by the persons referred to as the Valar (or Powers): angelic created beings appointed to the government of the world. The Elves naturally believed in them as they lived with them, But to explain all this would simply hinder my getting on with publishing it in proper form.

287 From a letter to Joy Hill, Allen & Unwin 10 May 1966

[Tolkien's telephone number was still in the Oxford directory, and he was sometimes bothered by calls from 'fans'.]

Thank you very much for your suggestions about my telephone number, which I will consider. Removing the number from the directory seems better than the method adopted by Major W. H. Lewis in protecting his brother, which was to lift the receiver and say 'Oxford Sewage Disposal Unit' and go on repeating it until they went away.

288 To Professor Norman Davis

[The English Faculty of Oxford University wished to acquire a bust of Tolkien by his daughter-in-law Faith. The bust was duly presented to them, and now stands in the English Faculty Library.]

10 May 1966   76 Sandfield Road, Headington, Oxford
Dear Norman,
   I feel much honoured, and so also does my daughter-in-law (the sculptress), by the Faculty's wish to place the bust of me in the English Library in some prominent position – if on second thoughts you do not think a storied urn would be better. I shall be most pleased to present it to the Faculty.
   It occurs to me that the plaster bust is rather fragile and very easily damaged. I suggest, therefore, that I should have it cast in bronze for presentation (at my own cost). I have already referred the matter to the sculptress who knows how these things are done. Once in bronze it would then be unaffected by any dignities or indignities offered to it. I often used to hang my hat on the Tsar of Russia's bust, which he graciously presented to Merton.
                                   Yours ever,
                                   Ronald.

289 From a letter to Michael George Tolkien   29 July 1966

Mirkwood is not an invention of mine, but a very ancient name, weighted with legendary associations. It was probably the Primitive Germanic name for the great mountainous forest regions that anciently formed a barrier to the south of the lands of Germanic expansion. In some traditions it became used especially of the boundary between Goths and Huns. I speak now from memory: its ancientness seems indicated by its appearance in very early German (11th c. ?) as *mirkiwidu* although the **merkw-* stem 'dark' is not otherwise found in German at all (only in O.E., O.S., and O.N.), and the stem **widu-* > *witu* was in German (I think) limited to the sense 'timber', not very common, and did not survive into mod. G. In O.E. *mirce* only survives in poetry, and in the sense 'dark', or rather 'gloomy', only in *Beowulf* 1405 *ofer myrcan mor*: elsewhere only with the sense 'murky' > wicked, hellish.

369

It was never, I think, a mere 'colour' word: 'black', and was from the beginning weighted with the sense of 'gloom'. . . . .

It seemed to me too good a fortune that Mirkwood remained intelligible (with exactly the right tone) in modern English to pass over: whether *mirk* is a Norse loan or a freshment of the obsolescent O.E. word.

290 From a letter to Michael George Tolkien   28 October 1966

[Tolkien's grandson was now a graduate student at Oxford.]

I am interested to hear what you say about your work, and your growing view of 'research' as applied to modern literature. I am myself and always have been sceptical about 'research' of any kind as part of the occupation or training of younger people in the language-literature schools. There is such a lot to *learn* first. It is often forced on students after schools because of the desire to climb on to the great band-waggon of Science (or at least onto a little trailer in tow) and so capture a little of the prestige *and* money which 'The Sovereignties and Powers and the rulers of this world' shower upon the Sacred Cow (as one writer, a scientist, has named it) and its acolytes. But many of those devoted to the Arts privately desire nothing more than a chance to read more.

Quite rightly. For there is a climacteric, at any rate in people of our N.W. race, occurring somewhere in the mid-twenties, before which knowledge acquired is retained (and digested); after which it becomes rapidly and increasingly evanescent. I should think seriously about the change to a B. Phil. if it contains subjects suitable to yourself. (It was established after my time, so, though I advocated something of its kind, I do not know how it's now arranged. After 40 years as both a slave and a deviser of them I cannot now look at University statutes or syllabuses without a sick-feeling.)

I did not warn you of my talk on Wednesday night. I thought you would be too busy. I did not give a talk in fact, but read a short story recently written and yet unpublished; and that you can read when you have time: *Smith of Wootton Major*: if I have not already inflicted on you. Though the title is intended to suggest an early Woodhouse [*sic*] or story in the B[oys'] O[wn] P[aper], it is of course nothing of the kind.

The event astonished me altogether, and also the promoters of the series: the Prior of Blackfriars and the Master of Pusey House. It was a nasty wet evening. But such a concourse poured into Blackfriars that the Refectory (a long hall as long as a church) had to be cleared and could not contain it. Arrangements for relay to passages outside had to be hastily made. I am told that more than 800 people gained admittance. It became very hot, and I think you were better away.

291 To Walter Hooper

[Hooper had sent Tolkien a new volume of Lewis's writings, which he had edited.]

22 November 1966   76 Sandfield Road, Headington, Oxford
My dear Hooper,
    Thank you very much for the copy of *Of Other Worlds*. I read it with great interest, particularly those things I hadn't seen before.
With best wishes,
Yours sincerely,
J. R. R. Tolkien.

Too brief. But I am snowed up. I noticed, for the first time consciously, how dualistic Lewis' mind and imagination [were], though as a philosopher his reason entirely rejected this. So the pun Hierarchy/Lowerarchy. And of course the 'Miserific Vision' is rationally nonsense, not to say theologically blasphemous.

292 To Joy Hill, Allen & Unwin

[Tolkien had been sent details of a proposed 'sequel' to *The Lord of the Rings* that a 'fan' was going to write himself.]

12 December 1966   76 Sandfield Road, Headington, Oxford
Dear Miss Hill,
    I send you the enclosed impertinent contribution to my troubles. I do not know what the legal position is, I suppose that since one cannot claim property in inventing proper names, that there is no legal obstacle to this young ass publishing his sequel, if he could find any publisher, either respectable or disreputable, who would accept such tripe.
    I have merely informed him that I have forwarded his letter and samples to you. I think that a suitable letter from Allen & Unwin might be more effective than one from me. I once had a similar proposal, couched in the most obsequious terms, from a young woman, and when I replied in the negative, I received a most vituperative letter.
With best wishes,
Yours sincerely,
J. R. R. Tolkien.

293 From a letter to William Foster 29 December 1966

[Foster had asked if he might interview Tolkien for *The Scotsman*.]

Thank you for your interest in me. I have, however, had a surfeit of visits and interviews during the present year. I have found none of them pleasant, nearly all of them a complete waste of time, even from the point of view of sales. But your request is, I admit, probably worth taking note of. *The Scotsman* is a highly reputable paper and you are, I am sure, better equipped than some of the interviewers let loose on me by the London Press. I am, however, now desperately in need of time, and I have with the assent of my publishers decided in no circumstances to give any more interviews until I have brought out another book. [1]

294 To Charlotte and Denis Plimmer

[The Plimmers had recently interviewed Tolkien for the *Daily Telegraph Magazine*, and had now sent him a draft of their article, the finished version of which was published in the issue of 22 March 1968.]

8 February 1967   76 Sandfield Road, Headington, Oxford

Dear Mr and Mrs Plimmer,

Thank you for your courtesy in sending me a copy of the preliminary draft of your article. It is evident that I presented some difficulties to you during the interview: by my swift speech (which is congenital and incurable), my discourtesy in walking about, and my use of a pipe. No discourtesy was intended. I suffer from arthritis and my knees give me pain if I sit for long. It is one alleviation of being interviewed if I can stand. I should forgo smoking on these occasions, but I have found being interviewed increasingly distasteful and distracting, and need some sedative.

The copy came to this address the day before I returned hoping to get on with my proper work; I have now found time to consider it. There are one or two points which I should prefer to see altered, and some inaccuracies and misunderstandings that have, no doubt partly by my own fault, crept into the text. Among my characteristics that you have not mentioned is the fact that I am a pedant devoted to accuracy, even in what may appear to others unimportant matters. I have not had time to state these points clearly and legibly, and I hope that the revision and cutting of your article can still wait a day or two. I will try to send them off to reach you by Friday.

In one point I fear that I shall disappoint you. I am informed that the *Weekend Telegraph* wishes to have your article illustrated by a series of pictures taken of me at work and at home. In no circumstances will I agree to being photographed again for such a purpose. I regard all such intrusions into my privacy as an impertinence, and I can no longer afford the time for it. The irritation it causes me spreads its influence over a far greater time than the actual intrusion occupies. My work needs concentration and peace of mind.

Yours sincerely

J. R. R. Tolkien.

[The following are extracts from Tolkien's commentary, sent to Charlotte and Denis Plimmer, on the draft text of their interview with him. The passages in italics are quotations from their draft.]

the cramped garage that he uses as a study
May I say that it is not a 'study', except in domestic slang: in happier days I had one. It was a hastily contrived necessity, when I was obliged to relinquish my room in college and provide a store for what I could preserve of my library. Most of the books of value have since been removed, and the most important contents are the rows of orderly files kept by my part-time secretary. She is the only regular user of the room. I have never written any literary matter in it. . . . .

My present house and its location were forced on me by necessity; few even of its furnishings afford me any pleasure. I am caught here in acute discomfort; but the dislocation of a removal and the rearrangement of my effects cannot be contemplated, until I have completed my contracted work. When and if I do so, if I am still in health, I hope to go far away to an address that will appear in no directory or reference book.

If you wonder why I received you, two courteous and charming people, in such a hole, may I say that my house has no reception room but my wife's sitting-room, filled with her personal belongings. This was contemptuously described in the *New Yorker* (by a visitor),[1] and we both suffered ridicule (and worse: commiseration) when this was quoted in the London papers. Since then she has refused to admit anybody but personal friends to the room. I myself do not intend to admit anyone (certainly no photographer) to the 'bedsitter' where, in the company of the books that I really use and the files of unpublished material, I spend most of my days at home, and do such writing as I am allowed time for.

Tolkien, tall and strongly built
I am not in fact tall, or strongly built. I now measure 5 ft 8½, and am very slightly built, with notably small hands. For most of my life I have been very thin and underweight. Since my early sixties I have become 'tubby'. Not unusual in men who took their exercise in games and swimming, when the opportunities for these things cease.

Tolkien let a few of his Oxford friends read The Hobbit. *One, the Mother Superior of a girls' hostel, lent it to a student, Susan Dagnall....*

The Rev. Mother was superior of a convent (of the order of the Holy Child) at Cherwell Edge, which among other functions kept a hostel for women undergraduates. But as I know it the story runs so: Miss M. E. Griffiths (now one of the senior members of the English Faculty) was beginning her work as a tutor in English Language; she had been a pupil of mine, and was a friend of my family. I lent her the typescript of *The Hobbit*. She lent it to Susan Dagnall, a pupil of hers, who lived in the hostel.[2] Susan lent it to the Rev. Mother to amuse her during convalescence from influenza. Whether it amused her or not, I never heard, so she is a side-track in the journey of the MS. Neither of the loans, to Susan or to the Rev. Mother, were authorized by me[3] – I did not think the MS. important – but they proved the foundation of my good fortune in connecting me with Allen and Unwin. I have always been undeservedly lucky at major points. It is sad that Miss Dagnall, to whom in the event I owe so much, was, I believe, killed in a car-accident not long after her marriage.

[The Silmarillion] *was turned down [by Allen & Unwin] as being too dark and Celtic.*

A & U's readers were quite right in turning it down; not (I hope) because it was, as they said 'too dark and Celtic for modern Anglo-Saxons', since it retains the character thus misdescribed, as does much of *The Lord of the Rings*; but because it needed re-writing and more thought. Most of it was very early work, going back to 1916 and in inception earlier.

Middle-earth grew out of Tolkien's predilection for creating languages....

This reference to 'invention of Language' has become, I think, confused. My fault, in introducing too casually complex matters and personal theories, better not touched on unless at greater length than would be suitable (or interesting) in such an article. For the matter is not really pertinent: the amusement of making up languages is very common among children (I once wrote a paper on it, called *A Secret Vice*), so that I am not peculiar in that respect. The process sometimes continues into adult life, but then is usually kept a secret; though I have heard of cases where a language of this sort* has been used by a group (e.g. in a pseudo-religious ritual).

In your paragraph there is a missing link, more important (I think) for

*That is, one in which inventing a language for pleasure was the main motive. I am not concerned with slangs, cants, thieves' argot, Notwelsch, and things of that sort.

the purpose than what I said, or should have said, about 'invention'. Namely: how did linguistic invention lead to imaginary history? So that I think the passage would be more intelligible if it ran more or less so: 'The imaginary histories grew out of Tolkien's predilection for inventing languages. He discovered, as others have who carry out such inventions to any degree of completion, that a language requires a suitable habitation, and a history in which it can develop.'

'When you invent a language,' he said, 'you more or less catch it out of the air. You say boo-hoo and that means something.'

I have of course no precise memory of just what I said, but what is here written seems to me odd, since I think it unlikely that I should intentionally have said things contrary to my considered opinions. I do *not* think that an inventor catches noises out of the air. If said it was a conversational bit of 'short-talk', possibly intelligible at the moment, but not in cold print – meaning that he utters an articulate sound-group *at random* (so far as he is aware); but it comes of course out of his linguistic equipment and has innumerable threads of connexion with other similar-sounding 'words' in his own language and any others that he may know. Even so, if he said *boo-hoo* it would not mean anything. No vocal noises mean anything in themselves. Meaning has to be attributed to them by a human mind.* This may be done casually, often by accidental (non-linguistic) associations; or because of a feeling for 'phonetic fitness' and/or because of preferences in the individual for certain phonetic elements or combinations. The latter is naturally most evident in private invented languages, since it is one of their main objects, recognized or unconscious, to give effect to these likings. It is these preferences, reflecting an individual's innate linguistic taste, that I called his 'native language'; though 'native linguistic potential' would have been more accurate, since it seldom comes to effect, even in modifying his 'first-learnt' language, that of his parents and country.

Middle-earth . . . . corresponds spiritually to Nordic Europe.

Not *Nordic*, please! A word I personally dislike; it is associated, though of French origin, with racialist theories. Geographically *Northern* is usually better. But examination will show that even this is inapplicable (geographically or spiritually) to 'Middle-earth'. This is an

---

*My *hobbit* is a case. Showing how peculiar to an individual this attribution may be (often obscure to the perpetrator of the 'noise' and not discoverable by others). If I attributed meaning to *boo-hoo* I should not in this case be influenced by the words containing *bŭ* in many other European languages, but by a story by Lord Dunsany (read many years ago) about two idols enshrined in the same temple: Chu-Bu and Sheemish. If I used *boo-hoo* at all it would be as the name of some ridiculous, fat, self-important character, mythological or human.

old word, not invented by me, as reference to a dictionary such as the Shorter Oxford will show. It meant the habitable lands of our world, set amid the surrounding Ocean. The action of the story takes place in the North-west of 'Middle-earth', equivalent in latitude to the coastlands of Europe and the north shores of the Mediterranean. But this is not a purely 'Nordic' area in any sense. If Hobbiton and Rivendell are taken (as intended) to be at about the latitude of Oxford, then Minas Tirith, 600 miles south, is at about the latitude of Florence. The Mouths of Anduin and the ancient city of Pelargir are at about the latitude of ancient Troy.

Auden has asserted that for me 'the North is a sacred direction'. That is not true. The North-west of Europe, where I (and most of my ancestors) have lived, has my affection, as a man's home should. I love its atmosphere, and know more of its histories and languages than I do of other parts; but it is not 'sacred', nor does it exhaust my affections. I have, for instance, a particular love for the Latin language, and among its descendants for Spanish. That it is untrue for my story, a mere reading of the synopses should show. The North was the seat of the fortresses of the Devil. The progress of the tale ends in what is far more like the re-establishment of an effective Holy Roman Empire with its seat in Rome than anything that would be devised by a 'Nordic'.

[Of C. S. Lewis's comments on *The Lord of the Rings*:] '*When he would say, "You can do better than that. Better, Tolkien, please!" I would try. I'd sit down and write the section over and over. That happened with the scene I think is the best in the book, the confrontation between Gandalf and his rival wizard, Saruman, in the ravaged city of Isengard.*'

I do not think the Saruman passage 'the best in the book'. It is much better than the first draft, that is all. I mentioned the passage because it is in fact one of the very few places where in the event I found L's detailed criticisms useful and just. I cut out some passages of light-hearted hobbit conversation which he found tiresome, thinking that if he did most other readers (if any) would feel the same. I do not think the event has proved him right. To tell the truth he never really liked hobbits very much, least of all Merry and Pippin. But a great number of readers do, and would like more than they have got. (If it is of interest, the passages that now move me most – written so long ago that I read them now as if they had been written by someone else – are the end of the chapter Lothlórien (I 365–7), and the horns of the Rohirrim at cockcrow.)

His taste for Nordic languages stems from the fact that he had German ancestors who migrated to England two centuries ago.

This is the reverse of the truth. Not Nordic: this is not a linguistic term. Germanic is the received term for what appears to be meant. But my taste for Germanic languages has no traceable connexion with the history of my surname. After 150 years (now 200) my father and his immediate kin were extremely 'British'. Neither among them nor others of the name whom I have since met have I found any who showed any linguistic interests, or any knowledge of even modern German. My interest in languages was derived solely from my mother, a Suffield (a family coming from Evesham in Worcestershire). She knew German, and gave me my first lessons in it. She was also interested in etymology, and aroused my interest in this; and also in alphabets and handwriting. My father died in South Africa in 1896. She died in 1904. Two years before her death I had with her sole tuition* gained a scholarship to King Edward VI School in Birmingham.

Dante . . . . 'doesn't attract me. He's full of spite and malice. I don't care for his petty relations with petty people in petty cities.'
  My reference to Dante was outrageous. I do not seriously dream of being measured against Dante, a supreme poet. At one time Lewis and I used to read him to one another. I was for a while a member of the Oxford Dante Society (I think at the proposal of Lewis, who over-estimated greatly my scholarship in Dante or Italian generally). It remains true that I found the 'pettiness' that I spoke of a sad blemish in places.

'I don't read much now, except for fairy-stories.'
  For 'except' read 'not even'. I read quite a lot – or more truly, try to read many books (notably so-called Science Fiction and Fantasy). But I seldom find any modern books that hold my attention.† I suppose because I am under 'inner' pressure to complete my own work – and because of the reason stated [in the interview]: 'I am looking for something I can't find.'

---

*except in geometry which I was taught by her sister. That was the aunt whose last years I cheered and amused by composing and selecting *The Adventures of Tom Bombadil*, and consulting her about the book, which she had asked for. She died in her 92nd year soon after it was published.[4]

†There are exceptions. I have read all that E. R. Eddison wrote, in spite of his peculiarly bad nomenclature and personal philosophy. I was greatly taken by the book that was (I believe) the runner-up when *The L. R.* was given the Fantasy Award:[5] *Death of Grass*.[6] I enjoy the S.F. of Isaac Azimov. Above these, I was recently deeply engaged in the books of Mary Renault; especially the two about Theseus, *The King Must Die*, and *The Bull from the Sea*. A few days ago I actually received a card of appreciation from her; perhaps the piece of 'Fan-mail' that gives me most pleasure.

'I'm always looking for something I can't find. . . . . Something like what I wrote myself. There's nothing like being vain, is there?'

An apology for seeming to speak out of vanity. Actually this arose in humility, my own and Lewis's. The humility of amateurs in a world of great writers. L. said to me one day: 'Tollers, there is too little of what we really like in stories. I am afraid we shall have to try and write some ourselves.' We agreed that he should try 'space-travel', and I should try 'time-travel'. His result is well known. My effort, after a few promising chapters, ran dry: it was too long a way round to what I really wanted to make, a new version of the Atlantis legend. The final scene survives as *The Downfall of Númenor.*⁷ This attracted Lewis greatly (as *heard* read), and reference to it occurs in several places in his works: e.g. 'The Last of the Wine', in his poems (*Poems*, 1964, p. 40). We neither of us expected much success as amateurs, and actually Lewis had some difficulty in getting *Out of the Silent Planet* published. And after all that has happened since, the most lasting pleasure and reward for both of us has been that we provided one another with stories to hear or read that we really liked – in *large* parts. Naturally neither of us liked all that we found in the other's fiction.

Tolkien . . . is among the 'principal collaborators' of the newly-translated Jerusalem Bible.

Naming me among the 'principal collaborators' was an undeserved courtesy on the part of the editor of the *Jerusalem Bible*. I was consulted on one or two points of style, and criticized some contributions of others. I was originally assigned a large amount of text to translate, but after doing some necessary preliminary work I was obliged to resign owing to pressure of other work, and only completed 'Jonah', one of the shortest books.

295 To W. H. Auden

[Auden had written to praise Tolkien for the poem in Anglo-Saxon which Tolkien had contributed (together with a version in modern English) to the journal *Shenandoah* as part of a *festschrift* for Auden's sixtieth birthday. (It was published in the Winter 1967 issue (Vol. XVIII no. 2, pp. 96–7).) In his letter, Auden had praised Tolkien's poem 'The Sea-bell' ('Frodo's Dreme'), which he called 'wonderful'.]

29 March 1967   76 Sandfield Road, Headington, Oxford
Dear Wystan,

I was equally delighted by your letter. It arrived very quickly (on Good Friday) and it did much to restore my spirits, as by the same post I received a very distressing letter.[1] I was greatly cheered not only by your pleasure in having an Old English poem (I thought this would be appropriate) but also by your praise of *Frodo's Dreme*. That really made me wag my tail. I hope we can meet again soon.

Yours ever,

[signature not on carbon]

P.S. Thank you for your wonderful effort in translating and reorganising *The Song of the Sibyl*.[2] In return again I hope to send you, if I can lay my hands on it (I hope it isn't lost), a thing I did many years ago when trying to learn the art of writing alliterative poetry: an attempt to unify the lays about the Völsungs from the Elder Edda, written in the old eight-line fornyrðislag stanza.[3]

296 To Rayner Unwin

21 July 1967   Hotel Miramar, Bournemouth

My dear Rayner,

I feel deeply grateful for your kindness to me on Wednesday, and all the trouble you took in looking after me and my affairs. I thought you looked very tired (and no wonder) before we parted. I am singularly fortunate in having such a friend. I feel, if I may say so, that our relations are like that of Rohan and Gondor, and (as you know) for my part the oath of Eorl will never be broken, and I shall continue to rely on and be grateful for the wisdom and courtesy of Minas Tirith. Thank you very much indeed. . . . .

Yours ever

Ronald Tolkien.

297 Drafts for a letter to 'Mr Rang'

[At the top, Tolkien has written: 'Some reflections in preparing an answer to a letter from one *Mr Rang* about investigations into my nomenclature. In the event only a brief (and therefore rather severe) reply was sent, but I retain these notes.' Tolkien has added the date: 'Aug. 1967.']

I am honoured by the interest that many readers have taken in the nomenclature of *The Lord of the Rings*; and pleased by it, in so far as it shows that this construction, the product of very considerable thought and labour, has achieved (as I hoped) a verisimilitude, which assists probably in the 'literary belief' in the story as historical. But I remain puzzled, and indeed sometimes irritated, by many of the guesses at the 'sources' of the nomenclature, and theories or fancies concerning hidden meanings. These seem to me no more than private amusements, and as such I have no right or power to object to them, though they are, I think, valueless for the elucidation or interpretation of my fiction. If published,* I do object to them, when (as they usually do) they appear to be unauthentic embroideries on my work, throwing light only on the state of mind of their contrivers, not on me or on my actual intention and procedure. Many of them seem to show ignorance or disregard of the clues and information which are provided in notes, renderings, and in the Appendices. Also since linguistic invention is, as an art (or pastime) comparatively rare, it is perhaps not surprising that they show little understanding of the process of how a philologist would go about it.

It must be emphasized that this process of invention was/is a private enterprise undertaken to give pleasure to myself by giving expression to my personal linguistic 'æsthetic' or taste and its fluctuations. It was largely antecedent to the composing of legends and 'histories' in which these languages could be 'realized'; and the bulk of the nomenclature is constructed from these pre-existing languages, and where the resulting names have analysable meanings (as is usual) these are relevant solely to the fiction with which they are integrated. The 'source', if any, provided solely the sound-sequence (or suggestions for its stimulus) and its purport *in the source* is totally irrelevant except in case of Earendil; see below.

Investigators seem commonly to neglect this fundamental point, although sufficient evidence of 'linguistic construction' is provided in the book and in the appendices. It should be obvious that if it is possible to compose fragments of verse in *Quenya* and *Sindarin*, those languages (*and* their relations one to another) must have reached a fairly high degree of organization – though of course, far from completeness, either in vocabulary, or in idiom. It is therefore idle to compare chance-similarities between names made from 'Elvish tongues' and words in exterior 'real' languages, especially if this is supposed to have any bearing on the meaning or ideas in my story. To take a frequent case: there is no linguistic connexion, and therefore no connexion in significance, between *Sauron* a contemporary form of an older *θauronð-derivative of an adjectival *θaurā (from a base √THAW) 'detestable', and the Greek σαύρα 'a lizard'.

Investigators, indeed, seem mostly confused in mind between (a) the meaning of names *within,* and appropriate to, my story and belonging to a fictional 'historic' construction, and (b) the origins or sources in my mind, *exterior* to the story, of the forms of these names. As to (a) they are of course given sufficient information, though they often neglect what is provided. I regret it, but there is no substitute for me, while I am alive. I have composed a commentary on the nomenclature for the use of

*E.g. in a nonsensical article by J. S. Ryan.

380

translators;[1] but this is directed primarily to indicating what words and names can and should be translated into L(anguage) of T(ranslation) which takes over the function from English of representing the C(ommon) S(peech) of the period, it being understood that names not in or derived from mod. English should be retained without change in translation, since they are alíen both to the original C.S. and to the L.T Desirable would be an *onomasticon* giving the meaning and derivation of all names and indicating the languages that they belong to. Also of interest to some, and agreeable to me, would be an historical grammar of *Quenya* and *Sindarin* and a fairly extensive etymological vocabulary of these languages of course far from 'complete', but not limited to words found in the tales. But I do not intend to engage in these projects, until my mythology and legends are completed. Meanwhile dealing piecemeal with guesses and interpretations only postpones and interferes with this work. . . . .

In illustration of my strictures, I will offer some comments on your specific queries and guesses. *Theoden* and *Gimli*. The reason for using 'Anglo-Saxon' in the nomenclature and occasional glimpses of the language of the *Eorlingas* – as a device of 'translation' – is given in Appendix F. From which it follows that 'Anglo-Saxon' is not only a 'fertile field', but the sole* field in which to look for the origin and meaning of words or names belonging to the speech of the Mark; and also that A-S will *not* be the source of words and names in any other language† – except for a few (all of which are explained) survivals in Hobbit-dialect derived from the region (The Vale of Anduin to the immediate north of Lórien) where that dialect of the Northmen developed its particular character. To which may be added *Déagol* and *Sméagol*; and the local names *Gladden River*, and *the Gladden Fields*, which contains A.S. *glædene* 'iris', in my book supposed to refer to the 'yellow flag' growing in streams and marshes: sc. *iris pseudacorus*, and not *iris foetidissima* to which in mod. E. the name *gladdon* (sic) is usually given, at any rate by botanists. Outside this restricted field reference to A-S is entirely delusory.‡

---

*With the possible exception of the name (of a king) *Gram*. This is, of course, a genuine A-S word, but not in recorded A-S used (as it is in Old Norse) as a noun = 'warrior or king'. But some influence of the Northern language upon that of the *Eorlingas* after their removal northward is not unlikely. It is in fact paralleled by clear traces of the influence upon one another of the (poetic) language of Old Norse and A-S.

†The only (but a major) exception is *Eärendil*. See below.

‡The word *Warg* used in *The Hobbit* and the *L.R.* for an evil breed of (demonic) wolves is not supposed to be A-S specifically, and is given prim. Germanic form as representing the noun common to the Northmen of these creatures. It seems to have 'caught on' – it appears in *Orbit* 2 p. 119, not as a word in [a] strange country, but in an official communication from Earth to a space-explorer. The story is by a reader of the *L.R.*

As stated in the Appendices the 'outer' public names of the northern Dwarves were derived from the language of men in the far north *not* from that variety represented by A.S., and in consequence are given Scandinavian shape, as rough equivalents of the kinship *and* divergence of the contemporary dialects. A-S will have nothing to say about *Gimli*. Actually the poetic word *gim* in archaic O.N. verse is probably not related to *gimm* (an early loan < Latin *gemma*) 'gem', though possibly it was later associated with it: its meaning seems to have been 'fire'.

Legolas is translated *Greenleaf* (II 106, 154) a suitable name for a Woodland Elf, though one of royal and originally Sindarin line. 'Fiery locks' is entirely inappropriate: he was not a *balrog*! I think an investigator, not led astray by my supposed devotion to A-S, might have perceived the relation of the element *-las* to *lassi* 'leaves', in Galadriel's lament, *lasse-lanta* 'leaf-fall' = autumn, III 386; and *Eryn Lasgalen* III 375. 'Technically' Legolas is a compound (according to rules) of S. *laeg* 'viridis' fresh and green, and *go-lass* 'collection of leaves, foliage'.

Rohan. I cannot understand why the name of a country (stated to be Elvish) should be associated with anything Germanic; still less with the only remotely similar O.N. *rann* 'house', which is incidentally not at all appropriate to a still partly mobile and nomadic people of horse-breeders! In their language (as represented) *rann* in any case would have the A-S form *rǫn* (<*rǫnn* <*rǽzn* <*razn*; cf. Gothic *razn* 'house'). The name of [the] country obviously cannot be separated from the Sindarin name of the Eorlingas: *Rohirrim*. *Rohan* is stated (III 391, 394) to be a later softened form of *Rochand*. It is derived from Elvish **rokkō* 'swift horse for riding' (Q. *rokko*, S. *roch*) + a suffix frequent in names of lands. *Rohirrim* is a similarly softened form of *roch* + *hîr* 'lord, master', + *rîm* (Q. *rimbe*) 'host'.

Nazgul. There is no conceivable reason why a word from the Black Speech should have any connexions with A-S. It means 'Ring-wraith', and the element *nazg* is surely plainly identical with *nazg* 'ring' in the fiery inscription on the One Ring. I do not know any O.E. compound *gael-naes*, but in any case an inventor, engaged in rational linguistic constructions would not supplement a failure in inventiveness by reversing the order of elements in a word of a totally unconnected language, which had no appropriate meaning!

Moria. Your remarks make me suspect that you are confusing *Moria* with *Mordor*: the latter was a desolate land, the former a magnificent complex of underground excavations. As to *Moria* you are told what it means, III 415, and that is an Elvish (actually Sindarin) name = Black Chasm. Does it not plainly contain the √MOR 'dark, black', seen in *Mordor, Morgoth, Morannon, Morgul* etc. (technically √MOR: **mori* 'dark(ness)' = Q. *more*, S. *môr*; adj. **mornā* = Q. *morna*, S. *morn* 'dark'.) The *ia* is from Sind. *iâ* 'void, abyss' ($\sqrt{\text{YAG}}$: **yagā* > S. *iâ*).

As for the 'land of Morīah' (note stress): that has no connexion (even 'externally') whatsoever. Internally there is no conceivable connexion between the mining of Dwarves, and the story of Abraham. I utterly repudiate any such significances and symbolisms. My mind does not work that way; and (in my view) you are led astray by a purely fortuitous similarity, more obvious in spelling than speech, which cannot be justified from the real intended significance of my story.

This leads to the matter of 'external' history: the actual way in which I came to light on or choose certain sequences of sound to use as names, *before* they were given a place inside the story. I think, as I said, this is unimportant: the labour involved in my setting out what I know and remember of the process, or in the guess-work of others, would be far greater than the worth of the results. The spoken forms would simply be mere audible forms, and when transferred to the prepared linguistic situation in my story would receive meaning and significance according to that situation, and to the nature of the story told. It would be entirely delusory to refer to the sources of the sound-combinations to discover any meanings overt or hidden. I remember much of this process – the influence of memory of names or words already known, or of 'echoes' in the linguistic memory, and few have been unconscious. Thus the names of the Dwarves in *The Hobbit* (and additions in the *L.R.*) are derived from the lists in *Völuspá* of the names of *dvergar*; but this is no key to the dwarf-legends in *The L.R.* The 'dwarves' of my legends are far nearer to the dwarfs of Germanic [legends] than are the Elves, but still in many ways very different from them. The legends of their dealings with Elves (and Men) in *The Silmarillion*, and in *The L.R.*, and of the Orc-dwarf wars have no counterpart known to me. In *Völuspá*, *Eikinskjaldi* rendered *Oakenshield* is a separate name, not a nickname; and the use of the name as a surname and the legend of its origin will not be found in Norse. *Gandalfr* is a dwarf-name in *Völuspá*!

Rohan is a famous name, from Brittany, borne by an ancient proud and powerful family. I was aware of this, and liked its shape; but I had also (long before) invented the Elvish horse-word, and saw how Rohan could be accommodated to the linguistic situation as a late Sindarin name of the Mark (previously called *Calenarðon* 'the (great) green region') after its occupation by horsemen. Nothing in the history of Brittany will throw any light on the Eorlingas. Incidentally the ending *-and* (*an*), *-end* (*en*) in land-names no doubt owes something to such (romantic and other) names as *Broceliand(e)*, but is perfectly in keeping with an already devised structure of primitive (common) Elvish (C.E.), or it would not have been used. The element *(n)dor* 'land', probably owes something to say such names as *Labrador* (a name that might as far as style and structure goes be Sindarin). But *not* to Scriptural *Endor*. This is a case in reverse, showing how 'investigation' without knowledge of the real events might go astray. *Endor* S. *Ennor* (cf. the collective pl. *ennorath* I 250) was invented as the Elvish equivalent of Middle-earth by combining the already devised *en(ed)* 'middle' and *(n)dor* 'land (mass)', producing a supposedly ancient compound Q. *Endor*, S. *Ennor*. When made I of course observed its accidental likeness to *En-dor* (I Sam. xxviii), but the congruence is in fact accidental, and therefore the necromantic witch consulted by Saul has no connexion or significance for *The L.R.* As is the case with *Moria*. In fact this first appeared in *The Hobbit* chap. 1. It was there, as I remember, a casual 'echo' of *Soria Moria Castle* in one of the Scandinavian tales translated by Dasent. (The tale had no interest for me: I had already forgotten it and have never since looked at it. It was thus merely the source of the sound-sequence *moria*, which might have been found or composed elsewhere.) I liked the sound-sequence; it alliterated with 'mines', and it connected itself with the MOR element in my linguistic construction.*

I may mention two cases where I was *not*, at the time of making use of them, aware of 'borrowing', but where it is probable, but by no means certain, that the names were nonetheless 'echoes'. *Erech*, the place where Isildur set the covenant-stone. This of course fits the style of the predominantly Sindarin nomenclature of Gondor (or it would not have been used), as it would do historically, even if it was, as it is now convenient to suppose, actually a pre-Númenórean name of long-forgotten meaning. Since naturally, as one interested in antiquity and notably in the history of languages and 'writing', I knew and had read a good deal about Mesopotamia, I must have known *Erech* the name of that most ancient city. Nonetheless at the time of writing *L.R.* Book V chs. II and IX (originally a continuous narrative, but divided for obvious constructional reasons) and devising a legend to provide for the separation of Aragorn from Gandalf, and his disappearance and un-expected return, I was probably more influenced by the important element ER (in Elvish) = 'one, single, alone'. In any case the fact that *Erech* is a famous name is of *no* importance to *The L.R.* and no connexions in my mind or intention between Mesopotamia and the Númenóreans or their predecessors can be deduced.

nazg: the word for 'ring' in the Black Speech. This was devised to be a vocable as distinct in style and phonetic content from words of the same meaning in Elvish, or in other real languages that are most familiar: English, Latin, Greek, etc. Though actual congruences (of form + sense) occur in unrelated real languages, and it is impossible in con-

---

*Already well advanced 20 years before *The Hobbit* was written. The legends of the past before the time of *The Hobbit* and *The L.R.* were also largely composed before 1935.

structing imaginary languages from a limited number of component sounds to avoid such resemblances (if one tries to – I do not), it remains remarkable that *nasc* is the word for 'ring' in Gaelic (Irish: in Scottish usually written *nasg*). It also fits well in meaning, since it also means, and prob. originally meant, a *bond*, and can be used for an 'obligation'. Nonetheless I only became aware, or again aware, of its existence recently in looking for something in a Gaelic dictionary. I have no liking at all for Gaelic from Old Irish downwards, as a language, but it is of course of great historical and philological interest, and I have at various times studied it. (With alas! very little success.) It is thus probable that *nazg* is actually derived from it, and this short, hard and clear vocable, sticking out from what seems to me (an unloving alien) a mushy language, became lodged in some corner of my linguistic memory.

The most important name in this connexion is *Eärendil*. This name is in fact (as is obvious) derived from A-S *éarendel*. When first studying A-S professionally (1913 –) – I had done so as a boyish hobby when supposed to be learning Greek and Latin – I was struck by the great beauty of this word (or name), entirely coherent with the normal style of A-S, but euphonic to a peculiar degree in that pleasing but not 'delectable' language. Also its form strongly suggests that it is in origin a proper name and not a common noun. This is borne out by the obviously related forms in other Germanic languages; from which amid the confusions and debasements of late traditions it at least seems certain that it belonged to astronomical-myth, and was the name of a star or star-group. To my mind the A-S uses* seem plainly to indicate that it was a star presaging the dawn (at any rate in English tradition): that is what we now call *Venus*: the morning-star as it may be seen shining brilliantly in the dawn, before the actual rising of the Sun. That is at any rate how I took it. Before 1914 I wrote a 'poem' upon Earendel who launched his ship like a bright spark from the havens of the Sun. I adopted him into my mythology – in which he became a prime figure as a mariner, and eventually as a herald star, and a sign of hope to men. *Aiya Eärendil Elenion Ancalima* (II 329) 'hail Earendil brightest of Stars' is derived at long remove from *Éala Éarendel engla beorhtast*. But the name could not be adopted just like that: it had to be accommodated to the Elvish linguistic situation, at the same time as a place for this person was made in legend. From this, far back in the history of 'Elvish', which was

---

*Its earliest recorded A-S form is *earendil (oer-)*, later *earendel, eorendel*. Mostly in glosses on *jubar=leoma*; also on *aurora*. But also in *Blick[ling] Hom[ilies]* 163, *se niwa éorendel* appl. to St John the Baptist; and most notably *Crist* 104, *éala! éarendel engla beorhtast ofer middangeard monnum sended*. Often supposed to refer to Christ (or Mary), but comparison with Bl. Homs. suggests that it refers to the Baptist. The lines refer to a *herald*, and divine messenger, clearly not the *soðfæsta sunnan leoma*=Christ.

beginning, after many tentative starts in boyhood, to take definite shape at the time of the name's adoption, arose eventually (a) the C.E. stem *AYAR 'Sea'*, primarily applied to the Great Sea of the West, lying between Middle-earth, and *Aman* the Blessed Realm of the Valar; and (b) the element, or verbal base (N)DIL, 'to love, be devoted to' – describing the attitude of one to a person, thing, course or occupation to which one is devoted for its own sake.† *Earendil* became a character in the earliest written (1916–17) of the major legends: *The Fall of Gondolin*, the greatest of the *Pereldar* 'Half-elven', son of *Tuor* of the most renowned House of the Edain, and *Idril* daughter of the King of Gondolin. *Tuor* had been visited by *Ulmo* one of the greatest *Valar*, the lord of seas and waters, and sent by him to Gondolin. The visitation had set in Tuor's heart an insatiable sea-longing, hence the choice of name for his son, to whom this longing was transmitted. For the linking of this legend with the other major legends: the making of the Silmarils by Fëanor, their seizure by Morgoth, and the recapture of one only from his crown by *Beren* and *Lúthien*, and the coming of this into Earendil's possession so that his voyages westward were at last successful, see I 204–6 and 246–249. (The attempt of *Eärendil* to cross *Ëar* was against the Ban of the Valar prohibiting all Men to attempt to set foot on *Aman*, and against the later special ban prohibiting the Exiled Elves, followers of the rebellious Fëanor, from return: referred to in Galadriel's lament. The Valar listened to the pleading of *Eärendil* on behalf of Elves and Men (both his kin), and sent a great host to their aid. Morgoth was overthrown and extruded from the World (the physical universe). The Exiles were allowed to return – save for a few chief actors in the rebellion of whom at the time of the *L.R.* only *Galadriel* remained.‡ But *Eärendil*, being in part descended from Men, was not allowed to set foot on Earth again, and became a Star shining with the light of the Silmaril, which

---

*Q. *ëar* S. *aear* (see I 250).

†This provides the key to a large number of other Elvish Q. names, such as *Elendil* 'Elf-friend' (*eled+ndil*), *Valandil*, *Mardil* the Good Steward (devoted to the House, sc. of the Kings) *Meneldil* 'astronomer' etc. Of similar significance in names is -(*n*)*dur*, though properly this means 'to serve', as one serves a legitimate master: cf. Q. *arandil* king's friend, royalist, beside *arandur* 'king's servant, minister'. But these often coincide: e.g. Sam's relation to Frodo can be viewed either as in status -*ndur*, in spirit -*ndil*. Compare among the variant names: *Eärendur* '(professional) mariner'.

‡At the time of her lament in Lórien she believed this to be perennial, as long as Earth endured. Hence she concludes her lament with a wish or prayer that Frodo may as a special grace be granted a purgatorial (but not penal) sojourn in *Eressëa*, the Solitary Isle in sight of *Aman*, though for her the way is closed. (The Land of Aman after the downfall of Númenor, was no longer in physical existence 'within the circles of the world'.) Her prayer was granted – but also her personal ban was lifted, in reward for her services against Sauron, and above all for her rejection of the temptation to take the Ring when offered to her. So at the end we see her taking ship.

contained the last remnant of the unsullied light of Paradise, given by the Two Trees before their defilement and slaying by Morgoth. These legends áre deliberately touched on in Vol. I as being the chief ones in the background of *The L.R.*, dealing with the relations of Elves and Men and Valar (the angelic Guardians) and therefore the chief backward links if (as I then hoped) the *Silmarillion* was published.

I relate these things because I hope they may interest you, and at the same time reveal how closely linked is linguistic invention and legendary growth and construction. And also possibly convince you that looking around for more or less similar words or names is not in fact very useful even as a source of sounds, and not at all as an explanation of inner meanings and significances. The borrowing, when it occurs (not often) is simply of *sounds* that are then integrated in a new construction; and only in one case *Eärendil* will reference to its source cast any light on the legends or their 'meaning' – and even in this case the light is little. The use of *éarendel* in A-S Christian symbolism as the herald of the rise of the true Sun in Christ is completely alien to my use. The Fall of Man is in the past and off stage; the Redemption of Man in the far future. We are in a time when the One God, Eru, is known to exist by the wise, but is not approachable save by or through the *Valar*, though He is still remembered in (unspoken) prayer by those of Númenórean descent.

[The text ends with a brief discussion of Númenórean religion.]

298 To William Luther White

[This letter was printed, apparently without permission, with Tolkien's address and private telephone number at the head of it, in White's book *The Image of Man in C. S. Lewis* (1969).]

Oxford 61639   76 Sandfield Road
                                                      Headington
                                                         Oxford
                                              11 September, 1967.

Dear Mr. White,

I can give you a brief account of the name *Inklings*: from memory. The Inklings had no recorder and C. S. Lewis no Boswell. The name was not invented by C.S.L. (nor by me). In origin it was an undergraduate jest, devised as the name of a literary (or writers') club. The founder was an undergraduate at University College, named Tangye-Lean,—the date I do not remember: probably mid-thirties. He was, I think, more aware than most undergraduates of the impermanence of their clubs and fashions, and had an ambition to found a club that would prove more lasting. Anyway, he asked some 'dons' to become members.

C.S.L. was an obvious choice, and he was probably at that time Tangye-Lean's tutor (C.S.L. was a member of University College). In the event both C.S.L. and I became members. The club met in T.-L.'s rooms in University College; its procedure was that at each meeting members should read aloud, unpublished compositions. These were supposed to be open to immediate criticism. Also if the club thought fit a contribution might be voted to be worthy of entry in a Record Book. (I was the scribe and keeper of the book).

Tangye-Lean proved quite right. The club soon died: the Record Book had very few entries: but C.S.L. and I at least survived. Its name was then transferred (by C.S.L.) to the undetermined and unelected circle of friends who gathered about C.S.L., and met in his rooms in Magdalen. Although our habit was to read aloud compositions of various kinds (and lengths!), this association and its habit would in fact have come into being at that time, whether the original short-lived club had ever existed or not. C.S.L. had a passion for hearing things read aloud, a power of memory for things received in that way, and also a facility in extempore criticism, none of which were shared (especially not the last) in anything like the same degree by his friends.

I called the name a 'jest', because it was a pleasantly ingenious pun in its way, suggesting people with vague or half-formed intimations and ideas plus those who dabble in ink. It might have been suggested by C.S.L. to Tangye-Lean (if he was the latter's tutor); but I never heard him claim to have invented this name. *Inkling* is, at any rate in this country, in very common use in the sense that you quote from C.S.L.'s writings. (I remember that when I was an undergraduate there was, briefly, an undergraduate club called the *Discus*, suggesting a round-table conference, and *discuss*: it was a discussion club.)

With best wishes,

Yours sincerely,

J. R. R. Tolkien.

299 To Roger Lancelyn Green

[Green, an old friend, had reviewed *Smith of Wootton Major*, which was published in October 1967. He wrote: 'To seek for the meaning is to cut open the ball in search of its bounce.']

12 December 1967   76 Sandfield Road, Headington, Oxford
My dear Roger,

Best wishes to you and all your family. Thank you for your most gracious review (esp. for comment on the search for source of bounce!). Though I have been much better treated than I expected. But the little tale was (of course) *not* intended for children! An old man's book, already weighted with the presage of 'bereavement'. (I am sorry that I cannot remember your address. I have rung up Merton.) But Merton comes in. Our present admirable little chef (with a v. tall hat) is, at least pictorially, the original of Alf.

All graces and cheer at Christmas

Ronald Tolkien.

300 From a letter to Walter Hooper   20 February 1968

[With reference to C. S. Lewis's verse 'We were talking of dragons, Tolkien and I / In a Berkshire bar . . . .' This short poem, first printed in Lewis's *Rehabilitations* (1939), p. 122, tells how a workman in the bar claimed to have seen dragons himself.]

The lines which Jack[1] gives as examples are not unfortunately entirely accurate examples of Old English metrical devices. The occasion is entirely fictitious. I have never seen a dragon, nor ever seen a man who said that he has. I don't wish to see either. A remote source of Jack's lines may be this: I remember Jack telling me a story of Brightman, the distinguished ecclesiastical scholar,[2] who used to sit quietly in Common Room saying nothing except on rare occasions. Jack said that there was a discussion on dragons one night and at the end Brightman's voice was heard to say, 'I have seen a dragon.' Silence. 'Where was that?' he was asked. 'On the Mount of Olives,' he said. He relapsed into silence and never before his death explained what he meant.

301 From a letter to Donald Swann   29 February 1968

[The BBC made a documentary programme, *Tolkien in Oxford*, which was filmed in early February and televised on 30 March 1968. Swann, whose musical setting of some of Tolkien's poems, *The Road Goes Ever On*, had been published the previous year, had written to Tolkien about the television programme.]

Thank you for trying to cheer me up. But I am not cheered. You are too optimistic. In any case your kind of performance is quite different from mine – as a writer. I am merely impressed by the complete 'bogosity' of the whole performance. The producer, a very nice, very young man and personally equipped with some intelligence and insight, was nonetheless already so muddled and confused by BBCism that the last thing in the world he wished to show was me as I am/or was, let alone 'human or lifesize'. I was lost in a world of gimmickry and nonsense, as far as it had any design designed it seemed simply to fix the image of a fuddy not to say duddy old fireside hobbitlike boozer. Protests were in vain, so I gave it up, & being tied to the stake stayed the course as best I could. I am told that the picture results were v.g. – at which my blood runs cold: it means they've got what they wanted, and that my histrionic temperament (I used to like 'acting') betrayed me into playing ball (the ball desired) to my own undoing. I was not lifted up in a helicopter, though I am surprised one was not substituted for an eagle: they appeared completely confused between ME and my story, and I was made to attend a firework show: a thing I have not done since I was a boy. Fireworks have no special relation to me. They appear in the books (and would have done even if I disliked them) because they are part of the representation of *Gandalf*, bearer of the Ring of Fire, the Kindler: the most childlike aspect shown to the Hobbits being fireworks.

302 From a letter to Time-Life International Ltd. 2 May 1968

Your ideas of the natural and mine are different, since I never in any circumstances do work while being photographed, or talked to, or accompanied by anybody in the room. A photograph of me pretending to be at work would be entirely bogus.

303 From a letter to Nicholas Thomas 6 May 1968

As for knowing Sarehole Mill,[1] it dominated my childhood. I lived in a small cottage almost immediately beside it, and the old miller of my day and his son were characters of wonder and terror to a small child.

304 From a letter to Clyde S. Kilby 4 June 1968

My domestic situation came at the end of April and the beginning of May to a point at which something had to be done quickly. I am now leaving Oxford and going to live on the south coast. As things are at present arranged I shall be removing at the end, or very soon after the end, of this month. For my own protection I shall remove my address from all books of reference or other lists. By arrangement with them, my address will be c/o Messrs. Allen & Unwin, and they will not inform enquirers of my actual address. When this is finally settled, I will let a few persons know – those who I can trust not to publish it abroad.

[On 17 June, while preparing to move house, Tolkien fell downstairs and injured his leg. This letter was written from hospital in Oxford.]

I am beginning to come to my senses. I believe I am making a fairly good and quick physical recovery and may hope to be about on crutches about July 8th, but not sooner. My fall has, all the same, proved disastrous for my work and arrangements at this time, and even with good luck I cannot hope to emerge from chaos now till the end of August at the earliest.

306 **From a letter to Michael Tolkien**

[At the top, Tolkien has written: 'Found among my scattered papers. Not sent or finished for reasons now forgotten. JRRT. 11/Oct/68.' But the letter was eventually sent to Michael Tolkien. It was begun at 76 Sandfield Road (Tolkien noted) 'sometime after Aug. 25, 1967' and was finished at 19 Lakeside Road, the new house, whose postal address was Poole, Dorset, but which was in effect in a suburb of Bournemouth.]

I am . . . . delighted that you have made the acquaintance of Switzerland, and of the very part that I once knew best and which had the deepest effect on me. The hobbit's (Bilbo's) journey from Rivendell to the other side of the Misty Mountains, including the glissade down the slithering stones into the pine woods, is based on my adventures in 1911*: the *annus mirabilis* of sunshine in which there was virtually no rain between April and the end of October, except on the eve and morning of George V's coronation. (Adfuit Omen!)†[1]

Our wanderings mainly on foot in a party of 12 are not now clear in sequence, but leave many vivid pictures as clear as yesterday (that is as clear as an old man's remoter memories become). We went on foot carrying great packs practically all the way from Interlaken, mainly by mountain paths, to Lauterbrunnen and so to Mürren and eventually to

---

*Though the episode of the 'wargs' (I believe) is in part derived from a scene in S. R. Crockett's *The Black Douglas*, probably his best romance and anyway one that deeply impressed me in school-days, though I have never looked at it again. It includes Gil de Rez as a Satanist.

†Which I remember, since (*omen* again) the OTCs[2] of that day were specially privileged and I was one of 12 sent down from K[ing] E[dward's] S[chool] to help 'line the route'. We were camped for a wettish night in Lambeth Palace and marched to our stations early on a dull morning that soon cleared up. I was actually standing outside Buck. Palace great gates to the right, facing the palace. We had a good view of the cavalcades, and I have always remembered one little scene (unnoticed by my companions): as the coach containing the royal children swept in on return the P[rince] of W[ales] (a pretty boy) poked his head out and knocked his coronet askew. He was jerked back and smartly rebuked by his sister.

the head of the Lauterbrunnenthal in a wilderness of moraines. We slept rough – the men-folk – often in hayloft or cowbyre, since we were walking by map and avoided roads and never booked, and after a meagre breakfast fed ourselves in the open: cooking utensils and quantities of 'spridvin' (as the one uneducated French-speaking member of the party both called and wrote it, for 'methylated spirit'). We must then have gone eastward over the two Scheidegge to Grindelwald, with Eiger and Mönch on our right, and eventually reached Meiringen. I left the view of *Jungfrau* with deep regret: eternal snow, etched as it seemed against eternal sunshine, and the *Silberhorn* sharp against dark blue: the *Silvertine* (*Celebdil*) of my dreams. We later crossed the Grimsell Pass down on to the dusty highway, beside the Rhône, on which horse 'diligences' still plied: but not for us. We reached Brig on foot, a mere memory of noise: then a network of trams that screeched on their rails for it seemed at least 20 hrs of the day. After a night of that we climbed up some thousands of feet to a village at the foot of the Aletsch glacier, and there spent some nights in a châlet inn under a roof and in beds (or rather under them: the *bett* being a shapeless bag under which you snuggled). I can remember several incidents there! One was going to confession in Latin; others less exemplary were the invention of a method of dealing with your friends the harvestmen spiders, by dropping hot wax from a candle onto their fat bodies (this was not approved of by the servants); also the practice of the beaver-game which had always fascinated me. A wonderful place for the game, plenty of water at that altitude coming down in rills, abundant damming material in loose stones, heather, grass and mud. We soon had a beautiful little 'pond' (containing I guess at least 200 gallons). Then the pangs of hunger smote us, and one of the hobbits of the party (he is still alive) shouted 'lunch' and wrecked the dam with his alpenstock. The water soared down the hill-side, and we then observed that we had dammed a rill that ran down to feed the tanks and butts behind the inn. At that moment an old dame trotted out with a bucket to fetch some water, and was greeted by a mass of foaming water. She dropped the bucket and fled calling on the saints. We lay more doggo than 'men of the moss-hags' for some time, and eventually wound our way round to present ourselves grubby (but we were usually so on that trip) and sweetly innocent at 'lunch'. One day we went on a long march with guides up the Aletsch glacier – when I came near to perishing. We had guides, but either the effects of the hot summer were beyond their experience, or they did not much care, or we were late in starting. Any way at noon we were strung out in file along a narrow track with a snow-slope on the right going up to the horizon, and on the left a plunge down into a ravine. The summer of that year had melted away much snow, and stones and boulders were exposed that (I suppose) were normally covered. The heat of the day continued the melting and we were alarmed to see many of them starting to roll down the slope at gathering speed: anything from the size of oranges to large footballs, and a few much larger. They were whizzing across our path and plunging into the ravine. 'Hard pounding,' ladies and gentlemen. They started slowly, and then usually held a straight line of descent, but the path was rough and one had also to keep an eye on one's feet. I remember the member of the party just in front of me (an elderly schoolmistress) gave a sudden squeak and jumped forward as a large lump of rock shot between us. About a foot at most before my unmanly knees. After this we went on into Valais, and my memories are less clear; though I remember our arrival, bedraggled, one evening in Zermatt and the lorgnette stares of the French bourgeoises dames. We climbed with guides up to [a] high hut of the Alpine Club, roped (or I should have fallen into a snow-crevasse), and I remember the dazzling whiteness of the tumbled snow-desert between us and the black horn of the Matterhorn some miles away.

I do not suppose all this is very interesting now. But it was a remarkable experience for me at 19, after a poor boy's childhood. I went up to Oxford that autumn. . . . .

'Trends' in the Church are . . . . serious, especially to those accustomed to find in it a solace and a 'pax' in times of temporal trouble, and not just another arena of strife and change. But imagine the experience of those born (as I) between the Golden and the Diamond Jubilee of Victoria. Both senses or imaginations of security have been progressively stripped away from us. Now we find ourselves nakedly confronting the will of God, as concerns ourselves and our position in Time (*Vide* Gandalf I 70 and III 155).[3] 'Back to normal' – political and Christian predicaments – as a Catholic professor once said to me, when I bemoaned the collapse of all my world that began just after I achieved 21. I know quite well that, to you as to me, the Church which once felt like a refuge, now often feels like a trap. There is nowhere else to go! (I wonder if this desperate feeling, the last state of loyalty hanging on, was not, even more often than is actually recorded in the Gospels, felt by Our Lord's followers in His earthly life-time?) I think there is nothing to do but to pray, for the Church, the Vicar of Christ, and for ourselves; and meanwhile to exercise the virtue of loyalty, which indeed only becomes a virtue when one is under pressure to desert it. There are, of course, various elements in the present situation, which are confused, though in fact distinct (as indeed in the behaviour of modern youth, part of which is inspired by admirable motives such as anti-regimentation, and anti-drabness, a sort of lurking romantic longing for 'cavaliers', and is not necessarily allied to the drugs or the cults of fainéance and filth).

The 'protestant' search backwards for 'simplicity' and directness – which, of course, though it contains some good or at least intelligible motives, is mistaken and indeed vain. Because 'primitive Christianity' is now and in spite of all 'research' will ever remain largely unknown; because 'primitiveness' is no guarantee of value, and is and was in great part a reflection of ignorance. Grave abuses were as much an element in Christian 'liturgical' behaviour from the beginning as now. (St Paul's strictures on eucharistic behaviour are sufficient to show this!) Still more because 'my church' was not intended by Our Lord to be static or remain in perpetual childhood; but to be a living organism (likened to a plant), which develops and changes in externals by the interaction of its bequeathed divine life and history – the particular circumstances of the world into which it is set. There is no resemblance between the 'mustard-seed' and the full-grown tree. For those living in the days of its branching growth the Tree is the thing, for the history of a living thing is part of its life, and the history of a divine thing is sacred. The wise may know that it began with a seed, but it is vain to try and dig it up, for it no longer exists, and the virtue and powers that it had now reside in the Tree. Very good: but in husbandry the authorities, the keepers of the Tree, must look after it, according to such wisdom as they possess, prune it, remove cankers, rid it of parasites, and so forth. (With trepidation, knowing how little their knowledge of growth is!) But they will certainly do harm, if they are obsessed with the desire of going back to the seed or even to the first youth of the plant when it was (as they imagine) pretty and unafflicted by evils. The other motive (now so confused with the primitivist one, even in the mind of any one of the reformers): *aggiornamento*: bringing up to date: that has its own grave dangers, as has been apparent throughout history. With this 'ecumenicalness' has also become confused.

I find myself in sympathy with those developments that are strictly 'ecumenical', that is concerned with other groups or churches that call themselves (and often truly are) 'Christian'. We have prayed endlessly for Christian re-union, but it is difficult to see, if one reflects, how that could possibly begin to come about except as it has, with all its inevitable minor absurdities. An increase in 'charity' is an enormous gain. As Christians those faithful to the Vicar of Christ must put aside the resentments that as mere humans they feel – e.g. at the 'cockiness' of our new friends (esp. C[hurch] of E[ngland]). One is now often patted on the back, as a representative of a church that has seen the error of its ways, abandoned its arrogance and hauteur, and its separatism; but I have not yet met a 'protestant' who shows or expresses any realization of the reasons in this country for our attitude: ancient or modern: from torture and expropriation down to 'Robinson'[4] and all that. Has it ever been mentioned that R[oman] C[atholic]s still suffer from disabilities not even applicable to Jews? As a man whose childhood was darkened by persecution, I find this hard. But charity must cover a multitude of sins! There are dangers (of course), but a Church militant cannot afford to shut up all its soldiers in a fortress. It had as bad effects on the Maginot Line.

I owe a great deal (and perhaps even the Church a little) to being treated, surprisingly for the time, in a more rational way. Fr Francis obtained permission for me to retain my scholarship at K[ing] E[dward's] S[chool] and continue there, and so I had the advantage of a (then) first rate school and that of a 'good Catholic home' – 'in excelsis': virtually a junior inmate of the Oratory house, which contained many learned fathers (largely 'converts'). Observance of religion was strict. Hilary[5] and I were supposed to, and usually did, serve Mass before getting on our bikes to go to school in New Street. So I grew up in a two-front state, symbolizable by the Oratorian Italian pronunciation of Latin, and the strictly 'philological' pronunciation at that time introduced into our Cambridge dominated school. I was even allowed to attend the Headmaster's classes on the N[ew] T[estament] (in Greek). I certainly took no 'harm', and was better equipped ultimately to make my way in a non-Catholic professional society. I became a close friend of the H[ead] M[aster] and his son, and also made the acquaintance of the Wiseman family through my friendship with Christopher Luke W. (after whom my Christopher is named). His father was one of the most delightful Christian men I have met: the great Frederick Luke W. (whom Fr Francis always referred to as The Pope of Wesley, because he was the President of the Wesleyan Methodist Conference). . . . .

Oct. 1968.
A part of this letter seems to have got lost in the general confusion of my papers during the move. My bedroom-study at 76 was full of papers and half written works – which I knew where to lay my hand. I ran down-stairs on the afternoon of June 17 and fell. I was picked off the floor of the hall and transported to the Nuffield [Orthopaedic Centre] as I was and never went back again – never saw my room, or my house, again. In addition to the shock of the fall and the operation, this has had a queer effect. It is like reading a story and coming to a sudden break (where a chapter or two seems missing): complete change of scene. For a long time I felt that I was in a (bad) dream and should wake up perhaps and find myself back in my old room. It also made me feel restless & uncomfortable – and 'suspicious'. I could not mentally settle in the new home, as if it was something unreal & might vanish! Also I am still – since no one seems able to help me, and I have been too lamed to help myself for long without weariness – searching for vanished or scattered

395

notes; and my library is still a wilderness of disordered books. . . . .

My 'poetry' has received little praise – comment even by some admirers being as often as not contemptuous (I refer to reviews by self-styled literary blokes). Perhaps largely because in the contemporary atmosphere – in which 'poetry' must only reflect one's personal agonies of mind or soul, and exterior things are only valued by one's own 'reactions' – it seems hardly ever recognised that the verses in The L.R. are all dramatic: they do not express the poor old professor's soul-searchings, but are fitted in style and contents to the *characters* in the story that sing or recite them, and to the situations in it. . . . .

I have only *since* I retired learned that I was a successful professor. I had no idea that my lectures had such an effect – and, if I had, they might have been better. My 'friends' among dons were chiefly pleased to tell me that I spoke too fast and might have been interesting if I could be heard. True often: due in part to having too much to say in too little time, in larger part to diffidence, which such comments increased.

I never gave the customary 'inaugural' when taking up either of my 'chairs' – because I was too frightened of a don-audience. I substituted a 'valedictory' in 1959: and to my surprise it was packed out. But the University press refused to publish it (though they always publish inaugurals) because it was not an 'inaugural'![6] Yet many people wrote approving my choice. Julian Huxley said it was an excellent innovation that should be followed. ('Inaugurals' are largely addressed to small audiences, casually assembled (but probably containing some professional ill-wishers who favoured some other candidate), and are either dull, or off the point, or occasionally pompous announcements of changes of policy and what the new professor intends to do.)

307 From a letter to Amy Ronald 14 November 1968

I said to my wife (about 3 p.m. today): 'there's a man coming to the back door with a box, but it is not from our people so it must be a mistake. Don't get up! I'll deal with it.'

So it was that I received 4 Ports and 3 Sherries, from a cheery fellow, who laughed: 'It's all right, you'll find. Just a nice present from somebody.'

I should say it *is* a nice present: and not just from Somebody. I cannot think why youbody* treat us with such magnificence. But it is very delightful. And, of course, being from you, well-timed. We are fairly snug now in our new home, having learned how to manage the central heating that was unfamiliar; but even here in a sheltered woodland

*A nice singular which I feel hobbits must have used, with a distinctive pl[ural] '*youbodies*'.

(though within sound of the sea) nights, and days, grow chill. Port and a good sweet sherry are great warmers.

Elde is me istolen on ... ich am eldre than i was a wintre and ek a lore:[1] so wrote a moralist (c. AD 1200 or earlier). It did not touch me until recently. I *hope 'ek a lore'* (sc. also in *learning*, which seems to include the learning of experience, justifying the giving of advice!) is true. But I doubt it.

308 To Christopher Tolkien

2 January 1969   [19 Lakeside Road, Branksome Park, Poole]

Dearest C.

This is hardly 'correspondence'; but I must just write to wish you good fortune in 1969. . . . .

My library is now in order; and nearly all the things that I thought were lost have turned up. (Also some things which I thought were lost before the move!) Joe Wright's *Gothic Gram[mar]* first edn. has vanished; but it is of no importance, except sentimental. It was the acquisition of this by accident that opened my eyes to a window on 'Gmc. philology'. No doubt it contributed to my poor performance in Hon. Mods.; though it guided me to sit at the feet of old Joe in person. He proved a good friend and adviser. Also he grounded me in G[reek] and L[atin] philology. (It was only many years later that I discovered and met the angelic examiner who gave me $\alpha+$ in Gk. Philol. and so saved my 'bacon', by squeaking into a 'second' instead of merited 'third', with the consequence that I did not lose my 'exhibition', and was allowed by a generous college – Farnell, my tutor and then Rector, had a respect for philology and was one of the dons who in the days of Yorke Powell and Vigfusson had become aware of Northern learning – to transfer to 'English' avowedly as a pure philologue with no liking at all for English.) . . . .

I have horrible arthritis in the *left* hand, which cannot excuse this scrawl, since, mercifully, my right is not yet affected! Love to you both. I wish you were not so far away. (But it is very comfortable here!) . . . .

309 From a letter to Amy Ronald 2 January 1969

Now, my dear, as to my name. It is *John*: a name much used and loved by Christians, and since I was born on the Octave of St John the Evangelist, I take him as my patron – though neither my father, nor my mother at that time, would have thought of anything so Romish as giving me a name because it was a saint's. I was called John because it was the custom for the eldest son of the eldest son to be called John in my family. My father was Arthur, eldest of my grandfather John Benjamin's second family; but his elder half-brother John had died leaving only 3 daughters. So John I had to be, and was dandled on the knee of old J.B., as the heir, before he died. (I was only *four* when he died at 92 in 1896.)[1]

My father favoured John Benjamin Reuel (which I should now have liked); but my mother was confident that I should be a daughter, and being fond of more 'romantic' (& less O[ld] T[estament] like) names decided on Rosalind. When I turned up, prematurely, and a boy though weak and ailing, Ronald was substituted. It was then a much rarer name in England as a Christian name – I never in fact knew any of my contemporaries at school or Oxford who had the name – though it seems now alas! to be prevalent among the criminal and other degraded classes. Anyway I have always treated it with respect, and from earliest days refused to allow it to be abbreviated or tagged with. But for myself I remained John. Ronald was for my near kin. My friends at school, Oxford and later have called me John (or occasionally John Ronald or J. Rsquared). . . . .[2]

As for an 'Elvish' name: I could of course invent one. But I do not really belong *inside* my invented history; and do not wish to!

As for Master: I am not one. In high uses it would be presumptuous and profane to adopt such a title; in lower uses it is conceited. I am a 'professor' – or was, and occasionally in more inspired moments deserved the title – and it is now at any rate (though not in Oxford of the generation before mine) a customary social title.

So what? I think if for private reasons *John* or *Ronald* is not pleasing for you to use (I quite understand that the collocation John Ronald is so) then we must fall back on 'Professor'. (And I shall call you Lady!)

Of course there is always *Reuel*. This was (I believe) the surname of a friend of my grandfather. The family believed it to be French (which is formally possible); but if so it is an odd chance that it appears twice in the O[ld] T[estament] as an unexplained other name for Jethro Moses' father-in-law. All my children, and my children's children, and their children, have the name.

I think I shall call you Aimée, which I like better than its anglicization, and suits your love & knowledge of French. . . . .

[As a postscript to the letter:]

> J. R. R. Tolkien
> had a cat called Grimalkin:
> once a familiar of Herr Grimm,
> now he spoke the law to him.

[Rayner Unwin's daughter Camilla was told, as part of a school 'project',
to write and ask: 'What is the purpose of life?']

20 May 1969   [19 Lakeside Road, Branksome Park, Poole]
Dear Miss Unwin,

I am sorry my reply has been delayed. I hope it will reach you in time.
What a very large question! I do not think 'opinions', no matter whose,
are of much use without some explanation of how they are arrived at;
but on this question it is not easy to be brief.

What does the question really mean? *Purpose* and *Life* both need
some definition. Is it a purely human and moral question; or does it refer
to the Universe? It might mean: How ought I to try and use the life-span
allowed to me? OR: What purpose/design do living things serve by
being alive? The first question, however, will find an answer (if any)
only after the second has been considered.

I think that questions about 'purpose' are only really useful when
they refer to the conscious purposes or objects of human beings, or to
the uses of things they design and make. As for 'other things' their value
resides in themselves: they ARE, they would exist even if we did not.
But since we do exist one of their functions is to be contemplated by us.
If we go up the scale of being to 'other living things', such as, say, some
small plant, it presents shape and organization: a 'pattern' recognizable
(with variation) in its kin and offspring; and that is deeply interesting,
because these things are 'other' and we did not make them, and they
seem to proceed from a fountain of invention incalculably richer than
our own.

Human curiosity soon asks the question HOW: in what way did
this come to be? And since recognizable 'pattern' suggests design, may
proceed to WHY? But WHY in this sense, implying reasons and
motives, can only refer to a MIND. Only a Mind can have purposes in
any way or degree akin to human purposes. So at once any question:
'Why did life, the community of living things, appear in the physical
Universe?' introduces the Question: Is there a God, a Creator-Designer,
a Mind to which our minds are akin (being derived from it) so that It is
intelligible to us in part. With that we come to religion and the moral
ideas that proceed from it. Of those things I will only say that 'morals'
have two sides, derived from the fact that we are individuals (as in some
degree are all living things) but do not, cannot, live in isolation, and have
a bond with all other things, ever closer up to the absolute bond with our
own human kind.

So morals should be a guide to our human purposes, the conduct of
our lives: (a) the ways in which our individual talents can be developed

without waste or misuse; and (b) without injuring our kindred or interfering with their development. (Beyond this and higher lies self-sacrifice for love.)

But these are only answers to the smaller question. To the larger there is no answer, because that requires a *complete* knowledge of God, which is unattainable. If we ask why God included us in his Design, we can really say no more than because He Did.

If you do not believe in a personal God the question: 'What is the purpose of life?' is unaskable and unanswerable. To whom or what would you address the question? But since in an odd corner (or odd corners) of the Universe things have developed with minds that ask questions and try to answer them, you might address one of these peculiar things. As one of them I should venture to say (speaking with absurd arrogance on behalf of the Universe): 'I am as I am. There is nothing you can do about it. You may go on trying to find out what I am, but you will never succeed. And why you want to know, I do not know. Perhaps the desire to know for the mere sake of knowledge is related to the prayers that some of you address to what you call God. At their highest these seem simply to praise Him for being, as He is, and for making what He has made, as He has made it.'

Those who believe in a personal God, Creator, do not think the Universe is in itself worshipful, though devoted study of it may be one of the ways of honouring Him. And while as living creatures we are (in part) within it and part of it, our ideas of God and ways of expressing them will be largely derived from contemplating the world about us. (Though there is also revelation both addressed to all men and to particular persons.)

So it may be said that the chief purpose of life, for any one of us, is to increase according to our capacity our knowledge of God by all the means we have, and to be moved by it to praise and thanks. To do as we say in the *Gloria in Excelsis*: Laudamus te, benedicamus te, adoramus te, glorificamus te, gratias agimus tibi propter magnam gloriam tuam. We praise you, we call you holy, we worship you, we proclaim your glory, we thank you for the greatness of your splendour.

And in moments of exaltation we may call on all created things to join in our chorus, speaking on their behalf, as is done in Psalm 148, and in The Song of the Three Children in Daniel II. PRAISE THE LORD . . . all mountains and hills, all orchards and forests, all things that creep and birds on the wing.

This is much too long, and also much too short – on such a question.

With best wishes
J. R. R. Tolkien.

400

I was delighted to get your letter of 27th today, and felt very unhappy about my own silence. I begin to feel a bit desperate: endlessly frustrated. I have at last managed to release the demon of invention only to find myself in the state of a man who after a strong draught of a sleeping potion is waked up and not allowed to lie down for more than a few consecutive minutes. Neither in one world or another. Business – endless – lies neglected, yet I cannot get anything of my real work finished. Then came this latest stroke of malice. I was assailed by very considerable pain, and depression, which no ordinary remedy would relieve. Three weeks ago last Tuesday Tolhurst came and 'gave me the works', and diagnosed an inflamed/or diseased gall-bladder. Took me at once off all fats (including butter) and all alcohol. Usually a cheerful and encouraging doctor, he was alarmingly serious, and the prospect looked dark. We (or at least I) know far too little about the complicated machine we inhabit, and (like the totally unmechanical to whom 'carburettor' is the name of a small part of the engine of minor and little known function) underestimate the gall-bladder! It is a vital part of the chemical factory, and apart from all else can cause intense pain, if it goes wrong; and if it is 'diseased': well you are 'for it'. – I do not know why one wants to talk about illnesses, espec. since details are intricate and boring: cutting short, I was treated with great civility by the X-ray-man. He cut out all protocol, and after second bout he developed the plates at once, and came back to me with a smile, saying 'the plates will go to your doctor who will report and advise you but I can say, though the plates are still wet, that your g-b is in its right place and is functioning, and I can see no gall-stones or growths. I should go now and have a good lunch.' Tolhurst came yesterday, and took me off diet: butter and alcohol 'in moderation'. I feel quite well: i.e. as well as I did before the outset. But life is not easy. The Parke[1] has gone sick. Mummy is ailing, and I fear slowly 'declining'. Also I feel very cut off. . . . .

312   From a letter to Amy Ronald   16 November 1969

I meant to write to let you know how much I am perturbed by and sorry for your afflictions: poor dear. I pray for you – because I have a feeling (more near a certainty) that God, for some ineffable reason which to us may seem almost like humour, is so curiously ready to answer the prayers of the *least* worthy of his suppliants – if they pray for others. I do not of course mean to say that He only answers the prayers of the unworthy (who ought not to expect to be heard at all), or I should not now be benefitting by the prayers of others. What a dreadful, fear-darkened, sorrow-laden world we live in – especially for those who have also the burden of age, whose friends and all they especially care for are afflicted in the same way. Chesterton once said that it is our duty to keep the Flag of This World flying: but it takes now a sturdier and more sublime patriotism than it did then. Gandalf added that it is not for us to choose the times into which we are born, but to do what we could to repair them; but the spirit of wickedness in high places is now so powerful and so many-headed in its incarnations that there seems nothing more to do than personally to refuse to worship any of the hydras' heads. . . . .

I have greatly enjoyed the Cape Flower Book.[1] Quite fascinating in itself and in its general botanical and indeed paleo-implications. I have not seen anything that immediately recalls *niphredil* or *elanor* or *alfirin*: but that I think is because those imagined flowers are lit by a light that would not be seen ever in a growing plant and cannot be recaptured by paint. Lit by that light, *niphredil* would be simply a delicate kin of a snowdrop; and *elanor* a pimpernel (perhaps a little enlarged) growing sun-golden flowers and star-silver ones on the same plant, and sometimes the two combined. *Alfirin* ('immortal') would be an immortelle, but not dry and papery: simply a beautiful bell-like flower, running through many colours, but soft and gentle. . . . .

All illustrated botany books (or better, contact direct with an unfamiliar flora) have for me a special fascination. Not so much the rare, unusual, or totally unrelated specimens, as in the variations and permutations of flowers that are the evident *kin* of those I know – but not the same. They rouse in me visions of kinship and descent through great ages, and also thoughts of the mystery of pattern/design as a thing other than its individual embodiment, and recognizable. How? I remember once in the corner of a botanical garden growing (unlabelled and unnamed) a plant that fascinated me. I knew of the 'family' Scrofulariceæ, and had always accepted that the scientific bases of grouping plants in 'families' was sound, and that in general this grouping did point to actual physical kinship in descent. But in contemplating say Figwort and the Foxglove, one has to take this on trust. But there I saw a 'missing link'. A beautiful 'fox-glove', bells and all – but also a figwort: for the bells were brown-red, the red tincture ran through the veins of all the leaves, and its stem was angular. One of the 17 species (I suppose) of Digitalis which we do not possess in Britain. But such botany books as I have do not comment on such 'links' between the *branches* of the family (Scrofularia & Digitalis). Just occasionally one actually sees a change take place – which might in favourable circumstances become permanent. In a former garden I had a border planted with garden daisies (mostly red); but they seeded into the lawn, where in the struggle

402

for life they reverted to ordinary daisies and conducted their battle with the grass like their ancestors. Some seeds, however, managed to reach a place where an enormously rich soil had developed (rotting grass and deep black bonfire ash). One hardy adventurer tried to do something about it – but could only do it in daisy fashion: it grew four times the size with a flower the size of a half-crown. I said 'magnificent; but a little coarse? No real improvement on *bellis perennis.*' It or Something may have heard. Next morning it had put out from its flower, on delicate stalks rising in a ring out of the rim of the disc, six pink-tipped little elvish daisies like an airy crown. Far more graceful and patterned than any hen-and-chickens development I had – or have – seen. (I had not the time or skill to perpetuate it.)

313 From a letter to Michael Tolkien 25 November 1969

I wish I had time to produce an elementary (! both languages are, of course, extremely difficult) grammar and vocabulary of 'elven': sc. Quenya and Sindarin. I am having to do some work on them, in the process of adjusting 'the Silmarillion and all that' to The L.R. Which I am labouring at, under endless difficulties: not least the natural sloth of 77+.

314 From a letter to Christopher Tolkien 15 December 1969

As to your last paragraph! I am wholly in favour of the 'dull stodges'. I had once a considerable experience of what are/were probably England's most (at least apparently) dullest and stodgiest students: Yorkshire's young men and women of sub-public school class and home back-grounds bookless and cultureless. That does not, however, necessarily indicate the actual innate mental capacity – largely unawakened – of any given individual. A surprisingly large proportion prove 'educable': for which a primary qualification is the willingness *to do some work* (to learn) (at any level of intelligence).* Teaching is a most exhausting task. But I would rather spend myself on removing the 'dull' from 'stodges' – providing some products of β to β + quality that retain some sanity – a hopeful soil from which another generation with some higher intel-ligence could arise. Rather – rather than waste effort on those of (apparently at any rate) higher intelligence that have been corrupted and

*This willingness usually connotes some degree of humility. In Yorkshire its first impulse was the desire to 'get on'. But that does not remain the sole objective. Cupboard-love is a frequent preliminary to actual love.

disintegrated by school, and the 'climate' of our present days.* Teaching an organized subject is simply not the instrument for their rehabilitation – if anything is. Give me one little stubby root, which possibly in a better soil will send out some leaves, and even eventually produce some seed, rather than a large pink root rotten with carrot fly! Amen. But I am old, and probably unable to envisage the appalling situation now existing. Worse even than the soft roots rotten with disease, are (I imagine) the inferior ones that in my time would have been probably sound, but are now equally rotten, but meaner and nastier.

315 From a letter to Michael Tolkien 1 January 1970

I am *not* getting on fast with *The S*. The domestic situation, Mummy's gallant but losing fight against age and disability (and pain), and my own years – and all the interruptions of 'business' do not leave much time. I have in fact so far been chiefly employed in trying to co-ordinate the nomenclature of the very early and later parts of the *Silmarillion* with the situation in The L.R. 'Stories' still sprout in my mind from names; but it is a very difficult and complex task.

When you pray for me, pray for 'time'! I should like to put some of this stuff into readable form, and some sketched for others to make use of. Also I should dearly love to defeat the Inland Revenue and survive beyond the iniquitous 7 years.[1] (Also I should like time to set down what I know or remember of my childhood and my kin on either side.)

316 From a letter to R. W. Burchfield 11 September 1970

[The *Oxford English Dictionary* staff, under Dr Burchfield, were compiling an entry for *hobbit* in their Second Supplement. Tolkien's help was sought, particularly on the question of whether he had invented the word, or whether there had been an older story with the same title (see no. 25).]

The matter of *hobbit* is not very important, but I may be forgiven for taking a personal interest in it and being anxious that the meaning intended by me should be made clear.

Unfortunately, as all lexicographers know, 'don't look into things, unless you are looking for trouble: they nearly always turn out to be less simple than you thought'. You will shortly be receiving a long letter on *hobbit* and related matters, of which, even if it is in time, only a small part may be useful or interesting to you.[1]

For the moment this is held up, because I am having the matter of the

*Not to mention 'drugs'

etymology: 'Invented by J. R. R. Tolkien': investigated by experts. I knew that the claim was not clear, but I had not troubled to look into it, until faced by the inclusion of *hobbit* in the Supplement.

In the meanwhile I submit for your consideration the following definition:

> One of an imaginary people, a small variety of the human race, that gave themselves this name (meaning 'hole-dweller') but were called by others *halflings*, since they were half the height of normal Men.[2]

This assumes that the etymology can stand. If not it may be necessary to modify it: e.g. by substituting after 'race'

> ; in the tales of J. R. R. Tolkien said to have given themselves this name, though others called them . . .

If it stands, as I think it will even if an alleged older story called 'The Hobbit'[3] can be traced, then the '(meaning "hole-dweller")' could be transferred to the etymology.

317 From a letter to Amy Ronald All Hallows 1970

I have expended your wonderful gift. I felt like a wise man setting out on a long voyage, and storing his craft with the most useful and necessary things:– I still feel this house is a ship or ark: it looks like one (from the garden), contented and quiet but at the same time still a bit surprised, as if it had been dumped here by a wave while asleep, and did not feel sure where it was.

Alas I did not buy any good brandy. My palate has never learned to appreciate it as it deserves. But I have laid in some burgundy – some port which we both like,* and some good sherry, some liqueurs, and one bottle of champagne (with a view to Christmas).

318 From a letter to Neil Ker 22 November 1970

[Ker had sent Tolkien a copy of an article on A. S. Napier (1853–1916), who was Professor of English Language & Literature at Oxford when Tolkien became an undergraduate.]

I am most grateful for your kindness in sending me an offprint of your work on Napier. I have been deeply interested in it. Naturally. I entered the English School in T[rinity] T[erm] 1913 at my own request: I had

---

*Not 'vintage'. But I like port (v. much) as a mid-morn. drink: warming, digestible, and v. good for my throat, when taken (as I think it should be) by itself or with a dry biscuit, and NOT after a full meal, nor (above all) with desert!

discovered its existence in the Examination Statutes. I was not as surprised as I ought to have been by the generosity of Exeter College in allowing me to do this without depriving me of my classical exhibition, but your essay confirms my guess that this was due to Farnell.[1]

At any rate he wrote me an introduction to Napier, and I called on him at his house in Headington. I recall that I was ushered into a very dim room and could hardly see Napier. He was courteous, but said little. He never spoke to me again. I attended his lectures, when he was well enough to give them. But alas! I came too late. His illness must have been already far advanced.

But this was compensated by a piece of singular good fortune: Sisam[2] became my tutor. I think I certainly derived from him much of the benefit which he attributes to Napier's example and teaching. To these things Sisam's own great talents were evidently very responsive, and his feelings warmed by affection for a great man in his decline. His teaching was, however, spiced with a pungency, humour and practical wisdom which were his own. I owe him a great debt and have not forgotten it. . . .

Incidentally the foundation of my library was laid by Sisam. He taught me not only to read texts, but to study second-hand book catalogues, of which I was not even aware. Some he marked for me.

319 From a letter to Roger Lancelyn Green   8 January 1971

The Ox. E. D. has in preparation of its Second Supplement got to *Hobbit*, which it proposes to include together with its progeny: *hobbitry*, *-ish*, etc. I have had, therefore, to justify my claim to have invented the word. My claim rests really on my 'nude parole' or unsupported assertion that I remember the occasion of its invention (by me); and that I had not *then* any knowledge of *Hobberdy*, *Hobbaty*, *Hobberdy Dick* etc. (for 'house-sprites');* and that my 'hobbits' were in any case of wholly dissimilar sort, a diminutive branch of the human race. Also that the only E. word that influenced the invention was 'hole'; that granted the description of *hobbits*, the trolls' use of *rabbit* was merely an obvious insult, of no more etymological significance than Thorin's insult to Bilbo 'descendant of rats!' However, doubt was cast on this as far back as 1938.[1] A review appeared in *The Observer* 16 Jan 1938, signed *'Habit'* (incidentally thus long anticipating Coghill's perception of the similarity of the words in his humorous adj. 'hobbit-

*I have now! Probably more than most other folk; and find myself in a v. tangled wood – the clue to which is, however, the belief in *incubi* and 'changelings'. Alas! one conclusion is that the statement that *hobgoblins* were 'a larger kind' is the reverse of the original truth. (The statement occurs in the preliminary note on Runes devised for the paperback edition, but now included by A & U in all edns.)

forming' applied to my books). 'Habit' asserted that a friend claimed to have read, about 20 years earlier (sc. c. 1918) an old 'fairy story' (in a collection of such tales) called *The Hobbit,* though the creature was very 'frightening'. I asked for more information, but have never received any; and recent intensive research has not discovered the 'collection'. I think it is probable that the friend's memory was inaccurate (after 20 years), and the creature probably had a name of the *Hobberdy, Hobbaty* class. However, one cannot exclude the possibility that buried child-hood memories might suddenly rise to the surface long after (in my case after 35–40 years), though they might be quite differently applied. I told the researchers that I used (before 1900) to be read to from an 'old collection' – tattered and without cover or title-page – of which all I can now remember was that (I think) it was by Bulwer Lytton, and con-tained one story I was then very fond of called *'Puss Cat Mew'*. They have not discovered it. I wonder if you, the most learned of living scholars in this region, can say anything.[2] Esp. for my own satisfaction about *Puss Cat Mew* – I do not suppose you have found a name precisely *hobbit* or you would have mentioned it. Oh what a tangled web they weave who try a new word to conceive!

320 From a letter to Mrs Ruth Austin   25 January 1971

I was particularly interested in your remarks about Galadriel. . . . . I think it is true that I owe much of this character to Christian and Catholic teaching and imagination about Mary, but actually Galadriel was a penitent: in her youth a leader in the rebellion against the Valar (the angelic guardians). At the end of the First Age she proudly refused forgiveness or permission to return. She was pardoned because of her resistance to the final and overwhelming temptation to take the Ring for herself.

321 From a letter to P. Rorke, S.J.   4 February 1971

[With reference to the Caverns of Helm's Deep in *The Lord of the Rings.*]

I was most pleased by your reference to the description of 'glittering caves'. No other critic, I think, has picked it out for special mention. It may interest you to know that the passage was based on the caves in Cheddar Gorge and was written just after I had revisited these in 1940 but was still coloured by my memory of them much earlier before they became so commercialized. I had been there during my honeymoon nearly thirty years before.

As far as my work goes, things are looking more hopeful now than they have done for some time and it is possible that I may be able to send an instalment of the *Silmarillion* to Allen & Unwin later this year.

323   To Christopher Tolkien

Begun about June 2nd. 1971.   [19 Lakeside Road]
My dearest C.

I am sorry that I have been so silent. But only a long 'tale of woe', of which you know the main outlines, wd. fully explain it. Here we are June 2nd, and May, one of the best of my experience, has escaped, without a stroke of 'writing'. Not all 'woe' of course. Our brief holiday to Sidmouth, which was what Dr Tolhurst's advice boiled down to, was very pleasant indeed. We were lucky in our time – in fact the only week available at the hotel – since May was such a wonderful month – and we came in for a 'spring explosion' of glory, with Devon passing from brown to brilliant yellow-green, and all the flowers leaping out of dead bracken or old grass. (Incidentally the oaks have behaved in a most extraordinary way. The old saw about the oak and the ash, if it has any truth, would usually need wide-spread statistics, since the gap between their wakening is usually so small that it can be changed by minor local differences of situation. But this year there seemed a month between them! The oaks were among the earliest trees to be leafed equalling or beating birch, beech and lime etc. Great cauliflowers of brilliant yellow-ochre tasseled with flowers, while the ashes (in the same situations) were dark, dead, with hardly even a visible sticky bud). . . . .

The Belmont proved a v.g. choice. Indeed the chief changes we observed in Sidmouth was the rise of this rather grim looking hotel (in spite of its perfect position) to be the best in the place – especially for *eating*. . . . . Neither M nor I have eaten so much in a week (without indigestion) for years. In addition our faithful cruise-friends (Boarland) of some six years ago, who recently moved to Sidmouth, and were so anxious to see us again that they vetted our rooms [at] the Belmont, provided us with a car, and took us drives nearly every day. So I saw again much of the country you (especially) and I used to explore in the old days of poor old JO, that valiant sorely-tried old Morris.[1] An added comfort was the fact that Sidmouth seemed practically unchanged, even the shops: many still having the same names (such as Frisby, Trump, and Potbury). Well that is that, & now, alas, over! I am, of course, still in the doldrums as far as my proper work goes – with time leaking away so fast.

June 10th. At this point I was interrupted – as usual. But among other things, both M and I have been afflicted with what may be either a 'virus', or food-poisoning of which the risk is steadily mounting in this polluted country of which a growing proportion of the inhabitants are maniacs. . . . .

I am longing to see you. I am sure there are many more things, which I shall remember as soon as this is posted, that I wished to say. But what I personally need, prob. more than anything, is two or three days general consultation and interchange with *you*. Though I think the course of events ran in an inescapable succession, I now regret daily that we are separated by a distance too great for swift interchange, and I am so immoveable. . . . .

324   From a letter to Graham Tayar   4–5 June 1971

[Tayar had asked about the use of the name 'Gamgee' in *The Lord of the Rings*, and whether the name 'Gondor' had been suggested by Gondar in Ethiopia.]

In the matter of *Gondar/Gondor* you touch on a difficult matter, but one of great interest: the nature of the process of 'linguistic invention' (including nomenclature) in general, and in *The Lord of the Rings* in particular. It would take too long to discuss this – it needs a long essay which I have often in mind but shall probably never write. As far as *Gondor* goes the facts (of which I am aware) are these: 1) I do not recollect ever having heard the name *Gondar* (in Ethiopia) before your letter; 2) *Gondor* is (a) a name fitted to the style and phonetics of *Sindarin*, and (b) has the sense 'Stone-land' sc. 'Stone (-using people's) land'.* Outside the inner historical fiction, the name was a very early element in the invention of the whole story. Also in the linguistic construction of the tale,† which is accurate and detailed, *Gondor* and *Gondar* would be two distinct words/names, and the latter would have no precise sense. Nonetheless one's mind is, of course, stored with a 'leaf-mould' of memories (submerged) of names, and these rise up to the surface at times, and may provide with modification the bases of 'invented' names. Owing to the prominence of Ethiopia in the Italian war *Gondar* may have been one such element. But no more than say *Gondwana-land*

*This meaning was understood by other peoples ignorant of Sindarin: cf. *Stoningland* (1 vol. edn. 882), and in particular the conversation of *Théoden* and *Ghân* 864f. In fact it is probable within the historical fiction that the Númenóreans of the Southern kingdom adopted this name from the primitive inhabitants of *Gondor* and gave it a suitable version in Sindarin.

†The remark in the foreword to the 1 vol. paper-back p. 7 that the whole thing was 'primarily linguistic in inspiration' is strictly true.

(that rare venture of geology into poetry). In this case I can actually recollect the reason why the element *gon(o), *gond(o) was selected for the stem of words meaning stone, when I began inventing the 'Elvish' languages. When about 8 years old I read in a small book (professedly for the young) that nothing of the language of primitive peoples (before the Celts or Germanic invaders) is now known, except perhaps *ond* = 'stone' (+ one other now forgotten). I have no idea how such a form could even be guessed, but the *ond* seemed to me fitting for the meaning. (The prefixing of g- was much later, after the invention of the history of the relation between *Sindarin* & *Quenya* in which primitive initial g- was lost in Q: the Q. form of the word remained *ondo*.) . . . .

Gamgee is quite a different matter. In my early days *gamgee* was the word we used for what is/was more generally called 'cotton-wool'. . . . . Recently in the English Place Names Society volumes on Gloucester-shire (vol. iii) I came across forms that could conceivably explain the curious *Gamgee* as a variant of the not uncommon surname *Gamage* (*Gammage, Gammidge*). This name is ultimately derived from a surname *de Gamaches* . . . . but early records of the forms of this name in England, as *Gamages, de Gamagis, de Gemegis*, might well provide a variant *Gamagi* > *Gamgee*.

Your reference to *Samson Gamgee* is thus very interesting. Since he is mentioned in a book on Birmingham Jewry, I wonder if this family was also Jewish. In which case the origin of the name might be quite different. Not that a name of French or Francized form is impossible for a Jewish surname, especially if it is one long established in England. We now associate Jewish names largely with German, and with a colloquial Yiddish that is predominantly German in origin.* But the lingua franca of mediæval Jewry was (I was told by Cecil Roth, a friend of mine) of French or mixed French-Provencal character.

325 From a letter to Roger Lancelyn Green 17 July 1971

The 'immortals' who were permitted to leave Middle-earth and seek *Aman* – the undying lands of *Valinor* and *Eressëa*, an island assigned to the *Eldar* – set sail in ships specially made and hallowed for this voyage, and steered due West towards the ancient site of these lands. They only set out after sundown; but if any keen-eyed observer from that shore had watched one of these ships he might have seen that it never became hull-down but dwindled only by distance until it vanished in the

---

*Possibly the reason why my surname is now usually misspelt TOLKEIN in spite of all my efforts to correct this – even by my college-, bank-, and lawyer's clerks! My name is Tolkien, anglicized from *To(l)kiehn* = *tollkühn*, and came from Saxony in the 18th century. It is not Jewish in origin, though I should consider it an honour if it were.

twilight: it followed the straight road to the true West and not the bent road of the earth's surface. As it vanished it left the physical world. There was no return. The Elves who took this road and those few 'mortals' who by special grace went with them, had abandoned the 'History of the world' and could play no further part in it.

The angelic immortals (incarnate only at their own will), the *Valar* or regents under God, and others of the same order but less power and majesty (such as Olórin = Gandalf) needed no transport, unless they for a time remained incarnate, and they could, if allowed or commanded, return.

As for *Frodo* or other mortals, they could only dwell in *Aman* for a limited time – whether brief or long. The *Valar* had neither the power nor the right to confer 'immortality' upon them. Their sojourn was a 'purgatory', but one of peace and healing and they would eventually pass away (*die* at their own desire and of free will) to destinations of which the Elves knew nothing.

This general idea lies behind the events of *The Lord of the Rings* and the *Silmarillion*, but it is not put forward as geologically or astronomically 'true'; except that some special physical catastrophe is supposed to lie behind the legends and marked the first stage in the succession of Men to dominion of the world. But the legends are mainly of 'Mannish' origin blended with those of the Sindar (Gray-elves) and others who had never left Middle-earth.

326 From a letter to Rayner Unwin   24 July 1971

[Since the death of Sir Stanley Unwin, Rayner had been Chairman of Allen & Unwin.]

I do miss seeing you very much, though it is inevitable since your accession to the throne: + of course all the care of men: uneasy lies the head that wears the father's bowler.

327 From a letter to Robert H. Boyer   25 August 1971

[Answering a question about his acquaintance with W. H. Auden.]

I did not know Auden personally as a young man and in fact I have only met and spoken to him very few times in my life.

So far as his interest in Old English Poetry was due to me, this was derived from my public lectures and was mainly due to his own natural talents and the possession of an 'open ear' among the majority of the deaf.

I am, however, very deeply in Auden's debt in recent years. His support of me and interest in my work has been one of my chief encouragements. He gave me very good reviews, notices and letters from the beginning when it was by no means a popular thing to do. He was, in fact, sneered at for it.

I regard him as one of my great friends although we have so seldom met except through letters and gifts of his works. I tried to repay him and express part of my feelings by writing a commendatory poem in Old English, which appeared in a volume of *Shenandoah* celebrating his sixtieth birthday.

328 To Carole Batten-Phelps (draft)

[Autumn 1971]   [19 Lakeside Road]
Dear Miss Batten-Phelps,

I am sorry that your letter (written on August 20th) was delayed in reaching me, and has then again waited so long for an answer. I am harassed by many things and the endless 'business' of my affairs; and I am in constant anxiety owing to my wife's failing health. . . . .

I was much interested in your references to M. R. Ridley.[1] We of course knew one another well at Oxford. . . . . Not until I got your letter did I learn that he had done me the honour of placing the works of his old colleague in the ranks of 'literature', and gaining me intelligent and well-equipped readers. Not a soil in which the fungus-growth of cults is likely to arise. The horrors of the American scene I will pass over, though they have given me great distress and labour. (They arise in an entirely different mental climate and soil, polluted and impoverished to a degree only paralleled by the lunatic destruction of the physical lands which Americans inhabit.) . . . .

I am very grateful for your remarks on the critics and for your account of your personal delight in *The Lord of the Rings*. You write in terms of such high praise that [to] accept it with just a 'thank you' might seem complacently conceited, though actually it only makes me wonder how this has been achieved – by me! Of course the book was written to please myself (at different levels), and as an experiment in the arts of long narrative, and of inducing 'Secondary Belief'. It was written slowly and with great care for detail, & finally emerged as a Frameless Picture: a searchlight, as it were, on a brief episode in History, and on a small part of our Middle-earth, surrounded by the glimmer of limitless extensions in time and space. Very well: that may explain to some extent why it 'feels' like history; why it was accepted for publication; and why it has proved readable for a large number of very different kinds of people. But it does not fully explain what has actually happened. Looking back

on the wholly unexpected things that have followed its publication –
beginning at once with the appearance of Vol. I – I feel as if an ever
darkening sky over our present world had been suddenly pierced, the
clouds rolled back, and an almost forgotten sunlight had poured down
again. As if indeed the horns of Hope had been heard again, as Pippin
heard them suddenly at the absolute *nadir* of the fortunes of the West.
But How? and *Why?*

I think I can now guess what Gandalf would reply. A few years ago I
was visited in Oxford by a man whose name I have forgotten (though I
believe he was well-known). He had been much struck by the curious
way in which many old pictures seemed to him to have been designed to
illustrate *The Lord of the Rings* long before its time. He brought one or
two reproductions. I think he wanted at first simply to discover whether
my imagination had fed on pictures, as it clearly had been by certain
kinds of literature and languages. When it became obvious that, unless I
was a liar, I had never seen the pictures before and was not well
acquainted with pictorial Art, he fell silent. I became aware that he was
looking fixedly at me. Suddenly he said: 'Of course you don't suppose,
do you, that you wrote all that book yourself?'

Pure Gandalf! I was too well acquainted with G. to expose myself
rashly, or to ask what he meant. I think I said: 'No, I don't suppose so
any longer.' I have never since been able to suppose so. An alarming
conclusion for an old philologist to draw concerning his private amusement. But not one that should puff any one up who considers the
imperfections of 'chosen instruments', and indeed what sometimes
seems their lamentable unfitness for the purpose.

You speak of 'a sanity and sanctity' in *the L.R.* 'which is a power in
itself'. I was deeply moved. Nothing of the kind had been said to me
before. But by a strange chance, just as I was beginning this letter, I had
one from a man, who classified himself as 'an unbeliever, or at best a
man of belatedly and dimly dawning religious feeling . . . but you', he
said, 'create a world in which some sort of faith seems to be everywhere
without a visible source, like light from an invisible lamp'. I can only
answer: 'Of his own sanity no man can securely judge. If sanctity
inhabits his work or as a pervading light illumines it then it does not
come from him but through him. And neither of you would perceive it
in these terms unless it was with you also. Otherwise you would see and
feel nothing, or (if some other spirit was present) you would be filled
with contempt, nausea, hatred. "Leaves out of the elf-country, gah!"
"Lembas – dust and ashes, we don't eat that."

Of course *The L.R.* does not belong to me. It has been brought forth
and must now go its appointed way in the world, though naturally I take
a deep interest in its fortunes, as a parent would of a child. I am

comforted to know that it has good friends to defend it against the malice of its enemies. (But all the fools are not in the other camp.) With best wishes to one of its best friends. I am

Yours sincerely
J. R. R. Tolkien.

329 From a letter to Peter Szabó Szentmihályi (draft)
[October 1971]

I have no time to provide bibliographical material concerning criticisms, reviews, or translations.

The following points, however, I should like to make briefly. (1) One of my strongest opinions is that investigation of an author's biography (or such other glimpses of his 'personality' as can be gleaned by the curious) is an entirely vain and false approach to his works – and especially to a *work of narrative art*, of which the object aimed at by the author was to be *enjoyed* as such: to be read with literary *pleasure*. So that any reader whom the author has (to his great satisfaction) succeded in 'pleasing' (exciting, engrossing, moving etc.), should, if he wishes others to be similarly pleased, endeavour in his own words, with only the book itself as his source, to induce them to read it for literary pleasure. When they have read it, some readers will (I suppose) wish to 'criticize' it, and even to analyze it, and if that is their mentality they are, of course, at liberty to do these things – so long as they have *first* read it with attention throughout. Not that this attitude of mind has my sympathy: as should be clearly perceived in Vol. I p. 272: Gandalf: 'He that breaks a thing to find out what it is has left the path of wisdom.'

(2) I have very little interest in serial literary history, and no interest at all in the history or present situation of the English 'novel'. My work is *not* a 'novel', but an 'heroic romance' a much older and quite different variety of literature.

(3) Affixing 'labels' to writers, living or dead, is an inept procedure, in any circumstances: a childish amusement of small minds: and very 'deadening', since at best it overemphasizes what is common to a selected group of writers, and distracts attention from what is *individual* (and not classifiable) in each of them, and is the element that gives them life (if they have any). But I cannot understand how I should be labelled 'a believer in moral didacticism'. Who by? It is in any case the exact opposite of my procedure in *The Lord of the Rings*. I neither preach nor teach.

330 From a letter to William Cater 1 November 1971

[During this month, Cater visited Tolkien to interview him for the *Sunday Times*. The interview was published on 2 January 1972, as part of an eightieth birthday tribute to Tolkien.]

I am v. sorry about this: your letter of 19th October is still unanswered, although it was one of the most kind and encouraging letters I have received from any one. I must ask you to believe that *letters* (of any length) to an isolated man are like bread to a prisoner starving in a tower.

331 To William Cater

29 November 1971   [Miramar Hotel, Bournemouth]
My dear Cater,
    I am grieved to tell you that my wife died this morning. Her courage and determination (of which you speak truly) carried her through to what seemed the brink of recovery, but a sudden relapse occurred which she fought for nearly three days in vain. She died at last in peace.
    I am utterly bereaved, and cannot yet lift up heart, but my family is gathering round me and many friends. There will be notices in *Times* and *Telegraph*. I am glad that you saw her still undimmed on Thursday (18th I think), before she fell ill on Friday night (19). I shall treasure your letter of 26th, especially for its last lines.
Yours ever sincerely
Ronald Tolkien.

332 To Michael Tolkien

[Merton College, of which Tolkien had been a Fellow from 1945 to 1959, had offered him accommodation now that his home in Poole was being given up.]

24 January 1972   West Hanney[1]
Dearest Mick,
    . . . . I think the news will comfort and please you. By an act of great generosity – in spite of great internal difficulties – Merton has now provided [me] with a very excellent flat, which will probably accommodate the bulk of my surviving 'library'. But wholly unexpected 'strings' are attached to this! (1) The rent will be 'merely nominal' – which means what it implies: something extremely small in comparison with actual market-value; (2) All or any furniture required will be provided *free* by the college – and a large Wilton carpet has already been assigned to me, covering the whole floor of a sitting room having nearly

415

the same floor-space as our big s[itting]-r[oom] at 19 Lakeside Road (it is a little shorter and a little broader). (3) Since 21 M[erton] St. is legally part of the college, domestic service is provided *free*: in the shape of a resident care-taker and his wife as housekeeper: (4) I am entitled to *free* lunch *and* dinner throughout the year when in residence: both of a very high standard. This represents – allowing 9 weeks absence – an actual emolument of between £750 and £900 a year from which the claws of the I. Taxgatherers have so far been driven off. (5) The college will provide free of rent two telephones: (a) for *local* calls, and calls to extensions, which are *free*, and (b) for long distance calls, which will have a private number and be paid by me. This will have the advantage that business and private calls to family and friends will not pass through the over-worked lodge; but it will have the one snag that it will have to appear in the Telephone book, and cannot be ex-directory. But I had already found in Poole that the disadvantages of an ex-directory number (which are considerable) really outweigh its protection. If it proves a nuisance I shall have a telephone answerer installed, that can be switched on at need. (6) No rates, and gas and electricity bills at a reduced scale; (7) The use of 2 beautiful common-rooms (at a distance of 100 yards) with free writing paper, free newspapers, and mid-morning coffee. It all sounds too good to be true – and of course it all depends on my health: for it has, quite justly and rightly, been pointed out to me that it is only my apparent good health and mobility for my age that makes this arrange-ment possible. I do not myself feel very secure on this point since my illness in October (in which in a week or so I lost over a stone), that did not really lose its head until after Christmas. But the feeling of insecurity is possibly (and I hope) due mainly to the maiming effect of the bereave-ment we have suffered. I do not feel quite 'real' or whole, and in a sense there is no one to talk to. (You share this, of course, especially in the matter of letters.) Since I came of age, and our 3 years separation was ended, we had shared all joys and griefs, and all opinions (in agreement or otherwise), so that I still often find myself thinking 'I must tell E. about this' – and then suddenly I feel like a castaway left on a barren island under a heedless sky after the loss of a great ship. I remember trying to tell Marjorie Incledon[2] this feeling, when I was not yet thirteen after the death of my mother (Nov. 9. 1904), and vainly waving a hand at the sky saying 'it is so empty and cold'. And again I remember after the death of Fr Francis my 'second father' (at 77 in 1934)*, saying to C. S. Lewis: 'I feel like a lost survivor into a new alien world after the real world has passed away.' But of course these griefs however poignant (especially the first) came in youth with life and work still unfolding. In

*He was actually of almost exactly the same age as my real father would have been: both were born in 1857, Francis at the end of January, and my father in the middle of February.

1904 we (H[ilary] & I) had the sudden miraculous experience of Fr Francis' love and care and humour – and only 5 years later (the equiv. of 20 years experience in later life) I met the Lúthien Tinúviel of my own personal 'romance' with her long dark hair, fair face and starry eyes, and beautiful voice. And in 1934 she was still with me, and her beautiful children. But now she has gone before Beren, leaving him indeed one-handed, but he has no power to move the inexorable Mandos, and there is no *Dor Gyrth i chuinar*, the Land of the Dead that Live, in this Fallen Kingdom of Arda, where the servants of Morgoth are worshipped. . . . .

333 To Rayner Unwin

16 March 1972   Merton College
Dear R.
    Everything you do for me fills me with gratitude.
    I am now at last since Tuesday, IN but not 'settled' in. The weather (which seems a slice of our normal 'wedding-day weather' come too early) contributes to my comfort. The great bank in the Fellows' Garden looks like the foreground of a pre-Raphaelite picture: blazing green starred like the Milky Way with blue anemones, purple/white/yellow crocuses, and final surprise, clouded-yellow, peacock, and tortoiseshell butterflies flitting about.
    I hope in less than a week's time to have ordered my 'flat', except for the last labour – recalling my library from store. I have a faint hope that perhaps you and your wife could soon pick a fine day and visit me.
    Excuse scrawl.
                                        Yours ever
                                        J. R. R. T.

334 To Rayner Unwin

[Tolkien received the C.B.E. at Buckingham Palace on 28 March 1972. Rayner Unwin held a dinner in his honour at the Garrick Club, and Allen & Unwin put him up at Brown's Hotel in London.]

30 March 1972   Merton College
My dear Rayner,
    I cannot thank you adequately for your kindness and generosity, on my own behalf and for John and Priscilla, for all that you did for us to make March 27th and 28th both memorable and delightful.
    I enjoyed the party immensely, not least because as I looked round everyone else seemed to be doing so too. I slept peacefully (in the great

comfort of Brown's), but briefly, waking at 6 a.m. to hear wind and rain; but feeling my luck to be in, I was not surprised to have brilliant sunshine for the occasion.

Owing to the skill and kindness of your driver both journeys were accomplished without hitch. Inside the Palace the ceremonies were, especially for 'recipients', accompanied by some tedium (with a few touches of the comic). But I was very deeply moved by my brief meeting with the Queen, & our few words together. Quite unlike anything that I had expected. But I will say no more about that now. Perhaps I shall have a chance of seeing you, while the memory is fresh? . . . .

Yours ever
Ronald Tolkien.

Would it be possible for you to use my Christian name? I am now accepted as a member of the community here – one of the habits of which has long been the use of Christian names, irrespective of age or office – and as you are now a v. old friend, and a very dear one, I should much like also to be a 'familiaris'.   R.

335 From a letter to Michael Salmon   18 May 1972

Thank you for your most kind letter and for your general interest in my work. I am however now an old man struggling to finish some of his work. Every extra task however small diminishes my chance of ever publishing *The Silmarillion*. So I hope you will understand why I feel it impossible to spend time making any comments on myself or my works.

336 From a letter to Sir Patrick Browne   23 May 1972

Being a cult figure in one's own lifetime I am afraid is not at all pleasant. However I do not find that it tends to puff one up; in my case at any rate it makes me feel extremely small and inadequate. But even the nose of a very modest idol (younger than Chu-Bu and not much older than Sheemish)[1] cannot remain entirely untickled by the sweet smell of incense!

337 From a letter to 'Mr Wrigley'   25 May 1972

I fear you may be right that the search for the sources of *The Lord of the Rings* is going to occupy academics for a generation or two. I wish this need not be so. To my mind it is the particular use in a particular situation of any motive, whether invented, deliberately borrowed, or unconsciously remembered that is the most interesting thing to consider.

418

[Answering the question: did the Ents ever find the Entwives?]

As for the *Entwives*: I do not know. I have written nothing beyond the first few years of the Fourth Age. (Except the beginning of a tale supposed to refer to the end of the reign of Eldaron about 100 years after the death of Aragorn. Then I of course discovered that the King's Peace would contain no tales worth recounting; and his wars would have little interest after the overthrow of Sauron; but that almost certainly a restlessness would appear about then, owing to the (it seems) inevitable boredom of Men with the good: there would be secret societies practising dark cults, and 'orc-cults' among adolescents.) But I think in Vol. II pp. 80–81[1] it is plain that there would be for Ents no re-union in 'history' – but Ents and their wives being rational creatures would find some 'earthly paradise' until the end of this world: beyond which the wisdom neither of Elves nor Ents could see. Though maybe they shared the hope of Aragorn that they were 'not bound for ever to the circles of the world and beyond them is more than memory.' . . . .

In dealing with Greek I feel like a renegade, resident wilfully for long years among 'barbarians', though I once knew something about it. Yet I prefer Latin. I feel like Theodore Haecker[2] – or like an eminent philologist (Bazell) once a pupil of mine who is now expert in such 'barbaric' tongues as Turkish, who once wrote to me about some language recently discovered: 'It is of a kind that you and I both feel to be normal, in a central human mode – it indeed resembles Latin.'

339   To the Editor of the *Daily Telegraph*

[In a leader in the *Daily Telegraph* of 29 June 1972, entitled 'Forestry and Us', there occurred this passage: 'Sheepwalks where you could once ramble for miles are transformed into a kind of Tolkien gloom, where no bird sings . . .' Tolkien's letter was published, with a slight alteration to the opening sentence, in the issue of 4 July.]

30 June 1972   Merton College, Oxford
Dear Sir,

With reference to the Daily Telegraph of June 29th, page 18, I feel that it is unfair to use my name as an adjective qualifying 'gloom', especially in a context dealing with trees. In all my works I take the part of trees as against all their enemies. Lothlórien is beautiful because there the trees were loved; elsewhere forests are represented as awakening to consciousness of themselves. The Old Forest was hostile to two legged creatures because of the memory of many injuries. Fangorn Forest was old and beautiful, but at the time of the story tense with hostility because it was threatened by a machine-loving enemy. Mirkwood had fallen under the domination of a Power that hated all living things but was restored to beauty and became Greenwood the Great before the end of the story.

It would be unfair to compare the Forestry Commission with Sauron because as you observe it is capable of repentance; but nothing it has done that is stupid compares with the destruction, torture and murder of trees perpetrated by private individuals and minor official bodies. The savage sound of the electric saw is never silent wherever trees are still found growing.

Yours faithfully,
J. R. R. Tolkien.

340 From a letter to Christopher Tolkien   11 July 1972

I have at last got busy about Mummy's grave. . . . . The inscription I should like is:

EDITH MARY TOLKIEN
1889–1971
Lúthien

: brief and jejune, except for *Lúthien*, which says for me more than a multitude of words: for she was (and knew she was) my Lúthien.*

July 13. Say what you feel, without reservation, about this addition. I began this under the stress of great emotion & regret – and in any case I am afflicted from time to time (increasingly) with an overwhelming sense of bereavement. I need advice. Yet I hope none of my children will feel that the use of this name is a sentimental fancy. It is at any rate not comparable to the quoting of pet names in obituaries. I never called Edith *Lúthien* – but she was the source of the story that in time became the chief part of the *Silmarillion*. It was first conceived in a small woodland glade filled with hemlocks at Roos in Yorkshire (where I was for a brief time in command of an outpost of the Humber Garrison in 1917, and she was able to live with me for a while). In those days her hair was raven, her skin clear, her eyes brighter than you have seen them, and she could sing – and *dance*. But the story has gone crooked, & I am left, and *I* cannot plead before the inexorable Mandos.

I will say no more now. But I should like ere long to have a long talk with *you*. For if as seems probable I shall never write any ordered biography – it is against my nature, which expresses itself about things

*She knew the earliest form of the legend (written in hospital), and also the poem eventually printed as Aragorn's song in LR.

deepest felt in tales and myths – someone close in heart to me should know something about things that records do not record: the dreadful sufferings of our childhoods, from which we rescued one another, but could not wholly heal the wounds that later often proved disabling; the sufferings that we endured after our love began – all of which (over and above our personal weaknesses) might help to make pardonable, or understandable, the lapses and darknesses which at times marred our lives – and to explain how these never touched our depths nor dimmed our memories of our youthful love. For ever (especially when alone) we still met in the woodland glade, and went hand in hand many times to escape the shadow of imminent death before our last parting.

15 July. I spent yesterday at Hemel Hempstead. A car was sent for me & I went to the great new (grey and white) offices and book-stores of Allen & Unwin. To this I paid a kind of official visitation, like a minor royalty, and was somewhat startled to discover the *main* business of all this organization of many departments (from Accountancy to Despatch) was dealing with my works. I was given a great welcome (& v.g. lunch) and interviewed them all from board-room downwards. 'Accountancy' told me that the sales of *The Hobbit* were now rocketing up to hitherto unreached heights. Also a large single order for copies of *The L.R.* had just come in. When I did not show quite the gratified surprise expected I was gently told that a single order of 100 copies used to be pleasing (and still is for other books), but this one for *The L.R.* was for 6,000.

341 **From a letter to Marjorie Incledon** 17 September 1972

I feel the truth (now very much) of what you say about the desire, indeed necessity, of escaping from 'community life', at intervals. The college has treated me with the greatest kindness and generosity: they have provided me with a beautiful flat with 2 large rooms & a bathroom in one of their houses in Merton Street, which has a caretaker (and his wife) who look after my domestic needs. They have made me a residential Emeritus Fellow with all the privileges of a Fellow (such as free lunch & dinner at the common table) but no duties. I am as far as they are concerned purely 'ornamental'. The Fellow and members of Common Room are now 3 times as many, and their standard has risen v. greatly since I was an active Fellow (1945–59): they cover almost all branches of learning & science, and are nearly all (in various degrees) very good companions, though mostly very hard-working and busy. Nonetheless – I often feel very lonely, and long for a change! After term (sc. when the undergraduates depart) I am all alone in a large house with only the caretaker & his wife far below in a basement, and since I am (especially on my return to Oxford) a marked man, and troubled with many intruders and some nefarious persons, I live behind locked doors.

I have managed to get away occasionally. And I am, of course, 'legally' able to go and come as I wish. But I do have some obligations of courtesy as a Fellow (and of gratitude for my rescue from the despair of my situation in Jan. & Feb): and one of the chief of these occasions is the meeting of all the Fellows on the Wednesday before Full Term in October (this year October *11th* before Oct. 15th). I had already assured the Warden of my presence on Oct. 11, before I received your letter. If I seem to have prolonged the uncertainty too long, do forgive me! I am very fortunate*, but I am not in fact yet 'happily settled': I am still in considerable confusion.

342 From a letter to Mrs Meriel Thurston   9 November 1972

I am honoured by your letter, and quite willing that you should use the name of Rivendell as a herd prefix, though in my ignorance I don't think the actual valley of Rivendell would have been suitable for herd breeding.

I should be interested to hear what names you eventually choose (as individual names?) for your bulls; and interested to choose or invent suitable names myself if you wish. The elvish word for 'bull' doesn't appear in any published work; it was MUNDO.

343 From a letter to Sterling Lanier   21 November 1972

I am glad to know that you were awarded a prize, but not surprised that it proved useless. I had a similar disappointment when a drinking goblet arrived (from a fan) which proved to be of steel engraved with the terrible words seen on the Ring. I of course have never drunk from it, but use it for tobacco ash.

344 From a letter to Edmund Meskys   23 November 1972

[On the subject of numerals in *The Lord of the Rings*.]

With regard to the numerals: the use of duodecimals, especially such main figures as 12 and 144, has no reference to fingers at all. The English

*Owing to Christopher – when I was looking in vain for somewhere to live he wrote 'off his own bat' to the Warden of Merton College and said that his father was wandering looking in vain for a home, & could the College help? So I was amazed to receive a letter from the Warden saying that he had called a special meeting of the Governing Body, and it had unanimously voted that I should be invited to be a residential Fellow!

use duodecimals and have special words for them, namely *dozen* and *gross*. The Babylonians used duodecimals. This is due to the elementary mathematical discovery, as soon as people stop counting on their fingers and toes, that 12 is a much more convenient number than 10. I did devise numeral signs to go with the Fëanorian alphabet accommodated to both a decimal nomenclature and a duodecimal, but I have never used them and no longer hold an accurate memory of them. I am afraid the folder containing the numeral systems is not available and may be locked away in a strongroom. I remember that the numerals were written according to a positional system like the Arabic, beginning at the left with the lowest number and rising to the highest on the right.

345 To Mrs Meriel Thurston

[See no. 342 for the circumstances of this letter.]

30 November 1972   Merton College, Oxford
Dear Mrs Thurston,

Thank you for your letter. Personally I am rather against giving strictly human and noble names to animals; and in any case Elrond and Glorfindel seem unsuitable characters, for their names which meant (1) 'The vault of stars' and (2) 'Golden hair' seem inapt. I recently played with the notion of using the word for bull I gave you, which introduced in the form *-mund* gives a fairly familiar sound (as in Edmund, Sigismund, etc.), and adding a few Elvish prefixes, producing names like Aramund ('Kingly bull'), Tarmund ('Noble bull'), Rasmund ('Horned bull'), Turcomund ('Chief of bulls'), etc. I wonder what you think of these?

Arwen was not an elf, but one of the half-elven who abandoned her elvish rights. Galadriel ('Glittering garland') is the chief elvish woman mentioned in *The Lord of the Rings*; her daughter was Celebrían ('Silver queen'). There was also Nimrodel. But I shouldn't really like these names to be given to heifers or cows. If you care for the Aramund type, I could invent a few female names. But though it is made on classical models rather than elvish, wouldn't the name of Farmer Giles' favourite cow – Galathea (in *Farmer Giles of Ham*) – be useful? which as it stands might be interpreted 'Goddess of milk'.

Yours sincerely,
J. R. R. Tolkien.

[A reply to a reader who had asked for Tolkien's help with an academic project concerning his works.]

See *Lord of the Rings* Vol. I, p. 272: 'He that breaks a thing to find out what it is has left the path of wisdom' (/or she) – Gandalf. I should not feel inclined to help in this destructive process, even if it did not seem to me that this exercise was supposed to be your own private work without assistance. . . . . It is also said (I p. 93) 'Do not meddle in the affairs of Wizards, for they are subtle and quick to anger.' I am sorry if this letter sounds grumpy. But I dislike analysis of this kind.

347 **To Richard Jeffery**

[A reply to the following questions: (1) Does 'Speak, friend, and enter' (the inscription over Moria Gate) mean 'Speak as a friend', i.e. in a friendly voice? (2) None of the Kings of Gondor and Arnor has a name ending in a vowel, as most Quenya names do. Is this to make them less strange in a Sindarin context, whereas the descendants of Castamir, who presumably regarded the later kings as halfbreeds, asserted their pure blood with 'aggressively Quenya names'? (3) Only men, not Elves, seem to use Quenya at all in Middle-earth for names. Elendil and his sword Narsil are Quenya; Gil-galad and his spear Aiglos are Sindarin, though he was King of the High-elves. Is this related to the absence of artificial pomp among elves? (4) Does *tyelpe* (the name of the letter *ty*) correspond to *celeb*, silver? (5) Could Aragorn mean 'tree-king' (with lenition of **gorn* to *orn* in Celeborn, etc.), and Arathorn possibly 'Two-trees-king', with reference to the Two Trees?]

17 December 1972   Merton College, Oxford
Dear Richard,

Forgive me for not answering your interesting letter (of Aug. 14) much sooner. . . . . As you probably know, I am an old man, and slower at work than I used to be; but I am still burdened with a great many affairs, that constantly interrupt my efforts to publish at least some of my other legends. I have also often been unwell during the last 3 months.

All your questions are interesting, but I am afraid satisfactory answers require in many cases reference to linguistic and legendary matters that would take far too long to deal with in a letter.

1. *pedo mellon.* I do not know why you are not satisfied with G[andalf]'s own interpretation, I p. 321–2, *Say 'friend'*: i.e. utter the word 'friend'. Because it makes G. seem rather dense? But he admits that he was, and he explains why – adequately for those who realize what a burden of responsibility, haste, and fear he bore.

2. *Q[uenya]* *names of Kings, etc.* Q. was known to the learned in Gondor at least as well as Latin still is in W. Europe. Its use was honorific, and there was no reason to accommodate the Q. names to Sindarin. And none of the Q. names in the lists (III 315–8–9) are accommodated: all are in *form* entirely suitable to Quenya. Q. permitted, indeed favoured, the 'dentals' *n, l, r, s, t* as final consonants: no other final consonants appear in the Q. lists. *Angamaitë* 'Ironhanded', and *Sangahyando* 'Throng*-cleaver', were good Q. but no more so than the other names, and there was no need to assert their royal descent, as that was clear. They were, however, possibly 'aggressive' in being personal warrior names (or nicknames), whereas the other (few) warlike Q. names, like *Rómendacil*, were 'political': assumed by a king in celebration of victories against a public enemy.

3. *High-elvish* and *Sindarin.* The mixture may seem curious to us, but it was entirely in accordance with the history of the First and Second Ages, briefly alluded to in III append. A 313–7. Also III 363. At the time of the L.R. (see III 106) Quenya had been a 'dead' [language] (sc. one not inherited in childhood, but learnt) for many centuries (act. about 6,000 years). The 'High-Elves' or exiled Noldor had, for reasons that the legend of their rebellion and exile from Valinor explains, at once adopted Sindarin, and even translated their Q. names into S. or adapted them. *Galadriel* though beautiful & noble enough in form is not a Q. name, any more than *Gil-galad*, which contains the S. word *galad*; and *Celeborn* is a transl. of the orig. name *Telporno*; though said to be a kinsman of King Elu Thingol he was so only afar off, for he too came from Valinor. It may be noted that at the end of the Third Age there were prob. more people (Men) that knew Q., or spoke S., than there were Elves who did either! Though dwindling, the population of Minas Tirith and its fiefs must have been much greater than that of *Lindon, Rivendell*, and *Lórien*.† In Gondor the generally used language was 'Westron', a lang. about as mixed as mod. English, but basically derived from the native lang. of the Númenóreans; but Sindarin was an acquired polite language and used by those of more pure N[úmenórean] descent, esp. in *Minas Tirith*, if they wished to be polite (as in the cry *Ernil i Pheriannath* III 41 cf. 231, and Master *Perian* 160). *Narsil* is a name composed of 2 basic stems without variation or adjuncts: $\sqrt{NAR}$ 'fire', & $\sqrt{THIL}$ 'white light'.It thus symbolised the chief heavenly lights, as enemies of darkness, Sun *(Anar)* and Moon (in Q) *Isil.*‡ *Andúril* means Flame of the West (as a region) not of the Sunset.

*Sc. a closely formed body of enemy soldiers.
†The Silvan Elves of Thranduil's realm did not speak S. but a related language or dialect.
‡The difference between this and S. *Ithil* is due to a change of $\bar{p}$ (th) >*s* in Q. of the Exiles. But there was a stem $\sqrt{SIL}$ as in *Silmarilli*. Cf. also *sila lúmenna omentielvo.*

4. You are of course right in seeing that the words for 'silver' point to an orig.: *kyelepē*: Q. *tyelpe* (with regular syncope of the second *e*): S. *celeb*: and Telerin *telepi* (in T. the syncope of second vowel in a sequence of 2 short vowels of the same quality was not regular, but occurred in words of length such as *Telperion*). Though *tyelpe* remained in Q., *telpe* (with Q. syncope) became the most usual form among the Elves of Valinor, because the Teleri in their lands, to the north of the Noldor, found a great wealth of silver, & became the chief silversmiths among the Eldar.

5. *Aragorn* etc. This cannot contain a 'tree' word (see note).* 'Tree-King' would have no special fitness for him, and it was already used by an ancestor. The names in the line of Arthedain are peculiar in several ways; and several, though S. in form, are not readily interpretable. But it would need more historical records and linguistic records of S. than exist (sc. than I have found time or need to invent!) to explain them. The system by which all the names from *Malvegil* onwards are trisyllabic, and have only one 'significant' element† (*ara* being used where the final element was of one syllable; but *ar* in other cases) is peculiar to this line of names. The *ara* is prob. derived from cases where *aran* 'king' lost its *n* phonetically (as *Arathorn*), *ara-* then being used in other cases.

I have not bothered to explain the S. lenitions in the Appendices, already overloaded, because I am afraid they would have been passed over, or have been felt unintelligible and tiresome, by practically all readers, since that is the normal attitude of the English to Welsh. (The lenitions or 'mutations' of S. were deliberately devised to resemble those of W[elsh] in phonetic origin and grammatical use;‡ but are not the *same* in either p[honetic] o[rigin] or g[rammatical] u[se].) Thus *ost-giliath* 'fortress of the stars' in which the second noun functions as an uninflected genitive shows no mutation. Cf. *ennyn Durin*. In S. this absence of mutation is maintained (a) in compounds and (b) when a noun is actually virtually an adjective, as in *Gil-galad* Star (of) brilliance. In S. initial *g* was retained in composition, where a contact *n* + *g* occurred. So *born*

*Note: 2 ancient words in Elvish for 'tree': (1) *galadā* <√GAL 'grow' intr[ansitive]; and (2) *ornē* from the v[ery] f[requently] used√OR/RO rise up, go high (cf. *ortani* 'raised'). (1) > Q. *alda*, S. *galadh*. (2) > Q. *orne*, S. *orn*.

(1) is not connected in origin with the name *Galadriel*, but it does [occur] in *Calas Galadhon, Galadhrim*. Before I discovered that many readers like you wd. be interested in language-details, I thought people would feel *dh* uncouth, and so wrote *d* (for ð & *dh*) in names. But *galadhon, -dhrim* is now in text.

†If indeed all were so; some may have been merely coinages in the general style; or alterations of old names arising domestically. As in our Robert > Robin, Dobbin, Hob, Bob etc.

‡Your use of *lenited* indicates that you know these, so I need not say any more; except to observe that though of *phonetic* origin, they are used *grammatically*, and so may occur or be absent in cases where this is not phonetically justified by descent.

'hot, red' + *gil* to *borñgil*; *morn* 'black' + *dor* to *morñdor*; the tricon-sonantal group then being reduced to *rg*, *rd*. t>|þ(th) is the nasal mutation, and so appears after the plural article in: *thiw*, *i Pheriannath*. *palan-tîriel* should phonetically > *-thíriel*, past participle 'having gazed afar'; but grammatically before actual forms of verbs, the soft mutation only was normally used in later S., to avoid the confusion with other verb stems, and the soft mut. of *m>v̂>v* was also often used for the same reason. *Palantír* is Q. < *palantīră* with continuative stem of TIR watch, gaze at etc. *tíro* is S. but a mistake in printing for *tĭro* imperative (of all persons) in S. (I have appended a good many notes on the Elvish S. verses to Donald Swann's musical settings in *The Road Goes Ever On*. This includes a note on *ath*.)

ath: Though it cd. be an S. form of Q. *atta* '2', it is not in fact related, nor a sign of a dual. It was a collective or group suffix, and the nouns so formed [were] originally singulars. But they were later treated as pl[ural]s, especially when applied to people(s).* The S. duals of nouns or pronouns early became obsolete, except in written works. A case occurs in *Orgalaðad* 'Day of the Two Trees', but since these S. nouns were all derived from Quenya names of the 6-day week, brought from Valinor, it may be due to an attempt to imitate Q. duals, such as *ciriat 2* ships.† In any case *-d* was later lost, and so we have *argonath*‡ 'the group of (two) noble stones instead of **argonad*. *Orbelain* is certainly a case of 'phonological' translation (of which the Noldor were quite capable), since *Valanya* (adj.) must be from older **Balaniă* which would > S. **Belain*, but no such form existed in S.

The intrusion of a suffix *ath* in *Arathorn* is not possible. The name contains an abbreviated form of þ*orono* (thorono) 'eagle', seen in *Thoron- dor*, *Thorongil*: Q. þ*orno* / *sorno*. No human or elf could be called Two-tree King, with ref. to the Two Trees of Valinor. They were made & owned by the Valar, but both had perished, in the Darkening of Valinor.

I am afraid it is unfair on linguistically minded readers not to provide them with more material. I should like to. But though I may leave behind me sufficiently ordered matter, at 81 I have no time – not if I am ever to produce any more 'legends'.

Well it is a long while now since Aug. 14! And I have only been able to compose all this at intervals. But I hope it may reach you as a sort of

---

*e.g. *Periannath* the Hobbit-folk, as distinguished from *periain* hobbits, an indefinite number of 'halflings'.

†Original[ly] the Q. duals were (a) purely numerative (element *ata*) and pairs (element *ŭ* as seen in Aldūya); but they were normally in later Q. only usual with reference to natural pairs, and the choice of *t* or *u* [was] decided by euphony (e.g. *ŭ* was preferred after d/t in stem.

‡from *arn(a)gon -ath*.

427

Christmas Present – though it may alas! be like some of such, not quite (or at all) what you wanted.

Very best wishes for Yule.

J. R. R. Tolkien

An instance of how difficult it is to keep books correct – mine & the index are full of mistakes – you sign yourself *Jeffery*, but *Jeffrey* is the spelling in the [University] Residents' List. I am nearly always written to as *Tolkein* (not by you): I do not know why, since it is pronounced by me always *-keen*.

I am afraid this is largely illegible, and though longwinded and complicated, leaves much to be explained. And not all the words or names can be 'explained': i.e. regularly referred to older forms of known meaning. In living languages (including Elvish langs.!) new words could be invented without any precise origin, or made up of existing elements in compounds that did not follow older phonetic habits. And in such cases 'euphony' (or what seemed 'euphonious' to a language and people at a given time) will then play a part. Also it has to be remembered that the *author* invented a very great number of names over a long period of time, and though he knew well enough the 'styles' of the supposed languages, at an early period in this labour their phonetic history was not so precise in his mind as it is now!

For instance we have *Arnor* and *Gondor*, which he has retained because he desired to avoid *Ardor*. But it can now only (though reasonably) be explained after invention as due to a blending of Q. *arnanóre* / *arnanor* with S. *arn(a)dor* > *ardor*. The name was in any case given to mean 'royal land' as being the realm of *Elendil* and so taking precedence of the southern realm.

348 From a letter to Mrs Catharine Findlay 6 March 1973

Galadriel, like all the other names of elvish persons in *The Lord of the Rings*, is an invention of my own. It is in Sindarin form (see Appendices E and F) and means 'Maiden crowned with gleaming hair'. It is a secondary name given to her in her youth in the far past because she had long hair which glistened like gold but was also shot with silver. She was then of Amazon disposition and bound up her hair as a crown when taking part in athletic feats.

349 From a letter to Mrs E. R. Ehrardt 8 March 1973

I do not understand why you should wish to associate my name with TOLK, an interpreter or spokesman. This is a word of Slavonic origin that became adopted in Lithuanian (TULKAS), Finnish (TULKKI) and in the Scand. langs., and eventually right across N. Germany (linguistically Low German) and finally into Dutch (TOLK). It was never adopted in English.

350 To C. L. Wiseman

[Christopher Wiseman, Tolkien's friend from schooldays and 'The T.C.B.S.' (see no. 5), now lived at Milford-on-Sea, near Bournemouth.]

24 May 1973   Merton College, Oxford

My dear Chris:

I have (of course) meant many times, since you drew me from my lair in Bournemouth and took me to Milford, to write to you; and now I am dismayed by the speed of the passing of time. . . . . The immediate reason for actually writing is this: in sorting some piles of letters and marking a few for keeping, I came across a letter (received in *May '72*) from whom? None other than C. V. L. Lycett, and from Los Angeles! . . . . His letter . . . . [is] full of reminiscences of K[ing] E[dward's] S[chool]. . . . . Here is an excerpt from his letter: 'As a boy you could not imagine how I looked up to you and admired and envied the wit of that select coterie* of J.R.R.T., C. L. Wiseman, G. B. Smith, R. Q. Gilson, V. Trought, and Payton. I hovered on the outskirts to gather up the gems. You probably had no idea of this schoolboy worship.' . . . .

Well: here I am now established in Merton; still fairly lively and active though I have had a longish bout of poor health since my 81st birthday party on Jan 3rd (a mere sequel in time & not due to the party!). After having my inside X-rayed extensively (with on the whole v.g. reports) I am now deprived of the use of *all* wines, and on a somewhat restricted diet; but am allowed to smoke & consume the alcoholic products of barley, as I wish.

If you care to take up the glove, and reply I shall be delighted.

With my very kind regards & good wishes to your wife. Your most devoted friend.

Yrs.
JRRT. TCBS.

351 To Christopher Tolkien

[Postmarked 29 May 1973]   [Merton College]

My dearest Chris.

I was very glad to get your letter of May 17 (p.m. 18). For I guessed that something untoward, beyond some vagary of the French posts,

---

*This we certainly never meant to be.

must have happened. I can deeply sympathize with the horror of your arrival – having several times in my earlier days suffered similar things, especially in the period from John's birth in 1917 to 1925 incl., which now in retrospect seems like a long nomadic series of arrivals at houses or lodgings that proved horrible – or worse: in some cases finding none at all! . . . . You went away about the same time as Prisca went to Crete. This seems to have been the most successful jaunt she has ever made. She came back looking and feeling really well and full of delight, but you must hear of that at first hand. For the first time since '68 I felt a real tug of desire to go and 'see places' or this one at any rate. But I am afraid I must now live on travellers' tales.

A lot of course has been happening to me since Easter – but mainly of the sort that takes longer to report in writing than it is worth: chiefly a record of unending pressure: social, literary, professional & financial. . . . . I fled from the overcrowded days of the summer term to Bournemouth from May 16–22 incl., and returned much the better. I had some good plain food, a room with a private balcony, and saw a good deal of my dear friends the Tolhursts; and I had good weather (which Oxford did *not* get). . . . . How long are you staying at Bargemon? All will I hope go on well or better while you are there. You are *all* in my constant thoughts, and this place seems rather empty without you. Much love my dearest Chris & Baillie & + A[dam] & + R[achel]. Daddy.

Since you left (I think in each case), Warnie,[1] Tom Dunning,[2] R. B. McCallum, Rosfrith M.[3] have died. (Warnie had a very warm obit. in the Times.)

352   **From a letter to Ungfrú Aðalsteinsdottir**   5 June 1973

I am very pleased to know that an Icelandic translation of *The Hobbit* is in preparation. I had long hoped that some of my work might be translated into Icelandic, a language which I think would fit it better than any other I have any adequate knowledge of.

353   **From a letter to Lord Halsbury**   4 August 1973

You pile Weathertop on Erebor, as Bilbo might have said, with your other generosities. The whisky will be welcomed whenever it comes: it will be quite safe if sent to college, whether I am here or briefly away. When you retire I shall certainly beg your help. Without it, I begin to feel that I shall never produce any part of *The Silmarillion*. When you were here on July 26, I became again vividly aware of your invigorating effect on me: like a warm fire brought into an old man's room, where he sits cold and unable to muster courage to go out on a journey that his heart desires to make. For over and above all the afflictions and obstacles I have endured since *The Lord of the Rings* came out, I have lost confidence. May I hope that perhaps, even amid your own trials and the heavy work which must precede your retirement, you could come again before so very long and warm me up again? I particularly desire to hear you read verse again, and especially your own: which you make come alive for me. Also I may send you ere long some copies of things which I have written to clarify my mind and imagination on such things as the relations of Elves the longeval and Men the short-lived – but which you need not let trouble you, not even to return.

I meant right away to deal with Galadriel, and with the question of Elvish child-bearing – to both of which I have given much thought. But I must not delay longer to send you this letter of gratitude. . . . .

Galadriel was 'unstained': she had committed no evil deeds. She was an enemy of Fëanor. She did not reach Middle-earth with the other Noldor, but independently. Her reasons for desiring to go to Middle-earth were legitimate, and she would have been permitted to depart, but for the misfortune that before she set out the revolt of Fëanor broke out, and she became involved in the desperate measures of Manwe, and the ban on all emigration.

354 To Priscilla Tolkien

[Written, from the home of Dr Denis Tolhurst, four days before Tolkien died at the age of eighty-one.]

Wed. Aug. 29th. 1973   at 22 Little Forest Road, Bournemouth.
Dearest Prisca,

I arrived in B'th. about 3.15 yesterday, after a successful drive with most traffic going north not seawards, & a curry-lunch shared by Causier,[1] Mrs C. and David. It was v. v. hot here & crowded. The Cs. then went off to find 'accommodation' for 2 nights, and departed necessarily with all my luggage on what looked like a hopeless quest. They dropped me on the East Overcliff by the Miramar[2] which nostalgically attracted me; but I went into the town & did some shopping, including having a hair trim. I then walked back to the Miramar at 4.45 – and things then began to go wrong. I was told Causier had called to find me about 4 p.m. which made me afraid that he was in difficulties. I also found that I had lost my Bank Card & some money. 'Reception' were surprised but welcoming, comforted me with a good tea. Also assuming that I had been looking for something more than a tea, they told me they could have done nothing at all for me, but for a cancellation which would allow them to take me in on Tuesday Sep. 4 – but I said I would see. I took a taxi to 22 L.F.R. (which promptly lost its way) and arrived late to find the house crowded & lively – only the Dr. was away till evening. (Happy go-lucky folk.) Then I waited anxiously for Causier. It was nearly 7 before he (and Mrs C. & D) turned up – I suspect he too had lost his way – and said it had only taken him 15 mins to find v. g. rooms for 2 nights! In the meanwhile Martin Tolhurst (formerly of N[ew] College), now grown to an immensely tall, charming, and efficient man, had by telephone located my Bank Card etc. at *The Red Lion* Salisbury. So all was well, for the present. But I have accepted the *Miramar* offer, and shall not return to Oxford till Sep. 11. For various reasons: the chief being I wish to give Carr plenty of time to clean my rooms, which, and I too, were much neglected latterly; I wish v. much to visit various people here, also Chris Wiseman at Milford, and I am old enough to much prefer familiar surroundings.

My dearest love to you.

Daddy.

It is stuffy, sticky, and rainy here at present – but forecasts are more favourable.

NOTES
INDEX

Notes

[1] 1. A Shakespeare and L. L. H. Thompson of Exeter College. 2. Father Francis Morgan (1857–1934) of the Birmingham Oratory, the Catholic priest who became Tolkien's guardian after the death of his mother in 1904. 3. L. R. Farnell, Rector (i.e. head) of Exeter College, 1913–28. 4. Kenneth Sisam (1887–1971), who in 1914 was a research student and assistant to Professor A. S. Napier. He acted as Tolkien's tutor; see no. 318. 5. Thomas Wade Earp, then an undergraduate at Exeter College; he later became known as a writer on modern painters. See no. 83 for Tolkien's reference to him as 'T. W. Earp, the original twerp'; since Partridge's *Dictionary of Slang* records the first use of 'twerp' as *circa* 1910, it is possible that Earp's name and initials may have given rise to the word. Earp was one of the editors of *Oxford Poetry 1915*, in which one of Tolkien's first published poems, 'Goblin Feet', was printed. 6. Tolkien's reworking of one of the *Kalevala* stories, 'The Story of Kullervo', was never finished, but proved to be the germ of the story of Túrin Turambar in *The Silmarillion*. For Tolkien's account of this, see no. 163. 7. Tolkien usually signed his letters to Edith Bratt 'Ronald' or 'R.', though he sometimes used his first Christian name, John.

[2] 1. Tolkien wrote a poem entitled 'The Voyage of Earendel the Evening Star' in September 1914. The first stanza is quoted in *Biography* p. 71.

[4] 1. Apparently a reference to an early form of the Elvish language Quenya, first invented by Tolkien probably during undergraduate days. For an example of a stanza written in it, and dated 'November 1915, March 1916', see *Biography* p. 76.

[7] 1. Henry Bradley (1845–1923) was in charge of the Oxford Dictionary while Tolkien worked on the staff.

[10] 1. Tolkien was at this time the holder of a Leverhulme Research Fellowship. 2. A black and white illustration included in the first British and American editions of *The Hobbit* as an illustration to Chapter 8, but not used in subsequent printings. It is reproduced alongside the note to no. 37 in *Pictures*. 3. As well as the maps, Tolkien had initially offered only the two illustrations mentioned earlier in this letter, both of which were in black and white. The six more now submitted were presumably most of the remaining monochrome drawings which were used in the first edition.

[13] 1. This was the painting entitled 'Beleg finds Gwindor in Taur-nu-Fuin', reproduced as no. 37 in *Pictures*, where a note gives its history.

[14] 1. C. S. Lewis, Fellow of Magdalen College, and a friend of Tolkien since 1926. 2. Russell Meiggs, Fellow of Keble College and later of Balliol, who at this time edited the *Oxford Magazine*, in which Tolkien's poems 'The Dragon's Visit' and 'Iumonna Gold Galdre Bewunden (The Hoard)' were published in February and March 1937. 3. One of these pictures was 'Beleg finds Gwindor in Taur-nu-Fuin', q.v. in note 1 to no. 13 above. Tolkien refers to it later in this letter as 'The Mirkwood picture . . . . [which] illustrates a different adventure', i.e. an episode in *The Silmarillion*. The other paintings were probably 'Glórund sets forth to seek Túrin' and 'Mount Everwhite', which were the only other substantial and finished paintings relating to Middle-earth in existence at this time; they are reproduced as nos 38 and 31 in *Pictures*. As Tolkien pointed out, the three *Silmarillion*

illustrations were not intended for publication in *The Hobbit*, and were sent merely as samples of his work.

[15]   1. The publishers wrote in the blurb on the dust-jacket of *The Hobbit*: 'Professor Tolkien – but not his publishers – still remains to be convinced that anybody will want to read his most delightful history of a Hobbit's journey.' 2. George Gordon, formerly Professor of English Literature at Leeds (see no. 46) and then holder of the same chair at Oxford. By 1937 he was President of Magdalen College. 3. R. W. Chambers (1874–1942), Professor of English at London University.

Commentary on jacket-flap: 1. Elaine Griffiths of St Anne's College, Oxford, who worked with Tolkien as a research student during the 1930s. For her part in the publication of *The Hobbit* see no. 294. 2. 'To say that Bilbo's breath was taken away is no description at all. There are no words left to express his staggerment, since Men changed the language that they learned of elves in the days when all the world was wonderful.' (*The Hobbit*, Chapter 12.) 3. Owen Barfield, friend of C. S. Lewis and author of *Poetic Diction* (1928), an account of the development of language from its early roots in mythology. 4. Sir Walter Raleigh, Professor of English Literature at Oxford, 1904–22. 5. A *viva voce* is the oral part of Oxford University examinations.

[16]   1. At the Oratory School the equivalent of 'studies' at other public schools were known as 'flats'. 2. Tolkien's eight-year-old daughter Priscilla, and John Binney, a family friend.

[17]   1. C. S. Lewis reviewed *The Hobbit* in *The Times* on 8 October 1937 and in the *Times Literary Supplement* on 2 October 1937. Both reviews were unsigned. 2. *Gnome* was a term used at this period by Tolkien for the Noldorin Elves; see no. 239. 3. Latin, 'thus it is hobbited to the stars': an allusion to *Aeneid* IX. 641, 'sic itur ad astra'. 4. R. M. Dawkins, who was a member of Tolkien's informal Icelandic reading club, the Coalbiters (see *Inklings* p. 27). 5. Parker's bookshop in Broad Street, Oxford.

[19]   1. 'The Adventures of Tom Bombadil', first published in the *Oxford Magazine* in 1934. 2. i.e. in the reprint of *The Hobbit*. 3. On 1 January 1938 Tolkien lectured on 'Dragons' as part of a series of lectures for children at the University Museum, Oxford. 4. Unwin had told Tolkien he was going abroad. 5. Tolkien gave a talk on 'Anglo-Saxon Verse' on the BBC on 14 January 1938. The duration was 13 minutes, and the talk was part of the series 'Studies in National Inspiration and Characteristic Forms'.

[20]   1. For an account of the first draft of the opening chapter of *The Lord of the Rings*, see *Biography* p. 185. 2. Arthur Ransome, whose books were much admired by Tolkien's children, wrote to Tolkien, describing himself as 'a humble hobbit fancier', and complaining about Gandalf's use of the term 'excitable little man' as a description of Bilbo. He cited other, similar uses of 'man' or 'men' to describe dwarves and goblins.

[22]   1. Christopher Tolkien was confined to bed with irregularities of the heart, a condition which caused him to be a total invalid for several years.

[23]   1. The Long Vacation is the summer vacation at Oxford. Tolkien's research fellowship ended in September 1938.

[24]   1. This indicates that in the original draft of *Out of the Silent Planet* the hero was named Unwin; in the published book his name is Ransom. 2. For another account of this,

see no. 294. **3.** Tolkien's unfinished story of time-travel, 'The Lost Road', was shown to Allen & Unwin in November 1937, and was returned by them with the comment that it did not seem likely, even if it was finished, to be a commercial success. For a description of the story, see no. 257, and *Biography* pp. 170–1.

[26] **1.** Possibly no. 24, which may have been sent as an enclosure with this letter. **2.** *Land Under England* by Joseph O'Neill (1935). **3.** A phrase used in the reader's report. **4.** *Voyage to Arcturus* by David Lindsay (1920).

[28] **1.** Besides his duties at Oxford, Tolkien often acted as an external examiner for other universities, and marked Higher Certificate papers, as he was in need of the extra income. **2.** It is not clear precisely to which works Tolkien was referring. Possibly he had in mind the Middle English *Ancrene Wisse* and *Pearl*, the former of which he was editing for the Early English Text Society, and the latter of which he was working on with E. V. Gordon – though in fact neither of these projects was near completion. The work in Old English was probably the revision of Clark Hall's translation of *Beowulf*, of which Tolkien was reading the proofs, and to which he was supposed to be contributing an introduction; see no. 37. The work in Old Norse to which he refers was probably an edition of *Víga-Glúms Saga*, edited by G. Turville-Petre (Oxford University Press, 1940); this was one of the Oxford English Monographs, of which Tolkien was joint editor with C. S. Lewis and D. Nichol Smith. **3.** Fox was Dean of Divinity of Magdalen College and an early member of the Inklings.

[29] **1.** German, 'confirmation'.

[30] **1.** German, 'descent, genealogy'.

[31] **1.** A society at Worcester College, Oxford.

[33] **1.** For an account of this sequel, see no. 36, and *Biography* p. 166. **2.** 'The King of the Green Dozen' is the story of the King of Iwerddon, whose hair and the hair of his descendant's twelve sons is coloured green. The story, which is set in Wales, parodies the 'high' style of narrative. Tolkien never completed it.

[34] **1.** E. V. Gordon, Tolkien's collaborator on the edition of *Sir Gawain and the Green Knight*.

[35] **1.** In January 1939 Tolkien was asked whether in the event of a national emergency (i.e. war) he would be prepared to work in the cryptographical department of the Foreign Office. He agreed, and apparently attended a four-day course of instruction at the Foreign Office beginning on 27 March. But in October 1939 he was informed that his services would not be required for the present, and in the event he never worked as a cryptographer.

[37] **1.** Tolkien injured himself while gardening. **2.** John Tolkien was studying for the Catholic priesthood at the English College in Rome. **3.** H. S. Bennett (1889–1972) of Emmanuel College, Cambridge, medievalist and literary historian.

[38] **1.** 20 Northmoor Road was damaged by burst water-pipes during the winter of 1939–40. **2.** i.e. the revised edition of Clark Hall contained (at this stage) no introductory material apart from an 'argument' or summary of the story of *Beowulf*, and ten lines of information about the manuscript. **3.** The section of Tolkien's introduction entitled 'On Metre'.

[42] 1. R. E. Havard (a general medical practitioner). 2. C. S. Lewis and his brother Major W. H. Lewis. 3. (Sir) Basil Blackwell, bookseller and publisher. 4. H. V. D. ('Hugo') Dyson, friend of Lewis and Tolkien, at this time a lecturer at Reading University. 5. On 10 January 1941 Germany signed a new treaty with Russia as an indication of the mutual understanding that supposedly existed between them at this time. 6. The daily newspaper of the British Communist Party.

[43] 1. Tolkien's guardian, Father Francis Morgan, disapproved of his clandestine love-affair with Edith Bratt. 2. Tolkien was excited during schooldays to discover the existence of the Gothic language; see no. 272. 3. Classical Honour Moderations, in which Tolkien was awarded a Second Class. 4. The actual date of Tolkien's Channel crossing with his battalion was 6 June 1916. The poem he refers to, dated 'Étaples, Pas de Calais, June 1916', is entitled 'The Lonely Isle', and is subtitled 'For England', though it also relates to the mythology of *The Silmarillion*. The poem was published in *Leeds University Verse 1914–1924* (Leeds, at the Swan Press, 1924), p. 57. 5. Tolkien inherited a small income from his parents, derived from shares in South African mines.

[44] 1. Tolkien's mother died of diabetes; Tolkien believed her condition had been made worse by his relatives' intolerance of her conversion to Catholicism. 2. Tolkien's mother had rented rooms for a summer holiday in a cottage occupied by a postman and his wife.

[45] 1. The final examination taken by undergraduates at Oxford. 2. During the war, Tolkien organised a syllabus for naval cadets reading English at Oxford. 3. A. H. Maxwell was Tobacco Controller for the British Government during the war.

[46] 1. During 1926, Tolkien continued to lecture at Leeds while already holding the chair of Anglo-Saxon at Oxford. 2. Lascelles Abercrombie became Professor of English Literature at Leeds in 1922, after Gordon's return to Oxford. 3. Gordon was a Fellow of Magdalen College, Oxford, from 1907 to 1913. 4. F. W. Moorman, Professor of English Language at Leeds, died in the summer of 1919; after his death, the post was reduced to the status of a Readership. 5. The salary appears to have been £500 per annum. 6. Probably not true; Gordon makes no mention of Kenneth Sisam in his (published) letters discussing the appointment, but writes to R. W. Chapman on 26 June 1920: 'I may take Tolkien from you; but only, I hope, to give him the leisure to do texts.' (Tolkien was at that time working in the Dictionary department of the Oxford University Press.) 7. See note 4 to no. 15 (commentary on jacket-flap).

[47] 1. During 1942 Tolkien began to serve as an Air Raid Warden. 2. In the first draft of *The Lord of the Rings* the chapters were numbered continuously. XXXI was 'Flotsam and Jetsam', which became Book III, Chapter 9.

[48] 1. Presumably a lecture on the Arthurian matter. 2. This initial is meant to stand for 'Tollers', Lewis's usual name for Tolkien.

[49] 1. The text of *Christian Behaviour* was later incorporated into Lewis's book *Mere Christianity*. 2. Over *permanent* is written *lifelong*. This and subsequent alterations are in pencil; the text of the letter is in ink. 3. Altered to read *total human health*. 4. Altered to *with*. 5. *all* is underlined in pencil. 6. *permanent* is again altered to *lifelong*. 7. 'Social Morality' was the title of an earlier chapter in the book. 8. *elaborate* is replaced by *defend*. 9. Lewis suggested that if an audience were to watch not a striptease, but a cover being slowly lifted off a dish of bacon, then one would conclude that 'something had gone

wrong with the appetite for food'. **10.** Reno, Nevada, famed for its instant divorces. **11.** Latin, 'To hold an opinion with the Church.'

[50] **1.** An office manned by Air Raid Wardens for the North Oxford area.

[52] **1.** Latin, 'I do not wish to be made a bishop.' **2.** Two lines from Tolkien's unpublished poem 'Mythopoeia', written for C. S. Lewis.

[53] **1.** Charles Williams, who was now living in Oxford. **2.** The Teheran Conference, held in November 1943, was attended by the British, American and Russian leaders. **3.** i.e. Winston Spencer Churchill. **4.** 'Collie' Knox, a writer and popular journalist. **5.** The dash is in the original letter; no name is given.

[54] **1.** Anglo-Saxon, '[The] father's counsel [to] his son.'

[55] **1.** Anglo-Saxon, '[The] father [to] his third son.' **2.** Reader in Old Icelandic at Oxford. **3.** The Air Raid post mentioned in no. 50. **4.** Reader in Jewish Studies at Oxford. **5.** i.e. from the fishmonger. **6.** A pub in Broad Street. **7.** The Tolkiens were now keeping hens, and this is a pun on 'fowls'. **8.** Latin, '[The] Father to his Son[,] Born the youngest (but not at all in other respects [the least]).' **9.** Anglo-Saxon, '[The] Father to his own son, the youngest [but] by no means the least loved.' **10.** A Polish officer who had consulted Tolkien a few weeks earlier.

[56] **1.** Tolkien spent the first three years of his life in South Africa, where his father was a bank manager in Bloemfontein. See also no. 163.

[58] **1.** A method of sending letters to servicemen overseas. The text was photographed by the postal authorities, and was delivered to the addressee in the form of a small bromide print which could then be read with the aid of a magnifying glass.

[60] **1.** Dutch, 'Opened by the Censor.' **2.** i.e. 'Mummy and Priscilla'. **3.** C. S. Lewis's brother Warren H. Lewis. **4.** Lord David Cecil, Fellow of New College and an occasional attender at the Inklings. **5.** Sarah Connaughton, a family friend. **6.** David Nichol Smith was Professor of English Literature at Oxford, 1929–46. **7.** Elaine Griffiths; q.v. in note 1 to no. 15 (commentary to jacket-flap). **8.** i.e. proofs of University of Wales examination papers.

[61] **1.** Christopher Tolkien sailed to South Africa on the S.S. *Cameronia*. Conditions on board were so unpleasant that he and his companions nicknamed it the *Altmark*, after the German prison-ship of that name. **2.** Heaton Park Camp, Manchester, where Christopher Tolkien had been stationed. **3.** *Beowulf* 1395–6: 'For this day have thou patience in every woe, even as I know thou wilt.' **4.** *Beowulf* 1386–8: 'To each one of us shall come in time the end of life in this world; let him who may earn glory ere his death.' (This and the above are taken from Tolkien's translation of the poem.) **5.** Frank Pakenham, later Lord Longford, was Tutor in Politics at Christ Church, 1934–46. **6.** Mary Salu, a graduate pupil of Tolkien's, who later published a translation of the *Ancrene Riwle* with a preface by Tolkien. **7.** Latin, 'Keep a calm mind, restrain the tongue.'

[63] **1.** i.e. the air-raid siren. **2.** The Mitre Hotel in Turl Street. **3.** Tolkien was an executor of the will of Joseph Wright, who died in 1930. **4.** 'fellow-Christians'. **5.** Anglo-Saxon, 'God alone knows.' **6.** Mabel Tolkien was on 'home leave' in England when her husband died, and was not able to return to Bloemfontein for the funeral.

[64] 1. An early title for *The Silmarillion* was 'The History of the Gnomes' – i.e. of the Noldorin elves. See no. 239.

[66] 1. A priest at the Birmingham Oratory. 2. Alexander Buchan (1829–1907), a meteorologist who foretold certain periods of cold weather as being of annual occurrence, and gave his name to the cold spell of May 9–14, which is known as 'Buchan's winter'.

[67] 1. Leonard Rice-Oxley, Fellow of Keble College. 2. R. B. McCallum, Fellow of Pembroke College, who at this time was tutoring Michael Tolkien, who had returned to Oxford to read History.

[69] 1. Father Douglas Carter, parish priest of St Gregory's Catholic Church in Oxford. 2. 'Who Goes Home' was later re-titled *The Great Divorce*. 3. i.e. of Tolkien's story 'Leaf by Niggle', first published in the *Dublin Review*, January 1945.

[71] 1. Anglo-Saxon, 'on earth and in heaven'. 2. *Gaudy Night* by Dorothy Sayers (1935).

[72] 1. H. L. Drake, Walter Ramsden and L. E. Salt, Fellows of Pembroke College, where Tolkien held a Professorial Fellowship. 2. i.e. Hugo Dyson. 3. Examination papers for the naval cadets reading English at Oxford. 4. Proprietor of a bicycle repair shop. 5. Latin, 'Ah! triumph'. 6. An annexe to Lincoln College built in Turl Street. 7. Censor (i.e. head) of St Catherine's Society, Oxford. 8. H. G. Hanbury, Fellow of Lincoln College and Lecturer in Law.

[73] 1. E. R. Eddison [sic], author of *The Worm Ouroboros* and other romances. This was his second visit to the Inklings (see *Inklings* p. 190). 2. W. H. Lewis held the rank of Captain in the Royal Army Service Corps until his promotion to Major at the outbreak of the Second World War. 3. *The Mezentian Gate*, which remained incomplete at Eddison's death in 1945, though a text was edited by his brother C. R. Eddison and published in 1958.

[74] 1. After some weeks in the Transvaal, Christopher Tolkien was moved to an air training school at Kroonstad. 2. Michael Tolkien had been judged unfit for further military service as a result of 'severe shock to nervous system due to prolonged exposure to enemy action'. 3. An edition of *The Hobbit* was issued by Foyles of London in 1942; see no. 47.

[75] 1. Tolkien owned a Hammond typewriter with interchangeable typefaces, one of which was very small. 2. American servicemen, who were in the Oxford area in large numbers. 3. The translation by W. H. Kirby, published in the Everyman series in 1907. 4. Classical Honour Moderations; see note 3 to no. 43.

[76] 1. While on holiday with his family at Lamorna Cove in Cornwall in 1932, Tolkien amused the children by giving the nickname 'Gaffer Gamgee' to a local 'character'. See no. 257. 2. At the Oxford Playhouse.

[77] 1. News had come of Allied Advances in Normandy; meanwhile von Papen, the German ambassador to Turkey, had cut short his holiday and returned to Ankara following reports that the Turkish government might break off diplomatic relations with Germany. 2. Latin, 'Carthage must be destroyed' (Plutarch, *Life of Cato*).

[79] 1. A nickname for the Eagle & Child pub.

[81] 1. Another letter to Christopher Tolkien, dated 22 September 1943, refers to Lewis's 'new translation in rhymed alexandrines of the Aeneid'. It was not published. 2. Tolkien had promised his translation of *Pearl* to Blackwell, who wanted to publish it, and had the text set up in type. But Tolkien failed to provide an introduction to the book, and the project was eventually abandoned.

[83] 1. C. S. Lewis was known to his friends as 'Jack'; 'Warnie' was the nickname of his brother Warren. 2. 'Trotter' was the original name of the character Strider in *The Lord of the Rings*. 3. Sir William Walton (b. 1902). 4. A colleague of Tolkien's in the English Department at Leeds University, and the author of many books of poetry. 5. Father Martin D'Arcy, S.J., Principal of Campion Hall, Oxford, 1932–45. 6. Old Icelandic, 'world-doom'.

[89] 1. Also known as the Forty Hours' Devotion. The Blessed Sacrament is exposed on a throne in a monstrance and the faithful pray before it, in turns, throughout forty hours; this length of time was probably fixed on as the period during which Christ's body rested in the tomb. 2. Greek ἀνάγκη, 'necessity, constraint'. 3. Elizabeth Jennings, later to become well known as a poet; her family were friends of the Tolkiens.

[91] 1. This 'final chapter' was written in the form of an Epilogue to *The Lord of the Rings*, which Tolkien eventually decided not to publish.

[92] 1. Lewis's next published novel after *That Hideous Strength* and *The Great Divorce* was *The Lion, the Witch and the Wardrobe*. Tolkien is, however, almost certainly referring to some other book of Lewis's that was never completed. Tolkien's 'dimly projected third' may have been 'The Notion Club Papers': see *Biography* pp. 171–2. 2. Lewis told Chad Walsh, who visited him in the summer of 1948, that this book was to be called 'Language and Human Nature' and was to be published the following year by the Student Christian Movement Press; but this never happened. In 1950, Lewis wrote to a friend: 'My book with Tolkien – any book in collaboration with that great, but dilatory and unmethodical man – is dated I fear to appear on the Greek Calends' (*Letters of C. S. Lewis*, p. 222).

[94] 1. 22 Northmoor Road, in which Tolkien lived from 1926 to 1930. 2. i.e. Mr Anthony Eden, speaking in the House of Commons.

[96] 1. Professor of English Language and Literature at Oxford. 2. i.e. the Merton Professorships of English Language and Literature and of English Literature. 3. A reference to a celebrated poster advertising the 'bracing' air of the sea-resort of Skegness, on which there appeared a cheery-looking fisherman clad entirely in oilskins. 4. This was probably the essay 'Myth became Fact', first published in *World Dominion*, September/October 1944, and reprinted in Lewis's book *Undeceptions* (American title: *God in the Dock*). 5. Greek, 'would that I were'; quoted, as are the words that follow, from Rupert Brooke's 'The Old Vicarage, Grantchester'. 6. Latin, 'singly, separately'.

[98] 1. A second cousin of Rayner Unwin; his real name was Harold. 2. Christopher Tolkien was never officially a pupil of his father, but he did receive some informal tuition from him during his year as an undergraduate (1942–3) before joining the R.A.F. 3. It is impossible to say what Tolkien had in mind. Perhaps he was alluding to the embryonic story referred to at the end of no. 69. 4. This footnote carries no indication, in the original letter, as to which part of the text it refers to. Its placing here is therefore conjectural.

5. The Tolkien/d'Ardenne edition of the Western Middle English MS. *Katerine*, which was never completed. 6. Tolkien's edition of the MS. *Ancrene Wisse*, not in fact completed until 1962. 7. British Daylight Saving Time.

[103] 1. Tolkien wanted to rent a college house, because 20 Northmoor Road was proving too large for his family's present needs. 2. Hugo Dyson was elected a Fellow of Merton and was admitted to the college at the same time as Tolkien.

[105] 1. 'The Lay of Aotrou and Itroun'. 2. 'The Notion Club Papers': see *Biography* pp. 171–2.

[107] 1. Nothing is known of this person's identity. 2. Tolkien had arranged to rent this house from Merton College.

[108] 1. C. H. Wilkinson was the English tutor at Worcester College.

[109] 1. See note 1 to no. 128. 2. The first three people in this list were probably Owen Barfield, R. E. Havard and W. H. Lewis; the others cannot certainly be identified, though the artist may have been Tolkien's first cousin Marjorie Incledon, who was a painter. 3. An earlier name for Fredegar or Fatty Bolger. 4. ' "Policemen never come so far, and the map-makers have not reached this country yet. They have seldom even heard of the king round here. . . . . ." ' (*The Hobbit*, Chapter 2.) This passage was greatly changed in a later revision. 5. These pages contain references to the Necromancer. 6. The Unwins were travelling to Switzerland.

[111] 1. S. R. T. O. d'Ardenne.

[112] *Transcription* (pairs of letters in italics are represented by one character in the runes):

*TH*RE MANOR RO*A*D

SUNDAY NOV[E]MBER

*TH*E *TH*IRTIE*TH*

D*EA*R MRS FARRER: OF COURSE I WILL SIGN YO

UR COPY OF *TH*E HOBBIT. I AM HONOURED BY *TH*E

RECWEST. IT IS GOOD NEWS *TH*AT *TH*E BOOK IS OBTAIN

ABLE AGAIN. *TH*E NEXT BOOK WILL CO[N]TAIN MORE D

ETAILED INFORMATION ABOUT RUNES AND O*TH*ER

ALFABETS IN RESPO[N]SE TO MANY ENCWIRIES. IN

*TH*E M*EA*NTIME WHILE *TH*E GR*EA*T WORK IS BEI*NG* FINIS[H]

ED I WONDER IF YOU WOULD LIKE A PROPER

KEY TO THE SPECIAL DWARVIS[H] ADAPTATION

OF *TH*E E*NG*LIS[H] RUNIC ALFABET ONLY PART OF

WHICH *A*PPEARS IN *TH*E HO*BB*IT INCLUDI*NG* *TH*E COVER.

WE ENIOYED LAST MONDAY EUENI*NG* VERY MU

CH AND HOPE FOR A RETURN MATCH SOON.

YOURS SINCERELY

J. R. R. TOLKIEN

[113] 1. *Sir Gawain*, line 2363, 'the most faultless knight'. 2. It appears that Hugo Dyson had been putting it about that Tolkien objected to Lewis's 'loud' manner in the Inklings. 3. Archaic, 'if'. 4. Bird and Baby, i.e. Eagle and Child pub.

[114] 1. Hugh Brogan had been a pupil at the school.

[115] 1. An Elvish sage in Tol Eressëa from whom the mariner Aelfwine heard the legends that make up *The Silmarillion*; see *Biography* pp. 90, 169.

[118] *Transcription* (in the runic passage, pairs of letters in italics are represented by one character in the runes; the letter 'Z' is used for the voiced 'S'):

> *DEAR HUGH* THIS [I]Z JUST TO *WISH YOU* A HA*PP*Y *CH*RISTMAS IN DWARF RUN*EZ*.
>
> dear hugh: this iz just to wish you a very happy christmas
> in two styles of elvish script: i am sending some explanations,
> and hope you wont find them too complicated.

The third inscription repeats the wording of the second, inserting the word 'I' between 'and' and 'hope'.

[124] 1. Tolkien was overestimating the combined length of the two works by several hundred thousand words. 2. i.e. the planned sequel to *Farmer Giles of Ham*.

[126] 1. Another Merton College house, not far from 3 Manor Road, which had proved too small for the Tolkiens' needs.

[127] 1. Unwin's second letter was an acknowledgement of Tolkien's note of 2 April. 2. Tolkien's anger with Allen & Unwin is shown by the much more strongly-worded draft for this letter, which is quoted in *Biography* p. 210, in the passage beginning 'i.e. that you may be willing to take . . . .'

[128] 1. In the original version of Chapter 5 of *The Hobbit*, Gollum really does intend to give Bilbo the Ring when the hobbit wins the riddle-game, and is deeply apologetic when he finds that it is missing: 'I don't know how many times Gollum begged Bilbo's pardon. He kept on saying: "We are ssorry; we didn't mean to cheat, we meant to give it our only present, if it won the competition." He even offered to catch Bilbo some nice juicy fish to eat as a consolation.' Bilbo, who has the Ring in his pocket, persuades Gollum to lead him out of the underground passages, which Gollum does, and the two of them part company in a civil manner.

[130] 1. The note, which was included in the second edition of *The Hobbit*, explained the change of text in Chapter 5: 'There the true story of the ending of the Riddle Game, as it was eventually revealed (under pressure) by Bilbo to Gandalf, is now given according to the Red Book, in place of the version Bilbo first gave to his friends, and actually set down in his diary. This departure from truth on the part of a most honest hobbit was a portent of great significance. It does not, however, concern the present story, and those who in this edition make their first acquaintance with hobbit-lore need not trouble about it. Its explanation lies in the history of the Ring, as set out in the chronicles of the Red Book of Westmarch, and it must await their publication.'

[131] 1. See introductory note to no. 19. 2. Noumenon, neuter of the present participle of νοεῖν (noein), to apprehend, conceive; introduced by Kant in contrast to 'phenomenon', and given the meaning 'an object of purely intellectual intuition, devoid of all phenomenal attributes'. 3. The text of this letter is taken from a typescript made, at

Milton Waldman's instigation, by a professional typist (there are a number of misspellings of names, which Tolkien has corrected); it appears that here the typist has omitted some words from Tolkien's MS. **4.** Tar-Calion (the Quenya name for Ar-Pharazôn) was originally the thirteenth ruler of Númenor; in later developments of the history of Númenor he became the twenty-fifth (usually recorded as the twenty-fourth, but see *Unfinished Tales* p. 226, note 11). **5.** As earlier letters in this book show, *The Lord of the Rings* was in fact begun in December 1937.

[132] **1.** C. L. Wrenn succeeded Tolkien as Professor of Anglo-Saxon at Oxford.

[133] **1.** Rayner Unwin's letter of 29 [sic] November said that he was 'hoping that I might get the chance of seeing *Silmarillion*. Believe it or not I am still quite certain that you have something most important for publication in this book and *The Lords of the Ring*! [sic]' **2.** Maurice Bowra, Warden of Wadham College and, at this time, Vice Chancellor of Oxford University. **3.** In a later letter on the subject of the oral transmission of 'Errantry', Tolkien noted that 'a curious feature was the preservation of the word *sigaldry*, which I got from a thirteenth-century text'. (To Donald Swann, 14 October 1966.) **4.** See *Inklings* p. 57. **5.** Sir John Burnett-Stuart [sic] commanded the 1st Battalion of the Rifle Brigade in the Second World War. **6.** i.e. 'Authorised Version' and 'Revised Version'. **7.** Russell Meiggs, who edited the *Oxford Magazine* in the 1930s, is uncertain which member of the Nowell Smith family was among his predecessors. **8.** It may appear at a first glance that Tolkien did write another poem in this metre, 'Eärendil was a mariner', which appears in Book II Chapter 1 of *The Lord of the Rings*. But this poem is arguably a development of 'Errantry' rather than a separate composition.

[134] **1.** Michael Tolkien was teaching at the Oratory School in Berkshire and had a cottage nearby. **2.** The offices of Allen & Unwin, near the British Museum. **3.** For more about these tape-recordings, some of which were issued on gramophone records in 1975, see *Biography* p. 213.

[135] **1.** Tolkien's contribution to *Essays & Studies* was 'The Homecoming of Beorhtnoth Beorthelm's Son', which was published in this journal in 1953. **2.** The lecture, given in Glasgow on 15 April 1953, consisted of a discussion of *Sir Gawain and the Green Knight* with particular attention to Gawain's temptation to commit adultery with the Lady, and his confession in the chapel at Bercilak's court before going out to meet the Green Knight. **3.** The first British atomic bomb test took place in the Monte Bello Islands, off Australia, on 3 October 1952.

[136] **1.** A list of contents to *The Lord of the Rings* written by Tolkien and included in the manuscript of that book at Marquette University, Milwaukee, U.S.A., has a different set of titles: Vol. I *The First Journey* and *The Journey of the Nine Companions*; Vol. II *The Treason of Isengard* and *The Journey of the Ringbearers*; Vol. III *The War of the Ring* and *The End of the Third Age*.

[137] **1.** A note on Volume I of the first edition of *The Lord of the Rings* promised that Volume III would contain 'some abridged family-trees . . . . an index of names and strange words with some explanations . . . . [and] some brief account . . . . of the languages, alphabets and calendars'. The 'index of names' did not, in the event, appear in the first edition of Volume III. **2.** The inscription around the West Gate of the Mines of Moria. **3.** Tolkien had planned to include facsimiles of the damaged pages of the 'Book of Mazarbul', but these had to be omitted because of cost (they were in several colours). They are reproduced as no. 23 in *Pictures*. **4.** The subject of his W. P. Ker Lecture; see note 2 to no. 135 above. **5.** Tolkien is here referring to his long letter to Milton Waldman (no. 131).

[140] 1. In a subsequent letter to Rayner Unwin (no. 143), Tolkien is more definite that the Two Towers are 'Orthanc and the Tower of Cirith Ungol'. On the other hand, in his original design for the jacket of *The Two Towers* (see no. 151) the Towers are certainly Orthanc and Minas Morgul. Orthanc is shown as a black tower, three-horned (as seen in *Pictures* no. 27), and with the sign of the White Hand beside it; Minas Morgul is a white tower, with a thin waning moon above it, in reference to its original name, Minas Ithil, the Tower of the Rising Moon (*The Fellowship of the Ring* p. 257). Between the two towers a Nazgûl flies.

[143] 1. The Appendices to Volume III.

[144] 1. ' "*Uglúk u bagronk sha pushdug Saruman-glob búbhosh skai.*" ' 2. ' "... all the gardens of the Entwives are wasted: Men call them the Brown Lands now." ' 3. ' "My grand-dad, and my uncle Andy after him, ... he had a rope-walk over by Tighfield many a year." ' 4. ' "Why, to think of it, we're in the same tale still! It's going on. Don't the great tales never end?" ' 5. Naomi Mitchison's house in Scotland.

[145] 1. Bannister, a Senior Scholar of Merton College, was the first person to run a mile in under four minutes, a record that he achieved at Oxford on 6 May 1954.

[148] 1. Allen & Unwin wished to publish Tolkien's translation of *Sir Gawain and the Green Knight*, which had been broadcast on the BBC Third Programme in a dramatised version in December 1953, with a repeat (referred to by Tolkien in this letter) in September 1954.

[149] 1. Peter Green, the biographer of Kenneth Grahame, wrote in the *Daily Telegraph* on 27 August 1954: 'I presume it is meant to be taken seriously, and am apprehensive that I can find no really adequate reasons for doing so. .... And yet this shapeless work has an undeniable fascination: especially to a reviewer with a cold in his head.' 2. Edwin Muir wrote in the *Observer* on 22 August 1954: 'This remarkable book makes its appearance at a disadvantage. Nothing but a great masterpiece could survive the bombardment of praise directed at it from the blurb. .... *The Fellowship of the Ring* is an extraordinary book. .... Yet for myself I could not resist feeling a certain disappointment. Perhaps this was partly due to the style, which is quite unequal to the theme. .... But perhaps it was due more to a lack of the human discrimination and depth which the subject demanded. 3. J. W. Lambert wrote in the *Sunday Times* on 8 August 1954: 'Whimsical drivel with a message? No; it sweeps along with a narrative and pictorial force which lifts it above that level. A book for bright children? Well, yes and no.' 4. A. E. Cherryman wrote in *Truth* on 6 August 1954: 'It is an amazing piece of work. .... He has added something, not only to the world's literature, but to its history.' 5. Howard Spring wrote in *Country Life* on 26 August 1954: 'This is a work of art. .... It has invention, fancy and imagination. .... It is a profound parable of man's everlasting struggle against evil.' 6. H. l'A. Fawcett wrote in the *Manchester Guardian* on 20 August 1954: 'Mr Tolkien is one of those born story-tellers who makes his readers as wide-eyed as children for more.' 7. The *Oxford Times* review, signed 'C.H.H.', was printed on 13 August 1954, and described the book as 'extraordinary and often beautiful'.

[150] 1. See note 1 to no. 137 above.

[151] 1. Tolkien made two finished designs for *The Fellowship of the Ring*, both of which survive. In that referred to here, the Ruling Ring, surrounded by the fiery letters of its inscription, and the Red Ring (Narya) above it, were represented exactly as in the other

design, which was adopted, and which is still seen in enlarged form on the jackets of the three-volume hardback and paperback editions published by Allen & Unwin; but in the design referred to here there appeared below to left and right the White Ring (Nenya) and the Blue Ring (Vilya), with their gems turned towards the Ruling Ring in the centre.

[153]   1. One would expect 'three cases': cf. *The Lord of the Rings* III 314: 'There were three unions of the Eldar and the Edain: Lúthien and Beren; Idril and Tuor; Arwen and Aragorn. By the last the long-sundered branches of the Half-elven were reunited and their line was restored.' 2. ' "Don't you know my name yet? That's the only answer. Tell me, who are you, alone, yourself and nameless?" ' 3. i.e. the poem 'The Adventures of Tom Bombadil' was first published in that magazine in 1934. 4. ' "We look towards Númenor that was, and beyond to Elvenhome that is, and to that which is beyond Elvenhome and will ever be. Have you no such custom at meat?" '

[154]   1. Naomi Mitchison reviewed *The Fellowship of the Ring* in the *New Statesman* on 18 September 1954. She called it 'extraordinary, terrifying and beautiful'. 2. German, 'realities, technical facts'. 3. sic, here and elsewhere in the letter. 4. Mentioned in Mrs Mitchison's review.

[155]   1. Greek γοητεία (γόης, sorcerer); the English form *Goety* is defined in the O.E.D. as 'witchcraft or magic performed by the invocation and employment of evil spirits; necromancy.' 2. Alongside the final paragraph, Tolkien has written: 'But the Númenóreans used "spells" in making swords?'

[156]   1. Peter Hastings; see no. 153. 2. Greek, 'messenger'. 3. See note 4 to no. 131.

[157]   1. Trinity College, of which Katherine Farrer's husband Austin was Chaplain, had reduced the fees for the education of Tolkien's sons when they were undergraduates there. 2. Perhaps C. S. Lewis's review of *The Fellowship of the Ring* in *Time & Tide*, 14 August 1954. 3. i.e. 'New York Sunday Times'. Auden reviewed *The Fellowship of the Ring* in the *New York Times Book Review* on Sunday 31 October 1954, and in *Encounter*, November 1954. 4. Edwin Muir, reviewing *The Two Towers* in the *Observer* on 21 November 1954, wrote of the Ents: 'Symbolically they are quite convincing, yet they are full of character, too, as formidable and strange as a forest of trees going to war.'

[163]   1. Auden used the term 'trilogy' in his letter; for Tolkien's dislike of it as applied to *The Lord of the Rings* see nos. 149 and 165. 2. From the Anglo-Saxon poem *The Wanderer*, 87: '*eald enta geweorc idlu stodon*', 'the old creations of giants [i.e. ancient buildings, erected by a former race] stood desolate.' 3. The reviewer, Maurice Richardson, wrote: 'It is all I can do to restrain myself from shouting . . . . "Adults of all ages! Unite against the infantilist invasion." . . . . Mr Auden has always been captivated by the pubescent world of the saga and the classroom. There are passages in *The Orators* which are not unlike bits of Tolkien's hobbitry.' (18 December 1954.) 4. Tolkien's second son Michael. 5. 'The Fall of Gondolin' was in fact read to the Exeter College Essay Club not in 1918 but in 1920, as is recorded in the club's minute book: '. . . on Wednesday March 10th at 8.15 p.m. . . . . the president passed to public business, and called upon Mr J. R. R. Tolkien to read his "Fall of Gondolin". As a discovery of a new mythological background Mr Tolkien's matter was exceedingly illuminating and marked him as a staunch follower of tradition, a treatment indeed in the manner of such typical romantics as William Morris, George Macdonald, de la Motte Fouqué etc. . . . . The battle of the contending forces of good and evil as represented by the Gongothlim [sic, for Gondothlim, the name for the people of

Gondolin in the original 'Fall of Gondolin'; see *Unfinished Tales* p. 5] and the followers of Melco [sic, for Melko, an early name for Melkor] was very graphically and astonishingly told.' Among those at the meeting were Nevill Coghill and Hugo Dyson. 6. Latin, 'who has put down the mighty from their seat and has exalted the humble'; from the *Magnificat*. 7. A potentially misleading statement. While he was writing *The Lord of the Rings*, Tolkien laboured at revising and rewriting a great part of *The Silmarillion*. On the other hand, *The Silmarillion* was in existence before 1936, and cannot be regarded as having originated between that year and 1953. 8. 'He is surer of finding the way home in a blind night than the cats of Queen Berúthiel.' (Aragorn of Gandalf in *The Lord of the Rings*, Book II, Chapter 4.) See *Unfinished Tales* pp. 401–2. 9. An episode from Tolkien's childhood in Bloemfontein; see *Biography* p. 13.

[165] 1. The English meaning of *tollkühn*. 2. His mother's maiden name was Suffield. 3. See *Biography* pp. 168–9. 4. E. R. Eddison.

[168] 1. i.e. *Enedwaith*. For the history of this region see *Unfinished Tales* pp. 262–4.

[171] 1. Second person singular of 'I wot', with an optional 'double negative'.

[172] 1. Tolkien's lecture 'English and Welsh', the first of the O'Donnell Lectures, was delivered in Oxford on 21 October 1955, and was published in *Angles and Britons: O'Donnell Lectures*, University of Wales Press, 1963.

[174] 1. See note 8 to no. 163.

[177] 1. This professorship at Oxford had fallen vacant with the end of C. Day Lewis's term of office, and nominations were being invited for his successor. W. H. Auden was eventually elected.

[180] 1. International languages, invented during the nineteenth and twentieth centuries. 2. See no. 211, and also *Unfinished Tales* pp. 389–90, 393–4. 3. See note 4 to no. 163.

[181] 1. But see note 5 to no. 131. 2. A reference to the proposal for a 'relief' road through Christ Church Meadow.

[188] 1. The 1947 Swedish translation, published under the title *Hompen*.

[190] 1. A term signifying an imaginary 'rustic' county. 2. i.e *cane*, 'duck', + *étang*, 'pool, pond'.

[191] 1. 'Wherefore let him that thinketh he standeth take heed lest he fall. There hath no temptation taken you but such as is common to man: but God is faithful, who will not suffer you to be tempted above that ye are able; but will with the temptation also make a way to escape, that ye may be able to bear it.'

[192] 1. ' "Pity? It was Pity that stayed [Bilbo's] hand. Pity, and Mercy: not to strike without need. And he has been well rewarded, Frodo. Be sure that he took so little hurt from the evil, and escaped in the end, because he began his ownership of the Ring so. With Pity." ' 2. ' "Behind that there was something else at work, beyond any design of the Ring-maker. I can put it no plainer than by saying that Bilbo was *meant* to find the Ring, and *not* by its maker." ' (Gandalf to Frodo.)

[193] 1. 'She [Morwen] bore him three children in Gondor, of whom Théoden, the second, was his only son.'

[195] 1. The reference is to a passage in 'The Scouring of the Shire' (Book VI, Chapter 8) where Frodo tells Pippin: ' "There is to be no slaying of hobbits, not even if they have gone over to the other side. . . . . No hobbit has ever killed another on purpose in the Shire, and it is not to begin now. And nobody is to be killed at all, if it can be helped." '

[199] 1. Eddison in fact read from *The Mezentian Gate*; see no. 73. **2.** 'You may like or dislike his invented worlds (I myself like that of *The Worm Ouroboros* and strongly dislike that of *Mistress of Mistresses*) but there is no quarrel between the theme and the articulation of the story.'

[200] 1. There is perhaps a contrast here to *Unfinished Tales* p. 254: 'The probability is that Sauron was in fact one of the Aulëan Maiar, corrupted "before Arda began" by Melkor.' On the 'attachment' of Olórin to Manwë, see *Unfinished Tales* p. 393.

[203] 1. The text of this letter is taken from an article in *Mallorn* 10, p. 19, with silent emendation of the uncharacteristic 'that's', 'there's', etc., to 'that is', 'there is', which was Tolkien's normal usage.

[204] 1. Almqvist & Wiksell Förlag AB, Stockholm, one of Tolkien's Swedish publishers. **2.** The translator of the Swedish edition of *The Lord of the Rings*. **3.** The translator of the Dutch edition. **4.** *Björnavad*: 'Bear-ford'. *Gamleby*: 'Old village'. *Månbergen*: 'Moon-mountains'. *Ljusa slätterna*: 'Bright plains'. In fact *Månbergen* seems not to have been used, but the River Lune and the Gulf of Lune were translated *Månfloden, Mångolfen.*

[205] 1. Christopher Tolkien said in his lecture: 'In the hosts of Attila there went men of many Germanic peoples. . . . . Indeed, his name itself appears to be Gothic, a diminutive of *atta*, the Gothic for "father".' **2.** 'A star shines on the hour of our meeting' (*The Lord of the Rings*, Book I, Chapter 3). The reading in the letter, *omentielmo*, is the same as in the first edition of the book, but Tolkien later changed it to *omentielvo*. The Elvish language Quenya makes a distinction in its dual inflexion, which turns on the number of persons involved; failure to understand this was, Tolkien remarked, 'a mistake generally made by mortals'. So in this case. Tolkien made a note that the 'Thain's Book of Minas Tirith', one of the supposed sources of *The Lord of the Rings*, had the reading *omentielvo*, but that Frodo's original (lost) manuscript probably had *omentielmo*; and that *omentielvo* is the correct form in the context. (The Ballantine paperback edition of *The Lord of the Rings* has the erroneous reading 'omentilmo'.)

[206] 1. The publishers of the Dutch edition of *The Lord of the Rings*. **2.** Professor Piet Harting of Amsterdam University, a friend of Tolkien for many years. **3.** See further *Biography* pp. 225–6.

[207] 1. Forrest J. Ackerman, agent for the film company; see no. 202.

[210] 1. 'Gandalf was shorter in stature than the other two; but his long white hair, his sweeping silver beard, and his broad shoulders, made him look like some wise king of ancient legend. In his aged face under great snowy brows his dark eyes were set like coals that could leap suddenly into fire.' **2.** i.e. in the inn at Bree. **3.** 'The darkness was breaking

447

too soon, before the date that his Master had set it.' **4.** The slaying of the Lord of the Nazgûl by Éowyn. **5.** 'The *lembas* had a virtue without which they would long ago have lain down to die. . . . . It fed the will, and it gave strength to endure, and to master sinew and limb beyond the measure of mortal kind.' **6.** 'But here and there bright sunbeams fell in glimmering shafts from the eastern windows, high under the deep eaves.' 'The sunlight was blotted out from the eastern windows; the whole hall became suddenly dark as night.'

[211] **1.** This reading was adopted in later printings. **2.** In Appendix A to *The Lord of the Rings* (III. 315) the King of Númenor preceding Ar-Adûnakhôr was Tar-Calmacil; the mention here of Tar-Atanamir seems to be no more than a slip. See further *Unfinished Tales* pp. 226–7. **3.** Elsewhere Tolkien called the other two wizards Ithryn Luin, the Blue Wizards; see *Unfinished Tales* pp. 389–90. **4.** In the Index to *The Silmarillion* the names *Elrond, Elros,* and *Elwing* are translated 'Star-dome', 'Star-foam', and 'Star-spray'. These interpretations of the names are later than those in the present letter. **5.** This paragraph is taken from another text of the letter (a draft). The version sent is more brief on this point. **6.** 'The regions in which Hobbits then lived were doubtless the same as those in which they still linger: the North-West of the Old World, east of the Sea.'

[212] **1.** In *The Silmarillion* (pp. 43–4) there is no mention of the 'six mates'.

[214] **1.** Mr Nunn's letter called Tolkien 'a model of scholarship'. **2.** See *The Lord of the Rings* III 413 (Appendix F). **3.** A derivative of Anglo-Saxon *byrd,* 'birth'. **4.** Two *Pontos* are named in the family tree of *Baggins of Hobbiton* (*The Lord of the Rings* III 380), the first being an ancestor of Peregrin Took and Meriadoc Brandybuck. **5.** *Lalia the Great* is not mentioned in *The Lord of the Rings,* but her husband *Fortinbras II* appears in the family tree of *Took of Great Smials* (*The Lord of the Rings* III 381).

[220] **1.** Federated Superannuation Scheme for Universities. **2.** As an examiner to the National University of Ireland.

[224] **1.** Latin, 'therefore I will keep silent'.

[228] **1.** Åke Ohlmarks, translator of the Swedish edition of *The Lord of the Rings*; he had included a biographical article about Tolkien in his translation of the book.

[229] **1.** Swedish, 'mastery, masterly skill'.

[230] **1.** 'I am . . . . of the race of the West [i.e. Númenor] unmingled' (III 249). **2.** 'Laurelindórean lindelorendor malinornélion ornemalin.' **3.** 'Taurelilómëa-Tumbaletaurëa Lómëanor.' **4.** From Glorfindel's greeting to Aragorn: 'Ai na vedui Dúnadan! Mae govannen!' (I 222). **5.** 'A vanimar, vanimálion nostari!' (III 259). **6.** The following lines are translated by Tolkien in the letter. Line 2: 'Cuio i Pheriain anann! Aglar'ni Pheriannath!' Line 4: 'Daur a Berhael, Conin en Annûn! Eglerio!' Line 6: 'Eglerio!' Line 7: 'A laita te, laita te! Andave laituvalmet!' Line 9: 'Cormacolindor, a laita tárienna!'

[232] **1.** i.e. in the tales of 'Saki' (H. H. Munro). **2.** A story entitled *Woorroo,* published by Joyce Reeves under the name of Joyce Gard (Gollancz, 1961). She had sent a copy to Tolkien.

[234] **1.** 'with silver tipped at plenilune / his spear was hewn of ebony' (*The Adventures of Tom Bombadil* p. 27). 'At plenilune in his argent moon / in his heart he longed for Fire'

(ibid., p. 36). **2.** Jane Neave had written to Tolkien: 'The Pied Piper *never* palls! It is asked for every day of every visit when the children are here. But yours would be so much more welcome.' **3.** Probably not a poem included in *The Adventures of Tom Bombadil*; most of the verses in that book were composed some years before it was published.

[235] **1.** 'However good in themselves, illustrations do little good to fairy-stories. The radical distinction between all art (including drama) that offers a *visible* presentation and true literature is that it imposes one visible form. Literature works from mind to mind and is thus more progenitive.' ('On Fairy-Stories', Note E.)

[236] **1.** The paragraph in Appendix F beginning 'It is to mark this that I have ventured to use the form *dwarves* . . .' **2.** The printers of the Puffin edition. **3.** The printers of *The Lord of the Rings* (3-volume hardback, first and second editions). **4.** Founder and Chairman of Penguin Books, of which Puffin is a division.

[237] **1.** ' "Your mother if she saw you, / she'd never know her son, unless 'twas by a whisker." ' (*The Adventures of Tom Bombadil*, p. 19.) Cf.: 'The Aesir handed over the treasure to Hreidmar, stuffed the otterskin full and set it on its feet. Then the Aesir had to pile the gold alongside and cover it up. When that was completed, Hreidmar went up and saw a single whisker, and told them to cover that.' (*Völsungasaga*, Chapter 14; translation by R. G. Finch.) **2.** 'queer tales from Bree, and talk at smithy, mill, and cheaping'. (*The Adventures of Tom Bombadil*, p. 21.) Cf.: 'From mulne ant from chepinge, from smiððe ant from ancre hus me tidinge bringeð.' ('From mill and from market, from smithy and from anchor-house one hears the news.') (*Ancrene Wisse*, edited by J. R. R. Tolkien, Early English Text Society, 1962, p. 48; translation from *The Ancrene Riwle* by M. B. Salu, Burns and Oates, 1955, p. 39.)

[238] **1.** American critic, who visited Tolkien and Unwin in the summer of 1962. **2.** The broadcast was actually on 7 August 1936. It was initiated by Guy Pocock, who had seen the MS. of Tolkien's translation while he was with the publishing house of Dent, to whom it was offered. Pocock later joined the staff of the BBC. **3.** The poem is 'The Nameless Land', published in G. S. Tancred (ed.), *Realities, an anthology of verse* (Leeds, at the Swan Press; London, Gay & Hancock, 1927), p. 24. It is written in the *Pearl* stanza, and begins:

> There lingering lights do golden lie
> On grass more green than in gardens here . . . .

[239] **1.** Two words are in question: (1) Greek *gnōmē*, 'thought, intelligence' (and in the plural 'maxims, sayings', whence the English word *gnome*, a maxim or aphorism, and adjective *gnomic*) – and (2) the word *gnome* used by the 16th-century writer Paracelsus as a synonym of *pygmaeus*. Paracelsus 'says that the beings so called have the earth as their element . . . . through which they move unobstructed as fish do through water, or birds and land animals through air' (*Oxford English Dictionary*, s.v. *Gnome*[2]). The O.E.D. suggests that whether Paracelsus invented the word himself or not it was intended to mean 'earth-dweller', and it discounts any connection with the other word *Gnome*.

[240] **1.** 'suddenly . . . . there appeared above the reeds an old battered hat with a tall crown and a long blue feather stuck in the band'. **2.** 'He made no secret that he owed his recent knowledge to Farmer Maggot, whom he seemed to regard as a person of more importance than they had imagined.' **3.** Sir Thomas Browne, *Vulgar Errors*, III Chapter 10: 'That a Kingfisher, hanged by the bill, showeth where the wind lay.' **4.** See note 1 to no. 237. **5.** See note 2 to no. 237.

[241] 1. On p. 3 of 'English and Welsh' Tolkien writes: '[A] story . . . . which I first met in the pages of Andrew Boord [sic], physician of Henry VIII . . . . tells how the language of Heaven was changed. St Peter, instructed to find a cure for the din and chatter which disturbed the celestial mansions, went outside the Gates and cried *caws bobi*, and slammed the Gates to again before the Welshmen that had surged out discovered that this was a trap without cheese.' 2. 'My college . . . . was shocked when the only prize I ever won . . . . the Skeat Prize for English at Exeter College, was spent on Welsh.' ('English and Welsh', p. 38.) 3. '. . . . not presuming to enter the litigious lists of the accredited Celtic scholars . . . .' 4. Lady Agnew, a resident of Northmoor Road. 5. But in the foreword to *Tree and Leaf* (1964), Tolkien wrote: 'It was suddenly lopped and mutilated. . . . . It is cut down now.'

[242] 1. The book was reviewed in the *Times Literary Supplement* on 23 November 1962 (p. 892) and in the *Listener* on 22 November 1962 (p. 831). The latter review was very enthusiastic, and talked of Tolkien's 'superb technical skill . . . . something close to genius'.

[244] 1. 'Faramir . . . . held out a white rod; but Aragorn took the rod and gave it back, saying: "That office is not ended, and it shall be thine and thy heirs' as long as my line shall last." '

[246] 1. 'And there was Frodo, pale and worn, and yet himself again; and in his eyes there was peace now, neither strain of will nor madness, nor any fear. . . . . "The Quest is achieved, and now all is over," [said Frodo].' 2. Paragraphs 3 and 4 of the first page of the chapter 'Many Partings' (Book VI Chapter 6); and this passage: 'We can't go any quicker, if we are going to see Bilbo. I am going to Rivendell first, whatever happens.' 3. Elrond's blessing to Frodo at the end of Book VI Chapter 6. 4. 'His mind was hot with wrath. . . . . It would be just to slay this treacherous, murderous creature. . . . . But deep in his heart there was something that restrained him: he could not strike this thing lying in the dust, forlorn, ruinous, utterly wretched.' 5. 'Wild fantasies arose in his mind; and he saw Samwise the Strong, Hero of the Age, striding with a sword across the darkened land, and armies flocking to his call as he marched to the overthrow of Barad-dûr.'

[247] 1. This account, 'The Quest of Erebor', is printed in *Unfinished Tales*.

[248] 1. The pagination is that of *Essays Presented to Charles Williams*, and the passage cited is: 'It is easy for the student to feel that with all his labour he is collecting only a few leaves, many of them now torn or decayed, from the countless foliage of the Tree of Tales, with which the Forest of Days is carpeted.' 2. 'The Christian . . . . may now, perhaps, fairly dare to guess that in Fantasy he may actually assist in the effoliation and multiple enrichment of creation.'

[249] 1. Sir James Murray (1837–1915) founded the *Oxford English Dictionary*.

[250] 1. Possibly a reference to Pius X's recommendation of daily communion and children's communion. 2. The Second Vatican Council (1962–6). 3. Tolkien's guardian, Fr Francis Morgan. 4. Tolkien's home from 1926 until 1930. 5. Latin, 'Blessed is he who comes in the name of the Lord.' (From the Communion service.) 6. The general practitioner who attended Tolkien during his visits to (and, later, residence in) Bournemouth. 7. Tolkien's grandson, Michael's son, then at St Andrews University studying English. 8. See note 5 to no. 19, which gives details about this broadcast. 9. James Callaghan, Shadow Chancellor of the Exchequer in the Labour opposition party at this time. The Labour Party came to power in 1964. 10. i.e. before 1931, implying that *The Hobbit* was written in this year. (But see *Biography* p. 177.)

[251]   1. James Dundas-Grant, one of the Inklings. 2. Lewis's stepson. 3. Professor of English at Keele University and a former pupil of Lewis.

[252]   1. The words 'We were separated . . . . long after the event' are struck through in the draft. 2. See note 3 to no. 24.

[253]   1. See Tolkien's drawing 'The Tree of Amalion', no. 41 in *Pictures*.

[254]   1. R. W. ('Dickie') Reynolds; see *Biography* p. 47. 2. Wiseman became headmaster of Queen's College, Taunton. 3. Headmaster of King Edward's.

[257]   1. 'Light as Leaf on Lindentree', *The Gryphon*, new series VI no. 6 (June 1925), p. 217. 2. '. . . . to be the bride-price of Lúthien to Thingol her father.' (Misprinted as 'bride-piece' in all editions for many years, and only recently corrected.) For an account of this poem, see *Inklings* pp. 29–30. 3. See introductory note to no. 9. 4. In Cornwall, on the coast not far from Penzance. This holiday was in the summer of 1932. 5. Tolkien lived in Duchess Road from 1908 until 1910. 6. *Brummagem* is the local (and very old) form of the name of Birmingham.

[261]   1. Bailey wrote: 'From the very first tutorial, Lewis consistently mistook me for Geoff Dutton, an Australian and an excellent student, and Dutton for me.'

[267]   1. Latin, 'in this city the solemn light.'

[268]   1. ' "In him one of the mighty steeds of old has returned." ' ' "Were the West Wind to take a body visible, even so would it appear." ' 'These were the *mearas*. . . . . Men said of them that Béma (whom the Eldar call Oromë) must have brought their sires from West over Sea.'

[269]   1. ' "The Shadow that bred them can only mock, it cannot make: not real new things of its own. I don't think it gave life to the orcs: it only ruined them and twisted them." '

[270]   1. The offices of the Houghton Mifflin Co. are in Boston, Mass.

[274]   1. 'They waded the stream, and hurried over a wide open space, rush-grown and treeless, on the further side. Beyond that they came again to a belt of trees: tall oaks, for the most part, with here and there an elm tree or an ash.'

[275]   1. Sir Cyril Norwood (1875–1956), President of St John's College, Oxford, and author of the Norwood Report on education.

[276]   1. In fact at least three people beside C. S. Lewis had read the mythology: Christopher Tolkien, Rayner Unwin, and Lord Halsbury.

[278]   1. Tolkien's remark is certainly enigmatic, because in *Light on C. S. Lewis* (Bles, 1965), Owen Barfield makes a number of comments on Lewis's personality. Possibly Tolkien was referring to Barfield's puzzlement about 'the great change that took place in [Lewis] between the years 1930 and 1940 – a change that roughly coincided with his conversion . . . but which did not appear, and does not appear in retrospect, to be inevitably or even naturally connected with it' (p. ix). Barfield continued: '*Was* there something, at least in his impressive, indeed splendid, literary personality, which was somehow – and with no taint of insincerity – *voulu*? . . . . some touch of a more than

merely *ad hoc* pastiche?' (p. xi). Alternatively, Tolkien may have been alluding to Barfield's remark (p. xvi) about Lewis's 'distinctive combination of an almost supreme intellectual and "phantastic" maturity, laced with moral energy, on the other hand, with . . . . a certain psychic or spiritual immaturity on the other'.

[281] 1. This drawing is reproduced as no. 19 in *Pictures*. 2. ' "You don't really suppose, do you, that all your adventures and escapes were managed by mere luck, just for your sole benefit?" ' (Gandalf to Bilbo).

[293] 1. Tolkien apparently relented, for Foster's interview with him was published in *The Scotsman* on 25 March 1967.

[294] 1. W. H. Auden; see no. 284. 2. See introductory note to no. 9. 3. According to Tolkien's friend Elaine Griffiths, the MS. was in fact lent by Tolkien to Susan Dagnall, who had heard about it from Miss Griffiths. 4. For Tolkien's correspondence with Jane Neave, the aunt here mentioned, see nos. 231, 234, 238 and 241. 5. See no. 202. 6. By John Christopher, first published in 1956. 7. See also no. 24 for an account of this.

[295] 1. It is not known to what letter Tolkien was referring. 2. Auden had sent Tolkien a typescript of the translation he and Paul B. Taylor had made of the *Völuspá* or 'Song of the Sibyl'. It was eventually published in a collection of their translations from the Edda, under the title *The Elder Edda: A Selection* (Faber & Faber, 1969); this book was dedicated to Tolkien. 3. A long unpublished poem entitled 'Volsungakviða En Nyja', probably written in the late 1920s or early 1930s. Tolkien described it, in a letter to Auden dated 29 January 1968, as 'written in fornyrðislag 8-line stanzas in English: an attempt to organise the Edda material dealing with Sigurd and Gunnar'. *Fornyrðislag* is the Old Norse stanzaic metre, very closely resembling in its lines those of Old English poetry, in which most of the narrative poems of the Edda were composed.

[297] 1. This commentary was published, after Tolkien's death, in Jared Lobdell (ed.), *A Tolkien Compass* (La Salle, Illinois, Open Court, 1975), pp. 153–201.

[300] 1. Nickname for C. S. Lewis. 2. F. E. Brightman (1856–1932), Fellow of Magdalen College.

[303] 1. Tolkien lived with his mother and younger brother in a cottage opposite this mill, in a hamlet outside Birmingham, during his early childhood.

[306] 1. Latin, 'that was an omen'. 2. Officers' Training Corps. 3. ' "You have been chosen, and you must therefore use such strength and heart and wits as you have." ' ' "It is not our part to master all the tides of the world, but to do what is in us for the succour of those years wherein we are set." ' 4. Bishop J. A. T. Robinson, Author of *Honest to God* (1963). 5. Tolkien's younger brother (1894–1976). 6. The lecture, delivered on 5 June 1959, was eventually published in *J. R. R. Tolkien, Scholar and Storyteller*, ed. M. B. Salu & R. T. Farrell (Cornell University Press, 1979).

[307] 1. 'Old age has stolen upon me . . . I am older than I was both in winters [i.e. years] and in learning [i.e. wisdom].'

[309] 1. J. B. Tolkien (1807–96) was in fact 89 when he died. 2. But see no. 334, one of many letters signed 'Ronald' (never 'John' except to his wife in the days of their courtship), and in which he asks Rayner Unwin to call him this.

[311]   1. Mrs Parke, who acted as driver and general help to the Tolkiens for several hours a week.

[312]   1. *Wild Flowers of the Cape Peninsula* by Mary Maytham Kidd (Oxford University Press, 1950).

[315]   1. Tolkien had made over the greater part of his literary income to his sons and daughter; if he survived for seven years after doing so, the gift would be free of death duties.

[316]   1. This letter was never received by the Dictionary Department, and was probably never sent. 2. This definition was used, prefaced by the words 'In the tales of J. R. R. Tolkien (1892–1973)', in the 1976 *Supplement* to the Dictionary. 3. See no. 25.

[318]   1. See note 3 to no. 1; also no. 308. 2. See note 4 to no. 1.

[319]   1. See no. 25. 2. Green informed Tolkien that the author was E. H. Knatchbull Hugessen and the book was *Stories For My Children* (1869).

[323]   1. The Morris car which the Tolkiens owned in the 1930s bore a registration plate which began with the letters JO.

[328]   1. Fellow of Balliol College.

[332]   1. Tolkien was staying with his son Christopher and family in the village near Oxford where they then lived. 2. Tolkien's first cousin.

[336]   1. Idols in a story by Lord Dunsany; see no. 294.

[338]   1. The song of the Ent and Entwife in the chapter 'Treebeard'. 2. German philosopher and writer on Kierkegaard; 1879–1945.

[351]   1. W. H. Lewis. 2. T. P. Dunning, C.M., of University College, Dublin; scholar in Anglo-Saxon. 3. Rosfrith Murray, daughter of Sir James Murray. See no. 249.

[354]   1. The driver of the hired car by which Tolkien travelled to Bournemouth. 2. The Bournemouth hotel where Tolkien and his wife had often stayed.

Index

Compiled by Christina Scull & Wayne G. Hammond

Figures in *italics* indicate letters addressed to the person, etc. indexed. For names and epithets of persons, places, objects, and languages in Tolkien's works the list of page references includes any citations also given by topic. For other entries general and miscellaneous references precede, and are distinct from, citations by topic. Figurative uses of names or words are cited separately. In general, names within titles of works are not indexed. Titles of Tolkien's works are **boldfaced**. *The Lord of the Rings* is generally abbreviated *LR*. Subjects to which Tolkien alludes are indexed by their actual names, titles, or literary sources. His manner of referring to elements of his mythology by different names and in varying degrees of specificity is reflected in the grouping of related entries, e.g. *Valinor* and *Valimar* under *Aman*. Space does not permit indexing of every passing reference by Tolkien; priority has been given to details about his writings, with cross-references from familiar alternate forms of names (but not every variant form or spelling), and to those references most important in the context of Tolkien's life, times, work, and interests. The editor's notes are indexed only selectively.

Although the compilers have tried to be comprehensive and consistent, omissions are inevitable in a work so complex, and at times consistency has been sacrificed for increased usefulness, in the selection and arrangement of entries and sub-entries. A more extensive index of references to the Elvish languages in Tolkien's letters, compiled by the late Taum Santoski, was published in the journal *Vinyar Tengwar* for November 1991.

Andersen, Hans Christian 311; *The Ugly Duckling* 232

Anduin 156, 157, 179, 376, 381; Great River 157, 158, 231

Andúril 273, 425

Andvari 314

Angamaitë 425

Angband, fortress of the Devil 376; Gates of Hell 193; stronghold 148, 149, 150, 307

Angelic beings *see* Ainur

Angels, guardian 66, 99, 159, 288; *see also* Fall (of angels)

Angerthas *see* Runes

Anglo-Saxon *see* Old English

Anglo-Saxon England (Stenton) 108

Aotrou and Itroun 118, 441

Applicability *see* Allegory

Ar-Adûnakhôr 279, 448

Aragorn 104, 160, 161, 180, 193, 200, 206, 237, 246, 247, 258, 267, 272, 273, 286, 307, 323–4, 327, 332, 334, 344, 346, 347, 384, 419, 420, 424, 426, 445, 446, 448, 450; Strider 216, 273, 346, 347, 440; Thorongil 427; Trotter 95, 97, 440; meaning of *Aragorn* 426; healing power 200; longevity 193, 307; Númenórean descent 160, 307, 448; Sauron's opposite 180; could not have withheld Ring from Sauron 332; death 267, 286, 419; descendants 344; unknown to Tolkien when introduced 216

Aragorn and Arwen, Tale of see The Lord of the Rings: Appendices

Arathorn 424, 426, 427

Archeology, in Middle-earth 196

Archet 263

Arda 283, 285, 417, 447; Earth 150, 193, 194, 197, 198, 283, 411; world 150, 154, 156, 186, 195, 259, 283, 386, 411; flat world changed to round 154, 156, 186, 194, 197–8, 206, 386, 411; end of the world 149, 207, 284, 285, 325, 419; circles of the world 156, 206, 286, 287, 325, 354, 386, 419; and our own world 224, 283; Arda

Unmarred 328; meaning of *Arda* 283; 'Arda' used figuratively 417

Ardizzone, Edward 130

Ariosto, Ludovico 181, 184

Arms and the Man (Shaw) 94

Arnor 157–8, 199, 347, 424, 428; North Kingdom 199, 281; meaning of *Arnor* 428; diadem of 281; 'North Kingdom' used figuratively 223

Ar-Pharazôn 205–6, 277, 279, 443; Tar-Calion 155–6, 443

Art, by Tolkien *see* Tolkien, J.R.R.: Artistic abilities

Art, pictorial 223, 413

Arthedain 426

Arthur, King, matter of 59, 199, 241, 280; anachronisms in 133; British, not English 144; poem by Tolkien 219

Arvedui 199

Arwen (Undómiel) 160, 161, 180, 193, 198, 237, 327–9, 423, 445; not reincarnation of Lúthien 193; and Frodo's journey into West 198, 327–9

Asfaloth 211, 277, 279

Asimov, Isaac 377

Assisi 223

Aðalsteinsdottir, Ungfrú 430

L'Atlantide et le règne des géants (Saurat) 198

Atlantis, myth used in Tolkien's writings 151, 175, 186, 197–8, 206, 213, 232, 303, 342, 347, 361, 378; *see also* Númenor

Atomic bomb 116, 165, 303, 443

Atomic power 246

Attila 264, 447

Auden, W.H. 211–17, 355, 359, 367–8, 378–9, 452; 96, 322, 376, 446; *About the House* 367–8; *The Elder Edda* (trans. Auden and Taylor) 379, 452; *The Orators* 212, 445; reviews of *LR* 208, 211, 238–44, 412, 445; BBC talk on *LR* 211–17, 229; comments on Tolkien's house 367–8, 373; Tolkien's appreciation of Auden 411–12

Beowulf (trans. Tolkien) 438
Beowulf and the Finnesburg Fragment
see Prefatory Remarks . . .
Beowulf: The Monsters and the
Critics 350
Beren 149, 180, 193, 204, 221, 282,
334, 345, 347, 386, 445; Tolkien
as Beren 417
Beren and Lúthien, versions of tale
see The Silmarillion
Berkshire 65
Bernardus Silvestris 34
Berúthiel 217, 228, 231, 446
Bestiaries 343
Betjeman, John 184, 322
Beveridge, William Henry 91
Bible: Corinthians 252, 394, 446;
Daniel 400; Ephesians 370; Genesis
109–10; Gospels 100, 237, 338,
393; John 338; Jonah 378; Luke
99; New Testament 109, 358, 395;
Old Testament 398; Psalms 400;
Samuel 384; Jerusalem Bible 378
Bilbo Comes to the Huts of the
Raft-elves 19, 27
Bilbo Woke with the Early Sun in
His Eyes 19, 27, 34, 35
Bill the pony 104
Binney, John 23, 47, 89, 435
Biography, literary 257, 288, 305,
321, 367, 414
Bird and Baby see Eagle and Child
Birmingham 7, 54, 69–70, 96, 179,
218, 219, 235, 245, 348, 410, 451,
452; Brummagem (Brum) old form
of name 69, 348, 451; changed
since Tolkien's boyhood 70;
Beaufort Road 348; Bristol Road
70; Duchess Road 348, 451;
Edgbaston 348; Edgbaston Park
Road 70; New Street 395
Birmingham, University of 245
Birmingham Oratory 7, 395, 434
Birnam Wood 212
The Black Douglas (Crockett) 391
Black Gate see Morannon
Black Riders see Ringwraiths
Black Speech 175, 178, 382,
384–5, 444
Blackfriars, Oxford 115, 370

Blackwell, Basil 47, 94, 114, 437, 440
Blackwell's Bookshop, Oxford 47
Blake, William, Milton 90
Blasphemy 97–8
Blickling Homilies 385
Bloemfontein 75, 213, 219
Blunderbuss 133
Blyton, Carey 350
Blyton, Enid 312
Boarland family 408
Boffin family 31
Bolger family 31
Bolger, Belisarius 120, 122
Bolger, Fredegar (Fatty) 441
Bolger, Hamilcar 120, 122
Bombadil, Tom 26, 104, 174, 178–9,
187, 191–2, 216, 228, 267, 272,
307, 308, 315, 318–19, 445, 449;
spirit of (vanishing) Oxford and
Berkshire countryside 26; inserted
into LR 315, 318–19; function in
LR 178–9, 192; intentional enigma
174; not improved by philosophiz-
ing about 192; exemplar of natural
science 179, 192; and pacifist view
179; Eldest in Time 191; no fear or
desire of possession or domination
192; 'He is' 187, 191–2; and the
Entwives 179
Bombadil Goes Boating 315, 318–19,
449
Book of Mazarbul 168, 170, 171,
186, 248, 443
Boorde, Andrew 320, 450
Boromir 79, 197, 266, 323
Bournemouth 316, 335–6, 391,
429, 430, 431, 450; East Overcliff
431; Little Forest Road 431, 432;
see also Tolkien, J.R.R.: Homes
Bowen, R. 259–60
Bowra, Maurice 162, 443
Boyer, Robert H. 411–12
Boys' Own Paper 184, 370
Bracegirdle family 31
Bradley, Henry 12, 434
Brainwashing 234, 252, 253, 327
Brandy Hall 294, 358
Brandybuck family 31
Brandybuck, Meriadoc (Merry)
246, 276, 334, 376, 448

Bratt, Edith *see* Tolkien, Edith
Bree 158, 216, 303, 360, 361, 447, 449
Breit, Harvey 217–18, 219
Bretherton, Christopher *344–9*
Brightman, F.E. 389, 452
Britain, and England 65, 107; and firearms 133; 'air' of 144; *see also* England
British (Celtic language) 214, 219; British-Welsh 176
British Broadcasting Corp. *187, 253–5; 63, 93, 164; talk on Anglo-Saxon verse 27, 340, 435, 450; broadcasts of Homecoming of Beorhtnoth* 187, 219; broadcast of *Pearl* 317, 449; dramatization of *Sir Gawain and the Green Knight* 183, 444; dramatization of *LR* 228, 229, 244, 253–5, 257; talk on *LR* 211, 229; film *Tolkien in Oxford* 389–90
British Commonwealth 65
Brittany 383
Broceliande 383
Brogan, Hugh *129, 131–2, 185–6, 224, 225–6, 230;* 442
Bromsgrove 54
Brooke, Rupert, *The Old Vicarage, Grantchester* 110, 440
Brooke, V.J. 84, 439
Browne, Patrick *418*
Browne, Thomas, *Vulgar and Common Errors* 319, 449
Browning, Robert, *The Pied Piper* 311, 449
Brown's Hotel, London 417–18
Bruinen, Ford of 263
Buchan, Alexander 79, 439
Buckingham Palace 391, 417–18
Buckinghamshire 130
Buckland 296
Bucklebury Ferry 358
Buildings, modern 70, 84, 91, 439; slums and gas-works, shabby garages, arc-lit suburbs 96; houses north of old Oxford 230; reconstruction of Rotterdam 265
The Bull from the Sea (Renault) 377
Bumpus 217

Burchfield, R.W. *404–5*
Burn, J. *251–2*
Burne-Jones, Edward 128
Burnett-Stuart, John 162, 443
Burrowes family 31
Busman's Honeymoon (Sayers) 82
Butler, Samuel, *Erewhon* 88
Butterbur, Barliman 272; used figuratively 181
Bywater 31

Calas Galadhon 426
Calenarðon 383
Callaghan, James 340, 450
Cambridge 44, 124
Cambridge, University of 74, 164, 351
Campbell, Roy 95–6; *Flaming Terrapin* 95; *Flowering Rifle* 95
Canada 36, 73, 218
The Canterbury Tales (Chaucer) 39–40
Carcharoth 193
Carmelites, Barcelona 95–6
Carr, Charlie 416, 421, 432
Carroll, Lewis 21–2; *Alice's Adventures in Wonderland* 21, 22, 25; *Hiawatha's Photographing* 22; *Sylvie and Bruno* 22; *Through the Looking-Glass* 22, 94
Carryl, Charles E., *Davy and the Goblin* 104
Cars 82, 89, 109, 343; destroying Oxford for motor-cars 235, 446; traffic 165, 344–5; Tolkien's car 'JO' 408, 453; 'infernal combustion' engine 77
Carter, Douglas *419;* 80, 99–102, 439
Cat 343
Cater, William *408, 415*
Catholic Church, anti-Catholic feelings 52, 83–4, 95–6, 354, 394–5; Catholics and evil ends 190; habit of calling priests *father* 191; apparent failings in Church 337–9, 354; Second Vatican Council 339, 450; changes in the Church 393–5; pictured as a tree 394
Catholic Herald 112

460

205; a race doomed not to leave the world 246; immortal not etenal 146, 189, 204, 236–7, 267, 285–6, 325; deathlessness a burden 146, 147, 236, 325; and reincarnation 147, 187–9, 236, 286; childbearing 431; not wholly good or in the right 197; hostility between Elves and Dwarves 152, 159; friendship of Elves of Eregion with Dwarves of Moria 152, 190; High Elves had no religious practices in Middle-earth 204; belief in God 243; called on Varda-Elbereth 206; monotheists 253; did not know fate at end of Arda 285, 325; departure into the West 176, 177, 198; 'Elves' used figuratively 78; *see also* Children of God, Halfelven, Mortality, Rings of Power

Elvish languages 129, 143–4, 145, 146, 175, 178, 219, 248, 282, 380, 385–6, 403, 428; Elvish roots/stems 178, 224, 277, 278, 281, 282, 303, 308, 347, 361, 380, 382–3, 384, 386, 423, 425, 426, 427; plurals 178; names and words in *k* rather than *c* 247; two related Elvish languages 26, 143, 175; Primitive/Common Elvish 278, 281, 282, 383, 386, 410; Telerin 425, 426; and Númenóreans 154; at end of Third Age more Men than Elves knew Quenya or spoke Sindarin 425; Tolkien would have liked more Elvish in *LR* 216; would have preferred to write *LR* in Elvish 219; Elvish languages represent his linguistic tastes 143, 175–6, 214, 231, 264, 380; his most absorbing interest 247; tape-records some pieces of Elvish 164; *see also* Tengwar

Quenya (High-elven, *including examples and translated names*) 148, 150, 151, 156, 176, 178, 180, 189, 194, 202, 204, 206, 207, 219, 224, 265, 277–9, 281, 282, 283, 284, 303, 307–8, 343, 347, 361, 380, 381, 382–4, 385, 386, 403,

410, 422, 423, 424, 425–8, 434, 447, 448; nonsense fairy language 8, 434; and Latin 176, 343; and Finnish 176, 214; and Greek 176, 343; Elven-latin 176; archaic language of lore 176; 'dead' language 425; abandoned by Noldor for Sindarin 425; and Treebeard's lament 307–8; *omentielmo* vs. *omentielvo* 447

Sindarin (Grey-elven, *including examples and translated names*) 152, 158, 176, 178, 199, 219, 223, 224, 247, 263, 277, 278–9, 281, 282, 283, 308, 380, 381, 382–3, 384, 392, 402, 403, 409–10, 417, 423, 424, 425–8, 448; and Welsh 219; fits 'Celtic' legends and stories 176; and Quenya 219, 425; living language of the Western Elves 176; Gnomish dialect 106; Woodland dialect 282, 425; 'A Elbereth Gilthoniel' explained 277–8; predominant nomenclature in Gondor 175, 178, 224, 384, 409, 424, 425; pronunciation in Gondor 178

Elwin 347

Elwing 150, 193, 282, 334, 448

Emma (after Austen) 83

Encounter 208, 211, 445

Endor *see* Middle-earth

Endor, Witch of 384

Enedwaith 224, 446

Enemy 146; *see also* Morgoth, Sauron

Engels, Horus 119

England 56, 65, 89, 90–1, 106, 281, 305, 410; class distinctions 69; Anglo-Saxon period 108; mythology for 144–5, 231; scope left for others to develop the mythology 145; 'Shire' based on rural England 235, 250; *LR* is English 250, 299

English and Medieval Studies Presented to J.R.R. Tolkien (ed. Davis and Wrenn) 322–3

English and Welsh 227, 228–9, 319–20, 446, 450

English Dialect Dictionary (Wright) 11

English language, modern 107, 254, 370; shame spoken so widely 65; accents 69–70, 253–4; pronunciation 72–3; and archaism 187, 225–6; grammatical question 300; learned by Tolkien at school 213; remote from his personal taste 214; and Black Speech 384; and Westron 425; see also Middle English, Old English

English literature, Tolkien not nourished by 172; did not learn at school 213; not interested in English novel 414

English Literature in the Sixteenth Century (C.S. Lewis) 125, 128

Entish language 269, 307–8

Ents 104, 160, 178, 179, 208, 211–12, 223, 231, 275, 276, 277, 334–5, 419, 445; Onodrim 178, 223–4; Shepherds of the Trees 160; origin of *Ent* 208, 212; origin of concept 212; and Great Birnam wood 212; oldest of living rational creatures 160; and Dwarves 334; Entmoot 97; Tolkien did not consciously invent them 211–12, 231, 334; does not know what happened to them 104; Entwives 179, 335, 419; 'male' and 'female' attitudes to wild things 212; 'Ent' used figuratively 340

Eorl, House of 177, 216; oath of, used figuratively 379

Eowyn 161, 323, 324, 448

Epstein, Jacob 96

'Erebor' used figuratively 430

Erech 384

Ered Luin (Mountains of Lune) 196, 263, 334

Eregion 152, 190, 360

Erendis 360

Eressëa see Aman

Erewhon (Butler) 88

Errantry 161–3, 309, 310, 443, 448; and oral tradition 162, 443; and *Earendil was a Mariner* 443

Eru 190, 194, 204, 206, 335, 345, 387; Authority 202, 203; Creator 147, 189, 203, 237, 259–60, 280, 283, 285, 286, 287, 345; Eru Ilúvatar 205; God 146, 147, 155, 156, 191, 194, 201, 204, 205, 206, 207, 235, 236, 243, 285; God the Creator 279; Ilúvatar 155, 204, 285, 287; The One 149, 155, 190, 194, 204, 235, 243, 253, 277, 280, 283, 284, 285, 287, 345; One God 189, 235, 387; Other Power 253; Teller 284; True God 206, 207, 243; Writer of the Story 253; meaning of *Eru Ilúvatar* 204; has no embodiment in the world 235, 237, 283; remote 204, 235, 387; reserves right to intervene 235; has sole right to divine honour 243; gave world secondary reality 259; see also Children of God, Creation

Escapism 85, 120

Esperanto 231, 446

Essays Presented to Charles Williams (ed. C.S. Lewis) 118, 209, 216, 220, 258, 297, 450

Essex 187

Eucatastrophe 100–1

Europe, and Tolkien's mythology 144, 283, 376; elves and fairies of 176; dress of 280; tradition of men out of the sea 212, 303; and Fastitocalon 344

Everett, Caroline 257–9

Evesham 218, 377

Evil 75–6, 80, 127, 252, 280; things not evil may serve evil ends 190; no Absolute Evil 243; see also Good and Evil, Torture

Evil, in Tolkien's mythology, arises from apparently good root 146; and power of creation 187, 190–1, 195; Shadow 207, 296; hang-over from one age to another 180; after Third Age Evil not incarnate 154, 160, 207, 252; and Orcs 355; see also Good and Evil, Morgoth, Power, Sauron

Examination Schools, Oxford 353

Exeter Book 66, 102–3

Exeter College, Oxford 12, 52, 214–15, 406, 434, 450

to Frodo 329–30, 386; treats
Gollum like Caliban by Ariel 77;
and Gollum's failure to repent 110,
221, 235, 329–30; heroic character
161, 244, 329; chief hero 161;
most closely drawn character 105;
successor to Bilbo 105; jewel
among hobbits 88; most representative hobbit 329–30; irritates
some readers 329
Gamgee tissue 88, 245, 348, 410
Gandalf 24, 28, 31, 42, 79, 94, 104,
110, 119, 120, 121, 159, 180, 181,
182, 200, 201–3, 207, 217, 225,
228, 231, 232, 236–7, 243, 253,
271, 273, 276, 277, 289–90, 291,
293, 296, 307, 327, 328, 329,
332–3, 334, 346, 348, 349, 354,
365, 376, 383, 384, 390, 393, 402,
411, 413, 414, 424, 435, 442, 446,
447, 452; Olórin 259, 411, 447;
White Rider 79; origin of Gandalf
31, 383; Odinic wanderer 119; was
always old 182; sense of humour
271; avuncular attitude to hobbits
271; person of high and noble
authority 271; angelic being 202–3,
237, 243, 354; emissary 182, 202,
237, 327, 354, 365; had been
attached to Manwë 259, 447; his
function especially to watch human
affairs 159; opposed to Sauron
180, 202–3, 327; only wizard who
fully passed tests 202; death and
return from death 201–3, 237;
enhanced powers 202, 203, 237;
as Ringbearer 236–7, 327, 390;
if he had taken the Ring 332–3;
use of magic 200; and fireworks
390; and inscription on the Doors
of Durin 424; and Saruman 202,
271, 277; and Shadowfax 354; and
Frodo's journey to the West 327,
328; his return to the West 236–7,
327, 354; see also Ainur, Wizards
Gard, Joyce see Reeves, Joyce
Gardeners' Arms, Oxford 87
Gardner, Ava 353
Garm 130–1
Garrick Club 417

Gasch, Pauline see Baynes, Pauline
Gaudy Night (Sayers) 82, 439
Gebers Förlag 304
Genesis A 314
Geology, in Middle-earth 248
Geometry 377
George (Georgius, Prince, son of
Giles) 43, 133
George V 391
George Allen & Unwin see under A
German, Germanic languages 37–8,
93, 178, 218, 263, 269–70, 314,
340, 358, 369, 376–7, 381, 385,
410; Early German 369; Low
German 429; Old Germanic lan-
guages 12, 377; Primitive German
369, 381; Germanic philology 12,
218; German translation of The
Hobbit 37–8, 44, 119; see also
Dutch, English, Gothic, Old
English languages, Runes
German Mythology Applied (Ryan)
380
Germanic legend 144
Germany 37–8, 48, 55, 89, 90, 111;
German people 65, 93, 229;
'Germanic' ideal 55–6
The Gest of Beren and Lúthien see
The Silmarillion
Ghân-buri-Ghân 409
Ghosts 103
Giant (Farmer Giles of Ham) 131
Giant, in The Lord of the Rings 42
Gielgud, John 102
Gift of Men see Mortality
Giles, Farmer 131, 423
Gil-galad 152, 153, 154, 156, 157,
190, 260, 273, 279, 280, 424, 425,
426; meaning of name 279, 426
Gilson, Robert C. 52, 343, 395, 451
Gilson, Robert Q. 8–10, 395, 429
Gimli 198, 229, 288, 381, 382;
source of name 382; and his father
229; passes to Elvenhome 198
Gladden Fields 263, 381
Gladden River 381
Glasgow, University of 164, 165, 167
Glittering Caves 282, 407
Glóin 229
Glorfindel 277, 279, 423

Glórund Sets Forth to Seek Túrin
19, 434
Gnome (word) 318, 449
Gnomes see Elves
Goblins see Orcs
God 9–10, 49, 51, 54, 66, 73, 76, 94,
99, 105, 110, 116, 126, 127, 128,
191, 234, 288, 326, 340, 393,
399–400; Creator 188, 189, 192,
399, 400; Great Author 215; Judge
234; supreme Artist and the Author
of Reality 101; Writer of the Story
252; Light of 99; Will of 191;
Finger of 204; belief in personal
God 400
God, in Tolkien's mythology see Eru
Gods see Ainur
Goebbels, Joseph 93
Goldberry 187, 191–2, 228, 272
Golden Hall 254, 275–6
The Golden Key (MacDonald) 351
Gollum 32, 42, 70, 71, 76, 77, 81,
110, 119, 121, 124, 161, 164, 217,
221, 232, 233, 234–5, 252, 255,
286, 289, 296, 307, 313, 326, 327,
330, 334, 442; Sméagol 201, 34–5,
289–2, 381; and original version
of *The Hobbit* 121, 161, 442; and
Déagol 290–2; and grandmother
293, 296; and the Stoors 289, 290;
'Sméagol' not fully envisaged at
first 201; pitiable but ended in persistent wickedness 234; courage
and endurance 234; and Frodo
234–5, 326, 330; and temptation
233–5; failure to repent 110, 221,
234–5, 252, 255, 330; treatment by
Sam 77, 110, 221, 234–5, 330; like
Caliban to Sam's Ariel 77; Tolkien
tape-records Gollum passages 164
Gondar, Ethiopia 409
Gondolin 21, 150, 158, 193, 346,
386, 445–6; chief Elvish stronghold
150; fall of 21, 158, 346
Gondor 79, 104, 157–8, 168, 175,
178, 185, 196, 197, 216, 217, 224,
241, 244, 248, 254, 259, 277, 281,
323–4, 334, 347, 384, 409–10,
424, 425, 428, 447; South
Kingdom 281, 409; Stoningland

409; one surviving Númenórean
state 323; origin of *Gondor* 409–
10; crown 277, 281; kings 424,
425; Stewards 158, 217, 324;
Great Council 324; government
104, 323–4; economy 196; history
157–8; compared to Byzantium
157; people of (Gondorians,
Númenóreans) 77, 175, 197,
244, 281, 344, 409; compared to
Egyptians 281; compared to Jews
281; restored kingdom like Holy
Roman Empire 376; and Common
Speech 175; predominantly Elvish
nomenclature 175, 178, 224, 384,
409, 424, 425; Gondorian boys
play at being Orcs 344; 'Gondor'
used figuratively 223, 379
Gondwanaland 409–10
Good and Evil, on both sides in war
10, 82, 197; evil labours in vain,
always preparing soil for good to
sprout in 76; and Nazi Germany
93; goodness depends on values
independent of a particular conflict
242–3; evil not finally resistable by
incarnate creatures, however 'good'
252–3; see also Evil
Good and Evil, in Tolkien's mythology, evil arises from apparently
good root 146; *LR* not just a fight
between Good and Evil 178–9,
197, 243–4, 262; see also Evil
Gordon, E.V. 41, 42, 114; *Sir Gawain
and the Green Knight* (ed. Tolkien
and Gordon) 11, 436
Gordon, George S. 20, 56–7, 435,
437
Gordon, Ida, *Pearl* (ed.) 36, 114, 436
Gothic language 12, 264, 357–8, 382,
447; Tolkien discovered while at
school 213, 214, 345, 357, 397,
437; contributed to difficulty in
winning award to Oxford 52;
inscriptions in books 356–8
Goths 357
Government 63–4
Grace 75, 80, 126, 172, 326
Grace, in Arda 120, 326; at meat
(Númenórean) 194, 201, 281

470

The Hoard 312; *Iumonna Gold Galdre Bewunden* 18, 434
Hobberdy (Hobbaty, Hobberdy Dick) 406, 407
The Hobbit 14–32, 34–8, 41, 42, 44, 58, 86, 98, 101, 117, 120, 122, 123, 124, 125, 129, 131, 135, 136–7, 145, 149, 151, 152, 153, 158–9, 160, 161, 178, 187, 191, 215, 216, 218, 297–8, 309, 314, 334, 344, 346, 348, 355, 364–5, 383, 384, 385, 406–7, 434, 435, 441, 442, 450

Writing: first sentence 215, 219, 406; history of writing 14, 32, 215, 344, 348, 450; for children 21, 145, 215, 298, 346; Tolkien regrets style and tone 159, 191, 215, 218, 297–8, 310, 346; read before publication 14, 21, 36, 135, 215, 346, 374, 452

Publication: came to attention of Allen & Unwin 14, 215, 346, 374, 452; preparation for publication 14–22; illustrations and maps 14–20, 27, 434 (*see also individual titles*); dust-jacket 16–17; jacket blurb 20–2, 232, 435; publication date 18–19, 20; sales, income 20, 24, 36, 43, 85, 421; errata (various eds.) 28, 34, 123, 313, 435

American edition (1938): 17–20, 34, 36; payment for illustrations 20; dust-jacket 181; wins prize 36

Reprints and later editions: reprinted (1937) 19, 27; stocks burnt in air-raid 58; reprinted (1942) and Children's Book Club ed. 58, 86; second ed. (1951), and revised ch. 5 124, 141, 142, 161, 442; Puffin Books ed. (1961), reluctance to cheapen the old Hobbit 302; Puffin Books 'corrections' to text 312–13; Ballantine Books ed. (1965), cover art 362–3; Unwin Books ed. (1966) 364–5, 406; extract in *School Magazine* 314; music based on 350

Reviews and responses: 18, 23–5, 30, 32, 41, 98, 435; request for

a sequel 23–6; not meant to have a sequel 24, 29, 38; 'new Hobbit' *see The Lord of the Rings*

Translations: German 37–8, 44, 119; Icelandic 430; Spanish 318; Swedish 249, 251, 446; *hobbit* must not be translated 251

Sources: Old English literature 21; Icelandic literature 21, 31, 175, 382, 383; Northern myth 22; *Beowulf* 30–1; George MacDonald 31, 178; epic, mythology, and fairy-story 31; *warg* from primitive German 381; holiday in Switzerland 309, 391–3; *The Black Douglas* 391; *The Marvellous Land of Snergs* 215; *Soria Moria Castle* 384

And The Silmarillion 158, 218, 232, 318; adventures on outskirts of the mythology 17; intruded into the mythology 21, 24; drawn into edge of the mythology 26; drawn into the mythology against Tolkien's will 38; torn at random out of world in which it already existed 122; frequent allusion made in *The Hobbit* to the mythology 31; independently conceived, Tolkien did not know as he began that it belonged 145; taken as matter from the great cycle susceptible of treatment as a 'fairy-story' 159; originally unconnected, inevitably drawn into greater construction and modified it 215, 346; shadow of *Silmarillion* deep on later parts 136; background to *The Hobbit* 122, 151–2, 216

Miscellaneous: only philological remark 22, 435; presence of terrible gives it verisimilitude 24; includes Tolkien's favourite motifs and characters 29; riddles 32, 123; and eucatastrophe 101; study of simple ordinary man against high setting 159; story and sequel about achievements of specially graced and gifted individuals 365; tone and style change in course of story 159, 298; virtually human point of

view 145; Tolkien tape-records parts 164; *see also* Runes
'Hobbit dinner' 265–6
Hobbiton 31, 294, 376
Hobbits 23, 24, 26, 27, 30–1, 34, 35, 36, 38, 42, 77, 79, 83, 88, 120–1, 146, 147, 149, 155, 158, 159, 160, 179, 180, 184, 185, 186, 193, 196, 197, 200, 202, 215, 228, 232, 233, 240, 244, 246, 250, 251, 255, 262, 265, 271, 278, 280, 289–96, 299, 303, 305, 328, 329, 343, 365, 375, 376, 381, 390, 396, 404–5, 406–7, 427, 448; Halflings 308, 405; Little Folk 158; Pheriain, Pheriannath 425, 427; Shire-folk 290, 292, 293; Stoors 289–90, 296; possible sources of invention 30–1, 34–5, 406–7; word *hobbit* 375, 404–5; definition of *hobbit* in *Oxford English Dictionary* 404–5, 453; not pygmies 30, 34–5; not rabbits 30, 35, 406; not a Utopian vision 197; not allegorical 233; branch of the human race 158, 406; names 31, 83, 88, 196; language 31, 180, 278, 290, 299, 381, 448; appearance, stature 30, 35, 158, 365; clothes 35, 280; Tolkien's illustrations of 35; history 158; birthday customs 289–93; marriage, kinship, inheritance 291–6; hobbit-children 179; had no worship or prayer 193; tobacco industry 79; 'hobbitry' 158, 184, 228; comic, amusing 26, 38; courage, heroism at a pinch 120–1, 158, 196–7; free from ambition or greed 158; unimaginative, vulgar 158, 160, 232, 240, 329, 365; sloth and stupidity of 262; slow to change 290; no bloodsports 197; in touch with nature 158, 197; exceptional hobbits 329, 365; 'wheels of the world' turned by the apparently small and weak 149, 160, 246; ennoblement of 215, 220, 232, 237; Tolkien is fond of hobbits 121, 329; sometimes irritated by them 329; 'hobbit talk' amuses him more than adventures

36; Tolkien as a hobbit 227, 265, 288–9, 315; 'hobbit' used figuratively 24, 78, 115, 170, 201, 247, 227, 288–9, 314, 361, 365, 390, 392, 406–7, 435
Holderness peninsula 221, 345
Holland 250, 265–6
Hollin 77
Holy Trinity church, Headington Quarry, Oxford 341
Holywell Street, Oxford *see* Tolkien, J.R.R.: Homes
The Homecoming of Beorthnoth, Beorthelm's Son 165, 306, 443; no dialect tone or rural quality needed in broadcast 187; deals with heroism and chivalry 219, 350
Homer 154, 159, 172, 201
Honest to God (Robinson) 394, 452
Hooper, Walter *371, 389*
Hopkins, Gerard Manley 127–8
Hornblower family 31
Hornburg 276
Houghton Mifflin *35, 217–21, 237–8, 349–52, 358;* 17–18, 19–20, 21, 34, 36, 123, 181, 208, 352, 355, 363, 451
The Hound of Heaven (Thompson) 340
The House of the Wolfings (Morris) 303
Hudson, C.H. 185, 444
Hughes, Richard 23, 24, 181
Humber Garrison 345, 420
Huxley, Aldous 96
Huxley, Julian 30, 34–5, 62, 396
Hymns Ancient and Modern 103

Icarus 88
Icelandic languages and literature, dwarf names from 21, 31, 175, 382, 383; Old Icelandic 12, 13, 21, 31, 134; Old Norse 36, 175, 214, 269, 306, 314, 358, 369, 370, 381, 382, 436; Icelandic translation of *The Hobbit* 430; *see also titles of works in Old Norse etc.*
Ido 231, 446
Idril 193, 345, 361, 386, 445

Illustration, and fairy-stories 312
Ilúvatar see Eru
Imladris see Rivendell
Immortal lands see Aman
Immortality see Elves, Mortality
Imperialism 115
Imrahil of Dol Amroth 323–4
Incledon, Marjorie 421–2; 122,
　416, 453, 441
Income tax 69, 256, 316, 340–1,
　363, 416
Indick, Benjamin P. 366
Indo-European languages 267,
　269–70
Indo-Iranian languages 37
Inklings (Tangye Lean) 162, 387–8
Inklings, meetings of (including
　generally meetings with Lewis,
　Williams, et al. in pubs, Magdalen
　College, etc.) 29, 36, 47, 59, 63,
　67, 68, 71, 72, 73, 74, 76, 77, 79,
　80, 81, 82, 83, 84, 92–3, 94, 95–6,
　102, 103, 105, 108, 109, 116, 117,
　125, 128–9, 161, 209, 258, 320,
　349, 351, 387–8, 436, 438, 439,
　441, 451; origins 387–8; purpose
　29, 388; club of practising poets
　36; Tolkien reads The Hobbit to
　36; reads LR to 71, 72, 73, 76, 79,
　81, 209; reads Leaf by Niggle to
　320; and criticism 125–9; planned
　victory celebration 94; ham-feast
　161
International Congress of Linguists
　164
International Fantasy Award 261, 377
Invention, LR seemed to write itself,
　as if the truth comes out 104, 231;
　stories arose as 'given' things 145;
　feeling of not inventing but report-
　ing, wait till 'what really happened'
　came through 145, 212, 231; Ents
　not consciously invented 211–12,
　231; Tolkien the 'chosen instru-
　ment' for writing LR 413; parts
　of his mythology seem revealed
　through rather than by him 189
Ireland (Eire), visits by Tolkien 140,
　184, 219, 278, 289, 359; finds air
　wholly alien 219; fond of it and

(most of) its people 289
Irish languages 26, 134, 219, 289;
　Gaelic 219, 385; Gaelic nasc
　and Black Speech nazg 385
Iron Crown 148, 149, 150
Isengard 170; used figuratively 235
Isildur 156–7, 198, 206, 384
Israel 109
Istari see Wizards
Italian language 214, 223, 288,
　377, 419
Italy, Italians 66, 223, 409
Ithilien 76, 79, 97, 323
Iwerddon, King of 436
Ixion, Ixion Cycles 88

Jairus's daughter 99
James, Saint, mother of 338
Japan 89, 90, 116
Jarrold and Sons 169, 183, 222, 313
Jeffery, Richard 223–4, 424–8
Jennings, Elizabeth 101, 440
Jerusalem Bible 378
Jesus Christ 97, 99, 127, 128, 237,
　338–9, 340, 385, 387, 393–4;
　Resurrection 100–1, 286; Ascen-
　sion 286; only just literary critic
　128
Jews, praised 37, 410; and Nazi
　Germany 37–8, 93; Tolkien rejects
　Nazi race-doctrine 37–8; woken
　by Jew to go to mass 67; Númen-
　óreans compared to 204, 281;
　Dwarves compared to 229; Roman
　Catholic disabilities compared to
　Jews' 394–5; Jewish names 410
Joad, C.E.M., The Recovery of
　Belief 63
Johannesburg 75, 91
John the Baptist, Saint 385
John the Evangelist, Saint 397
John Inglesant (Shorthouse) 348
Jonah (trans. Tolkien) 378
Jones, John Morris see Morris-Jones,
　John
Joseph, Saint 101
Journey, in story-telling 239–40
Judas Iscariot 338
Judith (Old English text) 314
Julius Agricola 107

random 219, 379; a name comes first and the story follows 219; derivation of invented names 380–4; some elements possibly absorbed from memories 384–5, 409; borrowing of sounds 387; invention of names, and euphony 428; *see also names of languages,* Dale, Gondor, Hobbits, Long Lake, *The Lord of the Rings, The Silmarillion*

Lanier, Sterling 422

Last Alliance 129, 157, 179

Latin language 66, 172, 213, 214, 219, 263, 268–70, 354, 358, 361, 376, 382, 384, 393, 395, 397, 419, 425; and Quenya 176, 343

Lawlor, John 341, 451

The Lay of Aotrou and Itroun 118, 441

The Lay of Beren and Lúthien see The Silmarillion

The Lay of Leithian see The Silmarillion

Lazarus 286

Leach, Lyle 424

Leaf by Niggle 81, 111, 320–2; originally *The Tree* 257; arose suddenly and almost complete 113, 257, 320; written just before the War 320; in *Dublin Review* 97, 112, 320; in *Tree and Leaf* 335; escaped grasp of *Silmarillion* 145; sources 257, 321, 450; meaning 195; allegorical 195; not an 'allegory' so much as 'mythical' 320–1; similar stories 113, 117

'Leaf-mould' of memories 409

Lean, Edward Tangye 162, 387–8

Learning 336–7, 370

Leeds (city) 306, 340, 345–6

Leeds, University of 13–14; 305–6, 346; English School under Gordon 56–8; students 11–13, 57, 305, 403–4; Tolkien's interview for job 56; as Reader in English Language and Professor 11, 12–14, 56–7, 219, 345; for one year held both Leeds and Oxford chairs 56, 437

Legendarium 149, 189, 197, 214

Legends, in general 144, 193, 255, 264, 383; ignorance of 88; legends and myths largely made of 'truth' 147; interdependence with language 143–4, 231, 345, 375; men out of the sea 212, 303; corn and culture heroes 347; of Golden Age of the North 224; *see also* Myth

Legolas 180, 198, 277, 282, 382

Lembas 274–5, 288, 448

Letters to Malcolm (C.S. Lewis) 352

Lewis, C.S. 59–62, 125–9; 23, 29, 32–4, 36, 47, 52, 63, 65, 67, 68, 71, 72, 73, 74, 76, 77, 79, 80, 81, 83, 84, 92–3, 95–6, 102, 103, 105, 109, 161, 209, 256, 257, 258, 302, 341–2, 349, 350–1, 361, 362, 371, 377, 378, 387–8, 389, 416, 434, 436, 437, 438, 440

    Works by: Aeneid (trans.) 93, 440; *Christian Behaviour* 59–62, 437–8; *English Literature in the Sixteenth Century* 125; *Essays Presented to Charles Williams* (ed.) 118, 209, 216, 220, 258, 297, 450; *The Great Divorce (Who Goes Home?)* 71, 80, 83, 439; *Letters to Malcolm* 352; *Myth Became Fact* 109, 440; *Of Other Worlds* 371; *Out of the Silent Planet* 29, 32–4, 36, 89, 342, 347, 361, 378, 435; Tolkien speaks favourably of *OSP* to Stanley Unwin 29, 32–4; Tolkien found blend of *vera historia* and *mythos* in *OSP* irresistible 33; *Perelandra* 89, 342, 361; Priscilla Tolkien preferred *Perelandra* to *OSP* 89; *Poems* 378; Ransom trilogy 209, 303, 342; Tolkien as model for Ransom 29, 89; *Rehabilitations* 389; *The Pilgrim's Regress* 349; *The Screwtape Letters* 108, 342; *Studies in Words* 302; *That Hideous Strength* 224, 342, 361; influence of Charles Williams spoiled *THS* 342, 361; Lewis on committee revising Ancient and Modern Hymnal 103; planning story about descendants of Seth and Cain 105, 440

Life and character: energetic and jolly 68; getting too much publicity 68; put away three pints and said was going short for Lent 68; good deal of Ulster in him 95, 350–1; bias against Catholics 95–6; and criticism 125–9, 388; excites animosity in certain quarters 184; passion for hearing things read aloud 303, 361, 388; wrote to authors who pleased him 209; generosity and friendship 350, 362; and Owen Barfield 103, 341, 363, 451–2; and Roy Campbell 95; and the Inklings 387–8 *and see* Inklings; mutual influence by Lewis and Charles Williams on their writings 341–2, 349, 361; impressionable man 362; dualism of his mind and imagination 371; and Oxford Professorship of Poetry 36, 351; and Merton Professorship of English Literature 108, 117; Clarke Lecturer in Cambridge 74; Professor at Cambridge 350–1; marriage 256, 341, 349; death 341–2, 349; obituaries do not do him justice 341–2, 350–1

Friendship with Tolkien: from about 1927 to 1940 Tolkien's closest friend 349; never called each other by Christian name 365; read Dante together 377; Tolkien refutes allegation that he criticized Lewis for loudness 128, 441; shall have to write themselves the kind of books they want to read 209, 378; agreed that Lewis was to write on space-travel and Tolkien on time-travel 29, 342, 347, 378; planned book on language together 105, 440; Lewis used names from Tolkien's works in his own 33, 113, 151, 224, 303, 361, 378; Narnia outside Tolkien's sympathy, as much of his work was outside Lewis's 352; 'We were talking of dragons, Tolkien and I' 389; *Light on C.S. Lewis* 363, 451–2; Lewis encouraged Tolkien as writer 184,

303, 362, 366; Lewis reads, reviews *The Hobbit* 14, 18, 23, 32, 41, 124, 346, 435; hears, approves *LR* 34, 41, 58, 68, 71, 72, 73, 77, 79, 80, 81, 83, 84, 103, 122, 209, 303, 362; criticizes *LR* 36, 38, 169, 376; blurbs for *LR* 166, 181, 184; reviews *LR* 184, 208, 445; audience for *The Silmarillion* 21, 24, 130, 224, 361; his death like an axe-blow near the roots 341; lack of closeness in later years 341, 349

Lewis, W.H. 47, 67, 68, 74, 84, 92, 95, 102, 103, 117, 437, 439, 441; *The Splendid Century* 71, 83, 84, 92–3; and the Inklings *see* Inklings; enjoyed *LR* 122; protected brother on telephone 369; not at brother's funeral 341; death 430

Liège, University of 124, 181, 185, 219

Life, purpose of 399–400

Life of Cato (Plutarch) 89, 439

Light, in Tolkien's mythology 120, 121, 148, 386–7

Light as Leaf on Linden Tree 346, 420, 451

Light on C.S. Lewis (ed. Gibb) 363, 451–2

Lincoln College, Oxford 84, 439

Lincolnshire 124

Lindon 425

Lindsay, David, *A Voyage to Arcturus* 34, 436

The Listener 322, 450

Literature, in general 50

Lithuanian language 429

Little Delving 250

Little Forest Road *see* Bournemouth

Little Kingdom 39, 42, 43, 113, 133, 137, 139; heart has gone out of 113

Liverpool Street Station, London 265

London 9–10, 254, 261, 320; Museum Street 164, 261, 443; Tooting a Hobbit-sounding place 245

Lonely Isle *see* Aman (Eressëa)

The Lonely Isle 53, 437

Long Lake, language of 175

477

Longbottom, used humourously
359, 361
Longbottom Leaf 266
'Lord Nelson' 84, 102
The Lord of the Rings 23–9, 38–9,
40–4, 47, 58, 79, 86, 94, 97, 98,
104, 105, 110, 112–14, 118, 119–
23, 124, 129, 130, 131, 132, 134,
135–42, 143, 151, 153, 159–61,
163–203, 208–12, 215–17, 219–
41, 243–67, 270–84, 288–90,
297–301, 303–8, 310, 313, 315,
318–19, 321–2, 323–34, 342,
346–9, 354–6, 358, 360, 364,
365–7, 371, 374, 376, 377, 379–
87, 396, 409–11, 412–14, 422,
423, 431, 437, 440, 443, 444,
445, 447, 448, 451

Writing: sequel to *The Hobbit*
wanted 23–6, 215–16; first chapter
27–9, 435; used up ideas in *The
Hobbit* 29, 38; too much 'hobbit
talk' 36, 38, 376; read, heard,
approved by friends, family 29, 34,
36, 38, 41, 42, 44, 58, 68, 71, 72,
73, 77, 79, 80–1, 83, 91, 92, 94,
103, 105, 106–7, 110, 112–13,
119–21, 122, 124, 131, 135, 137,
140, 209, 362, 366, 376; written
with Christopher Tolkien in mind
91, 94, 103, 104, 112–13, 118;
Tolkien reports progress to Christopher 69, 70, 71, 72, 73, 74, 76–
7, 79, 80–1, 82, 83, 88, 89, 91, 92,
94, 97, 98, 101, 103–4, 105, 106–
7, 113, 118, 216, 321; problems
with moons, synchronization 74,
80–1, 97, 258; need to know how
to stew a rabbit 74; early sketches
for conclusion no longer suitable
80–2, 104; reports progress to
Allen & Unwin 29, 34, 36, 38–9,
40–4, 58, 86, 113–14, 118, 119–
23, 124, 129; not a sequel to *The
Hobbit*, darker, more adult 41, 42,
44, 58, 86, 120, 134, 135, 136,
137, 138; not written for children
249, 310; references to length 41–
2, 44, 58, 73, 86, 90, 113, 131,
134, 136, 138, 139, 160, 165;

Tolkien has epic temperament in
age devoted to snappy bits 90;
doubts value of *LR* 135; *LR* better
than *The Hobbit* 40, 42, 134; best
of entire cycle 159; great (though
not flawless) work 164; Tolkien
considered every word 42, 160;
written in his life-blood 122;
cannot substantially alter 122,
137, 160; linking with *The Hobbit*
120–2, 124, 141–2, 161, 216, 334,
346–7; would be easier to write if
Silmarillion were published first
130, 161, 163; Rayner Unwin
never felt lack of *Silmarillion*
140; labour by Tolkien of writing,
typing 83, 89, 114, 132, 133, 136,
163, 164, 209, 247, 321, 344;
Christopher Tolkien typed much of
LR 70, 79, 86, 112, 114; rewriting
and revision 41, 44, 80, 81, 82, 86,
94, 97, 114, 124, 131, 136, 141,
160, 164, 209, 321; completion
anticipated 42–3, 44, 58, 86, 118,
119, 129; brought to successful
conclusion 131, 134; prospective
readers 120, 121–2, 138, 165;
those that like this kind of thing
like it very much 121–2

Collins episode: Collins offer to
publish both *LR* and *The Silmarillion* 134–5; *LR* the continuation
and completion of *The Silmarillion*
136–7; together the Saga of the
Jewels and the Rings 138, 139; *LR*
interdependent with *Silmarillion*
143–61; Tolkien extricates self
from obligation to Allen & Unwin
134–41; Rayner Unwin suggests
that *LR* be published as prestige
book, *Silmarillion* dropped 140–1;
ultimatum to Allen & Unwin 141;
delays 143; Collins withdraw 161

Publication: Tolkien accepts
publication of just *LR* 163; Rayner
Unwin costs, agrees to publish in
three volumes 163–5; revision for
press 164, 166, 167, 168, 173,
174; preparation for publication
165–71, 173, 181–3, 184–5,

478

261; criticizes film script 261, 266–7, 270–7

Considered by Tolkien in retrospect: recalls writing 215–16, 258–9, 321–2; seemed to write itself 104; ceased to invent, waited until what really happened came through 212, 231; as if written by someone else 211–12, 278, 356, 376; wrote slowly and with great care for detail 412; 'chosen instrument' for writing *LR* 413; started with a map and made the story fit 177; had calendar to keep track of characters and events 258; drawing together separate threads 258; had general idea in mind from early stage 258; rough sketches of events seldom of much use 258, 321, 325; astonished *LR* was ever completed 257; caught up visions of most things he most loved or hated 257; favourite passages 110–11, 221, 376; pages blotted with tears 321; finds it good 'in parts' 349; would have liked more Elvish in *LR* 216; would have preferred to write *LR* in 'Elvish' 219; modernities and silly names of hobbits a mistake 196; inconsistencies, errors, weaknesses 188, 191, 196, 279, 289, 448

Contents, author's intentions: written to please himself 211, 412; written to amuse, excite, move reader 232–3, 414; a fairy-story for adults 209, 232–3; attempt to induce literary or secondary belief 233, 379, 412; an exciting story of the sort Tolkien enjoys 267, 297; experiment in arts of long narrative 412; not a novel, but a heroic romance 414; attempt to create world in which a form of language agreeable to his personal aesthetic might seem real 264–5; largely an essay in 'linguistic aesthetic' 220; no 'message' intended 267; not an allegory 41, 121, 212, 220, 239, 246, 262; does not 'objectify'

Tolkien's experience of life 239; primary symbolism of the Ring, as the will to mere power 160; not an allegory of Atomic power, but of Power 246; Power and Domination not at centre 246, 262, 284; centre is not in strife and war and heroism but in freedom, peace, ordinary life and good liking 105; journey of Ringbearers heart of the tale 271; deeds of the small, humble, their ennoblement or sanctification 160, 215, 220, 232, 237, 246, 365; the Quest in 105, 191, 233–4, 238–9; *LR* in terms of good and evil 119–20, 121, 178–9, 197, 207, 243–4, 262; real theme is death and immortality 246, 262, 267, 284; mainly concerned with relation of Creation to making and subcreation, and related matter of 'mortality' 188; fundamentally religious and catholic work 172; cut out practically all references to 'religion' 172, 220; theological implications in 187–95, 233–5, 355; monotheistic world of 'natural theology' 220; sanity and sanctity in *LR*; Ring verse as leit-motif of *LR* 153; poetry in 169, 186, 396; verses fitted in style and contents to characters and situations 396; archaism in 225–6; vocabulary 249; deliberately left some things unexplained 174, 190; Tolkien does not himself know all the answers 278; better not to state everything, more like real history 354; must concentrate on small part so much will be left out 192; frameless picture, searchlight on brief episode 412; need to omit and compress 289, 293; blends Elvish and human point of view 145; seen mainly through eyes of Hobbits 160, 200, 237, 246; love stories in 160–1, 227, 323–4; importance of seasons in 271–2; its end like the re-establishment of a Holy Roman Empire with seat in Rome 376

Sources 208, 212, 303, 418; for names etc. 379–87, 409–10, 418; main idea not a product of World War II 216; no post-war references 235; his mythology 227, 231

Lord's Prayer 233, 252

Lórien see Lothlórien

The Lost Road 25, 105, 118, 347, 436; Tolkien and Lewis to write themselves the kind of books they want to read 209, 378; agreed that Tolkien to write on time-travel 29, 342, 347, 378; Númenor-Atlantis theme 342, 347, 378; and LR 342, 347; and The Downfall of Númenor 378

Loth, Joseph 320

Lothlórien (Lórien) 176, 203, 216, 261, 273, 274, 349, 381, 386, 419, 425; no word of it had reached Tolkien till he came there 216; beautiful because there the trees were loved 419; Lórien as name of house 349

Louis XIV 71, 83

Lourdes 100

Love 100, 324; see also Marriage

Lovelace Society 39, 119, 133, 436

Luke, Saint 99

Lúthien (Tinúviel) 149, 150, 180, 193, 194, 204, 206, 221, 282, 334, 345, 346, 347, 386, 445, 451; a mere maiden, if an elf of royalty 149; allowed to become mortal, a direct act of God 193–4; Edith Tolkien as Lúthien 417, 420

Lycett, C.V.L. 429

Lytton, E.G.L.B., Lord 407

Macbeth (Shakespeare) 212

McCallum, R.B. 79, 430, 439

MacDonald, George 31, 351; and goblins 178, 185; The Golden Key 351; The Princess and the Goblin 178, 185

Machines 218, 288, 349, 401, 420; attempts to actualize desire and so create power 87–8; labour-saving machinery only creates endless and worse labour 88; mechanism and evil 110; World War II first War of the Machines 111; machine related to magic and power 145–6, 152, 165, 190, 200; and the Elves of Eregion 190; dynamiting factories and power-stations 64; 'infernal combustion' engine 77; see also Airplanes, Atomic bomb, Cars, Noise, Pollution

Madras, University of 299

Magdalen College, Oxford 18, 56, 63, 71, 82, 84, 92, 95, 96, 103, 108, 117, 258, 321, 341, 388, 389

Maggot, Farmer 265, 319, 449; 'Maggot Soup' 265

Magic, and desire for power 145–6, 152, 200; corruptible into evil 152; magia and goeteia 199, 445; in LR 199–200; basic motive is immediacy 200

Magnificat 66, 215, 446

Maiar see Ainur

Maldon 187

Mallorn 248

Mallos 248

Malory, Thomas 181

Malvegil 426

Malvern College 164, 168

Mâmuk 79

The Man in the Moon 309, 310, 448–9

Manchester Guardian 184, 186, 444

'Mandos' used figuratively 417, 420

Mankind, relations between men and women 48–52; proper study of Man anything but Man 64; bossing other men most improper job of any man 64; mass and weight of human iniquity 80; no genuine Uruks, folk made bad by intention of maker 90; moral and intellectual status declining 116; development of character 240; moral failure 326–7; boredom of Men with the good 344, 419; 'male' and 'female' attitudes to wild things 212

Manners 72

Manor Road see Tolkien, J.R.R.: Homes

481

Manwë 259, 278, 280, 282–3, 285, 335, 431, 447; Elder King 259, 277, 283; Lord of the Valar 283; meaning of name 283; high or Elder King of Arda 283; lieutenant of One in Eä 285

Mardil 386

The Mariner's Wife 360

Marriage, advice to Michael Tolkien 48–52; and *Christian Behaviour* (C.S. Lewis) 59–62, 437–8; Elf-Human *see* Elves *or* Men

Mars (god) 269

Marshall, Dora 209

The Marvellous Land of Snergs (Wyke-Smith) 215

Mary, Virgin 49, 172, 288, 340, 354, 385, 407; Assumption 286

Mary I (Bloody Mary) 354

Mary, Princess Royal 391

Masefield, John 39–40; *East Coker* 353

Mass production *see* Standardization

Materialism 110

Mathew, Gervase 115

Maxwell, A.H. 55, 437

Medea (Barfield) 103

Mediterranean 280, 376

Meiggs, Russell 18, 20, 434, 443

Melko, Melkor *see* Morgoth

Memory 85, 409

Men, in Tolkien's mythology 147–8, 149, 150–1, 153, 154, 155, 156, 157, 159, 160, 176, 179, 189, 194, 195, 196, 197, 200, 202, 203–5, 228, 235–6, 244, 260, 267, 274, 280, 282, 284, 285, 286, 325, 345, 383, 386, 387, 411, 419, 431; Big Folk 158; Dúnedain 282; Edain 282, 386; Followers 147, 176; Northmen 381; Second Race of the Children 189; Successors 345; Three Houses 149, 150, 204, 282; akin to Elves 176, 205, 236; biologically one race with Elves 189; Elves and Men different aspects of the Humane 236; art and poetry of Man dependent on Elven blood 149; Elf-Human marriage 149, 176, 188, 189, 192–3, 445; enter-

ing into Men of Elven-strain part of Divine Plan for ennoblement of Human Race 194; destined to replace Elves 194; fall of 147–8, 154–6, 203–5, 286, 387; 'Men' used figuratively 78; *see also* Children of God, Dominion of Men, Gondor, Half-elven, Mortality, Númenóreans, Rohirrim

Meneldil 386

Meneldur 360

Meneltarma (Pillar of Heaven) 194, 204, 206

Mercury (planet) 220

Mercy 243, 252, 253, 326, 446

Mere Christianity (C.S. Lewis) 437

Merlin (name) 182

Merton College, Oxford 133, 140, 369, 389, 418; College meetings 116, 201; College housing 116, 119, 140, 344, 441, 442; Tolkien admitted to 116; lunches, dines at 116–17, 353; room at 116, 181–2, 373; inspects College estates 124; a residential Emeritus Fellow 415–16, 421–2, 429

Merton Professorship of English Language and Literature 108, 114, 116, 117, 216

Merton Professorship of English Literature 108, 117

Merton Street, Oxford *see* Tolkien, J.R.R.: Homes

Meskys, Edmund 422–3

Mesopotamia 384

Metals, in Middle-earth 196

The Mezentian Gate (Eddison) 84, 258, 439, 447

Micara, Cardinal 223

Michel Delving, used humourously 361

Middle-earth 148, 150, 151, 152, 153, 154, 155, 156, 176–7, 180, 182, 186, 193, 194, 196, 197, 198, 202, 203, 205, 206, 220, 224, 236, 237, 239, 244, 272, 277, 283, 328, 360, 368, 374, 375–6, 384, 386, 410, 411, 424, 431, 434; Endor, Endoré, Ennor 224, 383–4; origin of *Middle-earth* 186, 220, 239,

482

283, 375–6; North-west of 148, 154; actual Old World of our planet in imaginary period 220, 239, 244, 283, 375–6; familiarity of 239

Middle English language and literature (in general) 11, 12, 36, 74, 213, 218, 225, 268, 283, 302, 317, 322, 352, 364, 436; used in Tolkien's mythology 220, 239, 283, 361

A Middle English Vocabulary 11

Midlands *see* West Midlands

A Midsummer Night's Dream (Shakespeare) 143, 300

Milford-on-Sea 429, 432

Millennium 110

Miller (*Farmer Giles of Ham*) 131

Milton, John 344

Milton (Blake) 90

Mimesis (Auerbach) 238–9, 241–2

Minas Ithil 76, 323, 444

Minas Morgul 76, 79, 80, 323, 444

Minas Tirith 104, 158, 170, 173, 203, 254, 258, 290, 334, 376, 425; meaning of name 158; and Common Speech 254; population at end of Third Age 425; 'Minas Tirith' used figuratively 379

Minchin, H. Cotton 247–8

Mindolluin 206

Ministry of Information 93

Miracles 99–100, 101, 235

Miramar Hotel, Bournemouth 335–6, 431, 432

Míriel 286

Mirkwood 158, 176, 369–70, 420; Eryn Lasgalen 382; Great Wood 158; Greenwood the Great 158, 420; sources of *Mirkwood* 369–70

Mirkwood 15, 17, 19, 434

Mr. Bliss 15, 25, 28–9, 39, 42

Mistress of Mistresses (Eddison) 258, 447

Misty Mountains 152, 180, 271, 391; Hithaeglin 180

The Misty Mountains Looking West 15, 434

Mitchison, Naomi *133–4, 173–81, 196–200, 217, 228–9, 300*; read

page-proofs of *LR* 173; blurb for *LR* 181; review of *The Fellowship of the Ring* 196, 445

Mithril coat 104

Mitre Hotel, Oxford 68, 74, 103, 108, 438

Mohammedans 60

Möllendorf, Willamowitz 343

Monarchy 63–4

Moon, in Tolkien's mythology 148, 425; Isil 425; Ithil 425; Light of Sun and Moon 148

Moorman, F.W. 56, 437

Morality 326, 399–400

Morannon 97, 178, 303, 382; Black Gate 104, 178; Gates of the Land of Shadow 73; Gates of Mordor 71, 72, 76, 79; sources for approaches to 303

Mordor 71, 76, 77, 81, 83, 104, 106, 153, 154, 157, 158, 175, 178, 228, 234, 241, 259, 307, 321, 330, 344, 382; Black Land 152, 178; Land of Shadow 73; why placed in east 307; 'Mordor' used figuratively 82, 88, 165, 166, 235, 300; *see also* Morannon

Morgan, Francis 7, 52, 213, 340, 354, 395, 416–17, 434, 450; and Tolkien's romance with Edith Bratt 52–3, 437; death 416

Morgoth 78, 85, 155–6, 190, 194, 195, 202, 243, 282, 283, 285, 287, 334, 382, 386, 387; Beginner of Evil 146; Melko 446; Melkor 147, 259, 283, 284, 285, 446, 447; Dark Lord 187, 190, 195, 205; Dark Power 176, 178, 180; Devil 376; Diabolus 191, 195, 283; Enemy 146, 148, 149, 150, 151, 267; Prime Dark Lord 190, 198, 199, 204, 205; Rebel 190, 259; Shadow 191, 451; eldest of the Valar 205; and power of creation 178, 195; fall of 146, 195, 286–7; power of Evil still visibly incarnate 148; thrust into the Void, never to reappear in incarnate form 150; 'Morgoth' used figuratively 417

Moria 177, 178, 190, 334, 346, 382, 424; meaning, source of name 178, 382–3, 384; Mines of Moria 129, 152, 159, 216, 443; and Moriah 383; Bridge of Khazad-dûm 202

Morris, William 7; *The House of the Wolfings* 303; *The Roots of the Mountains* 303

Morris-Jones, John, *A Welsh Grammar* 320

Mortality, in Tolkien's mythology, Elves and Men represent problem of Death 236; Men doomed to leave the world, Elves doomed not to leave it 147, 246; mortal or immortal nature could not be altered except by the One 151, 194, 204, 411; death and the nature of Man 205, 237, 285; men must accept death 145, 154–6, 205, 286; a good man dies of free will 205, 286; death is not a punishment 205, 286; death as doom or gift of God to Men 147, 151, 155, 189, 205, 267, 285, 286; death is freedom from the circles of the world 147, 286, 325; longevity 151, 154, 193, 204, 206, 307; natural mortal life-span cannot be increased 155; mortals allowed to go to Elven-home eventually die 198–9, 411; real theme of *LR* is death and immortality 246, 262, 267, 284; *see also* Elves, Half-elven

Morthond 178

Morwen (mother of Théoden) 447

Motor-cars *see* Cars

Mount Doom 104, 152–4, 325, 330; Cracks of Doom 325, 331; Mountain of Fire 153; Sammath Naur 331; 'Sammath Naur' used figuratively 252

The Mountain-path 15, 434

Mountains of Lune *see* Ered Luin

Muir, Edwin 184, 208, 229–30, 444, 445

Murasaki, Shikibu, *The Tale of Genji* 139

Murdoch, Iris 353

Mure, Geoffrey 181–2

Murray, James 133, 171, 336, 450

Murray, K. 84

Murray, Robert *171–3, 200–7, 267–70*

Murray, Rosfrith 336, 430, 453

Music, in Middle-earth 196

Music of the Ainur see The Silmarillion

Myth 144, 147, 153, 224, 231, 279, 282, 345, 347, 361; of Eden 109–10; myth and fairy-story must contain moral and religious truth 144; legends and myths largely made of 'truth' 147; Tolkien not 'learned' in matters of myth 144; expresses himself in tales and myths 420–1; *LR* exhibits 'myth' passing into history 207; mythology for England, *see* England; *see also* Fairy-story, Legends

Myth Became Fact (C.S. Lewis) 109, 440

Mythopoeia 64, 438

The Nameless Land 317, 449

Nandungorthin 180

Napier, A.S. 405–6, 434

Nargothrond 282

Narnia 352

Narog 282

Narsil 424, 425

Narya *see* Rings of Power

Nasturtians 183

National Research Development Corp. 227

National University of Ireland 300, 448

Natural History Museum *see* University Museum, Oxford

Nauglamir 334

Nazgûl *see* Ringwraiths

Neagle, Anna 83

Neave, Jane *308, 309–11, 315–18, 319–22; 308–9, 449, 452;* suggests book with Tom Bombadil 308; taught Tolkien geometry 377

Necromancer *see* Sauron

Neldoreth 334

Nenya *see* Rings of Power

Netherlands *see* Holland
New College, Oxford 432
New English Dictionary see
  Oxford English Dictionary
New Republic 232
The New Shadow 344, 419
New Statesman 296–9; 212, 445
New Testament *see* Bible
New Theatre, Oxford 102
New York Herald Tribune 36
New York Times Book Review
  208, 211, 217–8, 238, 445
New Yorker 367, 368
New Zealand Honours Examinations
  41, 42, 43
Newspapers, standards of 68, 368,
  372
Nibelung legends, Norse versions
  306, 314, 315, 319
Nibelungen Ring 306
Nichol Smith, David 71, 436, 438
Niggle 111, 113, 114, 128, 321, 352
Niggle's Parish 111
Nimrodel 423
Níniel 150
Niphredil (nifredil) 106, 248, 402
Noble, and simple 220
Nobottle 360
Noise 77, 82, 164–5, 344–5
Noldor *see* Elves
North, northern atmosphere in
  The Hobbit 21; Hitler ruined
  the noble northern spirit 55–6;
  Chesterton knew nothing about
  the 'North' 92; appeal to Tolkien
  of atmosphere of North-west
  144, 212–13, 376
North Kingdom *see* Arnor
North Sea 347
Northey, A.P. *354*
Northfolk 187
Northmoor Road *see* Tolkien, J.R.R.:
  Homes
Norwood, Cyril 359, 451
The Notion Club Papers 105, 118,
  440, 441
Novial 231, 446
Nowell Smith family 162, 443
Nuffield Orthopaedic Centre, Oxford
  395

Númenor (Númenóre) 151, 154–7,
  160, 175, 186, 193, 194, 197, 198,
  204, 205, 206, 224, 260, 279, 280,
  303, 307, 322, 333, 347, 359, 360,
  361, 386, 443, 445, 448; meaning
  of name 151, 224, 303, 361;
  Atlantis isle 151, 175; Land of the
  Star 204; Númenor-Atlantis 186,
  206, 342; Westernesse 151, 186,
  204, 303, 361; ban on 204; corruption by Sauron 205; rebellion
  of 194; downfall of 154, 186, 198,
  260, 360, 333, 386; version of
  Atlantis myth 197–8, 303, 347,
  361; originally unrelated to
  Silmarillion mythology 347;
  see also Atlantis, *The Downfall
  of Númenor, The Lost Road,*
  Númenóreans
Númenórean language *see* Adûnaic
Númenóreans 151, 154–7, 193–4,
  198, 204–7, 229, 243, 253, 279,
  280, 282, 286, 307, 323, 324,
  384, 386, 445; evil Númenóreans,
  Sauronians 206; Kings of Men 156,
  198, 204; history and fall 154–7,
  204–6, 279; longevity 151, 154,
  193, 204, 206, 307; long life aids
  achievements in art and wisdom
  154; longing for immortality
  154–5, 205; knowledge of heredity
  307; tradition of men out of the sea
  155, 303; used 'spells' in making
  swords 445; religion 193–4, 204,
  206, 243, 253, 279, 281, 387;
  compared to Jews 204; religion
  introduced by Sauron 155–6, 194,
  205, 206; calendar 229; *see also*
  Gondor
Numerals 422–3
Nunn, A.C. *289–96;* 448
Nursery rhyme books 123

Oakenshield, Thorin *see* Thorin
  Oakenshield
Observer 30–2; 34–5, 184, 229,
  406–7, 444, 445
Odin 119
O'Donnell Lecture in Celtic Studies
  227, 228–9, 446

Pelennor, Battle of the 258, 272
Pembroke College, Oxford 24;
  Tolkien dines at 69, 79, 83, 84;
  meeting at 74; criticism of 108,
  116–17
Pengolod 130, 442
Penguin Books 313
Perelandra see Lewis, C.S.
Peter, Saint 203, 339, 450
'Peterborough' 68
Philology see Language
Pickwick Papers (Dickens) 349
Picture Post 91
The Pied Piper (Browning) 311, 449
The Pilgrim's Regress (C.S. Lewis)
  349
Pipe-weed 79, 122, 266
Pity 191, 193, 234, 252, 253, 326,
  330, 446
Pius X 339, 450
Pius XII 84
Place Names of Gloucestershire
  (A. Smith) 410
Plimmer, Charlotte and Denis 372–8
Plotz, Dick 359–62
Plutarch, Life of Cato 89, 439
Pocock, Guy 449
Poema Morale 397
Poems (C.S. Lewis) 378
Poetic Diction (Barfield) 22, 435
Poetry, in general 213, 317; by
  Tolkien see Tolkien, J.R.R.: Poetry
Poland, Poles 68, 93
Polish language 67–8; translation of
  LR 299
Pollution 165, 409, 412
Poole see Tolkien, J.R.R.: Homes
Poptawski 67–8, 438
Porter (Leaf by Niggle) 321
Potter, Beatrix, The Tale of Jemima
  Puddle-Duck 251; The Tale of
  Mrs Tiggywinkle 251
Powell, Frederick Yorke 397
Power, ominous and sinister word
  except as applied to the gods 152;
  attempts to defeat evil power by
  power 121; desire for 145–6; and
  domination 152, 237, 243, 246;
  rights and wrongs of power and
  control 179; powerful must have,

depend upon subjects 279;
  see also Rings of Power
Prancing Pony 95
Prefatory Remarks on Prose
  Translation of Beowulf (introd.
  Tolkien) 36, 43–6, 436
Prehistory 105, 282, 283
Pre-Raphaelites 417
Primary World 189
Primer of the Gothic Language
  (Wright) 357, 397
The Princess and the Goblin
  (MacDonald) 178, 185
Propaganda 89, 93
Proudfoot family 31
Pterodactyl 277, 282
Puffin Books 302, 312–13
Pusey House, Master of 370
Pusey Street see Tolkien, J.R.R.:
  Homes
Puss Cat Mew (Knatchbull-Hugessen)
  407, 453
Pygmies 30, 35, 233

Quendi see Elves
Quenta Silmarillion see
  The Silmarillion
Quenya see Elvish
The Quest of Erebor 334, 450

Racism 37–8, 73, 93, 375
Rackham, Arthur 261, 312
Radagast 231, 266, 271;
  see also Wizards
Radcliffe Infirmary, Oxford 101
Radio see British Broadcasting Corp.,
  Wireless
Ragnarök 96, 149
Raleigh, Walter 22, 56, 95, 435
Ramsden, Walter 83, 84, 439
Rang, Mr 379–87
Ransome, Arthur 28, 435
Rawlinson and Bosworth
  Professorship of Anglo-Saxon
  see Oxford University: Tolkien
  as Professor
Reade, Vincent 78, 439
Reason 101, 148, 246
Recordings see Elvish languages,
  The Hobbit, The Lord of the Rings

Saurat, Denis, *L'Atlantide et le règne des géants* 198

Sauron 26, 104, 129, 151–7, 176, 177, 178, 179, 180, 188, 190, 194, 197, 201, 202, 203, 205, 206, 207, 236, 237, 243–4, 259, 260, 272, 277, 279–80, 281, 284, 285, 286, 307, 327, 330, 331, 332, 333, 380, 386, 419, 420, 447; Dark Lord 151, 153, 157, 159, 216, 332; Dark Throne 159; Enemy 146, 199, 200, 202, 273; Ring-maker 201, 446; Sauron Redivivus 158; Shadow 151, 158; derivation of *Sauron* 380; history 151–7; and Morgoth 151, 155–6, 176, 180, 190, 194, 202, 205, 243, 259, 285, 447; angelic being 205, 243, 259; incarnate forms 190, 332; rebuilding of body after defeat 157, 260, 280; could not rebuild after destruction of Ring 260; incarnation of Evil 151, 154, 160, 190, 207, 252; represents wholly evil will 243; stages of fall 151, 190, 243–4; desired to be god-king 155, 243–4; taken prisoner to Númenor 205, 279; defeated by Gil-galad and Elendil 280; Gandalf and Aragorn's opposite 180; no mortal with Ring could have withstood him 332; Necromancer (Sauron in *The Hobbit*) 24, 26, 42, 129, 152, 158, 159, 164, 216, 346, 441; function of in *Hobbit* 346; no connection with Ring, stood only for ever-recurrent evil 216; 'Sauron' used figuratively 78; *see also* Ainur, Evil, Rings of Power

Sayer, George 164, 168, 341

Sayers, Dorothy L., *Busman's Honeymoon* 82; *Gaudy Night* 82

Scandinavian languages 214, 429

Scandinavian legend 144

Schiro, Herbert 262

School Magazine 314

Schuchart, Max 263, 447

Scilly Isles 353

Scotland 42, 106, 219, 336

The Scotsman 372, 452

Scott, Nan C. *358*

The Screwtape Letters (C.S. Lewis) 108, 342

Sea 104, 176, 180, 198, 237, 281, 328; Great Sea of the West 386; passage over the Sea 104, 105, 176, 198, 237, 281, 327–9

The Sea-Bell 312, 378–9

Second Age 150–7, 159, 177, 188, 190, 199, 213, 220, 224, 228, 243, 283, 303, 361, 425; history of 150–7

Second World War *see* World War II

Secondary world 87

A Secret Vice 374

Selby, Mr 135–6

Serbian language 173

Severn, David *see* Unwin, David

Sex 48–52, 60–2, 285

Shadow *see* Evil, Morgoth, Sauron

Shadowfax 354; name of hydrofoil 349

Shakespeare, A. 7, 434

Shakespeare, William 201, 320; *Hamlet* 88, 102; *Macbeth* 212; *A Midsummer Night's Dream* 143, 300; *The Tempest* 77; folly of reading Shakespeare except as concomitant of seeing plays 88; and fairies 143; and debasement of *elves* 185; Tolkien disliked reading at school 213

Sharkey *see* Saruman

Shaw, George Bernard, *Arms and the Man* 94

Sheaf (Shield Sheafing) 347

Shelley, Norman 228

Shelob 81, 82, 180, 217; Shelob's lair 235, 330

Shenandoah 378–9, 412

Sherring, Zillah *356–8*

The Shire 104, 105, 158, 175, 186, 196, 230, 235, 240–1, 246, 250, 271, 280, 283, 290–4, 299, 315, 328, 358, 360–1; in what is now called Europe 283; based on rural England 235, 250; Warwickshire village of period of the Diamond Jubilee 230, 235, 288; place-names devised according to English

163, 174, 228; demands that Allen & Unwin publish both *Silmarillion* and *LR* 134–41; Collins accepts, rejects both books 134–5, 139–40, 143, 161; *Silmarillion* part of Saga of the Jewels and the Rings 138, 139; interdependent with *LR* 143–61

Work after The Lord of the Rings: The Silmarillion wanted by Allen & Unwin after success of *LR* 174, 217, 220, 224, 228, 232, 237–8, 296, 303, 333, 373; delays 228, 229, 238, 252, 256, 261, 296, 301, 302, 303, 317, 322, 333, 342, 355, 359–60, 363, 367, 372, 401, 403, 404, 408, 418, 424, 430–1; trying to make publishable 252; needs copies made of all the copyable material 262; progressing with help of secretary 301; needs to rework *Silmarillion* to agree with *LR* 264, 333, 360, 403, 404; needs some shape or frame 333, 360; in a confused state owing to alteration and enlargement at different dates 333, 359, 366, 374, 404; needs help of friend and adviser 366, 430–1; Tolkien fears it will not have the appeal of *LR* 228, 238, 303, 333; to visit background of *LR* is to destroy the magic 333; estimates completion 360, 408 see also *The Downfall of Númenor*, England (mythology for), *The Rings of Power*

Silmarils 26, 148–50, 282, 334, 386, 425; Jewels 139, 148, 150; Primeval Jewels 148; Three Jewels 138, 303; meaning 148; history 148–50; are in Tolkien's heart 26
Silvertine (Celebdil) 392
Simbelmynë *see* Symbelmynë
Sindar *see* Elves
Sindarin *see* Elvish
Singing, in one's bath 102
Sir Gawain and the Green Knight (anon.) 128, 228, 317–18, 441
Sir Gawain and the Green Knight (ed. Tolkien and Gordon) 11

Sir Gawain and the Green Knight (trans. Tolkien) 183, 301, 302, 316–18, 322, 333, 342, 348, 352, 355, 363, 364, 444
Sir Gawain and the Green Knight (W.P. Ker Memorial Lecture) 164, 165, 167, 168, 443
Sisam, Kenneth 7, 11, 56, 353, 406, 434, 437
Sitwell, Edith 261
Skeat Prize 320, 450
Skegness fisherman 108–9, 440
Skibniewska, Maria 299
Slavonic languages 173, 428
Sloth 55, 340
Smaug 14, 27, 31, 32, 35, 134, 364; origin of name 31; conversation with Bilbo indebted to Fáfnir 134
Sméagol *see* Gollum
Smial 292
Smith, A.H., *Place Names of Gloucestershire* 410
Smith, Geoffrey Bache, 8–10; 429
Smith of Wootton Major 351, 355, 370–1, 388–9; read at Blackfriars 370–1; title meant to suggest Wodehouse or *Boy's Own Paper* 370; not intended for children 388–9; an old man's book 389; Alf based on chef at Merton College 389
Snow Hill 70
Socialism 110
Somme, Battle of the 9–10, 53, 221, 303
Song of the Sybil (trans. Auden and Taylor) 379, 452
Sons of Fëanor *see* Fëanor (Sons of)
Soria Moria Castle 384
South Africa 68, 69, 73, 75, 90, 95, 321, 377, 438, 446; Tolkien's memories of 68, 82, 85, 213, 219; longs to see again 82, 90; Mother hated, father liked 90; South African shares, patrimony 53, 437; racism in 73
Southern Star 266
Southfolk 187
Southrons *see* Haradrim
Spanish Civil War 95–6

315, 316, 367, 401, 404, 409, 412;
death 415–17, 420–1; grave 420
Tolkien, Faith 223, 245, 261; 369
Tolkien, Hilary 122, 395, 417, 452
Tolkien, John Benjamin 398
Tolkien, John Francis Reuel 161; 11,
53, 74, 133, 430; part of original
audience for The Hobbit 21, 58;
at Dragon School 129; approved
LR 42, 44, 58; study in Italy for
priesthood 44, 436; accompanied
father to investiture 417
Tolkien, John Ronald Reuel
Life and character: autobiographical accounts 12–13, 52–3,
212–16, 217–21, 288–9, 395; in
fact a hobbit in all but size 288;
Christian names 357, 397–8; form
of address 120, 365–6, 397–8, 418,
434, 437, 452; appearance 74, 373;
clothes 70, 108, 289; handwriting
222, 247, 311, 325, 336, 344,
358, 377, 397; letter-writing 336;
writes in books 357–8; simple
sense of humour 289; swift speech
372; does not remember dates
56; pessimism 401–2; romance,
marriage 7, 11, 52–3, 420–1,
437; bereavement on death of
wife 415–17, 420–1; children,
birth of 11, 53, 76, 430; domestic
duties 11, 58, 69, 73, 79, 80, 83,
86, 107, 108, 109, 114, 119; rides
bicycle 69, 83, 86–7, 99, 101,
108–9; interviews 372–3; refuses
to be photographed 372–3, 390;
not a critic 126; employment see
Leeds University, New Zealand
Honours Examinations, Oxford
English Dictionary, Oxford
University, University College
Dublin, Wales (University of);
awarded D.Litt., Liège 181;
awarded D.Litt., Dublin 181, 219;
receives C.B.E. 417–18; see also
especially World War I, World
War II
Artistic abilities: 14–20, 28–9,
35, 42–3, 167, 186, 364–5; the
author cannot draw 15; casual

and careless pastime products 19;
easier to write a story than draw
29; can only draw imperfectly what
he can, and not what he sees 186;
pattern-designing 342
Food and drink 69, 70, 74, 87,
102, 108, 265, 288–9, 314, 396–7,
401, 405, 408, 429, 430
Gardening 54, 71, 73, 74, 79,
83, 102, 107, 402–3, 436
Health 14, 22, 26, 40, 42, 43,
44, 45, 117, 132, 135, 138, 163,
166, 173, 196, 227, 229, 256, 297,
299, 316, 325, 334, 335, 340, 367,
372, 391, 395, 397, 401, 409, 416,
424, 429, 436; not being able to
use pen or pencil as defeating as
loss of her beak would be to a
hen 335
Homes: nomadic series of
arrivals at houses or lodgings
430; Pusey Street (Alfred Street),
Oxford 95; No. 22 Northmoor
Road, Oxford 340, 440; No. 20
Northmoor Road, Oxford 45,
321, 344, 436, 441; Manor Road,
Oxford 119, 321–2, 344, 441, 442;
Holywell, Oxford 138, 140, 164,
344, 442; Sandfield Road, Oxford
166, 167, 261, 306, 344–5, 367,
368, 373, 391, 395; garage not
really a study, works in 'bedsitter'
373; Lakeside Road, Poole
(Bournemouth) 390, 391, 396–7,
405, 415, 416; problems of move,
putting library in order 390,
395–6, 397; Merton Street,
Oxford 415–17, 421–2
Income 24, 94, 208, 256, 336,
363–4, 416, 437; South African
shares 53, 437; need to supplement
income by examining, correcting
papers, etc. 24, 36, 42, 163, 215,
436; pension 163, 256, 300, 316,
363; from writing 20, 43, 85, 186,
232, 245, 256, 300, 302, 315–16,
322, 363–4, 367; taxes, duties 256,
316, 340–1, 363, 404, 416, 453;
made over greater part of literary
income to his children 404, 453

Turgon 193, 386
Túrin Turambar 150, 434
Turville-Petre, Gabriel 67, 182, 438
Turville-Petre, Merlin Oswald 182
The Two Towers see The Lord of
the Rings
Two Trees 148, 387, 427
Tyndall, Denis 342-3
Typewriter, Hammond model 86,
439; Tolkien dreams of electric
model with Fëanorian script 344

The Ugly Duckling (Andersen) 232
Ulmo 386
Ulster 95, 350
Umbar 205
Ungoliante 180
Union of Soviet Socialist Republics
47, 63, 89, 111, 115; Russian
revolution 307; Samoyedes 64
United States of America, Americans
89, 115, 238, 261, 355, 356, 362,
364; American illustration 17;
sanitation, morale-pep, feminism
and mass production 65; precon-
ceptions about British 69; accents
69-70; servicemen 69-70, 87, 95,
439; imperialism 115; different
mental climate and soil, polluted
and impoverished 412; lunatic
destruction of the physical lands
which Americans inhabit 412;
U.S. copyright see Copyright
University College Dublin 219
University College, Oxford 91, 162,
387-8
University Museum, Oxford 27, 435
University Parks, Oxford 115
Unwin, Camilla 399-400
Unwin, David (David Severn) 112,
113, 117
Unwin, Harold 'Chris' 112, 440
Unwin, Merlin 181-2
Unwin, Rayner 161-71, 173, 181-2,
184-5, 208, 209-10, 229-30,
249-51, 256-7, 260-1, 262-4,
265-7, 301-2, 309, 312-15, 342,
349, 355-6, 362-3, 364-5, 379,
391, 411, 417-18; 25, 112, 117,
123, 124, 163, 170, 335, 361, 441,

443, 451; original reader of The
Hobbit 23-4, 131, 135, 215, 346;
reads, criticizes, approves LR 29,
34, 36, 38, 119-22, 124, 131, 135,
137, 140; naval cadet at Oxford
85-6, 112; at Trinity College,
Oxford 131; recommends publication of LR 140; LR would not
have been published without him
215, 256; becomes head of Allen
& Unwin 411; helps arrange festschrift for Tolkien 322-3; Tolkien
likes very much 135; asks him to
drop Professor 365; asks him to
use his Christian name 418; thanks
him for kindnesses, friendship 379;
thanks him for arrangements when
Tolkien received C.B.E. 417-18;
see also The Lord of the Rings
Unwin, Stanley 23-7, 29, 32-5, 36-7,
41, 43-6, 58, 85-6, 112-14, 117-
23, 124, 135-9, 140-1, 142, 322,
335; 14, 21, 27, 28, 123, 140, 139,
140, 141, 261, 316, 346, 411, 435,
441, 442; Tolkien gives him manuscripts to consider 25-6; congratu-
lates him on knighthood 117;
agrees to drop courtesy titles 120;
has friendly personal relations with
but does not much like him 135;
the one most often to make Tolkien
apprehensive 348; The Truth about
Publishing 348; see also The Lord
of the Rings
Uppsala 306
'Urukhai' used figuratively 78, 90
Utumno, fortress of the Devil 376

Valandil 386
Vale of Anduin 381
Valedictory Address 396, 452
Valimar see Aman
Valinor see Aman
Varda 206, 278, 282-3; Elbereth 193,
206, 278, 282-3, 288; Queen of
the Blessed Realm 206; Fanuilos
278; meaning of names 278, 282-3
Vendryes, Joseph 25
Venice 223
Venus (planet) 385

Verdi, Giuseppe, *Rigoletto* 223
Vergil 201; *Aeneid* 93, 435, 440
Victoria (Queen) 230, 235, 393
Viga-Glúms Saga (ed. G. Turville-Petre) 36, 436
Vigfusson, Guðbrandur 397
Viking Club, Leeds 13
Villalba Rubio, José 96
Vilya *see* Rings of Power
Virgin Mary *see* Mary, Virgin
Void 150, 155
Volapük 231, 446
Volsungakviða En Nyja 379, 452
Völsungs 379
Völuspá 379, 383, 452
Voorhoeve en Dietrich 265, 267
The Voyage of Earendel the Evening Star 8, 385, 434
A Voyage to Arcturus (Lindsay) 34, 436
Vulgar and Common Errors (Browne) 319, 449

Wainriders 248
Waldman, Milton *134–5, 139–40, 143–61*; *see also The Lord of the Rings*: Collins episode
Waldron, Molly *228*
Wales 130, 219, 289, 319–20; never walked in Wales in his youth 307; Welsh people 450
Wales, University of, Cardiff 67, 114; examination papers 68, 71, 438
Walloping Window-blind 104
Walton, William 95, 440
The Wanderer (Old English text) 212, 445
War 46, 73, 75–6, 78; one war enough for any man 54; sympathy for the plain soldier 54–5; martial glory and true glory 79; in real life good and bad on both sides 82, 90; and feeling of *Delenda est Carthago* 89; wars are always lost, and The War always goes on 116; 'victors' never can enjoy 'victory' 235; *see also* Spanish Civil War, World War I, World War II
Wargs *see* Wolves
Warlock, Peter 96

Warwick 8
Warwickshire 230, 235
Wayland Smith 307
Weathertop 273, 331; name used figuratively 430
Webster, Deborah *288–9*
Wells, H.G., *The Time Machine* 121
A Welsh Grammar (Morris-Jones) 320
Welsh language 12, 26, 134, 178, 214, 218–19, 289, 320, 345, 426, 450; English attitude to 426; British-Welsh 176; Welsh scholarship and philology a faction-fight 320; language of heaven 320, 450; and *Welsh rabbit* 320; Tolkien did not learn any Welsh until an undergraduate 213; saw Welsh names on coal-trucks 213; abiding linguistic-aesthetic satisfaction with 213; and Sindarin 176, 219
Welsh Marches 218, 307
Welsh Review 118
Wesleyan Methodist Conference 395
West, peoples opposed to Sauron 179, 413; *see also* Aman
West Midlands, Tolkien and his family West-Midlanders 54, 108, 213, 218; and Battle of Maldon 213
Westernesse *see* Númenor
Westron *see* Common Speech
The Whale (Old English text) 343–4
White, William Luther *387–8*
White Council 122
White Horse (pub), Oxford 67, 74
White Tree 206, 217
Who is Who 305
The Wild 31
Wild Flowers of the Cape Peninsula (Kidd) 402, 453
Wilderland 290, 296
Wilderland 14–15
Wilhelm II, Kaiser 55
Wilkinson, C.H. 119, 441
Willesden 63
William (troll) 187, 191
Williams, Charles 65, 67, 71, 72, 74, 84, 92–3, 94, 95, 102, 103, 105–6, 118, 122, 209, 339, 341, 342, 349,

in Pacific 115; atomic bomb 116, 303; War of the Machines 111; cryptographical department of Foreign Office 42, 436; Tolkien permanently reserved 55; air raid warden 58, 63, 67, 71, 74, 81, 82, 115, 437, 438; virtual head of English department at Oxford with outbreak of war 44; increased workload 45, 58, 117; organized English syllabus for naval and air cadets at Oxford 54, 59, 71, 83, 85, 86, 94, 112, 437, 439; concern, sympathy for sons 46, 54–5, 71, 72, 73, 76, 77, 78, 86, 90, 105, 112, 115; evacuee family billeted with Tolkiens 46; keeps hens 67, 73, 74, 82, 87, 102, 438; stock of *Hobbit* burnt 58; hatred of war in the air 105, 115; rejects propaganda 93; rejects justification for genocide 93; criticizes gloating over defeated 111; wonders and fears what peace will bring 48, 89, 91; and *LR* 216, 235

The Worm Ouroboros (Eddison) 84, 220, 258, 377, 439, 447

Wormings 137

Wormtongue 201

Worskett, Col. *333–5*

Wrenn, C.L. 43, 46, 161, 238; succeeded Tolkien as Professor of Anglo-Saxon 117, 238, 443; *English and Medieval Studies Presented to J.R.R. Tolkien* (ed. Davis and Wrenn) 322–3

Wright, E.M. *11*; 74, 438

Wright, Joseph 11, 22, 336, 397, 438; *English Dialect Dictionary* 11; *A Grammar of the Gothic Language* 357; *Primer of the Gothic Language* 357, 397

'Wrigley', Mr *418*

Wyke-Smith, E.A., *The Marvellous Land of Snergs* 215

Wyld, H.C.K. 108, 114

Xerxes 64

Yavanna 285, 335

Yiddish language 410

Young, Brigham 51

Youth, modern 393

Zimmerman, Morton Grady 266–7, 270–7